proceedings of the united nations conference on trade and development

third session

santiago de chile, 13 april to 21 may 1972

volume II
merchandise trade

united nations
new york, 1973

, Conference on Trade and Development.

NOTE

Symbols of United Nations documents are composed of capital letters combined with figures. Mention of such a symbol indicates a reference to a United Nations document.

* *

The designations employed and the presentation of the material in this publication do not imply the expression of any opinion whatsoever on the part of the Secretariat of the United Nations concerning the legal status of any country or territory or of its authorities, or concerning the delimitation of its frontiers.

* *

For the recommendations adopted by the United Nations Conference on Trade and Development at its first session, see *Proceedings of the United Nations Conference on Trade and Development*, vol. I, *Final Act and Report* (United Nations publication, Sales No. 64.II.B.11), pp. 17-65. For the resolutions, declarations and decisions adopted by the Conference at its second session, see *Proceedings of the United Nations Conference on Trade and Development, Second Session*, vol. I, and Corr.1 and 3 and Add.1-2, *Report and Annexes* (United Nations publication, Sales No. E.68.II.D.14), annex I, pp. 27-58.

TD/180, vol. II

UNITED NATIONS PUBLICATION

Sales No. E.73.II.D.5

Price: $U.S. 7.00

(or equivalent in other currencies)

CONTENTS

PART ONE

Commodities

PART TWO

Manufactures

ABBREVIATIONS

ACC	Administrative Committee on Co-ordination
AfDB	African Development Bank
AsDB	Asian Development Bank
BIRPI	United International Bureaux for the Protection of Intellectual Property
BTN	Brussels Tariff Nomenclature
c.i.f.	Cost, insurance, freight
ECA	Economic Commission for Africa
ECAFE	Economic Commission for Asia and the Far East
ECE	Economic Commission for Europe
ECLA	Economic Commission for Latin America
ECSC	European Coal and Steel Community
EDF	European Development Fund of EEC
EEC	European Economic Community
EFTA	European Free Trade Association
FAO	Food and Agriculture Organization of the United Nations
f.a.s.	Free alongside ship
f.o.b.	Free on board
GATT	General Agreement on Tariffs and Trade
GDP	Gross domestic product
GNP	Gross national product
GSP	Generalized system of preferences
IBRD	International Bank for Reconstruction and Development
ICC	International Chamber of Commerce
IDA	International Development Association
IDB	Inter-American Development Bank
IFC	International Finance Corporation
ILO	International Labour Organisation
IMF	International Monetary Fund
ISIC	International Standard Industrial Classification of all Economic Activities
ISO	International Organization for Standardization
ITC	UNCTAD/GATT International Trade Centre
LAFTA	Latin American Free Trade Association
LTA	Long-Term Arrangement regarding International Trade in Cotton Textiles
m.f.n.	Most-favoured-nation
n.e.s	Not elsewhere specified
OAU	Organization of African Unity
OECD	Organisation for Economic Co-operation and Development
SITC	Standard International Trade Classification
UNCTAD	United Nations Conference on Trade and Development
UNDP	United Nations Development Programme
UNESCO	United Nations Educational, Scientific and Cultural Organization
UNESOB	United Nations Economic and Social Office in Beirut
UNIDO	United Nations Industrial Development Organization
UNITAR	United Nations Institute for Training and Research
WHO	World Health Organization
WIPO	World Intellectual Property Organization

EXPLANATORY NOTES

Unless otherwise stated:

References to "dollars" ($) indicate United States dollars.

References to "tons" indicate metric tons.

An oblique stroke (/) between years, e.g., 1965/66, indicates a season or a crop or fiscal year.

A hyphen (-) between years, e.g., 1965-1966, signifies the full period involved, including the beginning and end years.

The term "billion" signifies 1,000 million.

The following symbols have been used in the tables throughout this volume:

Two dots (..) indicate that the data are not available or are not separately reported.

A dash (—) indicates that the amount is nil or negligible.

A minus sign (−) indicates a decrease, unless otherwise stated.

A plus sign (+) has been used in some of the tables showing percentage changes to indicate an increase.

Use of parentheses around a figure, e.g. (25.0), indicates that the figure is an estimate.

Details and percentages in tables do not necessarily add to totals, because of rounding.

Part one
COMMODITIES

THE DEVELOPMENT OF INTERNATIONAL COMMODITY POLICY

Progress report by the UNCTAD secretariat*

[Original text: English]

CONTENTS

Chapter I

Developments in international commodity policy since the second session of the Conference

1. The desirability of evolving an integrated international commodity policy was considered in some depth at the second session of the Conference on the basis of a study by the secretariat.[1] That study, which discussed the possibility of alternative remedial policy "packages" for the various short-term and long-term problems faced by developing countries in international commodity trade, provided a single analytical framework within which international actions on different aspects could be related to one another. The time did not, however, appear ripe by the date of the second Conference for the evolution of such an integrated international commodity policy, as was also shown by the Conference's failure to reach a consensus on the need for a general agreement on Commodity arrangements embodying the main principles of such an integrated policy.[2]

2. The main achievement of the second Conference in the commodities field was the elaboration of an action programme covering some twenty individual commodities of export interest to developing countries. Its resolution 16 (II) set out in some detail an action programme for the consideration of the problems faced by each commodity and the determination of appropriate remedial measures. What was envisaged was a series of commodity-by-commodity consultations or negotiations either within existing Study Groups or in *ad hoc* meetings, or arranged specially for this purpose by the Secretary-General of UNCTAD.

3. So far, however, this action programme has had only very limited success.[3] A new International Sugar Agreement was concluded at the end of 1968, but this was more the culmination of a long series of consultations dating back to 1966, than the result of resolution 16(II). Considerable progress towards a new international agreement for cocoa has been achieved, but so far an agreement has not been concluded. Progress has been achieved also in relation to tea, for which informal export regulation schemes were negotiated for 1970 and 1971/72 under the auspices of the FAO Consultative Committee on Tea, which has also been considering—in its Standing Exporters Group—the principles of a possible long-term agreement for this commodity.

---

* The text of this report was circulated to the Conference as document TD/113, dated 3 March 1972.

[1] See the study by the UNCTAD secretariat entitled "The development of an international commodity policy" (TD/8/Supp.1), in *Proceedings of the United Nations Conference on Trade and Development, Second Session*, vol. II, *Commodity Problems and Policies* (United Nations publication, Sales No. E.68.II.D.15), p. 1.

[2] See the report of the First Committee, in *Proceedings of the United Nations Conference on Trade and Development, Second Session*, vol. I and Corr.1 and 3 and Add.1 and 2, *Report and Annexes* (United Nations publication, Sales No. E.68.II.D.14), annex VII A, paras. 16 and 17.

[3] For a more detailed review of the action taken under Conference resolution 16 (II), see the reports by the UNCTAD secretariat entitled "Problems and international action concerning commodities covered by Conference resolution 16 (II)" (TD/113/Supp.1 and Add.1 and 2). (For TD/113/Supp.1, see p. 61 below.)

4. For most of the other commodities covered by resolution 16 (II) very little remedial international action has been achieved, despite intensive studies and inter-governmental consultations on the problems of many of these commodities. The reasons for this general lack of progress may be traced to the inherent economic and technical complexities of many primary commodity markets, the nature of the existing intergovernmental consultative machinery relating to individual commodities, and the lack of political will on the part of interested governments.[4]

5. There seems little doubt that, for these reasons, negotiations on a commodity-by-commodity basis are inevitably complicated and time-consuming. This fact raises an important issue for the Conference, since—on the basis of past experience—a continuation of the existing approach to the problems of primary commodities cannot be expected to result in effective international remedial actions covering the whole range of commodities listed in resolution 16 (II) until nearer the end of the century. What now seems to be urgently required, in order to deal effectively with the varied problems affecting a wide range of primary commodities by the end of the present decade is that at least two new elements should be added to the existing approach. First, a higher degree of priority should be given by the governments concerned with trade in particular problem commodities to the need for concluding new international agreements embodying appropriate remedial measures. In some cases, such action would require a more positive attitude to such agreements on the part of importing countries; in other cases, it would involve additional efforts by exporting countries to reach a mutually acceptable arrangement concerning market shares.[5]

6. Second, consideration needs to be given to evolving new international measures which could be applied in a general way to primary commodity trade, or at least to trade in certain well defined groups of commodities of particular export interest to developing countries. Such measures would, if effective, alleviate the market problems of a wide range of commodities and so complement efforts to negotiate new international agreement for individual commodities.

7. As the Secretary-General of UNCTAD has pointed out in his report to the third session of the Conference entitled "The International Development Strategy in action: the role of UNCTAD"[6] the continuing machinery of UNCTAD has become increasingly concerned in recent years with reaching agreement on a number of general approaches to the problems of primary commodity markets. Agreed resolutions have been adopted by the Committee on Commodities on a number of important

general aspects, including diversification, competition from synthetics and substitutes, the marketing and distribution system for primary commodities, and special measures for the least developed countries,[7] all subjects which appear on the provisional agenda for the third Conference. Moreover, by its resolution 73 (X), the Trade and Development Board provided a basis for further consideration of action in the fields of market access and pricing policy.[8]

8. The documents submitted by the secretariat under the various sub-headings of item 13 of the provisional agenda are generally based on the agreements so far reached in UNCTAD bodies, but since these agreements are very largely couched in terms of general principles, the secretariat's objective has been to explore alternative ways in which such general principles might best be made operational.

Chapter II

Access to markets and pricing policy

A. RELATION BETWEEN MARKET ACCESS AND PRICING POLICY

9. Measures designed to achieve a significant improvement, over the longer term, in the earnings of developing countries from exports of primary commodities can influence the volume of these exports, or their prices, or both. Such measures, to be successful, must take into account the underlying economic and technological factors which influence the long-term trends in the various commodity markets, as well as the impact of national economic and trade policies.

10. The rate of economic growth in the developed countries—still the preponderant markets for the commodity exports of developing countries—is a major factor determining the rate of growth in world demand for primary commodities. However, the process of economic growth is associated with a number of structural changes which tend to act as constraints on the expansion in the demand for the traditional exports of developing countries. One of the principal changes, arising from rapid scientific and technological progress in the petrochemical industries of developed countries, has been a continuing, and relatively fast, expansion in the output of new types of synthetic materials. This, in turn, has had a substantial adverse impact on the growth in developing countries' earnings from exports of a range of important agricultural

---

[4] For a more detailed analysis, see document TD/113/Supp.1. (See p. 61 below.)

[5] For the related discussion, see document TD/113/Supp.1, paras. 30-35 (see p. 66 below) and the report by the UNCTAD secretariat entitled "Pricing policy, including international price stabilization measures and mechanisms" (TD/127), paras. 22-24. (See p. 43 below).

[6] See TD/99 and Corr.2, chap. III.

[7] See "Special measures for the least developed among the developing countries: action programme submitted by the Secretary-General of UNCTAD" (TD/135) for a discussion of an action-oriented programme of special measures relating to primary commodities in favour of the least developed among the developing countries. (See *Proceedings of the United Nations Conference on Trade and Development, Third Session*, vol. IV, *General Review and Special Issues* (United Nations publication, Sales No. E.73.II.D.7).

[8] Action on the general aspects mentioned is also envisaged in General Assembly resolution 2626 (XXV) of 24 October 1970 on the International Development Strategy for the Second United Nations Development Decade, paras. (21)-(29).

raw materials, in that a downward pressure was exerted on prices of the natural materials concerned, though the volume of demand has also been affected, to varying extents, by their displacement by synthetic substitutes in particular end-uses.

11. Two other structural tendencies, of a long-term character, act as constraints on the growth of demand in the developed countries for this group of commodities. First, the pattern of industrial output changes markedly with economic growth; in particular, the relative importance of the chemical and engineering industries increases, while that of the textile, clothing, timber and other consumer industries—based largely on agricultural raw materials— decreases. Second, the degree of fabrication of primary materials generally increases as the production process becomes technically more sophisticated, and consequently over the long term the volume of raw materials used per unit of manufactured output declines.

12. Owing to the combination of these several elements, a particular rate of economic growth in the developed countries does not lead to a commensurate beneficial expansion in their demand for the agricultural raw material exports of developing countries. Appropriate remedial measures which could be taken on an international basis are discussed in chapter III below.

13. Another structural change, closely associated with the process of economic growth, is that as real income rises the pattern of consumer demand undergoes certain changes of a systematic nature. These changes, which are reflected in differences between the income-elasticities of demand for various products, can be traced with a fair degree of precision in both developed and developing countries. In developed countries, however, the demand for certain foods and beverages—particularly cereals, dairy products, sugar and coffee, cocoa and tea—is generally inelastic with respect to increases in real income.

14. Where such commodities are produced wholly or mainly in developing countries—as are the beverage crops and other tropical agricultural products—the relatively slow growth in demand often tends to be associated with a faster growth in exportable production in developing countries, partly as a result of the application of scientific methods to improve yields, and partly because they become useful cash crops for a widening circle of peasant producers. This conjunction of circumstances leads to a fall in prices, of greater or lesser severity. For tree crops, such as coffee, cocoa and tea, a price decline, if it persists, is followed after some time-lag by a reduction in the volume of supplies as marginal units cease production or turn to other crops. The reduced level of production results in a recovery in prices which, again after a time-lag, engenders a renewed expansion in supply. Hence, a cyclical movement in prices is superimposed on a relatively static or declining trend, prices at the cyclical turning points often being either abnormally high or unprofitably low for most producers. These swings in market prices are often accentuated by uncertainties surrounding the magnitude of the next crop and by the consequential speculation on the terminal markets.

15. For this group of commodities, remedial action must be sought essentially through a pricing policy. Restrictions on access to markets exist, but these, in the form of revenue charges imposed in a number of developed market economy countries, are an incidental feature of national taxation systems, rather than important impediments to the expansion of consumption. There would, however, appear to be scope for measures to expand the volume of consumption—and hence of imports from developing countries—in the socialist countries of Eastern Europe. The policy proposals made in the relevant secretariat document are summarized in section B below, as regards improving market access, and section C relating to pricing policy.

16. Where, however, commodities for which demand is inelastic with respect to income changes are produced in substantial amounts in developed countries as a result of a policy of protection for domestic producers against competing imports, the problem is essentially one of improving market access for lower-cost products available for importation. This group of protected primary commodities consists essentially of temperate-zone agricultural products, such as sugar, vegetable oilseeds, meat, cereals and tobacco, in all of which developing countries have an important export interest.

17. As a result of price support, given in various ways to maintain the real income of the farm community at a reasonable level in relation to that of other sectors of the economy, there is the paradoxical situation in which the internal prices of these agricultural products in many developed market economy countries are maintained at levels considerably higher than those obtaining in the world market. The prevailing systems of income support for the domestic farm population of these countries thus operate, in effect, to restrict—by protective devices—access to their internal markets for lower-cost supplies available elsewhere, including sources in developing countries; and, by incidentally diverting such lower-cost supplies to third markets, these support schemes result in a lower level of prices in those markets than would otherwise obtain.

18. For this group of temperate-zone agricultural commodities, therefore, market access and pricing policy aspects are closely interlinked. Measures which reduce the level of domestic price support will, by discouraging domestic production, thereby improve the conditions of access for lower-cost competing products from developing countries. Such measures, by encouraging consumption in the developed countries of the commodities concerned, as well as by discouraging high-cost domestic production, will also raise the level of world prices, at least over the short and medium term. Improvements in market access are thus likely to benefit the earnings of developing countries from exports of these commodities, because of increases in both volume and prices. Policy proposals designed to result in improved market access for temperate-zone agricultural commodities are summarized in section B below.

19. Measures to improve the earnings of developing countries from exports of this group of commodities can also be conceived in terms of pricing policies alone. These are considered in section C. Such measures, while they may undoubtedly benefit the export revenue of developing countries would, however, leave untouched the underlying problem of the misallocation of world resources used in the production of these commodities.

20. Finally, there is an important group of commodities for which demand is, in effect, income-elastic. This group consists predominantly of minerals and metals, which are indispensable for industrial expansion. For this reason, also, there are generally few impediments to free access to the markets of developed countries for the minerals and crude metals produced in developing countries.[9] Owing to the industrial expansion of the developed countries demand for most non-ferrous ores and metals has been outrunning supply, with consequential increases in both volume and prices of exports of these commodities from developing countries. For ferrous ores—iron and manganese—the opposite has, however, occurred for a variety of reasons, and prices have been on a downward trend for the past decade. The implications for remedial action in the field of pricing policy are discussed in section C below.

B. IMPROVING ACCESS TO MARKETS[10]

21. Little, if any, progress has been achieved since the second session of the Conference in improving access for primary commodities to the markets of industrialized countries. Measures in these countries in support of domestic production, particularly of temperate-zone agricultural commodities, remain widespread, often at relatively high cost to both consumers and taxpayers. The adverse effects of such support policies on exports from lower-cost producers, including developing countries, have been aggravated, in the case of certain commodities, by the export of surpluses which are often disposed of with export aids on the world market.

22. The case for a concerted effort by the industrialized countries to reduce or remove existing protection, or other support measures, for high-cost domestic production is now generally accepted in principle. Such an effort would yield direct benefits to lower-cost producers, including developing countries, and would enable developed importing countries to adapt their resources to a more productive pattern of economic activity. It would also reduce the budgetary burden of support in the developed countries, as well as reducing the cost to the consumer.

23. At the same time, it must be recognized that existing farm support policies in developed countries have primarily a social objective; that is, they have been devised to provide the farm community with a real income standard comparable with that of the urban areas. Any substantial reduction in the degree of support may well have implications for the size and structure of the agricultural sector and for the rate of emigration from the land to the towns. Changes in existing support policies must, therefore, be considered in a wider context of social and economic policy.

24. Nonetheless, the time appears ripe for a reconsideration of these support policies in the light of the heavy

real costs which they involve, not only to the developed countries themselves, but also to the export position and potential of the developing countries. Support measures and other protective devices for such important commodities as sugar, rice, beef and veal, tobacco, citrus fruits and vegetable oilseeds result in a misallocation of world resources for the production of commodities in which developing countries often have a marked comparative advantage. A further access problem is created in some developed countries by the imposition of revenue charges on tropical foods and beverage crops.

25. Significant progress towards improved market access for primary commodities would require considerably more purposeful action by the international community than has been taken in the past. One major prerequisite for such action would seem to be a generally greater political conviction of the merits of policies to improve access. Another would be a greater willingness by Governments of developed countries to change their existing methods of agricultural support so as to minimize their adverse effects on the trade of low-cost producing countries. In view of the meagre results achieved in recent years through unilateral actions to reduce barriers to trade in agricultural commodities, it would appear essential that future moves to improve access should be taken on a multilateral basis within an appropriate consultative, or negotiating, framework. In this context, it is envisaged that specific commitments concerning the improvement of access to their domestic markets would be undertaken by both developed market economy countries and socialist countries.

26. A new initiative on these lines should have as its principal objective the improvement of market access for the commodities of special export interest to developing countries, though the interests of developed countries heavily dependent on primary commodity exports should also be taken into account. The appropriate forum for the proposed consultations would be one in which the political momentum, and the chances of practical results emerging, would be greatest, account being taken of breadth of membership, the priority accorded to the interests of developing countries and the character of the consultations. The consultations should not be regarded as implying reciprocity—as is usual in tariff negotiations—but rather as being designed to elicit meaningful offers from individual developed countries concerning improvements in access to their markets for particular commodities.

27. The Conference may wish to consider the possibility of establishing such consultative, or negotiating, machinery, as well as the degree of priority which should be accorded to action in this respect, the nature of the objectives to be pursued, and a possible time-table for the consultations.

C. PRICING POLICY[11]

28. Over the past decade a major problem in the export trade of developing countries has been posed by declining

---

[9] Protective tariffs are, however, general for semi-fabricated metals and manufactured metal goods.

[10] For a fuller discussion of the problems and policy issues involved, and for more detailed proposals for future progress in this field, see the report by the UNCTAD secretariat entitled "Access to markets" (TD/115). (See p. 11 below.)

[11] For a more detailed discussion of problems and possible remedial policies relating to pricing policy, see the report by the UNCTAD secretariat on the subject (TD/124). (See p. 104 below.)

or stagnant price trends for two major groups of primary commodities, namely agricultural products facing increasing competition from synthetic materials, and tropical foods and beverages, for many of which demand grows but slowly and which tend to be in persistent surplus on the world market. Developing countries heavily dependent on such commodities for the bulk of their export earnings have generally suffered from stagnation or inadequate growth in these earnings. Trends in the world market for products competing with the protected agricultural output of developed countries have likewise not been favourable for developing countries. Prospects for the remainder of the present decade do not hold out much hope for a reversal of these unfavourable trends, in the absence of remedial international action.

29. The problem of excessive short-term market instability will no doubt persist for a number of important primary commodities, both agricultural and mineral, unless a higher degree or priority is given by the international community to the conclusion of appropriate stabilization arrangements.

30. The strategy adopted so far to achieve stable, remunerative and equitable prices for primary commodities has been to conduct a series of negotiations on a commodity-by-commodity basis. This strategy, however, has had only very limited success in view of the complex and time-consuming character of the negotiations relating to individual commodities. Hence, the Conference may wish to consider strengthening and supplementing the existing strategy so that more effective action can be taken in respect of a broader range of commodity price problems. More specifically, it might recommend that Governments most concerned with particular problem commodities should give a higher degree of priority than that accorded hitherto to the need for concluding new international stabilization agreements.[12]

31. In addition, new measures seem to be needed to deal with the particular pricing problems of each of the main groups of commodities, to supplement the existing commodity-by-commodity approach. A number of possible alternatives exist in the field of fiscal policy. For example, developing countries exporting tropical agricultural products for which there are no direct substitutes in consumption might impose a uniform *ad valorem* export tax, or enforce a minimum level of export prices. On the part of developed importing countries, the alternatives include the refunding to producing countries of a proportion of revenue charges collected on the import or internal sale of tropical products; the adoption of compensatory payments arrangements under which all, or part, of the difference between actual prices and agreed reference prices would be credited to exporting countries; and the extension of existing systems of preferential prices for a few commodities (now benefiting only certain developing countries) to all developing countries supplying them, as well as to other commodities.

32. The Conference may wish to consider the need for assigning a higher degree of priority to the conclusion of international price stabilization arrangements, and the merits of preparing feasibility studies of alternative forms of international fiscal co-operation to offset a longer-term deterioration or stagnation in the trend of commodity prices. Consideration might also be given to the desirability of including in such new arrangements—as well as in existing commodity agreements—provisions designed to offset sudden, unforeseen changes in the terms of trade of developing producing countries due, for example, to changes in currency valuation.

Mineral production from the sea-bed

33. A special aspect of pricing policy relates to the potential production of minerals from the sea-bed beyond national jurisdiction in competition with like minerals produced from land-based sources, including the developing countries.[13] The latter group of countries accounts for the bulk of world exports of most of the minerals which are considered to be the most likely to be commercially exploitable from sea-bed resources in the foreseeable future (copper, cobalt, manganese, nickel, petroleum and natural gas). These resources have been recognized by the General Assembly in its resolution 2750 A (XXV) of 17 December 1970 as "the common heritage of mankind", and as available for exploitation by the international community "for the benefit of mankind as a whole, taking into account the special interest and needs of the developing countries". In these special circumstances, the international community itself has a decision-making role as to the conditions, including the pricing policy, to be applied to any minerals produced from the sea-bed.

34. Since the sea-bed would constitute a completely new source of supply, such production would tend to reduce the market prices of the minerals concerned below the levels that would otherwise obtain and to displace marginal output from land sources. The net result of these price and volume effects would be that export earnings of developing producing countries might decline from present levels; in any event, they would be smaller than they would have been in the absence of production from the sea-bed. Moreover, if these countries were obliged to reduce their mineral production, additional social costs would arise from a fall in employment or a re-allocation of the labour force. It is, therefore, important that firm arrangements should be made in advance of the production of minerals from the sea-bed in order to ensure that such new production will not adversely affect the interests of developing producing countries.

35. The main alternative approaches to the problem of protecting the interests of developing producing countries appear to be either the adoption of measures designed to ensure that these countries do not incur losses, or the provision of financial compensation for losses when they arise. By means of the preventive approach, the rate of production from the sea-bed, or the rate of disposal of such output, or the relevant selling price, would be strictly

---

[12] In this connexion, reference should be made to a report by the Secretary-General of UNCTAD entitled "Effectiveness of commodity agreements" (TD/129 and Corr.1).

[13] For a fuller discussion of the issues of international commodity policy raised by mineral production from the sea-bed, see the report by the UNCTAD secretariat entitled "Mineral production from the area of the sea-bed beyond national jurisdiction: issues of international commodity policy" (TD/113/Supp.4). (See p. 67 below.)

controlled by the international authority, which it is envisaged will be established in order that market prices for the minerals concerned should not be depressed below levels declared by the international community as being remunerative and equitable.

36. Under the alternative compensatory approach no restriction would be placed on sea-bed mineral production, so that the adverse effects on the export earnings of developing countries, mentioned earlier, can be expected to arise, but these adverse effects would, in principle, be offset by compensatory payments from the net revenue of the international authority derived from royalties or profits. However, if the net revenue was a modest proportion of the selling price, it would be insufficient to compensate developing exporting countries for export proceeds lost as a result of sea-bed production, if the loss were regarded as including the growth of export earnings which would otherwise have taken place. It would therefore be necessary to obtain a prior commitment from consuming countries and/or the international financial institutions to make good the difference so as to provide the full amount of financial compensation required.

37. If, by contrast, the compensation for loss of export proceeds was related to any shortfall from an historical level, say that of 1972, then the net revenue of the authority might well be sufficient for the purpose. However, this approach would make no allowance for the potential expansion in export earnings which developing producing countries would otherwise attain in an expanding market.

38. The Conference may wish to give some consideration to the implications of these alternative approaches, and to express its views on the commodity policies which would be appropriate in this new field of endeavour, bearing in mind both the international ownership of sea-bed minerals and the potential impact of their exploitation on the export position and prospects of many developing countries.

D. MARKETING AND DISTRIBUTION SYSTEMS

39. The impact of the marketing and distribution system on the operation of particular primary commodity markets constitutes, in a sense, a special aspect of international pricing policy. The need for a series of analyses of the marketing and distribution systems for primary commodity exports of developing countries, covering the entire distributive chain between the points of production and consumption, was agreed upon at the third session of the Committee on Commodities in 1968.[14] The purpose of such analyses, as elaborated in later documents prepared by the UNCTAD secretariat for the Committee on Commodities,[15] would be to determine whether and to what extent inefficiency, or excess profit, exists in the present marketing and distribution systems for primary commodities; and to assess the scope for potential gains

from improvements in the existing system. Since information available from published sources is generally inadequate for this task, it would seem essential—if meaningful progress is to be made—to undertake studies in depth of individual commodities.

40. A study in depth of the marketing and distribution system operating for cocoa has already been commenced.[16] Apart from considering the internal marketing system in producing countries, the study will pay particular attention to the structure and operation of the cocoa terminal markets in major consuming countries, and to assessing their influence, if any, on the course of cocoa prices and on the relative position of consumers and producers in the market. The relative position of consumers and producers is also influenced by their ability to act in unison within their own group, and by the physical and financial facilities available for stockholding. It is hoped that sufficient information will be forthcoming about these various aspects to make possible an evaluation of the costs and benefits of the present marketing system for cocoa.

41. Though the cocoa study could be of importance as a guide to possible improvements in present marketing arrangements for that commodity, it cannot be used in relation to other commodities, for which the marketing and distribution structure may be very different from that of cocoa and which may, indeed, stand to gain more from possible improvements. The marketing and distribution systems operating for both tea and tobacco, for example, are based predominantly on auctions held in major producing and/or consuming countries. As regards tea, account would have to be taken of production in plantations owned by large enterprises which blend, pack and market tea in consuming countries; while in the case of tobacco, State monopolies for marketing manufactured tobacco operate in many developed countries in order to produce tax revenue. Other agricultural crops, such as bananas, are marketed by vertically-integrated enterprises of developed countries; these enterprises own plantations in developing countries, export the crop in their own ships, and sell it in developed countries through their own wholesale distributive units.

42. In the minerals field, certain types of marketing system assume major importance. A noteworthy phenomenon in recent years has been the rapid growth of sales by mining enterprises in developing countries on long-term contracts to metal-making concerns in developed countries. It has been estimated, for example, that in 1968 about one-third of the world trade in iron ore was transacted under long-term agreements, which may be valid for periods up to twenty years; another one-third was accounted for by transfers from mines in developing countries to parent firms in developed countries, leaving the remaining one-third to be sold on the residual free market. The relative importance of vertically-integrated concerns owning, or partially controlling, both mining facilities in developing countries and marketing outlets in developed countries is even greater for a number of other

---

[14] See *Official Records of the Trade and Development Board, Eighth Session, Supplement No. 3* (TD/B/202/Rev.1), para. 44.

[15] Reports by the UNCTAD secretariat entitled "Marketing and distribution systems for primary commodities" (TD/B/C.1/85) and "Proposals for studies in depth of marketing and distribution systems for primary commodities" (TD/B/C.1/111).

[16] Report by the UNCTAD secretariat entitled "Marketing and distribution systems for primary commodities: progress report on a study in depth regarding cocoa" (TD/113/Supp.3).

minerals than it is for iron ore. For such minerals, it might be useful to examine the problems which might arise if production were placed under national control.

43. It would therefore seem desirable that the series of studies in depth envisaged by the Committee on Commodities should cover a number of commodities, which together would involve detailed consideration of the operation of the various major types of marketing and distribution systems. The Conference may wish to consider this matter with a view to deciding upon some guidelines for future work in this field.

Chapter III

Competitiveness of natural products[17]

44. A number of natural raw materials exported from developing countries, principally rubber, the textile fibres (cotton, wool, jute and hard fibres), leather and lauric oils, have faced increasingly serious competition from synthetic materials in recent years. The rapid growth of production of synthetics and their substitution for natural products have resulted in an appreciable narrowing of markets for natural products and downward pressure on prices. The prospects are for an intensification of competition between natural products and synthetic materials, and for further encroachment by synthetics on the markets for natural products.[18]

45. For each of these natural materials, an appropriate long-term strategy needs urgently to be devised within which agreed measures can be adopted to meet the challenge posed by synthetics. In such a strategy, depending on the nature of the competition, the emphasis may be on productivity improvement, on short-term price stabilization, on access to markets, on the improvement of quality and technical characteristics, on the development of new end-uses, on promotion, on diversification, or on a combination of several of these measures. However, the essential element in a viable long-term strategy for all these natural materials must be the improvement in their competitive position as regards both price and technical characteristics. To achieve significant progress towards this objective, it is imperative to mount well-conceived research and development programmes of adequate size.

46. For certain of these natural materials—cotton, wool and rubber—producers are already co-operating for purposes of research. For other natural materials of importance in the export trade of developing countries no such international co-operation exists at present. Moreover, except possibly in the case of wool, the scale of existing research and development efforts is quite inadequate in relation to the seriousness of the competition from synthetic substitutes. For all these materials—again,

apart from wool—there is an urgent need, first, to devise appropriate long-term strategies including the required research and development programmes; and, second, to mobilize financial support for these programmes.

47. As regards programmes for research, development and promotion, these could best be worked out by an appropriate intergovernmental body for each natural material, as has already been done in the case of cotton by the International Institute for Cotton. Where bodies specifically concerned with the international co-ordination of research and development and promotion do not exist, the interested governments could consider establishing them. The FAO intergovernmental commodity groups for jute and hard fibres, for example, are encouraging the study of the possibilities for establishing such research and promotion bodies, and similar bodies for other natural materials could also be considered. For natural materials not covered by intergovernmental commodity groups, such as hides, skins and leather and essential oils, UNCTAD in co-operation with other agencies such as FAO and UNIDO could arrange consultations among interested governments with a view to establishing the appropriate research and promotion bodies.

48. Once the required research and development programmes have been agreed at the intergovernmental level, they should not be held up for lack of the necessary finance. The Conference may, therefore, wish to consider recommending that assistance for such programmes should be accorded high priority by the international financial institutions, including any necessary support from UNDP; to be effective, such action might call for the establishment of consultative machinery for considering specifically the financing requirements of research and development programmes for these natural materials. Individual countries with a particular interest in the research and development programme proposed for any natural material should also consider making voluntary contributions to its financing, even if they do not participate in the intergovernmental body co-ordinating the research and development programme concerned.

49. The Conference may also wish to endorse the role of the Permanent Group on Synthetics and Substitutes as the body primarily responsible for stimulating and reviewing progress in the various intergovernmental bodies concerned with improving the competitive position of natural products and, in particular, progress in any direction recommended by the Conference in this field.

Chapter IV

Diversification

50. The urgent need for accelerating the diversification of the economies of developing countries has received general support in UNCTAD bodies, as well as in other international forums. The need for developed countries to "give increased attention within the framework of bilateral and multilateral programmes to supplementing the resources of the developing countries in their endeavour to accelerate the diversification of their economies"

---

[17] For a fuller discussion of the main issues, see the reports by the UNCTAD secretariat entitled "The competitiveness of natural products" (TD/117) and "The competitiveness of natural products: research and development" (TD/117/Supp.1). (For TD/117, see p. 73 below.)

[18] See the report by the UNCTAD secretariat entitled "Trends in commodity trade in the 1960s and prospects for the 1970s" (TD/113/Supp.2 and Corr.1).

is also recognized in paragraph (28) of the International Development Strategy.

51. This subject has been intensively discussed in UNCTAD bodies since the second session of the Conference, and a detailed programme for further work was set out in decision 5 (VI) of the Committee on Commodities at its sixth session in July 1971.[19] The areas in which practical international action might be concentrated, as envisaged in decision 5 (VI), can be grouped under the following four headings:

(a) Collection and dissemination of information;

(b) Harmonization of diversification programmes;

(c) Technical and financial assistance for commodity diversification;

(d) Special assistance for countries heavily dependent on "problem" commodities.

52. As regard the existing arrangements in the United Nations system for the collection and dissemination to governments of information relevant to decisions affecting diversification, the Conference may wish to consider a number of improvements that appear to be required.[20] It is suggested, for example, that the international agencies concerned should make widely known the type of information they provide in their publications or on request; should consider jointly the scope for the collection and dissemination of additional information, and should jointly recommend measures for obtaining local information now lacking in developing countries. Proposals for improving the effectiveness in this field of the existing activities of each of the agencies would also merit the attention of the Conference.[21]

53. As regard the need for harmonizing the diversification programmes of developing countries, there appears to be a need for closer consultation between Governments providing bilateral assistance for particular projects and the appropriate international agencies on the national and international implications of such projects, so as to ensure such harmonization. A more active and purposeful role in this connexion should also be considered for the specialized intergovernmental commodity bodies.[22]

54. Improvements can also be envisaged in the existing arrangements for technical and financial assistance for commodity diversification.[23] Such assistance, from all sources, needs to be more specifically adapted, both in volume and in type, to appropriate long-term diversification strategies for developing countries with unfavourable export structures. The Conference may also wish to consider the desirability of establishing procedures for evaluating on a regular basis the effectiveness of technical and financial assistance to developing countries for diversification. Finally, a concerted effort appears to be required on the part of the various international agencies to strengthen the statistical systems of developing countries and to raise the technical level of their economic planning work.

55. Developing countries in need of special international assistance for diversification can be classified into those dependent largely on the export of "problem" commodities in actual or potential surplus on the world market, or facing significant competition from synthetics; those whose exports are excessively concentrated in a single commodity; and those whose need for diversification arises for particular *ad hoc* reasons. For such countries, the immediate need is the adoption of appropriate long-term diversification strategies, or the revision of existing unsuccessful strategies. The Conference will wish to consider the desirability of inaugurating a series of studies in depth of the diversification problems of a number of such developing countries, with a view to elaborating appropriate long-term diversification strategies. On the basis of these studies—which could be made, at the request of the Governments concerned, by inter-agency teams of experts co-ordinated by UNCTAD—proposals could be made for practical action by the Governments concerned and, where appropriate, for supporting action by the international community.

---

[19] See *Official Records of the Trade and Development Board, Eleventh Session, Supplement No. 4* (TD/B/370), annex I.

[20] For a full discussion of suggested improvements, see the report by the UNCTAD secretariat entitled "International action relating to commodity diversification" (TD/109). (See p. 79 below.)

[21] *Ibid.*, para. 65 (a).

[22] *Ibid.*, para. 66.

[23] *Ibid.*, para. 67.

ACCESS TO MARKETS

Report by the UNCTAD secretariat*

[*Original text: English*]

CONTENTS

---

* The text of this report was circulated to the Conference as document TD/115, dated 27 January 1972, and TD/115/Corr.1, dated 15 March 1972.

Introduction

1. In international discussions of commodity problems and policies during the first United Nations Development Decade, much attention was devoted to the question of improving access to markets for primary commodities, especially commodities of interest to developing exporting countries. This concern reflected a growing awareness of the benefits which a more rational economic distribution of the world's primary production would bring to both the developing and the industrial countries and, more specifically, a growing recognition of the great contribution which the improvement of access to markets in developed areas would make to the realization of the international community's objective of stimulating the export earnings and economic growth of the developing areas.

2. The principal international discussions which provide a basis for future consideration within UNCTAD of the question of improving access to primary commodity markets are described briefly in the passages which follow. At the first session of the United Nations Conference on Trade and Development, in 1964, the principal recommendation adopted in the field of international commodity trade—the recommendation on international commodity arrangements and removal of obstacles and expansion of trade contained in annex A.II.1 to the final Act—called for a variety of measures to improve access to markets in developed areas.[1] At the second session of the Conference, in 1968, various proposals for the liberalization of trade in commodities were discussed but no substantive agreement was reached.[2] However, the proposals were referred to the permanent machinery of UNCTAD and, after considerable discussion in the Committee on Commodities and in the Trade and Development Board, the latter, in September 1970, adopted resolution 73 (X) on "Commodity problems and policies: pricing policy and liberalization of trade", which included guidelines for the liberalization of trade in primary commodities of particular export interest to developing countries.[3] Subsequently, in October 1970, discussions concerning objectives in the Second United Nations Development Decade culminated in the adoption by the General Assembly of an International Development Strategy for the Decade, which called (in paragraphs 25 and 26) for more favourable economic and commercial policies on the part of developed countries and included certain policy measures for the improvement of access to developed countries for primary products of export interest to developing countries.

3. In 1964 the Conference envisaged the improvement of access to primary commodity markets in developed areas as involving a series of measures which might be summarized as follows:

(*a*) A standstill on all trade barriers;

(*b*) The removal or reduction of direct obstacles, such as quantitative restrictions, tariffs, and internal fiscal charges;

(*c*) The modification of domestic policies which stimulate uneconomic production and adversely affect trade;

(*d*) Guarantees ensuring to developing countries fair and reasonable shares of markets and market growth;

(*e*) The avoidance of subsidization of exports of primary commodities in a manner injurious to the exports of developing countries;

(*f*) The exercise of special care in the disposal of agricultural surpluses; and

(*g*) Equivalent positive measures by the socialist countries of Eastern Europe to expand imports of primary commodities from the developing countries, for example, by taking into account the trade needs of the developing countries when determining economic policies and/or fixing quantitative targets in long-term economic plans.

4. The substantive measures concerning access to primary commodity markets which are proposed in Board resolution 73 (X) and in the International Development Strategy are stated in less detail than those in the recommendation in annex A.II.1 of the 1964 Conference, and the relevant provisions omit explicit reference to certain elements of the latter. Nevertheless, it is notable that all three agreed texts include the two elements—a standstill on trade barriers, and the removal or reduction of barriers affecting trade in primary commodities of interest to developing countries. In Board resolution 73 (X), it was envisaged that the socialist countries of Eastern Europe should continue to foster the growth of commodity imports from developing countries and to this effect the measures envisaged in Conference resolution 15 (II) should be taken.

5. As regard the manner in which the intent of these resolutions should be translated into concrete action, the 1964 Conference proposed that action should be taken mainly through international commodity agreements or through appropriate national measures by developed countries, without an expectation of reciprocity by developing countries. The Board, in resolution 73 (X), envisaged that Governments and competent international institutions would take action to the fullest extent possible "either as an international co-operative endeavour or unilaterally", and paragraph 26 or the International Development Strategy requires that the agreed measures be implemented by Governments through international joint action or unilateral action. Both the Board's resolution and the International Development Strategy

---

[1] Although the Conference adopted the recommendation in annex A.II.1 formally without dissent, reservations were expressed by a number of delegations in the course of consideration of the subject in committee or in plenary meetings. For a brief account of these reservations see *Proceedings of the United Nations Conference on Trade and Development*, vol. I, *Final Act and Report* (United Nations publication, Sales No. 64.II.B.11) annex B to the Final Act, p. 66, and annex D to the report of the Conference, paras. 79-82.

[2] See *Proceedings of the United Conference on Trade and Development*, *Second Session*, vol. I and Corr.1 and 3 and Add.1 and 2, *Report and Annexes* (United Nations publication, Sales No. E.68.II.D.14), pp. 360-363.

[3] For the substance of comments and objections by certain delegations with respect to some of the provisions of Trade and Development Board resolution 73 (X) see *Official Records of the General Assembly*, *Twenty-fifth Session*, Supplement No. 15, part two, annex II.

call for the intensification of international consultations with the aim of reaching concrete and significant trade liberalization results early in the 1970s.

6. In the prefatory paragraph of resolution 73 (X)—which it considered was a step that could lead to the adoption of an international policy on primary commodities—the Board requested the Secretary-General of UNCTAD to submit to the Conference at its third session "proposals for future work" relating to the liberalization of trade in primary commodities (as well as pricing policy). The present report by the UNCTAD secretariat has been prepared accordingly. It follows a series of report by the UNCTAD secretariat on the subject of access to markets for primary commodities of interest to developing countries, some of which were submitted to the Conference at its first and second sessions[4] and others, on particular aspects or commodities, to the Committee on Commodities at certain of its sessions.[5]

7. In determining the scope and emphasis of this report, the secretariat has endeavoured to take account of a number of factors. First, in recent years practical measures to improve access to markets have been very limited in relation to the potential scope, and other developments or actions have tended to restrict access. Secondly, apart from the over-riding problem of the persistent foreign trade difficulties of developing countries, a number of new factors point to the rising economic costs

---

[4] See *Proceedings of the United Conference on Trade and Development*, vol. III, *Commodity Trade* (United Nations publication, Sales No. 64.II.B.13), "International Commodity Problems": Study by the Bureau of General Economic Research and Policies, United Nations Secretariat, chap. I; and *ibid.*, *Second Session*, vol. II, *Commodity Problems and Policies* (United Nations publication, Sales No. E.68.II.D.15), "The development of an international commodity policy: study by the UNCTAD secretariat (TD/8/Supp.1), chaps. V and VI, "Programme for the liberalization and expansion of trade in commodities of interest to developing countries: report by the UNCTAD secretariat" (TD/11/Supp.1), and "Trade barriers and liberalization possibilities in selected commodities: report by the UNCTAD secretariat" (TD/11/Supp.2).

[5] See, for example, "Study on certain temperate zone products: Market sharing-note by the UNCTAD secretariat" (TD/B/C.1/93); "Trends in markets of selected temperate zone products in five importing areas: note by the UNCTAD secretariat" (TD/B/C.1/108 and Corr.1).

of protectionism and, conversely, the increasing benefits to be derived by the international community from practical action to improve access to primary commodity markets. These include the increasing degrees of self-sufficiency in many developed importing countries with regard to major protected commodities, the likely effects on international commodity trade of the prospective enlargement of EEC, the opportunities created by the "green revolution", the increasing burdens borne by consumers and/or taxpayers in developed countries supporting high-cost domestic primary production, and the contribution which liberalization could make to checking the increasing rate of inflation in many developed countries. Thirdly, the limited progress so far achieved in improving access appears to indicate either that the political conviction of the merits and urgency of action has been insufficiently strong, given the undoubted difficulties which often stand in the way, or that arrangements have been deficient for the translation into practical measures of resolutions which have been adopted with very widespread, if not universal, agreement.

8. In these circumstances, the main objective of this report is to re-state the case for liberalization—now stronger than ever—from the standpoints of both protectionist developed countries and exporting developing countries—and, taking into account experience in this field to date, to explore ways and means by which concrete progress might be stimulated. Chapter II of the present report gives a brief account of major developments concerning access to primary commodity markets since the second session of the Conference; chapter III outlines the forms, extent and consequences of existing protective measures affecting trade in primary commodities; chapter IV re-examines the case for action to improve conditions of access; chapter V discusses alternative approaches to the problem of protectionism; chapter VI examines the problem of revenue duties and chapter VII reviews the question of equivalent measures by the socialist countries of Eastern Europe. For the reader's convenience, chapter I includes a summary of the factual and analytical content of the report and presents the secretariat's conclusions and proposals for future work toward improving access to primary commodity markets.

CHAPTER I

Summary, conclusions and proposals for future work

9. The factual information and the accompanying analysis presented in chapters II to VII of this report point to certain conclusions about the nature, importance and urgency of the problem of improving access to markets for primary commodities of export interest to developing countries; and they carry implications concerning the specific objectives and modalities of any future concerted efforts by the international community to deal with this long-standing problem.

10. As regards the character of the problem and the need for urgent international action to solve it, some relevant considerations which emerge from chapters II to VII are the following:

(a) Little, if any, over-all progress in improving access to primary commodity markets in industrial countries has been achieved since the second (or, indeed, since the first) session of the Conference, certain positive actions having been offset by negative actions or results (see chapter II, in which some national and international actions are reviewed).

(b) Measures in support of the domestic production of importable primary commodities remain very widespread in the industrial countries (see paragraphs 52 to 56, below). Such policies have involved increasing outlays by the taxpayers and consumers in these countries: for example, in four developed market economies, such outlays range from $21 to $24 billion a year, of which about $13 to $15 billion consists of budgetary outlays a sum far exceeding the rate of official aid flows to developing countries and the annual value of imports by all developed market economy countries, from developing countries, of agricultural commodities competing with protected domestic output of the commodities concerned (see paragraphs 57 to 61). The margins of protection are known to have increased in certain instances (see paragraph 68).

(c) The adverse trade effects of protectionism, arising from consequential reductions in consumption and increases in domestic output and self-sufficiency, have been compounded by the emergence (or increase) of exportable surpluses of protected commodities, which are often disposed of with export aids on third markets that are also of interest to developing exporting countries (see paragraphs 64, 65 and 67).

(d) The range of primary commodities the international trade in which is substantially affected by protectionism in developed areas includes nearly all the commodities produced in those areas—sugar, rice, other cereals, meats, oilseeds, oils and fats, tobacco, wine, fish, wool cotton and petroleum (see tables 1 to 3, annex).

(e) The potential benefits of action to improve access to primary commodity markets are very impressive, both for the developing exporting countries (see paragraphs 74 to 76) and for the liberalizing countries (see paragraphs 78 to 80). Some quantitative illustrations of the possible export gains for the developing countries of certain actions to provide improved access are given in paragraph 75, one calculation—based on the assumption of the complete removal of protection—giving a figure as high as $10 billion a year, and another—based on specified market-sharing arrangements—a figure of over $4 billion a year by 1980.

(f) Although the developing countries would benefit from any appreciable general expansion of international primary commodity trade, it would seem prudent that precautions should be taken in order to ensure that the developing countries receive a more-than-proportionate share of the benefits of any programme of action to improve access, with the intention that any such trade initiative should have a preferential character—one designed to benefit principally, although not exclusively, the developing exporting countries. Certain steps to this end, outlined in paragraph 85, include the selection of commodities in which the developing countries enjoy a large measure of competitiveness, and the adoption of a market-sharing approach involving the reservation of assured shares of consumption requirements in developed countries for developing countries. Certain techniques discussed in paragraph 85 also appear suitable for the purpose of according to the least developed among the developing countries more than proportionate benefits.

(g) The case for action to improve access to markets is reinforced by considerations related to the prospective enlargement of EEC (to include countries that are currently less protectionist than the Community in regard to primary commodities) and to the spread of the "green revolution", which accentuates the need for access to protected markets for cereals in developed countries (see paragraphs 72 and 73).

(h) Because of the stimulus which a given margin of protection can provide to the continuation of a trend towards increasing self-sufficiency in a protectionist country, a mere standstill on trade barriers, however valuable as a starting point, could quite possibly result in reduced scope for imports into that country; hence, a more positive approach is required in order to ensure export gains to supplying developing countries.

(i) Revenue duties charged by certain developed countries on imports of tropical beverage crops, and on certain other commodities not produced in those countries, impair the export earnings of the developing countries concerned; this situation calls for an approach which takes consideration of the fact that the revenues collected by the importing countries are typically greater than the value of the potential trade results from the removal of the duties (see chapter VI and table 4, annex).

A. Objectives of future work

11. If the necessary political will can be summoned by the whole international community, especially potential liberalizing countries, the general objective of future work on the problem of improving access to primary commodity markets might be to translate the general intent of existing resolutions on this subject (referred to in paragraphs 2 to 5, above) into practical arrangements for each commodity in each protectionist developed country, and the efficacy and value of such arrangements might be judged according to the degree of the country's commitment in concrete terms, in each instance, to the improvement of the market opportunities for developing supplying countries (due regard being paid to the interests of all competitive producing countries).

12. As regards protected commodities, attention should be concentrated on the desired trade results themselves rather than on the required adjustments in protective devices—which would vary from country to country, commodity to commodity and time to time, and which should be left for each Government to determine as it saw fit. The essential aim in respect of all protected primary commodities might be, as recommended by the Pearson Commission, "to assure that over time an increasing share of domestic consumption [in protectionist developed countries] is supplied by imports from developing countries".[6]

13. For each of those protected commodities in respect of which it is feasible to lay down target ratios of the volumes of consumption requirements to be imported, the developed countries concerned would, in a multilateral framework, determine and announce the specific proportions to be reserved, in the remaining years of the 1970s, for domestic producers and for imports and, within the latter category, for developing countries. The greatest benefits for developing supplying countries would arise from a gradual reduction of the volume of protected output; however, the developing countries would still benefit, and the volume of domestic output in the devel-

---

[6] See *Partners in Development: report of the Commission on International Development* (London, Pall Mall Press, 1969), p. 97, recommendation 2.

oped countries would not need to be reduced, if an increasing proportion of future consumption growth were reserved for developing countries. In order to overcome the problem posed by seasonal fluctuations in crops and imports requirements, performance might be measured according to the average relationship of imports to consumption over more than one year.

14. Such a market-sharing approach would seem applicable to several important primary commodities, including sugar, rice, beef and veal, unmanufactured tobacco, citrus fruits and possibly also oilseeds, oils and fats. All of these commodities are subject to significant trade impediments, and the developing countries account for either a dominant or an appreciable share of the collective imports of each of them into protectionist developed countries. In the case of sugar, a further circumstance which might obviate the need for any special measured additional to those outlined above is that not only do developing countries account for the bulk of world trade, but their share is largely protected through the export quota provisions of the International Sugar Agreement.

15. Developed countries which are net exporters of protected commodities with the aid of export subsidies might, in recognition of the fact that they thus pre-empt markets which might otherwise be supplied by developing countries, agree to freeze either the volume of subsidized exports to the markets of developed countries of the sums expended on such subsidies.

16. In instances in which the setting of targets expressed as ratios of the volumes of consumption to be supplied by imports from developing countries was found to be inapplicable for insuperable technical reasons, the developed countries concerned might undertake to seek to ensure that the values of imports of the commodities or commodity group in question increase at least at the same rates as the gross values of domestic output of competing commodities or commodity groups.

17. Progress in the liberalization of the protection, usually afforded through tariffs, of domestic processing of imported primary commodities in developed countries might be achieved through the inclusion of semi-processed and processed primary commodities within the scope of the GSP.

18. As regards the problem of revenue duties charged on imports of (non-competing) primary commodities from developing countries, governments might consider adopting one of the alternative approaches set out in paragraph 106, envisaging either the removal of the duties, or the refunding of part or all of the revenue proceeds as compensation for the export earnings "lost" by the developing countries (see chapter VI, below).

19. The socialist countries of Eastern Europe, in recognition of the *de facto* protection which they may provide for domestic production of importable primary commodities, might undertake explicit commitments concerning the equitable sharing of their consumption requirements between domestic sources and developing exporting countries. These countries might also undertake to reduce any undue differentials between the international c.i.f. prices of imported tropical products and the domestic

prices charged for such commodities, and increase imports accordingly (see chapter VII, below).

B. Some pre-conditions for substantial progress

20. Significant progress in the improvement of access implies the taking of concrete actions for the purpose of increasing imports, mostly in competition with domestic output, and would require much more resolute action to that end than Governments have been willing to contemplate in the past.

21. Some of the prerequisites for the achievement of substantial progress in improving access are the following. First, a greater realization of the irrationality, from an economic standpoint, of present protectionist policies and a greater political conviction as to the merits of liberalization—both for internal and external reasons—appear to be required. Second, greater willingness on the part of the Governments of protectionist countries to change methods of agricultural support—so as to minimize the adverse trade effects of existing policies—and to improve the availability of adjustment assistance for marginal producers adversely affected by trade liberalization, would be most helpful. Third, the vestiges of the traditional expectation of reciprocal concessions by beneficiary developing countries need to be discarded, whether any access commitments are envisaged within or outside the context of international commodity agreements. Fourth, the concept of "equality of sacrifice" on the part of liberalizing countries should cease to have an important influence in moves to improve access and, to the extent that Governments continue to attach importance to it, the concept should not be limited to actions concerning access or even to actions in the whole field of primary commodities. Finally, given the meagre results achieved in recent years through unilateral actions to reduce barriers to trade in primary commodities, it appears virtually essential that future moves to improve access should be taken to the maximum possible extent as an international co-operative endeavour within an appropriate consultative framework. Such a co-operative approach would help to ensure that Governments devote, on a continuing basis, that full measure of attention to the problem which agreed statements of principle seem to require.

C. Organizational arrangements for future work

22. Both the International Developemnt Strategy and Board resolution 73 (X) envisage the intensification of intergovernmental consultations, concerning access to primary commodity market, with the object of reaching concrete and significant results early in the 1970s. The nature of the arrangements to be made for such intensified consultations—a question which merits consideration by the Conference—should presumably reflect the importance and complexity of the task and the need for continuing discussions over a lengthy period.

23. Because of inter-relationships among various commodities and the advantages of a unified consultative framework, all primary commodities of special export

interest to developing countries for which access to markets in industrial countries is impeded should be included in any new initiative. The existence of specialized commodity bodies concerned with certain of those commodities would not seem to constitute sufficient reason for the exclusion of the commodities concerned from the scope of any consultative arrangements under such a broad-ranging trade initiative during the life of the initiative (for example, the Kennedy Round of negotiations between the contracting Parties to GATT covered a wide range of agricultural commodities, including several dealt with in specialized bodies). Specialized commodity bodies typically do not concentrate upon the problem of trade barriers and, if they administer an international commodity agreement, are usually preoccupied with aspects of the operation of the agreement. (For example, export quotas and prices—rather than trade barriers—are expected to be the chief issues for the next conference which is to review the operation of the current International Sugar Agreement.)

24. The appropriate forum for such intensive consultations would be one in which the political momentum and the likelihood of concrete results would be the greatest, account being taken of the breadth of membership, the priority accorded to the interests of developing countries and the character of the consultations. As far as developing exporting countries are concerned, these would not be negotiations, implying reciprocity, but discussions designed to elicit meaningful offers from prospective liberalizing countries concerning access to their markets for primary commodities of special export interest to developing countries.[7]

25. If Governments decided that the intensification of intergovernmental consultations concerning access to primary commodity markets should be undertaken within the framework of UNCTAD, any arrangements made should include provision for the establishment of several *ad hoc* consultative groups on selected commodities or groups of commodities—each of which might find it necessary to meet several times in the course of its work—and for the designation or establishment of an intergovernmental body which, at a senior level, would oversee the consultations on individual commodities, receive reports of their results, and examine certain general problems relating to access.

26. More specifically, and by way of illustration, either a special committee on access to primary commodity markets might be established, or the Committee on Commodities might meet in a series of special sessions devoted exclusively to the important and complex problem of improving access to markets. This body would set up *ad hoc* intergovernmental consultative groups on selected commodities which would presumably include, but not necessarily be limited to, sugar, rice, beef and veal, unmanufactured tobacco, citrus fruits, oilseeds, oils and fats, and tropical beverage crops; it would itself undertake the examination of common problems (such as export subsidies) and of primary production and support policies in each protectionist developed country, and it might also review the observance of the principle of standstill on trade barriers (after establishing criteria and procedures for such reviews).

27. The essential objective of the commodity groups, the membership of which would include the major developed market economy, socialist and developing countries concerned, would be to explore liberalization possibilities in respect of each commodity with a view to determining market-sharing arrangements or other specific measures for improving access, or at least assisting the potential liberalizing countries subsequently to formulate and announce such specific measures.

28. At an appropriate stage (say, within one to two years from the commencement of consultations), a high-level meeting of the Committee concerned might be held with a view to receiving the conclusions of protectionist countries regarding the specific steps which they proposed taking, in the light of the prior consultations, in order to improve access to their markets for each protected primary commodity of export interest to developing countries. The commodities covered by any such offers should be all the protected commodities, whether or not it had been found possible to have them examined by specialized groups within the consultative framework.

29. From an institutional standpoint, a new initiative launched in 1972 would have the advantage of the impetus to action which will no doubt be provided by the fact that FAO will concentrate attention upon the problem of agricultural adjustment in the course of 1972 and 1973, and of the valuable experience which the Governments of some developed market economy countries have gained in the course of the work recently carried out in various GATT groups, especially the discussions, on a problem-by-problem basis, within the GATT Agriculture Committee.

D. Principal policy issues

30. In the light of the present re-examination of the problem of improving access to primary commodity markets and, in particular, the conclusions set out in this chapter, it would appear that the principal issues concerning future moves to improve market access which merit the attention of the Conference are:

(*a*) The degree of priority which should be accorded by Governments to action for dealing with the problem;

(*b*) The extent to which efforts to improve access should be undertaken jointly as part of an international co-operative endeavour;

---

[7] Recent proposals by certain developed countries for the inauguration of intensive multilateral negotiations concerning agricultural trade barriers offer, from the standpoint of developing exporting countries, a potential opportunity for international co-operative action which could bring them important trade benefits. At the same time, they pose a serious risk that, if problems of access are tackled chiefly with a view to the negotiation of reciprocal concessions among interested developed countries, the interests of the developing countries would receive only cursory attention. Very careful consideration would therefore appear to be required on the part of Governments with a view to determining the appropriate framework for the particular kind of trade initiative proposed in this report, if this is considered to merit acceptance, or for any alternative programme of action which might be adopted.

(c) The specific substantive objectives of, and approaches to be followed in, future co-operative work; and

(d) The nature of any operational arrangements which should be made, and the time-table, for such work.

The secretariat's purpose in preparing the present report is to provide a basis—consisting of factual information, analysis and tentative suggestions—for such an "action-oriented" review by the Conference.

CHAPTER II

Developments since the second session of the Conference

31. In the period since March 1968, as formerly, national actions—taken by the developed countries essentially in the light of international considerations—rather than multilateral actions have constituted the main influences on conditions of access to primary commodity markets. One notable exception is the GSP, which has been established as an international co-operative endeavour, although it needs to be borne in mind that it is of marginal applicability to primary commodity trade.

A. Some national actions

32. The basic policy of supporting domestic primary production, which is common to the major industrial countries and is the mainspring of the impediments to imports of primary commodities into these countries, was maintained during the period under review, the principal change being the decision of the United Kingdom Government gradually to change its system of agricultural support to that used by EEC.

33. In EEC, the coverage of the Common Agricultural Policy was extended to additional commodities—notably wine, tobacco and fishery products[8]—and the levels of the support prices of the main agricultural commodities were increased on several occasions during the period. In continuation of a long-term trend, the budgetary cost of support of agricultural markets increased in step with the rising levels of support prices and the growth of agricultural production, leading to surpluses in certain commodities[9] and a consequential increase in the cost of export subsidies. Government expenditures in support of agricultural markets in the Community increased from about $500 million in 1960 to $1,500 million in 1967 and $2,400 million in 1969. Total government expenditure for agriculture in EEC (including, in addition to market support, structural and other measures and social benefits) rose from $2,100 million in 1960 to $5,100 million in 1967 and about $6,250 million in 1969.[10] As a result of a growing recognition within EEC of the problems associated with

the Common Agricultural Policy, prolonged deliberations on the reform of agriculture—on which the Commission of the European Communities had presented proposals[11]—culminated in the adoption by the EEC Council of Ministers, in March 1971, of an agricultural adjustment programme which included novel elements, such as assistance for persons leaving farming and assistance to enable selected farmers to expand the size of their operations. However, it was found necessary in the circumstances prevailing at the time to announce increases in the levels of support prices for 1971 in conjunction with the agricultural adjustment programme.

34. In the United Kingdom, where for over twenty years agriculture has been supported through a system of free market prices accompanied by government deficiency payments to farmers to bring unit returns to guaranteed levels,[12] the Government announced in October 1970 that it would aim "to adapt the present system of agricultural support to one relying increasingly on import levy arrangements, under which the farmer will get his return increasingly from the market".[13] A system of minimum import prices, backed as necessary by variable import levies, had been introduced in 1964 in respect of cereals, and the Government's intention, as announced in October 1970, was to introduce as soon as possible interim levy schemes in respect of beef and veal, of mutton and lamb and of milk products other than butter and cheese, and to modify the existing scheme for cereals. Such a change in the method of price support implies higher market prices for agricultural commodities, involving greater outlays by consumers, with consequential economies in government payments. In November 1968, the United Kingdom Government had announced that it would continue to 1972/73 its policy of selective expansion of agriculture and that priority would continue to be given to wheat and barley, beef and pigmeat.[14] Accordingly, the guaranteed prices of these commodities were raised appreciably (by amounts varying between 17 and 34 per cent) between the 1967/68 and the 1971/72 seasons. The estimated cost of Exchequer support of agriculture by means of deficiency payments and production grants and subsidies has remained in recent years at a level equal to about $650 million a year, equivalent on average, in the last three

---

[8] In addition, in the period under review, common prices throughout EEC came into effect in respect of a number of commodities—notably sugar, beef and veal, and milk products—for which a common market organization had been introduced before 1968.

[9] The EEC does not maintain production controls on the major agricultural commodities, with the sole exception of sugar.

[10] See Secretariat General of the Commission, *Memorandum on the Reform of Agriculture in the European Economic Community, Supplement No. 1 (1969) of the Bulletin of the European Communities,* annex 21; Commission of the European Communities "The Agricultural Situation in the EEC", *Newsletter on the Common Agricultural Policy,* No. 1, January 1971 (66/X/71-E); The Atlantic Institute, "A Future for European Agriculture", *The Atlantic Papers 4* (Paris, 1970), p. 57.

[11] Secretariat General of the Commission, op cit.

[12] As exceptions to the general rule, the cost of the guarantees for milk and sugar was borne by the consumer as a result of fixed market prices.

[13] See United Kingdom, Ministry of Agriculture, Fisheries and Food, *Annual Review and Determination of Guarantees 1971,* Cmnd. 4623 (London, H.M. Stationery Office, March 1971), p. 5.

[14] See United Kingdom, Ministry of Agriculture, Fisheries and Food, *Annual Review and Determination of Guarantees 1969,* Cmnd. 3965 (London, H.M. Stationery Office), p. 5.

completed financial years, to a little over one-tenth of farmers' total gross receipts and nearly one-half of the "net income of agriculture", as officially defined.

35. Japan has, by and large, maintained its system of protection of many temperate zone products through quantitative import restrictions and/or State monopoly trading and internal support prices. About two-thirds of the value of total agricultural output was affected by price support and/or stabilization measures in 1966,[15] and it is likely that this proportion has been at least sustained in more recent years. Direct public expenditure for agriculture totalled $2,120 million in 1968,[16] most of this being devoted to the support of agricultural prices. The budgetary cost of support of agricultural prices, which amounted to $90 million in 1960 and $446 million in 1965, rose to $1,530 million in 1968; it then fell to $1,210 million in 1969. The main individual commodity which accounted for this sharp increase was rice,[17] of which the support price—the highest in the world[18]—was raised by 26 per cent between 1965 and 1968. No doubt as a result of the high degree of official support for the rice industry, Japan changed from the position of a net rice importer in 1966 to that of a net rice exporter by 1970 and accumulated vast surplus rice stocks. However, the Government decided to set a limit to its rice purchases as from the 1971 crop[19] and is aiming to diversify agriculture to certain other crops, such as fruits and vegetables, dairy products and livestock. Another important objective of agricultural policy in Japan is to reduce the number of farming households and to expand the size of the average farm.

36. Certain liberalization measures taken in Japan in the course of 1971 resulted in the removal of the quantitative restrictions which previously applied to tungsten ore, certain fruits and vegetables, live animals, pigmeat, black tea, and to several oilseeds, oils and oilcakes of interest to developing countries—namely groundnuts and oil, cottonseed oil and sunflower seed oil. These measures constitute significant progress in the improvement of access for primary commodity imports. However, a number of important comodities—notably rice, beef and veal, dairy products, oranges and tangerines, and fish—remain subject to measures of support of domestic production and/or limitation of imports.

37. United States commodity policies affecting conditions of access for primary commodities of interest to developing countries changed little during the period under review. The broad pattern of domestic agricultural support, typically involving price supports accompanied by quantitative import restrictions and provision for the payment of export subsidies, was maintained. However, the policy trend toward restraining output in surplus commodities was reinforced by linking certain subsidies to controls on supplies.[20] Total government expenditure on agriculture and rural development rose from about $5,000 million a year in the mid-1960s to over $6,000 million a year in 1969 and 1970, although the rate of expenditure has declined somewhat since. The cost of "farm income stabilization"—included in the totals just cited—has recently amounted to between $4,000 million and $5,000 million per year. With regard to sugar, the United States, which is the world's leading importer and pays premium prices for imports, maintained its system of allocating import quotas on a country-by-country basis, combined with the reservation of about three-fifths of total requirements for domestic suppliers. The Act embodying the United States sugar régime was extended for a period of three years, until the end of 1974, without major changes other than a reduction in the national reserve for Cuba.[21]

38. Between about mid-August and mid-December 1971, the United States Administration applied a temporary surcharge on dutiable imports not subject to quantitative restrictions, generally at a rate of 10 per cent *ad valorem* (on f.o.b. prices). The surcharge, which applied to many unprocessed and processed agricultural products as well as certain minerals and metals—including copper, lead and zinc—was removed after the adoption of new exchange parities for certain currencies, including the United States dollar.

B. International action and discussions

39. Multilateral discussions regarding barriers to trade in primary commodities continued in the principal international bodies concerned, comprising UNCTAD, GATT, FAO and autonomous international commodity bodies.

40. After the meagre results of the Kennedy Round of trade negotiations in improving conditions of access to markets for primary commodities—non-tariff barriers and agricultural support policies were unaffected—GATT has been examining, principally through its Agriculture Committee, ways and means of achieving progress in this field. This work represents "... a renewed effort ... in GATT to

[15] See OECD, *Agricultural Policies in 1966: Europe, North America, Japan* (Paris, 1967), p. 343.

[16] See OECD, *Inflation: The Present Problem—Report by the Secretary-General* (Paris, 1970), p. 99.

[17] See Japan, Economic Planning Agency, *Economic Survey of Japan (1969-1970)* (Tokyo, 1970), p. 175.

[18] See FAO, *Report of the Fifteenth Session of the Study Group on Rice to the Committee on Commodity Problems* (CCP 71/5, May 1971), para. 59.

[19] *Ibid.* The impact of this move on the total output of rice might be rather limited since producers were permitted to sell rice on the free market.

[20] Thus, it has been stated that "more than half of the wheat payments and almost all feed grain payments in 1970 were judged to be necessary to prevent burdensome supplies at current price support levels" (United States Commission on International Trade and Investment Policy (Chairman: Albert L. Williams): *United States International Economic Policy in an Interdependent World: Report to the President* (Washington, D.C., Government Printing Office, July 1971), pp. 158-159). (This report is hereinafter referred to as the "Williams Commission report".) However, with respect to cotton—another commodity subject to controls on supply—the Commission reported an estimate "that in 1970 nearly the entire $900 million of payments to cotton producers was an income subsidy which did not serve to control supply. With smaller payments, it is likely that less, not more cotton would have been produced" (*ibid.*, p. 158).

[21] The Williams Commission had recommended in July 1971 "that the United States take advantage of the expiration of the Sugar Act at the end of 1971 to modify its provisions to open a larger share of our market to imports and at the same time lower the price of sugar to U.S. consumers" (*ibid.*, p. 162).

lay the basis for negotiations directed towards the liberalization of trade in farm goods. In this area, a great amount of time and effort has been spent over the past three years in determining the facts, appraising their significance in trade terms, and in exploring possible mutually acceptable solutions to the principal problems. Here the work has focussed not only on the area of import restraints and export aids, but also on what has become clear to all is probably the most important area: production policies.[22] The agriculture Committee has approached its task on a problem-by-problem rather than a commodity-by-commodity basis (the latter having been the approach until the conclusion of the Kennedy Round).

41. Apart from the Agriculture Committee, several other GATT bodies—notably the Committee on Trade and Development, the Group on Residual Restrictions, the Joint Working Group on Import Restrictions and the Special Group on Tropical Products—have responsibilities with respect to the reduction or elimination of barriers to trade in primary commodities and have been endeavouring, through intergovernmental discussions, to promote concrete action. Both the Group on Residual Restrictions and the Joint Working Group on Import Restrictions have been concerned with identifying the import restrictions applicable to a group of products of interest to developing countries and have been examining, on a product-by-product basis, the grounds on which restrictions are maintained and the possibilities of achieving the removal or relaxation of existing barriers. The Special Group on Tropical Products, which was reactivated in November 1967, has been concerned mainly with exploring the possibility of achieving the elimination or reduction of import duties, internal charges and quantitative restrictions affecting the major groups of tropical products, such as tea, coffee, cocoa, bananas, spices and vegetable oils and oilseeds.

42. Within FAO, the specialized commodity groups—now numbering eleven—which report to the Committee on Commodity Problems have tended to address themselves more closely to policy problems, especially supply/demand adjustments, and have increasingly discussed problems arising from trade barriers. Although not all of these FAO study groups (recently re-named intergovernmental commodity groups) are concerned with commodities confronting significant trade barriers, many of them are, and the possibilities of trade liberalization have been discussed in recent meetings of the Groups dealing with oilseeds, oils and fats, bananas, rice and meat. However, in keeping with the broad terms of reference of the groups and the characteristic attitude of their members to the discussion of policy proposals, the groups concerned have tended to deal with numerous aspects of the production, consumption, marketing, trade in and prices of each of the commodities under review and have not concentrated specifically upon the exceedingly difficult policy problems of improving access to markets.[23]

43. A decision by the FAO Conference in 1971 to accept a proposal by the Director-General that the subject of international agricultural adjustment should be a major theme of the FAO Conference in 1973 represents a new FAO initiative which should promote a greater appreciation by the international community of the need for action to improve conditions of access to markets for agricultural products. This decision follows agreement at the 1969 Conference that there was an urgent need for adjustment, including supply management, in international and national policies. It is stated that "The aim would be to reach at the 1973 Conference Session a consensus among FAO member Governments on the main aspects of the problem of agricultural adjustment, the main lines of approach at the international level, and the further concrete action to be taken by FAO itself."[24]

44. The GSP, concluded under UNCTAD auspices and already implemented by the beginning of 1972 by most of the principal industrial countries, represents a signal advance in trade liberalization for development. However, its benefits to developing countries apply essentially to manufactures and semi-manufactures; it concerns only tariffs and applies to relatively few primary commodities, and, in any event, non-tariff barriers constitute the principal impediments to commodity trade. In determining their offers, the preference-giving countries conceived of the System as not applying in principle to primary commodities—mainly items in BTN chapters 1 to 24. Nevertheless, nearly all countries have included selected processed and semi-processed agricultural products covered by BTN chapters 1 to 24 within their referential arrangements—for example, copra, cocoa paste and butter, preparations of flour and certain vegetables and fruits and fruits juices—although none of these items has been included by all preference-giving countries and some items have been included by a few countries only. Moreover, certain minerals and metals, which are subject to import duties in certain developed market economy countries—for example, phosphatic fertilizers and ferromanganese—are covered by the GSP although they fall within BTN chapters 25 to 99, but petroleum and petroleum products are specifically excluded from the GSP by leading preference-giving countries. As explained elsewhere,[25] the GSP

---

meeting in November 1970. Its report on this aspect provides a good illustration of the typical outcome of international discussions to date, whether in FAO or elsewhere, on non-tariff barriers to trade in primary commodities produced in both developed and developing countries; the relevant passage reads: "*Reduction of trade barriers:* The Working Party considered the suggestion that trade barriers on imports of rice should be reduced in developed countries so as to ensure free access to exports from developing countries. It concluded that this approach would not be generally acceptable to all countries. The removal of tariff and other barriers, although desirable in principle, would not be possible within the existing institutional framework in several countries, and as they were considered necessary by some countries as an indispensable measure of self-protection of the domestic rice industry". (*Report of the Fifteenth Session of the Study Group on Rice*..., annex D, para. 10, ii.) On the other hand, the Study Group on Bananas, in its report on its fourth session, held in May 1971, noted that discussions on barriers to imports had produced useful results (see FAO document CCP 71/6), para. 36.

[24] See FAO, *Perspective Study of World Agricultural Development and International Strategy for the Second Development Decade* (C 71/41), para. 7.

[25] See (TD/124, p. 104 below).

---

[22] Gardner Patterson (Assistant Director-General of GATT), "Current GATT Work on Trade Barriers", Williams Commission report, *Papers I*, p. 640.

[23] For example, an *Ad Hoc* Working Party on International Action on Rice set up by the FAO Study Group on Rice considered reduction of trade barriers as one of 15 possible lines of action at a

initially has a limited duration and the preferences accorded under it are variable in depth and are subject to certain safeguards and other conditions.

45. Discussions of the problem of trade barriers in the context of international commodity agreements and autonomous commodity study groups continued to be characterized by a lack of apparent concrete results, although the International Sugar Agreement of 1968 included novel provisions concerning access to markets.

46. Under the terms of the International Sugar Agreement of 1968, which entered into force on 1 January 1969, certain developed importing countries—notably Canada, Japan and the United Kingdom—made commitments concerning access for sugar imports. Canada undertook to operate its internal policies so as not to provide incentives to sugar production beyond a level representing 20 per cent of domestic consumption; Japan undertook to import not less than 1,500,000 tons a year and, in addition, a quantity equivalent to 35 per cent of the future growth of its annual domestic consumption over 2,100,000 tons; and the United Kingdom stated that it would import each year not less than 1,800,000 tons of sugar. However, these commitments remained well within the limits of past import performance and did not constitute an improvement on previous degrees of access. For example, in the three years 1966-1968, Canada's degree of self-sufficiency in sugar averaged 14 per cent and Japan's net imports averaged 1,698,000 tons, representing 75 per cent of average consumption of 2,256,000 tons.

47. The Wheat Trade Convention 1971, like all international wheat agreements concluded as from 1959, contains no obligations concerning policies, such as production policies, affecting access to markets.[26] In contrast, the first three international wheat agreements concluded after the Second World War (in 1949, 1953 and 1956) incorporated a system of guaranteed purchases by member importing countries which would be applicable when prices on the international market fell to the minima of the price ranges incorporated in the agreements.[27] The text of the International Coffee Agreement as renegotiated in 1968 retained the substance of an article regarding the removal of obstacles to increased trade in, and consumption of, coffee and the International Coffee Council has continued to discuss the problem of trade barriers from time to time. The International Olive Oil Agreement does not contain any provisions relating to access to markets.

48. Of the autonomous commodity study groups, the International Lead and Zinc Study Group decided at its session in 1969 to collate and examine information on tariffs and non-tariff barriers affecting world trade in lead and zinc, and has further discussed this subject at its subsequent sessions.

49. The next chapter gives an account of the existing protective measures affecting trade in primary commodities, the over-all extent and incidence of which—as is apparent from the foregoing outline of recent developments—have not diminished and have probably increased, since the second session of the Conference, certain positive actions having been offset by other actions or influences.

[26] Indeed, the Wheat Trade Convention of 1971, unlike immediately preceding international agreements on wheat, contains no price provisions or related rights and obligations.

[27] However, as prices did not fall to the specified minima, this provision did not become effective.

CHAPTER III

Existing protection: forms, extent and consequences

50. In any examination of the problem of improving access to markets in industrial countries for primary commodities of export interest to developing countries, governmental measures maintained in the former for the purpose of protecting domestic production from import competition assume prime importance; they are the subject of this chapter. Trade in certain commodities is also impeded by measures taken essentially for revenue-raising purposes; these are discussed in chapter VI.

51. Impediments to trade may also arise from certain measures taken without commercial policy objectives—such as food regulations maintained on grounds of health or safety, or compulsory technical specifications[28] or other administrative rules—or from technical problems.[29]

[28] See, for example, R. W. Middleton, "Technical Specifications—a Case Study of Non-tariff Barriers to Trade", *EFTA Bulletin*, vol. XII, No. 2, March 1971, p. 4, and No. 3, April 1971, p. 6.

[29] For example, in relation to improved forms of natural rubber, problems of identifying them correctly and classifying them accurately and explicitly in the tariff schedules of many countries appear to have led to the application of higher rates of duties in some instances than the improved rubbers would attract if they were correctly classified (see " Barriers to trade in raw, semi-processed and improved forms of natural rubber: note by the UNCTAD secretariat"

Health regulations governing imports can have serious restrictive effects upon imports, especially of meat and livestock. Apart from the possibility that such regulations may in some instances set unduly high standards, the lack of uniformity among importing countries in the standards laid down and the fact that they are liable to unpredictable changes in themselves constitute trade impediments. The remedy would appear to be largely the international harmonization of the standards concerned. Because such barriers to trade are presumably inadvertent, because of their highly technical nature and because they are not, on the whole, nearly as serious as commercial policy impediments, they are not further examined in the present study. In a few instances—for example, in respect of bananas in the United Kingdom—import restrictions are maintained for the purpose of safeguarding the trade of preferred trading partners. Nevertheless, the distinction drawn in paragraph 50 between protective and (non-protective) revenue-raising measures seems a valid and useful one for analytical and policy purposes, because it covers almost

(TD/B/C.1/SYN/24 and Corr.1) and "Removal of barriers to trade in raw, semi-processed and improved forms of natural rubber" (TD/B/C.1/ SYN/53).

the whole range of existing impediments maintained for purposes of economic policy.

A. Purposes and forms of protective measures

52. The essential purpose of governmental measures in the industrial countries to protect primary industries against competition from imports is to support the levels of employment and, in particular, the incomes of producers in those industries at levels higher than would prevail in the absence of governmental intervention. It is frequently the specific purpose to eliminate or reduce the gap between incomes in the agricultural sector and those in the rest of the economy.

53. Although having essentially similar objectives, the systems of support for domestic primary industries used in the industrial countries vary in the extent to which Governments intervene in the market place and in the extent to which the costs of support are borne by the Government or by consumers. In the United Kingdom, the traditional method of support has been to interfere with the free market as little as possible—by avoiding taking actions directly affecting the prices of imported commodities—and to supplement the unit returns of producers from the market with deficiency payments, to bring them to guaranteed levels. On the other hand, the established method of support in EEC, while also involving the determination of target unit returns, embraces measures controlling the prices of imports, by the maintenance of a system of variable import levies designed to ensure that imports are not available for less than the frontier equivalents of the internal target prices, and the acquisition by official agencies of surplus quantities of domestic output. Hence, in EEC, consumers pay for much of the cost of agricultural support as a result of the maintenance of internal market prices at high levels, whereas in the United Kingdom the citizens pay for most of the cost as taxpayers. The extent of official intervention in agricultural markets in the United States and Japan is intermediate between that prevailing in the United Kingdom and that in EEC.[30] However, the Governments of all major industrial countries provide subsidies, to varying degrees, for selected inputs or services utilized by the farm sector, and for structural improvements in farming.

54. The main elements in the systems of support of primary production practised in industrial countries are apparent or may be deduced from the foregoing paragraph. They are internal measures controlling or influencing domestic market prices of primary commodities, the granting of deficiency payments and other subsidies and grants to producers and—as concomitants of the policies of support—restraints at the frontier affecting either the volumes or prices, or both, of importable primary commodities which compete with domestic output, often accompanied by export aids to divert surplus output to external markets.

55. More specifically, protective measures at the frontier take the following forms: (a) quantitative import restrictions—which determine the volumes of imports irrespective of price changes; (b) variable import levies—which are varied so as to support domestic market prices at pre-determined levels, with the result that the scope for imports becomes residual and more unpredictable; and (c) tariffs expressed in *ad valorem* or specific terms, or a mixture of these. Measures (a) and (b), under which the volume of imports is determined or closely affected by administrative decisions, present the main obstacle for unprocessed primary commodities, although tariff barriers assume importance in relation to commodities which have undergone some processing.

56. The extent and general nature of the non-tariff barriers applying to imports of primary commodities into the leading industrial countries are shown in annex, table 1, and tariffs on selected primary and processed commodities are listed (after conversion of specific duties into estimated *ad valorem* equivalents) in table 2. Since variable levies have a tariff-like effect in so far as the admitted volume of imports is concerned, EEC's variable levies can be expressed in *ad valorem* equivalents; this has been done for recent years in table 3. (The incidence of trade barriers by commodities is discussed in paragraphs 66-70.)

B. Extent of support

57. The economic burden imposed on taxpayers and/or consumers in the protectionist developed countries through policies of agricultural support is enormous, amounting—in respect of EEC, Japan, United Kingdom and United States—to about $21 to $24 billion annually.

58. In a report to the 1964 Conference, it was estimated that, in the year 1962, the taxpayers or consumers in EEC, the United Kingdom and the United States devoted an estimated $10 billion in support of domestic agriculture through direct subsidies to producers or through the payment of managed prices above the levels prevailing in free markets.[31] This estimate now needs to be raised to reflect the increases which have occurred since then in the financial outlays of Governments (see paragraphs 33-37 above) in the levels of protection and in the volumes of output of which the prices are managed.

59. The components of the present estimate of over $21 to 24 billion of outlays by taxpayers and/or consumers are itemized below:

(a) EEC — budgetary outlays of $6.2 billion in 1969, from which $2.0 billion, collected in variable import levies, may be deduced, leaving $4.2 billion; outlays by consumers estimated in the range of $6 to 8 billion; making a total of $10.2 to 12.2. billion[32] (equivalent to

---

[30] It is significant, however, that limitations on the volumes of output which are eligible for price support have been increasingly applied in the United States, in contrast to the situation in EEC and the United Kingdom.

[31] See *Proceedings of the United Nations Conference on Trade and Development*, vol. III, *Commodity Trade* (United Nations publication, Sales No. 64.II.B.13), p. 26.

[32] Account has been taken of the following recent estimates. The secretariat of the Commission of the European Communities has estimated the total value of support of farm income in EEC at $9.6 billion in the year 1967 ("Comparison of Agricultural Support Systems in the United States and the Community", *Newsletter on the Common Agricultural Policy*, No. 5, May 1971); The Atlantic Institute has estimated that "... to seven thousand million dollars of public expenditure must be added six to eight thousand million dollars additional burden which the consumers of the Community

(Continend on next page.)

between 2.4 and 2.9 per cent of the Community's GNP in 1969).

(b) Japan — budgetary outlay of $2.1 billion in 1968.

(c) United Kingdom — budgetary outlay of $0.66 billion in 1969/70; outlays by consumers estimated at $0.40 billion,[33] making a total of $1.1 billion.

(d) United States — budgetary outlay of $6.2 billion (of which $4.6 billion was devoted to stabilization of farm incomes) in the 1970 fiscal year; outlays by consumers of possibly $2.0 billion (in respect of sugar and certain other commodities subject to quantitative import restrictions); making a total of $8.2 billion.

60. The foregoing estimates, although incomplete so far as the developed areas of the world are concerned, provide substantial evidence of the great importance which major developed countries attach to the objective of achieving or sustaining standards of living considered reasonable for their own primary producers. It is significant that, in a study carried out by the secretariat of the European Communities, it was concluded that "if direct agricultural support were withdrawn, farm income in the United States would decline by about 44 per cent and farm income in EEC by about 50 per cent".[34]

61. The magnitude of the annual budgetary outlay of $13.2 billion (or $15.2 billion before deduction of the proceeds of variable import levies)[35] and the total outlay of about $21 to $24 billion in support of domestic agriculture in the major developed market economy countries may be seen in perspective when compared with

(a) The net official flow of financial resources from all developed market-economy countries to multilateral institutions and to developing countries, amounting to $7.0 billion in 1969 and $7.7 billion in 1970;

(b) The total annual value (about $9 billion in 1969) of imports by all developed market economy countries, from

developing countries, of agricultural commodities in competition with domestic production of like or competing natural commodities, whether protected or not; and

(c) The total annual value (estimated at about $5 billion in 1969) of imports by all developed market economy countries, from developing countries, of agricultural commodities in competition with protected domestic output of the commodities concerned.

These imports were, of course, less than they otherwise would have been, owing to the measures maintained in support of primary industries in the developed countries concerned, for most of these measures served to stimulate domestic production and so displace imports—subject to the qualification that part of the budgetary outlays in the United States was payable on condition that limitations as to areas harvested or volumes produced or marketed were observed by farmers.

C. Consequences

62. The main effects of protection upon market outlets available to external suppliers are twofold. First, consumption of the commodities concerned is reduced, particularly in respect of items for which demand is readily affected by price changes or the prices of which are greatly increased as a result of the trade barriers. Second, domestic production of the commodities concerned is stimulated and, to that extent, the potential market for (lower-cost) imports is pre-empted. The associated transfer costs in the protectionist countries are represented by the financial outlays mentioned in paragraph 59.[36]

63. Although the price elasticity of demand for many agricultural products is quite low, for some—for example, meats and fruits—demand is appreciably affected by the price increases in question, and for others—for example, sugar (as in Japan)—the prices are so much higher that the effect on consumption can become significant.[37]

64. However, the stimulus given to production has, generally speaking, a more adverse effect on international trade than does the consumption effect, in that it raises the degree of self-sufficiency or sustains it in circumstances in which it might have declined. The data in table 5 in the annex show that the degree of self-sufficiency have indeed risen for a number of important commodities in major

---

(Footnote 32 continued.)

bear in the form of inflated prices. The tax levies which raise the import prices help to finance public expenditure which, however, amounts to some two thousand million dollars, and this latter sum should not be included both in higher prices and in public support expenditures. With that correction the burden appears to be in the range of eleven to thirteen thousand million dollars per year" (The Atlantic Institute, op. cit., p. 9); Richard W. Howarth has estimated the total agricultural support in EEC (borne by taxpayers and consumers) at $10.5 billion in 1968-69 (*Agricultural Support in Western Europe*, The Institute of Public Affairs, Research Monographs 25, London, 1971, pp. 40 and 44).

[33] Concerning one element of consumer subsidy, see Richard W. Howarth, op. cit., p. 34.

[34] See "Comparison of Agricultural Support Systems in the United States and the Community", *Newsletter on the Common Agricultural Policy*, No. 5, May 1971.

[35] This sum is broadly consistent with the figure of $14 billion of "direct public expenditure for agriculture" in 1968 (or 1968/69) which is given by the OECD for a group of countries which is roughly comparable, excluding some members of the EEC but including certain other members of the OECD. It is stated that "For the eleven Member countries for which figures are available for 1968, total public expenditure on agricultural policies amounted to $14 billion, or on average, about one per cent of GNP... If, in addition, the indirect cost to the consumer from protection at the frontier could be quantified, the total cost of present agricultural policies would be seen to be substantially higher". OECD, *Inflation...*, para. 158.

[36] The complete removal of protection by all developed countries would, of course, result in increases in the free market prices of practically all of the commodities concerned, and to that extent the transfer costs of protection aggregated for those countries tend to overstate the real costs for them as a group. However, for each country and for each decision whether to maintain existing protection or to liberalize trade—that is, at the practical level—the existing price at which imports could be obtained is the relevant one, not that which would exist under hypothetical conditions of completely free trade throughout the world. Seen in this light, the transfer costs cited in paragraph 59 remain valid indicators of misallocations of resources and carry practical implications for policy.

[37] The system of deficiency payments to agricultural producers which has been traditionally followed in the United Kingdom (and which the Government is now in the process of abandoning) thus has the relative advantage of not discouraging consumption of the commodities concerned.

industrial countries and, where the reverse has happened, it may reasonably be assumed that, in the absence of protection, the share of consumption met by imports would have increased more than it did. In some instances, protectionism results in the emergence for the first time in a formerly net importing country,[38] or in the increase, of exportable surpluses, which are frequently disposed of with the aid of export subsidies on other markets of interest to developing countries.

65. It follows that, as a result of protectionism in industrial countries, the market opportunities of developing (and other) exporters of primary commodities are adversely affected in the markets of the protectionist countries and in the commercial markets of third countries to which the affluent countries send any surpluses. These impediments thus limit the growth of the over-all export earnings of the developing countries, they often circumscribe the scope for the diversification of the exports of these countries,[39] and thus compound their foreign trade difficulties which arise out of such uncontrollable factors as the relatively slow growth of world requirements of foodstuffs and the competition which some natural products face from synthetics and substitutes.

D. Commodities principally affected

66. The commodities the international trade in which is substantially affected by protective measures in industrial countries include foodstuffs such as sugar, cereals—wheat, coarse grains and rice—meats, citrus fruits, dairy products, fish and wine; and raw materials such as oilseeds, oils and fats, tobacco,[40] cotton, wool and petroleum (see annex, table 1). The trade impact of protective measures is wider in scope than appears at first sight, given, for example, the interchangeability which exists among certain fats and oils and such indirect impediments as that affecting hides and skins as a consequence of the stimulus given to livestock production. Hence, among the commodities which are affected by trade barriers are some which are of actual or potential export interest to all of the developing countries, including the least developed and land-locked developing countries.

67. As can be seen from column B of table 1, the commodities exports of which are frequently subsidized or sold on concessional terms include most of those just mentioned, the most important ones in this context being rice, other cereals, sugar, tobacco, cotton and oilseeds, oils and fats. The effects of such export aids on the export trade of developing countries are particularly adverse because these countries are not in a position to match the easy terms offered by the affluent countries.

68. The margins of (nominal) protection in EEC—for which information is most readily available—represented by the excess of domestic prices over import prices—increased markedly between the periods 1956/57-1968/59 and 1970/71 for several major commodities—including sugar (from a range of 2 to 45 per cent, among the individual members of the Community, to 110 per cent for the Community as a whole), wheat (from a range of $+41/-24$ per cent to 89 per cent), and barley and butter.[41]

69. The current margins of (nominal) protection for the principal commodities are very substantial in both EEC[42] and in Japan,[43] and somewhat lower in the United Kingdom[44] and the United States.[45]

70. The degree of effective protection for domestic production and processing of primary commodities if often much higher than the nominal levels of protection would indicate. This can be the consequence of non-tariff barriers, which have been shown to result in extremely high effective protection in certain instances,[46] and of the

---

[38] For example, the FAO secretariat has reported that "As a result of Japan turning from one of the world's largest importers [of rice] to the fifth biggest exporter, the combined effect on the international trade has been considerable, i.e. in the region of 1.4 million tons between 1966 and 1970. While the cessation of imports has created problems for some of its traditional suppliers, the increase in concessional exports from Japan at a time when world markets are already weak has created additional problems for the traditional exporting countries". (*Report of the Fifteenth Session of the Study Group on Rice...*, para. 59.) Moreover, EEC as a whole had emerged for the first time in 1970 as a net rice exporter on a small scale (*ibid.*, para. 64).

[39] The Advisory Committee to the Board and to the Committee on Commodities, reporting on its special (sixth) session, held in March-April 1971 and devoted to the subject of diversification, "emphasized that while diversification required the application of vigorous and coherent policies by the developing countries concerned, its scope would be severely limited without effective concomitant action on the part of developed countries. The first requirement was a significant improvement in the conditions of access to the markets of the industrial countries. It was agreed that important opportunities for horizontal diversification would be opened up for developing countries if there was a reduction in the protection given in developed countries to production of temperate zone agricultural commodities such as rice, sugar, oils and fats, meat, cotton and tobacco. It was noted that such products were excluded from the generalized system of preferences recently agreed in UNCTAD, and it was felt that a new international initiative was needed to bring about some progress on this issue". See *Official Records of the Trade and Development Board, Eleventh Session, Annexes*, agenda item 7, document TD/B/348, para. 41.

[40] See "Principal problems of international trade in tobacco and guidelines for possible action: note by the UNCTAD secretariat" (TD/B/C.1/106).

[41] Represents the results of a comparison of the calculations in table 3 in the annex with estimates prepared by the secretariat of ECE (*Economic Survey of Europe in 1960* (United Nations publication, Sales No. 61.II.E.1), pp. 51-64).

[42] As table 3 in the annex does not present data for oilseeds, it is of interest that the secretariat of the European Communities estimated the Community price of this commodity group as being double the world market price in 1967/68 (*Newsletter on the Common Agricultural Policy*, No. 11, November 1968).

[43] In Japan the margins of protection (excess of domestic prices over import prices) were calculated to be as follows in the year 1968: rice, 80 per cent; wheat, 108 per cent; soybeans, 63 per cent; beef, 136 per cent; and butter, 169 per cent (*Economic Survey of Japan (1969-1970)...*, p. 88).

[44] See *Annual Review and Determination of Guarantees 1971...* The unit values of production grants and subsidies should be added to the deficiency payments shown at p. 38.

[45] See Harry H. Bell, "Some Domestic Price Implications of U.S. Protective Measures", Williams Commission report, *Papers I*, p. 465.

[46] See Larry J. Wipf, "Tariffs, Nontariff Distortions, and Effective Protection in U.S. Agriculture", *American Journal of Agricultural Economics*, vol. 53, No. 3, August 1971, p. 423.

tendency—evident from table 2 in the annex—for tariffs to rise as the degree of processing of the commodity increases.[47] This situation reflects policies of protection of

processing industries the purpose of which is to appropriate the benefits of the value added at the processing stage.

---

[47] For additional illustrations of tariff differentials between raw materials and processed items, as well as a fuller statement of this problem, see the report by the UNCTAD secretariat entitled "Increases in tariff differentials between raw materials, semi-manufactures and manufactures at different stages of processing resulting

from the Kennedy Round of tariff reductions" (TD/B/C.2/92). For a discussion of this problem, see Herbert G. Grubel, "Effective tariff protection: a non-specialist introduction to the theory, policy implications and controversies", *Effective Tariff Protection: Proceedings of a conference sponsored by GATT and the Graduate Institute of International Studies, Geneva, 17-20 December 1970* (Geneva, 1971).

CHAPTER IV

The case for action to improve access to markets

71. The case for action to improve access to primary commodity markets can be briefly stated since it is the obverse of the arguments, advanced in preceding parts of this report, concerning the adverse effects of protectionism on the economic welfare of both the developed countries maintaining trade barriers and the developing countries whose exports are hampered. The strong classical economic case for reducing such trade distortions has grown stronger as the levels and over-all costs of protection have increased over the years, and it is now powerfully reinforced by the universally recognized urgent need for more favourable economic and commercial policies on the part of developed countries to promote the economic growth of the developing countries.

72. In the field of primary commodity trade, the potentially adverse consequences for developing countries of the prospective enlargement of EEC without a prior or concurrent modification of commercial policies accentuate the need for measures to safeguard or advance the interests of developing exporting countries, particularly as the expanded Community would account for over 40 per cent of world trade in agricultural commodities. The entry of the principal acceding country, the United Kingdom, into the Community would result in (a) a rise in the prices received by producers of agricultural goods—which would tend to stimulate the expansion of production,[48] (b) a sharp increase in the prices paid by consumers for some commodities (principally sugar, beef and dairy products)— which would tend to retard the growth of consumption,[49] and (c) the granting of preferential entry to imports into the United Kingdom from other countries in the enlarged Community to the disadvantage of external suppliers, who would face new barriers to their exports.[50] In the light of

these considerations, the conclusions of one academic analyst that "It now seems quite certain that, if the United Kingdom, Ireland, Denmark and Norway joined EEC, barriers to trade will increase beyond those envisaged in a simple extrapolation of recent trends"[51] appears to be quite acceptable. It is consonant with a recently expressed view by the Secretary-General of OECD that "Self-sufficiency in formely importing countries has been wholly encouraged, and the enlargement of EEC, involving the application of the common agricultural policy to the United Kingdom and other European countries, seems likely to limit still more the scope for food imports from low-cost producing countries".[52]

73. The "Green revolution" is another new factor accentuating the need for action to improve access to markets. The rapid spread of the green revolution, in consequence of the transfer of seed and fertilizer technology from developed to developing countries, is resulting in increasing self-sufficiency of certain developing countries in wheat, rice and maize, and these countries hope to increase their exports cereals to the markets of developed countries. The Pearson Commission noted that "The dramatic advances in cereal output in several developing countries... make it likely that some of them might in the future become large-scale exporters of grains".[53] Accordingly, action to facilitate access to currently protected markets in developed countries appears to be necessary—

---

[48] In a White Paper on the question of joining the Community, the United Kingdom Government stated: "British farm output is on a rising trend and it has been the policy of the Government to encourage this. In the enlarged Community British farmers generally can expect better overall returns for their produce despite higher feed costs... Thus, as a result of our entry, home agricultural output can be expected to expand more quickly. The Government expects additional expansion of some eight per cent overall on this account by 1977". (*The United Kingdom and the European Communities*, Cmnd. 4715 (London, H.M. Stationery Office, July 1971), pp. 22-23).

[49] According to an official statement, "it is estimated that membership will affect food prices gradually over a period of about six years with an increase of about 2.5 per cent each year in retail prices" (*ibid.*, p. 23).

[50] Sugar, with regard to which the Community's offer is regarded by the United Kingdom Government and the other Commonwealth Governments concerned "as a firm assurance of a secure and continuing market in the enlarged Community on fair terms for the

quantities of sugar covered by the Commonwealth Sugar Agreement in respect of all its existing developing member countries..." (*ibid.*, p. 29), is potentially a substantial—although incomplete—exception to this generalization so far as the developing countries are concerned. Much will depend on the practical outcome of the assurance given by the Community. The exception is incomplete since the proposed arrangements would involve a reduction in the over-all degree of assured access for external sugar suppliers (unless concurrent measures were taken to modify the protection accorded to beet sugar production in the Community so as to ensure a corresponding expansion of the enlarged Community's sugar requirements from the free market). Such a reduction in access would be to the immediate disadvantage of the developed country concerned. However, this in turn would seem likely to have adverse effects on the opportunities for developing countries in third markets, since the displaced sugar supplies would become available for the free market, as article 34 of the International Sugar Agreement provides that if there is any significant change in the position of a Member under a special arrangement, there shall be compensating adjustments to its export quota in the free market.

[51] See D. Gale Johnson, "Agricultural Trade—A Look Ahead—Policy Recommendations", Williams Commission report, *Papers I*, p. 882.

[52] See OECD, *Inflation...*, para. 150.

[53] See *Partners in Development...*, p. 84.

as is the taking of special care by these countries to minimize the adverse effects of the distribution of food surpluses on terms which cannot be matched by new exporters—if the green revolution is to be a force for development in the widest sense.

A. Benefits of improved access for developing countries

74. The improvement of access to primary commodity markets in the developed countries would augment the export proceeds of developing countries by increasing the volumes or prices—or, most frequently, both the volumes and the prices—of their commodity exports to the liberalizing countries and to any third markets which might be relieved of pressure of supplies from developed countries. The trade significance of measures to improve access would, of course, depend upon their precise nature and their geographical scope and commodity coverage.

75. Although attempts to quantify the trade significance of measures to improve market access need to be viewed with caution, the following estimates serve to illustrate the possible orders of magnitude of the results of various actions:

(a) The complete removal of protection, in all its forms, for agricultural commodities in all countries would bring export gains to the developing countries amounting—according to a calculation which is highly qualified by the authors—to $10 billion in 1980.[54] (However, the complete removal of agricultural protection represents an extreme assumption and is not proposed in the present report.)

(b) If the high-income countries (including, in the study concerned, the developed market economy countries and the socialist countries of Eastern Europe) maintained their degrees of self-sufficiency in certain selected agricultural commodities—coarse grains, rice, fats and oils (excluding butter), sugar, beef and veal and citrus fruits—at levels which prevailed in 1964-1966 in place of projected 1980 levels, the export opportunities for the developing countries would be greater by around $4.1 billion.[55] (Even more significant results would be achieved if the levels of self-sufficiency prevailing in an earlier period were chosen.)

(c) If the policies of support were adjusted in some leading industrial countries (EEC, Japan, United Kingdom and United States) so as to reduce the output of major protected agricultural commodities by the equivalent of 5 per cent of their domestic consumption, the value of the increased trade opportunities thereby created for other (including developing) countries would amount to about $2.2 billion per year, calculated at recent rates of consumption and unit values.

(d) In the case of sugar, it has been estimated that in 1959, in the absence of protection, the free market price of sugar would have been 4 to 4½ cents per pound (f.a.s. Cuba) instead of the prevailing price of about 3 cents per pound.[56] It has been further estimated that the removal of sugar protection in the major Western European protectionist countries, taking into account the substitution of imports for protected production as well as the price effect, would increase the annual export earnings of the developing countries by about $0.75 billion.[57]

76. An argument occasionally advanced for the maintenance of protection in developed countries is that the expansion of exports from developing countries may be hampered by supply limitations, as in the case of beef and veal and coarse grains. However, if they were assured of increased market opportunities at improved prices, developing exporting countries would no doubt be willing and able to undertake appropriate programmes for the expansion of exportable production of the items concerned, and their supply potentials should be taken into account in any arrangements taking the form of a quantitative sharing of markets. In any event, any supply limitations would directly lead to higher world prices, which would benefit developing exporting countries and would tend to bring over-all supply and demand into balance, with a reduced degree of trade distortion. The argument certainly does not justify the maintenance of the *status quo* in protectionist countries, especially where—as is so often the case—the levels of protection are high.

B. Effects on the economies of liberalizing countries

77. Social and political difficulties would arise for developed countries which attempted a large measure of liberalization of primary commodity imports. The seriousness of these difficulties would depend greatly on the rate at which imports were increased and by the scale and appropriateness of any accompanying internal measures, especially in the field of adjustment assistance.

78. Since what is proposed in this report, and what is realistic to contemplate, is a moderation of protectionism rather than the complete dismantling of all protective measures, and since any programme for improving market access would undoubtedly be implemented in stages, it should not be beyond the ingenuity of the governments of liberalizing countries to promote the necessary internal social and economic adjustments with reasonable harmony, especially as real economic gains would flow to their economies in the process. As is explained in chapter V below, much could be done by the Governments concerned to ease any social problems arising from

---

[54] See "A world price equilibrium model", Projections Research Working Paper No. 3 (CCP 71/WP.3, November 1971), prepared jointly by the secretariats of FAO and UNCTAD and forming part of the FAO study, *Agricultural Commodity Projections, 1970-1980* (CCP 71/20), Rome 1971. This calculation, and other applications of the world price equilibrium model, are described by the authors as being "demonstrations which, while using actual data and those of the main projections study to the maximum possible extent, should not, because of severe data gaps and the degree of aggregation of the model as it now stands, be interpreted as substantive projections or forecasts. Rather, they foreshadow how a more fully evolved model of this type could be used in a context of projections or policy analysis, provided more adequate information, especially on supply relationships, was available" (para. 5.2).

[55] See FAO, *Agricultural Commodity Projections, 1970-1980 ...*, vol. I, para. 198.

[56] See R. H. Snape, "Some Effects of Protection in the World Sugar Industry", *Economica*, vol. 30, No. 117, February 1963, p. 67.

[57] See Harry G. Johnson, *Economic Policies Towards Less Developed Countries* (London, Allen and Unwin, 1967), appendix D.

liberalization measures. Moreover, the sectoral problems associated with increased competition from imports would be essentially of a short-term nature, and in the longer run real gains would accrue to the economy as a whole. The transfer of resources out of protected (hence relatively inefficient) sectors to sectors with a higher productivity would make a significant contribution to real national income, especially in those cases where the level of protection is high. As a result, the fundamental balance-of-payments position of the liberalizing country would be strengthened because of the more rational allocation of resources in the economy. It should also be borne in mind that the resultant increased capacity of beneficiary developing countries to import from the rest of the world would enhance the export opportunities of the liberalizing countries.

79. The real costs of protection in industrial countries are recognized in the recent report of the Williams Commission in the United States, in the following terms: "Import restrictions applied to particular products... almost always have the effect of shifting resources from more-economic to less-economic production, thereby reducing the income of the economy as a whole... Protection causes not only a general reduction of productivity and income, but also a transfer of income from the rest of the population to the protected industry.[58]

80. More liberal import policies, by reducing the cost of foodstuffs and other essential goods, could make a contribution towards reducing the rate of inflation, which has accelerated in recent years in a number of developed countries and which causes them considerable concern. This consideration would seem to merit wider appreciation in the present situation.[59]

81. It follows that the concept of equality of sacrifice on the part of liberalizing countries, which is often raised in connexion with proposed programmes of trade liberalization, is an irrational and irrelevant concept, since the associated expansion of trade would be in each liberalizing country's own interest. Nevertheless, concerted action by as many countries as possible to moderate impediments to trade would bring the greatest benefits all round and would be preferable for this reason and, to the extent that countries may continue to attach importance to the concept of equality of sacrifice, account needs to be taken of it in any multilateral move to reduce trade barriers.

C. Share of developing countries in benefits from measures to improve market access—need for special precautions

82. A question of importance is whether any programme of measures taken to improve access to primary commodity markets principally with a view to benefiting developing exporting countries would in fact give the latter an appropriate share of the intended benefits in the absence of special arrangements to that end. The developing countries are minority suppliers of many primary commodities or commodity groups to the industrial countries (18 out of the 28 listed in the annex, table 6), and their share of world primary commodity trade has been declining.[60] These factors indicate a strong possibility that the developing countries might not be the principal beneficiaries of unselective ("across-the-board") measures to improve access, and this would be particularly true if the traditional approach of concentrating upon the reduction of the levels of protection were followed.

83. On the other hand, the developing countries still account for over 50 per cent of the value of imports of all primary commodities (and 42 per cent excluding petroleum) into the industrial countries and, in particular, are pre-eminent or important suppliers of several highly protected commodities—including sugar, rice, cotton, oilseeds and oils and fruits. They may, therefore, be confidently expected to benefit from an appreciable general expansion of international primary commodity trade. Moreover, it is significant that the recent FAO agricultural commodity projections for 1970-1980 indicate that the developing countries' share of world agricultural trade could rise between 1970 and 1980 and that the commodities contributing to this rise would include sugar, rice, beef and veal, citrus fruit, fish, tobacco and cotton.[61] Furthermore, an FAO study indicates that the export gain accruing to developing countries as a result of the complete removal of protection would be impressive, and would exceed that of the developed countries taken as a group.[62] An additional consideration is that a greater degree of restraint in the subsidization of exports of primary commodities by industrial countries, which would be a by-product of effective liberalization, should contribute to the maintenance of the share of the developing countries in the trade in the commodities concerned.

84. Notwithstanding the considerations just mentioned, it would seem prudent—in view of the contrary considerations referred to in paragraph 82, above—that the international community should take all necessary precautions in order to ensure that the developing countries receive a more-than-proportionate share of the benefits of any

---

[58] See Williams Commission report, p. 60. Making a similar point, an official agency in Japan has stated that "there is no denying the fact that restrictions still imposed on a large number of agricultural imports are having an adverse effect on the moves to make the economy more efficient." (*Economic Survey of Japan (1969-1970)*..., p. 175).

[59] This was one of the principal points made by the Secretary-General of OECD in his report on inflation (see foot-note 52). He suggested in that report that "The admission of low-cost food imports could make an important contribution to relieving inflationary pressures... Many agricultural exporting countries, both inside the OECD and outside, have been obliged to cut back production well below their potential, even though they could profitably sell at prices much lower than those guaranteed to farmers in importing countries" (para. 160 (3)). He recommended that "The rise in food prices should be held back by containing the rise of agricultural support prices and where possible reducing them for products in surplus" (para. 15 (7)).

[60] Another notable feature which emerges from the annex, table 6 is that the share of a group of developed primary exporting countries identified in table 6 also fell between 1955 and 1969 but that, conversely, the share of world primary commodity trade represented by trade among industrial countries rose in the case of 21 out of the 28 commodities listed therein. Regional economic groupings among developed countries no doubt contributed to an important extent to this result.

[61] See FAO, *Agricultural Commodity Projections, 1970-1980*..., vol. I, para. 194.

[62] See FAO, "A World Price Equilibrium Model" (CCP 71/WP.3), loc. cit.

programme of action to improve access to markets, with the intention that any such trade initiative should have a preferential character—one designed to benefit principally, although not exclusively, the developing exporting countries.[63]

85. Accordingly, it is considered that the following elements should form part of any programme of action to improve market access, with a view to ensuring that the developing exporting countries receive the fullest possible therefrom:

(*a*) Priority might be given to commodities in the world trade in which the developing countries account for a large or appreciable share and in respect of which they have demonstrated a large measure of competitiveness—as in the case of sugar, rice, cotton, citrus fruits and tobacco—with the virtually certain consequence that in this way, without the need for any accompanying measures, the main benefits would in fact flow to the developing countries.

(*b*) For reasons related both to the question here at issue and for other, general considerations—as discussed in paragraphs 88 to 90, below—arrangements designed to improve access should be focussed directly on the desired trade results themselves rather than on modifications in the instruments or levels of protection. Thus, if the approach to the problem of improving access to markets were (as recommended in chapter V) one involving the reservation of certain shares of consumption requirements in developed countries for imports, such shares might be established solely for the developing countries or, alternatively, if global shares were established in the first place,

---

[63] It is assumed that, in accordance with the provisions of Trade Board resolution 73 (X), full account would be taken of the desirability of improving competitiveness and due regard would be paid to the interests of all producing countries, including those which rely heavily on export earnings from primary commodities.

the amounts allocated specifically to the developing countries as a group could be established at appropriate levels.

(*c*) In instances in which the traditional approach—envisaging the reduction of barriers as such—was found to be the only applicable approach, preferential adjustments to trade barriers might be made in favour of developing countries with a view to increasing the share of domestic consumption met by imports from developing countries.

(*d*) Advantage might be taken of a variety of other circumstances which would permit action to be taken to ensure that the developing countries secure a more than proportionate (or at least a proportionate) share of the benefits of improved access. In instances in which exports of the commodity concerned were regulated under an international commodity agreement (as in the case of sugar), the share of developing countries could be readily protected or increased. In other cases, in which imports were regulated under a quota system, the share of the developing countries could be readily increased or at least sustained in any deliberate increase in imports. The high degree of government supervision of imports involved by the system of variable import levies would also seem to provide opportunities for influencing the sources of imports.

D. Share of the benefits for the least developed among the developing countries

86. The approaches and techniques outlined in paragraph 85 appear equally suitable for the purpose of according more than proportionate benefits to the least developed among the developing countries. The latter countries, including land-locked countries, have an actual or potential export interest in a wide range of primary commodities subject to trade impediments.

CHAPTER V

Alternative approaches to the problem of protectionism

87. Until recently, the international community's approach to the problem of improving access to primary commodity markets has concentrated upon the objective of liberalizing the instruments and level of protection rather than upon achieving arrangements, such as the sharing of protected markets, expressed in terms of the desired end-results themselves. These constitute the two principal approaches to the problem of improving market access for internationally traded commodities which compete with protected production in developed countries.

A. Focus on instruments and levels of protectionism

88. The essence of the traditional approach—adopted in both GATT and UNCTAD—embraces the principle of standstill (no new tariff or non-tariff barriers or increases in existing barriers) and the principle of the elimination or reduction of existing duties and other barriers against imports of primary commodities of export interest to developing countries—normally subject to the reservation

of "whenever possible". Although the economic arguments, from the standpoints of both developed protectionist countries and developing exporting countries, for the active pursuit of this approach have gained increasing strength, it has brought very modest results to date. For potential liberalizing countries, the dismantling of protective devices, or the reduction of levels of support, poses the problem of a possible disruption of the agricultural sector, although more than is realized could be done to alleviate any transitional problems of adjustment (see paragraph 97, below). On the other hand, for potential beneficiary developing countries, this traditional approach does not carry an assurance of improvements in access to markets in concrete, measurable terms. For example, a very substantial reduction in the margin of protection would be required in most cases in order to improve the scope for imports appreciably, and a "frozen" margin of support can easily result in an increasing degree of self-sufficiency and a diminishing scope for imports. Hence the need to explore alternative approaches.

89. However, before alternative approaches are discussed, it should be noted that, to the extent that the traditional approach is followed, special arrangements would seem to be required for keeping under close intergovernmental attention the observance of the principles which it reflects. Such arrangements would presumably include provision for detailed reporting of relevant actions concerning protected commodities and for consultations in the event of alleged breaches. In order that any such arrangements might be workable, prior agreement would seem to be required on the applicability of the basic principles to a wide variety of measures. For example, would the substitution of an import levy system for a system of deficiency payments constitute a new barrier? And how would one classify an increase in the margin of protection or in the unit amount of export subsidy arising, variously, from a fall in the free market price or an increase in the domestic support price; or an increase in the subsidy paid on a specific agricultural input? And so on. The whole exercise would indeed become a very complicated one—which is another reason why a more direct approach seems preferable wherever possible.

B. Focus on trade results

90. Arrangements assuring developing countries of the opportunity of filling agreed shares of the present and future consumption requirements of developed countries in respect of commodities protected by the latter would bring valuable trade benefits if they were applied to important commodities so as to provide increasing shares to developing countries or, at least, safeguarded their historical shares. This approach might also appeal to the developed countries concerned, because they would not be required either to abandon their policies or techniques of agricultural support or to accept commitments to modify particular instruments of protection in specific ways; they would be left free to achieve the agreed trade results through any combination of measures suited to their own circumstances. These measures might well include adjustments of the levels of commodity support prices and/or the volumes of supported output, or direct controls on the volume of production without any accompanying reduction of support prices, or special disincentives for overproduction.

91. Certain developed countries have utilized the market-sharing approach successfully in relation to several primary commodities,[64] and it would seem to be applicable to such important commodities as sugar, rice, cotton, tobacco, beef and veal, citrus fruits, wheat and coarse grains.

92. In a comparable recommendation, the Pearson Commission proposed "that developed countries should draw up plans in respect of protected commodities designed to assure that over time an increasing share of domestic consumption is supplied by imports from developing countries".[65]

93. With regard to primary commodities to which the market-sharing approach may be found to be inapplicable, the traditional approach, which envisages the reduction of trade barriers as such, might continue to be applied. However, the measures taken should be designed to have a sufficient impact so as to achieve the result, as recommended by the Pearson Commission, of increasing the share of domestic consumption filled by imports from developing countries. To this end, preferential adjustments to trade barriers in favour of the developing countries would appear to be required.

94. As the widespread subsidization of exports of surplus output of protected commodities in developed countries seriously restricts the market opportunities for developing countries, a strong case would appear to exist for the limitation or gradual phasing out of subsidies for any such exports to developed importing countries. Such subsidies by developed exporting countries compound the foreign trade difficulties faced by developing exporting countries as a result of increasing degrees of self-sufficiency in developed importing countries, and are probably inconsistent with a long-standing provision of the General Agreement on Tariffs and Trade (article XVI).[66]

C. Methods of support and adjustment assistance

95. Whatever the approach adopted to the problem of improving access, there appear to be certain actions which, if taken by potential liberalizing countries, would greatly facilitate, and widen the scope for, measures of trade liberalization.

96. First, the methods of agricultural support might be modified so as to reduce the stimulus given to domestic output of protected commodities. In most protectionist developed countries, the essential purpose of protective devices is to sustain the incomes of small farms rather than to stimulate the over-all volume of output. However, the usual method of support—the fixing of high support prices, which benefit mainly the larger-scale, prosperous farmers—often fails to achieve its social objective[67] and gives an unintended impetus to output. An incipient trend

---

[64] See "Study on certain temperate zone products: Market sharing—note by the UNCTAD secretariat" (TD/B/C.1/93), paras. 21-27.

[65] See *Partners in Development* ..., p. 97, recommendation 2.

[66] GATT, *Basic Instruments and Selected Documents*, vol. IV.

[67] This basic defect of existing methods of agricultural support has received increasing notice in recent years. For example, the Williams Commission report noted that "Most of the benefits of U.S. farm programmes have gone to farmers with the higher gross incomes who presumably have the least need for income support" and expressed its belief "that present U.S. farm programmes have been less effective than they might have been in helping low-income farmers and agricultural labourers. To promote desired resource adjustments and reduce conflicts between farm programmes and trade policy objectives, we recommend the adoption of programmes related to the income needs of a farmer—not to his actual or potential production." pp. 158-159.) Similarly, the Secretary-General of the OECD has stated in para. 159 of his report on inflation (see foot-note 52) that "... the farm income problem remains unresolved, and in this respect the heavy and increasing reliance on price support is open to criticism, since most of the benefit goes to the larger farms". It is also notable that the Vedel Commission (France) pointed out that the existing system was unjust since, by benefiting mainly the big producers, it resulted in a transfer from the least favoured (low-income consumers burdened by unduly heavy food costs) to the most favoured (big producers) (see *Perspectives à long terme de l'agriculture française 1968-1985*, Paris, 1969, p. 29).

towards an increasing degree of direct income support in the developed countries, if accelerated, could make a useful contribution to any programme for improving the scope for imports. The complete replacement of systems of indirect support (through market prices) by direct income support would, of course, markedly reduce the stimulus to output if the income support were selective and not linked to the volume of output. However, it is most unlikely that such a change will come about in the foreseeable future.[68]

97. Secondly, arrangements to improve the availability of adjustment assistance, from public sources, for the retraining and re-employment of, or for granting other assistance to, marginal producers adversely affected by increased imports would greatly facilitate measures of trade liberalization. Such a move has been strongly recommended in the United States by the Williams Commission to "... facilitate the transfer of resources from import-impacted industries without undue hardship to employers or employees, and ... permit the country as a whole to benefit from increased efficiency and lower prices. Without adequate programmes of this type, some of the more serious trade barriers may not be amenable to negotiation in the near future." The Commission noted that "in no sector of our economy is this concept of potentially greater significance than in agriculture".[69]

D. Commodity-by-commodity or multi-commodity approach?

98. The international approach generally adopted to the solution of commodity problems is the commodity-by-commodity approach, because of the differing circumstances of various commodities and because of the problems experienced in past attempts to achieve progress on a broad front. This approach could appropriately be adopted for the purpose of any international consultations aimed at improving access to primary commodity markets.

However, it would seem desirable that several major commodities should be dealt with either concurrently in separate consultative groups or singly in quick succession in recognition of the interrelationships of commodities and the need to include several major commodities so as to achieve "concrete and significant trace liberalization results early in the 1970s", in accordance with Trade Board resolution 73 (X), part B, paragraph 3(e).

E. Monetary compensation — a second-best solution

99. If, despite any intensified consultations aimed at the improvement of access to markets in developed countries for primary commodities of export interest to developing countries, concrete and significant progress was not achieved or was not clearly in prospect, there would be an urgent need for considering any novel approaches, including second-best solutions. One such approach would start from the premise that, as protectionism in the developed countries gravely reduced the export earnings of the developing countries, the developed countries concerned should compensate the developing exporting countries for the damage thus caused to their trade; hence the protectionist developed countries might transfer sums calculated according to some simplified agreed formula—for example, the equivalent of half of the increase, from an agreed base period, in the gross value of the domestic production of protected commodities. Such transfers would need to be regarded as being additional to existing official financial flows to the developing countries.

F. Protection of processing

100. The processing of imported primary commodities in developed countries is protected mainly through tariffs. An essential element in any liberalization programme would be the reduction of such protection, possibly through the inclusion of semi-processed and processed primary commodities within the scope of the GSP.[70] Possible action along these lines will be discussed by the Conference under item 14 (a) of the provisional agenda.

---

[68] A change in the form of protection to one relying solely on deficiency payments represents a variant of the first approach (para. 88), which focusses on instruments and levels of protection. Although the degree of stimulus it provides to production is not intrinsically different from that provided by a system of high producer prices, it has the relative advantages of not hampering consumption and of making "visible", through the budget, the total cost of agricultural support.

[69] See Williams Commission report, pp. 72 and 159.

[70] It is significant that the Williams Commission report has recommended that "in a future review of the generalized preference system, consideration be given to including a greater number of processed and specialty agricultural products..." (p. 244).

Chapter VI

The problem of revenue duties

101. Revenue-raising measures, which incidentally impede imports from developing countries, are maintained by some developed countries with respect to certain primary commodities that are not produced at all or on a substantial scale in those countries. The commodities in question are the tropical beverage crops—coffee, cocoa and tea—and bananas and spices. Certain other primary commodities, which are produced in both groups of countries—tobacco, petroleum, wine and sugar—also are

subject to taxation in developed countries, but in these instances the taxes usually apply to domestic output at the same rates as to imports.[71]

---

[71] One notable exception is the imposition, by state trading monopolies in certain European countries, of discriminatory taxes on imported blends of tobacco, which are reflected in higher prices for the products concerned.

102. A compilation prepared from national official sources (annex, table 4) shows that, in 1969, the four major developed market economies (EEC, Japan, United Kingdom and United States) collected about $0.6 billion from revenue charges on the tropical beverage crops ($0.5 billion in 1965), about $0.1 billion from charges on bananas, and $26.0 billion from charges on tobacco and petroleum and petroleum products ($19.1 billion in 1965). The last-mentioned sum includes an estimated amount of $1.34 billion derived from taxes charged on tobacco and petroleum imported from developing countries ($9.4 billion in 1965). It will be noted that the proceeds from these taxes increased very substantially between 1965 and 1969.

103. Because the removal of the taxes on petroleum, tobacco and wines would have a marked impact on the budgetary situations in most developed countries, and since the taxes on tobacco and wine may be based partly on social considerations, they are not further considered in the present context. Of the other commodities subject to revenue duties, sugar seems to be a special case in that in certain leading consuming countries the duties are closely linked to their systems of protection of domestic production and provide the wherewithal for the payment of premium prices for imports. However, in other instances the domestic prices of sugar are augmented through revenue duties without any offsetting benefit to developing countries, and if these duties were removed the increase in consumption and trade would be appreciable. The FAO secretariat estimated in 1967 that "If retail prices of more than 25 cents per kg were reduced to that level, the result might be an immediate increase of consumption of around two million tons."[72]

104. The remaining comodities, of which the most important are beverage crops, are all tropical export products. Bananas are subject to revenue charges at the frontier or internally, the profits made by State monopolies being equivalent to internal revenue taxes, and moderate tariffs apply to spices.

105. Because the price elasticity of demand for these comodities is relatively low, the adverse effects of the existing duties on demand and imports (hence the potential export gains of the supplying countries from the removal of the duties) are small in comparison with the revenues collected by the taxing authorities.[73] However, the fact that imports are impeded to some extent and the additional consideration that the taxes—falling on consumers rather than taxpayers—are regressive, provide good reasons favouring the removal of the taxes. An alternative to removing the taxes would be to refund to supplying countries part or all of the associated revenue proceeds.

106. There would appear to be, altogether, four possible approaches to the problem of revenue duties which merit consideration by Governments:

(a) The developed countries concerned might abolish the revenue charges (and, if they found it necessary, recoup the budgetary losses through alternative taxes);

(b) The principle might be accepted that refunds should be made by the importing countries concerned for the purpose of compensating developing supplying countries for the estimated export earnings lost as a result of the application of the duties;

(c) In order to avoid the difficulties of estimating trade damage, associated with alternative (b), refunds might be made of agreed proportions of ascertained revenue receipts—say 10 per cent, initially at least. On the basis of the latter percentage and at rates of consumption and revenue duties prevailing in recent years, this approach would imply that refunds totalling $50 to $60 million a year would be made in respect of the tropical beverage crops by the developed market economy countries covered in the annex, table 4;

(d) A further possibility would be that amounts corresponding to any future increases in total proceeds from revenue duties would be refunded to the supplying countries concerned.

107. As all the trade benefits of action taken along the lines of any of the foregoing possible courses of action would accrue to the developing countries, including many of the least developed among them, the case for the removal or reduction of existing revenue duties (or for equivalent, compensatory action) appears to be a particularly strong one.[74] The technical problems associated with some of these possible actions, such as estimating total refunds and apportioning them among the various supplying countries, would not be insuperable and might be explored and settled after an agreement has been reached in principle concerning the particular policy approach to be adopted.[75]

---

[72] See *Proceedings of the United Nations Conference on Trade and Development, Second Session*, vol. II, *Commodity Problems and Policies* (United Nations publication, Sales No. E.68.II.D.15), p. 119.

[73] See, for example, estimates of the effects of alternative fiscal policies, concerning revenue duties, on the export earnings of the main producing countries (*ibid.*, pp. 48-49).

---

[74] The Advisory Committee to the Trade Board and to the Committee on Commodities, in the report on its second session, made suggestions corresponding to (a) to (c) in paragraph 106 of the present report. The Committee recommended that any refunds "should be regarded not as a form of aid, but essentially as compensation—independent of existing financial assistance—for export earnings forgone as the result of the imposition of such charges" (see *Official Records of the Trade and Development Board, Fifth Session, Annexes*, agenda item 5, document TD/B/127, para. 20).

[75] It is of interest that Denmark introduced arrangements in 1968 under which part of the proceeds from customs duties on imports of coffee (rising to a statutory maximum of 50 per cent by 1972) are contributed to a (non-profit) fund for industrialization of the developing countries.

CHAPTER VII

Equivalent measures by the socialist countries of Eastern Europe

108. The broad concept of a rational international division of labour, and the essence of the more specific concept of improved access to markets for primary commodities of interest to developing countries, are equally applicable to the socialist countries of Eastern Europe as to the developed market economy countries, despite differences in economic and trading systems. Whereas the degree of access to markets in developed market-economy countries is widely impeded by identifiable governmental measures taken at the frontier and/or internally, market opportunities in the socialist countries are largely determined by policy and administrative decisions concerning both imports and the conditions affecting domestic output of commodities produced in competition with imports.

109. Thus, *de facto* protection of domestic production of importable commodities can exist in the socialist countries and can result in a stimulus to the output of such commodities as sugar, rice, tobacco and oilseeds, with consequential increases in self-sufficiency,[76] to the disadvantage of developing exporting countries.

110. Under Conference resolution 15 (II), the socialist countries of Eastern Europe undertook to adopt a wide range of measures to expand further their trade with developing countries, and these included "taking duly into consideration the trade needs of the developing countries when quantitative targets are fixed in their long-term economic plans" and taking "into account the production and export potential of developing countries in drawing up their plans". Valuable as such undertakings might prove to be in practice, the commitment concerning the equitable sharing of consumption requirements (in the socialist countries) between domestic sources and developing exporting countries appears to be no more concrete than that represented by assurances about access given by the developed market economy countries in the Conference recommendation in annex A.II.1 to the Final Act of the first session and in Trade Board resolution 73 (X).

111. The national economic plans of the socialist countries typically include quantitative targets for domestic output of major primary commodities, including many of interest to developing exporting countries (for example, sugar cotton and ferrous and non-ferrous metals in the Economic Development Plan of the USSR for 1971-1975), but they do not include equally explicit provisions about imports. The case for a greater degree of specific commitment concerning the shares of the total requirements of various commodities to be met by developing countries would therefore appear equally strong as the case, already put forward in paragraphs 90-92, for such market sharing arrangements in the developed market economy countries.[77]

112. The foregoing considerations relate to commodities produced in both developing countries and socialist countries—that is, commodities which are known to be, or may be, protected against competition from imports. As regards tropical products, the socialist countries of Eastern Europe have been importing increasing quantities, especially of tropical beverage crops, from the developing countries. However, the concept of incidental impediments to consumption, hence to the scope for imports, which arise from revenue-raising measures in the developed market-economy countries is also partly applicable to the socialist countries to the extent that the domestic prices of any such commodities may be set at unduly high levels in relation to international c.i.f. prices. Any measures which would serve to reduce such differentials and to permit the resultant increases in consumer demand to be reflected in the flow of imports would make a valuable contribution to enlarging market outlets for developing countries; this is especially true because of the marked scope for increases in the levels of consumption per person in the socialist countries of Eastern Europe.

---

[76] A study by the UNCTAD secretariat indicates that the degrees of self-sufficiency of the USSR in certain primary commodities increased markedly between the periods 1959-61 and 1967-69: rice, from 27 per cent to 67 per cent; sugar, from 82 per cent to 94 per cent; and tobacco, from 70 per cent to 81 per cent (see "Trends in markets of selected temperate zone products in five importing areas: note by the UNCTAD secretariat" (TD/B/C.1/108 and Corr.1), chap. III, section E).

[77] For institutional reasons, market-sharing arrangements for imported commodities could be implemented more directly by the Governments of socialist countries than by those of developed market-economy countries.

ANNEX

TABLE 1

Primary commodities: non-tariff barriers to imports into major industrial countries, 1971

Commodities	EEC A	EEC B	Japan A	Japan B	United Kingdom A	United Kingdom B	United States A	United States B
Food, beverages and tobacco								
Wheat	CMA	Se	QM	S	—	Sd	Q	Se
Rice	CMA	Se	QM	S	—	—	—	Se
Barley	CMA	Se	QM	S	—	Sd	—	Se
Maize	CMA	Se	—	—	—	—	—	Se
Sugar	CMA	Se	—	S	Q	S	Q	S
Beef and veal	CMA	Se	Q	—	—	Sd	Q[a]	—
Pigmeat	CMA	Se	M	S	q	Sd	—	—
Mutton and lamb	q[b] m[b]	—	—	—	—	Sd	Q[a]	—
Poultry	CMA	Se	—	—	—	—	—	—
Eggs	CMA	Se	—	O	—	Sd	—	—
Butter/Milk	CMA	Se	QM	Sd	Q	S	Q	Se
Fish	CMA	—	q	—	—	S	—	—
Citrus fruit	CMA	Se	q	—	q	—	—	—
Bananas	Q[b]	—	—	—	—	Q	—	—
Spices	—	—	—	—	—	—	—	—
Coffee	—	—	—	—	—	—	—	—
Cocoa	—	—	—	—	—	—	—	—
Tea	—	—	—	—	—	—	—	—
Wine	CMA	S	—	—	—	—	—	—
Tobacco	CMA m[b]	Se	M	—	—	—	—	Se
Oilseeds, oils and fats								
Soya beans and oils	—	—	—	Sd	—	—	—	Se
Groundnuts and oil	—	—	—	—	—	—	q	Se
Cottonseed-oil	—	—	—	—	—	—	—	S
Rapeseed and oil	CMA	S	—	Sd	—	—	—	—
Linseed and oil	CMA	S	—	—	—	—	—	S
Sunflower seed and oil	CMA	S	—	—	—	—	—	—
Olive oil	CMA	Sd	—	—	—	—	—	—
Palm kernels and oil	—	—	—	—	—	—	—	—
Palm oil	—	—	—	—	—	—	—	—
Coconut oil	—	—	—	—	—	—	—	—
Copra	—	—	—	—	—	—	—	—
Castor oil and seed	—	—	—	—	—	—	—	S
Marine oils	—	—	—	—	—	—	—	—
Animal oils, fats	—	—	—	—	—	—	—	—
Oilseed cake	—	—	—	—	—	—	—	—
Fish meal	—	—	q	—	—	—	—	—
Agricultural raw materials								
Cotton	—	—	—	—	—	—	Q	Se
Wool	—	—	—	—	—	S	—	Sd
Jute and bagging	q[b]	—	—	—	q	—	—	—
Hard fibres	—	—	—	—	—	—	—	—
Natural rubber	—	—	—	—	—	—	—	—
Hides and skins	—	—	—	—	—	—	—	—
Fur skins	—	—	—	—	—	—	—	—
Timber	—	—	—	—	—	—	—	—
Ores and concentrates								
Iron	—	—	—	—	—	—	—	—
Copper	—	—	—	—	—	—	—	—
Tin	—	—	—	—	—	—	—	—
Lead	—	—	—	—	—	—	—[d]	—
Zinc	—	—	—	—	—	—	—	—
Bauxite	—	—	—	—	—	—	—	—
Manganese	—	—	—	—	—	—	—	—
Tungsten ore	—	—	—	—	—	—	—	—
Phosphates	—	—	—	—	—	—	—	—

TABLE 1 *(continued)*

Primary commodities: non-tariff barriers to imports into major industrial countries, 1971

	EEC		Japan		United Kingdom		United States	
Commodities	*A*	*B*	*A*	*B*	*A*	*B*	*A*	*B*
Metals								
Iron and steel (semi-processed) .	q^c	—	—	—	q^c	—	q^c	—
Copper, unwrought	—	—	—	—	—	—	—	—
Tin	—	—	—	—	—	—	—	—
Lead	—	—	—	—	—	—	—	—
Zinc	—	—	—	—	—	—	—	—
Aluminium	—	—	—	—	—	—	—	—
Petroleum, crude	Q^b M^b	—	—	—	—	—	Q	—

Sources: Commission of the European Communities, *Fourth General Report on the Activities of the Communities, 1970* (Brussels, February 1971);

United Kingdom, Ministry of Agriculture, Fisheries and Food, *Annual Review and Determination of Guarantees 1971*, Cmnd. 4623 (London, H.M. Stationery Office, March 1971);

United States, Office of the President, Commission on International Trade and Investment Policy, *United States International Economic Policy in an Interdependent World: Report to the President.* (Washington D.C., Government Printing Office, July 1971);

GATT documents prepared in connexion with the work of its Agriculture Committee and Committee on Trade and Development.

NOTE: *Column A* shows the general nature of the restraint at the frontier, a small letter indicating that the measure is applicable to only part of the item in question:
M,m   indicates state trading or trading by an authorized monopoly

Q,q   indicates quota restrictions
CMA   indicates commodity falling under Common Market arrangements.

Column B indicates the general nature of explicit official intervention on domestic markets, not including direct or indirect subsidies of inputs of the primary sector or fiscal privileges accorded to that sector:
O   indicates organization of the domestic market without official price fixation
S   indicates price supported or production subsidy paid
Sd   indicates price guaranteed by deficiency payment
Se   indicates support accompanied by provision for export subsidy.

^a Contingency quotas on beef and veal and mutton, authorized by legislation (not so far applied) accompanied by restraints by supplying countries.

^b Certain member States only.

^c Voluntary export restraint by certain supplying countries.

TABLE 2

Tariffs on selected primary and processed commodities in major industrial countries, 1971/72

NOTE. The tabulation is designed to show the broad picture as regards tariffs levied on primary commodities, including those of actual or potential interest to developing countries and those which have undergone some degree of processing. The secretariat has not had the opportunity of referring the table to Governments and some of the information might therefore not be completely up-to-date. However, the data should nevertheless be representative of the broad position in late 1971 or early 1972; the results of the Kennedy Round of tariff negotiations have been taken into account.

The commodities selected are specified in terms of the BTN classification at the four-digit level. In order to avoid showing wide tariff ranges for various items entering under a given BTN heading, a single commodity, defined as narrowly as possible, was retained with the intention of showing specific representative rates for international trade in various commodities.

The duties shown are those applied to non-preferential imports. The *ad-valorem* equivalents of specific duties, shown in brackets, were calculated from the official sources listed below, taking into account the average unit values of imports of the commodities concerned in the most recent twelve-monthly period for which data were readily available. For the United Kingdom, the Commonwealth preferential tariff is equal to zero for all the commodities listed, except refined sugar, roasted coffee, tobacco and rubber tyres for passenger cars. In the case of EEC, the preferences granted to Associated States are equal to the height of the common external tariff. This, however, is not the case for agricultural products covered by the EEC common organization of markets.

No attempt is made in this table to reflect any temporary suspension or reductions of tariffs, or to indicate the effects, in relation to certain items (principally semi-manufactures), of the GSP which had been implemented at the time of writing (January 1972) by EEC, Japan and the United Kingdom. (Several other preference-giving countries had also implemented their respective schemes.) The United States had not announced a proposed date of implementation.

Symbols used:

Parentheses () denote calculated *ad valorem* equivalents of specific duties.

VL denotes variable levies imposed on agricultural commodities subject, in the case of EEC, to common Market regulations. (See table 3 for the estimated tariff equivalents of certain EEC variable levies in recent periods.) At the time this tabulation was prepared, the United Kingdom was in course of introducing interim levy schemes in respect of beef and veal, of mutton and lamb and of milk products other than butter and cheese. No account is taken of any such levies, although a previously introduced levy scheme in respect of cereals is reflected in the tabulation.

Footnote ^a indicates that relevant information is given in the country notes which follow the table.

TABLE 2 *(continued)*

**Tariffs on selected primary and processed commodities
in major industrial countries, 1971/72**

BTN	Commodities	EEC	Japan	United Kingdom	United States
	FOOD, BEVERAGES AND TOBACCO				
	Cereals				
10.01	Wheat, unmilled, for human consumption .	VL	20	VL	(13.7)
10.05	Maize, for feeding purposes, other than seed	VL	0	VL	(10.8)
10.06	Rice, paddy	VL	15	0	. . [a]
10.06	Rice, glazed or polished, excluding broken .	VL	15	(4)	. . [a]
	Sugar				
17.01	Sugar, raw, of a polarization of 96°	VL	(110)	(7.3)[a]	(9.2)
17.01	Sugar, refined, of a polarization exceeding 99°	VL	(63)	(13.1)[a]	(10.2)
	Meat and dairy products				
02.01	Beef and veal, fresh, chilled or frozen . . .	20 & VL	25	5	(6)
16.02	Canned beef (corned beef)	26	25	15	7.5
02.01	Pigmeat, fresh, chilled or frozen	VL	10	10	(1.2)
02.06	Bacon, ham and other	VL	25	10	(2.4)
02.01	Mutton, fresh, chilled or frozen	20	7.5	(11.6)	(7.3)
02.01	Lamb, fresh, chilled or frozen	20	7.5	(7.1)	(4.6)
02.02	Chicken, fresh, chilled, etc., eviscerated . .	VL	20	(11.6)	(6.9)
02.02	Turkeys, fresh, chilled, etc., eviscerated . .	VL	15	(8.8)	(12.5)
04.05	Eggs in the shell, fresh	VL	20	(4.2)	(9.5)
04.03	Butter	VL	45	0	(10.9)[a]
	Fish				
03.01	Tuna, fresh, chilled or frozen	22	5	10	0
03.03	Frozen shrimps	12	5	10	0
16.04	Canned sardines, skinned or boned, in oil .	25	15	10	24
16.04	Canned tuna, in oil	24	15	8	35
16.04	Canned salmon	13	15	2.5	7.5
16.04	Canned anchovies	25	15	10	6
16.04	Caviar in airtight containers	30	10	30	15
16.05	Canned shrimps	20	15	7.5	0
	Fruits and edible nuts				
08.02	Oranges, in season	20[a]	40	5	(12.6)
08.02	Lemons, fresh	8	10	6	(9.2)
08.02	Grapefruit, fresh	6	20	(5.7)	(7.3)[a]
08.01	Bananas, fresh	20[a]	40 & 60	(11.9)	0
08.01	Pineapples, fresh	9	20	10	(18)
08.01	Coconuts in the shell	2	10	0	0
08.01	Brazil nuts	0	10	0	0
08.01	Cashew nuts	2.5	5	10	0
08.03	Figs, dried	10	10	(7)	(19.1)
08.04	Currants	6	5	(1.4)	(7)
08.04	Sultanas	6	5	(2.8)	(7)
20.07	Orange juice, not concentrated	19[a]	30[a]	0[a]	(17.7)
20.07	Orange juice, concentrated	42[a]	30[a]	0[a]	(81.5)
20.07	Grapefruit juice, not concentrated	15[a]	27[a]	0[a]	(28)
20.07	Grapefruit juice, concentrated	42[a]	27[a]	0[a]	(28)
20.07	Pineapple juice, not concentrated	19[a]	27[a]	5	(45.5)
	Spices				
09.04	Pepper of piper, not ground	10	0	0	0
09.04	Pepper of piper, ground	12.5	5	10	(6.1)
09.04	Pimento, not ground	10	0	10	0
09.04	Pimento, ground	12	5	10	(4.1)
09.05	Vanilla	11.5	0	10	0
09.06	Cinnamon, not ground	10	0	5	0
09.06	Cinnamon, ground	13	0	5	(3.7)
09.08	Mace, not ground	0	0	10	0[a]

TABLE 2 *(continued)*

**Tariffs on selected primary and processed commodities
in major industrial countries, 1971/72**

BTN	Commodities	EEC	Japan	United Kingdom	United States
09.08	Mace, ground	12.5	5	10	0[a]
09.08	Cardamoms, not ground	0	0	10	0
09.08	Cardamoms, ground	5	5	10	0
	Tropical beverages				
09.01	Coffee, raw	9.6	0	(1.2)	0
09.01	Coffee, roasted	15	35	(1.6)	0
18.01	Cocoa beans	5.4	0	0	0
18.03	Cocoa paste	15	20	0	0
18.04	Cocoa butter	12	0	0	3
18.05	Cocoa powder, unsweetened	16	35	0	(2.1)
09.02	Tea in bulk	9	35[a]	0	0
09.02	Tea in small containers	11.5	35[a]	0	0
	Oil-seeds and oils				
12.01	Groundnuts for oil extraction	0	0	10	(42)
15.07	Groundnut oil, edible, raw	10	(11.5)	15	(22)
15.07	Groundnut oil, edible, refined	15	(16)	15	(22)
12.01	Copra	0	0	10	(14.3)
15.07	Coconut (copra) oil, edible, raw	10	10	15	(23.1)[a]
15.07	Coconut (copra) oil, raw, for technical uses .	5	10	15	(23.1)[a]
15.07	Coconut (copra) oil, edible, refined	15	10	15	(7.7)[a]
12.01	Palm nuts and kernels	0	0	10	0
15.07	Palm kernel oil, edible, raw	10	8	10	(3.4)
15.07	Palm kernel oil, edible, refined	15	8	10	(3.4)
15.07	Palm oil, edible, raw	9	8	10	0
15.07	Palm oil, edible, refined	14	8	10	0
15.07	Palm oil, for technical uses, raw	4	8	10	0
15.07	Palm oil, for technical uses, refined	8	8	10	0
12.01	Soya beans, except certified seed	0	(6)	0	(18)
15.07	Soya bean oil, edible, raw	10	(18)	15	22.5
15.07	Soya bean oil, edible, refined	15	(25)	15	22.5
12.01	Linseed	0	0	10	(14.3)
15.07	Linseed oil, raw	5	10	15	(4.7)
15.07	Linseed oil, refined	8	10	15	(4.7)
12.01	Cotton seed	0	0	10	(9.5)
15.07	Cotton seed oil, edible, raw	10	(17.5)	10	(19.6)
15.07	Cotton seed oil, edible, refined	15	(17.5)	10	(19.6)
12.01	Castor oil seed	0	0	7.5	0
15.07	Castor oil, raw	0	10	12.5	7.5
15.07	Castor oil, refined	8	10	12.5	7.5
15.07	Olive oil, virgin	VL	0	10	(11.4)
15.07	Olive oil, refined	VL	0	10	(8.2)
	Meal and oilcakes				
12.02	Flour and meal of oil-seeds	0	15	10	(10.8)
23.04	Soy bean cake	0	5	10	(7.2)
23.04	Other vegetable oil cakes	0	0	10	(7.6)
23.01	Fish meal	2	2	10[a]	0
	Tobacco				
24.01	Tobacco leaf	15-23	355	(1 390)	19[a]
	AGRICULTURAL RAW MATERIALS				
	Fibres				
55.01	Cotton, raw, not bleached or dyed	0	0	0	..
	of a staple length under 1 1/8 inch	0	0	0	0
	1-1/8 to 1-11/16 inch	0	0	0	(8.5)
	over 1-11/16 inch	0	0	0	(4.3)
55.04	Cotton, carded or combed	1.5	0	5	(21.7)

TABLE 2 *(continued)*

**Tariffs on selected primary and processed commodities
in major industrial countries, 1971/72**

BTN	Commodities	EEC	Japan	United Kingdom	United States
55.05	Cotton yarn, not put up for retail sale, wholly of cotton	6[a]	5.5[a]	7.5	8.4[a]
55.05	of which sewing thread . . .	4	5.5	7.5	8.8
55.09	Cotton fabrics, woven, wholly of cotton . .	14	7	17.5	7.6[a]
53.01	Wool, greasy, other than merino, not over 40 strands	0	0	0	0
53.01	Wool, in the grease or washed, not sorted, finer than 44 strands	0	0	0	(33.5)
53.01	Wool, finer than 44 strands, scoured . . .	0	0	0	(39.6)
53.05	Wool, carded or combed	3	0	10	(19.6)
53.05	Wool tops	3	0	10	(36.2)
53.07	Wool, worsted yarn, wholly of wool	5	5	7.5	(30.9)
57.03	Jute, raw	0	0	0	0
57.06	Jute yarn, not polished or glazed	8	10	10	7.5
57.10	Jute, fabrics, woven	19	19	20	0
62.03	Jute, sacks and bags, new, not bleached, coloured, etc.	19	20	20[a]	(2.5)
62.03	Jute, sacks and bags, new, bleached and coloured	19	20	20[a]	(3.9)
57.04	Sisal and henequen, raw	0	0	0	0
57.04	Sisal and henequen, processed	0	0	5	8
57.02	Manila hemp (abaca), raw	0	0	0	0
57.02	Manila hemp, processed, but not spun . . .	0	0	5	4
59.04	Binder and baler twine of hard leaf fibres, not stranded	13	10	15	0[a]
	Rubber				
40.01	Natural rubber	0	0	0	0
40.05	Plates, sheets and strips of ungalvanized rubber	4	7.5	5	6
40.11	Rubber tyres for passenger cars	7.5	12.5	12	4
	Hides, skins and leather				
41.01	Bovine hides and skins (excluding buffalo), not split	0	0	0	0
41.02	Bovine cattle leather	8	20	12	9[a]
43.01	Fur skins, undressed, of lamb or kinds . .	0	0	0	0
43.02	Fur skins, dressed, plates, linings, strips, etc.	4.5	15	20	8.5
	Wood and products				
44.03	Tropical hardwoods, in the rough	0	0	0	0
44.04	roughly squared or sawn	0	0	0	0
44.14	Veneer sheets, Philippine mahogany	7	15	5	10
44.14	Veneer sheets, of teak, ebony rosewood and sandal wood	7	0	5	5
44.14	Veneer sheets, of other hardwood	7	15	5	5
44.15	Plywood (mahogany)	13	20	5	20[a]
	MINERALS AND METALS				
26.01	Iron ores and concentrates and roasted iron pyrites	0	0	0	0
73.01	Spiegeleisen	4	5	8	(0.8)
73.01	Pig iron	4	5	0	0
73.02	Ferro-manganese, containing not less than 4 per cent of carbon	4	12	8.4	(4.7)[a]
26.01	Copper ores and concentrates	0	0	0	(1.3)[a]
74.01	Copper matte, blister copper	0	0	0	(1.5)
74.03	Copper bars, sheets and strips in coils, unalloyed	8	15	8	(1.8)[a]
74.03	Wrought rods of copper, unalloyed	8	15	8	(1.5)[a]
74.03	Wire of copper, not coated or plated, unalloyed	8	15	8	(7)[a]

TABLE 2 *(concluded)*

**Tariffs on selected primary and processed commodities
in major industrial countries, 1971/72**

BTN	Commodities	EEC	Japan	United Kingdom	United States
26.01	Nickel ores and concentrates	0	0	0	0
75.01	Unwrought nickel, unalloyed	0	(10.5)	0	0
26.01	Bauxite ores and concentrates	0	0	0	0
76.01	Aluminium, unwrought, unalloyed	7	9	0	(4.4)[a]
26.01	Lead ores and concentrates	0	0	0	(7.7)
78.01	Lead, unwrought, unalloyed	(4.5)	7.5	0	(7.6)[a]
26.01	Zinc, ores and concentrates	0	0	0	(9)
79.01	Zinc, unwrought, unalloyed	(4.6)	2.5	(1.1)	(5)
26.01	Tin ores and concentrates	0	0	0	0
80.01	Tin, unwrought, unalloyed	0	0	0	0
26.01	Manganese ores and concentrates	0	0	0	(5.9)[a]
26.01	Chrome ores and concentrates	0	0	0	0
26.01	Tungsten ores and concentrates	0	0	0	(10.1)
81.01	Tungsten, unwrought, lumps grains and powders	6	5	12.5	(14.5)
81.04	Antimony, unwrought, unalloyed	8	10	25	(0.8)
25.10	Phosphates	0	0	0	0
31.03	Phosphatic fertilizers	4.8	10	11	0
	PETROLEUM AND PETROLEUM PRODUCTS				
27.09	Petroleum, crude, testing under 25° API . .	0	(13)	0[a]	(2.2)
27.09	Petroleum, crude, testing over 25° API . .	0	(12)	0[a]	(3.7)
27.10	Motor spirit	7	(2.3)	0[a]	(11.6)
27.10	Kerosene	7	(22)	0[a]	(2.9)
27.10	Gasoils	5	(30)	0[a]	(2.2)
27.10	Lubricating oils	6	10-15	0[a]	(7)

Sources: GATT: *Legal Instruments Embodying the Results of the 1964-67 Trade Conference* (Geneva, 30 June 1967); various documents prepared for the GATT Committee on Trade and Development.

EEC: *Tarif douanier des Communautés européennes,* July 1968, brought up to date to 21 September 1971.

United States of America: *Tariff Schedules of the United States, Annotated* (1971) (Washington, D.C., United States Tariff Commission 1970); *Concordance between the Tariff Nomenclature used by the United States (TSUS) and the Nomenclature used by the European Economic Community* arranged in the order of the BTN (Washington, D.C., United States Tariff Commission, March 1965).

United Kingdom: *H.M. Customs and Excise Tariff of the United Kingdom of Great Britain and Northern Ireland* (London, H.M. Stationery Office, 1970), as amended September 1971.

Japan: *Customs Tariff Schedules of Japan, 1971* (Tokyo, Japan Tariff Association).

COUNTRY NOTES

EEC

Beef and veal: Tariff of 20 per cent is bound on quota of 22 000 tons of frozen beef.

Tuna: Exemption within quota of 30 000 tons.

Oranges: Provision exists for the imposition under certain conditions of a compensatory tax in addition to the tariff.

Bananas: Duty free quota covers nearly entire German consumption.

Fruit juices: Additional duties are levied on the sugar content of fruit juices above specified levels.

Oilseeds and oils: For most items: provision exists for the imposition under certain conditions of a compensatory amount in addition to the tariff.

Cotton yarn: Duties range from 4 to 8 per cent.

Japan

Fruit juices: Tariffs shown relate to fruit juices containing added sugar. Those without added sugar are subject to duties of 22.5 and 25 per cent.

Tea: Duties shown relate to black tea, which constitutes around two thirds of tea imports. Duties on green tea are 20 per cent *ad valorem*.

Cotton yarn: Duties range from 3.5 per cent to 5.5 per cent.

Lead: Tariff position 78.01.1 (1).A.

United Kingdom

Sugar: Rates vary according to the degree of polarization from £2. 1s. 1/2d per long ton to £6. 18s. 0d per long ton, i.e. from (3.9) per cent to (13.1) per cent.

Citrus fruit juices: Citrus fruit juices containing more than 20 per cent by weight of added sweetening matter are subject to a tariff of 3 per cent.

Fish meal: Herring meal is duty-free.

Jute fabrics: Not containing silk or man-made fibres.

Petroleum and products: Excluding fiscal duties of 4s. 6d per gallon; fiscal charges on refined products ex-refinery are the same as those payable on the importation of refined products.

United States

Rice: Imports of paddy, brown rice and polished rice are nil or negligible. Imports of broken rice are subject to a levy of (6.5) per cent.

Butter: US tariff positions Nos. 116.00, 116.10 and 116.20. Rate applies to imports of butter within tariff quota. Tariffs outside of quota are double the quoted rate, around (22) per cent.

Grapefruit: US tariff position No. 147.10, applies to grapefruit entering the country between 1 August and 30 September.

Mace: Except Bombay or wild, on which rates were reduced from 100 to 50 per cent.

Coconut oil: Crude coconut oil imports from the Philippines covering total requirements enter duty-free within a quota or are subject to a levy of (8.3) per cent outside quota. There is no trade in refined coconut oil, on which the preferential rate for the Philippines is also zero.

Tobacco: Average incidence calculated by relating customs collection on raw tobacco to value of imports in 1970; 63 US tariff positions range from 0 to 381 per cent.

Cotton yarn: Average incidence of customs revenues in relation to imports in 1970, US tariff positions Nos. 301.00 to 302.00 and 302.20. Post-Kennedy range varies from 3.4 to 19.75 per cent *ad valorem* plus 3.6 per pound.

Cotton fabrics: US tariff position 320.10.

Binder and baler twine: Not of stranded construction, US tariff position No. 315.20.

Bovine leather: US tariff position No. 121.30.

Plywood: US tariff position No. 240.25.

Ferro-manganese: US tariff position No. 607.37.

Copper ores and concentrates: Duties are suspended on imports made before 30 June 1972.

Copper bars: US tariff position No. 612.31.

Copper rods: US tariff position No. 612.60.

Copper wire: US tariff position No. 612.72.

Aluminium: US tariff position No. 618.02.

Lead: US tariff position No. 624.03.

TABLE 3

Ad valorem **tariff equivalents of variable levies
in EEC, 1967-1971***

(Per cent)

Commodities	1967-1968	1968-1969	1969-1970	1970-1971
Soft wheat	90.7	95.4	114.4	89.3
Durum wheat	62.6	67.9	80.9	82.0
Rye	68.9	79.3	78.0	72.4
Barley	62.5	97.0	102.9	46.0
Oats	54.4	84.3	76.9	42.4
Maize	65.5	77.9	59.1	40.8
Sorghum	61.0	86.0	66.8	49.2
Rice, husked or polished, excluding broken	18.0	38.1	85.5	110.2
Rice, broken	0	18.5	46.9	60.4
Sugar, raw	—	232.4	169.2	110.0
Sugar, white	—	329.3	252.8	155.3
Olive oil	24.1	14.1	6.5	4.5[b]
Pigmeat	43.7	71.0	76.0	53.3
Eggs in the shell	34.2	52.0	53.2	37.2
Chicken, eviscerated	22.9	30.6	29.9	23.5
Turkeys, eviscerated	23.8	32.5	33.2	26.0
Butter	—	526.2	535.8	214.2
Fat cattle (excluding calves)[a]	—	43.3	22.4	20.7
Calves[a]	—	2.6	0	1.1

Source: Based on EEC, *Marchés agricoles, Prix,* various issues.

* As a rule, figures shown represent yearly averages of levies imposed, expressed as percentages of average c.i.f. prices of imports to which levies applied during the year. The yearly averages relate to the period 1 August-31 July, except for rice (1 September-31 August), sugar (1 July-30 June) and olive oil (1 November-31 October).

[a] Excluding *ad valorem* tariff of 16 per cent for live animals. (As regards beef and veal, an *ad valorem* tariff of 20 per cent—to which variable levies are added—is applied.)

[b] Average for first 10 months of year.

TABLE 4

Revenue proceeds from internal fiscal charges* and tariffs on specified commodities
in major industrial countries, 1969**

(Million dollars)

	Coffee	Cocoa	Tea	Bananas	Tobacco	Petroleum and petroleum products
EEC						
Internal charges	459	10	10	44	3 867	8 145
Tariffs	55	19	4	10	103	11
Belgium						
Internal charges	5	..	..	..	163	418
Federal Republic of Germany						
Internal charges	283	..	10	..	1 558	2 650
France						
Internal charges	51[a]	..	..[b]	..	758[c]	2 243
Italy						
Internal charges	120	10	—	44	1 153[c]	2 392
Netherlands						
Internal charges	..	..	..	..	235	442
Japan						
Internal charges	5	..	..	..	} 829[c]	1 227
Tariffs	—	1	4	59		226
United Kingdom						
Internal charges	..	..	..	..	} 2 801 }	3 069
Tariffs	2	—	—	..		
United States						
Internal charges	—	—	—	—	2 136	3 516
Tariffs	—	3	—	—	32	75

Sources: EEC: *Commerce extérieur 1969, Tableaux analytiques* (Statistical Office of the European Communities);

Belgium: *L'économie belge en 1970* (Brussels, Ministry of Economic Affairs, 1971);

Federal Republic of Germany: *Bundeshaushaltsplan für das Haushaltsjahr 1971* (Bonn, Government Printing Office);

France: *Statistiques et études financières*, Nos. 271-272, July-August 1971 (Paris, Ministry of Economy and Finance);

Italy: *Relazione generale sulla situazione economica del paese 1969* (Rome, Istituto Poligrafico dello Stato, 1970);

Netherlands: *Statistical Yearbook of the Netherlands 1969-1970* (The Hague, Netherlands Central Bureau of Statistics, 1971);

Japan: *Quarterly Bulletin of Financial Statistics, 3rd and 4th Quarters, 1970 Fiscal Year,* (Tokyo Research and Planning Division, Ministry of Finance, February 1971); *Monthly Statistics of Japan*, No. 118, April 1971 (Bureau of Statistics, Office of the Prime Minister); *Japan Exports and Imports 1969* (Japan Tariff Association);

United Kingdom: Central Statistical Office, *Financial Statistics*, No. 112, August 1971 (London, H.M. Stationery Office); *Overseas Trade Accounts of the United Kingdom, December 1969* (London, H.M. Stationery Office);

United States: *The Budget of the United States Government, Fiscal Year 1971* (Washington, D.C., Government Printing Office, 1970).

*   Excluding general turnover or sales taxes and taxes on value added in EEC.

** Tariff proceeds were generally estimated by applying *ad valorem* tariff rates ruling in 1969 to the value of dutiable imports in 1969.

[a] This figure relates to the year 1967, since when the single tax on coffee and tea has been replaced by taxes on value added. It includes revenue from indirect taxes on tea.

[b] Included in figure for coffee.

[c] The profits (or excess of revenue over expenditure) of the State trading monopoly in tobacco are regarded as internal charges in the context of this table.

TABLE 5

Selected primary commodities: ratio of net imports to consumption* in major industrial countries

(per cent)

Commodities	EEC		Japan		United Kingdom		United States	
	1954-1956	1967-1969	1954-1956	1967-1969	1954-1956	1967-1969	1954-1956	1967-1969
Food, beverage crops and tobacco								
Wheat[a]	16	−4	61	82	63	54	−56	−76
Rice	10	16	10	1	100	100	−140	−208
Barley	25	—	36	40	24	−2	−11	−3
Maize	32	46	79	99	100	100	−4	−14
Sugar, raw	−2	−4	90	76	60	67	47	45
Beef and veal[b]	3	7	2	7	34	24	−2	4
Mutton and lamb[b]	3	11	—	99	65	59	−1	12
Butter[c]	−1	−6	—	15	91	90	−15	−2
Oilseeds, fats and oils[c]	60	68	..	92	84	86	−21	−40
Citrus fruit	53	51	0	−1	100	100	−7	−3
Bananas	100	100	100	100	100	100	100	100
Coffee	100	100	100	100	100	100	100	100
Cocoa	100	100	100	100	100	100	100	100
Tea	100	100	−23	5	100	100	100	100
Tobacco	49	65	5	11	100	100	−21	−22
Agricultural raw materials								
Cotton, raw	100	101	100	99	100	100	−50	−39
Wool[d]	89	95	97	99	87	76	52	41
Rubber, total	102	25	101	40	100	47	37	12
of which:								
natural	102	112	100	108	100	102	100	89
synthetic	103	−33	108	−10	101	2	−10	−12
Bovine hides and skins	37	36	..	93	57	34	..	−58
Wood[e]	13	21	3	28	70	73	3	1
Minerals and metals								
Iron ore[f]	32	66	84	97	62	74	18	32
Copper ore	92	95	19	68	—	—	10	3
blister	76	75	..	27	92	100	19	17
refined	47	45	3	24	52	65	−1	4
Bauxite	36	48	100	100	100	100	75	87
Aluminium	13	34	−13	27	87	90	11	8
Lead ore	..	72	..	59	100	93	36	22
metal	16	11	15	6	73	33	39	33
Zinc ore	56	67	15	58	97	100	49	51
metal	−16	7	−2	−13	62	53	17	20
Tin concentrates	99	98	11	39	97	94	100	100
metal	−50	57	86	92	−3	−11	98	96
Crude petroleum	93	96	99	99	100	100	10	14
Petroleum products	−29	−16	22	15	4	11	3	12

Sources: United Nations, various issues of: *Commodity Trade Statistics, Statistical Papers, Series D; Yearbook of International Trade Statistics;* UNCTAD *Commodity Survey,* various issues.

FAO, various issues of: *Food Balance Sheets; Production Yearbook; Trade Yearbook; World Forest Products Statistics; Yearbook of Forest Products Statistics; Timber Bulletin for Europe;*

OECD, *Food consumption in the OECD countries; Foreign Trade Statistics Bulletins,* Series B and C, various issues; *The Hides, Skins and Footwear Industry in the OECD countries; Basic Statistics of Energy,* various issues;

EEC, *Statistique agricole,* various issues, (Statistical Office of the European Communities);

Commonwealth Economic Committee, *Wool Intelligence; World Trade in Wool and Wool Textile 1952-1963; Raw Hides and Skins; Iron and Steel and Alloying Metals;*

International Sugar Council, *Statistical Bulletin* and *Yearbook,* various issues;

International Lead and Zinc Study Group, *Lead and Zinc Statistics,* various issues;

British Bureau of Non-Ferrous Metal Statistics, *World Non-Ferrous Metal Statistics,* various issues;

Metallgesellschaft Aktiengesellschaft, *Metal Statistics* (Frankfurt-on-Main), various issues;

International Tin Council, *Statistical Bulletin,* various issues;

Petroleum Press Service, London, various issues.

International Rubber Study Group, *Rubber Statistical Bulletin,* various issues;

Monthly Statistics of Japan (Bureau of Statistics, Office of the Prime Minister), various issues.

* Actual consumption, taking into account changes in stocks, in the case of food, beverages and rubber. As regards other commodities, import ratios have been calculated by reference to apparent consumption (production plus net imports). A minus sign (−) denotes net exports.

a Including wheat equivalent of wheat flour.
b Allowance made for the meat equivalent of trade in live animals.
c Oil equivalent.
d Greasy basis.
e Production = removals; trade = wood, round and squared and partly worked.
f Estimated iron content.

Table 6

Imports of selected primary commodities into industrial countries* by area of origin, 1955 and 1969

Commodity	SITC code number	Total (million dollars) 1955	Total 1969	Intratrade* 1955	Intratrade* 1969	Group Iª 1955	Group Iª 1969	Group IIᵇ 1955	Group IIᵇ 1969	Socialist countries 1955	Socialist countries 1969
Food, beverage crops and tobacco											
Wheat and flour	041+046	1 077	1 295	34.9	53.0	42.6	36.9	19.7	4.3	2.8	5.8
Rice	042	266	119	27.8	62.6	3.5	2.3	61.2	30.7	7.4	4.4
Barley	043	287	359	35.5	74.5	41.2	17.3	21.7	5.4	1.4	2.8
Maize	044	330	1 195	52.3	67.4	15.3	6.0	27.1	25.0	5.2	1.6
Sugar	061	1 017	1 452	4.8	10.9	8.7	13.3	85.8	73.7	0.7	2.1
Live animals	001	268	982	43.3	42.1	42.9	21.2	9.3	13.1	4.5	23.6
Meat, fresh chilled or frozen	011	639	2 645	24.4	39.3	52.9	35.2	21.1	18.7	1.6	6.8
Butter	023	369	425	43.6	49.3	52.8	47.8	2.2	0.7	1.4	2.2
Other fats, oil-seeds and oils	091+22+4	1 672	2 608	34.2	45.0	6.0	9.5	55.6	37.0	4.2	8.5
Fresh fruit and edible nuts	051	1 025	2 391	25.6	26.1	28.2	25.7	46.0	46.9	0.3	1.3
Coffee	071	2 106	2 105	0.7	4.1	—	0.9	99.3	95.0	—	—
Cocoa	072	586	857	11.0	14.9	0.3	2.3	88.5	82.8	—	—
Tea and maté	074	450	320	2.7	5.9	—	2.0	96.8	90.7	0.5	1.4
Tobacco, unmanufactured	121	608	938	44.9	50.6	24.2	23.7	30.1	22.2	0.8	3.5
Sub-total		10 700	17 691	22.5	34.8	17.9	18.5	57.9	41.8	1.7	4.9
Agricultural raw materials											
Cotton	263	1 547	1 212	30.8	11.8	3.4	8.0	62.8	73.1	2.9	7.1
Wool	262	1 895	1 705	16.1	18.7	66.0	67.2	17.2	11.7	0.7	2.4
Crude rubber (including synthetic and reclaimed)	231	1 179	1 187	4.9	26.1	2.2	3.7	92.9	69.5	—	0.7
Hides and skins	211	351	679	29.9	36.9	30.2	32.8	39.6	27.1	0.3	3.2
Wood	242+243	1 685	3 991	31.9	30.0	41.2	25.9	17.5	30.2	9.4	13.9
Sub-total		6 657	8 774	22.3	25.3	32.0	29.0	42.5	37.6	3.2	8.1
Minerals and metals											
Iron-ore and concentrates	281	770	2 409	36.2	17.4	20.8	29.4	42.9	51.5	0.1	1.7
Non-ferrous ores	283	971	2 334	7.7	10.3	24.6	40.0	66.4	46.8	1.2	2.9
Copper	682	1 544	4 463	32.3	32.2	11.5	12.9	56.2	54.3	—	0.6
Aluminium	684	312	1 602	33.7	61.9	64.7	24.7	0.6	8.5	1.0	4.9
Lead	685	227	287	17.2	24.7	37.9	47.7	44.9	23.0	—	4.6
Zinc	686	139	277	44.6	35.7	39.6	37.5	13.7	15.9	2.2	10.9
Tin	687	224	472	39.3	15.9	—	0.6	60.7	80.7	—	2.8
Sub-total		4 187	11 844	27.4	28.2	22.0	24.1	50.2	45.4	0.4	2.3
Crude petroleum	331	2 863	11 115	0.8	1.1	1.5	5.1	97.5	92.3	0.2	1.5
Petroleum products	332	1 523	4 058	45.4	51.8	0.5	3.2	50.2	38.7	3.8	6.3
Total of commodities listed		25 930	53 482	22.2	26.0	19.3	17.5	56.6	52.2	1.9	4.3
Total excluding petroleum		21 544	38 309	23.4	30.6	23.1	22.7	51.6	42.0	2.0	4.7

Area of origin as percentage of total; Primary exporting countries comprise Group Iª and Group IIᵇ.

Sources: United Nations, *Commodity Trade Statistics, Statistical Papers, Series D,* various issues; OECD, *Foreign Trade Statistics Bulletin, Series C,* various issues.

* United States, Japan, EEC and EFTA excluding Portugal.

ª Canada, Australia, New Zealand, South Africa, Finland, Ireland, Iceland, Spain, Greece, Turkey and Portugal.

ᵇ All other primary exporting countries, elsewhere referred to as developing countries.

PRICING POLICY, INCLUDING INTERNATIONAL
PRICE STABILIZATION MEASURES AND MECHANISMS

Report by the UNCTAD secretariat*

[Original text: English]

The attached report, which deals specifically with questions of pricing policy in the field of international commodity trade, relates to only one part of item 13(a) of the provisional agenda. Its object is to clarify the issues involved in relation to international policies and actions affecting prices, which can in principle be envisaged as covering the whole range of primary commodities. The connexion between pricing policy and efforts to improve market access is not, however, overlooked. It concerns essentially that group of commodities for which impediments to imports exist in the markets of developed countries; and for this group the discussion in this report attempts to relate possible remedial actions designed to improve prices to those concerned with improving market access. Further discussion on the relationship between pricing policy and market access can be found in the progress report by the UNCTAD secretariat entitled "The development of international commodity policy" (TD/113).[1]

* The text of this report was circulated to the Conference as document TD/127, dated 7 February 1972.
[1] See p. 3 above.

CONTENTS

LIST OF TABLES

CHAPTER I

The background to the pricing problem

A. Secular trends in commodity prices and export earnings

1. Since the end of the boom in commodity prices associated with the Korean War in the early 1950s, the prices of primary commodities, and particularly those of commodities exported wholly or mainly by developing countries, have tended to decline. Overall measures of price trends, covering all countries and commodities, must however be used with caution since market trends have been very different for different groups of commodities.[2] This diversity of market trends in turn has been a major reason why there has been a great variety of experience as regards the trend in prices of exports from individual developing countries.

2. Over the past decade, the problem of deteriorating or stagnant price trends has affected essentially two major commodity groups: the natural agricultural products, which are facing increasing competition from synthetic materials, and the tropical foods and beverages, for many of which demand grows slowly and which tend to be in persistent surplus on the world market. In the course of the 1960s, the unit value of developing countries' exports of the first group—commodities competing with synthetics—fell by an average of about 3 per cent a year (equivalent to a decline of one-third over the full decade). This decline was slightly more than offset by an expansion in the volume of shipments, with the result that the export earnings of the developing countries concerned were virtually stagnant. In the second group—tropical foods and beverages—export prices declined by about 0.5 per cent a year, but, in consequence of an increase in volume, export earnings rose by 2.5 per cent a year (see table 1).

3. For both these groups, the expansion in export volume necessarily involved the use of additional productive resources in developing countries, and part of the growth in output reflected improvements in productive efficiency. These productivity improvements were, however, generally negated by the decline, or relative stagnation, in prices, and hence—to a greater or lesser extent—the benefit of productivity gains accrued to the importing, predominantly developed, countries.

4. Commodities produced in substantial amounts in both developing and developed countries, the production of which is usually protected in developed countries against lower-cost imports, constitute a third major group to be considered. For the major competing commodities, while there was a slight upward trend in export unit values (which rose, on average, by 1.5 per cent a year), the main contribution to the expansion in export earnings once

again came from increased volume (which rose by about 2 per cent a year). There were, of course, different price and volume movements within this group, the major price increase over the decade occurring in the case of meat, while average prices of vegetable oilseeds and oils declined.

5. The fourth major group distinguished in table 1—minerals and metals, other than fuels—experienced considerably more favourable market trends during the 1960s than any of the groups of agricultural products discussed above. The value of minerals and metals exported by developing countries over the decade rose, on average, by 9 per cent a year, and while the major contribution once again originated from an expansion in the volume of shipments, the rise in prices (by nearly 4 per cent a year) was substantial. Nonetheless, some important minerals within this group (iron ore and manganese ore) suffered from declining price trends.

6. These very divergent trends in export unit values over the past decade indicate that the pricing problem for developing countries' exports has been concentrated mainly in certain groups of commodities. Developing countries which are heavily dependent on such commodities for the bulk of their export earnings have tended generally to suffer from stagnation or inadequate growth in foreign exchange receipts from their merchandise trade. International action to achieve, and maintain, a more remunerative level of prices for such countries—provided that such action has no offsetting adverse effects on the volume of world demand—must inevitably be a major concern for the Conference.

7. Certain individual developing countries may nonetheless achieve a satisfactory rate of expansion in earnings from exports of commodities which face inelastic demand conditions, and which suffer from declining or stagnant price trends, provided that they can sufficiently expand their share of world exports. However, such an expansion in the market shares of some countries, which would reflect improvements in their relative competitive position, would be associated with inadequate growth rates in export earnings from such commodities by some other developing exporting countries, whose market shares would be declining. Thus, as the comparative advantage of certain countries for producing given commodities changes over time with differential rates of change in costs and productivity, the problem of sluggish growth in export earnings may shift from some developing countries to others.

8. Prospects for commodity prices during the rest of the 1970s cannot, of course, be assessed with any pretension to accuracy. Projections of the volume of exports from developing countries indicate, however, that much the same pattern of diversity among the various major commodity groups will probably recur in this decade as in the 1960s. If anything, the rate of growth in the volume of exports of agricultural commodities during the 1970s may well—on the basis of the latest FAO projections—be somewhat lower even than in the 1960s, if present policies

---

[2] For a more detailed analysis of movements in prices of commodity exports from developing countries, see the report by the UNCTAD secretariat entitled "Long-term changes in the terms of trade, 1954-1971" (TD/138 and Supp.1 and Supp.1/Corr.1) (for text, see *Proceedings of the United Nations Conference on Trade and Development, Third Session*, vol. IV, *General Review and Special Issues* (United Nations publication, Sales No. E.73.II.D.7)).

TABLE 1

Rates of change in unit value, volume and value of major
commodity groups exported from developing countries
(1959-1961 to 1967-1969)

	Unit value	Volume	Value	Value in 1967-1969
	(per cent per annum)			*(billion dollars)*
1. Natural materials facing competition from synthetics[a]	−3.0	3.9	0.7	3.56
2. Tropical foods and beverages[b]	−0.4	2.6	2.2	4.01
3. Competing agricultural commodities[c]	1.5	1.9	3.4	4.56
4. Minerals and metals (excluding fuels)[d]	3.8	5.0	9.0	4.70
Total of above	0.5	3.2	3.7	16.83
5. Fuels	..	..	8.6	14.86
TOTAL	..	..	5.7	31.69

Sources: FAO, *Commodity Review and Outlook, 1970-1971; Commodity Review, 1964, Special Supplement,* vol. 2; *Trade Yearbook; Yearbook of Forest Products Statistics;* and national statistics.

[a] Cotton, wool, natural rubber, tropical timber, jute and hard fibres.

[b] Coffee, cocoa, tea, bananas and pepper.

[c] Sugar, vegetable oilseeds and oils, cereals, beef and veal, citrus fruit and tobacco.

[d] Iron ore, copper, lead, zinc, tin, bauxite (including alumina and aluminium), manganese ore, tungsten concentrates and phosphate rock.

continue unchanged. Prices of agricultural raw materials seem likely to continue to decline as the competition of synthetics intensifies, while—in the absence of international agreement—prices of many major foods may also be under pressure. Prospects for exports of most minerals and metals from developing countries, on the other hand, will probably continue to be relatively promising.[3]

9. The problem of stagnant or declining prices for certain of the major commodities exported by developing countries would thus appear likely to remain in the course of the 1970s unless more vigorous, comprehensive and effective international remedial action is taken than has so far proved possible.

B. Short-term fluctuations in commodity prices and export earnings

10. The world markets for a wide range of primary commodities have continued to be subject, to varying extents, to short-term fluctuations in prices. Many developing countries have, as a result, also continued to experience considerable short-term fluctuations in their export earnings.

11. Short-term fluctuations in commodity prices are a reflection of complex interactions of temporary or random factors and seasonal and cyclical movements, both in production and in demand in major consuming markets. Of 11 primary commodities for which monthly price

movements exhibited substantial instability[4] in the second half of the 1960s, the majority—copper, pepper, rice, palm oil, cocoa, rubber and copra—suffered from greater instability than in the first half of that decade, as can be seen from table 2. On the other hand, instability was reduced, as between the first and second halves of the 1960s, for sugar, tungsten, lead and bananas. In a second group of primary commodities, described as exhibiting moderate price instability in the later 1960s, the majority suffered from a similar degree of instability—according to this classification—in the first part of the decade.

12. It is of interest, in principle, to distinguish, within the group of commodities suffering from short-term price instability, those for which prices are on a definite upward trend from those for which the trend in prices is either static or downward. For commodities which suffer from a downward price trend the market difficulties will be compounded if they also suffer from short-term instability. On the other hand, if the price trend is strongly upwards, this could diminish the adverse consequences of short-term price fluctuations for the export earnings of developing producing countries.

13. Only a minority of the commodities identified as suffering from substantial instability, however, exhibited definite upward trends in price in either the first or second halves of the past decade, viz. sugar, copper, cocoa, tungsten and lead, and among these, the trend was definitely upward in the second half of that decade only for sugar, cocoa and tungsten. The strong upward trend shown for sugar prices for the period 1960-1964 results from the abnormally high prices reached in 1963. Sugar prices

---

[3] For a more detailed discussion of the prospects for international commodity trade in the 1970s, see the report by the UNCTAD secretariat entitled "Trends in commodity trade in the 1960s and prospects for the 1970s" (TD/113/Supp.2 and Corr.1).

[4] As measured by the average percentage of deviations of monthly prices from a linear trend.

TABLE 2

Short-term price instability of selected primary commodities in relation to price trends, 1960-1970

	Instability indices[a]		Price trend[b]		Exports from developing countries (1967-1969 average)
	1960-1964	1965-1970	1960-1964	1965-1970	
	(per cent)		(per cent per annum)		(million dollars)
Group 1. Substantial instability[c]					
Sugar	35.0	21.8	+33.0	+13.5	1 523
Copper	13.3	15.3	+ 9.0	+ 0.7	2 143
Pepper	12.7	14.7	−11.4	+ 4.2	55
Rice	5.7	14.6	+ 2.0	+ 1.5	491
Palm Oil	3.5	14.3	+ 0.5	− 3.5	107
Cocoa	8.6	13.1	− 1.9	+14.2	668
Tungsten	22.5	12.5	−10.3	+17.8	33
Lead metal	17.3	12.4	+ 8.9	+ 0.1	58
Bananas	12.9	12.0	− 1.0	− 0.3	474
Rubber	7.4	10.6	−10.9	− 2.8	981
Copra	8.7	10.4	− 0.1	+ 0.7	207
Group 2. Moderate instability[d]					
Coffee	9.2	9.6	+ 5.8	+ 3.3	2 292
Groundnut oil	9.4	9.0	− 2.7	+ 3.2	104
Palm kernels	..	8.9	+ 3.0	− 0.9	59
Coconut oil	9.7	8.9	+ 0.7	+ 2.1	125
Groundnuts	6.7	8.9	− 2.6	+ 2.2	212
Sisal	12.3	8.0	+13.9	− 9.2	63
Tea	7.9	7.8	− 1.6	− 4.5	520
Tin	8.6	7.3	+10.5	− 1.4	405

Source: UNCTAD, *Monthly Commodity Price Bulletin*, various issues; FAO, *Commodity Review and Outlook*, various issues; national trade statistics.

[a] Average percentage deviation of monthly prices from linear trend.

[b] Linear trend calculated from monthly averages.

[c] Commodities for which instability indices exceed 10 per cent, for the period 1965-1970.

[d] Commodities for which instability indices fall between 7 and 10 per cent, for the period 1965-1970.

collapsed in 1964 and remained at very low levels in the following four years. The marked upward trend in sugar prices for the second half of the 1960s shown in table 2 reflects essentially the impact of the International Sugar Agreement of 1968 on the free market price in 1969 and 1970; for these two years only, the instability index is only 8.1 per cent. For cocoa, the sharp upward trend for 1965-1970 is misleading, since cocoa prices in 1965 were abnormally low; if 1966-1970 is taken as a more meaningful period, the upward trend is reduced to 9.8 per cent, the corresponding instability index being 12.5 per cent. Since the beginning of 1970, however, cocoa prices have fallen sharply, the downward trend being again accompanied by considerable short-term price variations. For tungsten, there is evidence of a cyclical movement, with prices generally declining up to mid-1963 and then rising until a peak was reached in early 1970; in both phases of the cycle, however, tungsten prices continued to show sharp variations, both on a monthly and on an annual basis.

14. At the other extreme, there were those commodities—natural rubber, sisal and tea—for which prices have tended persistently downward, at least in the later 1960s. Both rubber and sisal were under increasing pressure from alternative synthetic materials, and the instability in their prices was undoubtedly one element in their loss of competitive position in the world market. For natural rubber, the feasibility of an international arrangement to reduce the short-term fluctuations in natural rubber prices has not been seriously considered, yet it would seem reasonable, in the light of the above analysis, to include such an arrangement in the longer-term strategy for the natural rubber industry. For sisal, as for jute and abaca, informal price stabilization arrangements have been in operation under FAO auspices since 1968 or 1969.[5] Though the main need for these and other commodities facing serious competition from synthetics is to devise a viable long-term strategy—this is discussed in more detail in chapter II—such a strategy should include efforts to reduce short-term instability where such efforts would be feasible and appropriate.

15. The position so far as tea is concerned differs from that of the agricultural materials, since the short-term fluctuations of tea prices reflect very largely seasonal variations in the supply of the different grades and varieties. The major problem for tea is, rather, how to

---

[5] For further discussion of the problems of rubber and hard fibres, see chap. II below and the report by the UNCTAD secretariat entitled "Problems and international action concerning commodities covered by Conference resolution 16 (II)" (TD/113/Supp.1), p. 61 below.

devise longer-term policies to halt, and reverse, the downward price trend.[6]

16. Between these extremes are a number of primary commodities of importance in the export trade of developing countries for which the principal price characteristic appears to be short-term instability, rather than any definite upward or downward trend. The most important of these, in terms of export value, is copper. The upward trend of copper prices indicated in table 2 for the first half of the 1960s reflects almost entirely a sharp upward movement in the course of 1964, when prices reached a new, high, level; during the years 1960-1963 copper prices had, in fact, remained almost static as the result of informal pricing arrangements among producers. Since 1964, the copper market has been subject to sudden and substantial market variations around a virtually static trend. A number of vegetable oilseeds and oils also fall into this category, as do pepper, rice, bananas and lead (for coffee and tin international commodity agreements are in operation).

17. It should be emphasized that the commodities listed in table 1 (other than fuels) cover, in the aggregate, less than one-half of the value of primary commodity exports of developing countries. They are commodities for which price quotations are readily available, and the table should thus be taken as illustrative of the continuing importance of short-term price instability in world commodity markets, rather than as an attempt to identify all the commodities for which such instability remains a serious problem.

C. The problem before the international community

18. The objective of international action in regard to primary commodity prices, as set out in agreed form on many occasions, has been to secure stable, remunerative and equitable prices, with a view to increasing the foreign exchange earnings of developing countries. This formulation, which derives from the recommendation in annex A.II.1 to the Final Act of the first session of the Conference, was reaffirmed at the second session of the Conference,[7] and was incorporated in resolution 73 (X) of the Trade and Development Board and in paragraph 24 of the International Development Strategy for the Second United Nations Development Decade.

1. Price stability

19. As regards the objective of securing stable prices, the constraint has been, to a large extent, the technical problem of devising viable international market stabilization arrangements. By the end of 1971, formal international agreement designed, *inter alia*, to minimize short-term fluctuations in market prices were in operation for

coffee, olive oil, sugar, tin and wheat, while consultations on a draft agreement for cocoa were continuing.[8] In addition, informal price stabilization arrangements were operating, under FAO auspices, for jute and hard fibres.[9] The only other commodity for which an international market stabilization scheme has been under active consideration in recent years is the lauric acid group of vegetable oils.[10]

20. The position at the beginning of 1972 thus remains essentially unchanged from that prevailing at the time of the second session of the Conference, namely, that there are a number of important commodities subject to substantial short-term market instability for which international stabilization arrangements do net yet exist. It is for consideration whether a higher degree of priority should be accorded by the international community to devising such stabilization arrangements, on a commodity-by-commodity basis. On the basis of past experience, however, it would appear that the devising of suitable stabilization arrangements for additional individual commodities is likely to prove a difficult and time-consuming process.

2. Remunerative and equitable prices

21. Though there is general agreement on the objective of achieving a remunerative and equitable level of commodity prices, this formula is in too general terms to be effectively operational. Indeed, it would not be possible to devise criteria to determine, for any given commodity situation, a level of prices which could be expected to be accepted as both remunerative and equitable. Rather, the formula provides merely a general framework within which negotiations on particular prices, or price ranges, can be undertaken in the context of an international agreement or arrangement.

22. The strategy adopted so far in order to achieve the objective of remunerative and equitable prices has been to conduct a series of negotiations on a commodity-by-commodity basis. This would seem, in principle, to be a sound approach, since the different circumstances of each commodity market may well require different packages of remedial measures including, no doubt, somewhat different pricing policies. However, as indicated earlier, such negotiations, taking each commodity separately, are inevitably complex and time-consuming. So far, this strategy has had very limited success, whether one considers the range of commodities still suffering from

---

[6] For further discussion of the problems of the world tea market, see chap. II below and document TD/113/Supp.1, p. 61 below.

[7] See *Proceedings of the United Nations Conference on Trade and Development, Second Session*, vol. I and Corr.1 and 3 and Add.1 and 2, *Report and Annexes* (United Nations publication, Sales No. E.68.II.D.14), p. 236.

[8] The Wheat Trade Convention, 1971, attempts to stabilize prices by making market information available to member countries rather than by direct intervention. For more detailed discussion of the operation of commodity agreements, see the report by the Secretary-General of UNCTAD entitled "Effectiveness of commodity agreements" (TD/129 and Corr.1).

[9] An informal export quota arrangement for tea was also in operation under FAO auspices in 1970 and 1971, but this was designed to defend a price floor, rather than to even out short-term fluctuations.

[10] A feasibility study of a market stabilization arrangement for lauric oils was prepared in 1971 by the UNCTAD secretariat ("Feasibility of operating a supply stabilization scheme for the lauric oils market: returns, costs and financing" (UNCTAD/CD/Misc.41) and "an econometric model of the international lauric oils market: considerations for policy analysis" (UNCTAD/CD/Misc.43/Rev.1)).

substantial market instability, or those suffering from unfavourable price trends. In a sense, this situation creates a serious dilemma for the international community, since on the basis of past experience a continuation of the past strategy in this field cannot be expected to deal with the major remaining problems of commodity pricing within the Second Development Decade.

23. In the context of effort to achieve the agreed general objectives of international pricing policy with respect to a wide range of primary commodities by the end of the present decade, it would seem that at least two new aspects should be added to the existing strategy. First, a higher degree of priority must be given by the international community, and by the governments most concerned with particular "problem" commodities, to the need for concluding new international agreements, especially those including price provisions. In some cases, such higher priority would involve a more positive attitude to such agreements on the part of importing countries; in other cases, it would involve additional efforts by exporting countries to reach a mutually acceptable arrangement concerning market shares.

24. A second element in a commodity pricing strategy could be an identification of new measures which would support the traditional commodity-by-commodity ap-

proach. Are there any valid multi-commodity, or across-the-board measures in this area of policy? If so, to what extent are they likely to be negotiable, and what would be the costs and benefits to the various countries concerned? These are questions which would require considerable technical investigations before even approximate answers can be given, and they cannot therefore be considered in any detail in the present report.

25. However, a first step can be taken by considering the specific pricing problems of each of the broad commodity groups discussed earlier. The marked differences in price trends among these commodity groups reflect, to a considerable extent, underlying differences in market structures, and hence it is reasonable to expect that the appropriate pricing policy, designed to achieve remunerative and equitable prices in the sense of improving the trend in prices and in export earnings of developing producing countries, would be different for each group. If this proves to be the case, then the basic objective might be restated as the achievement of a pattern of price changes which would facilitate the rapid growth in the commodity export earnings of developing countries. Possible new approaches to the pricing problems of each of these broad commodity groups are explored in the following chapter.

CHAPTER II

Pricing problems of the main commodity groups

A. Natural materials facing competition from synthetics

26. The rapid expansion of the production of synthetic materials has been an outstanding factor in the industrial growth of the economically advanced countries since the end of the Second World War. The continuing emergence of new types of synthetics, often tailor-made for specific end-uses, reflects a vast investment of research and development resources. As a result, synthetic materials have been successfully evolved, on a large-scale commercial basis, which are often technically superior in particular uses to the natural materials traditionally produced for export in developing countries.

27. Moreover, with the benefit of substantial economies of scale accruing from the expanding output and size of plant, prices of major synthetics have been progressively reduced, thus forcing down prices of competing natural products. A further important competitive advantage of synthetic materials has been that, whereas prices of some competing natural products have shown considerable short-term fluctuations, it has been possible to maintain prices of synthetics reasonably stable over the short term.

28. During the 1960s, the competitive pressure of synthetic materials was steadily increasing in the world market over virtually the entire range of agricultural raw materials. The traditional natural textile fibres—cotton, wool, jute and hard fibres—suffered serious displacement in many important end-uses, as well as downward pressure on prices. The share of synthetic rubber in world consumption of elastomers grew from about 50 per cent in 1960 to about 65 per cent in 1970, while declining rubber prices

were associated with a relatively slow growth in the production of natural rubber. The sharpest expansion in the synthetics field, however, occurred in the production of plastic materials, reflecting in part the rapid growth in the petrochemical industries of developed countries. Plastic materials, which are produced in a large variety, substitute for a wide range of natural materials, including metals, leather, wood and paper, as well as textile fibres and rubber.

29. This growing competition between natural and synthetic materials must be expected to continue and, if anything, to intensify. It calls urgently for a viable long-term strategy for each of the natural materials affected. Within such a long-term strategy, pricing policy would necessarily have an important role, together with other remedial measures.

30. The major element in a long-term strategy for all the natural materials competing with synthetics would seem to be a greatly expanded research and development programme designed to improve their technical characteristics, to improve productivity so as to allow costs and prices to be reduced, and to find new end-uses.[11] Combined with intensive commercial promotion and agricultural extension work to diffuse the results of research and development, the progressive reduction of costs of production will remain an important policy objective, since this would improve the competitive position of natural

---

[11] For further discussion, see the report by the UNCTAD secretariat entitled "The competitiveness of natural products" (TD/117), p. 73 below.

materials in those end-uses where relative prices of natural and synthetic products are the major competitive factor, and at the same time enable production to be profitable even at lower prices.

31. Pricing strategy must, however, be linked with efforts to improve the technical characteristics of the natural product, since many synthetics have superior qualities for particular uses. The production of standard grades of natural rubber in recent years is an important example of the results of efforts to market a natural material with improved technical qualities, and these grades command a price premium over untreated natural rubber. The development of new end-uses, wherever practicable, as well as promotional activities, would assist in strengthening demand for the natural materials in question and so give support to a long-term marketing strategy.

32. A further element in a long-term strategy for these commodities would be to stabilize prices around the longer-term trend. The considerable fluctuations in the prices of these commodities have weakened their competitive position and helped to stimulate the expansion of production of competing synthetic materials. Prices would, however, have to be stabilized within a range (which would be subject to change), so that they are always maintained at levels fully competitive with the synthetic substitutes. The most feasible approach would seem to be the use of buffer stocks, either on an international basis or at a national level co-ordinated internationally, as the market structure is not suitable for traditional types of commodity agreements.

33. The objectives of pricing policy for this group of commodities can thus be restated as follows:

(a) To allow prices to remain fully competitive with those of competing synthetic materials through improvements in productivity and quality; and

(b) To minimize short-term fluctuations in prices for those natural materials for which such fluctuations are an important element in the competitive advantage of synthetic materials.

34. These objectives, as part of an over-all strategy, would be more readily attainable for some natural products than for others. For natural rubber, for example, the effect of any substantial reduction in production costs is likely to be to retard the installation of new capacity for the production of closely-competing synthetic rubbers. In the case of hard fibers, on the other hand, a decline in production costs cannot be expected, by itself, to maintain—let alone improve—their competitive position vis-à-vis the technically superior alternative synthetics becoming available in increasing amounts. Nonetheless, even for hard fibres, cost reductions would be an important element in an overall long-term strategy for the industry.[12] The degree to which prices of such natural products might be reduced in order to remain fully competitive with alternative synthetic materials will differ from one product to another; this is a topic which calls for further enquiry.

35. Further consideration also needs to be given to possible international arrangements for minimizing short-term price fluctuations. Among the commodities in this group, such fluctuations continue to be of importance particularly for natural rubber, jute and hard fibres and, to a lesser extent, for cotton.[13] The existing informal stabilization arrangements for jute and hard fibres, under FAO auspices, would seem to require strengthening, while the possibility of buffer stock operations for all these commodities—either on a national or on an international basis—would merit further examination.

B. Tropical foods and beverages

36. Because of the lack of direct substitutes in consumption, considerably greater scope exists for more positive international action on prices of tropical foods and beverages than in the case of products vulnerable to competition from synthetics.

37. For the major beverage crops—coffee, cocoa and tea—price behaviour tends to be complex, heavily influenced in the long term, as are most tree crops, by the considerable and changing lags in the response of production to changes in prices and, in the short term, by substantial seasonal variations in crop outturn and in other temporary factors on both the demand and supply sides of the market. For tea, the outstanding problem over the past decade has been a rapid expansion in exportable supplies, compared with a relatively slow growth in world import demand, with the consequence that prices have followed a marked downward trend.

1. EXPORT REGULATION AGREEMENTS

38. Because demand for the tropical beverages in the main import markets is generally inelastic, it is technically feasible to devise arrangements that regulate the total quantity coming on the world market so as to raise prices above the levels which would otherwise obtain. Since there is virtually no possibility, for most tropical products, of higher prices stimulating production in developed importing countries, such arrangements should result in a rise in prices, or in the prevention of a price decline that would otherwise have occurred, depending on the underlying market trends. Since 1963, such export regulation has been in force for coffee, with considerable benefits to the export earnings of the coffee producing countries.[14] Export regulation agreements for cocoa and tea have also been under active consideration by the countries concerned. For cocoa, the objective is essentially to stabilize the price within a pre-agreed range, whereas for tea the aim would be to halt the downward trend of prices and, to the extent possible, achieve a more remunerative level of prices than has existed in recent years.

---

[12] For a more detailed discussion of a possible long-term strategy for hard fibres, see "An evaluation of the informal stabilization arrangement for sisal and henequen" (TD/B/C.1/122).

[13] Lauric oils should also be considered in this connexion, since fluctuations in the market for this group of oils have been a factor in encouraging the use of synthetics in non-edible uses.

[14] One estimate put the net gain to coffee-exporting countries as high as $600 million a year during the period 1964-1967 (see *Foreign aid provided through the operations of the United States Sugar Act and the International Coffee Agreement: report to the Congress by the Comptroller General of the United States*, Washington, D.C., United States General Accounting Office, 23 October 1969).

39. These different objectives for cocoa and tea are reflected in differences in the market control measures under consideration. For cocoa, the consultations among interested governments within UNCTAD have considered a combination of measures, including export quotas and a buffer stock, while for tea, the discussions have focused on the possibility of a long-term export quota agreement only.

40. For the tropical beverage crops, demand is generally inelastic with respect to price changes unless prices rise to unusually high levels. Restriction of the growth in exports from developing countries would thus have a more than proportionate positive impact on prices, and the producing countries as a group would consequently receive a higher monetary return for a given investment of resources than would otherwise be the case. The difficulty in concluding such agreements arises rather from problems of reconciling the often divergent interests of particular countries, than from the approach itself. When world demand is increasing at a reasonably rapid rate, the problem of reconciling competing claims of producing countries is considerably easier than when demand is rising relatively slowly, as in the case of tea.

41. A corollary of an agreement which aims at raising prices to more remunerative levels by an export regulation scheme is that producing member countries will inevitably find it necessary to control their domestic production to avoid having to accumulate or destroy unwanted stocks. This control, in turn, logically demands diversification programmes which could, in principle, be financed in part from the proceeds of a levy on trade subject to export quotas.[15]

2. INTERNATIONAL FISCAL POLICY

42. An alternative approach to achieving a more remunerative level of prices for exports of tropical foods and beverages would be a co-operative arrangement by the trading countries concerned in the field of fiscal policy. This approach could be envisaged essentially as supporting and strengthening a series of export regulation arrangements, though for particular commodities—such as perishable foods—fiscal policy could be used where export regulation was not practicable.

(a) Action by exporting countries

43. Such fiscal arrangements can conveniently be divided into those enforced by exporting countries, and those enforced by importing countries. As regards the former, the simplest arrangement, in principle, would be a uniform ad valorem export tax. If applied simultaneously by all exporting countries, such a tax would not distort the relative price pattern for different grades and qualities of the commodity concerned, but would result in a higher level of prices for all grades and qualities.[16] In the case

of tea, however, this would probably be a difficult arrangement to negotiate, since certain major producers traditionally have taxed exports, while other producing countries have not.

44. A second possible arrangement, on the side of the exporting countries, would be an agreement to enforce a minimum level of export prices. Such an arrangement has been tried in the past for certain commodities.[17] However, in years of good crops, the enforcement of minimum prices necessarily involves involuntary accumulation of stocks by producers. This, in turn, could involve heavy expenditures, and financial loss if the quality of the crop in stock deteriorates. Thus, heavy pressure inevitably tends to arise for selling the entire exportable surplus, and this, in turn, tends to undermine a minimum export price arrangement.

(b) Action by importing countries

45. These various difficulties could be largely avoided by fiscal action on the part of importing countries. Here again, there are two major alternatives to be considered. The first would be the use of revenues from fiscal charges imposed on tropical products (import duties and/or internal sales taxes) for refunding to producing countries a proportion either (a) of the value of imports of tropical products, or (b) of the total of such fiscal revenues. Alternative (a) would be equivalent to a given percentage rise in prices of exports of these products from developing countries. Internal prices in importing countries would also rise, but since demand is inelastic in developed countries for most tropical products, the rise is not likely to have any substantial depressing effect on consumption. If, to take a purely hypothetical illustration, refunds of 20 per cent of imports of tropical beverage crops into developed countries had been made in 1970, the total transfers would have amounted to some $275 million for coffee, about $85 million for cocoa and about $65 million for tea.[18]

46. The application of such a scheme on a uniform basis by developed countries would, however, involve the imposition of new fiscal charges in those countries where no such charges at present exist, or increased charges where the revenue currently derived would be insufficient to pay for the transfer at the agreed rate.

47. Under alternative (b), no new fiscal charges would be involved, simply a transfer of a given percentage of existing revenue collected. The amounts involved are very considerable, particularly for coffee (for which fiscal charges yielded revenue in the region of $1,000 million in 1969 in the main developed market economy countries.[19] A transfer under this alternative—if made to individual exporting countries on a pro rata basis—would benefit most those countries which, for historical or other reasons, export wholly or mainly to developed countries with high fiscal charges.

---

[15] The Diversification Fund set up under the International Coffee Agreement, 1968, is so far the only example of this type of action. An alternative—which would, however, apply only in exceptional cases—would be to dispose of surplus stocks in non-traditional uses.

[16] Most of the tax would be borne by the consumer, since demand is inelastic with respect to price.

[17] For example, for cocoa and for sisal, for certain periods.

[18] In this calculation, the average price-elasticity of demand in developed importing countries was taken as −0.15 for coffee, −0.30 for cocoa and −0.05 for tea.

[19] See the report by the UNCTAD secretariat entitled "Access to markets" (TD/115), annex table 4, p. 40 above.

48. To avoid the need for imposing new fiscal duties, as well as an asymmetrical distribution of benefits to individual exporting countries, consideration might be given to the possibility of compensatory transfers being pooled in a central fund. The use of the fund's resources could then be supervised jointly by all the developing exporting countries concerned under pre-agreed guidelines (such as assisting in diversification programmes).[20]

49. It has often been argued that, since fiscal charges necessarily result in higher prices to consumers, they therefore restrict the market for tropical products exported by developing countries, and that developed countries imposing such fiscal charges should consider reducing or eliminating them. Recommendations to this effect were included in the recommendation in annex A.II.1 to the Final Act of the first session of the Conference, and also in resolution 73 (X) of the Trade and Development Board. However, the revenues collected by means of such duties are considerably higher than the additional export revenue which developing countries could earn as a result of the abolition of these fiscal charges.[21]

50. It was for this reason that one developed market economy country—Denmark—decided in 1967 to utilize the revenue from fiscal charges on coffee to assist the economies of developing countries, rather than to abolish the charges themselves. A Fund for the Industrialization of the Developing Countries was established, to assist investment projects by Danish firms in developing countries. Finance for the Fund is raised by the transfer of a progressively increasing proportion of the revenue raised by fiscal charges on coffee (the proportion so transferred rising from 20 per cent in 1968 to 50 per cent in 1972). The total amount to be transferred over the period 1968-1972 was envisaged as amounting to some $20 million.[22] The Danish scheme is, however, essentially a mechanism in the field of aid, rather than of trade. It does not aim at achieving a more remunerative price for developing countries exporting coffee, since its financial operations can relate to any developing country in which Danish private enterprise is contemplating new investment. Nonetheless, this is an interesting initiative which might point the way for similar action by other developed

countries, either on the same lines, or on lines discussed earlier in relation to the establishment of a fund under the supervision of the developing countries concerned.

51. The second alternative line of action which could be considered by developed importing countries for the purpose of achieving more remunerative prices for developing countries exporting tropical commodities would be a compensatory arrangement under which all, or part, of the difference between actual prices and an agreed reference price would be made up to the exporting countries. Such compensatory transfers could be financed, in principle, either from the proceeds of fixed or variable import levies, or direct from budgetary resources. Presumably, such transfers would need to be related to agreed quantities, or norms, in order to avoid an open-ended monetary commitment by the importing countries.[23] It may also be necessary to consider linking such transfers with diversification projects for transferring or diverting resources from the production of the commodities covered by the arrangement, where such diversification appears appropriate in particular developing countries.

52. Such compensatory arrangements should not necessarily be envisaged as purely alternative to an export regulation agreement. In some circumstances, compensation might also be used in support of export regulation, for example, in cases where export regulation can do little more than halt a persistent downward trend in prices over a period of years. Over the same period, importing countries could consider complementing the effects of the export regulation agreement by transfers which would, in effect, raise the net return to exporting countries to more remunerative levels, at least until the export regulation agreement can do so unaided.

3. IMPORTS BY DEVELOPING COUNTRIES

53. Consideration also needs to be given to avoiding increases in the prices of tropical foods and beverages purchased by developing importing countries, so as to relieve them of any additional costs which may arise from international action designed to achieve more remunerative prices for developing producing countries. Moreover, demand for tropical products in developing countries is believed to be generally more responsive to price changes than in developed countries, and any measures which avoided price increases for them would not therefore act as a brake on the growth of consumption.

54. The point arises essentially in connexion with the effects of an export regulation agreement, and of a uniform *ad valorem* tax on exports, as discussed above. In the former case, it might be possible to exempt exports to developing countries from export quotas; if this could be done, these countries would become residual markets in which prices would be lower than those paid by developed

---

[20] The idea of a central fund, based on import levies and administered jointly by the developing exporting countries to assist in the diversification and industrialization of their economies, formed an integral part of the proposals made by France at the first session of the Conference in relation to the organization of markets for temperate-zone foods (see *Proceedings of the United Nations Conference on Trade and Development*, vol. VI, *Trade expansion and regional groupings* (United Nations publication, Sales No. 64.II.B.16), p. 18), the same idea would appear equally applicable to tropical commodities.

[21] This follows from the fact that demand is inelastic with respect to price, so that a price decline resulting from the abolition of fiscal charges would result in only a relatively small increase in export value (for a more detailed consideration of this matter, see the study by the UNCTAD secretariat entitled "The development of an international commodity policy" (TD/8/Supp.1), in *Proceedings of the United Nations Conference on Trade and Development, Second Session*, vol. II, *Commodity problems and policies* (United Nations publication, Sales No. E.68.II.D.15), paras. 249-319.

[22] See *Proposed use of Denmark's coffee customs duties to aid developing countries*, International Coffee Organization, London, 12 June 1967 and 20 March 1968.

[23] A proposal on similar lines to offset the adverse effects of short-term price fluctuations on the export earnings of developing countries was made by Professor J. E. Meade at the first session of the Conference (see his paper entitled "International Commodity Agreements" in *Proceedings of the United Nations Conference on Trade and Development*, vol. III, *Commodity trade* (United Nations publication, Sales No. 64.II.B.13), p. 451).

countries.[24] In the latter case, the export tax would be applied only to shipments to developed countries. In either case, however, serious policing problems might arise in preventing such products exported to developing countries from being transhipped to higher-cost markets in developed countries.

C. Protected agricultural commodities

55. International trade in all the primary commodities in this group is affected to a substantial degree by protective measures in developed countries. Such measures limit the market outlets in these countries for competing agricultural products traditionally produced and exported by developing countries. They also give rise to production surpluses of certain commodities, which are frequently subsidized or sold on concessional terms by the developed countries concerned, a practice adding—at least to some extent—to the level of supplies coming on the world market, with consequential adverse effects on price levels.

56. Though the methods of protection of domestic agriculture vary widely among developed countries, the degree of protection remains very substantial, particularly in EEC and Japan.[25] Protection of domestic processing industries against competing imports is also general in all developed countries.

57. For a number of important commodities in this group the widespread use of protective devices has, in effect, resulted in the paradox of high internal prices in the markets of developed countries co-existing with relatively low prices received by developing countries exporting competing commodities.[26] A reduction in the degree of protection would not only result in improved market access—and thus have beneficial effects on the volume of exports of competing agricultural commodities from developing countries—but, to the extent that it reduced domestic production and/or stimulated consumption in the importing countries, would have the effect of raising world prices as well.

58. For certain competing commodities, special arrangements have been in force in a number of developed countries, designed to remove the paradox mentioned above, by providing guaranteed access for a given quantity of imports from certain developing countries at preferential prices. The most important example of such preferential arrangements relates to sugar. Imports into the United States, the United Kingdom and the USSR are either wholly or mainly transacted under such preferential arrangements,[27] at prices which are usually well above

those ruling on the free market.[28] In 1970, 59 per cent of the volume of net imports of sugar into the OECD countries came within the scope of preferential arrangements, and these represented 69 per cent of the total value of net sugar imports in that year.

59. Another example of imports at guaranteed prices was the arrangement between France and African franc-zone countries under which France guaranteed the purchase of given quantities of groundnuts and certain other vegetable oilseeds at prices well above world market levels.[29] This arrangement was superseded by the first Yaoundé Convention which entered into force in July 1967.[30] Under this Convention, deficiency payments were made to the Associated States when the prices of their principal oil and oilseed exports fell below agreed reference prices, such payments representing 80 per cent of the difference between the reference price and the market price, up to a maximum of $13 million for the period July 1967-April 1969. The Convention made provision, however, for the progressive elimination of the price premium, by financial aid designed to improve productivity and marketing methods in the Associated States. The deficiency payment system was not continued under the second Yaoundé Convention,[31] which instead provided for direct payments from the European Development Fund for productivity improvements and commodity diversification.

60. A more generalized approach to removing the price paradox for this group of commodities, with the object of achieving a higher net return for the exports of developing countries, could be pursued in either or both of two ways. The first would be to improve the net return received by exporting developing countries, either by extending the existing systems of preferential prices, or by initiating new compensatory payment systems. The second approach would consist of action to reduce internal prices in developed countries where these are excessively high in relation to world prices.

1. IMPROVING THE NET RETURN RECEIVED BY DEVELOPING COUNTRIES

61. One way in which a more remunerative level of prices could be achieved by developing countries for this group of competing commodities would be to extend the existing systems of preferential prices to all supplying developing countries, and to competing commodities not at present covered by such preferential arrangements. As

---

[24] A two-tier system is operated under the International Coffee Agreement, which exempts certain non-traditional markets, including the socialist countries of Eastern Europe, from quota restrictions.

[25] For details of the degree of protection accorded in the principal developed countries to the domestic production of particular agricultural commodities, see document TD/115, particularly chap. III and the tables in the annex, p. 20 above.

[26] The ratio of internal to external prices is one method of measuring the degree of protection.

[27] For details, see International Sugar Organization, *Statistical Bulletin*. Shipments into France and Portugal from their overseas Departments are also covered by preferential price arrangements.

[28] For example, the free market price (c.i.f., United Kingdom) averaged 6, 8 and 9.5 US cents per kg in 1968, 1969 and 1970, respectively, compared with a preferential price under the Commonwealth Sugar Agreement of 12.1, 11.2 and 11.6 cents respectively.

[29] For a brief description of the franc-zone market organization in the early 1960s, see the paper by Mrs. M. J. 't Hooft-Welvaars on "The organization of international markets for primary commodities", in *Proceedings of the United Nations Conference on Trade and Development*, vol. III, *Commodity Trade*, p. 458.

[30] Convention of Association between the European Economic Community and the African and Malagasy States associated with that Community, signed at Yaoundé on 23 July 1963.

[31] Convention of Association between the European Economic Community and the African and Malagasy States associated with that Community, signed at Yaoundé on 29 July 1969.

TABLE 3

Net imports of sugar by developed market-economy countries, 1965-1970

Year	From all preferential sources[a]			Free market supplies of sugar from developing countries			Hypothetical value of free market supplies from developing countries[e]	Difference between hypothetical and actual value
	Quantity (million metric tons)	Value (million dollars)	Average price[b] (cents per kg)	Quantity (million metric tons)	Value[c] (million dollars)	Average price[d] (cents per kg)	(million dollars)	(million dollars)
1965	5.32	706	13.3	2.12	125	5.9	273	148
1966	5.74	784	13.7	2.31	114	4.9	301	187
1967	5.90	835	14.2	2.40	128	5.3	316	188
1968	6.35	908	14.3	2.08	125	6.0	254	129
1969	6.14	883	14.4	2.35	190	8.0	267	77
1970	6.46	974	15.1	2.68[f]	252	9.5	315	63

Source: Based on data in International Sugar Council, *Statistical Bulletin*, various issues.

[a] Including imports from developed market-economy countries.

[b] Weighted average of negotiated price under Commonwealth Sugar Agreement (c.i.f., United Kingdom), and New York domestic contract price (c.i.f., net of duty).

[c] Quantity valued at corresponding average free market price.

[d] c.i.f., United Kingdom.

[e] Quantity of net imports of free market sugar from developing countries valued at corresponding negotiated price under the Commonwealth Sugar Agreement. No allowance has been made for the probable adverse effect on consumption of higher sugar prices in developed countries now importing wholly or mainly from the free market.

[f] In addition, 2.03 million tons were imported from developed market economy countries (for corresponding imports in earlier years, see International Sugar Council, *Statistical Bulletin*).

mentioned earlier, sugar is the outstanding example of the operation of such preferential price arrangements. Certain developed countries import sugar wholly or mainly at preferential prices, while others buy entirely from the residual free market. On infrequent occasions, the free market price rises to, or above, the preferential price range, because of temporary supply shortages. For example, over the past decade, the free market price exceeded preferential prices in 1963, and again in December 1971. On occasions when the free market price rises to the preferential levels, the situation is equivalent to one in which developed countries that import only from the free market were to agree to pay for these imports at preferential prices. For illustrative purposes, the additional import cost which would have been involved for such developed countries had they been importing sugar at preferential prices over the period since 1965 can be approximately estimated (see table 3).

62. In the period 1965-68, when the free market sugar price was very low, the additional cost of the arrangement discussed is estimated in table 3 to be in the range of $130 to $190 million a year. For simplicity, this calculation assumed that the countries which import sugar wholly or mainly from the free market would, in fact, have purchased the same quantities, in each year, under a régime of preferential prices. However, since there would have been some adverse reaction of higher prices on domestic demand, the figures shown are overstated to this extent. For 1969 and 1970, however, the additional cost of this hypothetical arrangement would have declined to only $60-80 million.[32] The principal burden of the additional

cost would fall on Japan, with the remainder falling on Canada and certain countries in Western Europe.

63. When free market prices rise to the level of preferential prices, the situation is, in effect, identical to that in which all developed countries agree to pay preferential prices for sugar imports from developing countries. The latter arrangement would, however, put a price floor—as well as a price ceiling—on the market.[33]

64. This arrangement would also allow developing importing countries to buy sugar at prices below the preferential levels, either through separate contractual arrangements with developing exporting countries, or on a free market basis. Since demand for sugar is considerably more responsive to price changes in developing than in developed countries, such an arrangement would not restrict the growth of consumption in developing countries.[34]

65. Such a system of preferential prices for imports into developed from developing countries, if viewed as an extension of the present preferential arrangements for sugar, would be based on bilaterally negotiated quotas

[32] Actually, the cost would be smaller because of the demand elasticity factor already mentioned.

[33] A similar result could also, in principle, be produced by an export regulation agreement of the type embodied in the International Sugar Agreement, but it would imply smaller basic quotas, and probably considerably more quota adjustment, than is the case under the present Agreement.

[34] Other approaches to organizing the world sugar market have also been suggested. For example, a recent study by the joint staffs of IMF and IBRD suggested a multilateral contract-type arrangement as meriting further consideration. A much more radical approach, involving the elimination of preferential prices for both imports and domestic production, while regulating the market by a combination of export quotas, a price range and a buffer stock, was also examined in this study (see IMF-IBRD, *The Problem of Stabilization of Prices of Primary Products—A Joint Staff Study (Part I)*, Washington, D.C., 1968).

for particular countries. While it would bring financial benefits to those developing countries that now rely wholly or mainly on the free market for their sugar exports, this type of arrangement would have certain drawbacks over the longer term. First, if considered as a self-contained policy divorced from measures to improve market access, it would leave untouched the underlying problem of the misallocation of world resources by the continued protection of high cost production in developed countries.

66. A second drawback would arise from the fact that all imports into developed countries would be subject to quotas arrived at independently by each importing country, rather than in a multilateral negotiation. The probable result, in practice, would be to introduce a considerable element of rigidity into the pattern of world trade, since there would be no multilateral mechanism to allow for quota changes reflecting shifts in productivity as between different supplying countries.

Price compensation

67. Moreover, a preferential price system would be more readily applicable to a homogeneous commodity like sugar than to a complex set of closely competing substitutes such as vegetable oils and oilseeds. For such less homogeneous commodities, an alternative approach to increasing the prices received by developing exporting countries would be the adoption of some method of price compensation, on the lines used by EEC under the first Yaoundé Convention.[35] A detailed examination of this approach was made in 1968 by a technical Working Party set up by the FAO Study Group on Oilseeds, Oils and Fats.[36] The Working Party examined *inter alia* the possibilities of compensating developing countries exporting vegetable oilseeds and oils by the use of levies on imports into developed countries, or by payments direct from national budgets of these importing countries.

68. As regards the levy system, the Working Party considered illustrative calculations, prepared by FAO in conjunction with UNCTAD, of the specific levies required to raise export earnings of developing countries by $20 per ton.[37] This increase could have been achieved (on the basis of 1961-1963 imports) if developed countries had imposed a levy of $10 a ton on all imports of fats and oils or, alternatively, a levy of about $3 a ton on total consumption. A later illustrative calculation by the FAO secretariat indicated that a variable levy, if applied throughout the period 1960-1967 and designed to make up 80 per cent of the difference between average world prices of tropical oils and oilseeds and the reference prices fixed by EEC for these products under the first Yaoundé Convention, would have varied between $11.5 per ton (if applied to imports) or $4.3 per ton (if applied to consumption) in 1961, and zero in 1964 and 1965.[38]

69. It would appear that the imposition of such levies would not result in any significant adverse impact on consumption, particularly if the levy was applied to total consumption rather than to imports, in view of the low elasticity of demand for fats and oils taken as a group.[39] Moreover, the small rate of import levy envisaged would be unlikely to result in a shift in demand in developed countries towards domestically-produced oilseeds; this possibility would, in any case, be avoided if the levy was related to total consumption.[40] A further potential problem would be how to prevent such compensatory payments from resulting in a stimulus to increased production, which would have the effect of reducing world prices, with a corresponding rise in compensation. This could be avoided by making the compensation available to governments, rather than to the individual producers, and by limiting the quantity of exports eligible for compensatory payments.

70. A compensatory payments approach would seem to be technically feasible for vegetable oils and oilseeds as a means of achieving a higher net return by developing exporting countries. As regards alternative financing methods, the FAO secretariat concluded that "budgetary financing would present fewer technical difficulties than arrangements based on specific levies, but specific levies also appeared to be technically feasible in certain circumstances".[41] Similar arrangements might also be appropriate for other primary commodity exports competing with domestic production in developed countries, and further technical studies would appear to be needed. If this approach should be feasible and desirable for a number of different competing products, a central compensatory fund might eventually be envisaged.

2. Reducing excessively high internal prices in developed countries

71. As indicated earlier, the second line of approach to reducing the differential in the prices received for competing commodities by producers in developed and developing countries would be action to reduce internal prices in developed countries where these are excessively high in relation to world prices. Such action, in turn, would imply a reduction in the degree of protection of domestic production of these commodities in relation to lower-cost imports.[42]

72. The effects of any given reduction in the internal price support for a particular commodity, such as beet sugar or vegetable oilseeds, on international trade would, however, be difficult to estimate. Much would depend on the potential of domestic producers to reduce their costs in

---

[35] See foot-note 30 above.

[36] See FAO, *Report of the Third Session of the Study Group on Oilseeds, Oils and Fats* (CCP 68/3), appendix II.

[37] *Ibid.*, appendix III.

[38] See FAO, "Compensatory arrangements" (CCP OF 68/5/3), December 1968.

[39] *Ibid.*, paras. 21 and 25.

[40] *Ibid.*, paras. 26-27.

[41] Report of the fourth session of the FAO Study Group on Oilseeds, Oils and Fats (CCP 69/3), para. 24. No agreement was, however, reached at that meeting (held in December 1968), and the proposals for a compensatory financing arrangement for vegetable oils and oilseeds have not been discussed since at the international level.

[42] For a more detailed discussion of the degree of protection of such commodities in individual developed countries, see document TD/115, chap. III, p. 20 above.

the face of a lower net return, and on the relative profitability of alternative crops, taking existing crop rotation systems into account, as well as on the reaction of domestic demand to price declines. In cases where the present degree of price support is relatively high, a small reduction in the support price is unlikely to have any substantial effect on import demand, particularly if there is an upward trend in productivity in domestic production. In such circumstances, there would not be any indirect positive effects on world prices. For any significant rise in world prices to materialize—at least over the short and medium term—there would need to be a reduction in the level of domestic price support large enough to result in a significant replacement of imported for domestic production.

73. Because of the uncertainty about the precise effects of a particular reduction in the price support accorded to specific commodities on the levels of production, consumption and imports, and on prices, it may not be very practical to envisage an "across the board" reduction in the levels of price support for commodities which compete with imports from developing countries. It has been argued elsewhere that a market-sharing approach would be a more reliable instrument for achieving an increase in exports of such commodities from developing to developed countries than would a standstill, or a given reduction, in protection.[43]

74. To this extent also, the market-sharing approach would be more effective in resulting, indirectly, in increases in world prices of competing agricultural products, than would an "across the board" reduction in price support levels. The two approaches are, of course, closely interrelated, since in order to achieve an agreed increase in the market share of consumption for developing country imports, it will normally be necessary to reduce the degree of domestic price support for particular commodities. But the market-sharing approach is more likely to ensure that the operation results, in practice, in an expansion in demand for developing country products.

75. For this group of commodities, therefore, pricing policy and market access questions are closely interconnected. The connexion can, perhaps, be further clarified by considering the approaches, discussed earlier, designed to achieve a more remunerative net return for exporters in developing countries by the use of a preferential price system, or by a system of compensation in relation to an agreed reference price. In the absence of simultaneous action to improve market access (and thus to reduce internal support prices), preferential price or compensation arrangements for developing country exports would, as indicated earlier, leave untouched the underlying problem of the misallocation of resources, on a world basis, in the production of particular commodities.

76. It would, however, be possible to envisage action on both prices and market access as mutually supporting efforts. For example, instead of relating preferential prices, or compensation payments, to a guaranteed quantity (based on past performance), they might be related to a progressively increasing quantity, as implied in any particular market-sharing arrangement. To the extent that market-sharing involves a reduction in internal support prices in developed countries, this reduction would presumably also imply the use of a lower reference price as a basis for a price compensation arrangement. Further, since world prices would tend to rise, at least in the short and medium term, the rate of price compensation would be narrowed. Nonetheless, the lower rate of compensation would be offset by expanding volume as the market-sharing principle began to take effect.

77. The details of such a combined approach would clearly be somewhat complicated, and fall outside the scope of the present report. However, if the developed countries would agree to an investigation of the potential of a market-sharing approach with a view to taking appropriate action, it should be possible to consider, in the same context, supporting action, of the type discussed above, which directly affects the prices received by developing countries for their exports of competing agricultural products.[44]

3. IMPORTS BY DEVELOPING COUNTRIES

78. As indicated earlier, action by developed importing countries to increase the net return per unit of exports to them from developing countries, by the extension of present preferential price systems, would not result in an increase in prices paid for the commodities concerned by developing importing countries.[45] The same is true for a system of price compensation operated by developed importing countries.

79. Another case, of importance to certain developing importing countries, concerns international agreements which regulate the world price of commodities, such as wheat, that are produced and exported mainly by developed countries. Where such international agreements attempt to raise prices to more remunerative levels for producers (mainly in developed countries), consideration needs to be given to some arrangement whereby developing importing countries can buy their requirements at lower prices than apply to developed importing countries.[46]

D. Minerals and metals

80. Though the market position and prospects of different mineral commodities vary considerably, they possess a number of important common features which justify a separate consideration of the pricing problems of this group of commodities. First, the characteristic which most clearly distinguishes mineral from agricultural commodities is their non-renewable nature. The long-term economic problem of developing countries which are

---

[43] *Ibid.*, chap. V, p. 20 above.

[44] While a joint consideration of pricing and movements in market access would seem desirable, it should not rule out the possibility of focusing action on either pricing policy, or on market access, should either course in isolation appear immediately negotiable.

[45] See para. 64, above. There might, however, be some indirect effects, depending on the reaction of production to additional preferential price arrangements.

[46] This would have been an important consideration for wheat-deficit developing countries had the price provisions of the Wheat Trade Convention, 1967, proved effective.

heavily dependent on mining for their economic development is essentially the replacement of a wasting natural asset by other capital assets of a more enduring character, in particular by the installation of productive physical capital and infrastructure, and by improved labour skills and know-how. Without such replacement, these countries will face particularly severe problems of readjustment as their mineral resources are depleted.

81. A second feature common to a wide range of minerals and metals is that world demand for them is relatively dynamic. The reason is that minerals are a basic input of modern industry, which is the focal point of economic growth in the developed countries. Though, as mentioned earlier,[47] prices of minerals and metals as a group shown have a marked upward trend over the past decade, for certain mineral ores—iron and manganese, in particular—prices have been under persistent downward pressure as a result of substantial expansion in mine capacity and ore supplies. Nonetheless, even for these minerals world demand has expanded at a substantially faster rate than for most agricultural commodities.

82. Third, the discovery and exploitation of mineral deposits require large capital investments and a high degree of technical skill and know-how, for which developing countries have had to rely heavily on large mining enterprises in developed countries. One consequence has been that the ownership or control of mineral resources and mineral exploitation in most developing countries is, to varying extents, in the hands of foreign enterprises.

83. Fourth, the expansion of mining industries in developing countries by vertical diversification through the establishment of smelters and refineries and the production of semi-finished and finished metal and engineering goods could play a major role in the process of industrialization, as well as increasing the value of their exports of minerals and mineral products. In this connexion, it is relevant to note that mineral processing gives rise to special environmental problems, a circumstance which may in the future favour a wider geographical dispersion of such industrial processes.

84. A pricing policy for minerals and metals must take account of these general features. However, its application to individual mineral markets will vary according to the special problems of each. These need detailed examination falling outside the scope of the present report. Nonetheless, it may be useful at this stage to consider how minerals might be grouped for this purpose according to the main features of their market structure.

85. At one extreme, there are those minerals for which demand is both price inelastic and relatively dynamic and for which developing countries have a very large share in total supply or, at least, in supplying the increment in demand. Petroleum is evidently the outstanding example of this kind of market structure, which has allowed the developing producing countries to exercise their quasi-monopoly power by acting in concert to obtain more remunerative prices (including taxes and royalties).

86. At the other extreme, are minerals (mica being one example) which face displacement in their traditional end-uses by synthetics or other substitute materials, or by new technologies which require different materials. The problem here—as for the corresponding group of agricultural products—is how to effect a sufficient reduction in costs and improvement in quality, which will make it possible for the natural material to remain competitive with potential substitutes.

87. Most mineral commodities fall in intermediate positions between these extremes. For minerals produced in substantial amounts by both developed and developing countries—such as copper, iron ore and manganese ore—the possibility of achieving more remunerative levels of prices could, in principle, be realized by close co-ordination among exporting countries (both developed and developing) of policies for moderating the over-all expansion in capacity and in exportable supplies. However, such action would prove ineffective in the longer term if prices were raised to levels which made it profitable for developed importing countries to expand their domestic production and/or to use cheaper substitutes. Where prices are on a declining trend, as has been the case for iron ore and manganese ore, action designed to restore prices to an earlier, more remunerative, level would be less likely to evoke production growth in importing countries or to stimulate substitution in the long term.

88. For minerals produced wholly or mainly in developing countries—tin being the major example—the scope for action designed to raise prices is limited essentially by the probability that such action would encourage consumers to turn to substitute materials for the production of particular end-products, or to develop new technologies which do not require such end-products. Plastic materials have become a major substitute for many metals in a great variety of end-products, while metals such as tin also compete with other metals, particularly aluminium, in a number of applications.

89. For certain minerals—manganese, nickel, cobalt and copper—consideration of possible international arrangements to achieve a more remunerative level of prices would have to take account of the probable exploitation of the mineral resources of the sea-bed outside the limits of national jurisdiction. A substantial addition to existing land-based production capacity might well involve adverse economic consequences for developing producing countries, unless adequate preventive measures were adopted by any central authority established to control sea-bed production.[48]

90. A further consideration is that many minerals occur jointly in the same ore bodies, and hence an expansion in production in response to a rise in the price of one mineral will tend to have repercussions on the supply—and consequently on the prices—of certain other minerals. Equally, an increase in the price of one metal will tend to call forth increased supplies of scrap for secondary production of that metal.

[47] See para. 5 and table 1, above.

[48] For further discussion of this issue, see the report by the UNCTAD secretariat entitled "The development of international commodity policy" (TD/113), p. 3 above. A detailed preliminary assessment of the problem is given in "Possible impact of sea-bed mineral production in the area beyond national jurisdiction on world markets, with special reference to the problems of developing countries: a preliminary assessment" (document A/AC.138/36).

91. Accordingly, because of the complex interactions in the markets for most minerals and metals, careful feasibility studies would be required before international export regulation arrangements for particular minerals or metals could be considered viable. Nonetheless, the possibility of devising such arrangements would seem to merit further consideration as regards those mineral commodities the prices of which have generally been on a downward trend.

1. SHORT-TERM MARKET INSTABILITY

92. Apart from the problems involved in achieving a more remunerative level of prices over the medium and long term for mineral and metal exports from developing countries, there remains the problem of continued short-term instability in the prices of many of these commodities. Such price instability has been particularly acute in the case of tungsten, copper and lead (see table 2). Demand for these metals is sensitive to changes in the level of industrial production, while supplies have also been subject to sharp and unpredictable changes.[49] An aggravating element, in the case of copper, has been the narrowness of the physical market on the London Metal Exchange, sales on which tend to set the level of copper prices used in most other transactions in this commodity.

93. Wide and unpredictable short-term fluctuations in price can be an important factor contributing to worsening the competitive position of particular minerals or metals. This observation would seem to apply to copper, since aluminium, its main competitor in a number of end-uses, has the advantage of relatively stable prices. Price fluctua-

tions affecting other non-ferrous metals, though they may not induce extensive substitution of more price-stable alternatives in the short run, may nonetheless encourage such substitution over a longer period.

94. More intensive intergovernmental consideration of possible market stabilization arrangements for such metals would now seem desirable. In particular, it would seem useful to undertake feasibility studies in regard to possible buffer stock schemes. One condition for the successful operation of a buffer stock, namely that the commodity in question must be capable of being stored at low cost, is fulfilled by each of the metals concerned. However, it would also be important to consider other conditions (such as that demand for the metal should be inelastic and that an effective and homogeneous market with well-defined grades should exist),[50] and to estimate the probable costs, and the possible sources of finance, for such stabilization schemes.

2. ROLE OF FOREIGN MINING ENTERPRISES

95. In view of the importance of foreign capital investment in the mineral sectors of developing countries, pricing policy in the widest sense would also need to be related to the general question of the part played by foreign mining and metal enterprises in the economies of developing countries. To arrive at mutually satisfactory arrangements, it would seem necessary to take into account the risks involved in foreign investment, as well as the need for progress in the mining sector to bring adequate rewards to the developing countries concerned. The techniques by which this might be ensured, however, fall outside the scope of the present report.[51]

---

[49] For more detailed consideration of the factors accounting for short-term price instability in the markets for these and other metals, see chap. II of the study by the UNCTAD secretariat entitled "The development of an international commodity policy" (TD/8/Supp.1), in *Proceedings of the United Nations Conference on Trade and Development, Second Session,* vol. II, *Commodity Problems and Policies* (United Nations publication, Sales No. E.68.II.D.15), pp. 8-24. For further discussion of the instability of tungsten prices, see the report by the UNCTAD secretariat entitled "Problems and international action concerning commodities covered by Conference resolution 16 (II)" (TD/113/Supp.1), p. 61 below.)

[50] For further discussion of the conditions for a viable buffer stock operation, see chap. II of document TD/8/Supp.1 (see foot-note 49, above).

[51] For an examination of some of these techniques (e.g. profit-sharing between foreign enterprises and the Governments of host countries), see "The exercise of permanent sovereignty over natural resources and the use of foreign capital and technology for their exploitation" (A/8058) especially chap. IV.

CHAPTER III

Special problems of the terms of trade

A. Trends in the terms of trade of developing countries

96. The problems created for developing countries by deteriorating or stagnant trends of the prices for their primary commodity exports have already been touched upon in chapter I. That these problems affected a considerable number of developing countries over the past decade is indicated by the fact that, out of 87 developing countries for which new export price series have been calculated, export prices in 1969-70 were, on average, about the same as they had been a decade earlier for 41

countries, while they were significantly lower for a further 11 countries.[52]

97. By contrast, the prices of imports—particularly of capital equipment and other manufactures—into developing countries exhibited a steady upward trend of about 1 per cent a year over the decade of the 1960s. By 1969-70, therefore, prices of imports into developing countries as a group were 11-12 per cent higher, on average, than in 1959-60. Towards the end of 1971, the devaluation of the

---

[52] TD/138 and Supp.1 and Supp.1/Corr.1 (see foot-note 2 above).

dollar resulted in an equivalent rise in the unit cost of imports from developed countries whose currencies had been revalued in dollar terms.

98. The majority of developing countries, therefore, have suffered a significant deterioration in their terms of trade[53] over the past decade. Even before allowance is made for the recent changes in currency valuations, the terms of trade had deteriorated between 1959-60 and 1969-70 for 49 out of the 87 countries for which the relevant indices are available, and of these the deterioration exceeded 1.0 per cent per annum, on average, for 22 countries.[54]

99. For most developing countries experiencing a decline in export prices over the past decade, the adverse effects on their export earnings were more than offset by increases in the volume of exports. Nonetheless, the deterioration in the terms of trade represented a real economic loss, since it involved a transfer of resources from developing to developed countries. The countries suffering the greatest relative loss in this sense included many heavily dependent on "problem" commodities, the prices of which declined significantly over the past decade. Indeed, the expansion in the volume of their primary commodity exports was itself one aspect of the process of transferring productivity gains from developing exporting countries to developed importing countries.[55]

B. The "indexation" issue

100. The generally deteriorating trend in developing countries' terms of trade over the past decade and, more particularly, the additional sharp deterioration which has occurred in the more recent period, have generated increasing interest in the possibility of linking the prices of commodity exports from developing countries with an index of the prices of their essential imports. The use in this way of an appropriate index of import prices for the purpose of maintaining the real purchasing power in world markets of a unit of exports has come to be known as "indexation".

101. The concept itself, however, is open to a number of different interpretations. First—and perhaps in its simplest version—it could be regarded as a link between the prices of commodity exports from developing to developed countries and those of imports into developing from developed countries. A provision on the lines of this interpretation was incorporated in the 1971 agreement between the Organization of Petroleum Exporting Countries and the international petroleum companies.[56]

102. A more general application of this concept, to cover in particular the prices of "problem" agricultural commodities exported by developing countries, would raise a number of difficult issues. One is that, for individual developing countries, the proportion of imports coming from different developed countries varies widely. It follows that, since prices can be expected to rise at different rates in different developed countries, the average rise in import prices might well differ significantly among developing countries over a given period. To allow for different rates of indexation for individual developing countries would, however, greatly complicate any arrangement. This difficulty could be overcome, to some extent, by using an index of export prices covering all products sold by developed to developing countries as a basis; or, more specifically, the price index could be related to exports to those developing countries heavily dependent on the problem commodities in question.[57]

103. Second, the concept could be regarded as relating the prices of primary commodities to the prices of the manufactured goods in which these primary commodities are incorporated. To take an illustrative example, it could be argued that it would be desirable to halt the downward trend in iron ore prices by an arrangement which would link these prices with those of finished steel. This approach would apply essentially to industrial raw materials, and would exclude most foods and beverages (which are not subject to any considerable degree of further processing).

104. One problem arising here is that increases in prices of the final product often reflect cost increases in both manufacturing and distributive stages. Corresponding increases in the price of the primary commodity concerned would not reflect the underlying supply and demand forces in the market for that commodity, and might tend to encourage an excess of production.[58] This problem would probably not be of importance if the linking were aimed at halting a downward price trend, and re-establishing an earlier, more remunerative, level of prices. If, however, the price trend was upward, it might be necessary to modify the link arrangement, so as to channel the additional resources to the Governments of producing countries rather than to the individual producers.

105. According to a third possible interpretation of the indexation concept, the prices of primary commodities would be related to changes in their cost of production. This idea is, in fact, the basis on which negotiated prices are arrived at in the context of the Commonwealth Sugar Agreement. One of the principles of that Agreement, first concluded in 1951, is that the negotiated price should be "reasonably remunerative to efficient producers".[59] At the last triennial review of the Agreement, in December 1971, significant increases were announced in the negoti-

---

[53] i.e. the ratio of the relevant export price to import price indices.

[54] See foot-note 52, above.

[55] Apart from problems arising from the longer-term trend in the terms of trade, there are also short-term difficulties which arise for individual developing countries as a result of a sudden deterioration in the terms of trade. Such changes, in so far as they result in short-term balance-of-payments difficulties can be largely offset by borrowing from the IMF under the compensatory financing facility.

[56] This agreement included the following provision: "Each of the companies will make a 2½ per cent upward adjustment of posted prices, for inflation, on 1 June 1971, and on the first of each of the years 1973-1975."

[57] A variant would be to use an index of prices of manufactured goods only exported from developed to developing countries.

[58] In some circumstances, this type of indexation might also encourage substitution of alternative materials in the manufacturing process for the commodity concerned.

[59] In addition, a special payment for the less developed exporting member countries, related inversely to the world price, has been made by the United Kingdom since the beginning of 1965.

ated price.[60] These increases were based essentially on cost data submitted by exporting member countries for the years 1968 to 1970.

106. Though the Commonwealth Sugar Agreement is an important example of this type of indexation, it should not be overlooked that it came into being mainly in order to provide a guaranteed market in Britain for Commonwealth producing countries, many of which operate at relatively high costs of production. If cost-indexation were more widely applied, there would need to be some provision for assisting high-cost producing countries to divert resources into other activities.

107. Finally, indexation could be related to changes in currency valuations. As mentioned earlier,[61] the recent devaluation of the dollar has involved a significant rise in average prices of developing countries' imports from developed countries as a group. The loss to petroleum exporting countries has already been offset by an agreement reached in January 1972 between the major international petroleum companies and six producing countries in the Middle East. Under this agreement, posted prices were increased with immediate effect,[62] while provision was also made for further adjustments, within the period covered by the existing marketing arrangement, based on an index of the relationship between the dollar and other major currencies. Other petroleum exporting countries, not parties to the above agreement, have undertaken to achieve a corresponding increase in export prices by unilateral action or by bilateral arrangements with the international petroleum companies.

108. Though, as indicated earlier, the petroleum producing countries are in a specially favourable bargaining position owing to their quasi-monopoly of supply, the idea of international arrangements which provide developing exporting countries with some guarantee against the loss of purchasing power resulting from currency revaluation would seem to merit consideration in a wider context.

109. However, the application of an indexation clause—in any of the various meanings discussed above—implies

that there exists some form of effective control over the world market for the commodities covered. Such control may be exercised through international commodity agreements covering both producing and consuming interests, through agreements among producing countries where appropriate or, in special cases, through the operations of multinational corporations acting in unison. Where there is no effective market control, indexation cannot be applied as part of an international commodity policy.

110. For commodities covered by international stabilization agreements, it is for consideration whether such agreements should, as a normal rule, include provision for a review—possibly on an annual basis—of their price objectives, on the basis of whichever from of indexation is considered by the commodity councils concerned as being most appropriate. Where the price objectives are stated in terms of a single currency, such provision would need to allow for the effects on import costs of developing member countries of any future currency realignments.

111. For commodities not covered by international agreements, some form of indexation can be envisaged—leaving aside the rather special case of petroleum—only where specific international fiscal arrangements have been adopted to increase the net return per unit of exports from developing countries. It was suggested earlier that, for tropical foods and beverages, and for competing agricultural commodities, there are a number of alternative approaches which might be envisaged, including *ad valorem* export taxes, partial refunds of the revenue from fiscal charges, compensation for the difference between an agreed reference price and actual prices on the world market, etc. Should any specific scheme on these lines be adopted, it would be feasible to consider incorporating an indexation provision similar to that suggested above for international commodity agreements.

112. For the remaining commodities exported by developing countries that are covered neither by agreements nor by fiscal arrangements, it is considerably more doubtful whether there is any scope for the application of indexation (apart, again, from petroleum). To the extent that such commodities bulk large in the export earnings of particular developing countries, remedial measures to offset unforeseen adverse changes in the terms of trade would need to be sought outside the realm of international commodity policy—for example by a scheme of supplementary financing.

---

[60] The negotiated price was increased by 15 per cent, from £43.5 to £50 per ton.

[61] See para. 97, above.

[62] The immediate rise, of 8.49 per cent, was intended to offset the net effect of the currency realignments on prices of imports into the petroleum producing countries concerned.

CHAPTER IV

Proposals for future work

113. Adverse trends in the terms of trade of many developing countries will probably remain an important constraint on the attainment of their economic development objectives, in the absence of internationally agreed remedial measures. Such measures should include action

designed to improve the export prices received by developing countries as part of a wider package of measures embracing, *inter alia*, improved access to markets, greatly expanded research in regard to products facing competition from synthetics, and accelerated diversification.

114. As regards measures designed specifically to improve the trend in prices, and to attain more remunerative levels for developing exporting countries within a range considered equitable by consumers, as well as to reduce excessive short-term market instability, it would appear desirable for the third session of the Conference to consider appropriate guidelines for further work in this field within the continuing machinery of UNCTAD. Such further work might perhaps be considered on the following lines:

(*a*) A higher degree of priority might be assigned to devising international stabilization agreements, or arrangements, for those commodities which still suffer from excessive short-term instability, or from a persistent stagnant or downward price trend, and for which such arrangements do not at present exist.

(*b*) For commodities for which such agreements or arrangements do not appear feasible, but which also suffer from short-term instability or long-term price stagnation or deterioration, feasibility studies might be envisaged of the costs and benefits of alternative forms of remedial

international fiscal policy to be applied jointly either by exporting or by importing countries.

(*c*) If a consensus is reached on the desirability of international action to improve the prices of commodity exports from developing countries in either, or both, of the ways mentioned above, consideration might also be given to the feasibility and desirability of channelling at least part of the additional revenues through an international fund, to be used for development purposes under the supervision of the developing countries concerned.

115. The consideration of guidelines for further work in relation to pricing policy should be coupled with consideration of how best to use the existing committee structure in UNCTAD to achieve desirable price objectives. As regards competing agricultural commodities, it would seem desirable to consider pricing policy within the framework of intergovernmental consultations of the kind envisaged in relation to market access.[63]

_____

[63] See TD/115, paras. 25-29, p. 16 above.

PROBLEMS AND INTERNATIONAL ACTION CONCERNING COMMODITIES COVERED BY CONFERENCE RESOLUTION 16 (II)

Report by the UNCTAD secretariat*

[Original text: English]

This report reviews in broad outline the implementation of Conference resolution 16 (II). It assesses the results achieved for different groups of commodities and attempts to draw certain conclusions from the experience gained.

Agricultural commodities and minerals and metals are the subject of two separate reports under the same title (TD/113/Supp.1/Add.1 and Supp.1/Add.2), which briefly discuss the problems faced by each commodity or group of commodities, international action taken since the second session of the conference, and further action that might be taken in respect of each commodity or group of commodities.

---

* The text of this report was circulated to the Conference as document TD/113/Supp.1, dated 22 February 1972.

CONTENTS

Chapter I

Summary of action taken under Conference resolution 16 (II)

1. Conference resolution 16 (II) is in the form of a programme of international action to deal with the urgent problems facing some twenty agricultural and mineral commodities of export interest to developing countries.[1] The essential problems relating to individual commodities covered in the resolution included short-term price instability, structural imbalance between supply and demand, severe competition from synthetic materials and appreciable trade barriers, depending on the commodities concerned. In view of the diversity and complexity of the issues involved, many of the recommendations set out specific remedial measures to be considered for individual commodities. The resolution collated these recommendations into a general programme, and established certain guidelines, priorities and procedures to be followed in its implementation. It was the first time that such an approach to international action on primary commodities was agreed upon at an international level, and it marked an important step towards the elaboration of an integrated international commodity policy.

2. For the purpose of assessing the results so far achieved in pursuance of the resolution, it is convenient to consider the commodities covered by the resolution in five groups.

---

[1] The value of the commodities specifically mentioned in the resolution accounted for about 40 per cent of total exports of primary commodities (excluding fuel) from developing countries in 1967.

A. Cocoa and sugar

3. For these two commodities, the resolution called for the convening of conferences in 1968 to conclude international agreements. A new International Sugar Agreement, for which preparations had been well advanced before the second session of the Conference, was concluded in September 1968 and came into force in January 1969. After the Agreement had been concluded, there was a substantial rise in the world market price of sugar despite the fact that some important consuming countries have not yet acceded to the Agreement. On the other hand, despite numerous consultations and strenuous efforts made since 1968, following preparations which had commenced much earlier, an international agreement on cocoa has so far not been concluded, though considerable progress towards that goal has been made. The need for a cocoa agreement remains real and urgent; all the more so since the failure so far to conclude such an agreement has had damaging consequences for a number of countries.

B. Oilseeds, oils and fats, natural rubber, hard fibres and jute

4. For each of these commodities, the resolution made specific proposals for action. With respect to oilseeds, oils and fats, it recommended that the Secretary-General of UNCTAD and the Director-General of FAO consider the necessity of setting up, at the earliest possible date, but not later than the end of 1968, an intergovernmental consultative committee on oilseeds, oils and fats to suggest short-term and long-term remedial measures. Extensive discussions on the implementation of this recommendation were held between the secretariats of UNCTAD and FAO and within UNCTAD and FAO bodies. Nonetheless, no agreement was reached among governments on the setting up of such an intergovernmental consultative Committee, even though at its special session in early 1970 the FAO Study Group[2] on Oilseeds, Oils and Fats had recommended consideration of a joint FAO/UNCTAD body. By a decision of the FAO Committee on Commodity Problems at its forty-fifth session, the terms of reference of the FAO Study Group on Oilseeds, Oils and Fats were expanded to include the work mentioned in resolution 16 C (II). The Study Group has undertaken an expanded programme of work, and set up a statistical sub-group to help prepare short-term market evaluations, and make policy recommendations. It has continued discussion of the longer-term problems, and of remedial policies, relating to this group of commodities. But international measures which would be of benefit to developing oilseed exporting countries have still to be agreed.[3]

5. So far as natural rubber is concerned, under resolution 16 D (II) the UNCTAD Permanent Group on Synthetics and Substitutes, in co-operation with the International Rubber Study Group was charged with the task of hastening the implementation of the measures for dealing with the problems of rubber indicated in the report of the UNCTAD Exploratory Meeting on Rubber held in December 1967.[4] Consultations have taken place in both UNCTAD and the Rubber Study Group on international action on rubber.[5] Some action has been taken by importing countries to eliminate duties on raw, semi-processed and processed forms of natural rubber. A survey of the research and development effort concerning natural rubber is being carried out under the auspices of the International Rubber Study Group at the request of the UNCTAD Permanent Group on Synthetics and Substitutes, with a view to assessing further research needs. However, decisions that could be of practical assistance to natural rubber producers have generally been few, there has been a continuing fall in the share of natural rubber in the total rubber market and natural rubber prices have fluctuated considerably in a declining trend.

6. With regard to hard fibres, the Conference requested the Secretary-General of UNCTAD and the Director-General of FAO to follow closely and evaluate the operation of the informal arrangement for sisal and henequen and for abaca (the object of which is to achieve the stabilization of prices at remunerative and equitable levels) and to consider further steps towards achieving the objectives of the informal understanding, including the possibility of a formal agreement. Since 1968, the informal arrangements have proved to have limitations as a means of stabilizing the market. In 1968 and 1969, the arrangement for sisal and henequen undoubtedly prevented losses in export earnings from being incurred by a number of developing countries.[6] A weakness of the arrangement in a situation of rapid stock accumulation in certain exporting countries, however, was shown in 1970 when no agreement could be reached on individual export quotas and on the minimum prices and differentials to be applied during 1970; prices, in turn, dropped to a post-war low. The reactivated informal arrangement for 1971 did not make provision for any specific minimum price, and market prices were substantially lower than indicative prices, which had been maintained unchanged.[7] The arrangement for abaca provides for indicative prices only, and in fact market prices fluctuated widely above the indicative level.

7. The Secretary-General of UNCTAD, pursuant to the request made in resolution 16 E (II), commissioned a report to evaluate the operation of the informal arrangement for sisal and henequen and to indicate a long-term strategy for this commodity. The report indicates the lines on which such a long-term strategy, covering price stabilization, diversification and the development of new and improved end-uses to improve the competitive position

---

[2] By decision of the FAO Conference in November 1971, all FAO study groups were renamed intergovernmental groups.

[3] For further details regarding international action on oilseeds, oils and fats see TD/113/Supp.1/Add.1, chap. VI, and TD/CONTR/2.

[4] See TD/39, paras. 23-24.

[5] See the report by the UNCTAD secretariat entitled "International action on rubber" (TD/B/C.1/121), and the report of the Expert Working Party on Rubber (TD/B/C.1/120).

[6] The Consultative Sub-Committee of the FAO Study Group on Hard Fibres, in its evaluations of the informal arrangements for sisal and henequen for 1968 and 1969, concluded that the informal arrangements had succeeded in bringing about a high degree of price stability, and in effectively supporting the sisal market in 1968 and 1969 at a level of prices which could not otherwise have been reached in the then existing supply/demand situation.

[7] For further details regarding international action on hard fibres, see TD/113/Supp.1/Add.1, chap. V, and TD/CONTR/2.

of sisal could be undertaken through international action. The report[8] will be circulated to interested Governments before the third session of the Conference to assist them in their consideration of further remedial action.

8. As regards jute, resolution 16 F (II) states that the informal arrangement on jute should be strengthened and that effective international action is necessary for the stabilization of the price of jute; the Conference recommended that the FAO Study Group on Jute, Kenaf and Allied Fibres, in consultation with the UNCTAD secretariat, should urgently explore the possibility of setting up an appropriate buffer stock scheme. Actually, the informal arrangement has been maintained but has not worked too effectively since 1967/68. In recent years, prices have fluctuated on an upward trend, and on occasion have risen well above the indicative limits set by the Consultative Committee of the Study Group. Moreover, while various proposals for the establishment of a buffer stock were put forward and discussed in the Study Group, no agreement has so far been reached on this matter.[9]

C. BANANAS, CITRUS FRUITS, COTTON, TUNGSTEN, TEA AND WINE

9. For these commodities, which are covered by specialized commodity groups or *ad hoc* meetings, the Conference requested the commodity bodies or *ad hoc* meetings concerned to identify the problems faced by the commodity; to determine the techniques appropriate for dealing with them; and to agree on appropriate remedial measures. By resolution 16 G (II) the Conference also requested the specialized commodity groups to examine the commodity concerned on the lines indicated above, in close cooperation with the Secretary-General of UNCTAD, and to transmit the results to the Committee on Commodities of UNCTAD for consideration and review. It further invited the Secretary-General of UNCTAD, taking into account the views of the commodity groups concerned, and after consulting with the interested member governments, to arrange for intergovernmental consultations.

10. This request has not, strictly speaking, been acted upon by the specialized commodity bodies concerned, in the sense that no specific examination in response to the resolution was carried out of the problems or of appropriate remedial measures. As a result, the specialized bodies did not transmit the results of any such examination to the Committee on Commodities for consideration and review. Moreover, certain of these bodies, when considering resolution 16 (II), agreed that they already provided an adequate forum for international consultations and that additional machinery was neither necessary nor desirable. Against this background, and taking into account the competence of the specialized commodity bodies, the Secretary-General of UNCTAD was not in a position to arrange for intergovernmental consultations concerning these commodities. It should be noted, however, that

regular consultations have been held within the specialized commodity groups, and various aspects of their work programmes broadly parallel the request made in the resolution. This work has in turn led, to an increasing degree, to policy recommendations on action in respect of the commodity markets concerned and, in some cases, to negotiations on informal stabilization arrangements.

11. The major problems of the world market for bananas and citrus fruits and possible international approaches to resolve them have been considered since 1968 by the specialized commodity bodies and a number of recommendations have been made, but it has not been possible to agree on international measures of a binding character.[10]

12. The problems facing cotton and the appropriate policies for dealing with them have been discussed since the 1950s in the specialized body concerned. The most concrete international effort made to improve the competitive position of cotton has been the research and promotion being carried out by the International Institute for Cotton, an organization financed by producing countries which was originally established under the auspices of the International Cotton Advisory Committee. In the case of tungsten, the prices of which are subject to wide fluctuations, the UNCTAD Committee on Tungsten has not, since the second session of the Conference, examined in depth the need and possibilities for international action to stabilize the tungsten market. However, the Committee's Working Group agreed at its 1970 session that its activities and those of the Committee on Tungsten represented a practical approach to the tasks envisaged in resolution 16 (II).

13. In the case of tea the FAO Consultative Committee on Tea held discussions broadly on the same lines as those contained in the request made in the resolution, and one result was the negotiation of an informal export quota scheme for 1970 and 1971/72 in order to achieve remunerative prices for the producing countries. The principles of a long-term agreement have also been discussed in the Committee, and two conciliators, from FAO and UNCTAD, have been holding discussions with exporting countries to facilitate reaching a consensus on these principles. With regard to wine, the FAO Study Group on wine and vine products established in 1968 has examined possible approaches to the problems confronting those products, and agreed on an action programme mainly relating to the provision of technical assistance in the production and marketing of wine.[11]

D. IRON ORE, MANGANESE ORE, PHOSPHATES, MICA, TOBACCO, PEPPER AND SHELLAC

14. In respect of these commodities, which are not covered by specialized commodity groups, the resolution likewise called for the identification of problems, for the determination of appropriate techniques for dealing with

[8] Note by the UNCTAD secretariat entitled "An evaluation of the informal stabilization arrangement for sisal and henequen" (TD/B/C.1/122).

[9] For further details regarding international action on jute, see TD/113/Supp.1/Add.1, chap. VI, and TD/CONTR/2.

[10] For further details regarding international action on bananas and citrus fruits, see TD/113/Supp.1/Add.1, chaps. I-II, and TD/CONTR/2.

[11] For further details regarding international action on tea and wine, see TD/113/Supp.1/Add.1, chaps. XIV and XVII respectively.

them, and for an agreement on appropriate remedial measures. The Secretary-General of UNCTAD, who, under the resolution, was requested to make such studies as may be appropriate and to arrange, after consulting with the interested member governments, the intergovernmental consultations he may consider necessary, convened an *ad hoc* meeting on iron ore in 1970, and arranged consultations on phosphates in 1972.[12] A further intergovernmental meeting on iron ore, and consultations on manganese ore, are scheduled to be held in February 1972. Consideration has also been given to the problems of tobacco and pepper in UNCTAD and FAO bodies, and to the problems of shellac and mica in the Permanent Group on Synthetics and Substitutes.

15. No international action involving producing and consuming countries has been taken to deal with the problems faced by these commodities. The discussions concerning iron ore have not so far resulted in general agreement on the nature of the main problems requiring international remedial action. The discussions on phosphates resulted in a consensus on the nature of the market problems facing the commodity, but the formulation and application of any remedial measures which might be appropriate require agreement, in a wider range of countries than were represented at the consultations held in Janauary 1972, on matters not sufficiently discussed at those consultations.

16. The question of establishing specialized commodity groups on tobacco and pepper has been under active consideration in FAO bodies, but no agreement among governments has been reached on their establishment so far.[13] As regards mica, the Permanent Group on Synthetics and Substitutes at its third session in 1969 agreed to include mica in the list of commodities to be covered by the factual survey of research and development to be undertaken by the UNCTAD secretariat. As regards shellac, the Group recommended to exporting countries that they consider the co-ordination of production, marketing, research and promotion; and to the international financial organizations that they give due consideration to making available financial and technical assistance for a research and development project to develop new and improved end-uses.[14]

E. TEMPERATE ZONE PRODUCTS

17. With regard to those temperature zone products not specifically mentioned in the resolution, the Secretary-General of UNCTAD was requested to continue to exchange information with FAO and GATT and other international agencies with the objective of making a comprehensive and continuing evaluation of the problems and of measures to be adopted for their solution. A major

development, though of limited benefit to developing exporting countries, was the entry into force in 1971 of the second Food Aid Convention under which food aid is given in the form of grains to developing importing countries. The current Wheat Trade Convention, which, like the Food Aid Convention, is part of the International Wheat Agreement, 1971, does not contain price control provisions or provisions concerning related rights and obligations but provides for international co-operation and consultation. Consultations on the problems of meat, rice and grains have also been held in the specialized bodies concerned with these commodities and, in certain cases, measures for their solution have been considered. However, remedial action, particularly in the form of measures to deal with the problems faced by developing countries exporting these commodities, has been limited.[15]

18. In response to the specific request addressed to the Secretary-General of UNCTAD concerning temperate zone products, two notes prepared by the secretariat[16] were submitted to the UNCTAD Committee on Commodities. The first note analysed the long-term trends for this group of commodities and proposed market-sharing as a possible approach to deal with the basic trade problems. The second note reviewed the trends in the markets of the major developed countries for temperate zone products and underlined the principal factors responsible for these trends.

Chapter II

Appraisal and conclusions

19. It is apparent from the foregoing summary that it has not generally been possible to attain the objectives of resolution 16 (II). Nor was it possible to adhere to the target dates where these were stipulated—except in the case of sugar—especially in respect of the recommendation (section G, para. 5) that studies and consultations should be held concurrently for a large number of commodities listed, and that they should aim at achieving practical results by the end of 1969. Although intensive consultations on individual commodities have been conducted there has, in fact, been a notable lack of success so far in the implementation of the resolution and in achieving practical results.

20. A number of conclusions can be drawn from the experience gained from attempts to give effect to resolution 16 (II). These can conveniently be discussed under three headings: those relating to (a) the economic and technical problems; (b) the consultative machinery, including the procedures for the execution and review of a programme of action on primary commodities; and (c) the political will on the part of governments to take remedial action. Such

[12] See the report of the *ad hoc* Meeting on Iron Ore (TD/B/C.1/75-TD/B/C.1/IRON ORE/1) and the report of the Consultations on Phosphates (TD/B/C.1/123-TD/B/C.1/PHOS/CONS./1).

[13] For further details regarding international action on pepper and tobacco, see TD/113/Supp.1/Add.1, chaps. IX and XV respectively.

[14] See *Official Records of the Trade and Development Board, Tenth Session, Supplement No. 3A* (TD/B/C.1/72/Rev.1-TD/B/C.1/SYN/34/Rev.1), paras. 39, 40 and 43.

[15] For further details regarding international action on meat, rice and wheat, see TD/113/Supp. 1/Add.1, chaps. VII, X and XVI respectively and (for rice) TD/CONTR/2.

[16] "Study on certain temperate zone products: market sharing" (TD/B/C.1/93) and "Trends in markets of selected temperate zone products in five importing areas" (TD/B/C.1/108 and Corr.1).

a grouping also makes it possible to distinguish more clearly the lines along which policies might usefully be directed in order to attain the objectives of an over-all strategy for improving the conditions of trade in primary commodities of interest to developing countries.

A. ECONOMIC AND TECHNICAL PROBLEMS

21. Because of the inherent problems affecting many commodities, it is often impossible to take rapid remedial international action.[17] The structures of the markets for the different primary commodities vary greatly. Some markets, for example that for fats and oils, which covers a group of competing commodities with a high degree of interchangeability among them and with synthetics, are extremely complex. Consequently, before feasible and practical international measures conforming to the peculiarities of the individual markets concerned can be agreed upon, difficult issues of an economic and technical and, in some cases, financial nature must first be studied. Such studies involve a great deal of analysis of the workings of the markets and a thorough investigation of the implications of alternative policies. Progress in such systematic studies is often slow and time-consuming because of gaps in existing knowledge and of deficiencies in available statistical data.

22. Experience has also shown that, even after intensive study and preparatory work for the establishment of international agreements, it takes a long time to resolve technical, economic and other issues at the stage of the negotiation of an agreement. The delay often arises as a result of the tendency to try to solve not only all the known basic problems involved but the potential ones as well before an agreement is concluded. A particular illustration has been given by the protracted successive consultations on cocoa during which considerable time was spent on very detailed technical questions.

23. It would seem necessary, when setting target dates for international action, to take fully into account the time required to resolve the underlying technical and economic problems. The question also arises whether there is a need to deal with all possible issues before concluding international commodity agreements or adopting other international measures, or whether some of them should be left to be dealt with at a later, more operational, stage and in the light of experience.

B. CONSULTATIVE MACHINERY

24. As regards consultative machinery, several important conclusions can be drawn from the experience of attempting to give effect to resolution 16 (II).

25. First, it would seem that existing machinery for consultations on individual commodities, both within UNCTAD and in the specialized commodity bodies concerned, has limitations as a means of achieving practical results of the type envisaged in the resolution. The institutional framework is, by and large, geared to deliberation, and not to the negotiation of binding commitments to take remedial action. In general, the existing institutional machinery is useful in that the specialized bodies offer a forum for the study and discussion of problems of the commodity concerned; for exchanging market intelligence and comparing policies; for reaching agreement on general conclusions and recommendations to be submitted to governments; and, in some cases, for establishing informal price stabilization arrangements. Usually, however, there are no procedures for giving effect to recommendations or for the enforcement of arrangements. In the light of experience it would seem that, although discussion in the specialized commodity bodies is of importance in bringing governments close to a consensus regarding suitable lines af action, while discouraging action having harmful effects, such discussion cannot by itself be expected to result in the adoption of concerted remedial actions for improving the conditions of trade of the commodities concerned. The adoption of such remedial actions requires political will on the part of governments (see paragraphs 30-35, below).

26. Secondly, it would seem that for most problem commodities what is urgently required is a consensus among producing and consuming countries on a longer-term strategy for dealing with the basic problems of the commodity concerned, and on a set of measures for early application which would operate within the framework of such a strategy. The major elements of a long-term strategy would differ from commodity to commodity to take account of the different problems and of diverse market structures. The longer-term policy aims might, for example, relate to facilitating market access (e.g. for competing agricultural commodities), diversification (e.g. for hard fibres), or a greatly expanded research and development programme (e.g. for agricultural raw materials).

27. For such a strategy to be meaningful and effective, agreement is necessary not only on priorities, but on a package of measures dealing specifically with long-term problems and also with immediate problems, such as short-term price fluctuations. In addition, procedures for carrying such measures into effect need to be agreed, including, where appropriate, financial support from both producing and consuming countries, as well as from international financial institutions.

28. The elaboration of such an international policy and programme of action for each commodity, and the review of its effectiveness, might be undertaken by specialized commodity groups where these exist. In particular cases, the scope of activities of commodity groups might need to be widened in order that they should be responsible for formulating and executing an effective strategy for the commodities concerned. It is desirable that such programmes be worked out in close co-operation with interested international agencies, especially with the international and regional financial institutions. In this connexion, it should be noted that, while all the important agricultural commodities entering world trade are covered by specialized international commodity bodies, the only such bodies dealing with minerals and metals are those concerned with tin, lead and zinc and tungsten.

29. Third, recent experience shows the weakness of

---

[17] Some of the complex problems involved, and possible approaches to overcome them, are discussed in various sections of TD/113/Supp.1/Add.1 and Supp.1/Add.2 and in other reports submitted to the Conference.

attempts to take remedial action for dealing with commodity problems narrowly or entirely on the basis of a commodity-by-commodity approach. When a number of commodities face similar or related problems, it would seem that a more fruitful approach would be to consider certain types of remedial action within a wider framework covering a number of commodities at the same time. The outstanding illustration of the need for a wider approach is the case of market access, which constitutes a major problem for a broad range of commodities.[18] Probably, market access could be more easily improved if it were considered in connexion with a wide range of commodities within a single framework. Within such a framework, differences in the circumstances of various commodities, and in the policies of the developed countries concerned, could be taken into account and national measures could be concerted so as to maximize the possibilities of trade expansion for the developing countries and facilitate any adjustments that may be required in developed countries. A similar multi-commodity approach might be required for designing programmes of research and development for natural products facing competition from synthetics, and for the mobilization of international financial and technical assistance to execute such programmes; or for a meaningful discussion of the question of special preferences at present accorded by certain developed countries to certain developing countries.

C. POLITICAL WILL ON THE PART OF GOVERNMENTS

30. Appropriate consultative machinery is essential; however, effective international remedial action depends ultimately on the policital will of the governments concerned and on their decisions. Where policital will has been shown, as in the case of sugar, agreement has been possible with substantial benefits derived therefrom. The experience of commodity consultations in the past few years does not, however, suggest that sufficient political will has been shown in respect of concrete international action on specific commodities.

31. Moreover, consultations on certain commodities mentioned in resolution 16 (II) have not so far resulted in general agreement on the nature and the scope of the problems requiring international remedial action, a major reason in the case of certain commodities being that market conditions widely recognized as having adverse effects on the interests of developing exporting countries having not been regarded by developed countries as general problems justifying action by the international community.

32. It would seem that the new emphasis brought to commodity trade policy as a result of the first session of the Conference is, by and large, not reflected in consultations relating to individual commodities. Remedial action still continues to be assessed by each country purely in commercial terms, and not as a common endeavour forming part of a broad strategy for contributing to the development of developing countries.

33. Equally, developing countries ought to display the political will to achieve practical results. Even for those commodities which are exported exclusively by developing countries and which do not face competition from synthetics and substitutes, effective action to improve prices and earnings by a co-operative effort to restrain the rate of expansion in exportable supplies has not usually been possible owing to conflicting national interests, particularly as regards the distribution of export quotas. Resolving such conflicts in an equitable manner requires a high degree of political will on the part of all developing exporting countries concerned.

34. To sum up, it would seem that the achievement of the agreed general objectives of international commodity policy—to improve the long-term rate of growth of the earnings of the developing countries from commodity exports and to reduce short-term fluctuations in those earnings, while taking into account the interests of consumers in importing countries—calls for a much higher priority to be given by the international community and by the governments most concerned with particular problem commodities, for a readiness to go beyond recommendations and conclusions with little or no practical consequences, and for a willingness to negotiate and conclude agreements, either on a commodity-by-commodity or on a multi-commodity basis, on various aspects which require remedial action such as price stabilization, market access, research and development and diversification. It would also be useful to fix agreed target dates for the achievement of practical results, though such dates would need to be set in a realistic manner.

35. A more vigorous strategy on commodities would require a far more positive attitude to negotiations and agreements on the lines mentioned above on the part of developed importing countries, and additional efforts by developing exporting countries to reach a mutually acceptable consensus among themselves on the major issues involved. Such efforts could be assisted by the existing permanent consultative machinery, strengthened as appropriate in the light of these objectives and taking into account the experience thus far gained.

---

[18] For a detailed discussion of the problems of improving market access, see the report by the UNCTAD secretariat entitled "Access to markets" (TD/115), p. 11 above.

MINERAL PRODUCTION FROM THE AREA OF THE SEA-BED BEYOND NATIONAL JURISDICTION: ISSUES OF INTERNATIONAL COMMODITY POLICY

Report by the UNCTAD secretariat*

[Original text: English]

The question of mineral production from the sea-bed first arose within UNCTAD as a result of General Assembly resolution 2750 A(XXV) of 17 December 1970, which requested the Secretary-General of the United Nations to co-operate with the United Nations Conference on Trade and Development (and other bodies) in order to:

"(a) Identify the problems arising from the production of certain minerals from the area beyond the limits of national jurisdiction and examine the impact they will have on the economic well-being of the developing countries, in particular on prices of mineral exports on the world market;

"(b) Study these problems in the light of the scale of possible exploitation of the sea-bed, taking into account the world demand for raw materials and the evolution of costs and prices;

"(c) Propose effective solutions for dealing with these problems."

The UNCTAD secretariat reported to the Committee on Commodities at its sixth session on its co-operation with the Department of Economic and Social Affairs of the United Nations Secretariat in the preparation of relevant studies pursuant to General Assembly resolution 2750 A (XXV).[1] In the discussion of this subject at the Committee's sixth session, representatives of developing countries stated that they attached great importance to the subject matter of General Assembly resolution 2750 A (XXV); that the co-operation envisaged in the resolution should be regarded as referring to UNCTAD at the intergovernmental as well as the secretariat level; that provision should be made for the Committee on Commodities to be informed of, and to discuss, developments in this field on a continuing basis; and that an opportunity should be provided for an examination of the matter at the third session of the Conference.[2] Similar views were expressed at the eleventh session of the Trade and Development Board.[3]

Accordingly, the secretariat has prepared the present report, which briefly discusses, in the light of information so far available on the subject, the main issues of international commodity policy arising from the potential production of minerals from the area of the sea-bed beyond the limits of national jurisdiction.

---

* The text of this report was circulated to the Conference as document TD/113/Supp.4, dated 7 March 1972. Parts of a preliminary version were incorporated in a report of the Secretary-General entitled "Possible impact of sea-bed mineral production in the area beyond national jurisdiction on world markets, with special reference to the problems of developing countries: a preliminary assessment" (A/AC.138/36), submitted to the Committee on the Peaceful Uses of the Sea-Bed and the Ocean Floor Beyond the Limits of National Jurisdiction.

[1] See the note by the UNCTAD secretariat entitled "Recent decisions by the Trade and Development Board and the General Assembly" (TD/B/C.1/115), paras. 8-12.

[2] See *Official Records of the Trade and Development Board, Eleventh Session, Supplement No. 4* (TD/B/370-TD/B/C.1/119), paras. 234-236.

[3] See *Official Records of the General Assembly, Twenty-sixth session, Supplement No. 15* (A/8415/Rev.1), part three, paras. 152-153.

Introduction

1. The possible exploitation of the mineral resources of the area of the sea-bed and the ocean floor, and the subsoil thereof, beyond the limits of national jurisdiction[4] raises novel issues of great complexity. For the first time, international resources recognized by the General Assembly in its resolution 2750 A(XXV) of 17 December 1970 as "the common heritage of mankind" are available for exploitation by the international community "for the benefit of mankind as a whole, taking into account the special interests and needs of the developing countries." The General Assembly has also affirmed, in the same resolution, that the development of these resources should by undertaken "in such a manner as to foster the healthy development of the world economy and balanced growth of international trade, and to minimize any adverse economic effects caused by the fluctuation of prices of raw materials resulting from such activities." In these special circumstances, the international community itself has a decision-making role as to the conditions to be applied to any production of minerals from the sea-bed.[5]

2. The following notes are designed to throw light on the nature of the economic effects, particularly upon world markets, of production of minerals from the sea-bed, and on the character of possible arrangements to obviate, remedy or minimize any adverse impact of such production on developing countries that are established land producers of the minerals concerned.

3. The mineral resources of the sea-bed which, in the light of present knowledge, are the most likely to be commercially exploitable in the foreseeable future are "manganese" nodules—containing copper, cobalt, manganese and nickel—and, less immediately, petroleum and natural gas.[6] Pilot-scale mining of manganese nodules has already been carried out, and it is reported that a syndicate expects to start exploiting particular nodule deposits in the Pacific Ocean within a few years.[7] The volume of manganese nodules on the sea-bed is reported to be vast, and to be growing at an estimated annual rate which exceeds the present annual consumption of the component metals.[8] The proportions of the various metals contained in manganese nodules differ from those of current world metal requirements as reflected in the composition of world production of 1968, as the following figures show:

	Metal in sea-bed nodules	Metal in world production
	(per cent)	
Manganese	90.0	56
Copper	4.5	40
Nickel	4.6	4
Cobalt	0.9	0.15
	100.0	100.0

The developing countries at present account for the bulk of international trade in manganese ore, cobalt and copper, but for only a small proportion of trade in nickel.

4. In considering the implications of production of minerals from the sea-bed, allowance should be made for the possibility of new major mineral discoveries on the sea-bed in the future, as well as for future improvements in the techniques of mining from the sea-bed, and thus for the possibility that production could occur on a larger scale, and cover a wider range of minerals, than can be foreseen at the present stage.

I. General nature of consequences

5. Since the sea-bed would constitute a completely new source of supply of whatever mineral was being produced, and since it can reasonably be assumed that such production would not occur unless it was competitive with output from land sources, sea-bed production would tend to have a depressing effect on the market price of the mineral concerned. The magnitude of the impact upon supplies and prices would depend upon the technical qualities of the sea-bed mineral, the particular circumstances of sea-bed production—the volume of additional supplies in comparison with land-based output, the costs of production and marketing, and taxation rates—as well as upon the conditions of supply and demand, including the responsiveness of prices to a given increment in supplies. If the pre-existing situation with regard to the mineral concerned was one exhibiting an upward trend in the mineral's price, the effect of sea-bed production would be to slacken or halt, or even reverse, the upward trend; if, on the other hand, the market price was constant or declining, the effect would be to bring about a decline or to accentuate a pre-existing decline. Generally speaking, therefore, although reliable quantification is not possible—both because of the absence of firm information on the circumstances of sea-bed production and because of the intrinsic difficulties of estimating market effects—the introduction of sea-bed production could be expected to result in a lower market price of the mineral(s) concerned than would otherwise have prevailed.

II. Consequences for consuming countries

6. It follows from the foregoing that the greater availabilities and presumed lower marginal costs associated with the production of minerals from the sea-bed

---

[4] Henceforth referred to, for the sake of brevity, as "the sea-bed". Final international agreement concerning the delimitation of the area beyond the limits of national jurisdiction has not yet been reached.

[5] The establishment of an equitable international régime, including international machinery, for the peaceful utilization of the sea-bed and its resources is envisaged in General Assembly resolution 2750 C (XXV). Discussions with a view to elaborating such an international régime are currently proceeding in the Committee on the Peaceful Uses of the Sea-Bed and the Ocean Floor Beyond the Limits of National Jurisdiction and are intended to culminate in agreement at a conference on the law of the sea scheduled to be convened in 1973.

[6] For a useful summary of available information on the prospects of exploitation of the mineral resources of the sea-bed, see document A/AC.138/36 (in particular, para. 10).

[7] A/AC.138/36, para. 139.

[8] *Ibid.*, para. 152.

would bring direct benefits to the consumers of the minerals concerned, who are, by and large, the mineral-using industries in developed countries. As is typical in primary production, the productivity gain resulting, in this case, from technological progress making lower-cost sea-bed production possible would be largely passed on to the consumers, in the form of lower prices, in the absence of any countervailing measures.[9]

III. Consequences for land producers

7. As mentioned in paragraph 5 above, sea-bed production would exert a downward pressure on the market prices of the minerals concerned. This would happen particularly in the case of those minerals, such as cobalt and manganese, which would be jointly mined with the more valuable minerals, nickel and copper, and which would be recoverable from manganese nodules in relatively greater proportions than those of world demand for the component metals.[10] The strong possibility of a sharp impact of sea-bed mining upon the market prices of certain minerals is indicated by illustrative calculations which show that five sea-bed mining operations, each harvesting 5,000 tons of nodules per day, would yield, annually, quantities of manganese equivalent to over one-half of the current annual rate of manganese exports of the developing countries as a group, and quantities of cobalt equivalent to the entire annual cobalt output of the developing countries.[11]

8. Secondly, because aggregate demand for many minerals is not very responsive to falls in their prices, output from the sea-bed would tend to displace marginal land production (or such land output as was previously marketed in the country in which the new supplies emanating from the sea-bed were consumed). This adverse quantitative effect would be compounded by the restrictive effects on land production of its diminished profitability and the accompanying decline in investment resources.

9. The over-all consequence of the price and volume effects mentioned in paragraphs 7 and 8 would be that the total earnings of land producers from the minerals concerned would decline or would grow less rapidly than they would have done otherwise—in any event, they would be smaller than in the absence of production from the sea-bed. The severity of the impact would vary among countries and producing enterprises according to relative efficiencies, patterns of trade and market structures.

10. However, as world demand for the minerals concerned is expected to continue growing, at rates of possibly 5 per cent or more per year, the addition of supplies from the sea-bed would not necessarily prevent established producers from land-based sources from expanding their own exports, and would not necessarily result in declines in market prices below pre-existing levels.[12] On the other hand, mineral sea-bed production could not be assumed to have such a moderate impact on world mineral markets unless the rates at which new supplies were marketed were strictly controlled by the international authority which it is envisaged should be established.

11. Although the most important effect of sea-bed production of minerals on world markets concerns the trend and level of prices of the commodities in question, such output might also accentuate short-term price fluctuations. This might occur if the flow of supplies from the sea-bed was irregular; it might also occur if the bulk of sea-bed production was undertaken by vertically integrated commercial enterprises, with the concomitant result that the world's "free market" for each mineral concerned would account for a declining proportion of total physical transactions, so becoming more of a residual market with greater price sensitivity to given changes in supply or demand.

12. The economic impact of competing production of minerals from the sea-bed, which might be expected to be adverse to varying extents for the export incomes of all established producers (in relation to the incomes that they would otherwise earn), might be particularly adverse for typical developing producing countries. This could be so for a variety of reasons:

(a) Developing producing countries typically depend more heavily on the minerals concerned (such as copper and manganese ore) for their export incomes and government revenues than do developed producing countries.

(b) The share of developing countries in world trade in certain minerals (notably manganese ore) has been declining owing to the more rapid progress made in the developed countries' production for export.

(c) The developing countries are likely to participate directly to only a small degree in the production of minerals from the sea-bed, for, because of its technically sophisticated nature and its high capital requirements, this production will no doubt be undertaken principally by interests from the affluent and technologically advanced countries.

(d) Developing countries, which are increasingly processing land minerals before export, would lose such potential export income to the extent that minerals produced from the sea-bed were processed on the mainland of the producing enterprise's "home country".

---

[9] Compare Nicholas Kaldor's remarks that "whereas the benefits of technical progress in manufacturing are largely retained by the producers (in the form of higher real wages and profits) the benefits of technological progress in primary production are largely passed on to the consumers in the form of lower prices, leaving little benefit to the producers in the form of a higher real income. (The exceptions to these are to be found in those cases—such as oil—where the distribution of the commodity is controlled by large international concerns.)" ("Stabilizing the terms of trade of under-developed countries" in ECLA, *Economic Bulletin for Latin America*, vol. VIII, No. 1, March 1963.

[10] The incremental cost of recovery of the mineral from the nodules, in relation to the prevailing market price, would be a further relevant factor.

[11] See A/AC.138/36, tables 1 and 17 and paras. 155-160.

[12] The more rapid the growth of world demand for a particular mineral, the greater is the possibility of concurrent increases in available supplies from both the sea-bed and land sources without a resultant decline in market prices. Thus, if cobalt were increasingly used as a substitute for nickel, world requirements of cobalt would increase much more rapidly than they would otherwise, and the impact of a given volume of marine production of cobalt on market prices would be moderated. (In that event, however, a given volume of nickel recovered from nodules would have a more severe impact on the market price of nickel than it would otherwise.)

Moreover, the stimulus that sea-bed production would undoubtedly impart to the existing technological trend towards the direct processing of mineral concentrates, and the avoidance of intermediate processes which are now partly carried out in developing producing countries, would aggravate the loss of potential export income on the part of developing countries.

(e) The need for large-scale capital investments for the exploration and mining of sea-bed resources might adversely affect the flow of private investment into similar activities in developing countries.

(f) Because fewer alternative investment and employment opportunities exist in developing than in developed countries, particularly heavy economic and social costs will be incurred in any re-allocation of resources that may be necessitated by the competition from sea-bed production.

IV. Some implications for policy

13. The essential problem that would arise from the production of minerals from the sea-bed would thus be the adverse impact of such production—in the absence of special arrangements—on the economic well-being of the developing producing countries concerned, and the consequential difference between the social costs and benefits of sea-bed production and its costs and benefits judged simply in terms of normal commercial criteria. The implication of this conclusion for international policy is that firm arrangements would be required in advance of the production of minerals from the sea-bed in order to ensure that such activity would not adversely affect the interests of developing producing countries or, better, would bring them, and other developing countries, positive benefits.

14. There would appear to be two possible approaches to the problem of protecting the trade interests of the developing countries that are established exporters of the minerals in question: an approach designed to obviate or minimize any potential adverse effects; and an approach under which the affected countries would receive compensation for the estimated adverse impact upon their export earnings.

A. THE PREVENTIVE APPROACH

15. The preventive approach would consist essentially of arrangements to ensure that output from the sea-bed will not result in prices that are not remunerative to reasonably efficient developing countries which are established producers of the minerals concerned (from land-based sources). For this purpose, it would be necessary that the rate of production from the sea-bed, or the rate of disposal of such output, or the selling prices or related terms of its disposal, should be strictly controlled by the proposed international authority, in order that the market prices for the minerals concerned are not depressed below levels declared by the international community as remunerative and equitable. Thus, an appropriate pricing policy might involve the setting of "floor" selling prices in respect of output from the sea-bed, supplemented by the

imposition as necessary of import levies by importing countries in order to forestall price-cutting by any private producers who might be permitted to operate under the international régime.[13] If such import levies were imposed, the proceeds would presumably be remitted to the sea-bed authority.

16. If the interests of established producing countries were protected through the setting of minimum selling prices for sea-bed minerals at levels designed to be remunerative to producers from land-based sources, a greater proportion of the net revenues of the sea-bed authority would become available to assist the economic development of non-producing developing countries, including land-locked countries, as envisaged by the General Assembly in its resolution 2750 (XXV).

B. THE COMPENSATORY APPROACH

17. Under the alternative, compensatory approach referred to in paragraph 14, compensation would be paid to developing exporting countries whose interests were adversely affected by production of minerals from the sea-bed. This compensation would be paid to the extent possible out of the net revenues accruing to the international authority from the exploitation of the sea-bed, either in the form of royalties, fees and taxes (if the international authority did not itself carry out the production activities), or in the form of profits (if the sea-bed authority engaged directly in the exploitation of the sea-bed). By means of this approach, an appropriate proportion of the net receipts of the sea-bed authority would be utilized for the purpose of compensating developing producing countries.

18. The formulation of workable compensation arrangements would, however, pose issues of considerable complexity. One issue relates to the criteria by which the extent of the "adverse impact" on the producing countries concerned would be measured: one possible yardstick might be the extent of any shortfall of proceeds from exports of the mineral(s) concerned below recent realized levels, or below the levels they might reasonably have been expected to reach in the absence of sea-bed production; allowance might or might not be made for the loss of benefits from any additional processing of the mineral suffered as a result of sea-bed production. Other issues are whether the arrangements should be on a commodity-by-commodity basis or should cover collectively all the minerals concerned; whether the arrangements should have a specified duration, and how frequently they should be reviewed. Regarding the apportionment of compensation funds, the amount of the compensation should presumably be assessed by reference to the potential export income lost as a result of sea-bed production, account being taken also of total foreign exchange availabilities, the degree of development of the country

---

[13] The arrangements should be kept as simple as possible. If, however, it became necessary to conclude comprehensive international commodity arrangements for the minerals concerned, in order effectively to protect the interests of producing developing countries, the operation of an international buffer stock of each relevant mineral by the international authority could, as in the case of the International Tin Agreement, be a useful adjunct to other measures for maintaining prices within any agreed ranges.

concerned and the scope for alternative employment of manpower and other resources.

19. A critical question relating to the compensatory approach is whether the net income of the sea-bed authority would be sufficient to implement a programme of compensation payments as outlined above. Although it is impossible to be precise on this point, it would seem that, in cases in which the developing countries account for most, or an appreciable part, of the international trade in the minerals in question, the net income accruing to the proposed international authority from sea-bed production would almost certainly fall short of the amount required to compensate developing producing countries for export proceeds lost as a result of sea-bed production, if the loss were regarded as including the growth of exports which would otherwise have taken place. This would be true in the case of cobalt, manganese ore[14] and copper, although probably not in the case of nickel, in the world exports of which the developing countries account for only a small proportion. There are two reasons why the loss in export earnings would probably exceed the net revenue of the sea-bed authority: first, the demand for most minerals is such that, other things being equal, an increase in available supplies often leads to a more than proportionate decline in prices, with a resultant fall in total proceeds; second, the net revenues of the sea-bed authority could not realistically be expected to exceed 10-30 per cent of the gross proceeds from the sale of sea-bed minerals, with the possible exception of petroleum. In these circumstances, in order to apply the compensatory approach, it would seem necessary that arrangements should be made to ensure that the shortfall in the required amount of financial compensation would be made good by consuming countries and/or the international financial institutions.

20. On the other hand, if developing exporting countries were to be compensated merely with a view to sustaining their historical export incomes from the minerals concerned, the net revenues of the sea-bed authority might well be sufficient for the purpose, although even this would be somewhat doubtful in respect of cobalt, manganese ore and copper. In any case, the latter, static approach would appear to be inconsistent with the International Development Strategy for the Second United Nations Development Decade, paragraph 19 of which envisages a positive contribution to meeting the trade and development needs of the developing countries through the formulation of a coherent set of international measures for development.

V. Other considerations

21. Whatever the nature of the arrangements made to protect the interests of the developing producing coun-

tries, a fundamental condition concerning sea-bed production should presumably be that no overt or disguised stimulus should be given to such production, since it would be at the expense of the mining industries on land, including those of the developing countries. As a corollary to this condition, if production activities were carried out by national enterprises, rather than directly by the international authority, provisions as to taxation and the conditions governing entry of the product into the home country of the producing enterprise should be such that supplies originating from the sea-bed should not receive preferential treatment by comparison with land production. Consideration would also need to be given to the possibility of avoiding the inbuilt "preference" for sea-bed production which would arise from the carrying out of such production by integrated enterprises based in developed countries.

22. In view of the possibility of market disruption, it would seem important to ensure, from the outset, that particular sea-bed mining projects would result in an over-all net gain to the international community, and especially to developing countries. The General Assembly, in resolution 2750 (XXV), envisaged the transfer to non-producing, including land-locked, developing countries of equitable shares of the benefits derived from the operations of the sea-bed authority, as well as the protection of the interests of producing developing countries. This particular objective would seem to call for the imposition of the maximum rates of royalties, taxation and fees that the traffic could bear in regard to sea-bed production, if the international authority did not itself carry out the production activities. The combined imposts should, at minimum, have an incidence at least equivalent to that of the average of national imposts on land production of the minerals concerned.

VI. Conclusion

23. The foregoing examination shows that the potential exploitation of the mineral resources of the area of the sea-bed beyond the limits of national jurisdiction has implications of great importance for international trade and development in the minerals sector and, in particular, for the export position and prospects of developing exporting countries. Bearing in mind both the potential effects of mineral sea-bed production and the international ownership of the resources concerned, the Conference may wish to express its views concerning: (a) generally, the commodity policies which would be appropriate in relation to the possible exploitation of the mineral resources of the sea-bed; and (b) in particular, the implications of alternative approaches to resolving potential problems arising from the production of minerals from the sea-bed, with special reference to the economic well-being of the developing countries.

---

[14] For example, in respect of manganese ore, it has been estimated that one sea-bed mining operation would result in a loss of potential export income to land-based producers of manganese ore amounting to about $15 million per year (see A/AC.138/36, annex II, para. 36).

THE COMPETITIVENESS OF NATURAL PRODUCTS

Report by the UNCTAD secretariat*

[*Original text: English*]

This report contains a number of suggestions for intensified international action to improve the competitiveness of natural products facing competition from synthetics. It takes into account the results to date of the survey of research and development efforts for these products initiated by the Permanent Group on Synthetics and Substitutes,[1] as well as the Group's conclusion, "that comprehensive programmes of international action aimed at the expansion of research and development efforts for natural products facing competition from synthetics were urgently required".[2]

---

* The text of this report was circulated to the Conference as document TD/117, dated 8 March 1972.

[1] These results are summarized in the report by the UNCTAD secretariat entitled "The competitiveness of natural products: research and development efforts and needs" (TD/117/Supp.1).

[2] See *Official Records of the Trade and Development Board, Eleventh Session, Supplement No. 4A* (TD/B/366-TD/B/C.1/112-TD/B/C.1/SYN/62), para. 32.

CONTENTS

Chapter I

The impact of synthetics

1. The seriousness of the competitive challenge to natural materials presented by synthetics is illustrated by the fact that, in terms of value at constant prices, the consumption of man-made fibres in OECD countries increased more than two and a half times between 1959-1961 and 1967-1969, while that of natural fibres declined. Jute was the only natural fibre whose consumption rose; use of cotton stagnated and that of wool and hard fibres fell in each case. Of the total increment in OECD consumption of elastomers in the same period, again in terms of value at constant prices, synthetic rubber accounted for 90 per cent and natural rubber for only 10 per cent. In 1971, the average price of natural rubber was less than half its level in 1960, and the prices of wool and

sisal were lower by 25 per cent and 34 per cent, respectively.

2. These movements underlay the declines in the earnings of developing countries from exports of rubber, wool and hard fibres, and the relative modesty of the increases in cotton and jute earnings, which occurred in the 1960s. In the case of wool, the position of developing countries exporting the commodity was also weakened by the fact that the developed countries as a group became less dependent on imports during the decade; on the other hand, developing countries exporters of cotton benefited to some extent from the fact that the developed countries, on balance, became less self-sufficient in cotton. The value of developing countries' total exports of agricultural raw materials, almost all of which are affected to varying extents by competition from synthetic substitutes, rose at an average rate of less than 1 per cent per annum during the 1960s. Thus in the First United Nations Development

Decade the production of agricultural raw materials for export, which absorbs large amounts of productive resources in developing countries, made virtually no net contribution to the expansion of export earnings which these countries urgently require for their development.

3. For developing countries heavily dependent on exports of agricultural raw materials, therefore, the competitive challenge of synthetics poses serious problems of resource allocation and development strategy. If competition from synthetics was entirely a matter of price, the response required from producers of natural materials would be clear; they would have to keep on improving productivity, or accept declines in the profitability of their operations which, sooner or later, would lead them to transfer resources from production of the natural material into more remunerative uses.

4. The policy issues facing producers of natural materials would be equally clear if competition from synthetics was based entirely on their possession of innately superior and inimitable quality and technical characteristics. If this were the case, producers of natural materials would indeed have to accept, as is sometimes claimed, that the displacement of natural materials by synthetics is the inevitable result of technological progress, and that diversification is the only answer to their problem.

5. In certain sectors of the markets for particular natural materials, either price or technical characteristics may, in fact, be the predominant factor in the competitive challenge from synthetics. For example, competition between cotton and rayon is almost entirely based on price, while the superior wearing qualities of synthetic rubber and plastics have been the main reason for the large-scale displacement of leather by these materials in the manufacture of footwear soles. In many cases, however, the natural material retains a clear technical advantage over the synthetic substitute (for example, natural rubber is superior to synthetic rubber for the manufacture of heavy duty vehicle tyres), and there are few cases where, independently of price, the technical characteristics of synthetic materials give them a decisive advantage. Moreover, in many of the cases where the characteristics of the synthetic material are superior to those of the corresponding natural material, the possibility of producing similar characteristics in the latter has not been adequately tested by research. An example of what can be achieved by such research is the progress that has been made in imparting to wool and cotton fabrics some of the easy-care properties responsible for much of the competition for these materials from man-made fibre fabrics. It should be noted, furthermore, that some of the inroads made by synthetics into the markets for natural materials are attributable neither to price nor to quality factors, but to intensive promotional campaigns designed to influence consumers' tastes, preferences and judgements.

Chapter II

The need for co-operation among producers

6. The defensive response which producers of natural materials need to make to meet the challenge of synthetics is therefore a complex and many-sided one, involving promotion, improvement of productivity and quality, and research and development (R and D) directed towards the reduction of costs in processing, the improvement of the technical performance of natural materials as well as of the goods made from them, and the discovery of new end-uses for these materials. There is every reason to believe that action in these areas could check the inroads being made by synthetics into the markets for natural materials, and might even enable the latter to recapture some of the ground they have lost.

7. Before such defensive action can be taken, however, producers of natural materials must first decide what is likely to be the most effective strategy for improving the competitive position of each material concerned (*i.e.*, the most effective combination of the measures mentioned above), and then mobilize the considerable resources required to translate that strategy into action. The difficulty which producers of natural materials have in taking these steps explains why, in general, their response to the challenge of synthetics has so far been inadequate.

8. The difficulty arises essentially from the fact that natural materials, in contrast to synthetics, are generally produced in large numbers of economically weak producing units. Many of these units, some of which may be peasant farms, are not large enough to benefit from economies of large-scale production, and most of them lack the resources to conduct their own research into ways of improving productivity. It is not economically possible, moreover, for any one unit producing, say, cotton, wool, jute, sisal, rubber or leather to work out an appropriate strategy for improving the competitive position of the material concerned on the world market and to finance its implementation.

9. Unless they co-operate, therefore, producers of natural materials cannot hope to offer an effective response to the threat from synthetics. In countries producing relatively large proportions of the total world supply of a particular material, co-operation at the national level may be highly effective. This is shown, for example, by the success of the Malaysian Rubber Research Institute in developing higher yielding rubber trees, methods for increasing the yields of rubber trees and improved forms of natural rubber. However, international co-operation can eliminate wasteful duplication of research efforts and can increase the total volume of resources available for research, development and promotion. In most cases, because of the economic weakness of the producing units, international co-operation has to be of an intergovernmental character.

10. For some natural materials, co-operative arrangements among producers already exist at both the national and the intergovernmental levels. The wool boards of Australia, New Zealand and South Africa, which represent both the wool-growers and the Governments of the countries concerned, have been collaborating since before the Second World War for the purposes of wool research, development and promotion through the International Wool Secretariat. Recently the wool growers of Uruguay have become associated with the work of that Secretariat. Within the last few years, the Governments of the principal cotton growing countries have established the International Institute for Cotton for similar purposes.

11. The rubber growers of Malaysia, the leading natural rubber producer, collaborate for purposes of production research through the Malaysian Rubber Research Institute and its dependent unit, the Natural Rubber Producers' Research and Development Board, but the functions of this body are confined to the maintenance of liaison between national research institutions; it does not itself plan or execute R and D activities. Co-operation among rubber producing countries at the intergovernmental level was established by the formation in 1970 of the Association of Natural Rubber Producing Countries, whose objectives are to promote co-ordination of production and marketing, technical co-operation and the attainment of fair and stable prices for natural rubber.

12. By contrast, for jute, hard fibres, leather, vegetable oils and essential oils, no co-operative international efforts by producers are at present being made in the fields of research, development or promotion. The need for such efforts, however, has been studied in FAO by the intergovernmental groups on jute, hard fibres and oilseeds, oils and fats, and in the Group of Experts on research and development for hides, skins and leather convened by UNCTAD in November 1971.[3] The last-mentioned body, in its report to the Permanent Group on Synthetics and Substitutes, recommended that the international co-ordination of expanded R and D and promotional activity for hides, skins and leather should be entrusted to an appropriate international body.[4] In the case of jute, a feasibility study carried out by UNDP at the request of the FAO Intergovernmental Group (formerly Study Group) on Jute, Kenaf and Allied Fibres, has recommended the establishment of an international jute research centre for the purposes of co-ordinating R and D and promotional activities for jute.

Chapter III

The need for expanded research and development

13. As was recognized by the Permanent Group on Synthetics and Substitutes, the main element in a strategy for the improvement of the competitive position of any natural material facing competition from synthetics must be an expanded programme of research and development. The surveys of current R and D efforts and needs in respect of cotton, jute, hard fibres, hides, skins and leather carried out at the request of the Group[5] indicate that current annual world expenditures on R and D for these materials are woefully inadequate in relation to the seriousness of the threat from synthetics. In the cases of jute, hard fibres and hides, skins and leather, these expenditures are estimated roughly at 0.5 per cent or less of the total annual value of world output of the raw material concerned, whereas corresponding expenditures on competing synthetics, it is believed, are many times greater in relative terms. The surveys also reveal that in some cases

existing research efforts are scattered and unco-ordinated, resulting in wasteful over-lapping, and that many important gaps exist in current R and D efforts.

14. For each natural material threatened by synthetics, therefore, a comprehensive programme of expanded research and development is urgently required. These programmes should provide for effective international co-ordination of research efforts and should aim at filling all the major gaps in current R and D work. When these programmes have been drawn up, however, the problem of mobilizing the necessary resources will arise. For cotton, a comprehensive international programme of research, development and promotion on the lines suggested has already been drawn up by the IIC, but it has not been possible to mobilize adequate resources from its member Governments.

15. Part of the resources problem is due to the fact that the industries which consume natural materials facing competition from synthetics cannot be expected to contribute to any great extent to the costs of R and D and of generic promotion for the natural materials, since they can choose either material and have no vested interest in the natural one. The problem is also due partly to the fact that production of natural materials takes place to a large extent (entirely in the cases of jute and hard fibres) in relatively poor countries. Moreover, the situation of producers of these materials is such that, when the need for defensive action against synthetic competition becomes urgent, the revenue out of which the action would have to be financed declines, owing to the fall in prices caused by the competition. There is little doubt, therefore, that international R and D promotional efforts for natural materials will remain inadequate unless substantial financial support for these efforts is forthcoming from international sources.

Chapter IV

The case for international financial support

16. The case for international financial support for efforts to improve the competitive position of natural materials vis-à-vis synthetics rests on the argument that the granting of such support would help to correct serious distortions in the allocation of world productive resources. Because of the enormous disparity between the amounts of resources devoted to R and D for natural materials on the one hand, and those devoted to synthetic substitutes on the other, the patterns of world resource allocation and income distribution are undergoing important changes. Resources used to produce natural materials that in developing countries cannot easily find alternative employments are earning diminishing returns, while scarce resources with high opportunity costs (including highly-trained scientists and engineers and expensive capital equipment) are being used on an increasing scale to develop and produce synthetic substitutes for these natural materials in developed countries.

17. It can be argued that the flow of resources into the development of synthetics is to some extent taking place

---

[3] *Ibid.*, para. 30.

[4] See the report of the Group of Experts (TD/B/C.1/SYN/63), para. 18.

[5] The results of the surveys are summarized in TD/117/Supp.1.

in response to a market demand for larger quantities, and improved types, of raw materials, and that some synthetic materials possess advantages which cannot be matched by natural materials (the strength of nylon, for example, which makes it superior to any natural fibres for certain purposes). This argument, however, ignores the possibility that if an equivalent, or even a much smaller, amount of resources had been devoted to R and D for the purpose of expanding the production of natural materials, adapting their properties to different manufacturing requirements and improving their performance in different end-uses, the greater part of the increasingly sophisticated demands of the market could have been equally well satisfied by natural materials, which could have been produced at a much lower real cost than the synthetic substitutes. The argument also ignores the fact that much of the "sophisticated demand" of the market for synthetic materials is in reality demand induced by intensive promotional campaigns designed to influence consumers' tastes, preferences and judgements.

18. Although the disproportionate flow of resources into the synthetic materials industries reflects the greater profitability of investments in the development and production of synthetics, compared with corresponding investments in natural materials, the differences in the private cost/benefit ratios of the two types of investment do not reflect the differences in the real social cost/benefit ratios if these are calculated on a global basis. In the case of investment in synthetics, the ratio of private costs to private benefits is undoubtedly more favourable than the ratio of global social costs to global social benefits, while in the case of investment in natural materials the reverse is true.

19. International support for R and D and promotional efforts to improve the competitive position of natural materials could help to correct these distortions in global resource allocation, which are seriously harming the interests of many developing countries, by ensuring that the apportionment of productive resources between natural and synthetic materials reflects more accurately the real advantages and potentialities, and the real social costs of production, of each type of material. Such support could be given by the international financial agencies, by individual donor Governments and by private research foundations.

Chapter V

Practical action required

20. For jute, hard fibres, rubber, lauric oils and hides, skins and leather, long-term strategies and related programmes of research, development and promotion should be drawn up for meeting the challenge of competition from synthetics. Since such strategies and programmes would have to be worked out by appropriate intergovernmental bodies, the interested Governments should consider establishing such bodies. In the cases of jute and hard fibres, the FAO intergovernmental groups for these commodities might take the initiative in sponsoring the establishment of appropriate organizations; for lauric oils

and natural rubber, the initiative might be taken by the Asian Coconut Community and by the Association of Natural Rubber Producing Countries, respectively. In the cases of hides, skins and leather and other natural materials for which no intergovernmental consultative groups exist, such as essential oils, the Conference might consider endorsing the suggestion that UNCTAD, in co-operation with other agencies (e.g. FAO and UNIDO), should convene consultations of interested Governments with a view to establishing appropriate research and promotion bodies.

21. For the R and D programmes to be drawn up for these commodities and, more immediately, for the programme which has already been drawn up for cotton by the IIC, there is a need for the mobilization of international financial support. Projects for research to be carried out in developing countries, or for research of benefit principally to these countries, whether carried out in developing or in developed countries, would normally be eligible for UNDP support. On the other hand, the financing of R and D projects in fields such as cotton processing or leather manufacture, the benefits of which might go in substantial measure to raw material producers and manufacturers in developed countries, as well as to those in developing countries, might be difficult for UNDP, since its statutes restrict its donor activities to the provision of aid for developing countries. The Conference might, therefore, wish to invite UNDP, in considering requests for assistance for R and D programmes for natural materials, to give a reasonably broad interpretation to the interests of developing countries, and to find ways and means of giving the maximum possible support to such programmes.

22. In June 1969, the Executive Directors of the IBRD announced a number of decisions relating to action which the World Bank Group intended to take in support of efforts to solve the commodity problems of developing countries.[6] The second of these decisions, concerning the strengthening of the competitiveness of primary products, stated, *inter alia*, that the World Bank Group would participate in financing research aiming at reduction of production costs and development of new uses for primary products. Early in 1971, the executive heads of IBRD, FAO and UNDP decided to sponsor a consultative group on international agricultural research with a view to attracting support from the main aid donors in order to cover major gaps or weaknesses in agricultural research of importance to developing countries that required a substantial multi-disciplinary effort for their solution and resources greater than those which could be mobilized by the developing countries alone. In addition to the three co-sponsoring agencies, the current membership of the Consultative Group includes three regional development banks, the Canadian International Development Research Centre, several major private foundations and a number of donor countries. The Group has established a Technical Advisory Committee of independent scientists for which FAO provides the secretariat.

---

[6] See IBRD, "Stabilization of prices of primary products: report of the Executive Directors", transmitted to the Trade and Development Board at its ninth session under a covering note (TD/B/274).

23. So far, however, the attention of the Consultative Group and of its Technical Advisory Committee has been concentrated mainly on research needs relating to food production. The Conference might, therefore, wish to request the Group to accord an equal priority to consideration of the need for assistance to research designed to improve the competitiveness of natural raw materials, including processing and end-use research as well as production research. For this purpose, the Group might consider establishing an additional Technical Advisory Committee of specialists on agricultural raw materials and their processing.

24. The Conference might also wish to invite donor Governments generally to support efforts to improve the competitive position of natural materials by participating in intergovernmental bodies for research, development and promotion, or by providing financial or technical assistance for the R and D activities of these bodies. Finally, the Conference might wish to endorse the role of the Permanent Group on Synthetics and Substitutes as the body primarily responsible for stimulating and reviewing progress in improving the competitive position of natural materials and, in particular, progress in implementing any action recommended by the Conference in this field.

INTERNATIONAL ACTION RELATING TO COMMODITY DIVERSIFICATION

Report by the UNCTAD secretariat*

[Original text: English]

In its decision 5 (VI) on diversification, taken at its sixth session in July 1971,[1] the Committee on Commodities requested the UNCTAD secretariat to prepare, on the basis of consultations with the international organizations concerned, reports on the following matters:

(*a*) Present arrangements in the United Nations system and in other international bodies for the collection and dissemination of information on progress in, assistance to, and plans for diversification programmes;

(*b*) Facilities available for harmonizing the diversification programmes of the developing countries;

(*c*) Provision of technical and financial assistance to countries undertaking diversification programmes.

The Committee envisaged that these reports would serve as bases for consideration of ways in which, on a mutually acceptable basis, future work on these three matters could best be pursued.

The present report is submitted in response to this request. In preparing it, the UNCTAD secretariat consulted closely with international organizations concerned, as requested by the Committee on Commodities. These consultations took place at two meetings convened by the Secretary-General of UNCTAD in October and December 1971, which were attended by representatives of the following organizations: FAO, IBRD, ILO, ITC, UNDP, UNIDO, AfDB, OECD (October meeting only) and the International Coffee Organization (October meeting only). Chapter III of the report and the annex, dealing with financial and technical assistance for diversification, are based largely on written statements contributed by the agencies and organizations concerned, describing their activities in this field.

---

* The text of this report was circulated to the Conference as document TD/109, dated 4 February 1972.

[1] See *Official Records of the Trade and Development Board, Eleventh Session, Supplement No. 4*, annex I.

CONTENTS

Introduction

1. In the report on its sixth session, devoted to diversification, the Advisory Committee to the Trade and Development Board and to the Committee on Commodities interpreted diversification to mean "widening, or reducing the degree of concentration in, the range of commodities and products, exported or not, on which a given country depended for its income". The Committee pointed out that, in this sense, "the problems of diversification were essentially those of economic development, which could be defined as the process of structural transformation associated with diversification of the commodities, products and services produced by the economy".[2]

2. The present report, however, does not attempt to discuss all the problems arising in connexion with the structural transformation of developing economies, but considers only those arising in connexion with commodity diversification. In this area the Advisory Committee noted that an important distinction was to be made between "horizontal" and "vertical" diversification.[3] By the former was meant widening the range of, or reducing the degree of concentration in, production or exports of primary commodities. By vertical diversification was meant processing in the country of domestically produced primary commodities.

3. Chapter I of the present report, dealing with the collection and dissemination of information, is concerned with both vertical and horizontal diversification. Chapter II, however, which deals with harmonization of diversification programmes, is concerned only with horizontal diversification, since it is in this area that the need for the harmonization of national diversification programmes is most urgent.

4. In chapter III and in the annex, the provision of technical and financial assistance for both horizontal and vertical commodity diversification is considered. It is naturally difficult, however, to establish a clear-cut divid-ing line between assistance for commodity diversification and assistance for development in general. For example, assistance given to developing countries for infrastructural development (roads, railways, training institutes, etc.) helps to stimulate not only commodity diversification but also the structural transformation of the economy in the wider sense. Moreover, while vertical diversification in a broad sense may be regarded as synonymous with industrialization,[4] assistance provided for the establishment of advanced manufacturing processes has more far-reaching effects on development than does assistance for setting up industries carrying out the earlier stages of processing of primary commodities.

Chapter I

Collection and dissemination of information

5. In its report on diversification, the Advisory Committee to the Board and to the Committee on Commodities emphasized the need for developing countries to adopt diversification strategies appropriate to their circumstances and to evaluate the private and social costs and benefits of individual diversification projects.[5] In view of the acuteness of under-employment and unemployment in many developing countries, the Committee considered that a major objective of diversification was to provide opportunities for productive employment and attached importance to the expansion of appropriate labour-intensive activities.[6] The Committee stressed also the need to ensure as far as possible the compatibility of national commodity diversification programmes.[7] For each of these purposes the basic requirement is that an adequate flow of information should be available to the Governments of developing countries regarding current and prospective demand and supply conditions for different primary and processed commodities, both in their domestic markets and in the world market as a whole, as well as

----

[2] *Ibid.*, *Eleventh Session*, *Annexes*, agenda item 7, document TD/B/348, para. 5.

[3] *Ibid.*, para. 6.

[4] *Ibid.*

[5] *Ibid.*, paras. 17 and 39.

[6] *Ibid.*, para. 11.

[7] *Ibid.*, paras. 45-51.

information about employment possibilities offered by alternative diversification projects. In order to minimize the inevitable delays involved in investment decision-making and to facilitate the making of rational decisions, it is important that such information should be readily available. It should be noted, however, that to some extent vertical and horizontal commodity diversification projects call for different kinds of information.

A. VERTICAL DIVERSIFICATION

6. Processing of a locally produced primary commodity may be undertaken by a developing country for the purpose of import substitution or export or both. In practice, import substitution may lead to export and, as suggested by the Advisory Committee,[8] this process should be encouraged, particularly in countries where the home market is mall.

7. In the case of a raw material which has to be processed before it can be consumed, a decision by a producing country to process the material in the country rather than to export it in its raw form does not in itself involve any increase in the total supply of the processed product on the world market. The decision-making authority does not therefore need to postulate an increase in demand for the product as a condition of the viability of the project. By contrast, in the case of foodstuffs which can be consumed in either raw or processed form (fruits and vegetables, for example), the authority planning to establish a processing industry will have to take account of the likely response of demand to an increase in the supply of the processed form of the food in question, whether on the home market or on export markets. In the case of most foodstuffs, however, demand for the processed form is often more income- and price-elastic than demand for the unprocessed form.

8. In each of the cases just described, therefore, the current and future trend of prices is likely to be determined mainly by trends in costs of production and the intensity of competition in the industry concerned. Hence it is information about these factors which is most required by authorities responsible for taking investment decisions in the field of vertical diversification, athough information is also needed about other factors likely to affect the competitive position of projected processing industries, notably information about tariff and non-tariff barriers in export markets and exchange rate policies at home and abroad, as well as information about factors affecting domestic and export demand.

9. With regard to prices of inputs in processing industries, the level of wages in developed countries is a particularly important factor in determining the competitiveness of labour-intensive industries in developing countries. In recent years, wage inflation in OECD countries has been exceptionally marked, and the continuation of the current trend could have important repercussions on the international division of labour between developed and developing countries.

10. At present, information about the matters mentioned above can be obtained by developing countries from the international financial and technical assistance agencies, either on request or in the context of project feasibility studies. In the latter context, moreover, information may be obtained about special factors likely to affect the viability of processing industries, such as possible future changes in technology and the possibility that industries in developed countries which now process raw materials exported by developing countries might turn to processing substitute raw materials if they met strong competition in their present activity.

11. Technical information and advice on the earlier stages of processing of agricultural commodities is provided to developing countries by FAO, while UNIDO provides similar assistance in connexion with more advanced industrial processing. Information about the earlier stages of marketing of processed agricultural commodities, including information relating to quality, packaging, shipping etc., is also provided by FAO, while information concerning the later stages of export marketing of semi-processed and manufactured commodities in general, including prices, trade barriers, actual or potential competition etc., is provided by the ITC. Furthermore, information supplied by the Centre relating to product promotion provides a basis for activities designed to stimulate consumption. The IBRD also contributes information relevant to decisions on vertical diversification projects, notably information on market trends and prospects. Information is provided both at the pre-investment stage, on request, and in the context of feasibility studies for particular projects in developing countries.

12. It would appear, therefore, that a developing country which is studying the possibilities for processing a locally produced primary commodity could, in principle, obtain most of the technical and market information it required from United Nations agencies. Some of the information might be available in published form. Journals containing information on technical and trade matters, and/or *ad hoc* studies and reports, are published by IBRD, FAO, UNIDO and the ITC.

13. Because of the highly specialized and detailed nature of the information required in connexion with vertical diversification, however, most of it has to be requested specifically much of it is provided only in the context of actual feasibility studies. Moreover, some data in the possession of international agencies (for example, data concerning costs of production in particular countries) might be confidential and could not be passed on to other countries. Again, such of the information required for decisions relating to vertical diversification is local information, relating to such matters as availability of skilled labour and managerial talent, impact of projects on employment, prices of inputs, local demand for the product concerned, exchange rate policy etc. in the country seeking to diversify its economy. Such information would have to be obtained locally by Governments or prospective investors, although the international agencies might be able to give help in establishing statistical services and procedures for obtaining it.

14. There would seem to be three main ways in which the present arrangements for the collection and dissemination of information relating to vertical diversification

---

[8] *Ibid.*, para. 38.

might be improved. First, since Governments, planning officials and prospective investors in developing countries do not always appear to know what information is available from international agencies and how to obtain it, it would be desirable that the agencies concerned should distribute to Governments:

(*a*) Particulars of their relevant publications, indicating the type of information contained in them; and

(*b*) A catalogue or list of the type of information obtainable on request, indicating how requests should be made. These lists and particulars should then be widely distributed by Governments to interested officials and businessmen.

15. Second, the international agencies concerned should consider jointly whether there might be any additional scope for the regular collection and publication of data relevant to decisions on vertical diversification, for example, data concerning prices, tariffs and consumption in different markets in respect of selected processed primary commodities, perhaps concentrating on the more homogeneous products of a labour-intensive nature. The agencies should at the same time consider which of them might undertake any such tasks considered to be worth while.

16. Third, the agencies should also jointly try to determine what are the principal types of local information relevant to decisions on vertical diversification that are most lacking in developing countries and should make appropriate joint recommendations to Governments to remedy the deficiencies. The agencies should at the same time consider what technical assistance activities might be necessary to improve the situation in this respect; this point is discussed further in chapter III below.

B. Horizontal diversification

17. Unlike world demand for processed foodstuffs and manufactured goods, demand for most primary commodities is relatively price-inelastic, with the consequence that prices of these commodities tend to be highly sensitive to changes in supply. The supply of primary commodities, moreover, is generally much less responsive than that of processed commodities to changes in prices in the short run. For these reasons, and also because of the influence of random factors such as variations in harvests, strikes etc., prices of primary commodities often show considerable fluctuations, both in the long and in the short term.

18. Information about factors likely to determine the future trend of prices of different primary commodities is therefore specially important for purposes of decisions on horizontal diversification. While such information is particularly crucial in connexion with investments involving long gestation and amortization periods, as in the case of tree crops or mining, it may also be important even in connexion with annual crops. Although cotton, for example, has to be planted every year, its cultivation may form part of a crop rotation system which cannot be changed from year to year in response to changes in market prices. A decision to grow cotton, therefore, might have to be regarded as a fairly long-term investment decision.

19. It is accordingly that planners concerned with horizontal diversification should have access to estimates of long-term price trends for a large number of primary commodities. Ideally, these estimates would be based on mutually consistent assumptions and would represent, to the extent possible, a consensus of expert opinion and judgement. In order to retain their usefulness, they would have to be revised at frequent intervals to take account of new developments.

20. However, even the most sophisticated price forecasts, based on adequate statistical data, are subject to a margin of error, since the effects of a number of factors will always be uncertain. Government policies, for example, are unpredictable, and future responses of producers to price changes may differ from those observed in the past. Announced production plans may not be fulfilled, and new production that was not allowed for in official plans or forecasts may be undertaken. For commodities facing competition from synthetics, it may be particularly difficult to project demand.

21. Whether or not any forecasts of price trends are available, therefore, economic planners in developing countries should at least have at their disposal projections of demand and supply for as many primary commodities as possible. These would enable them to make their own assessments of the future outlook for prices, and of the probable relative position of their country in the world market which would result from a given new investment. Ideally, such projections would also be based on mutually consistent assumptions, would be prepared by international bodies possessing expert knowledge of the commodities in question and would be revised at frequent intervals. The extent to which the need for this information is being filled under present arrangements within the United Nations system is considered in the following paragraphs.

1. *Projections of demand and supply*

22. Long-term projections of demand and supply for the principal agricultural commodities are prepared and published by FAO. They are revised and brought up to date at intervals of four or five years; if they could be revised more frequently their usefulness would be greatly enhanced. In respect of commodities for which FAO-sponsored intergovernmental commodity groups exist, the projections are reviewed by the groups concerned. None of the independent intergovernmental bodies dealing with agricultural or mineral commodities published regular long-term estimates of demand and supply, though some have prepared such estimates for *ad hoc* purposes.

2. *Price forecasts*

23. Price forecasts covering periods relevant for the purpose of making decisions concerning investment are prepared annually by the IBRD in respect of the principal primary commodities. The forecasts take account of work done by other bodies and individual experts, and those that concern commodities covered by specialized bodies benefit from formal consultations regarding the market implications of proposed investment projects with the

secretariats of the bodies concerned (including the FAO secretariat in the case of FAO-sponsored intergovernmental commodity groups). The price forecasts for these commodities as well as for those not covered by specialized bodies are the subject of informal consultations by the IBRD staff with interested bodies. Since UNCTAD has special responsibilities within the United Nations system for the study of problems concerning mineral commodities, there would appear to be scope for liaison between IBRD and UNCTAD in connexion with the preparation of market forecasts for these commodities. Although the IBRD's price forecasts are not published, they are available to the Governments of all States members of the Bank. While the projections prepared by FAO do not give price forecasts, they contain explicit discussion of the implications of the analysis for prices.

24. The UNCTAD secretariat has prepared econometric models of the world markets for certain primary commodities for *ad hoc* purposes and the results of the models, including the implications for future prices, have been discussed by the interested Governments of the countries members of UNCTAD. In the case of tea, for example, the results of the short-term price forecasting model prepared by the UNCTAD secretariat were taken into account in the negotiation of global export quotas in the informal stabilization arrangements for 1970 and 1971 concluded in the FAO Consultative Committee on Tea.

25. There are, however, relatively few commodity markets for which price forecasting models at present exist. In order to show the principal gaps, the UNCTAD secretariat is compiling an inventory of such models completed or under preparation in the various international agencies and in national research centres. It should then be possible, if this were considered desirable, for UNCTAD to co-ordinate international efforts to fill the gaps.

3. *Data requirements*

26. The collection of basic data and information necessary for the preparation of demand and supply projections for primary commodities is to a large extent a co-operative effort by the United Nations agencies concerned. For example, IBRD and FAO regularly exchange information about production plans, demand trends etc. collected by Bank missions and FAO experts visiting developing countries. Similarly, UNCTAD and FAO exchange data obtained from Governments or other sources in connexion with their projection work. In a number of respects, however, the quantity and quality of the agencies need to be improved.

27. In general, the greatest need is for strengthening the bases of supply projections for primary commodities. Published economic development plans may not contain details of commodity production projects, and Governments of developing countries may not be able to provide information concerning longer-term production prospects for individual commodities. The gap in the information relating to supply prospects does not exist only in developing countries; in developed countries also, information about the production intentions of farmers and mining

companies is often difficult or impossible to obtain, and Governments are often reluctant to indicate their future policy intentions. In both groups of countries, information relating to likely responses by producers to changes in price is seriously deficient.

28. Although in developed countries the demand for some primary commodities can be forecast or projected largely independently of price, this is not possible in most developing countries, where price-elasticities of demand, even for basic foodstuffs, are greater than in developed countries. In developing countries, moreover, demand for primary commodities shows a greater degree of elasticity with respect to income than in developed countries. Because of the lack of information relating to these factors, projections of demand for primary commodities in developing countries tend to be less soundly based than corresponding projections for developed countries.

29. Hence, in the case of developing countries there is a special need for more data concerning responses of demand, especially for domestically produced commodities, to changes in both prices and incomes. In these countries, it is particularly important to distinguish between urban and rural demand. Moreover, since promotional campaigns can increase the consumption of certain commodities, detailed information on consumer tastes and spending habits may be desirable to provide a basis for such campaigns.

30. In the case of natural commodities which face competition from synthetics, there are special problems in forecasting demand. Such forecasts involve first estimating total demand in the market in which the two types of product compete, and then estimating how the total demand will be shared between the natural and the synthetic product. Since this sharing will depend very largely on prices and on the technical characteristics of the synthetic products, there is a need for information—generally lacking at present—about the probable future costs of production and changes in technology in synthetics industries.

31. It will be noted from the foregoing paragraphs that, as in the case of vertical diversification, the provision of the additional data required in order to create better bases for decisions on horizontal diversification is the responsibility of Governments as well as of the international agencies. As far as developing countries are concerned, the new country programming procedures being established under the auspices of UNDP might provide an appropriate channel through which some of the additional information required (for example, information about commodity production plans) could be supplied to the United Nations system and brought to the attention of all the agencies concerned. Much of the additional information needed, however, is too detailed and too complex to be assessed and analysed in the context of country programming.

4. *The role of intergovernmental commodity groups*

32. A more appropriate channel through which additional information relating to demand and supply trends for primary commodities could be provided by Governments of both developed and developing countries would

be the various intergovernmental groups which are concerned with individual commodities. In principle, these bodies are the most appropriate ones to act as channels of information, since their members are in fact the Governments of the countries that are the main producers and consumers of the commodities in question. Moreover, these bodies are specially qualified to carry out the sifting and evaluation of information about production plans in individual countries which is required before the data can be aggregated and utilized in the preparation of global supply projections.

33. However, the extent to which the specialized bodies are involved in the preparation of demand and supply projections for the commodities with which they are concerned varies a great deal. The International Coffee Organization seems to have gone furthest in this direction, since one of its objects is to bring world coffee production into balance with demand in the longer term. For this purpose, each member country has been asked to prepare a national coffee production plan consistent with its quota under the International Coffee Agreement. The International Cotton Advisory Committee has begun an attempt to compile forecasts of cotton production and consumption for a period of five years ahead, while the FAO Study Group on Bananas has undertaken a similar project relating to bananas. *Ad hoc* forecasts of production and consumption have been prepared by the International Rubber Study Group and by the International Tin Council. The International Lead and Zinc Study Group, which holds regular discussions on long-term trends in the lead and zinc industry, has considered the possibility of preparing projects from econometric models. At present the Group is assembling information concerning the working of the lead and zinc economy which would be required for the construction of a model if this was considered desirable.

34. It would seem desirable that all the intergovernmental commodity bodies should carry this kind of work further, with the object of preparing medium-term and long-term projections of demand and supply (preferably in close consultation with IBRD, FAO and UNCTAD as appropriate), which would be revised at frequent intervals. In the case of those mineral commodities for which no specialized intergovernmental bodies exist, it would seem desirable that UNCTAD should expand its projections work, particularly in respect of commodities such as iron ore and manganese ore, the prices of which have experienced downward trends in recent years. The question of the possible need for the establishment of intergovernmental bodies for mineral commodities not yet covered by bodies is considered in chapter II of the present report.

Chapter II

Harmonization of commodity diversification programmes

A. THE MEANING OF HARMONIZATION

35. As was pointed out by the Advisory Committee to the Board and to the Committee on Commodities in its report on diversification, countries seeking to transfer or divert resources from the production of primary commodities which are actually or potentially in surplus on the world market, e.g. coffee, may divert resources into the production of other commodities which are in the same position, e.g. tea.[9] Such decisions may be taken in ignorance of the real situation on the world markets for the commodities in question. In this case, harmonization of horizontal diversification programmes can be promoted by ensuring as far as possible that such programmes are undertaken on the basis of adequate knowledge of probable future market trends for the commodities concerned. For this purpose, the collection and dissemination of information have to be improved on the lines suggested in chapter I above.

36. Actually, decisions to produce, under a diversification scheme, commodities of which there is a present or potential surplus may be taken quite deliberately and rationally, in full awareness of the further downward pressure on prices that they will generate, by countries whose "opportunity costs" of producing such commodities are low. By expanding their output, these countries expect to increase their income, despite any fall in price which may ensue. In such cases there will be a real conflict of interests between these countries and other producing countries, since the fall in price resulting from an increase in the supply on the world market, which may be severe if demand is inelastic, will inflict income losses on the other producing countries. In aggregate, moreover, these losses may well more than outweigh any gains accruing to the countries which expand their output.

37. In such situations, it may be possible to achieve some degree of harmonization of diversification programmes, in the sense of a reconciliation of the interests of the countries involved, by means of a formal or informal international commodity arrangement. Under such an arrangement, producing countries might accept national production or export quotas which, in aggregate, would ensure that the growth in world supply was kept in line with demand, thus avoiding further downward pressure on prices. A major problem in negotiating such quotas is how to ensure that low-cost producing countries obtain an increase in their share of the market, albeit a smaller increase than they would have obtained in the absence of such an arrangement. Such a harmonization of interests is in fact the objective of the existing international agreements for coffee, sugar and tin, whose effectiveness is examined in the report by the UNCTAD secretariat entitled "Pricing policy, including international price stabilization measures and mechanisms" (TD/127).[10]

38. Still, when horizontal diversification projects are undertaken for purposes of import substitution, any conflicts of interest arising as a result of the effects on the world market are less easy to reconcile by means of international arrangements than when export diversification only is involved. In such cases, and in other cases where international arrangements are not envisaged, the question arises, therefore, whether the harmonization of diversification programmes, for import substitution or export, can be promoted in any other ways.

---

[9] *Ibid.*, para. 46.
[10] See p. 43 above.

B. The role of aid-giving agencies and Governments

39. When requests for financial or technical assistance in connexion with horizontal diversification projects are made to organizations such as IBRD, the regional development banks and FAO, or to donor Governments, it is in principle possible for these organizations or Governments to take into account, in considering such requests, any conflicts of interest of the kind described above to which the execution of the project might give rise. Although the views of the international agencies or Governments in such cases may not always be decisive, they may influence decisions on diversification projects in a way that reconciles, at least to some extent, the different national interests involved.

40. In providing assistance in connexion with the production of commodities, IBRD always operates within the context of international commodity agreements where these are in force. In the case of projects for the production of other commodities not governed by such agreements, the Bank consults with any study groups or similar bodies which might be concerned before providing assistance and, in any case, gives careful attention to the probable impact on world markets of the proposed new projects. Where the impact is likely to be unfavourable, it tries to find suitable alternative ways of employing the productive resources. The application of this principle is being facilitated by the increasing emphasis which the Bank is giving in its lending policies to adaptive research, for the purpose of finding alternative opportunities for the use of productive resources, and to sectoral planning, intended to ensure that particular agricultural projects, for example, are considered not in isolation but in relation to the optimum allocation of resources in the agricultural sector as a whole. A final opportunity for the reconsideration of all Bank lending projects arises as a result of the fact that these projects have to be approved by all the Executive Directors of IBRD.

41. The FAO also takes account of the international impact of diversification programmes in its own technical assistance activity. The FAO is in fact giving increasing attention to the problems of international agricultural adjustment, which is to be one of the principal themes of the FAO Conference in 1973.

42. As has already been noted, both IBRD and FAO keep the current and prospective situation of individual primary commodities on the world market under study and maintain liaison, as appropriate, with specialized commodity bodies. The same is not necessarily true of regional development banks or of donor Governments acting singly or through aid consortia, or through such institutions as the EDF or the Colombo Plan. When these organizations and Governments are asked to assist horizontal diversification projects, their ability to take account of the repercussions of the projects on other producing countries may depend on whether they consult IBRD or FAO or any specialized body concerned. The holding of such consultations appears to be the normal practice of regional development banks and aid consortia, but in the case of bilateral assistance for commodity production projects consultation seems to be far from

systematic. In this connexion it may be noted that only about 10 per cent of all primary commodity production projects are supported by the technical and financial assistance agencies of the United Nations system. A much larger proportion of such projects is supported by donor Governments acting singly or in groups.

43. However, even if the appropriate United Nations agencies were given the opportunity to comment on all assisted projects for the production of commodities there would still remain the problem of projects, both in developing and developed countries, which receive no international assistance and which are executed on the basis of purely national criteria. To the extent that details of non-assisted projects were known, it would be possible for bodies such as IBRD and FAO to assess their international implications and to bring them to the attention of the Governments concerned. As already noted, however, information about non-aided projects is not always available to the international agencies.

44. So far as developing countries are concerned, the new procedures being instituted by UNDP for the purpose of programming technical assistance to individual countries in a more integrated and comprehensive framework (country programming) may provide a means by which fuller information about both aided and non-aided commodity production plans can be brought to the attention of the technical and financial assistance agencies of the United Nations system. Country programming involves consultations between government officials and representatives of the United Nations agencies and is designed to give each of the latter an opportunity to comment on a country's development plans and priorities in those sectors in which it has technical competence. The new procedures should therefore increase the amount of information about commodity production plans available to the agencies and at the same time provide increased opportunities to the agencies to influence these plans through discussion of their national and international implications. There would still be a need, however, for more systematic consultation between Governments providing bilateral assistance for commodity production projects and the international agencies and bodies concerned, with a view to promoting the harmonization of such projects.

C. The role of the specialized intergovernmental bodies

45. Any influence which the United Nations agencies can exert in the interests of the harmonization of horizontal commodity diversification projects can be brought to bear only in respect of projects in developing countries and only to the extent that details of such projects are known. Possibilities for promoting a greater degree of harmonization, falling short of an export regulation system, for some commodities would seem to exist within the various specialized intergovernmental commodity groups. Since these bodies usually include all the principal producing countries, they could do much to promote harmonization, if their members were willing, through discussions and intergovernmental consultations on the implications for prices and export earnings of current production programmes and of alternative rates of growth

of the production of the commodities concerned. This type of activity would be a logical extension of the work on demand and supply projections which, as was recommended in chapter I of this report, should be a regular responsibility of these bodies.

46. The specialized commodity bodies might also be able to promote the harmonization of diversification programmes through the adoption of principles or guidelines, covering such matters as production and export subsidies and access to markets, like the guidelines adopted for rice by the FAO intergovernmental group concerned with that commodity. A similar function could be performed in a regional context by the regional economic commission, as has been done by ECAFE, for example, in connexion with coconut products and pepper.

47. However, not every primary commodity is the concern of a specialized intergovernmental body, and there may be a need to establish more such bodies, particularly so far as minerals are concerned, for these are relatively less well covered in this respect than agricultural commodities. In the meantime, as regards mineral commodities for which no fully representative intergovernmental bodies exist, UNCTAD might be able to do more to promote the harmonization of diversification programmes through *ad hoc* intergovernmental consultations like those arranged for iron ore, manganese ore and phosphates for the purpose of examining problems of the world market for these commodities.

Chapter III

Technical and financial assistance for commodity diversification

A. THE UNITED NATIONS SYSTEM

48. The technical and financial assistance activities of the organizations within the United Nations family, both for commodity diversification and for the broader purposes of development, are part of an elaborate system in which, in principle, inter-agency co-operation is closely maintained from the highest level (through the ACC presided over by the Secretary-General of the United Nations) down to the level of field work in individual developing countries. In this system the UNDP has an essential role, since most of the activities of the agencies that involve technical assistance for commodity diversification and other purposes are formulated, financed and carried out within the framework of UNDP procedures. Illustrations of how the agencies most involved in the provision of financial and/or technical assistance for commodity diversification co-operate with each other and with other bodies are given in the following paragraphs.

49. The World Bank group (comprising IBRD, IDA and IFC) co-operates in a variety of ways with other United Nations agencies on matters related to economic diversification within and outside the primary commodity sector. This co-operation occurs at the informal and at the official level. Information is exchanged about market prospects for primary commodities, development plans and programmes of developing countries, research and pre-investment studies and the need for technical assistance for the preparation of projects. The Bank group's economic and sector missions always maintain close liaison with the UNDP Resident Representative and his team in every host country. In this way the Bank receives up-to-date information on the pre-investment and country programme studies being undertaken by other agencies. In addition, Bank missions quite frequently include members from United Nations agencies and especially FAO.

50. As already mentioned, the Bank has formal consultative arrangements with a number of international commodity bodies for the purpose of exchanging views about projects under consideration by the Bank which would increase world production of the primary commodities concerned. The Bank group specifically supports the diversification and stabilization activities of these bodies in several ways. Not only does it consult with them but it also communicates to them any information it may have concerning commodity prospects and plans. In the case of the Coffee Diversification Fund of the International Coffee Organization, the Bank group has provided technical assistance and offered to co-finance diversification projects.

51. The regional development banks the IDB, AfDB and AsDB also generally maintain close co-operation with other agencies. The AfDB, for example, has co-operative arrangements and working relations with IBRD, FAO, UNESCO, UNCTAD, ILO, WHO, UNIDO, UNDP, ECA and others. Other agencies sometimes provide funds to the AfDB for pre-investment studies. The AfDB also arranges joint missions with other agencies, particularly IBRD and FAO.

52. Since most of the projects specifically intended to promote diversification which are carried out by FAO are financed by the Special Fund component of UNDP, FAO co-operates with UNDP in determining the extent and nature of the assistance to be rendered. In the case of one such project in Malaysia, for example, the Consultative Group on Aid to Malaysia co-operated in selecting the project and IBRD collaborated in a similar scheme in Guatemala by providing assistance for the elaboration of a Coffee zone development plan. Further, during the last two years a close and growing co-operation has been established between FAO and the International Coffee Organization in diversification schemes. The FAO's assistance consists of the provision of experts for identification and appraisal missions, as well as for the implementation phase of projects financed through the Coffee Diversification Fund.

53. In implementing its technical assistance programmes UNIDO co-operates with other bodies as appropriate. This co-operation generally takes the form of co-ordinating selected projects in particular countries. Technical assistance programmes undertaken by the ITC can originate in the request of a developing country and occasionally are a sequel to missions carried out by other international agencies, or a result of recommendations made by meetings or conferences sponsored by other international agencies. At the implementation stage, close co-operation is maintained with other international agencies through regular co-ordination meetings or by

other means, particularly with FAO, UNIDO and the regional economic commissions. As a result, missions and programmes have been and will continue to be undertaken jointly with the above-mentioned agencies.

54. Among the regional economic commissions ECAFE, for example, has co-operated in its technical assistance activities with UNIDO, FAO, ILO, GATT, the ITC, the Customs Co-operation Council, IMF and the AsDB. In the planning and carrying out of its technical assistance activities, UNESOB maintains co-operation with other agencies concerned. Conversely, some agencies have sought the co-operation of that Office in carrying out their own technical assistance activities. For example, in 1971 that Office and UNIDO arranged joint missions to Iraq and Syria for the purpose of working out a programme of long-term technical assistance for industry in these two countries. More recently, the Office was requested to submit briefs on elected countries of its region to the United Nations Office of Technical Co-operation. These briefs will be used in the preparation of the various UNDP country programmes of technical assistance.

B. Country programming

55. In future, the technical assistance activities of the United Nations agencies are likely to be planned and executed to an increasing extent within the context of the new country programming procedures being introduced by UNDP. These procedures are designed to provide a more integrated and comprehensive framework for the programming of technical assistance and will progressively replace what hitherto has been mainly a project-by-project approach.

56. For each developing country, new country programming will seek to determine the needs for technical assistance, the priorities and an appropriate role for UNDP assistance, taking the various sectors together and relating them to the development of the country as a whole. Under the new system the beneficiary countries play an increasingly important part in determining priorities in their development and in planning the co-ordinated utilization of the technical assistance available to them from all sources. The participating and executing agencies, for their part, maintain close continuing contacts with the Resident Representative of UNDP who, at all stages in the formulation and implementation of the country programme, can and does call upon them for advice.

57. Country programming should, therefore, ensure both a closer study in developing countries of needs for diversification and a more effective co-ordination of technical assistance granted for diversification from all sources. As noted earlier, it should also improve the flow of information available to the international agencies concerning commodity production plans and thus facilitate the harmonization of these plans.

58. Since the new system has not yet come fully into operation, it is not yet possible to assess its effectiveness. Further experience of the new arrangements would seem to be necessary before suggestions can usefully be made on how they might be improved. The annex to the present report describes the technical and financial assistance for commodity diversification being provided at present to developing countries by the principal United Nations agencies concerned and by organizations outside the United Nations system, stating the nature and objectives of the assistance provided and the bases on which assistance programmes are determined.

C. Possible improvements in present arrangements

59. The object of the present organization of technical assistance within the United Nations system, as described above and in the annex to the present report, is to maximize the effectiveness of the aid operations of the various agencies by close co-ordination within a common framework provided by the UNDP. However, even if such co-ordination is successfully achieved in practice—by no means an easy task—this would not necessarily, in itself, secure an effective aid programme unless, at the same time, improvements were made in two important related areas.

60. First, while the present arrangements are designed to promote diversification in a general way in developing countries, it would seem to be desirable, in the case of countries, with unfavourable export structures, that technical and financial assistance from all sources should be more specifically adapted—both in volume and in type—to the requirements of an appropriate long-term diversification strategy. The problems of preparing such a strategy are discussed in the report by the UNCTAD secretariat entitled "Problems of commodity diversification in developing countries" (TD/119).[11]

61. Second, consideration should be given to whether some forum or mechanism is required within which the effectiveness of technical and financial assistance to individual developing countries for diversification could be regularly evaluated. Such an evaluation would be particularly necessary for those developing countries whose rate of export growth remains inadequate for financing their economic development programmes. It would be necessary to consider the appropriateness of existing diversification strategies and the modifications that might be required, as well as any deficiences in the technical and financial assistance activities of the various international agencies.

62. Another deficiency in both United Nations and bilateral assistance programmes is their neglect of statistical and economic services in developing countries. In many of these countries, the effective planning of diversification programmes is seriously hampered by the lack of adequate basic statistical data about the economic system, and by the weakness of the economic planning apparatus itself. Deficiencies in basic statistical knowledge can lead, for example, to serious misjudgments of the probable effects on the output structure of a particular pattern of new investment. It would seem most desirable that such statistical deficiencies should be remedied during the Second United Nations Development Decade, and a concerted effort by the appropriate United Nations agencies might be considered to strengthen the national

---

[11] See p. 93 below.

statistical systems of developing countries as part of their programmes of technical assistance.

63. As regards the economic planning apparatus, the objectives and institutional forms of economic planning must remain the responsibility of the Governments themselves. However, within this framework, the degree of technical competence of the planning officials, including an understanding of the relation between domestic investment decisions and the foreign trade balance, may well have a considerable influence on the degree of success of economic development programmes, including diversification schemes. The technical quality of economic planning can often be raised by the use of expatriate experts or teams working with local planning officials. In addition, there appears to be scope for the organization of multi-national symposia and seminars to enable the economic planning officials of developing countries to discuss common problems.[12]

Chapter IV

Summary of recommendations

64. For convenience of presentation, the various suggestions and recommendations made throughout the above discussion are summarized below. These suggestions and recommendations arose, in the main, during the detailed consultations on diversification held with the various international agencies, but the UNCTAD secretariat is alone responsible for submitting them for consideration by the Conference in their present form.

65. *Collection and dissemination of information*

(a) *Vertical diversification*

(i) The international agencies concerned should distribute to Governments details of their relevant publications, indicating the type of information contained therein; and also a list of the type of information obtainable on request, indicating how requests should be made (paragraph 14).

(ii) The agencies should consider jointly the possible scope for the additional regular collection and dissemination of data relevant to decision-making in regard to vertical diversification (paragraph 15).

(iii) The agencies should jointly try to determine what local information is now lacking in developing countries, and make appropriate joint recommendations to remedy the deficiencies (paragraph 16).

(b) *Horizontal diversification*

(i) The FAO should consider more frequent revision of its long-term projections of demand for and supply of agricultural commodities (paragraph 22).

(ii) The IBRD should consider establishing liaison with the UNCTAD secretariat in connexion with market forecasts for mineral commodities (paragraph 23).

(iii) The UNCTAD should consider initiating and co-ordinating a programme for the construction of econometric models of major commodity markets, for use in connexion with market forecasts (paragraph 25).

(iv) The specialized intergovernmental commodity bodies should aim, as part of their regular work, at preparing regular reviews or projections of the medium and long-term outlook for the supply of and demand for the commodities concerned, in consultation, as appropriate, with UNCTAD, FAO and IBRD (paragraphs 32-34).

(v) In the case of mineral commodities that are not the concern of specialized intergovernmental bodies, UNCTAD should expand its own work on projections (paragraph 34).

66. *Harmonization of diversification programmes*

(a) Governments providing bilateral assistance for commodity production projects should consult closely with the appropriate international agencies and bodies on the national and international implications of such projects with a view to promoting the harmonization of all the interests concerned (paragraph 44).

(b) The specialized intergovernmental commodity groups should:

(i) Discuss on a regular basis the implications of current production programmes for world prices and for the export earnings of the producing countries (paragraph 45);

(ii) Consider, where appropriate, the adoption of principles or guidelines designed to promote the harmonization of diversification programmes (paragraph 46).

(c) The need for additional specialized intergovernmental bodies, or additional *ad hoc* consultations, particularly as regards certain minerals, should be considered (paragraph 47).

67. *Technical and financial assistance for commodity diversification*

(a) In the case of developing countries with unfavourable export structures, technical and financial assistance from all sources should be more specifically adapted—both in volume and in type—to the requirements of an appropriate long-term diversification strategy (paragraph 60).

(b) Consideration should be given to whether some forum or mechanism is required to evaluate on a regular basis the effectiveness of technical and financial assistance to developing countries for diversification programmes (paragraph 61).

---

[12] An inter-regional seminar on those lines, dealing with the planning of the foreign trade sector, was organized by UNCTAD in September/October 1970 within the framework of UNDP.

(c) A concerted effort should be made by the appropriate United Nations agencies to strengthen the statistical systems of developing countries (paragraph 62).

(d) A continuing programme of symposia and seminars should be considered, with a view to raising the technical level of economic planning work in developing countries (paragraph 63).

ANNEX

Technical and financial assistance for diversification accorded by international agencies

The following descriptions of technical and financial assistance activities in support of diversification in developing countries—except the passage relating to the EDF are based on statements communicated to the UNCTAD secretariat in response to a request for such information addressed to all the agencies in the United Nations system concerned and to the International Coffee Organization. If any additional statements are received before the third session of the Conference they will be circulated as addenda to the present report.

A. WORLD BANK GROUP

Most World Bank group projects contribute in some degree to the broad objective of economic diversification in developing countries. Some investments have diversification as a specific objective, while others may contribute only in part and indirectly to this end. Bank group projects directed towards diversification (fairly broadly defined) in developing countries have in practice had one or more of the following objectives:

(a) *Reducing dependence on a small number of traditional export commodities.* Many Bank group investments are directed towards widening the export earning base of a country and thus reducing its vulnerability to adverse changes in the fortunes of one or two commodities.

(b) *Reducing dependence on imports of key staple foods.* Staple foods have in the past frequently pre-empted a substantial part of the foreign exchange earnings of some developing countries. The demand for these products is very inelastic, with the consequence that variations in domestic or world supplies have led to considerable fluctuations in foreign exchange expenditure on these products and thus made it difficult for a country to make reliable assumptions about foreign exchange availabilities for planning purposes.

(c) *Investment in infrastructure which will facilitate the realization of objectives* (a) *and* (b). Investments in irrigation and drainage schemes figure prominently in this category. Irrigation schemes serve not only to increase production but also to reduce variations in agricultural production.

(d) *Reducing dependence on agricultural production.* Investments in this category aim at increasing the proportion of earnings derived from processing and manufactures.

(e) *Infrastructure development related to tourism enterprises.*

(f) *Regional co-operation among developing countries.* Such co-operation is fostered particularly where it is likely to lead to an accelerated rate of development in secondary and tertiary industries.

(g) *Promotion (direct or indirect) of agricultural and other research which facilitates diversification.*

(h) *Technical assistance in programme and project preparation (including feasibility studies) aimed at encouraging diversification.*

Since the second session of the Conference (*i.e.* in fiscal years 1968 to 1971 inclusive) the Bank group has sanctioned loans totalling $7.8 billion[a] and the total capital cost of the projects financed

[a] Probably about one-tenth was for non-project assistance.

amounted to some $15.0 billion. Much of this investment will contribute directly or indirectly to economic diversification. Separate estimates of loans made for projects in categories (a) to (f) described above are provided in the following table:

Diversification projects financed by the World Bank group (financial years 1968 to 1971)

(In million dollars)

Type of diversification	IBRD loan	IDA credit	IFC loan or equity	Total Group loans	Total Capital cost
(a)	65	62		127	239
(b)	5	9		14	23
(c)	115	10		125	207
(d)	44	37		81	414
(e)	150	25	1	176	408
(f)	135	34	10	179	311
Mixed (a)-(f) . .	209	107		316	1,201
Total	723	284	11	1,018	2,803
Total operations	5,722	1,682	357	7,761	

In several Bank-sponsored agricultural projects a part of the loan is earmarked for adaptive research and development work. These are invariably projects introducing new enterprises and/or new agricultural technology to a country or region. Such funds are specifically directed towards facilitating diversification in a country's agriculture. Recent projects supported by IDA credits in Ecuador, Ethiopia, Indonesia, Madagascar and Tanzania are examples of this type. The Bank group has also played an active part in co-sponsoring a consortium for financing international agricultural research institutions. It seems probable that a substantial part of the research financed by the consortium will be devoted to finding new opportunities for agriculture in the tropics and sub-tropics.

A high proportion of the technical assistance accorded by the United Nations agencies in project preparation and feasibility studies is directed towards finding means of diversifying the economic activity of member countries. The Bank group plays an active part in this work in a variety of ways. The provision of technical assistance in project preparation is a regular part of the work of the Bank's permanent missions in East and West Africa and of its resident staff in Indonesia. In addition, technical help is frequently built into Bank-financed agricultural projects. Most of the work of the FAO/IBRD co-operative programme—which is substantially Bank-financed—is intended to assist member countries in preparing viable projects. IDA credits have also been used to finance project preparation and pre-investment studies, while the Bank staff may become directly involved in preparation and feasibility studies when the Bank acts as an executing agency for a UNDP project.

As the IBRD has increased its lending activities in the developing countries, it has devoted greater attention to its lending strategy, and in this matter the Bank's policies are still evolving. The Bank's economic mission performs a key function in determining the strategy for Bank lending to a developing country. The economic mission to a particular country will report on a number of subjects. These missions are becoming increasingly concerned with:

(1) Assessing the development strategy of the country in question;

(2) Its investment and foreign currency needs; and

(3) The priorities or emphasis that should be given to particular sectors in the country's development and investment programme.

A second type of economic mission that is being used increasingly by the Bank is the sector study mission. These missions normally consist of a few general economists and a number of "within sector" specialists. The missions concentrate on exploring the constraints on and opportunities for development within a sector that has already received special attention from the economic mission. These sector missions attempt to find investment possibilities within a sector such as agriculture, and also determine what pre-investment studies might have to precede project preparation. They also frequently indicate policy or institutional features which may need changing or amending to make a project feasible. In effect, they outline some of the conditions necessary for the success of a project.

In their reports the general economic and sector missions indicate to the Bank the strategy for development and associated lending which seems appropriate for the country concerned. The final reports and conclusions are always the products of an intensive dialogue and consultations between the Bank, the government officials of that country and the United Nations agencies operating in the field. They serve increasingly as a basis for the bank group's lending programme, and for scheduling missions for the purposes of pre-investment studies, project identification, and project preparation.

B. Regional development banks

Although the financial assistance provided by the regional development banks does not usually have diversification as an explicit objective, much of it in practice contributes to diversification in the wider sense and some of it contributes to commodity diversification. The AfDB, for example, has participated in the financing of six projects for the production of agricultural commodities, either to replace imports or for export. The export commodities in question— livestock and vegetables—were commodities with generally favourable prospects on the world market. Much of the AsDB's lending has also had the objective, directly or indirectly, of commodity diversification. Some of it has contributed to the expansion of rice, oil, palm fish and jute cultivation and some to the promotion of rice milling, cotton spinning, fertilizer manufacture and other forms of vertical diversification.

The technical and financial assistance activities of the regional development banks are determined on the basis of specific requests from member countries. The AfDB is currently giving priority to agriculture and transport in its lending operations, since it considers that agriculture must be the starting point for any realistic industrialization policy in Africa, and that economic growth generally depends largely on the development and modernization of transport. National diversification schemes carefully formulated in the form of specific agricultural projects will receive priority consideration for AfDB's financial assistance. The AfDB's appraisal of agricultural projects takes into account both relevant trends in world markets and the domestic circumstances of the borrowing country.

C. FAO

A substantial part of the whole work programme of FAO is concerned directly or indirectly with commodity diversification in the sense that it assists projects for the production of and trade in commodities and their processing. This is the case of a large number of projects for the development of land and water resources, specific regions within a country, crop and livestock production, farm management, marketing, agricultural processing and, particularly fisheries and forestry. Similarly, technical assistance provided for national, regional and sub-regional agricultural planning includes assistance in planning changes in the commodity composition of future output. At present, nearly forty developing countries and several regional or sub-regional schemes are benefiting from the advice of FAO agricultural planning experts. FAO has provided assistance for a number of specific diversification projects, e.g., diversification of uneconomic tea and rubber lands in Ceylon and marginal coffee-growing areas in El Salvador and Guatemala. Such projects include research as well as investment feasibility studies, and generally contain a component of agricultural extension, field demon-

stration and training. The research element in these projects includes technical surveys, studies and experiments as well as social and economic investigations to identify alternative production projects and to determine their technical and economic viability, including where necessary investigation of export prospects.

In addition to field projects, numerous studies and activities are carried out at FAO headquarters which have an important bearing on diversification as understood in the present report. Examples have been the Provisional Indicative World Plan for Agricultural Development,[b] long-term agricultural commodity projections, various commodity studies, and the activities of FAO bodies such as the Committee on Commodity Problems and its subsidiary intergovernmental commodity groups. It may be noted that the FAO programmes in the more general economic and social field are becoming increasingly oriented towards diversification. Agricultural adjustment has been chosen as a major theme for the 1973 FAO Conference, and supporting studies are under way or will be commenced shortly. The objective of this whole body of work is essentially to contribute to the economic and social development of developing countries and to promote a better allocation of resources in world agriculture. More specific objectives include the following: to assist developing countries in making decisions on agricultural policy, to raise productivity levels in agriculture, to improve nutrition, to widen the composition of exports, to reduce undue dependence on food imports, to establish an effective infrastructure for agriculture, and to contribute to the creation of employment opportunities in rural sectors.

The FAO has been rendering technical assistance for crop diversification under various programmes. In the first place, in response to direct requests from individual developing countries, FAO has been rendering assistance through its field programmes. These requests might be for a project identification mission, as in the case of Ceylon and Malaysia, or for research and investment projects. Although the assistance rendered is not explicitly part of a comprehensive programme of assistance for the particular country, the nature and justification of the requests are considered in the light of the country's needs and priorities. In addition, attention is given to the linking of diversification projects with other assistance schemes. For example, in countries like Ceylon, Malaysia, El Salvador and Guatemala, where crop diversification is an over-riding objective of agricultural development policy, the assistance rendered has been in fact part of a concerted effort to assist the agricultural development of the countries. In the future, with UNDP country programming, it may be expected that assistance for crop diversification will become part of a comprehensive programme for countries which are aiming at the diversification of their economies.

Secondly, FAO has been providing assistance in response to requests from regional and sub-regional groupings. Such assistance has been provided in Latin America for studies relating to the diversification of agriculture, the preparation and evaluation of specific programmes and projects at regional and sub-regional levels and the harmonization of agricultural policies. More specifically, the FAO Advisory Group on Central American Economic Integration has provided the Governments with specialized assistance in planning at the sub-regional level, the development of the agricultural sector and the promotion of a common market for agricultural products.

Thirdly, the World Food Programme (a joint FAO/United Nations agency) has been providing food aid in connexion with the diversification of the land-use pattern in some of the countries in the Near East and with schemes for replacing animal husbandry by other activities in some of the Latin American countries (e.g. the Agricultural Improvement and Diversification Project in Paraguay). Assistance to countries through studies of problems of diversification is also envisaged by FAO under the Perspective Study of World Agricultural Development and the study on international agricultural

---

[b] FAO, *Provisional Indicative World Plan for Agricultural Development: a synthesis and analysis of factors relevant to world, regional and national agricultural development*, Rome, 1970.

adjustment. These studies are being undertaken in response to recommendations or resolutions of FAO's governing bodies.[c]

D. UNIDO

Technical assistance provided by UNIDO is aimed at the expansion of export earnings and employment through industrialization generally, rather than at vertical diversification as such. Nevertheless UNIDO country missions, which have already served about twenty developing countries, pay due attention to finding opportunities for the processing of locally produced raw materials. The assistance given by UNIDO relates mainly to the pre-investment stage and is provided chiefly through industrial management programmes. These programmes may be short-term, involving a study of a particular industrial sector for four to six weeks by a team of consultants, or longer-term, involving the setting-up of a national industrial development corporation. One of the objectives of both types of programme is to find opportunities for the manufacture of new products, including possibilities for increasing the extent to which raw materials are processed, either for import substitution or export. Industrial management programmes include the provision of assistance in the over-all planning and organization of enterprises, both in the creation and expansion stage, as well as in productivity improvement, quality control and distribution. In some cases, technical assistance is provided by UNIDO in response to *ad hoc* requests; increasingly, however, it is being given in the context of comprehensive industrial development programmes.

E. ITC

The ITC helps to promote both vertical and horizontal diversification through its Trade Promotion Advisory Service, Training Service, Market Research Service, Export Promotion Techniques Research Service, Publishing Service and Documentation Service. Usually all the expertise available in the Centre, regardless of service, is drawn upon in implementing any particular export promotion project.

Until 1970 most of the technical assistance provided by the Centre was determined on an *ad hoc* basis in response to specific requests from or through Governments, trade organizations and private companies, and priorities for major projects were established by the Joint UNCTAD/GATT Advisory Group on the ITC. Since 1970, however, assistance has increasingly been planned and provided through integrated programmes involving all services of the Centre. Such comprehensive integrated programmes might be prepared as a consequence of a country's request through one of the Centre's fact-finding and programming missions, or they might form part of UNDP country programmes.

F. ILO

Technical assistance provided by the ILO relating to diversification comes under the headings of employment promotion, vocational training and management development. Under its World Employment Programme the high level inter-agency employment missions to Colombia and Ceylon organized by the ILO to assist these countries in formulating employment-oriented development strategies made specific recommendations on the diversification of exports, with emphasis on exports of commodities in processed and semi-processed form to reduce the role of "problem" commodities (viz. coffee in Colombia and tea and rubber in Ceylon). Employment missions to other developing countries in progress (Iran) and in preparation (Kenya) will give similar attention to commodity diversification. The ILO regional employment teams stationed in Asia and Latin America have likewise taken into consideration the employment implications of diversification in primary production in the advice given to Governments and in their studies of employment

problems and policies in the countries of these regions. Besides, technical assistance provided by the ILO to several countries for promoting rural employment and small-scale industries and handicrafts is directed to the creation of productive employment through commodity diversification, vertical and horizontal.

ILO technical assistance in connexion with vocational training and management is intended to ease the constraints on the diversification of production imposed by limitation of human resources. Some of the vocational training projects carried out by the ILO make provision for training in skills directly related to the processing of primary commodities for export, for example textiles and canned foods in Egypt. While vocational training schemes assisted by the ILO in many cases cover a cross-section of workers and craftsmen including those in export industries, greater emphasis is being placed on the improvement of skills in export industries in view of the growing need for the vertical diversification of exports from the developing countries. Rural vocational training projects undertaken by the ILO represent another type of training designed to teach farmers and craftsmen improved and new skills necessary for the diversification of their productive activities. ILO management projects, like its vocational training projects, have been devoted chiefly to the training of managerial and entrepreneurial skills for various economic sectors essential to economic diversification in the wider sense. A number of them have contributed to the vertical diversification of exports, in two related ways. First, several projects have worked out simple improved methods of processing locally produced materials for export, such as pottery in New Guinea and the replacement of imported yarn by locally made yarn from local wool for the hand-woven carpet industry in Syria. Secondly, the promotion of export products has been accorded increasing importance in these projects through training and consultative services rendered to government and industry in the matter of export marketing, improvement of quality standards, selection and use of appropriate production methods, and through other assistance. Moreover, export marketing management has been a regular feature of the training programme operated by the ILO International Centre for Advanced Technical and Vocational Training at Turin.

G. The regional economic commissions and UNESOB

Technical assistance for diversification is provided by the regional economic commissions and UNESOB in indirect ways, notably through research, training activities and advisory services. ECAFE, for example, assists its member countries to diversify their export sectors by means of surveys of markets for selected commodities and by the training of trade promotion personnel. The ECAFE Trade Promotion Centre collects and disseminates information about export opportunities and trade barriers and promotes international trade fairs and intra-regional trade promotion talks. A similar trade centre is attached to ECA. The ECAFE secretariat also renders technical assistance through project feasibility studies, advisory services to Governments of member States, training programmes, seminars and intergovernmental discussions on matters relating to trade and development. Assistance for diversification may be provided also through the regional economic research institutes which are sponsored by certain of the regional economic commissions, for example, the Latin American Institute for Economic and Social Planning sponsored by ECLA.

UNESOB undertakes research studies relating to diversification in countries of the region served by the Office and organizes seminars and training workshops for planning, trade promotion and marketing and aspects of industrial policy. Advisory services are rendered to Governments by regional advisers attached to the Office as well as by its regular staff. Sometimes the services are performed through participation of staff members in missions conducted by other agencies for the purpose of exploring, finding and evaluating alternative investment opportunities.

---

[c] See FAO, *Report of the Conference of FAO, Sixteenth Session*, Rome, 6-25 November 1971, paras. 76-87.

Assistance provided by regional economic commissions or UNE-SOB in the form of research, studies and training activities is normally determined by the organization's own judgment of the priority needs of the countries in the region in question and on the basis of consultations with Governments. Assistance in the form of advisory services, however, is provided in response to specific requests by Governments.

H. COFFEE DIVERSIFICATION FUND

Among institutions outside the United Nations family the Coffee Diversification Fund of the International Coffee Agreement is notable as being the only example so far of a fund constituted within the framework of an international commodity agreement for the purpose of assisting members to transfer or divert resources from production of a particular commodity in surplus on the world market. The Coffee Diversification Fund is designed specifically to help member countries to adjust their coffee production in the long term to their coffee export quotas under the Agreement.

Loans by the Coffee Diversification Fund are made for specific programmes or projects presented by participants for financing by the Fund. Programmes or projects must form part of an approved national coffee policy plan and are considered for financing in relation to the plan as well as to the most recent information on the coffee situation in the territory of the participant concerned. Each project submitted to the Board of the Fund for its approval is accompanied by a report of the Executive Director presenting his findings and recommendations.

From its inception the Diversification Fund of the International Coffee Organization has sought to maintain close co-operation with other international agencies in pursuance of the objectives of the Fund. International agencies have provided expert advice in connexion with the formulation of the Fund's policies and have made information and staff available to it. Co-operation with other international agencies has two purposes:

(a) To permit the Fund to co-ordinate its policies and its activities with those of other international organizations; and

(b) To encourage the joint financing of programmes and projects.

In view of the short life of the Fund, it has proved difficult to conclude satisfactory arrangements for the joint financing of programmes and projects with other international organizations. Of the six loans approved by the Fund, the loan to Tanzania is the only one which supplements financial resources made available by other financial agencies: the project in Tanzania is to be financed jointly by the Diversification Fund, IDA (which appraised the project) and the Norwegian Agency for International Development. It is the intention of the Fund to participate in co-operative arrangements whenever possible.

I. EDF

In the two Conventions of Association between the EEC and the Associated African and Malagasy States (the Yaoundé Conventions), explicit provision was made for the granting of technical and financial assistance to the Associated States by the EDF for the purpose of diversification. Under the first Convention, signed on 20 July 1963, assistance was provided specifically for commodity diversification, inasmuch as its object was to help the Associated States to adapt their production structures to the fact that marketing at world prices was to be progressively introduced for certain commodities previously marketed at privileged prices under special arrangements with States members of EEC.[d] However, under the second Convention signed on 29 July 1969, provision was made only for assistance for diversification in the wider sense, "with a view to diversifying the economic structure of the Associated States and, especially, to promoting their industrialization and their agricultural development" (Article 19).

---

[d] The commodities in question were: coffee, rice, sugar, oil-seeds and oleaginous fruit, desiccated coconut, pepper, palm oil, cotton, and gum arabic.

PROBLEMS OF COMMODITY DIVERSIFICATION IN DEVELOPING COUNTRIES

Report by the UNCTAD secretariat*

[Original text: English]

In its decision 5 (VI) on diversification,[1] taken at its sixth session in July 1971, the Committee on Commodities requested the UNCTAD secretariat "to present proposals for concrete action by the appropriate national and international bodies for the solution of urgent structural problems in specific fields of the commodity sector, and particularly in respect of countries heavily dependent on exports of a commodity facing structural marketing problems". The secretariat was also requested to bear in mind, in respect of its work on diversification, "that the aims should be to assist the Governments of the developing countries in the formulation and reconsideration of their diversification programmes, to assist the Governments of developed countries in framing their diversification policies and to identify the areas where additional international action is called for".

The attached report is submitted in response to these requests. In preparing it, the UNCTAD secretariat took into account views expressed at two inter-agency meetings on diversification convened by the Secretary-General of UNCTAD in October and December 1971. These meetings were attended by representatives of IBRD, FAO, UNIDO, UNDP, the ILO, ITC, AfDB, the International Coffee Organization (October meeting only) and OECD (October meeting only). None of these organizations, however, is necessarily committed to any of the views expressed in the present report, which is issued on the responsibility of the UNCTAD secretariat alone.

The review entitled "Main issues in agricultural commodity trade" (TD/CONTR/2), prepared by FAO for submission to the third Session of the Conference, should be read in conjunction with the present report, since it is intended to provide background information about problems of agricultural commodities, some of which might give rise to diversification problems in individual countries. A report by the UNCTAD secretariat on international action relating to commodity diversification, based on the discussions at the two inter-agency meetings referred to above, is contained in document TD/109.[2]

---

* The text of this report was circulated to the Conference as document TD/119, dated 9 February 1972, and TD/119/Corr.1, dated 18 April 1972.

[1] *Official Records of the Trade and Development Board, Eleventh Session, Supplement No. 4* (TD/B/370-TD/B/C.1/119), p. 35.

[2] See page 79 below.

CONTENTS

Chapter I

Diversification and economic development

1. The Advisory Committee to the Trade and Development Board and to the Committee on Commodities, in its 1971 report on this subject, interpreted diversification to mean "widening, or reducing the degree of concentration in, the range of commodities and products, exported or not, on which a given country depended for its income". In this sense, the Advisory Committee pointed out, "the problems of diversification were essentially those of economic development, which could be defined as the process of structural transformation associated with diversification of the commodities, products and services produced by the economy".[3]

2. The structural transformation which constitutes economic development involves not merely an increase in the variety of goods and services produced, but also the provision of certain specific types of services (such as services in the fields of banking, rural credit, industrial finance and trading), the creation of an infrastructure of transport, communications and educational facilities and governmental machinery and changes in ownership patterns. Economic development in this structural sense and diversification are, in fact, interdependent processes. When economic development has reached an advanced stage, however, the process of diversification becomes more a consequence than a cause of development, whereas in the earlier stages of economic development the reverse tends to be true. The higher the level of economic development, the more mobile its factors of production become, and the more automatic is the process of diversification in response to new demands and changes in consumers' tastes in home and export markets. In under-developed economies, by contrast, diversification is often the prime mover in the development process, especially when diversification is of the "vertical" type, i.e., the processing or further transformation of locally-produced primary commodities.

3. In this connexion, the Advisory Committee pointed out that diversification can contribute to structural change through backward and forward linkages, and possibilities for the development of new skills and knowledge or markets, associated with the introduction of new commodities in the pattern of production or export.[4] It referred also to the contribution diversification could make to the saving and earning of foreign exchange, required for the purchase from abroad of capital equipment and specialized, highly-skilled, services essential for development. Foreign exchange can be saved by means of import-substituting diversification (into domestic food production, for example), while export-oriented diversification can expand export earnings, especially if it takes place into products with favourable market prospects (such as processed commodities and manufactured goods). The Advisory Committee also drew attention to the importance of commodity diversification, particularly of the "vertical" type, in promoting economic development through the provision of employment for an expanding labour force.

Chapter II

Urgent problems of commodity diversification

4. When, as in the earlier stages of development, diversification is not an automatic process, it has to be actively promoted by governments through economic planning, the mobilization of resources and the provision of fiscal and other incentives to producers. For some developing countries, however, the promotion of commodity diversification may present special difficulties and necessitate special assistance from the international community.

5. There appear to be two main groups of developing countries in this situation. First, there are countries which are heavily dependent for their export earnings on one or more commodities for which world demand has been relatively stagnant and is likely to remain so. Second, there are countries where the export structure, and in some cases the production structure as well, is excessively concentrated in a single commodity; if the world market situation and prospects of the commodity concerned are unfavourable, the problem overlaps with that of the countries in the first category. However, even if the dominant export commodity is one for which world demand is relatively dynamic (for example, petroleum or copper), excessive dependence on such a commodity involves certain risks to the economy. In addition to these two categories of countries, there are some developing countries which have diversification problems of an *ad hoc* character. These different types of diversification problems are examined in more detail below.

---

[3] See *Official Records of the Trade and Development Board, Eleventh Session, Annexes*, agenda item 7, document TD/B/348, para. 5.

[4] *Ibid.*, paras. 7-14.

TABLE 1

Exports from developing countries of selected "problem" commodities

	Volume	Unit value		Value
	Average rate of change 1959-1961 to 1967-1969			1967-1969 (average)
	(per cent per annum)			(million dollars)
A. Commodities in actual or potential surplus on the world market				
Coffee	2.7	−0.2	2.5	2 292
Sugar	0.5	3.0	3.5	1 523
Tea	2.0	−3.2	−1.3	520
Rice	−3.6	5.6	1.9	491
B. Commodities facing serious competition from synthetics				
Cotton	4.2	−1.2	3.0	1 412
Rubber	3.0	−7.1	−4.3	981
Lauric oils	−0.6	−0.1[a]	−0.9	418
Jute	1.8	−0.5	1.3	205
Wool	−0.4	−2.0	−2.4	205
Hides and skins	..	..	−5.2	176
Sisal	0	−4.3	−4.3	71
Essential oils	..	..	4.6[b,c]	32[b,d]
Vanilla	7.4	−3.2	−4.0[e]	12

Sources: FAO, Commodity Review and Trade Yearbook; national trade statistics.

[a] Coconut oil only.

[b] Main developing exporters.

[c] 1959-1961 to 1966-1968.

[d] 1966-1968.

[e] 1961-1963 to 1967-1969.

A. UNFAVOURABLE EXPORT STRUCTURE

6. A list of "problem" commodities, i.e. those for which the world market situation and prospects are unfavourable, is contained in table 1, which is a revised version, brought up to date, of the corresponding table included in the Advisory Committee's report on diversification.[5] The table shows that during the 1960s the aggregate value of exports from developing countries of most of the principal commodities in actual or potential surplus on the world market, or facing serious competition from synthetics, either grew at a rate of less than 3.5 per cent per annum or actually fell, chiefly because of price declines. Although the reason for the sluggish growth in earnings of developing countries from exports of rice in the 1960s was inadequate production (rice prices actually rose strongly), rice has been included in the table because the world situation of this commodity, largely owing to the "Green Revolution", has now changed from one of shortage to one of surplus, and rice is likely to remain in substantial surplus for some time.

7. The latest projections for agricultural commodities prepared by FAO indicate that, from the point of view of developing exporting countries, world market conditions for most of the commodities listed in table 1 will probably be no better in the 1970s than they were in the 1960s, and

in some cases may well be worse.[6] The projections imply, therefore, that the rate of growth of developing countries' earnings from exports of each of the commodities concerned will continue to be unsatisfactory during the Second United Nations Development Decade.[7]

8. Table 2 gives information about the export performance during the 1960s of a sample of 13 developing countries which are dependent on the problem commodities listed in table I for 50 per cent or more of their total export earnings. In none of these countries did the average rate of growth of total export earnings in the 1960s exceed 5 per cent per annum, even though the increase in the aggregate value of exports of problem commodities achieved by certain countries (Ethiopia, Egypt, Sudan, Khmer Republic and Brazil) represented a better export performance than the average performance of all developing countries with respect to the "basket" of problem commodities concerned. In two cases (Ceylon and Burma) total export earnings actually declined.

9. For a number of countries (Mauritius, Cuba, the Dominican Republic, Burma and Haiti), export performance with respect to problem commodities was sub-

[5] Ibid., annex I.

[6] FAO, Agricultural Commodity Projections, 1970-1980, Rome, 1971.

[7] For further discussion of these projections, see the report by the UNCTAD secretariat entitled "Trends in commodity trade in the 1960s and prospects for the 1970s" (TD/113/Supp.2 and Corr.1).

TABLE 2

Export performance of selected developing countries heavily dependent on "problem" commodities

	"Problem" commodities[a]			Other commodities	Total exports		
	Share in total exports 1967-1969	Average rate of change in value 1959-1961 to 1967-1969					GDP 1969[d]
		Actual	Hypothetical[b]	Actual	Actual	Hypothetical[c]	
	(per cent)	(per cent per annum)					(billion dollars)
Mauritius	89	2.1	3.6	4.2	2.3	3.7	0.18
Ceylon	82	−1.9	−1.7	2.9	−1.2	−1.0	1.98
Cuba	79	−0.7	3.6	12.3	1.2	4.6	2.31
Colombia	71	2.0	2.0	3.8	2.5	2.5	6.18
Ethiopia	69	5.2	0.0	4.4	4.9	1.6	1.61
Madagascar	62	4.9	5.2	4.8	4.8	5.1	0.75
Dominican Republic	61	2.4	3.3	0.2	1.5	2.0	1.27
Egypt	60	1.0	−0.5	9.1	3.6	2.7	6.10
Sudan	60	3.7	0.4	1.7	2.9	1.0	1.73
Khmer Republic	59	1.1	−1.2	7.5	3.3	2.0	0.74
Burma	57	−10.4	1.8	−0.7	−7.4	1.2	1.99
Haiti	50	0.0	2.5	4.2	1.9	3.2	0.41
Brazil	50	2.0	1.1	9.1	5.0	4.6	31.16

Sources: As for table 1.

   [a] Exports of the commodities listed in table 1.

   [b] Assuming that the value of exports of each "problem" commodity exported by each country had increased at the same rate as the value of total exports of the same commodity from all developing countries.

   [c] Assuming that exports of "problem" commodities had increased at the hypothetical rates shown in the third column and taking the hypothetical rate for "other" commodities as equal to the actual rate.

   [d] GDP at factor cost expressed in current dollars.

stantially below average. It is significant, however, that even if the export performance of these countries had been fully up to average, the rate of growth of their total export earnings would still have failed to exceed 5 per cent per annum in every case, and for some countries the rate would still have been well below 5 per cent.

10. In the light of the unfavourable market prospects for the problem commodities concerned, these figures illustrate the seriousness and urgency of the diversification problems facing the countries listed in table 2. If account was taken of other commodities for which only a slow growth of world import demand is projected in the 1970s, e.g. wheat, cocoa, oilcakes, citrus fruits and bananas,[8] and if analyses were made of the export structures and performance of a larger number of developing countries, it would probably be possible to identify additional countries facing urgent diversification problems arising from the unfavourable composition of their exports.

B. EXCESSIVE CONCENTRATION OF EXPORTS

11. Table 3 gives examples of developing countries which are dependent for two-thirds or more of their total export earnings on a single commodity. In addition to the countries included in this table, there are a number of developing countries whose production and exports are largely concentrated in the petroleum industry (e.g. Libya,

Saudi Arabia, Iran, Iraq, Kuwait) and there are also many small islands whose economies are of the "monoculture" type, e.g. Barbados and Fiji (heavily dependent on sugar), and Windward Islands (bananas), or based on a single mineral, e.g. Nauru (phosphates).

12. Some of the commodities concerned, e.g. sugar and cotton, are among the "problem" commodities listed in table 1, and two of the countries mentioned in table 3 (Mauritius and Cuba), whose sugar export earnings showed an unsatisfactory trend in the 1960s, have already been identified in table 2 as countries with unfavourable export structures. For copper and petroleum, by contrast, the trend of demand and/or prices on the world market has been favourable and is likely to remain so. Whether prospects for future earnings from exports of these commodities are favourable or unfavourable, however, it is undesirable from the point of view of the countries concerned that their export structures should show such high degrees of concentration.

13. Where the prospects for future earnings are unfavourable the need for diversification is self-evident. Even where prospects seem favourable, however, undue concentration on a single commodity involves the risk of serious disruption of development plans, which depend crucially on export earnings, should there be an unexpected deterioration in the market situation and outlook. Moreover, where production of the principal export commodity makes a large direct contribution to the gross domestic product, as in Zambia, Mauritius, Mauritania, Surinam, Gambia, Liberia and Zaire (see table 3), a deterioration in

---

   [8] *Ibid.*

TABLE 3

Selected developing countries and territories heavily dependent

Country and principal export commodity	Value of exports of principal export commodity			GDP 1969[a]		Manufacturing production as proportion of GDP[b]
	As proportion of total exports 1969	As proportion of GDP 1969	Average rate of change 1959-1961 to 1967-1969	Total	Per head	
	(per cent)	(per cent)	(per cent per annum)	(billion dollars)	(dollars)	(per cent)
Zambia: Copper[c]	95	62	11.9	1.67	400	8
Mauritius: Sugar	94	33	2.1	0.18	225	13
Mauritania: Iron ore	87	39	[d]	0.17	150	..
Surinam: Aluminium[e]	87	49	15.4	0.24	615	13[f]
Chad: Raw cotton	82	11	7.8	0.24	70	..
Gambia: Groundnuts[g]	81	33	7.9	0.04	110	..
Chile: Copper[c]	78	15	11.0	6.16	645	28
Cuba: Sugar	76[h]	22	−0.7	2.31	280	..
Liberia: Iron ore	72	45	18.9	0.29	250	5
Ghana: Cocoa[i]	72	10	0.9	2.24	255	..
Sierra Leone: Diamonds	69	17	5.7	0.43	170	5
Zaire: Copper[c]	67	28	10.6	1.67	100	16
Senegal: Groundnuts[g]	66	10	−0.7	0.70	185	3

Source: FAO, *Trade Yearbook*; IMF, *International Financial Statistics*; United Nations, *Yearbook of International Trade Statistics* and *Yearbook of National Accounts*.

　a GDP at factor cost expressed in current dollars.
　b In latest year for which data are available (years range from 1965 to 1969).
　c Ore, blister and refined.
　d Exports commenced in 1963.
　e Bauxite, alumina and aluminium.
　f Including construction.
　g Including oil and cake.
　h 1968.
　i Including products.

market conditions for the key commodity could have a directly disruptive effect on the economy, while fluctuations in the commodity market concerned could have a seriously destabilizing effect. In general, therefore, countries excessively dependent on a single export commodity need to diversify their exports to insure against the risk of adverse long-term changes and short-term instability in the commodity market concerned.

14. A further reason for reducing excessive dependence on one or a small number of commodities arises from the growth-stimulating role of exports which was noted by the Advisory Committee.[9] When production of a single export commodity accounts for a high proportion of a country's GDP, as in the case of the countries mentioned in the preceding paragraph and the countries heavily dependent on petroleum mentioned in paragraph 11, this fact would seem to constitute *prima facie* evidence of under-development, inasmuch as it indicates inadequate diversification of the commodities, products and services produced by the economy. Even though a dominant export commodity such as petroleum or copper may be a buoyant source of export revenue to a country, the stimulus it provides to structural change through back-

ward and forward linkages may be weak. In such cases, therefore, diversification of the production and export structure may help to impact greater impetus to general economic development.

15. The fact that production of the dominant export commodity represents a comparatively small proportion of GDP in Chile, Chad, Ghana and Senegal, has a different significance in Chile from that in the other three countries. In Chile it reflects the relatively diversified and industrialized character of the production structure, which in turn implies a substantial degree of development. According to the criterion of GDP per head, or the share of manufacturing in GDP (see table 3), Chile is in fact considerably more developed than any of the other three countries mentioned. However, the high degree of concentration in the Chilean export structure might imply that too much emphasis had been given to import substitution in the country's industrial development. In this connexion, the Advisory Committee noted in its report on diversification that "if vertical diversification was to lead to faster economic growth it should be export-oriented, especially in smaller countries, since the possibilities of import substitution were limited by the size and rate of growth of the home market".[10] Even in countries which have already industrialized to a considerable extent, therefore, the

_____
[9] See *Official Records of the Trade and Development Board, Eleventh Session, Annexes*, agenda item 7, document TD/B/348, para. 80.

_____
[10] *Ibid.*, para. 38.

development of exports by industries originally established to serve the domestic market would create better prospects for economic growth.

16. In Chad, Ghana and Senegal, the comparatively low proportion of GDP accounted for by production of the dominant export commodity does not reflect, as it does in Chile, a substantially diversified production structure, but simply the relatively important role played by subsistence agriculture in these countries. In such cases also diversification of exports is needed to provide a stimulus to structural change and economic growth, as well as a stable and adequate flow of foreign exchange to pay for imports required for development.

C. AD HOC NEEDS FOR DIVERSIFICATION

17. At any time a relative deterioration in the long-term world market prospects for a commodity may lead planning authorities in developing countries to consider the desirability of a transfer or diversion of resources from production of the export commodity concerned, the urgency of the matter depending, *inter alia*, on the importance of the commodity in a country's exports. In certain circumstances, however, an urgent *ad hoc* need for diversification may arise for reasons unconnected with the over-all world market situation of a commodity. For example, after the establishment of EEC, a number of developing countries which were former colonies of certain EEC members lost the privileges of access on specially favourable terms which they had previously enjoyed in the metropolitan countries in respect of certain commodities. The preferential arrangements which were subsequently established under the Convention of Association negotiated between EEC and the Associated African and Malagasy States concerned (the Yaoundé Convention) did not in all cases provide an equivalent degree of protection. Accordingly, under the first Yaoundé Convention signed on 20 July 1963, provision was made for the granting of financial and technical assistance from the European Development Fund to help the Associated States to improve productivity in, or to diversify away from, the cultivation of crops which could not be produced economically at prevailing world market prices.[11] For similar reasons, special assistance for diversification may be required by some developing countries of the Commonwealth after the accession of the United Kingdom to the Treaty of Rome, establishing EEC.[12]

18. While a relative deterioration in the market prospects for a commodity, or the loss or partial loss of a country's privileged position in the market, may make it desirable for a country to transfer on divert resources from production of the export commodity concerned, it will not normally be obliged to do so. If no alternative employments are available for the resources involved, diversification will not normally take place, despite the losses of income suffered as a result of the change in market conditions. However, an unavoidable need may arise to transfer or divert resources from the production of a particular commodity as a result of a country's acceptance of a production or export quota in the context of an international commodity arrangement. If an actual cut in output was required, alternative employment for the land and/or labour released from production of the commodity in question would have to be found immediately. If adherence to the quota required only a halt to further expansion of output, no specific transfer of resources would be needed immediately; nevertheless, if productivity in the particular activity was rising, as might well happen if some or all of the production took place on an organized basis on plantations or in mines, a need for the redeployment of surplus factors of production would arise sooner or later.

19. Another example of a specific need to transfer or divert resources from the production of a particular commodity is that which may arise from a country's commitment to support international efforts to eliminate the illegal use of narcotic drugs and, eventually drug addiction itself, by putting an end to the illicit or uncontrolled cultivation of narcotic crops. The attainment of these objectives requires diversification away from narcotic plant cultivation in a number of developing countries, for example, the opium poppy in Thailand, the cocoa leaf in the Andes and cannabis in Lebanon.[13] In all the developing countries concerned, diversification away from narcotic crops presents a considerable problem because such cultivation has been traditional and provides an assured income, whether legal or illegal, and because the illegal traffic has a vested interest in opposing diversification.

Chapter III

National action required

20. Given the importance of an adequate growth of foreign exchange earnings for financing imports essential for development, *heavy dependence on exports of one or more commodities for which the world market situation and prospects are unfavourable* is the most serious and most urgent of the various types of diversification problem with which developing countries can be faced. The policy issues which arise in dealing with this problem include those arising for any developing country from a relative deterioration in the market prospects for any of its exports commodities, or from a loss or partial loss of its privileged position as an exporter of any commodity.

21. When the structure of a country's exports remains frozen in an unfavourable pattern for any length of time, this situation may be taken as evidence indicating that its general economic development has not yet reached the point where factors of production are able to respond spontaneously, without government intervention, to changes in market conditions and new opportunities, i.e.

---

[11] Aid for diversification was allocated in relation to production of certain crops: coffee, rice, sugar, oil-seeds and oleaginous fruit, desiccated coconut, pepper, palm oil, cotton, and gum arabic.

[12] Signed at Rome on 25 March 1957 (United Nations, *Treaty Series*, No. 4300, vol. 298, p. 11).

[13] Turkey has completely prohibited poppy-growing, which has hitherto been a licit activity, as from the autumn of 1972 and is engaged in drawing up a diversification programme.

the point where diversification becomes an automatic part of the development process. The solutions of the problem of unfavourable export structure cannot, however, await the attainment of a higher level of economic development. In fact, given the importance of export earnings and linkages, the attainment of such a higher level may depend on governmental action to promote diversification of the export structure; in other words, although general development and diversification are interdependent, this is one of the situations in which commodity or product diversification may be the primary engine of growth.

22. In its report on diversification, the Advisory Committee pointed out that there were no quick-acting panaceas for the problem of unfavourable export structure, and that, "What was required was that each country should adopt a diversification strategy appropriate to its circumstances".[14] Preparation of such a strategy would involve simultaneous study of a number of possible lines of action.

23. One subject of study would be the possibilities for the "horizontal" diversification of exports, i.e. the export of new primary commodities or of primary commodities already being produced but not exported. However, the Advisory Committee noted that the possibilities for successful diversification of this kind, "would depend chiefly on whether the resource endowment of a country enabled it to produce, on a competitive basis, products experiencing relatively dynamic demand conditions on the world market, such as livestock and fisheries products, fruits and vegetables, tropical timber, petroleum, coal and non-ferrous metals".[15] The Advisory Committee also pointed out that horizontal diversification might take place into commodities which were themselves actually or potentially "problem" commodities and might thus aggravate the market problems facing these commodities".[16] It emphasized, therefore, the need for harmonization, as far as possible, of diversification programmes.[17]

24. It sould be noted that, except in the case of diversification of the *ad hoc* type described earlier, horizontal diversification need not necessarily involve any transfer or diversion of resources from the production of traditional export commodities. If the factors employed in such production have no "opportunity costs", i.e. if there is ample unused or under-employed land and labour in the country, or if the factors so employed cannot be used in any other way, then there is no need to restrict production of the traditional commodities concerned. On the other hand, if any or all of the factors employed in traditional production are in short supply, diversification will require their transfer to more profitable employments. This may pose some difficult problems for decision-makers, because factors of production are employed in different proportions in different activities. For example, if agricultural land is fully used while much labour is unemployed, the transfer of, say, coffee land to a more profitable but less

labour-intensive use such as livestock rearing might increase export earnings at the cost of increased unemployment.

25. Wherever any of the resources employed in the production of traditional commodities with unfavourable market prospects have opportunity costs, it will also be necessary for Governments to consider, in conjunction with any projects involving the transfer of such resources, an appropriate long-term strategy for the traditional "problem" commodities concerned. In the light of the prospective world market trends for each commodity, it will be necessary to consider, for example, whether the country might be able to increase its share of the world market at the expense of other exporting countries by improving productivity and quality. In the case of commodities facing competition from synthetics, an assessment will have to be made of the chances of achieving a major improvement in the competitive position of the natural product through intensified research and development and increases in productivity.[18] In the case of commodities in actual or potential surplus on the world market, an assessment will have to be made of the possibilities for the conclusion of international stabilization or control arrangements. It might also be worthwhile to maintain production of a commodity if there was a good prospect of improvement in access to markets.

26. Since relatively few primary commodity markets offer dynamic export opportunities, and since unemployment or underemployment is a serious problem in many developing countries, particularly close study will have to be made by those responsible for planning diversification strategy of possibilities for "vertical" diversification, i.e. the processing for export of traditional or new commodities.[19] However, in developing countries where the resource endowment is limited and where unemployment is particularly acute, it may be necessary for planners to look beyond horizontal and vertical diversification to what might be called "diagonal" diversification, i.e. the processing of imported raw materials, or more advanced manufacturing using intermediate goods as inputs, as well as to the possibilities for the development of service activities such as tourism.

27. Where the diversification problem faced by a country arises from excessive concentration of exports, the national action required depends on whether the concentration has arisen in the context of the so-called "dual" economy, in which a relatively advanced sector, based on a single mineral or crop and often developed mainly by foreign interests, exists within a predominantly subsistence economy, or whether it has arisen in an economy which is already substantially industrialized. In the case of *export concentration in the "dual" economy*, the need is for government action to correct the imbalance in the pattern of development. It was mentioned earlier that economic development in the wider sense and diversification of the

---

[14] See *Official Records of the Trade and Development Board, Eleventh Session, Annexes*, agenda item 7, document TD/B/348, para. 17.

[15] *Ibid.*, para. 21.

[16] *Ibid.*, para. 46.

[17] The problem of harmonization is considered in some detail in document TD/109, chapter II (see p. 84 above).

[18] This issue is considered in detail in the reports by the UNCTAD secretariat entitled "The competitiveness of natural products" and "The competitiveness of natural products: research and development efforts and needs" (TD/117 and TD/117/Supp.1 respectively). (For document TD/117, see p. 73 above.)

[19] Some of the issues arising in this connexion are discussed in document TD/109, paras. 6-16.

commodities and products produced were interdependent and that at different stages of development either one or the other could be the primary "engine of growth". When development has been of the unbalanced kind under consideration, it seems probable that substantial corrective action, in the form of infrastructural development of various kinds, will be necessary before wider product diversification can be achieved.

28. In this connexion, the Advisory Committee emphasized that in situations of historically or institutionally determined concentration of the production structure, "it would be necessary for Governments to take the necessary steps to reform land tenure systems, to make the country's financial and marketing infrastructure more flexible and to provide training and encouragement for diversification of both a horizontal and a vertical character."[20] Through such action, it may be possible to bring about a rapid expansion in the production of cash crops which would lead to a greater "monetization" of the economy, and thus provide a stimulus to new productive activities. In this way, it might also be possible to introduce new commodities into the export pattern and to establish for new processing industries.

29. When the diversification problem confronting a Government is essentially one of *excessive export concentration in an economy whose production structure is already substantially industrialized and diversified*, the main need is to provide encouragement to exports and perhaps to new export-oriented industries. One of the options to be considered would be a modification of the exchange rate of the national currency. It might also be necessary, however, to modify the structure of existing subsidies and other incentives to industry with a view to correcting any distortions in the domestic price structure which might be hampering exports. For example, an industry with export potential might be rendered uncompetitive on the world market because of protection accorded to the manufacture at high-cost of one or more of its inputs in the country concerned.

30. Especially in small developing countries, where the size and rate of growth of the domestic market is limited, protection and encouragement should be given preferably to industries which have a chance, sooner or later, of becoming competitive on the world market. Care should be taken, moreover, that aids to industry do not actively discriminate in favour of home market sales as against exports. In general, the level of protection provided to any industry should be decided with care since, as the Advisory Committee pointed out, excessive protection bolsters inefficiency and tends to prevent industries from becoming competitive on the world market.[21]

31. The diversification problems arising from acceptance by a country of a quota under an international commodity arrangement, or from a country's efforts to reduce or eliminate production of a narcotic crop, give rise to policy issues somewhat different from those just discussed. The reason is that in these circumstances diversification, whether horizontal or vertical, involves *a specific need to transfer or divert resources from production of a particular commodity*, in conformity with an international commitment.

32. As already noted, even if no actual cut in production of the commodity was required, but only a limitation of further expansion, resources might still be released as a result of improved productivity. The improvement might be due to efforts by large-scale producers (estate companies or co-operatives) or by peasant farmers to increase their incomes, and is perhaps more likely to be achieved by the former than by the latter. In order to reduce production, or merely to curb further expansion, therefore, the Government may have to reduce the price received by the producer of the commodity. Unless opportunities and incentives for cultivating other cash crops or for engaging in alternative activities are provided, the result may be that marginal growers of the crop concerned, or workers dismissed from plantations or mines, will revert to subsistence farming or join the ranks of the unemployed seeking work in urban areas.[22]

33. In either of these circumstances, losses of income will be suffered by farmers and/or workers. If they arose in connexion with a country's participation in an international commodity arrangement, they would at least partially offset any gains accruing to the country from such participation. If they arose in connexion with the eradication of narcotic crops, for example, they would have to be regarded as part of the cost to the country of such eradication.

34. Such losses will be avoided only if alternative occupations are available for the released factors of production which provide an income comparable with that formerly obtained. The most favourable situation, from the point of view of economic development, would be one in which surplus labour could readily find employment in industry. In many developing countries, however, this is not likely to be possible, with the consequence that, where production of an agricultural commodity has to be restricted, efforts will have to be made sooner or later to re-employ released land and labour in the production of cash crops offering a more remunerative alternative than subsistence farming.

35. The facility with which such adjustments can be made will obviously depend to some extent on whether estate agriculture or peasant farming is chiefly involved. Peasant farmers will almost certainly require guidance and adjustment assistance from the Government. Problems for government policy may also arise if estate-owners choose to divert land to less labour-intensive uses which do not absorb all the labour released from the previous activity. In the case of foreign-owned estates, moreover, there is a possibility that released resources may leave the country rather than move into many alternative employment.

36. Given the adverse conditions on the world market for many agricultural commodities, and the relatively slow

---

[20] See *Official Records of the Trade and Development Board, Eleventh Session, Annexes*, agenda item 7, document TD/B/348, para. 20.

[21] *Ibid.*, para. 37.

[22] The Coffee Diversification Fund of the International Coffee Organization was established precisely in order to assist its member Governments to deal with these problems. An account of the Fund's activities is contained in document TD/109, annex, section H (see p. 92 above).

growth of world demand for others, the selection of alternative cash crops is likely to prove difficult.[23] In many cases, production of staple foodstuffs for the domestic market will deserve serious consideration, since increased production of this kind will make it possible to satisfy the rising cash demand for food associated with increasing industrial employment and incomes without recourse to additional imports. Since the pace of development is often uneven, however, domestic demand for food may show considerable fluctuations around its rising trend, and it may be necessary for Governments to establish stable, remunerative and guaranteed prices for locally-grown food in order to ensure that economic production expands at an appropriate rate.

Chapter IV

International action required

37. The international community can provide valuable support to the diversification efforts of developing countries by taking action over the whole field of international commodity policy, including action to stabilize individual commodity markets, to deal with the problems of particular commodities and to improve marketing and distribution systems.[24] There are three areas, however, in which international action can be particularly effective in support of diversification and where intensified efforts are principally required.

A. TECHNICAL AND FINANCIAL ASSISTANCE

38. One vitally important form of international action in support of diversification in developing countries is technical and financial assistance. Existing activities in this field are described in chapter IV of and the annex to the report by the UNCTAD secretariat entitled "International action relating to commodity diversification" (TD/109)[25], which also contains a number of suggestions for improving present arrangements. In addition to direct assistance for diversification, there is a need for international assistance for research and development aimed at improving the competitive position of natural products vis-à-vis synthetic and other substitutes, and at finding new uses for natural products. Needs in this respect are discussed in two reports by the UNCTAD secretariat, documents TD/117[26] and TD/117/Supp.1.

B. ACCESS TO MARKETS

39. In its report on diversification, the Advisory Committee agreed that important opportunities for horizontal diversification would be opened up for developing countries if there was a reduction in the protection and support given in developed countries to production of temperate-zone agricultural commodities.[27] The problems of improving access to markets for these products are discussed in detail in the report by the UNCTAD secretariat entitled "Access to markets" (TD/115).[28] The Advisory Committee also pointed out that the GSP approved in UNCTAD did not cover many items in the production of which developing countries enjoyed a comparative advantage, such as processed agricultural products and a variety of manufactured goods, and that it did not cover non-tariff barriers, which in some products represented the really effective barriers.[29] It may be noted also that many of the offers or commitments made by developed countries under the GSP are subject either to quantitative limitations or to escape clauses. Such reservations might seriously restrict the possibilities for industrial growth in developing countries with respect to the products affected.

40. While, therefore, the GSP is likely to make a valuable contribution to "vertical" diversification and economic development in developing countries, much greater diversification opportunities would be created for these countries if developed countries were prepared to move further towards a more rational international division of labour. If developed countries deliberately encouraged the gradual shift of their labour-intensive and simpler manufacturing industries to developing countries and their replacement by more technologically advanced industries, such a policy would in fact promote economic growth in both groups of countries. The reason is that in developed countries the advanced industries can make a much greater contribution to growth than the simpler industries, while the transfer of the latter industries to the developing world would greatly contribute to growth and development there.

C. THE NEED FOR STUDIES IN DEPTH

41. The fact that a substantial number of developing countries face urgent diversification problems of the types described in chapter II of the present report indicates that there is a need for the adoption of appropriate long-term diversification strategies, or for the revision of existing, unsuccessful, strategies, in the countries concerned. Until appropriate diversification strategies have been worked out in each case, it will not be possible to frame "proposals for concrete action by the appropriate national and international bodies", as requested by the Committee on Commodities in its decision 5 (VI).[30]

42. When such strategies have been prepared, however, they will provide a basis for determining specific measures to be applied by national authorities, or by the inter-

---

[23] Some of the problems of decision-making in the field of horizontal diversification including the problem of harmonization of national diversification programmes, are also discussed in document TD/109, chapter III (see p. 87 above).

[24] See the progress report by the UNCTAD secretariat entitled "The development of international commodity policy" (TD/113, p. 3 above).

[25] See p. 79 above.

[26] See p. 73 above.

---

[27] See *Official Records of the Trade and Development Board, Eleventh Session, Annexes*, agenda item 7, document TD/B/348, para. 41.

[28] See p. 11 above.

[29] See *Official Records of the Trade and Development Board, Eleventh Session, Annexes*, agenda item 7, document TD/B/348, para. 43.

[30] *Ibid., Supplement No. 4* (TD/B/370), annex I.

national community, in each case, and for a more effective application of technical and financial assistance from all sources. In this connexion, it is suggested in paragraph 67 of document TD/109[31] that technical and financial assistance provided to developing countries facing serious diversification problems should be adapted, both in volume and in type, to the requirements of an appropriate long-term diversification strategy.

43. The discussion in chapter III above of the complex issues which arise in preparing an appropriate diversification strategy indicates that such strategies can be prepared only on the basis of detailed studies in depth of the problems of each country concerned. It is suggested, therefore, that the United Nations agencies concerned should intensify their efforts to assist developing countries facing particularly serious and urgent diversification problems by carrying out such studies in depth. The studies could probably best be carried out, at the request of Governments, by inter-agency teams of experts in different fields. These teams, whose activities could be co-ordinated by UNCTAD, would work in the countries concerned and, on the basis of their studies, would make

---

[31] See p. 88 above.

recommendations to Governments regarding diversification strategy, with particular reference to the need to modify the existing pattern of exports to include commodities having more dynamic market opportunities and to reduce excessive dependence on a single commodity.

44. Since the proposed teams would concentrate primarily on the structure and performance of a country's exports, and not its progress in general or sectoral development, the function of the teams would be different from that of IBRD country or sector missions, and from that of the United Nations Development Advisory Teams. In recommending how a country's export structure might be changed over the longer term, the proposed teams would naturally have to consider the implications for over-all development planning. As mentioned earlier, however, general economic development and commodity diversification are not identical, though they are closely interdependent. Another important and distinctive function of the proposed teams would be to identify specific constraints on diversification in individual developing countries resulting from restrictions on access to markets in other countries, and to identify areas where more favourable diversification schemes could be adopted if such restrictions were removed or reduced.

Part two

MANUFACTURES

THE GENERALIZED SYSTEM OF PREFERENCES

Report by the UNCTAD secretariat*

[Original text: English]

CONTENTS

ANNEX

Average tariff protection in developed market-economy countries for 34 groups of industrial products arranged according to different stages of processing

---

* The text of this report was circulated to the Conference as document TD/124, dated 12 November 1971, and TD/124/Corr.1 dated 19 April 1972.

Introduction

1. At its second session held in New Delhi in early 1968, the Conference unanimously adopted resolution 21 (II) on preferential or free entry of exports of manufactures and semi-manufactures of developing countries to the developed countries in which the Conference recognized "the unanimous agreement in favour of the early establishment of a mutually acceptable system of generalized non-reciprocal and non-discriminatory preferences which would be beneficial to the developing countries".[1] It agreed that the objectives of the system of preferences should be to increase the export earnings of those coun-

tries, to promote their industrialization and to accelerate their rates of economic growth. To this end it established a Special Committee on Preferences to enable all the countries concerned to participate in the necessary consultations.

2. As a result of consultations held in the Special Committee[2] between the prospective preference-giving

---

[1] See *Proceedings of the United Nations Conference on Trade and Development, Second Session*, vol. I, *Report and Annexes* (United Nations publication, Sales No. E.68.II.D.14).

[2] The Special Committee met in four sessions between November 1968 and October 1970. For the reports on these sessions see *Official Records of the Trade and Development Board, Eighth Session, Supplement No. 4* (TD/B/218/Rev.1); *ibid., Ninth Session, Supplements Nos. 4* (TD/B/243/Rev.1) and *4A* (TD/B/262/Rev.1); *ibid., Tenth Session, Supplements Nos. 6* (TD/B/300/Rev.1) and *6A* (TD/B/329/Rev.1).

and preference-receiving countries on the basis of the substantive documentation submitted by the developed market-economy countries[3] and the joint declaration made by five socialist countries of Eastern Europe,[4] arrangements concerning the establishment of generalized, non-discriminatory, non-reciprocal preferential treatment for exports of developing countries in the markets of developed countries were drawn up and considered mutually acceptable to both groups of countries.

3. At its fourth special session held on 12 and 13 October 1970 the Trade and Development Board, by its decision 75 (S-IV), adopted the report[5] of the Special Committee on Preferences and took note of the agreed conclusions in that report. In proclaiming the Second United Nations Development Decade starting from 1 January 1971, the General Assembly at its twenty-fifth session included the preferential arrangements as an integral part of the International Development Strategy.

4. In line with paragraph 10 of section I of the agreed conclusions, the prospective preference-giving countries concerned submitted a formal application to the Contracting Parties to GATT for a waiver in accordance with article XXV:5 from their obligations under article I of the General Agreement, so as to permit the implementation of a generalized system of preferences.[6] By their decision of 25 June 1971, the Contracting Parties decided to waive the provisions of article I of the General Agreement for a period of ten years to the extent necessary to permit developed contracting parties to accord preferential tariff treatment to products originating in developing countries and territories.[7]

5. The EEC, Japan and Norway implemented their schemes of generalized tariff preferences on 1 July, 1 August and 1 October 1971 respectively.[8] Czechoslovakia, Hungary, Sweden and the United Kingdom indicated their intention to implement their respective schemes on 1 January 1972.[9] Several other Governments of preference-giving countries have introduced in their Parliaments the necessary legislation for implementation of their respective schemes.

6. The purpose of this paper is to describe the main features of the preferential arrangements drawn up in UNCTAD and of the schemes implemented so far by certain preference-giving countries, and to review the steps taken in UNCTAD in connexion with GSP. Specific trade data relating to the GSP are presented in the addendum to this report (see document TD/124/Add.1, p.123 below).

---

[3] The preliminary submissions were circulated in document TD/B/AC.5/24 and Add.1-11, and the revised submissions in documents TD/B/AC.5/34 and Add.1-10.

[4] See *Official Records of the Trade and Development Board, Tenth Session, Supplement No. 6A* (TD/B/329/Rev.1), part two, para. 192.

[5] The Special Committee's final report consists of the reports on the first and second parts of its fourth session (*Official Records of the Trade and Development Board, Tenth Session, Supplements Nos. 6* (TD/B/300/Rev.1) and *6A* (TD/B/329/Rev.1)), together with the substantive documentation submitted by the developed market-economy countries.

[6] See GATT document C/W/178, 19 May 1971.

[7] See GATT document L/3545, 28 June 1971.

[8] These schemes are contained in TD/B/373/Add.1 and annexes (EEC), TD/B/373/Add.7 and annex (Japan) and TD/B/373/Add.2 and annexes (Norway).

[9] See TD/B/373/Add.8 and annexes (United Kingdom) and TD/B/378/Add.2 (Czechoslovakia). Hungary announced its decision at the eleventh session of the Board. Sweden notified its decision on 20 September 1971.

CHAPTER I

Principal characteristics of the generalized system of preferences

A. Preferential arrangements by developed market-economy countries

7. Among the developed market-economy countries, 18 take part as preference-giving countries in the GSP: Austria, Canada, the States members of EEC (Belgium, Luxembourg, the Federal Republic of Germany, France, Italy and the Netherlands), Ireland, Japan, New Zealand, the Nordic countries (Denmark, Finland, Norway and Sweden), Switzerland, the United Kingdom and the United States of America.[10] The EEC, by virtue of the Treaty of Rome,[11] implemented a common scheme for its member States.

8. The main aspects of the preferential treatment envisaged or applied by the developed market-economy countries are summarized below:

1. PRODUCT COVERAGE

9. Generalized tariff preferences would apply in principle to manufactures and semi-manufactures in BTN chapters 25-99 generally with certain exceptions.[12] These exceptions are indicated mainly in the form of negative lists (exceptions lists) by individual preference-giving countries. The main products covered by the negative lists are textiles, petroleum and petroleum products and leather and leather goods.

10. Preference-giving countries have generally assumed that the GSP was not, in principle, intended to cover primary commodities. However, several preference-giving

---

[10] In 1966 Australia introduced a system of tariff preferences for developing countries on selected manufactures, semi-manufactures and handicraft products. See GATT "Australian tariff preferences for developing countries", Fourth annual report by the Government of Australia under the Decision of 28 March 1966 (L/3453).

[11] Treaty establishing the European Economic Community, Rome, 25 March 1957 (United Nations, *Treaty Series*, vol. 298 (1958), No. 4300).

[12] The definition for classes of goods employed in this report is based on the note by the Secretary-General of UNCTAD, "The definition of primary commodities, semi-manufactures and manufactures" (TD/B/C.2/3).

countries, namely Austria, Japan, the Nordic countries, Switzerland and the United Kingdom, have also provided for preferential treatment of primary commodities in BTN chapters 25-99, while Canada, New Zealand and the United States of America would extend such treatment to selected primary commodities falling within these chapters.

11. Preferential treatment would also apply to selected processed and semi-processed agricultural products in BTN chapters 1-24, including certain primary agricultural commodities falling within these chapters. These products are indicated in the positive lists of the preference-giving countries.

12. It should be noted that New Zealand submitted its preferential offer in the form of a positive list including selected products falling in BTN chapters 1-99, and that Ireland made no offers for agricultural products in BTN chapters 1-24.

(a) BTN chapters 25-99

13. A summary of the main products or product groups covered by the lists of exceptions (negative lists) is given below:

14. Austria would exclude starch products (38.19 and 39.06) falling under the Austrian starch law; manitol and sorbitol (ex 29.04); certain casein and albumin products (in chapter 35); certain chemical preparations (ex 38.12 and ex 38.19) subject to equalization charges; and cotton textiles coming under the provisions of the LTA.

15. The EEC scheme in force makes no initial exceptions. However, textiles and footwear are excepted with respect to certain beneficiaries under the scheme (see paragraph 82 below). In addition, preferential treatment is still under consideration for jute and coir products.[13]

16. Canada would exclude, through the operation of the safeguards clause, various textile products, gloves (Canadian tariff item 56830-1); elastic braid (56510-1); and electronic tubes (44542-1). In addition, certain categories of footwear may also be excluded.

17. Ireland would exclude superphosphates (31.03 and 31.05); egg albumin (ex 35.02) artificial sausage casings (certain tariff headings in BTN chapters 39 and 48); rubber tyres and tubes (40.11); leather (41.02/03); footwear (64.01/04); springs and leaves for vehicles (73.35A); sparking plugs and components (ex 85.08); electric filament lamps (ex 85.20); vehicles and parts thereof (chapter 87); brooms and brushes (96 01/02); hydrocarbon oils, perfumed spirits, matches and certain wines subject to revenue duties; and textiles goods.

18. Japan excludes petroleum oils, crude (27.09); petroleum spirits (27.10) and petroleum gases (27.11) subject to customs duties of a fiscal character; gelatin and glues derived from bones etc. (35.03); articles of apparel and clothing accessories of leather etc. (42.03); plywood (ex 44.15); raw silk (50.02-2); woven fabric of silk etc. (50.09); footwear with outer soles and uppers of rubber etc. (64.01); and parts of footwear of any material except metal (64.05).

19. The products considered by the Nordic countries to be susceptible to market disruption, and which therefore might be given special treatment, including initial exceptions by one or more of the Nordic countries are: cement (25.23); titanium oxides (28.25); rubber tyres and tubes (40.11); tableware of pottery (certain tariff headings in chapter 69); glassware (70.13); nails, tacks, staples, etc. (73.31); primary cells and primary batteries (85.03); cycles, motorized or not (87.09/10), certain furniture (94.01/03); slide fasteners (98.02); textile products (tariff headings in chapters 51, 53-58, 60, 61 and 62); some leather and leather products (tariff headings in chapters 41 and 42); and footwear (certain tariff headings in chapter 64). As was indicated above, most of these products are excluded from the scheme implemented by Norway. Products subject to duty of a fiscal nature are also excluded by Norway, namely, motors for vehicles (ex 84.06), motor vehicles (87.02), special motor lorries (87.03), chassis with engines (ex 87.04), and bodies for motor vehicles (ex 87.05).

20. Switzerland would exclude some petroleum products (tariff headings in chapters 27 and 29); cinematograph films (37.06/01); mixed alkylenes and mixed alkylaryls for use in engines (ex 38.19); internal combustion piston engines for automobiles (ex 84.06); motor vehicles, chassis and parts and accessories of motor vehicles (certain tariff headings in chapter 87), subject to duties of a fiscal character; casein and ovalbumine (35.01/02).

21. The United Kingdom would exclude perfumed spirits (33.06A); matches (36.05A and 36.06) and portable lighters (ex 98.10); hydrocarbon oils (certain tariff headings in chapters 27, 29, 32, 34, 36, 38 and 39) subject to revenue duties; and textiles (in chapters 50-63 and 65).[14]

22. The United States of America would exclude textiles, shoes, and petroleum and petroleum products.

(b) BTN chapters 1-24

23. The main items included in the positive lists of preference-giving countries are summarized below:

24. The Austrian positive list contains 52 items[15] including fish, fruit and nuts, coffee, tea, maté and spices; vegetable plaiting and carving materials; cocoa and cocoa preparations; mustard, sauces, soups etc.

25. Canada would provide preferential treatment for 45 agricultural items, 13 of which are primary commodities. The list includes canned meat, edible fruit and nuts; cocoa preparations and processed vegetables and fruit.

26. The EEC grants preferences for 50 items, 12 of which are primary commodities. The major items are: animal and vegetable fats and oils; some preparations of

---

[13] In its revised submission, EEC stated that customs exemption was envisaged for coir and jute products under specific measures to be arranged with the exporting developing countries. See document TD/B/AC.5/34/Add.1, annex I, p. 3.

[14] Some 42 textile items other than cotton are included in the United Kingdom offer.

[15] Here and in subsequent paragraphs the word "items" refers to BTN headings, some of which are only partially granted preferential treatment.

meat or fish, preparations of cereals, flour or starch; preparations of vegetables and fruit and preparations of chicory, coffee, tea, mustard, sauces, soups etc.

27. Japan grants preferences for 59 items, 19 of which are primary products. The major items are animal and vegetable fats and oils; preparations of meat and fish; cocoa preparations, processed vegetables and fruit, concentrates of coffee, tea or maté, beverages and spirits.

28. The positive list of New Zealand includes 34 agricultural items, 21 of which are primary commodities. The majority of these products are edible fruit and nuts and prepared or preserved fish.

29. The positive list of the Nordic countries includes 97 items,[16] 62 of which are primary products. All products falling in BTN chapters 5 (materials of animal origin, which are not normally used as food), 13 (raw vegetable materials), 14 (vegetable plaiting and carving materials), and 18 (cocoa and cocoa preparations except chocolate) are included in the list. Other products are fish; edible vegetables; edible fruit and nuts; coffee, tea, maté and spices; oil seeds; animal and vegetable fats and oils; preparations of vegetables and fruit and beverages. Norway grants preferences under its final scheme to 52 items, or all products in the common list to which this country applied duties.

30. The positive list of Switzerland contains 76 items, 40 of which are primary commodities. The major items are fish; vegetables, fruits and nuts; raw vegetable materials for use in dying and tanning, lacs etc.; animal and vegetable fats and oils; preparations of meat or fish; cocoa and cocoa preparations; preparations of cereals, flour or starch; preparations of vegetables and fruit; extracts or essences of coffee, tea or maté; mustard, soups etc.

31. The United Kingdom positive list consists of 69 items, 21 of which are primary commodities. The list includes roasted chicory; extracts of coffee, tea or maté; mustard, sauces, soups products, of the milling industries, malt and starches and preparations of cereals, flour or starch. Products covered only to a certain extent are preparations of vegetables, fruit, and residues and waste from food industries.

32. The United States of America would provide preferential treatment for 95 TSUS (Tariff Schedules of the United States) items, 45 of which are primary commodities. Among the major items are: fresh meat and fish; edible vegetables, fruit and nuts; products of the milling industry; preparations of meat or fish; preparations of cocoa; preparations of cereals, flour or starch; preparations of vegetables and fruit; and beverages.

2. DEPTH OF TARIFF CUT

33. With regard to products in BTN chapters 25-99 covered by their respective schemes, EEC, Japan and Norway apply duty-free treatment. Japan, however, applies a 50 per cent tariff reduction from most-favoured-nation rates in the case of 57 selected products. Duty-free

treatment is also envisaged by the United States of America, the United Kingdom and the other Nordic countries. The other preference-giving countries, namely, Austria, Canada, Ireland and Switzerland, envisage linear tariff reductions falling short of duty-free entry. New Zealand would grant varying degrees of tariff cuts.

34. With regard to BTN chapters 1-24, Norway applies duty-free treatment to products covered by its scheme and the same treatment is envisaged by the other Nordic countries, the United Kingdom and the United States of America. Varying degrees of tariff cuts are applied by EEC and Japan are also envisaged by the remaining preference-giving countries.

35. A summary of tariff reductions by individual preference-giving countries for products covered by generalized preferences is given below:

36. Austria would grant as a first stage, a 30 per cent preferential tariff reduction on goods falling within BTN chapters 25-99. Varying tariff reductions are provided for products in BTN chapters 1-24, including duty-free entry for some of the items.

37. In Canada, the products in BTN chapters 25-99 included in its offer and originating in beneficiary countries would be entitled to the lower of the following two rates: (a) a rate which is 33 1/3 per cent below the post-Kennedy Round MFN rate, or (b) the British (Commonwealth) preferential tariff rate of Canada. Some 300 tariff items covered by the offer enter duty-free under the British preferential rate and developing countries have already a trade interest in a fifth of these items. Of the 45 Canadian tariff items included in the positive list, 24 would enjoy duty-free treatment and the rest varying degrees of preferential cuts. The above tariff reductions would be the first step in liberalizing tariff treatment for developing countries and further reductions would be considered in the light of experience. These tariff reductions would be considered in the light of experience. These tariff reductions might be staged over a two-year period.

38. The EEC applies duty-free treatment to all industrial products in BTN chapters 25-99 covered by its scheme. Various duty reductions apply to processed agricultural products in the EEC positive list. Preferential treatment for these products consists of a reduction in the post-Kennedy Round tariff rates for products subject to tariff duties, or of a reduction in the fixed element of protection for products subject to the system of levies.

39. Ireland would reduce the full rate of customs duty by 33 1/3 per cent on goods in BTN chapters 25-99 covered by its offer.

40. Japan applies duty-free entry to goods in BTN chapters 25-99 covered by its scheme, except in the case of "selected products" consisting of 57 tariff items, on which a 50 per cent tariff reduction applies. Various duty reductions, including zero-duty treatment, apply to products in BTN chapters 1-24 covered by the positive list. A fourth of the tariff items in this list enjoy duty-free entry and most-favoured-nation rates are halved in the case of 40 per cent of the tariff items in the list.

41. New Zealand would grant for products covered by its positive list in BTN 1-99 various tariff reductions which will be in most cases to the British preferential level.

---

[16] Thirty-one of these items are already admitted duty free under most-favoured-nation treatment into all four Nordic countries.

Duties on eight items will be established at less than British preferential rates. Duty-free entry is envisaged for a few items.

42. The Nordic countries preferential offer provides for duty-free entry for all goods eligible for preferences. Accordingly, Norway applies duty-free entry to all products included in its scheme.

43. Switzerland's aim of duty-free treatment on products in BTN chapters 25-99 covered by its offer would be reached in two stages. During the first stage a linear reduction of 30 per cent of the prevailing tariffs would apply. In the second stage, coming after a two-year period, the Government will decide to what extent it will be necessary, in the light of the experience gained and the principle of equitable burden-sharing, to make special arrangements for certain products or to limit the preferential margin to the 30 per cent already granted or to a rate lying between 30 per cent and duty-free treatment. More than two-thirds of the agricultural products covered by the positive list would enter duty-free and for the rest a reduction of 30 per cent would be applied during the initial period.

44. The United Kingdom envisages duty-free entry for all products covered by its offer, except six items in the positive list to which a Commonwealth preferential duty falling short of duty-free entry would apply.

45. The United States of America would grant duty-free treatment to all products eligible for preferences.

46. The tariff cuts described above thus present a varying and complex picture. The margins for products in the positive list in BTN chapters 1-24 can be readily seen in the positive list of individual schemes or offers. In the case of products in BTN chapters 25-99 for which the extent of tariff cut is described in general terms, the task of determining preferential margins is more difficult, since it involves prior determination of most-favoured-nation rates from national tariff schedules. While it is impossible to give in this report the preferential margins envisaged or applied for all products in BTN chapters 25-99, an idea of the scope of these margins can be derived from the level of tariff protection which affects these products generally, keeping in mind the various tariffs cuts described above. This level is shown in the table annexed to the present report, which gives a simple arithmetic average of post-Kennedy Round tariff protection in Austria, Canada, the EEC countries, Japan, the Nordic countries, the United Kingdom and the United States of America, for 34 groups of products of export interest to developing countries, arranged according to different stages of processing.[17] The table shows average tariff protection in the first horizontal line and the range of tariff protection for each product group in the second horizontal line. Moreover, for each product group, the value of dutiable goods imported by the developed countries concerned

from developing countries is indicated in the second (product description) column of the table.[18]

47. An important conclusion to be drawn is that tariffs, and consequently preferential margins, generally tend to rise from low to high with the increase in the degree of processing.[19] The preferential elimination or reduction of tariffs would thus eliminate or substantially reduce the tariff differentials between products at different stages of processing, providing greater incentive to processing for export in the preference-receiving countries.

3. SAFEGUARD MECHANISMS

48. All preference-giving countries provide for certain safeguard mechanisms so as to retain some degree of control over the trade which might be generated by the new tariff advantages. Austria, EEC and Japan base their safeguard mechanisms on an *a priori* limitation formula while the other preference-giving countries envisage escape-type measures as the main safeguards at their disposal.

49. The conditions for applying these safeguards are stated in section III of the agreed conclusions. This section will review the safeguards included in the schemes which have been implemented.

(a) EEC

50. With respect to products in BTN chapters 25-99 covered by its scheme, EEC applies a limitation formula based on a system of Community ceilings.[20] For those products considered sensitive, preferential imports are regulated by means of tariff quotas.[21] With respect to products in chapters 1-24 of the BTN which are included in the scheme, the safeguard mechanism is of an escape-clause type.[22] The possibility of withdrawing preferential treatment in whole or in part also exists, for the correction of adverse situations which may arise in the associated countries as a result of implementation of the GSP.

---

[17] Leather, rubber, wood, paper, wool, cotton, jute, clothing, fertilizers, glass, precious stones, ores, iron and steel, copper, nickel, aluminium, lead, zinc, tin, metal manufactures, gas and petroleum, chemicals, non-electrical machinery, electrical machinery, transport equipment, scientific instruments, footwear and travel goods, photographic and cinematographic supplies, furniture, musical instruments, toys, works of art, stationery supplies and other manufactured articles.

[18] Imports in 1969 for Canada, in 1968 for Denmark and Switzerland, and in 1967 for all other preference-giving countries.

[19] In certain cases, however, tariffs are relatively high even on raw materials. For example for raw hides and skins in the United States of America, Canada, and Japan; for wool in the United States of America, Austria, Canada, the United Kingdom and Japan; for various unwrought non-ferrous metals in the United States of America, Canada, Japan, the United Kingdom and EEC.

[20] See document TD/B.373/Add.1. Products listed in EEC Council Regulation No. 1309, constituting the bulk of manufactures and semi-manufactures in BTN 25-99, in EEC Council Regulation No. 1311 consisting of twenty cotton textiles and substitutes coming under the LTA, in EEC Council Regulation No. 1313 consisting of sixty-five textiles other than cotton and four footwear products, and in Decision 233, consisting of four iron and steel products.

[21] *Ibid.* Products listed in EEC Council Regulation No. 1308, including certain petroleum products, fertilizers, certain rubber, leather, wood, paper and glass products, some copper and zinc semi-manufactures, sewing machines, certain electrical machinery, motors and apparatus, transistors, bicycles, furniture, dolls, etc.; in EEC Council Regulation No. 1310, including thirteen cotton textile products and two substitutes; in EEC Council Regulation No. 1312, including seventeen textile products other than cotton and four footwear products, and in Decision 232, including five iron and steel products.

[22] *Ibid.* Products listed in EEC Council Regulation No. 1314.

(i) Ceilings

51. The ceilings, expressed in units of account for each category of products, are equal to the sum of the c.i.f. value of imports by the Community in 1968 of the products in question from beneficiary countries and territories under the scheme, excluding those already benefiting from various preferential tariff régimes granted by the Community, and 5 per cent of the c.i.f. value of imports from other sources, including countries and territories already benefiting from such régimes.[23] Half the amount obtained under this formula is available for the six-month period of the validity of the scheme; i.e., from 1 July to 31 December 1971.

52. Preferential imports of products originating in any of the beneficiary countries and territories which are charged to the ceiling cannot as a general rule exceed a maximum Community amount corresponding to 50 per cent of this ceiling, except in the case of a few products for which the maximum amount is reduced to 30 per cent. The common external tariff may be re-established at any time until the end of 1971 by the Commission or by any member State, in the case of iron and steel products, on imports from all beneficiary countries or territories whenever Community preferential imports of products reach the ceiling, and on preferential imports originating in each country or territory concerned, whenever Community imports or imports under national quotas, in the case of iron and steel products, reach the maximum amounts.

(ii) Tariff quotas

53. In the case of sensitive products, preferential imports are administered by means of Community tariff quotas and, in the case of iron and steel products, by means of national tariff quotas. Community tariff quotas, expressed in value or in quantity (textiles) are allocated among member States according to the following fixed percentages: Federal Republic of Germany, 37.5 per cent; the Benelux countries, 15.1 per cent; France, 27.1 per cent and Italy 20.3 per cent. Each member State is responsible for managing, in accordance with its own regulations, its share of the Community tariff quota or its national tariff quotas, as the case may be.

54. The maximum amounts of preferential imports of sensitive products, amounting to 20, 30, 40 and 50 per cent[24] of the tariff quota, which can be admitted from any one beneficiary country or territory are specified in the scheme against each product subject to tariff quota.

55. Whenever preferential imports of products subject to Community tariff quotas reach the maximum amount, the Commission must immediately inform the member States of the date on which the normal tariff must be reimposed in respect of the country or territory concerned.

This information will be published in the *Journal officiel des Communautés européennes*. With regard to iron and steel products, each member State can resume collection of the suspended duties with regard to any beneficiary country or territory whenever it finds that imports under its national quota of the products concerned have reached the maximum amount. Such resumption will be notified immediately to the Commission, which will promptly inform the other member States.

(b) Japan

56. Preferential imports of products within BTN chapters 25-99 covered by the scheme can be made up to a ceiling set for each group of products. In addition, emergency tariff measures can be applied in respect of particular products. For products in the positive list, escape clause-type measures will apply.

(i) Ceilings

57. The ceiling for each group of products will be set for each fiscal year (April/March) and will be calculated as follows: the value (or quantity, as the case may be) of imports from beneficiaries in 1968 (basic quota) plus 10 per cent of the value (or quantity) of imports from sources other than beneficiaries in the year dating back two years from the year for which the ceilings are being set (supplementary quota). The supplementary quota will not be less than that of the previous year. Preferential treatment for a particular beneficiary will be suspended for a particular group of products in the course of a fiscal year if preferential imports from that beneficiary exceed 50 per cent of the ceiling for that group of products.

(ii) Operation and control of ceilings

58. The products subject to ceilings have been classified into 214 groups. Control of the ceiling quotas will be effected according to the following three methods, depending on the product group: daily control, monthly control or prior allotment. The value (or quantity) of preferential imports of each product group will be announced monthly in the Official Gazette.

59. Under the daily control method, preferential treatment will be granted on a first-come-first-served basis. The value (or quantity) of preferential imports will be computed daily and preferences will be suspended two days from the day when the aggregate value (or quantity) has exceeded the ceiling. The same will apply when the value (or quantity) of imports from a particular beneficiary exceeds 50 per cent of the ceiling. The product groups affected by this method of control total 95.

60. Under the monthly control method, preferential treatment will also be granted on a first-come first-served basis, and the value (or quantity) of preferential imports will be computed monthly. Preferences will be suspended on the first day of the month following the month after any month in which the aggregate value (or quantity) has exceeded the ceiling. The same will apply when the value (or quantity) of imports from a particular beneficiary exceeds 50 per cent of the ceiling. This method of control applies to 108 product groups.

---

[23] See document TD/B/AC.5/34/Add.1, annex 1, p. 2: "Subject to improvements in the basis of calculation after several years of operation, the basic quota will be a fixed amount corresponding to imports in a reference year. The supplementary quota will be variable and recalculated annually on the basis of the latest available figures without, however, resulting in a reduction in the ceiling".

[24] Ten per cent in the case of one product (BTN 46.03 basket-work, wickerwork and other articles of plaiting materials etc.).

61. Under the prior allotment method, preferential treatment will be granted within allocated limitations to importers to whom the Government of Japan has, in advance, allotted a certain value (or quantity) not exceeding the ceiling. Initially, 11 product groups will be covered by this method.[25]

62. Preferential treatment of particular imports up to the ceiling will be determined on the basis of the date of import declaration (the date of application for approval of entry into bonded warehouse or bonded manufacturing warehouse, if any).

(c) *Norway*

63. Norway has reserved the right to introduce the safeguard measures outlined in the agreed conclusions of the Special Committee on Preferences whenever preferential imports cause or threaten to cause market disruption.

4. RULES OF ORIGIN

64. The GSP calls for the application of rules of origin in order to ensure that only goods produced in preference-receiving countries will benefit from the system and enjoy preferential tariff treatment.

65. Consultations between prospective preference-giving and preference-receiving countries on rules of origin to be implemented for the GSP were completed in December 1970 in the Working Group on Rules of Origin established for this purpose.[26] The Group worked out agreed texts on a number of subjects concerning rules of origin[27] and designed appropriate forms for this purpose, i.e. combined declaration and certificate or origin (form A) and application for certificate of origin (form B).

66. Preference-giving countries agreed that, to the maximum extent possible, the rules of origin they would introduce would take fully into account these agreed texts. They also agreed to harmonize their rules to the greatest extent possible.

(a) *Main elements of rules of origin*

67. The main elements of rules of origin agreed by the Group are summarized below:

(i) *Conditions for admission to preference*

68. The main conditions for admission to preference of goods falling within a description of goods eligible for preference in the country of destination are that they:

Must, in general, be consigned directly to the preference-giving country from the preference-receiving country of exportation, transportation being effected without passing through the territory of any other country, or, alternatively, by passing through the territory of one or more countries, with or without trans-shipment or temporary storage, provided that the goods remain under customs transit control and do not enter into trade or consumption there and must comply with the origin criteria specified for those goods by the preference-giving country of destination.

69. In general, goods are considered to have originated in a preference-receiving country if they have been produced in that country either wholly or by substantial transformation from materials and/or components imported or of undetermined origin. The category of goods which are generally regarded as wholly produced has been specified by the Group.

70. With regard to goods which have undergone substantial transformation in the preference-receiving countries, Canada, New Zealand and the United States of America have indicated that they would base their requirements for substantial transformation on the value-added criterion, i.e., transformation is regarded as being substantial if the value of imported materials and/or components does not exceed 50 per cent in the case of New Zealand, 40 per cent of the ex-factory price of the exported article in the case of Canada, and, in the case of the United States, 50 per cent of the appraised value for Customs purposes of the exported article.

71. The other preference-giving countries would base their requirements for substantial transformation on the process criterion. For these countries the transformation must, in general, be such as to lead to the exported goods being classified under a BTN heading other than that relating to any of the materials and/or components imported of or undetermined origin used in production. In addition, special rules would be prescribed for various classes of goods in lists of qualifying and non-qualifying processes.

(ii) *Documentary evidence*

72. The claim that goods are eligible for preferential tariff treatment must be supported by appropriate documentary evidence as to origin and consignment. Documentary evidence consists of a declaration completed by the exporter of the goods in the preference-receiving country and certified by a governmental authority (Form A). By mutual arrangement between preference-giving and preference-receiving countries, certification may be performed by a non-governmental body approved for this purpose by the preference-receiving country concerned.

73. For preferential exports to New Zealand, the exporter in a preference-receiving country will be required to complete an origin declaration in a form prescribed by the New Zealand Customs Regulations.

(iii) *Verification*

74. While the combined declaration and certificate of origin would *prima facie* be acceptable for according

---

[25] These product groups include mostly textile products, i.e. BTN 51.04, woven fabrics of man-made fibres; 57.06, yarn of jute; 57.10, woven fabrics of jute; 58.05, cotton woven fabrics; 60.01, outer garments; 60.03, stockings; 60.04 undergarments; and 60.05 outer garments, knitted.

[26] See Report of the Working Group on Rules of Origin on its third session (TD/B/AC.5/38).

[27] These subjects are: wholly produced goods, minimal processes, consignments of small value, direct consignment, documentary evidence, verification sanctions, mutual co-operation, treatment of packing, unit of qualification and exhibitions and fairs.

preference, a preference-giving country may seek further evidence, information or verification pertaining to the entitlement to preference by means of correspondence with the trader concerned or with the authorities of the preference-receiving country concerned, or by means of other agreed arrangements.

(iv) *Mutual co-operation*

75. Countries participating in the GSP have agreed to establish close co-operation and to provide mutual assistance for the effective control and verification of origin and consignment.

(b) *Rules of origin applied*

76. The rules of origin applied by EEC, Japan and Norway for the implementation of their schemes of generalized preferences take into account the above-mentioned agreed texts and other agreements and under-standings reached by the Working Group.

77. Under the rules of origin applied by EEC, products originating in a beneficiary country are goods wholly produced in that country or products other than wholly produced which have undergone sufficient working or processing.[28] The requirements for sufficient working or processing have, as indicated above, been based on the process criterion, i.e. working or processing is considered sufficient if the resulting goods are subsequently classified under a tariff heading different from those covering any of the materials or components used. In addition, EEC has specified a number of working or processing operations, which result in a change of tariff heading without conferring the status of "originating" products on the products undergoing such operations, or conferring this status only subject to certain conditions (list A) and a number of working or processing operations which do not result in a change of tariff heading, but which do confer the status of "originating" products on the products undergoing such operations (list B).

78. The rules of origin applied by Norway are based on those introduced by EEC.[29] As regards lists of working or processing operations, Norway has adopted the EEC lists as far as products in chapters 25-99 are concerned, with the exception of printed fabrics in List B. For products in chapters 1-24 covered by its scheme, a special list of qualifying and non-qualifying operations has been established.

79. The rules of origin applied by Japan are similar to those applied by EEC.[30] However Japan's lists of qualifying and non qualifying working or processing operations differ to some extent from the EEC lists A and B. There are also certain variations in respect of documentary evidence and administrative requirements.

5. BENEFICIARY COUNTRIES AND TERRITORIES

80. With regard to beneficiaries, the developed market-economy countries would in general base themselves on the principle of self-election. With regard to this principle, reference should be made to the report by the OECD Special Group on trade with developing countries.[31] In this document it is stated, *inter alia*, that "Special tariff treatment should be given to the exports of any country, territory or area claiming developing status ... Individual developed countries might, however, decline to accord special tariff treatment to a particular country claiming developing status on grounds which they hold to be compelling. Such *ab initio* exclusion of a particular country would not be based on competitive considerations."

81. In line with the principle of self-election, the countries members of the Group of 77 declared in the Special Committee on Preferences that they considered themselves under Conference resolution 21(II) to be prospective beneficiaries under the GSP and, therefore, entitled to preferential treatment in the markets of all preference-giving countries. The representatives of Romania, Bulgaria, Cuba, Turkey, Israel, Greece, Malta and Spain also declared that their countries were entitled to benefit from the GSP. The representative of Mongolia reserved the right to define his country's position with respect to the question of beneficiaries at a later time. The representatives of the United Kingdom, New Zealand, Australia and the Netherlands made statements on behalf of the countries and territories for which they were responsible with regard to their inclusion among the beneficiaries of the GSP.

82. The EEC scheme recognizes as beneficiaries all developing countries members of the Group of 77 and dependent territories. However, in the case of cotton textiles and substitute products, preferences apply only to countries signatories to the LTA,[32] namely, Colombia, India, Jamaica, Republic of Korea, Mexico, Pakistan and the Arab Republic of Egypt. Moreover, dependent territories of third countries are excluded from preferential treatment for textiles and footwear. Developing countries members of the Group of 77 already benefiting from various preferential tariff régimes granted by the Community are recognized as beneficiaries of the EEC scheme of generalized preferences and continue to enjoy special preferences.

83. Japan grants preferences to 96 developing countries that are members of UNCTAD and have elected themselves as beneficiaries of the GSP. Those countries, however, which currently invoke article XXXV of the GATT against Japan will in principle lose their beneficiary status after three years from the entry into force of the scheme,

---

[28] The EEC rules of origin are reproduced in document TD/B/396 (see Regulation (EEC) No. 2862/71 of the Commission of 22 December 1971).

[29] The Norwegian rules of origin are reproduced in document TD/B/373/Add.2/Annex II and Corr.1 (Norway).

[30] The Japanese rules of origin are reproduced in document TD/B/373/Add.7/Annex (Japan).

[31] See *Proceedings of the United Nations Conference on Trade and Development, Second Session*, vol. III, *Problems and policies of trade in manufactures and semi-manufactures* (United Nations publication, Sales No. E.68.II.D.16), document TD/56, annex, part one, section A.

[32] In its revised submission, EEC stated that references may also be granted for the duration of the LTA, in accordance with terms and procedures to be agreed bilaterally, to countries which are beneficiaries under the GSP but not signatories to the LTA, which give similar undertakings *vis-à-vis* the Community to those given in the LTA (see TD/B/AC.5/34/Add.1, annex 1, p. 3).

if they have not discarded the discriminatory measures during the intervening period.

84. Thus, the beneficiaries include all the countries members of the Group of 77 (with the exception of Botswana, Jamaica, Lesotho and Swaziland), as well as the following countries not members of the Group of 77: Cuba, Fiji, Greece, Israel, Malta, Spain, Turkey and Western Samoa. The question of the inclusion of the rest of the self-elected countries, territories and areas is to be reviewed early in 1972.

85. Norway's scheme of preferences has been initially put into effect in favour of the countries at present members of the Group of 77. This list of beneficiary countries is preliminary, however, and will be reconsidered in the light of further international consultations on the subject and of decisions taken by other preference-giving countries.

86. Sweden would extend preferences in the first instance to the countries members of the Group of 77 and to Israel, Cuba, Mongolia and Western Samoa. The Government is further authorized to include in the list of beneficiaries non-European dependent territories of preference-giving countries and non-European countries for whose external relations a preference-giving country is responsible.

6. SPECIAL MEASURES IN FAVOUR OF THE LEAST DEVELOPED AMONG THE DEVELOPING COUNTRIES

87. When the GSP was drawn up the special need to, improve the economic situation of the least developed among the developing countries was recognized. It was considered important that these countries should benefit to the fullest extent possible from the system. In this connexion, the preference-giving countries agreed to consider to the greatest extent possible, on a case-by-case basis, the inclusion in the generalized system of preferences of products of export interest mainly to the least developed among the developing countries, and, as appropriate, greater tariff reductions on such products. The application of escape clause measures would remain exceptional and would be decided on, only after due account had been taken, within the limits of the legal provisions in force, of the interests of the least developed among the developing countries.

88. During the annual review of the operation of the GSP, special attention would be given by the institutional machinery to the effects of the system on the volume of exports and export earnings of the least developed countries and with respect to other objectives of Conference resolution 21 (II). This machinery would further investigate and consult on special measures in favour of those countries within the GSP (see paragraph 94 below).

89. It was recommended that priority attention should be given within UNCTAD to measures that would be related or complementary to the GSP, especially measures which would enable the least developed among the developing countries to participate fully in that system. In addition, the international efforts in this field should give priority to:

The identification of products with respect to which the GSP opens up new or improved export possibilities for the least developed countries;

Market studies for such products;

Assistance towards the improvement of export services and export promotion services or the establishment of new services for these purposes where appropriate.

90. In accordance with the Agreed conclusions of the Special Committee on Preferences the attention of other appropriate international organizations has been drawn to the importance of taking measures relating to the GSP. Such measures might include, as appropriate, financial technical assistance for the establishment and development of industries likely to further the export of products included in the GSP, as well as financial assistance for pre-investment studies for such industries. The report[33] by the UNCTAD secretariat submitted to the Trade and Development Board at its eleventh session contains summaries of or extracts from the replies of various international organizations on the measures they had adopted or intended to adopt in favour of the least developed countries with respect to the implementation of the GSP.

91. At its eleventh session, the Board adopted resolution 82 (XI) which requested the Secretary-General of UNCTAD "to work out a detailed and comprehensive action-oriented programme, within UNCTAD's competence, for the implementation of the relevant provisions of the International Development Strategy for the Second United Nations Development Decade in favour of the least developed among the developing countries and to present this programme, together with his suggestions on institutional arrangements within UNCTAD for further work on special measures in favour of the least developed among the developing countries, to the United Nations Conference on Trade and Development at its third session." This action programme, submitted to the Conference in a separate document,[34] contains a section on proposals for special measures to be taken in connexion with the GSP.

7. REVERSE PREFERENCES

92. In conformity with section II of the agreed conclusions, the Secretary-General of UNCTAD continued his contacts on the question of reverse preferences with the governments concerned with a view to finding appropriate and timely solutions.

8. DURATION

93. It was agreed that the initial duration of the GSP would be ten years. The EEC implemented its scheme for an initial period of six months in order to be able to remedy any drawbacks which might become apparent during this first experiment, and also for technical reasons

---

[33] "Special measures in favour of the least developed among the developing countries in relation to the Generalized System of Preferences" (TD/B/372 and Corr.1 and Add.1).

[34] See *Proceedings of the United Nations Conference on Trade and Development, Third Session*, vol. IV, *General Review and Special Measures* (United Nations publication, Sales No. E.13.II.D.7), document TD/135, "Special measurements for the least developed among the developing countries. Action programme submitted on the Secretary-General of UNCTAD", paras. 40-46.

connected with the method of allocation of Community tariff quotas.[35] Japan's scheme will remain effective up to March 1981.

9. INSTITUTIONAL ARRANGEMENTS

94. It was agreed in the Special Committee on Preferences that there should be appropriate machinery within UNCTAD to deal with questions relating to the implementation of Conference resolution 21 (II), bearing in mind Conference resolution 24 (II). The terms of reference of the appropriate UNCTAD body as set out on section VIII of the agreed conclusions provide, *inter alia*, that it will review the effects of the GSP on exports and export earnings, industrialization and the rates of economic growth of the beneficiary countries, including the least developed among the developing countries. It will also review the special measures in favour of the least developed countries, the effects on the export earnings of developing countries from the sharing of their existing tariff advantages with the rest of the developing countries as a result of the GSP and the complementary efforts made by developing countries to utilize as fully as possible the benefits from the potential trade advantages created by the system. The appropriate body will, further, review questions related to measures taken by the socialist countries of Eastern Europe with a view to contributing to the attainment of the objectives of Conference resolution 21 (II). The above-mentioned functions would be carried out by means of periodic reviews (annual and triennial reviews and a comprehensive review towards the end of the initial period) which would also provide opportunity for multilateral or bilateral consultations between preference-giving countries and beneficiary countries on the system as initially applied, on the modalities of its application and on subsequent changes as well as with respect to possible improvements in the system. The Special Committee on Preferences considered that there might also be a need for consultations of an *ad hoc* character on specific aspects of the system that required urgent consideration. Such consultations could be arranged in agreement with interested Governments of members States and with the assistance when desired of the Secretary-General of UNCTAD.

95. At its fourth special session, the Trade and Development Board, in approving the institutional arrangements proposed in section VIII of the agreed conclusions of the Special Committee on Preferences, decided (see decision 75 (S-IV)) to postpone until its eleventh session the decision concerning the appropriate body within UNCTAD to deal with the questions relating to the implementation of the GSP and in the meantime extended the existence of the Special Committee. At its eleventh session the Board decided (see resolution 80 (XI)) to extend further the existence of this Committee with the terms of reference set out in section VIII of the agreed conclusions and to postpone the decision concerning the appropriate body within UNCTAD to a date not later than its thirteenth session.

B. Preferential arrangements by the social countries of Eastern Europe

96. In their joint declaration[36] made in the Special Committee on Preferences, five socialist countries of Eastern Europe, namely, Bulgaria, Czechoslovakia, Hungary, Poland and the Union of Soviet Socialist Republics, expressed their belief that they could contribute to the attainment of the general objectives set forth in resolution 21 (II), and to the solution of the problem of promoting the export by the developing countries of manufactures and semi-manufactures, by granting tariff preferences to the developing countries and by taking a number of special measures of a preferential nature, designed specifically to expand their imports from the developing countries, in particular of manufactured goods.

97. In the light of their economic development prospects, these socialist countries of Eastern Europe intend, *inter alia*;

To take account, in the preparation of their plans, of the production and export potential of the developing countries;

To include in their economic plans, as far as possible, suitable measures designed to expand the range of goods and to increase imports from the developing countries, including manufactures and semi-manufactures;

To accord, in their procurement policies, a preferential treatment for imports from the developing countries;

To take, within the framework of their national economic policies, all practicable steps to create favourable conditions for imports from the developing countries and for the consumption of products imported;

To refrain from encouraging imports of raw materials from other sources whenever they are available on competitive terms in developing countries.

98. The socialist countries of Eastern Europe also intend to continue to take steps contributing to the creation, in the developing countries, of export production and to the marketing of such production. To this end, they intend, *inter alia*:

To accept, in partial repayment of credits granted in connexion with the delivery of complete plants and equipment to the developing countries, not only traditional exports, but also goods in demand in the socialist countries and produced by those plants;

To promote agreements on partial division of labour;

To grant the developing countries technical assistance in the construction of national industrial undertakings and in the training of national cadres.

---

[35] In its resolution of 9 June 1971 on the granting of generalized preferences by EEC, the European Parliament stated, *inter alia*, that it considered that in order to be able promptly to remedy any drawbacks which this first experiment might reveal, as well as for technical reasons connected with the method of allocation of Community tariff quotas, application of the scheme in accordance with the proposed regulations should be limited initially to the second half of the year 1971 (see *procés-verbal* of the meeting of 9 June 1971).

[36] See footnote 3 above.

99. These measures, in their view, can produce the desired results only if the developing countries themselves apply measures contributing to an expansion of their trade with the socialist countries.

100. The socialist countries concerned indicated that the measures referred to above would be extended not only to manufactures and semi-manufactures, but also to raw materials and processed agricultural products imported from the developing countries. They would apply these measures to developing countries, regardless of their social and economic systems, and would, in individual cases, consider the desirability of applying them to those countries which do not grant them trade conditions no less favourable than those they grant to developed market-economy countries. Finally, they consider that the tariff and other special supplementary measures listed above contain the elements necessary to take care of the special interests of the least developed of the developing countries.

101. Customs tariffs exist only in some of the socialist countries of Eastern Europe. For this reason, only those socialist countries of Eastern Europe which possess such tariffs have granted, or intend to grant, tariff preferences as a means of helping to expand the exports of the developing countries.

102. In pursuance of the recommendations of the conference at its first session, the Union of Soviet Socialist Republics introduced in 1965 a régime of duty-free imports for all products of developing countries. There was no provision for the reintroduction of the abolished duties or the adoption of any other measure of a protective character. Moreover, no time-limit was set for this preferential treatment.

103. Czechoslovakia has notified the text of its contribution to preferential treatment in favour of developing countries.[37] This contribution was made in conformity with the above-mentioned joint declaration. Czechoslovakia intends to implement its preferential scheme as of 1 January 1972 for a 10-year period. The preferential treatment would apply in principle to all agricultural and industrial products, including primary commodities contained in the Czechoslovak Customs Tariff, with a minimum of exceptions. These exceptions include the following products:

White sugar (tariff item 19), cigarettes (22b/4), poultry of all kinds, not including feathered game (73), beer (107), meat prepared, i.e. salted, dried, smoked,

pickled and boiled (117b), meat sausages (118), carpets other than handmade (218 and 237), hats (267-269), ready-made articles of textiles (274).

104. While the final aim should be duty-free treatment Czechoslovakia would, in the first stage, be prepared to grant a 50 per cent linear reduction of customs duties of the post-Kennedy Round m.f.n. rates on goods originating in developing countries. Further reductions are envisaged in the light of experience gained during the implementation of the preferential scheme.

105. Czechoslovakia is prepared to grant preferences to countries which claim developing country status, but might decline to accord such treatment to a particular country or countries, or to products originating in these countries, on grounds which it would consider to be justified. In general, Czechoslovakia would resort to safeguard measures exceptionally and only after taking due account of the interest of the developing countries, and in particular, of the interests of the least developed among the developing countries. Moreover, the escape-clause type measures would be governed by the same considerations as are contained in the Agreed conclusions of the Special Committee on Preferences. The rules of origin envisaged will be based on the process criterion.

106. Hungary has also notified the text of its contribution to the attainment of the objectives of Conference resolution 21(II)[38] It will introduce preferential customs tariffs in favour of exports from the developing countries as of 1 January 1972. Preferences will cover groups of products, both agricultural and industrial, falling within 584 tariff numbers and sub-numbers. As a first step, approximately 100 of these products will be accorded duty-free entry, and for other products the preferential tariff rates will be 50 to 90 per cent below the m.f.n. tariff rates. The preferential tariff rates will apply to products originating in those developing countries in Asia, Africa and Latin America whose *per capita* national income is lower than that of Hungary and which do not discriminate against Hungary, maintain normal trade relations with it and can give reliable evidence of the origin of products eligible for preferential tariff treatment.

107. Bulgaria has indicated that it is prepared to introduce, within the framework of a new customs tariff, preferential tariff rates for imports of primary commodities and manufactured and semi-manufactured products coming from and originating in developing countries.

---

[37] See document TD/B/378/Add.2 (Czechoslovakia).

[38] See document TD/B/378/Add.3 (Hungary).

CHAPTER II

Technical assistance in connexion with the generalized system of preferences

108. In addition to the steps taken by UNCTAD in connexion with rules of origin and special measures in favour of the least developed among the developing countries, the following programme of technical assistance has been prepared in order to assist preference-receiving countries in deriving maximum benefits from the GSP.

A. Training and advisory services in connexion with the GSP

109. The training and advisory services project in connexion with the GSP, financed by UNDP under the Special Fund component, will extend over a three-year

period and will consist of a series of regional and sub-regional seminars, to be held in co-operation with the regional economic commissions, UNIDO and ITC. The aim of these seminars is, *inter alia*, to promote full awareness of the advantages and implications of the GSP among competent government officials and professional organizations and associations in the production and export sectors; to identify areas where action should be taken at the national level in order to derive maximum benefits from the GSP, and to assist governments in formulating programmes of action or requests for additional assistance; to suggest appropriate measures for promoting industrialization, particularly export-oriented industrialization; to formulate export policies, including export incentives, to achieve the objective of expansion and diversification of exports of manufactures; and to suggest trade promotion policies and measures for expansion of present exports and of products produced but not yet exported, in particular with respect to opportunities created in new markets as a result of the GSP.

110. The project also calls for the provision, on the spot and/or through correspondence, of advisory services to help in solving specific problems encountered in the implementation of the GSP and in determining what measures might be taken to promote exports and industrialization, with a view to deriving maximum benefits from the GSP.

B. Joint country missions

111. A joint programme of action has also been formulated by UNCTAD, UNIDO and ITC to assist developing countries, at their request, in assessing the new export opportunities resulting from the GSP and to advise them on measures which they would need to undertake in order to take full advantage of this system. A joint mission from the three above-mentioned organizations visited Morocco, at that country's request, in February/March 1972. Requests have also been received from other interested governments.

ANNEX

Average tariff protection in developed market-economy countries for 34 groups of industrial products arranged according to different stages of processing[a]

BTN heading	Products, dutiable imports from developing countries	EEC	United States of America	Canada	Japan	United Kingdom	Sweden	Denmark	Norway	Finland	Switzerland	Austria
41.01; 41.09; 43.01	Raw hides and skins . . . . $1.4 million	0.0	25.7	17.5	10.0	0.0	0.0	0.0	0.0	0.0	0.2	0.0
		0	2-41	0-18	5-20	0	0	0	0	0	0-02	0
41.02-08; 41.10; 43.02	Semi-manufactured products of leather . . . . $61.5 million	5.0	6.4	13.1	15.1	10.3	4.9	7.1	9.2	13.3	3.2	6.1
		3-8	0-19	0-23	8-25	5-20	3-6	0-8	0-22	7-16	0-10	0-10
42.01; 42.03-05; 43.03-04	Manufactured articles of leather . . . . $13.4 million	8.7	17.5	19.7	15.0	15.3	8.4	12.7	16.9	11.5	5.2	12.4
		5-13	3-87	0-25	8-25	8-25	7-13	5-23	3-52	8-15	1-18	5-24
40.01-04	Raw rubber . . . . $3.0 million	3.3	8.2	7.1	7.2	5.0	0.0	0.0	15.0	0.0	0.2	7.0
		3-5	3-16	3-18	0-8	0-8	0	0	0-15	0	0-0.2	0-7
40.05-09; 40.15	Rubber, semi-manufactured products . . . . $0.8 million	6.3	11.0	16.6	7.5	8.7	6.3	6.7	11.0	7.7	2.3	11.2
		3-10	3-38	10-23	3-10	5-18	4-10	2-12	3-21	3-13	0-6	6-25
40.10-14; 40.16	Rubber, manufactured articles . . . . $62.7 million	8.3	8.7	16.6	10.8	11.1	11.0	10.3	15.4	17.7	3.3	17.7
		8-10	2-35	10-25	8-15	8-18	3-36	8-14	2-59	8-30	1-6	7-27
44.01-04; 45.01	Wood and cork in the rough . . . . $4.2 million	3.9	7.0	13.0	3.8	4.3	0.0	0.0	0.0	0.0	2.3	5.1
		0-7	0-12	0-18	0-10	0-5	0	0	0	0	1.7	0-13
44.15; 44.18	Wood based panels . . . . $70.5 million	12.7	12.6	13.8	18.0	10.8	3.3	6.7	11.0	2.5	18.7	17.0
		12-13	6-20	10-15	15-20	5-18	3-5	4-9	4-20	3-15	10-31	16-18
44.05-14; 44.16-17; 44.19; 45.02	Wood and cork, semi-manufactured products . . . . $30.7 million	5.3	6.6	10.2	9.0	6.2	2.1	2.5	6.6	3.7	4.9	7.1
		3-10	0-14	0-15	0-20	4-15	0-5	0-5	0-8	0-5	0-14	0-16
44.20-28; 45.03-04	Wood and cork, manufactured articles . . . . $21.8 million	7.9	10.4	16.2	11.4	8.0	3.9	5.2	6.1	5.4	7.0	10.5
		4-16	3-26	0-46	5-40	3-15	0-5	0-9	0-13	3-8	1-14	5-15
47.01-02	Paper pulp and paper waste . . . . $6.8 million	2.8	0.0	0.0	5.0	7.5	0.0	0.0	0.0	0.0	2.4	5.2
		2-3	0	0	0-5	5-10	0	0	0	0	0-7	0-8
48.01-09	Paper and paperboard . . . . $5.2 million	10.6	6.2	13.5	9.2	14.5	2.5	5.5	2.5	6.0	12.9	14.8
		3-14	1-34	0-20	3-20	10-18	0-3	0-12	0-8	3-10	1-32	0-32
49.01-11	Printed matter . . . . $0.8 million	8.4	4.8	16.8	7.5	9.8	4.0	8.5	9.2	10.6	8.3	13.4
		0-13	0-10	0-25	0-8	0-12	0-4	0-15	0-15	0-13	0-13	0-19
48.10-11; 48.13-21	Pulp and paper, manufactured articles . . . . $1.5 million	12.4	6.7	16.0	7.9	13.5	3.8	11.3	8.4	10.8	11.1	19.1
		8-15	1-14	8-20	5-15	10-18	2-5	0-18	1-53	3-15	3-20	10-26
53.01-05	Wool . . . . $39.0 million	2.3	14.9	7.5	5.0	7.0	0.0	0.0	4.3	0.0	0.5	9.3
		0-3	0-43	0-10	0-5	0-10	0	0	0-6	0	0-2	0-18
53.06-10	Wool yarns . . . . $0.9 million	6.8	16.8	13.5	5.5	10.3	5.5	5.0	7.6	7.5	4.9	9.2
		4-11	5-30	8-23	5-8	8-13	5-6	5	5-8	6-12	3-8	0-17
53.11-13	Wool fabrics . . . . $5.4 million	11.8	35.2	23.7	10.3	17.5	17.6	13.4	16.8	24.1	8.4	20.8
		8-18	9-100	0-36	8-16	17-5	14-27	13-16	2-25	22-33	1-17	18-24
55.01-04	Cotton . . . . $43.1 million	1.5	5.9	5.0	0.0	5.0	5.0	0.0	0.0	2.5	3.1	3.0
		0-2	0-9	0-5	0	0-5	0-5	0	0	0-3	0-11	0-4
55.05-06	Cotton yarns . . . . $29.2 million	7.4	11.6	14.2	7.8	10.3	8.9	5.0	5.0	10.9	5.6	11.2
		4-12	4-20	10-18	6-11	8-13	7-13	5	5	7-14	2-10	8-20

ANNEX *(continued)*

Average tariff protection in developed market-economy countries for 34 groups of industrial products arranged according to different stages of processing[a]

BTN heading	Products, dutiable imports from developing countries	EEC	United States of America	Canada	Japan	United Kingdom	Sweden	Denmark	Norway	Finland	Switzerland	Austria
55.07-09	Cotton fabrics $104.9 million	13.0 9-15	18.4 7-36	17.7 18-20	11.2 7-14	20.0 18-25	13.8 13	11.5 10-16	16.9 18-25	24.4 21-33	11.2 9-13	22.8 18-26
57.03	Jute $0.001 million	0.0 0	6.3 5-8	0.0 0	0.0 0	5.0 5	0.0 0	0.0 0	0.0 0	0.0 0	0.3 0-0.3	10.0 10
57.06	Jute yarns $0.6 million	8.0 8	10.4 7-13	18.8 18-20	10.0 10	13.3 10-15	8.0 8	4.0 4	0.0 0	12.6 12-13	8.8 1-18	16.0 16
57.10	Jute fabrics $12.8 million	19.0 15-22	8.5 3-23	0.0 0	20.0 20	20.0 20	9.5 8-10	0.0 0	0.0 0	21.2 20-22	9.1 1-20	28.0 28
60.02-06; 61.01-11; 65.01-05	Clothing and clothing accessories $417.8 million	11.6 5-20	22.6 3-65	22.9 0-28	17.3 10-30	19.4 5-25	14.6 10-57	16.1 2-30	22.8 0-40	36.7 0-120	10.3 2-36	30.2 0-115
25.10; 31.01	Crude fertilizers $0.4 million	0.0 0	0.0 0	0.0 0	0.0 0	5.0 0-5	0.0 0	0.0 0	0.0 0	0.0 0	0.1 0-0.1	8.0 0-8
25.01-04; 25.06-09; 25.11-13; 25.18-19; 25.24-32; 26.02; 26.04; 27.15; 71.04	Other crude minerals $24.9 million	5.2 0-19	5.6 0-36	12.4 0-20	7.6 0-13	5.5 0-10	2.5 0-3	1.1 0-1	0.0 0	10.0 0-10	2.0 0-18	5.7 0-14
31.02-05	Manufactured fertilizers $2.9 million	4.0 2-6	5.7 0-9	14.4 0-14	9.2 0-10	8.5 0-13	5.6 0.6	0.0 0	0.0 0	0.0 0	3.8 0-16	11.8 0-15
70.04-09	Flat glass and manufactures $4.7 million	8.1 5-11	11.3 2-26	11.1 5-20	10.0 5-18	9.4 8-15	9.1 8-10	8.4 0-14	8.4 2-15	28.3 8-47	6.8 3-11	14.7 5-30
70.01-03; 70.10-21	Other glass manufactures $8.1 million	8.8 4-16	15.5 2-50	17.1 0-32	9.5 0-20	11.1 5-20	8.8 0-12	12.5 0-20	11.6 0-40	24.5 0-62	5.4 0-16	15.0 0-30
71.01-03	Precious stones, pearls $121.6 million	2.9 0-4	7.4 3-21	0.0 0	6.8 3-20	6.7 0-10	0.0 0	0.0 0	0.0 0	0.0 0	0.3 0-0.3	3.0 0-3
71.05-11	Unworked or semi-manufactured precious metals $20.2 million	3.8 0-8	13.4 0-25	15.0 0-20	7.1 0-10	5.0 0-5	1.5 0-2	0.0 0	5.5 0-8	2.4 0-4	0.8 0-2	8.2 0-13
71.12-16; 72.01	Articles of precious stones and precious metals $15.4 million	8.2 0-18	16.7 0-35	19.4 0-25	19.1 0-25	11.9 0-15	5.0 0-5	15.0 0-15	5.9 0.26	13.1 0-25	2.0 0-7	14.6 0-26
26.01; 26.03; 73.03	Ores and metal waste $84.9 million	1.5 0-2	10.1 0-36	11.9 0-18	7.5 0-8	0.0 0	0.0 0	0.0 0	0.0 0	0.0 0	0.4 0-0.4	0.0 0
73.01; 73.04-07	Iron and steel unworked $56.9 million	3.9 3-5	4.5 0-10	12.5 0-18	5.5 5-6	11.3 0-25	3.4 0-4	0.0 0	12.8 0-16	5.4 0-8	0.1 0-30	5.3 0-7
73.02	Ferro-alloys $10.3 million	7.0 4-10	5.6 3-10	7.2 3-18	7.5 5-10	12.5 5-17	2.3 1-3	0.0 0	0.0 0	11.0 0	11.0 1-30	16.0 5-7
73.08-18	Iron and steel, semi-manufactured products $43.2 million	6.8 3-10	7.8 1-13	10.4 0-18	10.2 8-20	10.3 8-25	5.9 3-8	5.8 0-8	7.3 0-20	6.4 0-20	6.5 0-30	8.9 5-24

BTN heading	Product	Imports	1	2	3	4	5	6	7	8	9	10	11
74.01-02	Copper, unwrought	$496.1 million	0.0 / 0	3.9 / 2-11	9.2 / 0-18	7.4 / 3-15	7.5 / 5-10	0.0	0.0	0.0	0.0	0.1 / 0-0.1	2.0 / 0-2
74.03-08	Copper, semi-manufactures	$14.6 million	7.4 / 2-10	8.0 / 2-16	9.3 / 0-20	16.5 / 10-20	11.3 / 8-15	3.1 / 3-5	3.9 / 0-5	4.8 / 0-10	4.1 / 0-8	3.1 / 1-13	11.0 / 8-17
75.01	Nickel, unwrought	$0.2 million	0.0 / 0	4.9 / 2-9	17.5 / 17-5	18.7 / 11-23	5.0 / 5	0.0 / 0	0.0 / 0	0.0 / 0	0.0 / 0	0.1 / 0-0.1	0.0 / 0
75.02-05	Nickel, semi-manufactures	$0.3 million	5.1 / 1-8	8.9 / 2-16	16.0 / 0-18	14.5 / 0-23	8.5 / 8-10	1.5 / 0-2	3.0 / 0-3	5.0 / 0-7	2.0 / 0-2	1.7 / 0-3	8.7 / 4-13
76.01	Aluminium, unwrought	$10.4 million	6.0 / 4-9	4.5 / 4-5	2.9 / 3	6.8 / 3-9	5.0 / 5	0.0 / 0	0.0 / 0	0.0 / 0	0.0 / 0	11.2 / 11	6.7 / 6-8
76.02-07	Aluminium, semi-manufactures	$7.7 million	10.9 / 8-12	7.7 / 2-20	13.2 / 5-18	14.9 / 10-18	8.7 / 8-10	3.2 / 3-5	5.8 / 0-8	11.4 / 0-10	3.1 / 0-10	11.4 / 4-17	15.1 / 11-27
78.01	Lead, unwrought	$58.0 million	5.4 / 5	9.0 / 8-10	15.0 / 10-18	8.4 / 5-12	5.0 / 5	0.0 / 0	0.0 / 0	0.0 / 0	0.0 / 0	0.3 / 0-0.3	5.8 / 5-7
78.02-05	Lead, semi-manufactures	$0.5 million	9.2 / 3-11	7.8 / 5-15	11.3 / 0-18	15.6 / 10-20	9.0 / 8-10	0.0 / 0	1.5 / 0-2	5.0 / 0-5	1.8 / 0-3	4.2 / 1-7	13.0 / 10-18
79.01	Zinc, unwrought	$22.4 million	4.6 / 5	11.2 / 5-19	0.0 / 0	4.4 / 3-8	3.3 / 2-5	0.0 / 0	0.0 / 0	0.0 / 0	0.0 / 0	0.1 / 0-0.1	2.0 / 2
79.02-04	Zinc, semi-manufactures	$4.7 million	9.2 / 6-10	7.9 / 2-12	10.8 / 8-18	10.4 / 8-15	9.0 / 8-10	0.0 / 0	0.0 / 0	5.5 / 0-9	1.0 / 1	1.2 / 0.2	13.3 / 10-18
80.01	Tin, unwrought	$64.9 million	0.0 / 0	0.0 / 0	8.8 / 8-10	5.0 / 5	0.0 / 0	0.0 / 0	0.0 / 0	0.0 / 0	0.0 / 0	0.2 / 0-0.2	3.0 / 3
80.02-05	Tin, semi-manufactures	$0.03 million	4.8 / 3-7	7.8 / 5-18	12.5 / 0-18	6.3 / 5-8	9.0 / 8-10	1.5 / 0-2	0.2 / 0-3	5.0 / 0-5	1.8 / 0-3	1.3 / 0-5	9.3 / 7-15
82.01-07	Tools	$5.5 million	7.0 / 5-10	8.4 / 2-21	16.1 / 0-20	8.8 / 8-10	10.1 / 8-17	5.0 / 4-6	3.4 / 0-5	13.2 / 5-20	5.9 / 3-8	2.9 / 1-6	16.9 / 5-28
82.09-15	Cutlery	$2.8 million	9.3 / 5-19	17.9 / 4-50	18.4 / 0-25	12.2 / 9-20	17.1 / 6-26	6.1 / 4-8	12.8 / 0-15	13.8 / 1-39	6.4 / 6-8	4.2 / 1-19	13.3 / 5-25
73.38; 74.17-18; 76.15; 82.08; 83.06; 83.12	Household equipment	$9.6 million	7.8 / 7-10	10.0 / 4-26	17.1 / 0-20	14.0 / 8-25	11.3 / 10-17	5.3 / 4-6	9.9 / 0-15	6.9 / 2-17	9.0 / 3-20	5.4 / 1-11	24.0 / 8-35
73.22-24; 74.09; 76.09-11	Metal containers	$0.9 million	7.8 / 6-12	6.4 / 5-10	16.1 / 0-20	8.4 / 5-10	10.0 / 10	5.2 / 4-6	7.3 / 3-12	9.8 / 0-27	7.6 / 5-10	6.2 / 0-15	17.3 / 10-21
27.11	Gas	$31.3 million	1.5 / 2	0.0 / 0	11.4 / 9-13	15.3 / 11-20	5.0 / 5	4.1 / 1-7	0.0 / 0	15.0 / 15	0.0 / 0	0.0 / 0	4.0 / 3-5
27.09	Crude petroleum	$2,262.2 million	0.0 / 0	3.6 / 3-5	0.0 / 0	12.2 / 12	0.0 / 0	0.0 / 0	0.0 / 0	0.0 / 0	0.0 / 0	0.0 / 0	14.0 / 14
27.06-08; 27.10; 27.12-14; 27.16; 34.03; 38.04	Products derived from coal, petroleum or gas	$1,206.8 million	4.5 / 0-7	9.1 / 0-27	13.6 / 0-20	11.5 / 0-62	5.0 / 3-10	0.9 / 0-2	2.9 / 0-3	5.3 / 0-15	5.0 / 0-5	2.6 / 0-10	11.2 / 0-45
15.11; 29.01-37; 29.40; 29.43; 29.45	Organic chemicals	$34.0 million	8.1 / 2-20	12.3 / 1-46	11.9 / 1-18	10.9 / 3-30	9.2 / 5-13	9.0 / 0-9	7.2 / 0-19	14.3 / 0-15	17.1 / 0-25	2.1 / 0-27	11.6 / 0-34
27.05; 28.01-28	Chemical elements, inorganic acids, oxides and halogens	$58.8 million	5.4 / 2-12	6.7 / 0-36	12.9 / 0-18	7.7 / 0-15	7.0 / 4-25	4.5 / 0-10	0.9 / 0-9	13.0 / 0-23	5.6 / 0-10	1.8 / 0-11	10.2 / 0-22
28.29-58	Other inorganic products	$4.1 million	5.8 / 2-13	6.4 / 0-74	12.0 / 0-18	9.3 / 0-38	6.9 / 5-13	4.0 / 0-7	4.4 / 0-7	8.3 / 0-15	10.0 / 0-15	1.7 / 0-14	10.8 / 0-20

ANNEX (concluded)

Average tariff protection in developed market-economy countries for 34 groups of industrial products arranged according to different stages of processing[a]

BTN heading	Products, dutiable imports from developing countries	EEC	United States of America	Canada	Japan	United Kingdom	Sweden	Denmark	Norway	Finland	Switzerland	Austria
32.01-03	Tanning materials $6.4 million	6.7 / 4-9	6.5 / 3-19	15.0 / 0-15	6.5 / 0-10	5.0 / 5	3.0 / 0-3	1.3 / 0-1	12.5 / 0-15	0.0 / 0	0.5 / 0-0.5	10.0 / 0-10
32.04-07	Colouring materials $0.6 million	6.9 / 2-14	10.7 / 1-30	11.3 / 5-15	10.1 / 3-13	10.2 / 5-25	0.0 / 0	0.0 / 0	2.8 / 0-8	4.8 / 0-5	1.5 / 0-3	20.6 / 5-28
32.08-13	Paints, varnishes, etc. $0.2 million	6.8 / 3-9	10.6 / 2-34	15.2 / 10-18	9.1 / 4-13	7.7 / 5-15	5.8 / 0-9	5.9 / 0-12	10.3 / 0-15	8.5 / 0-15	5.5 / 0-18	13.5 / 9-26
29.38-39; 29.41-42; 29.44; 30.01-05	Medical and pharmaceutical products $47.0 million	7.0 / 2-17	10.6 / 0-29	17.3 / 13-80	10.9 / 0-25	10.4 / 5-13	9.5 / 0-12	4.2 / 0-5	8.4 / 0-15	10.0 / 0-15	1.8 / 0-9	12.9 / 0-25
39.01-06	Plastic materials $3.3 million	8.6 / 5-14	10.9 / 3-30	13.4 / 8-28	12.0 / 5-18	7.9 / 5-13	9.4 / 3-11	7.6 / 3-9	13.4 / 0-20	10.8 / 3-21	3.2 / 0-10	14.9 / 5-25
39.07	Articles of plastics $18.2 million	8.8 / 7-12	11.3 / 4-35	17.8 / 8-25	12.5 / 10-15	8.2 / 7-10	10.7 / 7-11	5.3 / 3-11	18.1 / 8-20	21.5 / 8-59	6.0 / 3-10	21.0 / 20-23
33.01-05	Essential oils, perfume materials $8.8 million	5.8 / 2-12	8.5 / 0-18	7.5 / 0-8	8.9 / 5-18	10.8 / 4-36	0.0 / 0	9.0 / 0-9	6.4 / 0-17	0.0 / 0	4.7 / 0-26	6.8 / 0-18
33.06; 34.01-02; 35.04-05	Perfumery, cosmetics soaps, cleaning preparations, etc. $0.6 million	6.8 / 5-20	8.2 / 3-20	16.0 / 3-25	14.5 / 5-25	10.3 / 5-20	6.7 / 0-9	6.9 / 3-12	16.9 / 2-63	25.8 / 0-87	6.4 / 2-13	12.9 / 5-30
35.04; 38.01-03; 38.05-10; 38.12 15; 38.19	Other chemicals semi-manufactured products $4.8 million	5.2 / 2-11	7.5 / 1-26	11.1 / 0-18	8.3 / 0-20	6.3 / 2-13	6.8 / 0-9	7.9 / 0-20	12.1 / 0-26	5.4 / 0-6	1.4 / 0-10	16.5 / 0-50
34.07; 35.03; 35.06; 36.01-05; 36.07; 38.11; 38.16-18	Other chemicals finished products $6.3 million	6.7 / 4-12	8.1 / 0-26	15.8 / 0-20	9.8 / 3-20	6.6 / 5-13	6.4 / 0-10	5.7 / 0-9	8.5 / 0-15	14.0 / 0-79	3.8 / 0-9	15.0 / 9-30
84.01-65; 73.36-37	Non-electrical machinery $53.5 million	6.2 / 3-14	7.0 / 0-23	14.8 / 0-36	10.8 / 5-25	9.0 / 4-20	5.1 / 3-10	6.2 / 0-15	8.7 / 1-20	7.9 / 0-15	2.1 / 0.9	10.0 / 0-42
85.01-28	Electrical machines and apparatus $149.1 million	8.4 / 4-20	8.4 / 1-35	15.2 / 0-20	10.5 / 8-25	11.1 / 5-45	6.2 / 0-13	8.7 / 0-18	7.6 / 0-29	9.7 / 0-27	3.2 / 0-19	13.3 / 1-49
86.01-09; 87.01.06; 87.09-12; 87.14; 88.01-03; 89.01-05	Transport equipment $40.3 million	8.9 / 0-22	8.0 / 0-21	15.5 / 0-25	11.9 / 0-30	11.9 / 0-22	8.1 / 0-15	5.2 / 0-20	12.9 / 0-25	8.4 / 0-18	4.7 / 0-31	15.8 / 0-34
90.01-18; 90.20-29; 91.01-11	Professional scientific and controlling instruments, photographic apparatus, clocks and watches $16.1 million	9.2 / 5-14	19.4 / 0-85	14.7 / 0-25	10.6 / 3-20	15.2 / 8-25	5.1 / 0-7	4.9 / 0-8	6.9 / 0-25	6.2 / 0-10	2.3 / 0-13	9.3 / 0-27
64.01-06	Footwear $48.8 million	11.1 / 7-20	10.6 / 3-38	21.5 / 0-25	17.4 / 8-30	11.8 / 5-35	12.1 / 7-14	17.4 / 9-25	17.1 / 1-50	14.2 / 9-28	8.7 / 5-16	17.9 / 5-30
42.02	Travel goods, handbags, etc. $30.0 million	11.3 / 8-15	12.8 / 4-21	18.9 / 18-20	13.3 / 10-20	11.9 / 10-14	9.7 / 5-10	15.0 / 15	21.4 / 10-24	14.4 / 8-18	8.4 / 2-15	19.5 / 17-22

BTN heading	Product											
37.01-08	Photographic and cinematographic supplies $3.4 million	5.4 2-9	5.7 2-18	13.8 0-18	18.0 2-40	8.1 0-11	4.0 0-5	2.8 0-5	3.1 1-11	4.1 0-7	1.0 0-2	6.6 0-13
94.01-04	Furniture $31.9 million	8.2 6-11	10.9 4-22	18.5 15-25	12.5 10-15	14.0 10-20	8.8 4-16	7.1 3-16	8.0 3-13	9.6 8-13	8.6 3-18	14.8 4-30
92.01-13	Musical instruments, sound recording or reproduction apparatus $5.5 million	7.7 4-11	8.8 3-20	14.5 8-20	9.0 6-15	11.4 5-17	6.3 0-8	11.1 0-14	5.9 0-20	10.8 4-20	4.1 1-17	12.0 5-30
97.01-08	Toys $66.7 million	11.3 5-19	11.4 0-43	17.5 5-25	10.8 10-15	13.6 4-34	5.4 3-10	8.3 0-14	8.8 1-15	10.8 5-25	6.5 0-14	17.3 5-28
99.01-06	Works of art and collectors' pieces $0.2 million	0.0 0	7.5 0-8	19.5 0-20	0.0 0	10.0 0-10	0.0 0	0.0 0	0.0 0	0.0 0	0.6 0-2	0.0 0
83.04-05; 98.03-09	Office and stationery supplies $0.8 million	7.2 2-14	10.4 0-61	17.0 0-25	12.7 8-32	8.6 5-14	5.2 4-8	6.9 0-18	5.5 0-13	5.3 2-13	4.1 1-8	14.9 2-28
27.17; 34.06; 35.01-02; 35.05; 36.06; 36.08; 42.06; 46.01-03; 48.12; 65.06-07; 66.01-03; 67.01-05; 87.13; 88.04-05; 90.19; 95.01-08; 96.01-06; 98.01-02; 98.10-16	Manufactured articles not elsewhere specified $136.2 million	8.2 2-17	13.5 0-180	18.0 0-32	12.8 8-20	11.4 3-30	7.0 0-34	7.2 0-15	11.7 0-46	11.8 0-47	6.1 0-39	14.4 0-40

Source: GATT, *Basic Documentation for Tariff Study*, July 1970. [a] For an explanation of this table see paragraph 46 of this report.

THE GENERALIZED SYSTEM OF PREFERENCES

Addendum to the report by the UNCTAD secretariat*

[Original text: English]

CONTENTS

---

* The text of this addendum was circulated to the Conference as document TD/124/Add.1, dated 9 March 1972, and TD/124/Add.1/Corr.1, dated 5 May 1972.

PREFACE

Since the issue of the foregoing report by the UNCTAD secretariat, "The generalized system of preferences" (TD/124), a number of other preference-giving countries have implemented or are now expected to implement their schemes of preferences. The EEC has adopted new regulations and decisions concerning the operation of its scheme for the year 1972. This addendum gives a summary of the newly implemented schemes and of the changes made in the EEC scheme.

As was indicated in paragraph 6 of document TD/124, the addendum also presents specific trade data relating to the GSP.

CHAPTER I

Principal characteristics of the generalized system of preferences

A. Preferential arrangements by developed market-economy countries

1. Among the developed market-economy countries, Denmark, Finland, New Zealand, Sweden and the United Kingdom implemented their respective schemes of generalized preferences in favour of developing countries on 1 January 1972.[1] Switzerland decided to implement its scheme as of 1 March 1972.[2] The main elements of these schemes are described below.

2. On 20 December 1971, the EEC adopted new regulations and decisions which constitute its scheme for 1972.[3] This scheme is basically the same as that applied in the second half of 1971, except for certain changes in the lists of non-sensitive and sensitive products for which,

in addition, annual ceilings and tariff quotas have, respectively, been set. Moreover, the origin requirements for some products have also been slightly modified. These changes are also summarized below.

3. Several other Governments of preference-giving countries are taking the necessary legislative action for implementation of their respective schemes. Austria, for instance, is expected to implement its scheme in the spring of 1972.

1. PRODUCT COVERAGE

(a) BTN chapters 25-99

4. The product coverage of the EEC scheme has undergone the following changes. The headings of several products have been altered to conform with amendments to the BTN which became effective in the EEC common tariff on 1 January 1972.[4] Duties have been suspended on a m.f.n. basis in respect of 15 tariff items[5] for an indefinite period and in respect of four tariff items[6] for a temporary period. Duties were abolished on a m.f.n. basis in the case of five tariff items.[7] Six tariff items were withdrawn from the scheme[8] and three others were added.[9]

---

[1] See documents TD/B/373/Add.2 (Denmark), TD/B/373/Add.2 (Finland), TD/B/373/Add.2/Annex (Sweden) and TD/B/373/Add.8 and Annexes 1, 2 and III (United Kingdom). No information was available on New Zealand's scheme at the time of preparation of this addendum. However, paragraphs 10, 12, 28, 41, 70 and 73 of document TD/124 above deal with specific elements of New Zealand's offer as contained in documents TD/B/AC.5/24/Add.10 and TD/B/AC.5/34/Add.10.

[2] The scheme of Switzerland, contained in document TD/B/Add.9, is identical with that country's revised submission (TD/B/AC.5/34/Add.9) with respect to product coverage, depth of tariff cut and safeguards. These aspects are discussed in paragraphs 10, 20, 30, 33, 43 and 48 of document TD/124 above and therefore will not be summarized again in this addendum. The scheme also specifies the preferential rates for each product, lists the beneficiary countries and spells out the rules of origin. The latter two aspects are dealt with in appropriate sections below.

[3] See the Scheme of the European Economic Community for 1972 (TD/B/396) containing EEC Council Regulations Nos. 2794/71 to 2800/71 which replace Regulations 1308/71 to 1314/71, and Decisions Nos. 71/403 and 71/404 which replace Decisions 71/232 and 71/233 respectively (cf. para. 50 of document TD/124 above).

[4] See Journal officiel des Communautés européennes, annex, Tarif douanier commun (COM (71) 1220), part two, No. L 1/15.

[5] 27.10AI, AII, BI, BII, CIa, CIb, CIIa, CIIb, CIIIa, CIIIb; 27.11BI; 27.12AI, AII; 27.13BIa, BIb. In the case of eight of these items the suspension will apply under certain conditions. See Tarif douanier commun, chapter 27, supplementary note 6.

[6] These items are ex 29.01DVI; ex 29.44C; ex 30.01B; and ex 59.17D.

[7] These items are 27.11AII; ex 28.28E; 47.01AI; 47.01BI, BII.

[8] These items are 28.05A, B, C, DI; ex 62.02; and 90.19A, B.

[9] These items are ex 29.06A IV; ex 56.01A; 89.02 BII. The last-mentioned product is now dutiable under the new tariff nomenclature.

5. Denmark grants preferences in respect of all products in BTN chapters 25-99, without exception. Finland, Sweden and the United Kingdom grant preferences in respect of these products with certain exceptions, as shown below.

6. Finland excludes from its scheme products subject to duty of a fiscal nature, i.e. gasoline (ex 27.10), passenger cars (ex 87.02) and motor cycles (87.09). It also excludes some agricultural products, i.e. caseins (35.01), dextrins (35.05), glazings (38.12) and artificial resins (39.06); and other products falling under 55 tariff headings, 25 of which are made up of textile items and the rest of which comprise rubber articles, leather and leather products, footwear, electrical machinery and equipment and toy articles.

7. Sweden excludes products subject to agricultural regulation, i.e. egg white (ex 35.02), dextrins (35.05), glazings (ex 38.12), foundry core binders (38.19) and starches (ex 39.06); textiles[10] (17 tariff headings in chapters 51, 55-57, 60-62); articles of leather (42.03) and footwear (64.01-02).

8. The United Kingdom excludes most textiles (in BTN chapters 50-63 and 65) and products subject to revenue duties[11] under separate legislation, namely, perfumed spirits (33.06A), matches (36.05A and 36.06), portable lighters (ex 98.10) and hydrocarbon oils (certain tariff headings in BTN chapters 27, 29, 32, 34, 36, 38 and 39). It also excludes casein (35.01B), certain kinds of leather (41.02B and 41.08), pig iron (73.01) and unwrought zinc (79.01).[12]

(b) *BTN chapters 1-24*

9. As a result of the new Regulations, the following changes were made in the EEC scheme's product coverage in BTN chapters 1-24. The duty was suspended for one tariff item on a m.f.n. basis[13] and another two items were withdrawn.[14]

10. Denmark grants preferences in respect of 15 items[15] in BTN chapters 1-24. These items include various tropical fruits, i.e. avocadoes, mangoes, melons; and juices thereof,

nuts, roasted coffee substitutes, sauces and other mixed condiments.

11. Finland grants preferences in respect of 43 items, the major ones being various vegetables, fruits, cocoa preparations, roasted coffee substitutes, sauces, soups, non-alcoholic beverages and unmanufactured tobacco.

12. Sweden grants preferences in respect of 29 items, among them fruits, fruit juices, vegetables, preserved fish, cocoa preparations, soups, sauces and spirituous beverages.

13. The United Kingdom grants preferences in respect of 65 items, including meat and meat extracts, preserved fish, chocolate and cocoa preparations, preserved fruits and vegetables, extracts of coffee, tea or maté, mustard, sauces, soups and beverages.

2. DEPTH OF TARIFF CUT

14. Finland and Sweden accord duty-free entry without quantitative limitations for all products covered by their respective schemes. In general, all products covered by the United Kingdom scheme enjoy duty-free entry, except four items[16] in the case of which Commonwealth preferential rates apply and two other items[17] where the rate applicable is equal to 50 per cent of the full duty. Moreover, for products in BTN chapters 25-99 subject to both revenue and protective duties, the reliefs include any protective duty charged under the Import Duties Act of 1958 on these goods.[18] Denmark accords unlimited duty-free entry in respect of preferential imports of products in BTN chapters 25-99 and tariff reductions varying between 6 and 100 per cent in respect of those in BTN chapters 1-24.[19] In addition, all products enjoying preferences are exempt from the Danish temporary import surcharge introduced on 21 October 1971.

3. SAFEGUARD MECHANISMS

15. Following the adoption of the new EEC Regulations, 10 items have been added to the category of sensitive products subject to tariff quotas.[20] Two tariff items have been transferred from the category of sensitive to that of non-sensitive.[21]

16. With regard to the formula normally[22] used to calculate ceilings and tariff quotas, 1968 has been maintained as reference year for determining the basic quota, whereas, for the supplementary quota, 1969 has generally been used. However, for cotton and other textiles and for

[10] Special regulations have been introduced whereby duty-free entry may be accorded by Royal Decree for specific handloom fabrics of cotton which are accompanied by relevant certificates of origin. Under this procedure, duty-free entry has been accorded to imports from India as from 1 September 1968. See GATT document COM.TD/60/Add.2 and para. 35c of the Swedish Customs Tariff Proclamation (1960:392).

[11] See also paragraph 14 below.

[12] These items have been excluded in accordance with the reservation made in the revised United Kingdom offer (TD/B/AC.5/34/Add.8).

[13] This item is ex 12.07K. See also the note referring to this item in *Tarif douanier commun*, annex II.

[14] These items are 09.10 0I, 21.05 B.

[15] Here, and in subsequent paragraphs, the word "items" refers to BTN headings, some of which are only partially granted preferential treatment. In the preliminary offer submitted by the Nordic countries to the Special Committee on Preferences (TD/B/AC.5/24/Add.2), Denmark was prepared to grant preferences in respect of 33 of the dutiable items in BTN chapters 1-24 included in the common positive list.

[16] Coffee (09.01); dried chicory roots (12.05); roasted chicory and other extracts (21.01); and essences or concentrates of coffee (21.02).

[17] Meat extracts (16.03) and canned tuna (16.04).

[18] This is an added benefit with respect to the revised offer (TD/B/AC.5/34/Add.8).

[19] In their preliminary offer the Nordic countries, including Denmark, had also envisaged duty-free treatment for the items falling under BTN chapters 1-24 included in the common positive list.

[20] These items are 28.16; 31.02B; ex 59.04; 62.02; 73.18; 85.15CIII; 90.05; 90.12; 92.11A; 92.12.

[21] These items are 62.03; 84.41 AIa; 84.41 AII.

[22] Apparently, for a number of products, including certain textiles, ceilings are not calculated according to this general rule (see TD/124, para. 51).

two aluminium products (76.02 and 76.03) the ceilings and tariff quotas for 1972 are the same as those for 1971 but expressed on an annual basis, since the EEC scheme was valid only for the second half of 1971. This means that, for these products, 1968 has been used as reference year instead in 1969, in the calculation of the supplementary quota, whenever applicable.

17. For a number of sensitive products, maximum amounts have been further reduced to 30 or 20 per cent.[23] For several non-sensitive products maximum amounts have also been further reduced to 30 or 20 per cent.[24]

18. Finland reserves the right to introduce safeguard measures in line with the agreed conclusions of the Special Committee on Preferences.[25]

19. Sweden will base its safeguard measures on the standard escape clause. These measures can be introduced against imports from that country or those countries whose exports cause or threathen to cause market disruption or against all beneficiary countries.

20. The application of safeguard arrangements by the United Kingdom entails the withdrawal or modification of the preferences but will not affect goods eligible for Commonwealth Preference, or those enjoying duty-free entry on a most-favoured-nation basis.

4. RULES OF ORIGIN

21. The rules of origin in Commission Regulation No. 2862/71 governing the EEC scheme of preferences for 1972 correspond in the main to those originally prescribed in Commission Regulation No. 1371/71. However, article 31 of the latter Regulation which allowed subsequent submission of a Combined Declaration and Certificate of Origin (Form A) issued retroactively by the relevant government authority of the exporting beneficiary country has been omitted from the new rules. This means that goods originating in and consigned from a beneficiary country are eligible for preferences only if they are accompanied by a certificate of origin.

22. Furthermore, the lists of qualifying and non-qualifying working or processing operations (lists A and B), as well as the lists of products excluded from the scope of the Regulations (list C), have been modified with respect to a number of tariff headings in order to conform with the amendments to the Brussels Tariffs Nomenclature referred to above.

23. The rules of origin applied by the United Kingdom, Sweden, Denmark, Finland and Switzerland are similar to those applied by EEC. However, their lists of qualifying and non-qualifying working or processing operations (lists A and B) differ to some extent from the EEC lists. There are also certain variations in respect of conditions

for obtaining origin, including documentary evidence and administrative requirements.

5. BENEFICIARY COUNTRIES AND TERRITORIES

24. The beneficiary countries of the 1972 EEC scheme remain the same as under the 1971 scheme, except for some changes of a formal nature. The Community is still examining the requests of other countries to be added to the list of beneficiaries and was expected to reach a decision as soon as possible in the first half of 1972.

25. Beneficiaries of the Danish scheme include all the countries members of the Group of 77,[26] except Bahrain, Bhutan, Cuba, Fiji and Qatar.

26. Finland grants preferences to all countries members of the Group of 77, with the exception of the Republic of Viet-Nam and the Republic of Korea. The list of beneficiary countries is preliminary and will be expanded, taking into account, among others, the principle of burden sharing.

27. Beneficiaries of the Swedish scheme include all the countries members of the Group of 77, as well as the Democratic People's Republic of Korea, the Democratic Republic of Viet-Nam, Israel, Mongolia, the United Arab Emirates, Western Samoa and dependent territories of third countries.

28. Switzerland grants preferences to all the countries members of the Group of 77, as well as to Greece, Israel, Malta, Spain, Turkey and dependent territories of third countries. However, in the case of textiles and shoes (in BTN chapters 50-64) preferences do not apply to Hong Kong, the Republic of Korea and Macao.

29. The United Kingdom grants preferences to all countries members of the Group of 77 except Bhutan and Cuba. Other beneficiaries include Malta, the Kingdom of Tonga, the United Arab Emirates, Western Samoa and dependent territories whose external relations are conducted by third countries.

6. DURATION

30. The validity of the EEC scheme has been extended to 31 December 1972, while the United Kingdom scheme is valid up to 1 January 1973. It should be noted that both dates coincide with the date set for the United Kingdom's accession to the European Economic Community.

B. Preferential arrangements by the socialist countries of Eastern Europe

31. Czechoslovakia implemented its scheme of tariff preferences on 1 January 1972. The details of this scheme, however, were not available at the time of preparation of this addendum.[27]

---

[23] Out of 96 items considered sensitive, 16 are subject to a normal maximum amount of 50 per cent, 40 to a maximum amount of 30 per cent, 39 to a maximum amount of 20 per cent and 1 to a maximum amount of 10 per cent.

[24] The maximum amount is 30 per cent for 10 items and 20 per cent for 5 other items.

[25] See *Official Records of the Trade and Development Board, Tenth Session, Supplement No. 6A* (TD/B/329/Rev.1), part one.

[26] For a list of countries members of the Group of 77 see annex II to this addendum.

[27] The preferential treatment envisaged by Czechoslovakia was described in paragraphs 103-105 of document TD/124 above.

32. Hungary clarified certain elements of its preferential arrangements described in paragraph 106 of document TD/124. Preferential treatment applies to 299 tariff headings or sub-headings in BTN chapters 1-99, consisting of 580 tariff lines. Duty-free entry is accorded in respect of 101 tariff lines and the remainder enjoy preferential duty reductions varying from 50 per cent to 90 per cent on the most-favoured-nation rates.

33. The beneficiary countries include 57 countries[28] members of the Group of 77, namely, Afghanistan, Algeria, Argentina, Bolivia, Brazil, Burma, the Khmer Republic, *Cameroon*, *Central African Republic*, Ceylon, *Chad*, Chile, Colombia, *Congo*, Costa Rica, Cuba, *Dahomey*, Ecuador, *Egypt*, Ethiopia, *Gabon*, Ghana, Guinea, Honduras, India, Indonesia, Iran, Iraq, *Ivory Coast*, Jordan, Kenya, Laos, Lebanon, Liberia, *Madagascar*, Malaysia, *Mali*, *Mauritania*, Mexico, Morocco, Nepal, Nigeria, Pakistan, Peru, *Senegal*, Singapore, *Somalia*, Sudan, Syrian Arab Republic, Tunisia, Uganda, United Republic of Tanzania, Uruguay, Yemen, Upper Volta, Zaire and Zambia. The countries whose names are printed in italics enjoy preferential treatment provisionally, pending further notice by their Ministers of

Foreign Trade, on the assumption that these developing countries will eliminate special/reverse preferences not later than 31 December 1975 in accordance with the relevant resolutions of UNCTAD.

34. Under the safeguard mechanism, the government concerned may increase or reduce the preferential rates, individually or collectively, for a determined period, or may suspend their application provisionally.

35. Hungary bases its origin requirements on the value-added criterion. Goods are generally considered to have originated in the preference-receiving country of export if they have been produced wholly in that country or if the value of imported materials or components used in the manufacture of the goods does not exceed 50 per cent of the value of the goods.

36. Documentary evidence as to the origin of the goods consists of a declaration completed by the exporter of the goods in the exporting preference-receiving country and certified by the competent authority of that country. The form for the certificate of origin to be used is basically the same as that agreed by the Working Group on Rules of Origin, except for some minor modifications. Goods eligible for preferential tariff treatment must be imported directly from the preference-receiving country into Hungary. Import licences required for customs clearance constitute sufficient evidence of direct importation.

---

[28] For the criteria for selection of beneficiary countries see document TD/124 above, para. 106.

CHAPTER II

Trade data relating to the generalized system of preferences

A. General coverage of the GSP

37. The purpose of this part of the addendum is to provide some general information on the trade between the preference-giving countries and the developing countries which are claiming beneficiary status under the GSP. This is not an attempt to make an ex-ante evaluation of the effects of the schemes nor is it an attempt to enable a comparative analysis of the various schemes. The purpose is, rather, simply to illustrate the general range of magnitude of imports covered by the various schemes, by examining import data in a recent year under the assumption that the schemes had been in force during that year. This addendum covers trade data for those countries which implemented schemes in 1971 (the EEC countries, Japan and Norway) and on 1 January 1972 (Denmark, Finland, Sweden and the United Kingdom)[29] and the United States of America, which, because of the significance of its market, will be considered on the basis of its preliminary submissions.[30]

38. The immediate benefits which those developing countries recognized as beneficiaries are likely to receive

under the GSP will depend basically upon two factors; the current trade flows of the developing countries (the volume and product composition of their exports) and the scope and nature of the GSP schemes, especially the product coverage, GSP margins of preference and safeguard mechanisms embodied in the various schemes. All the schemes which have been implemented grant preferential duty-free entry in respect of manufactured and semi-manufactured products in BTN chapters 25-99.[31] Schemes implemented by the above-mentioned developed market-economy countries, except the EEC countries, cover all dutiable industrial raw materials included in BTN chapters 25-99. Selected agricultural products, both in processed and primary form, in BTN chapters 1-24, have also been included under the schemes and the preferential treatment consists sometimes of only a few percentage points of *ad valorem* duty. As a result, the bulk of the immediate benefits which the developing countries are likely to derive from the GSP will come from their exports of manufactured and semi-manufactured products in BTN chapters 25-99. These benefits might, however, be somewhat limited by the safeguard mechanisms, and, especially the ceiling systems in the schemes of EEC and Japan.

39. The immediate benefits accruing to the developing countries will depend on their ability to supply the products covered by the schemes, namely, manufactured

---

[29] New Zealand also implemented its scheme on 1 January 1972. However, owing to data limitations this scheme will not be covered.

[30] The details of the preliminary submissions by the United States of America are given in "Substantive documentation on the generalized scheme of preferences: submission by the United States of America" (TD/B/AC.5/24/Add.5, 21 November 1969 and TD/B/AC.5/34/Add.5/Rev.1, 24 September 1970).

[31] Japan grants 50 per cent tariff reduction in respect of a selected list of 57 items.

TABLE A

Imports of selected preference-giving countries: 1968

(Million dollars)

Product groups	Combined developed market-economy countries imports from all countries claiming beneficiary status	Combined developed market-economy countries[a] imports from		EEC imports from		Japan imports from		United Kingdom imports from		United States imports from		Denmark imports from		Finland imports from		Norway imports from		Sweden imports from	
		Group of 77[b]	Other[c]	Group of 77[b]	Other[c]	Group of 77[b]	Other[c]	Group of 77[b]	Other[c]	Group of 77[b]	Other[c]	Group of 77[b]	Other[c]	Group of 77[b]	Other[c]	Group of 77[b]	Other[c]	Group of 77[b]	Other[c]
All products: primary commodities, semi-manufactured and manufactured products																			
1. BTN 1-99	36 332	28 785	7 547	11 836	2 649	4 371	1 053	4 085	1 284	7 316	2 164	311	98	105	32	217	78	544	189
2. BTN 1-24	10 838	8 472	2 366	3 209	1 083	528	297	1 126	418	3 174	428	122	33	68	24	67	28	178	55
(percentage of products in line 1)	(30)	(29)	(31)	(27)	(41)	(12)	(28)	(28)	(33)	(43)	(20)	(39)	(34)	(65)	(75)	(31)	(36)	(33)	(29)
3. BTN 25-99	25 492	20 311	5 181	8 627	1 566	3 843	756	2 959	866	4 142	1 736	189	6	35	8	150	50	366	134
(percentage of products in line 1)	(70)	(71)	(69)	(73)	(59)	(88)	(72)	(72)	(67)	(57)	(80)	(61)	(66)	(35)	(25)	(69)	(64)	(67)	(71)
Semi-manufactured and manufactured products																			
4. BTN 1-99	10 979	6 698	4 281	1 980	1 336	737	262	1 163	800	2 487	1 677	51	47	19	11	57	37	204	111
(percentage of products in line 1)	(30)	(23)	(57)	(17)	(50)	(17)	(25)	(28)	(62)	(34)	(77)	(16)	(48)	(18)	(34)	(26)	(47)	(38)	(59)
5. BTN 1-24[d]	1 162	466	696	49	418	24	37	150	107	229	108	3	5	1	3	1	4	9	14
(percentage of products in line 2)	(11)	(2)	(29)	(2)	(39)	(5)	(12)	(13)	(26)	(7)	(25)	(2)	(15)	(1)	(13)	(1)	(14)	(5)	(25)
6. BTN 25-99[e]	9 784	6 199	3 585	1 931	918	680	225	1 013	693	2 258	1 569	48	42	18	8	56	33	195	97
(percentage of products in line 3)	(38)	(31)	(69)	(22)	(59)	(18)	(30)	(34)	(80)	(55)	(90)	(25)	(65)	(51)	(100)	(37)	(66)	(53)	(72)

[a] The EEC countries, Japan, Denmark, Finland, Norway, Sweden, the United Kingdom and the United States.

[b] The 96 members of the Group of 77 are listed in annex II below.

[c] Countries claiming beneficiary status who are not members of the Group of 77 (see annex I).

[d] Processed and semi-processed agricultural products.

[e] Manufactured and semi-manufactured products.

and semi-manufactured products listed in BTN chapters 25-99. Table A presents the 1968 trade flows of all products together and of those involving manufacturing activity separately, with respect to BTN chapters 1-99, 1-24 and 25-99. These data cover the imports of selected developed market-economy countries from developing countries which are members of the Group of 77 (annex II below) and from developing countries and territories claiming beneficiary status (annex I) which are not members of the Group of 77. The selected developed market-economy countries are those preference-giving countries which have implemented their respective schemes, together with the United States of America. Of the combined imports of the developed market-economy countries from other countries and territories claiming beneficiary status ($36.3 billion), only 27 per cent ($9.8 billion) are manufactured and semi-manufactured products included in BTN chapters 25-99. Of the imports from the Group of 77, countries generally recognized as beneficiaries under all schemes, only 22 per cent manufactured and semi-manufactured products included in BTN chapters 25-99. Thus, only about a quarter of developing countries' exports comprise manufactured and semi-manufactured products which are, with notable exceptions, covered by the schemes. In view of the small share of the products listed in BTN chapters 25-99 in the exports of these countries, their immediate benefits from the GSP would be substantially increased if the product coverage under BTN chapters 1-24 were broadened.

B. Individual schemes under the GSP

40. The discussion of the individual schemes is based upon the country tables B-1 to B-8 below. A separate table for each preference-giving country shows the imports from all beneficiaries, including the least developed. Imports from the imports from all beneficiaries, including the least developed. Imports from the beneficiaries are also broken down into imports from beneficiaries in Africa, in Asia and in Latin America. Imports from the 25 beneficiaries identified as being in the category of the least developed among the developing countries are also presented separately. Imports from the countries claiming beneficiary status but not recognized as beneficiaries under each scheme are indicated. The trade flows of those beneficiary countries which have special arrangements with the United Kingdom, under Commonwealth Preferences, or with EEC, under an association agreement, are shown separately and not under the general beneficiaries heading in the tables relating to the schemes of the United Kingdom and EEC (tables B-7 and B-1). It is recognized that these countries have the full legal status of beneficiaries; however, their trade flows will not be affected by these schemes in the same way as the trade flows of the other beneficiaries.

41. The trade flows from each category of developing country to the preference-giving country are presented for three product aggregations: BTN chapters 1-99, 1-24 and 25-99. For products in BTN chapters 1-99 the trade flows are broken down according to customs treatment as follows: total imports, dutiable imports, imports of products included in the scheme and the shares of total imports admitted duty-free under m.f.n. treatment and under GSP treatment. In addition, tariff revenues collected on products included in the scheme are shown. For the two product categories BTN chapters 1-24 and 25-99, trade flow data are presented for total imports, dutiable imports, imports of products included in the scheme and imports of dutiable products excluded from the scheme.

42. There was only one significant problem in aggregating these figures. Under some of the schemes a number of products defined at the tariff line level were partly included in and partly excluded from the scheme. Consequently, the trade flows for these "ex" items could not be measured accurately. Instead or arbitrarily designating a certain share to be included in the scheme, it was decided to present two figures for imports included in the scheme; namely, an over-estimate (max.) which includes all of these "ex" items under the scheme and an under-estimate (min.) which excludes all of these "ex" items from the scheme. The true value of trade under the scheme will lie somewhere in between these two estimates.

43. The information used in compiling these tables was derived from computer tapes covering 1967 imports by the preference-giving countries concerned (1968 imports in the case of Denmark) broken down by source and by narrowly-defined product groups. These tapes, prepared by the GATT secretariat, were made available to the UNCTAD secretariat under permission granted by the preference-giving countries. The tariff rates in the tape data are post-Kennedy Round rates expressed in *ad valorem* equivalents.

1. The scheme of EEC

44. Data relating to the EEC scheme are presented in table B-1. In 1967, EEC imports from countries and territories recognized as beneficiaries amounted to $9.5 billion, 72 per cent of which was admitted duty-free under m.f.n. treatment.[32] Of the $2,703 million of dutiable imports from all beneficiary countries, 18 per cent ($475 million) is covered by the scheme and 82 per cent is excluded from it. For those countries identified as least developed among the developing countries, 9 per cent ($7 million) of their dutiable trade with EEC is covered by the scheme. EEC imports from countries claiming beneficiary status but not recognized as beneficiaries and not having other special arrangements with EEC amounted to $774 million, of which 44 per cent is dutiable. The imports of products covered by the scheme account for 27 per cent ($90 million) of EEC's dutiable imports from these non-beneficiaries.

45. The table below shows EEC imports from the beneficiaries of products in BTN chapters 25-99 which are covered by the EEC scheme, broken down into four groups and two designations (sensitive and non-sensitive), as provided for in the EEC scheme. However, not all imports of these products from the beneficiaries receive

---

[32] Those beneficiairies already benefiting from various preferential tariff régimes granted by the Community are excluded from these figures. These countries are legal beneficiairies and may be granted preferential treatment under the EEC scheme whenever such treatment is more favourable than treatment under other régimes.

preferential treatment for with respect to two product groups, "cotton textiles covered by LTA" and "other textiles and footwear", preferences are not granted to all beneficiaries. Trade excluded from preferential treatment for this reason is shown in the table in parentheses. For example, EEC imported $27 million worth of "cotton textiles covered by LTA", designated as "sensitive", from all beneficiaries. However, only those beneficiaries which are signatories to the LTA enjoy preferential status. Consequently, part of this $27 million worth of imports is not granted preferential treatment, i.e., those imports originating in beneficiary countries which are not signatories to the LTA. The imports not enjoying preferential treatment are shown in parentheses ($19.5 million in the above example). For "iron and steel covered by Treaty of Paris (ECSC)" and "other products in BTN chapters 25-99", all beneficiary countries enjoy preferential treatment and, consequently, no figures appear in parentheses for these product groups.

EEC imports from beneficiaries[a]
(Million dollars)

Product groups (for defining beneficiary countries)	Total	Imports by product designations[b]	
		Sensitive	Non-sensitive
Cotton textiles covered by LTA	123.3	27.0	96.3
	(112.3)	(19.5)	(92.8)
Other textiles and footwear	124.6	113.1	11.5
	(34.1)	(28.8)	(5.3)
Iron and steel products covered by Treaty of Paris (ECSC)[c]	7.4	5.5	1.9
Other products in BTN chapters 25-99	335.3	159.2	176.1
	590.6	304.8	285.8
	(146.4)	(48.3)	(98.1)

[a] The figures in parentheses indicate the value of EEC imports from recognized beneficiary countries and territories whose trade is excluded from preferential treatment under either one or two of the product groups for defining the beneficiary countries under the scheme.

[b] The product designations refer to products covered by the scheme and designated as sensitive or non-sensitive.

[c] Treaty of Paris of 18 April 1951 instituting the European Coal and Steel Community (United Nations, *Treaty Series*, vol. 261 (1957), No. 3729).

46. EEC's imports of dutiable products in BTN chapters 25-99 from the beneficiaries amount to $668 million. Of this, 88 per cent ($591 million) is covered by the scheme. Of the trade covered, 25 per cent ($146 million) is excluded from preferential treatment because of this narrower listing of beneficiaries. The products designated as sensitive and subject to a rigid limitation of preferential imports under the system of tariff quotas account for 58 per cent ($305 − $48 = $257 million) of the total dutiable imports in BTN chapters 25-99. The non-sensitive products, subject to less rigid control under the system of ceilings, account for the remaining 42 per cent of total dutiable imports.

47. A factor which complicates any analysis of the EEC scheme is the fact that some beneficiaries already benefit

from various preferential tariff régimes granted by the Community which are generally more favourable than the preferences under the EEC scheme. Furthermore, trade with these beneficiaries is not considered as beneficiary trade in the administration of the ceilings. Consequently, the trade of those countries having special trade arrangements with EEC has been presented separately and is not included in the beneficiary columns. EEC's imports, dutiable under the m.f.n. treatment, from the associated States in Africa amounted to $550 million, 4 per cent ($21 million) of which is covered by the Community's offer. Ten per cent ($27 million) of the Community's imports from Morocco and Tunisia ($257 million), dutiable under the m.f.n. treatment, is covered by the scheme. The figures indicate that the EEC scheme covers a relatively small share of these developing countries' current exports to the Community. This is of direct relevance to the question of their sharing their special tariff advantages in the EEC market with other developing countries recognized as beneficiaries under the EEC scheme. In this connexion it is also relevant that these countries associated with EEC receive or will receive new preferential tariff advantages in the markets of other preference-giving countries.

2. THE SCHEME OF JAPAN

48. Data relating to the scheme of Japan are presented in table B-2. In 1967 that country's imports from the beneficiaries amounted to $4,400 million, 43 per cent of which was admitted duty-free under m.f.n. treatment. Of the $2,500 million worth of dutiable imports from all beneficiary countries, 18 per cent ($450 million) is covered by the scheme and 82 per cent is excluded. Eighty-three per cent ($10 million) of Japan's dutiable imports from countries identified as least developed among the developing countries is covered by the Japanese scheme. Japan's imports from countries claiming beneficiary status but not recognized as beneficiaries under the Japanese scheme amounted to $377 million, of which 72 per cent is dutiable. The imports of products covered by the scheme account for 24 per cent ($64 million) of Japan's dutiable imports from these non-beneficiaries.

49. A significant factor which might limit the benefits under the scheme of Japan is the safeguard mechanism embodied in the scheme. For products in BTN chapters 25-99, the major safeguard mechanism is provided through a system of ceilings. The system provides for preferential duties (zero-duty except in the case of 57 items for which the preferential rate granted in 50 per cent of most-favoured nation rates) on imports up to the ceiling, administered under a set of 214 quota groups. Japanese imports in excess of these ceilings face m.f.n. tariffs. The total permissible value of preferential imports under the 214 quota groups combined in $326 million for the initial period (1 August 1971 to 31 March 1972). On an annual basis, these ceilings provide for a yearly total of GSP preferential imports of $489 million. Comparing this maximum with Japan's actual 1967 imports of products covered by the scheme ($431 million) reveals that the system of ceilings provides for a maximum expansion of preferential imports by $59 million or 12 per cent of 1967

imports. This permissible expansion, over a four-year period, provides for a growth in Japanese imports from the beneficiaries of approximately 3 per cent a year from 1967 to 1971.[33] Any additional imports from the beneficiaries will enter under m.f.n. rather than GSP preferential treatment.

3. THE SCHEMES OF THE NORDIC COUNTRIES

50. Data relating to the schemes of the Nordic countries Denmark, Finland, Norway and Sweden, are presented in tables B-3, B-4, B-5 and B-6 respectively. In 1967 the imports of the Nordic countries from the beneficiaries amounted to $1,100 million, 75 per cent of which entered duty-free under m.f.n. treatment. Of the $291 million worth of dutiable imports, 13 per cent ($36.4 million) is covered by the schemes and 87 per cent is excluded. However, these averages conceal great variations among these countries, for the schemes of Denmark, Finland, Norway and Sweden cover 20, 5, 45 and 11 per cent respectively of those countries' total dutiable imports. For dutiable products in BTN chapters 25-99 the coverage amounts to 100, 63, 51 and 23 per cent respectively. Ten per cent ($0.6 million) of the Nordic countries dutiable imports from countries identified as least developed among the developing countries is covered by the Nordic countries' schemes. Imports into the Nordic countries from countries claiming beneficiary status but not recognized as beneficiaries under the schemes amounted to $253 million, of which 39 per cent is dutiable. The imports of products covered by the schemes account for 47 per cent ($46.5 million) of the Nordic countries' dutiable imports from these non-beneficiaries.

4. THE SCHEME OF THE UNITED KINGDOM

51. Data relating to the scheme of the United Kingdom are presented in table B-7. In 1967 the United Kingdom's imports from the beneficiaries, excluding those enjoying Commonwealth preferences, amounted to $2,100 million, 86 per cent of which was admitted duty-free under m.f.n. treatment. Of the $285 million worth of dutiable imports, 25 per cent ($70 million) is covered by the scheme and 75 per cent is excluded. Fifty-three per cent ($3.5 million) of the United Kingdom's dutiable imports from countries identified as least developed among the developing countries is covered by the United Kingdom's scheme. United Kingdom imports from countries claiming beneficiary status but not recognized as beneficiaries under the United Kingdom scheme amounted to $507, million of which 64 per cent is dutiable. The imports of products covered by the

scheme account for 31 per cent ($98 million) of the United Kingdom's dutiable imports from these non-beneficiaries.

52. A factor which complicates any analysis of the scheme of the United Kingdom is the existence of the Commonwealth preference system. United Kingdom imports from beneficiaries which receive Commonwealth preferences are presented separately, even though these countries are beneficiaries under the scheme. Since virtually every product is granted some preferential treatment under the Commonwealth system, all of the dutiable exports of these countries previously received preferential treatment (primarily duty-free entry) in the United Kingdom markets. This preferential treatment was relative both to other developing countries and to other industrial countries not receiving Commonwealth preferences. The United Kingdom scheme will affect these beneficiaries in two ways. First, for those products which are covered by the scheme (27 per cent of United Kingdom dutiable imports from the Commonwealth beneficiaries) they will share their Commonwealth preferences with the other beneficiaries under the scheme. On the other hand, there are products for which GSP treatment is duty-free while Commonwealth preferences are limited to a reduction of m.f.n. rates. For such products, exports from Commonwealth beneficiaries will receive preferential treatment relative to those from industrial Commonwealth countries which are not beneficiaries under the scheme. It should also be recognized that developing countries enjoying Commonwealth preferences stand to benefit from preferential tariff treatment in markets of the other preference-giving countries.

5. THE SCHEME ENVISAGED BY THE UNITED STATES OF AMERICA

53. Data relating to the scheme envisaged by the United States of America are presented in table B-8. Since at the time of preparation of this addendum the United States had not implemented a scheme, these calculations are for illustrative purposes only, as neither the product coverage of the scheme nor the beneficiaries could be known with certainty. In 1967, United States imports from the supposed beneficiaries amounted to $6,200 million, 47 per cent of which was admitted duty-free under m.f.n. treatment. Of the $3,323 million worth of dutiable imports, 25 per cent ($843 million) is covered by the scheme and 75 per cent is excluded. Twenty-four per cent ($11 million) of the United States' dutiable imports from countries identified as least developed among the developing countries, is covered by the United States scheme. United States imports from other countries claiming beneficiary status amounted to $1,560 million, of which 87 per cent is dutiable. The imports of products covered by the scheme account for 39 per cent ($531 million) of total United States dutiable imports from these countries.

---

[33] During the three-year period 1967 through 1969, Japanese imports from the developing countries increased from $782 million to $1,294 million, an annual growth rate of 28 per cent.

TABLE B-1. SCHEME OF EEC

EEC imports in 1967 from beneficiaries under the scheme and non-beneficiaries claiming beneficiary status

(Million dollars)

| Product groups | Total | Beneficiaries excluding those enjoying special régimes[a] | | | Including from least developed countries[b] | Beneficiaries enjoying special régimes | | Non-beneficiaries | |
		Africa	Asia and Europe	Latin America and other		with[g] assoc. status	with limited assoc status[i]	with limited[j] assoc. status	without assoc. status[c]
BTN 1-99									
Total imports	9 540.1	2 784.4	3 932.6	2 823.1	308.3	1 409.0	417.7	1 044.2	774.1
Dutiable imports . . .	2 702.7	379.4	845.7	1 477.6	81.5	550.4	257.1	783.6	336.8
Imports included in the scheme:									
Max.[d]	475.4	44.4	294.2	136.8	7.4	21.2	26.8	181.2	89.8
Min.[e]	440.7	37.4	276.9	126.3	5.2	16.5	17.0	165.9	78.6
Tariff revenues from imports:									
included in the scheme:									
Max.[d]	45.7	4.1	32.1	9.5	0.9	1.8	3.7	16.3	8.4
Min.[e]	40.5	2.9	29.6	8.0	0.8	1.3	1.6	14.0	6.3
Share of total imports admitted duty-free:									
under GSP[f] . . .	5 per cent	2 per cent	7 per cent	5 per cent	2 per cent	1 per cent	5 per cent	17 per cent	11 percent
under m.f.n. . . .	72 per cent	86 per cent	78 per cent	48 per cent	74 per cent	61 per cent	38 per cent	25 per cent	56 per cent
BTN 1-24									
Total imports	2 737.5	648.9	565.4	1 523.2	161.5	623.9	238.6	589.0	273.2
Dutiable imports . . .	2 034.8	328.7	400.0	1 306.1	71.8	504.5	228.3	569.0	239.1
Imports included in the scheme:									
Max.[d]	31.4	7.5	12.5	11.4	2.3	5.1	10.5	15.2	11.0
Min.[e]	4.1	0.6	2.3	1.3	0.2	0.6	0.9	5.6	1.3
Dutiable imports excluded from the scheme:									
Min.[d]	2 003.5	321.1	387.6	1 294.8	69.5	499.4	217.8	553.8	228.1
Max.[e]	2 030.7	328.1	397.8	1 304.8	71.6	503.9	227.4	563.4	237.8
BTN 25-99									
Total imports	6 802.7	2 135.5	3 367.2	1 299.9	146.8	785.1	179.1	455.2	501.0
Dutiable imports . . .	667.9	50.7	445.7	171.5	9.7	45.9	28.8	214.6	97.7
Imports included in the scheme:									
Max.[d]	444.0	36.9	281.7	125.4	5.1	16.1	16.2	166.0	78.9
Min.[e]	436.6	36.9	274.7	125.0	5.0	15.9	16.1	160.3	77.4
Dutiable imports excluded from scheme:									
Min.[d]	223.9	13.8	164.0	46.1	4.6	29.8	12.6	48.7	18.8
Max.[e]	231.4	13.9	171.0	46.5	4.7	30.0	12.8	54.3	20.3

NOTE. For the footnotes to tables B-1 to B-8 see page 138.

TABLE B-2. SCHEME OF JAPAN

Japan's imports in 1967 from beneficiaries under the scheme and non-beneficiaries claiming beneficiary status
(Million dollars)

| Product groups | Total | Beneficiaries[a] | | | Including from least developed countries[b] | Non-beneficiaries claiming beneficiary status[c] |
		Africa	Asia and Europe	Latin America and other		
BTN 1-99						
Total imports	4 398.6	323.8	3 240.1	834.7	57.8	377.5
Dutiable imports under m.f.n.	2 500.2	185.5	2 098.7	216.0	12.0	270.8
Imports included in the scheme:						
Max.[d]	463.4	177.2	211.3	74.9	10.0	64.4
Min.[e]	442.6	177.0	190.8	74.8	10.0	63.3
Tariff revenues from imports included in the scheme:						
Max.[d]	32.2	11.7	15.7	4.8	0.7	4.7
Min.[e]	28.7	11.6	12.3	4.8	0.7	4.5
Share of total importants admitted duty free:						
under GSP[f]	9 per cent	54 per cent	5 per cent	8 per cent	17 per cent	11 per cent
under m.f.n.	43 per cent	43 per cent	35 per cent	74 per cent	79 per cent	28 per cent
BTN 1-24						
Total imports	682.1	59.4	388.5	180.2	16.2	116.3
Dutiable imports under m.f.n.	387.1	13.6	264.6	108.9	2.5	96.7
Imports included in the scheme:						
Max.[d]	32.9	7.3	23.7	1.9	0.5	1.8
Min.[e]	12.0	7.1	3.2	1.7	0.5	0.6
Dutiable imports excluded from the scheme:						
Min.[d]	354.2	6.3	240.9	107.0	2.0	94.9
Max.[e]	375.1	6.5	261.4	107.2	2.0	96.1
BTN 25-99						
Total imports	3 770.5	264.4	2 851.6	654.5	41.7	261.2
Dutiable imports under m.f.n.	2 113.2	172.0	1 834.1	107.1	9.6	174.1
Imports included in the scheme:						
Max.[d]	430.6	169.9	187.6	73.1	9.5	62.6
Min.[e]	430.6	169.9	187.6	73.1	9.5	62.6
Dutiable imports excluded from the scheme:						
Min.[d]	1 682.6	2.1	1 646.5	34.0	0.1	111.5
Max.[e]	1 682.6	2.1	1 646.5	34.0	0.1	111.4

NOTE. For the footnotes to tables B-1 to B-8 see page 138.

TABLE B-3. SCHEME OF DENMARK

Denmark's imports in 1968 from beneficiaries under the scheme and non-beneficiaries claiming beneficiary status
(Million dollars)

Product groups	Total	Beneficiaries[a]			Including from least developed countries[b]	Non-beneficiaries claiming beneficiary status[c]
		Africa	Asia and Europe	Latin America and other		
BTN 1-99						
Total imports	297.3	65.1	131.1	101.0	6.9	92.2
Dutiable imports under m.f.n.	58.7	2.2	15.8	40.6	0.9	24.5
Imports included in the scheme:						
Max.[d]	12.0	1.5	9.5	1.0	0.2	17.3
Min.[e]	11.6	1.4	9.2	0.9	0.2	16.4
Tariff revenues from imports included in the scheme:						
Max.[d]	1.6	0.1	1.4	0	0	2.7
Min.[e]	1.5	0.1	1.4	0	0	2.6
Share of total imports admitted duty free:						
Under GSP[f]	4 per cent	2 per cent	7 per cent	1 per cent	2 per cent	26 per cent
Under m.f.n.	80 per cent	97 per cent	88 per cent	60 per cent	87 per cent	73 per cent
BTN 1-24						
Total imports	121.8	20.0	28.5	73.2	5.6	34.7
Dutiable imports under m.f.n.	47.1	0.8	6.6	39.7	0.7	8.1
Imports included in the scheme:						
Max.[d]	0.4	0.1	0.3	0.1	0	0.8
Min.[e]	0	0	0	0	0	0
Dutiable imports excluded from the scheme:						
Min.[d]	46.7	0.7	6.3	39.6	0.7	7.3
Max.[e]	47.1	0.8	6.6	39.7	0.7	8.1
BTN 25-99						
Total imports	175.5	45.1	102.6	27.8	1.2	64.6
Dutiable imports under m.f.n.	11.6	1.4	9.2	0.9	0.2	16.4
Imports included in the scheme	11.6	1.4	9.2	0.9	0.2	16.4
Dutiable imports excluded from the scheme	0	0	0	0	0	0

NOTE. For the footnotes to tables B-1 to B-8 see page 138.

TABLE B-4. Scheme of Finland

Finland's imports in 1967 from beneficiaries under the scheme and non-beneficiaries claiming beneficiary status

(Million dollars)

Product groups	Total	Beneficiaries[a]			Including from least developed countries[b]	Non-beneficiaries claiming beneficiary status[c]
		Africa	Asia and Europe	Latin America and other		
BTN 1-99						
Total imports	122.9	17.3	38.9	66.7	3.4	30.8
Dutiable imports under m.f.n.	68.1	8.3	3.0	56.9	1.6	23.1
Imports included in the scheme	3.2	0.8	2.0	0.4	0.3	4.7
Tariff revenues from imports included in the scheme . .	0.3	0.1	0.2	0	0	0.4
Share of total imports admitted duty free:						
Under GSP[f]	3 per cent	5 per cent	5 per cent	1 per cent	9 per cent	15 per cent
Under m.f.n.	45 per cent	52 per cent	92 per cent	15 per cent	53 per cent	25 per cent
BTN 1-24						
Total imports	73.6	9.4	5.1	59.2	2.2	20.5
Dutiable imports under m.f.n.	65.5	7.4	1.4	56.7	1.5	17.2
Imports included in the scheme	1.6	0.7	0.6	0.2	0.2	3.1
Dutiable imports excluded from the scheme	63.9	6.7	0.8	56.5	1.3	14.1
BTN 25-99						
Total imports	49.2	7.9	33.8	7.52	1.2	10.4
Dutiable imports under m.f.n.	2.7	0.9	1.6	0.23	0.1	5.9
Imports included in the scheme	1.7	0.1	1.4	0.18	0.1	1.5
Dutiable imports excluded from the scheme	1.0	0.8	0.2	0.05	0	4.4

Note. For the footnotes to tables B-1 to B-8 see page 138.

TABLE B-5. Scheme of Norway

Norway's imports in 1967 from beneficiaries under the scheme and non-beneficiaries claiming beneficiary status

(Million dollars)

Product groups	Total	Beneficiaries[a]			Including from least developed countries[b]	Non-beneficiaries claiming beneficiary status[c]
		Africa	Asia and Europe	Latin America and other		
BTN 1-99						
Total imports	194.5	51.2	37.6	105.7	14.2	56.3
Dutiable imports under m.f.n.	10.0	3.1	3.3	3.6	0.1	28.0
Imports included in the scheme	4.5	2.3	2.0	0.3	0.1	14.0
Tariff revenues from imports included in the scheme . .	0.2	0	0.1	0.0	0.0	0.5
Share of total imports admitted duty free:						
under GSP[f]	2 per cent	4 per cent	5 per cent	0 per cent	1 per cent	25 per cent
under m.f.n.	95 per cent	94 per cent	91 per cent	97 per cent	99 per cent	50 per cent
BTN 1-24						
Total imports	67.3	10.7	7.6	49.0	1.9	26.1
Dutiable imports under m.f.n.	6.5	2.4	0.8	3.4	0	16.2
Imports included in the scheme	2.7	2.1	0.5	0.1	0	10.6
Dutiable imports excluded from the scheme	3.8	0.3	0.3	3.3	0	5.6
BTN 25-99						
Total imports	127.2	40.6	29.9	56.7	12.3	30.2
Dutiable imports under m.f.n.	3.5	0.7	2.5	0.2	0.1	11.8
Imports included in the scheme	1.8	0.1	1.5	0.2	0.1	3.4
Dutiable imports excluded from the scheme	1.7	0.6	1.0	0	0	8.4

Note. For the footnotes to tables B-1 to B-8 see page 138.

TABLE B-6. SCHEME OF SWEDEN

Sweden's imports in 1967 from beneficiaries under the scheme and non-beneficiaries claiming beneficiary status
(Million dollars)

Product groups	Total	Beneficiaries[a]			Including from least developed countries[b]	Non-beneficiaries claiming beneficiary status[c]
		Africa	Asia and Europe	Latin America and other		
BTN 1-99						
Total imports	528.8	80.7	209.4	283.7	7.0	73.4
Dutiable imports under m.f.n.	154.1	10.8	59.4	83.9	3.6	22.7
Imports included in the scheme:						
Max.[d]	17.1	0.5	14.2	2.4	0	11.1
Min.[e]	16.7	0.5	14.0	2.2	0	10.7
Tariff revenues from imports included in the scheme:						
Max.[d]	1.1	0	1.0	0.1	0	0.7
Min.[e]	1.1	0	1.0	0.1	0	0.6
Share of total imports admitted duty free						
under GSP[f]	3 per cent	0 per cent	6 per cent	1 per cent	0 per cent	15 per cent
under m.f.n.	71 per cent	87 per cent	72 per cent	70 per cent	49 per cent	69 per cent
BTN 1-24						
Total imports	182.9	21.6	38.3	123.0	5.6	39.3
Dutiable imports under m.f.n.	96.8	9.7	4.4	82.7	3.6	9.0
Imports included in the scheme:						
Max.[d]	3.6	0.2	2.2	1.2	0	1.7
Min.[e]	3.3	0.2	2.1	1.0	0	1.3
Dutiable imports excluded from the scheme:						
Min.[d]	93.2	9.5	2.2	81.5	3.6	7.3
Max.[e]	93.5	9.5	2.3	81.7	3.6	7.7
BTN 25-99						
Total imports	345.9	59.1	171.1	115.7	1.4	34.1
Dutiable imports under m.f.n.	57.3	1.1	55.0	1.3	0	13.7
Imports included in the scheme	13.4	0.3	11.9	1.2	0	9.4
Dutiable imports excluded from the scheme	43.9	0.8	43.1	0.1	0	4.3

NOTE. For the footnotes to tables B-1 to B-8 see page 138.

TABLE B-7. SCHEME OF THE UNITED KINGDOM

The United Kingdom's imports in 1967 from beneficiaries under the scheme and non-beneficiaries claiming beneficiary status

(Million dollars)

Product groups	Total	Beneficiaries[a]			Including, from least developed countries[b]	Common-wealth[h]	Non-beneficia-ries claiming beneficiary status[c]
		Africa	Asia and Europe	Latin America and other			
BTN 1-99							
Total imports	2 068.6	394.7	929.9	744.0	35.7	2 121.7	507.4
Dutiable imports under m.f.n.	285.1	36.9	72.0	176.2	6.6	1 051.9	322.6
Imports included in the scheme:							
Max.[d]	71.7	12.5	37.8	21.4	3.5	322.0	103.5
Min.[e]	68.2	11.8	36.3	20.1	3.5	247.3	93.3
Tariff revenues from imports included in the scheme:							
Max.[d]	6.1	0.9	3.1	2.1	0.2	36.5	7.5
Min.[e]	5.7	0.8	2.9	2.0	0.2	28.1	6.8
Share of total imports admitted duty free							
under GSP[f]	3 per cent	3 per cent	4 per cent	3 per cent	9 per cent	14 per cent	17 per cent
under m.f.n.	86 per cent	91 per cent	92 per cent	76 per cent	82 per cent	50 per cent	36 per cent
BTN 1-24							
Total imports	323.3	49.7	40.7	232.9	8.7	975.7	315.1
Dutiable imports under m.f.n.	217.3	26.2	31.5	159.6	3.5	614.0	230.1
Imports included in the scheme:							
Max.[d]	13.0	2.9	3.0	7.1	0.4	92.2	30.6
Min.[e]	9.4	2.2	1.4	5.8	0.4	18.5	20.5
Dutiable imports excluded from the scheme:							
Min.[d]	204.3	23.3	28.5	152.5	3.1	521.8	184.5
Max.[e]	207.9	24.0	30.1	153.8	3.1	595.5	209.6
BTN 25-99							
Total imports	1 745.2	345.0	889.2	511.0	27.0	1 146.0	192.3
Dutiable imports under m.f.n.	67.8	10.7	40.5	16.6	3.1	437.9	92.5
Imports included in the scheme:							
Max.[d]	58.8	9.6	34.9	14.3	3.1	229.8	72.9
Min.[e]	58.8	9.6	34.9	14.3	3.1	228.8	72.8
Dutiable imports excluded from the scheme:							
Min.[d]	9.0	1.1	5.6	2.3	0	208.1	19.6
Max.[e]	9.0	1.1	5.6	2.3	0	208.1	19.7

NOTE. For the footnotes to tables B-1 to B-8 see page 138.

TABLE B-8. THE SCHEME ENVISAGED BY THE UNITED STATES OF AMERICA

United States imports in 1967 from beneficiaries under the scheme and non-beneficiaries claiming beneficiary status
(Million dollars)

Product groups	Total	Beneficiaries[a]			Including from least developed countries[b]	Non-beneficiaries claiming beneficiary status[c]
		Africa	Asia and Europe	Latin America and other		
BTN 1-99						
Total imports	6 223.7	577.5	1 546.9	4 099.3	214.0	1 559.6
Dutiable imports under m.f.n.	3 323.3	156.7	764.9	2 401.7	46.1	1 353.8
Imports included in the scheme	842.6	74.7	243.1	524.8	10.9	531.0
Tariff revenues from imports included in the scheme . .	52.6	2.8	26.2	23.6	0.5	56.0
Share of total imports admitted duty free						
under GSP[f]	13 per cent	13 per cent	15 per cent	13 per cent	6 per cent	34 per cent
under m.f.n.	47 per cent	73 per cent	51 per cent	41 per cent	78 per cent	13 per cent
BTN 1-24						
Total imports	2 666.1	324.3	446.7	1 895.1	152.0	331.6
Dutiable imports under m.f.n.	978.7	25.1	238.3	715.3	10.7	230.6
Imports included in the scheme	103.5	9.9	23.7	69.9	1.5	14.5
Dutiable imports excluded from the scheme	875.2	15.2	214.6	645.4	9.2	216.1
BTN 25-99						
Total imports	3 557.6	253.2	1 100.2	2 204.2	62.1	1 228.0
Dutiable imports under m.f.n.	2 344.5	131.6	526.4	1 686.5	35.5	1 123.2
Imports included in the scheme	739.1	64.8	219.4	454.9	9.4	516.4
Dutiable imports excluded from the scheme	1 605.4	66.8	307.0	1 231.6	26.1	606.8

FOOTNOTES TO TABLES B-1 TO B-8

[a] Beneficiaries:

Of the United States of America: the 96 countries which are members of the Group of 77, except Bahrain, Bhutan, Cuba, Fiji and Qatar. This definition of beneficiaries is for computation purposes only and is not intended to indicate which countries are to be designated as beneficiaries under the official scheme of the United States of America.

Of Norway: the 96 countries which are members of the Group of 77, except Bahrain, Bhutan, Cuba, Fiji, and Qatar.

Of the United Kingdom: the 96 countries which are members of the Group of 77 except Bhutan and Cuba, plus Malta, Nauru, Tonga, United Arab Emirates, Western Samoa and territories for whose external relations another country is responsible excluding beneficiaries receiving Commonwealth preferences.

Of Sweden: the 96 countries which are members of the Group of 77, plus the Democratic People's Republic of Korea, the Democratic Republic of Viet-Nam, Israel, Mongolia, Western Samoa and territories for whose external relations another country is responsible, excluding Angola, Cape Verde Islands, Macao, Mozambique, Portuguese Guinea, Portuguese Timor, São Tomé and Principe, Gibraltar and Spanish North Africa.

Of Denmark: the 96 countries which are members of the Group of 77, except Bahrain, Bhutan, Cuba, Fiji and Qatar.

Of Japan: the 96 countries which are members of the Group of 77, except Bahrain, Bhutan, Botswana, Jamaica, Lesotho, Qatar and Swaziland, plus Greece, Israel, Malta, Spain, Taiwan, Turkey and Western Samoa.

Of Finland: the 96 countries which are members of the Group of 77, except the Republic of Korea and the Republic of Viet-Nam.

Of the EEC countries: The beneficiaries differ with the various product group definitions under the EEC Council Regulations authorizing the scheme of EEC. The beneficiaries and corresponding product groups are as follows:

Cotton textiles covered by the LTA and substitutes: Colombia, Egypt, India, Jamaica, Republic of Korea, Mexico and Pakistan.

Other textiles and footwear: the 96 countries which are members of the Group of 77, except Bhutan, Cuba and Fiji.

All products covered by the scheme in BTN chapters 1-24, iron and steel products covered by the Treaty of Paris (ECSC) and all other manufactured and semi-manufactured products in BTN chapters 25-99: the 96 countries which are members of the Group of 77 except Bhutan, Cuba and Fiji, plus United Arab Emirates, plus territories for whose external relations another country is responsible excluding beneficiaries from various preferential tariff régimes granted by EEC.

The 25 "hard core" countries which the Committee for Development Planning at its seventh session suggested (See *Official Records of the Economic and Social Council, Fifty-first Session, Supplement No. 7* (E/4990), para. 66.) should be classified among the least developed among the developing countries, namely: Botswana, Burundi, Chad, Dahomey, Ethiopia, Guinea, Lesotho, Mali, Malawi, Niger, Rwanda, Somalia, Sudan, Uganda, United Republic of Tanzania, Upper Volta, Afghanistan, Bhutan, Laos, Maldives, Nepal, Sikkim, Western Samoa, Yemen, and Haiti. In some cases the trade breakdown presented on the data tapes prevented the inclusion of all 25 of these "hard core" least developed countries.

[c] Non-beneficiaries claiming beneficiary status: the 96 countries which are members of the Group of 77, plus Bulgaria, Greece, Israel, Malta, Romania, Spain, Taiwan, Turkey, and the United Arab Emirates, plus territories for whose external relations another country is responsible which are not beneficiaries.

[d] Including "ex" items under the scheme (see paragraph 42).

[e] Excluding "ex" items from the scheme (see paragraph 42).

[f] Note that not all items under the schemes are granted duty-free treatment. The percentages are based upon the average of the "max." and "min". imports included in the scheme.

[g] Signatories of the Yaoundé Convention (Convention of Association between the European Economic Community and the African and Malagasy States associated with that Community, signed on 20 July 1963) and the Arusha Agreement (Arusha Association Agreement signed on 26 July 1968 between EEC and three East African States).

[h] Commonwealth Preference Area countries and territories, less Australia, Canada, New Zealand, Southern Rhodesia and South Africa. These are recognized as beneficiaries under the scheme of the United Kingdom.

[i] Morocco and Tunisia.

[j] Greece, Israel, Malta, Spain and Turkey.

ANNEXES

ANNEX I

Countries and territories claiming beneficiary status[a] under the GSP

The countries and territories claiming beneficiary status under the GSP comprise the following:

1. The 96 members of the Group of 77 listed in annex II;

2. Bulgaria, Greece, Israel, Malta, Romania, Spain, Taiwan, Turkey and the United Arab Emirates;

3. Territories for whose external relations another country is responsible (annex III).

---

[a] See *Official Records of the Trade and Development Board, Tenth Session, Supplement No. 6A* (TD/B/329/Rev.1), part two, paras. 242-252.

ANNEX II

List of the 96 members of the Group of 77

The Kingdom of Afghanistan
The Democratic and Popular Republic of Algeria
The Argentine Republic
The State of Bahrain[a]
Barbados
The Kingdom of Bhutan[a]
The Republic of Bolivia
The Republic of Botswana
The Federative Republic of Brazil
The Union of Burma
The Republic of Burundi
The Khmer Republic
The Federal Republic of Cameroon
The Central African Republic
Ceylon
The Republic of Chad
The Republic of Chile
The Republic of Colombia
The Republic of Costa Rica
The Republic of Cuba[a]
The Republic of Cyprus
The Republic of Dahomey
The Dominican Republic
The Republic of Ecuador
The Arab Republic of Egypt
The Republic of El Salvador
The Republic of Equatorial Guinea
The Empire of Ethiopia
Fiji[a]
The Gabonese Republic
The Republic of the Gambia
The Republic of Ghana
The Republic of Guatemala
The Republic of Guinea
The Republic of Guyana
The Republic of Haiti
The Republic of Honduras
The Republic of India
The Republic of Indonesia
The Empire of Iran
The Republic of Iraq
The Republic of the Ivory Coast
Jamaica
The Hashemite Kingdom of Jordan
The Republic of Kenya
The State of Kuwait
The Kingdom of Laos
The Lebanese Republic
The Kingdom of Lesotho
The Republic of Liberia
The Libyan Arab Republic
The Malagasy Republic
The Republic of Malawi
Malaysia
The Republic of Maldives
The Republic of Mali
The Islamic Republic of Mauritania
Mauritius
The United Mexican States
The Kingdom of Morocco
The Kingdom of Nepal
The Republic of Nicaragua
The Republic of the Niger
The Federal Republic of Nigeria
Pakistan
The Republic of Panama
The Republic of Paraguay
The People's Republic of the Congo
The Republic of Peru
The Republic of the Philippines
The State of Qatar[a]
The Republic of Korea
The Republic of Viet-Nam
The Rwandese Republic
The Kingdom of Saudi Arabia
The Republic of Senegal
Sierra Leone
The Republic of Singapore
The Somali Democratic Republic
The People's Democratic Republic of Yemen
The Democratic Republic of the Sudan
The Kingdom of Swaziland
The Syrian Arab Republic
The Kingdom of Thailand
The Togolese Republic
Trinidad and Tobago
The Republic of Tunisia
The Republic of Uganda
The United Republic of Tanzania
The Republic of the Upper Volta
The Eastern Republic of Uruguay
The Republic of Venezuela
The Yemen Arab Republic
The Socialist Federal Republic of Yugoslavia
The Republic of Zaire
The Republic of Zambia

---

[a] Joined the Group of 77, after the first schemes had been implemented, at the November 1971 meeting of the Group of 77 held in Lima, Peru.

Annex III

Territories for whose external relations another country is responsible

Afars and Issas (Territory of the)
Angola (including Cabinda)
Bahamas
Bermuda
British Honduras
British Indian Ocean Territory (Chagos Archipelago, Des Roches)
British Oceania (Territories under the jurisdiction of the Western Pacific High Commission, namely, Gilbert and Ellice Islands, British Solomon Islands, New Hebrides Condominium, Canton, Enderbury and Pitcairn Islands)
Brunei
Cape Verde Islands
Cayman Islands and dependencies
Comoro Islands
Cook Islands
Falkland Islands (Malvinas) and dependencies
French Polynesia
French Southern and Antarctic Territories
Gibraltar
Hong Kong
Macau
Mozambique
Netherlands Antilles

New Caledonia and dependencies
New Guinea (Australian) and Papua (see Papua)
Pacific Islands administered by the United States of America or under United States trusteeship. These include Guam, American Samoa including Swains Island, Midway Islands, Johnston and Sand Islands, Wake Islands and the Trust Territory of the Pacific Islands: the Caroline, Mariana and Marshall Islands
Papua—New Guinea
Portugese Guinea
Portugese Timor
St. Helena (including Ascension, Gough Island and Tristan da Cunha)
St. Pierre and Miquelon
São Tomé and Príncipe
Seychelles (including Amirantes)
Spanish Sahara (Rio de Oro, Saghiet-el-Hamra)
Surinam
Territories for which New Zealand is responsible (Niue Island, Tokelau Islands)
Turks and Caicos Islands
Virgin Islands of the United States (St. Croix, St. Thomas, St. John etc.)
Wallis and Futuna Islands
West Indies—Leeward Islands; Antigua, Montserrat, St. Kitts-Nevis-Anguilla, British Virgin Islands; Windward Islands: Dominica, Grenada, St. Lucia, St. Vincent

PROGRAMME FOR THE LIBERALIZATION OF QUANTITATIVE RESTRICTIONS AND OTHER NON-TARIFF BARRIERS IN DEVELOPED COUNTRIES ON PRODUCTS OF EXPORT INTEREST TO DEVELOPING COUNTRIES

Report by the UNCTAD secretariat*

[*Original text: English*]

CONTENTS

---

* The text of this report was circulated to the Conference as document TD/120/Supp.1, dated 31 January 1972, TD/120/Supp.1/Corr.1, dated 24 March 1972, and TD/120/Supp.1/Corr.2, dated 30 March 1972.

ANNEX

LIST OF TABLES

Introduction

1. The International Development Strategy for the Second United Nations Development Decade deals in paragraphs 33-35 with tariff and non-tariff barriers, as well as with adjustment assistance to facilitate the removal of these barriers.[1] Paragraph 33 provides that developed countries "will not, ordinarily, raise existing tariff or non-tariff barriers to exports from developing countries, nor establish new tariff or non-tariff barriers or any discriminatory measures, where such action has the effect of rendering less favourable the conditions of access to the markets of manufactured and semi-manufactured products of export interest to developing countries". Paragraph 34 states that "intergovernmental consultations will be continued and intensified with a view to giving effect early in the Decade to measures for the relaxation and progressive elimination of non-tariff barriers affecting trade in manufactures and semi-manufactures of interest to developing countries. Efforts will be made with a view to implementing such measures before 31 December 1972. These consultations will take into account all groups of processed and semi-processed products of export interest to developing countries."

2. UNCTAD has particular responsibilities in respect of non-tariff barriers affecting the trade of the developing countries, as was recognized in decisions 2 (III), 1 (IV)

---

[1] See also paragraphs 25 to 27 of the Strategy, as well as paragraph 4 of the statement by the representative of Belgium, on behalf of Group B, at the 74th meeting of the Committee on Manufactures. See *Official Records of the Trade and Development Board, Eleventh Session, Supplement No. 2* (TD/B/352), annex III, A.

and 1 (V)[2] of the Committee on Manufactures.[3] These decisions form the basis of a programme of work for UNCTAD in the field of non-tariff barriers, which provides for the identification, preferably on a product-by-product basis, of non-tariff barriers, including quantitative restrictions, of serious concern to developing countries as affecting their trade, and for the analysis of the effects of such barriers. As specified in decision 2 (III), the objective is to assist the Committee on Manufactures in identifying non-tariff barriers of concern to developing countries and in its consideration of recommendations aimed at the removal of such barriers.

3. In pursuance of Conference recommendation A.III.4 and of the decisions of the Committee on Manufactures, mentioned above, the UNCTAD secretariat prepared various studies concerning non-tariff barriers affecting products of particular export interest to the developing countries. However, while these studies were discussed in general terms at the second session of the Conference and at sessions of the Committee on Manufactures, they have not been considered in depth or followed up by any action in accordance with the suggestions contained in them.

4. In the context of the work programme of the Committee on Manufactures, the UNCTAD secretariat has since prepared a number of additional studies.[4] The present document contains only a summary of the facts and analyses presented in those studies. However, the full studies will be made available in due course to the Committee on Manufactures and to any subsidiary organ which may be established to deal with the question of non-tariff barriers.

5. The present document draws on the considerable volume of work concerning non-tariff barriers undertaken in UNCTAD since the first session of the Conference.[5]

It takes into account in particular the findings of the studies referred to above and also, as far as possible, the information available in GATT and other international organizations. Its main purpose is to facilitate consideration and adoption by the Conference of an action programme designed to reduce, and ultimately eliminate, quantitative restrictions and other non-tariff barriers on products of export interest to developing countries.

6. The report deals principally with the following subjects: (a) identification of non-tariff barriers of serious concern to developing countries on manufactures and semi-manufactures, including processed and semi-processed agricultural products, of particular interest to those countries; (b) possible approaches to a liberalization programme as regards standstill and measures for the reduction and removal, on a multilateral basis, of quantitative restrictions and other non-tariff barriers, including advance liberalization in favour of developing countries with respect to certain elements of the programme; (c) measures that could be taken in the context of the LTA; (d) special measures that might be taken in favour of the least developed among the developing countries; (e) the contribution of the socialist countries of Eastern Europe to the expansion of exports of manufactures and semi-manufactures from developing countries; and (f) the institutional framework within which the liberalization programme could be most effectively implemented.

7. The liberalization of international trade in cotton textiles is treated separately in this report in view of the special arrangements under which the trade is carried out. For the same reason, cotton textiles are not included either in the inventory mentioned in paragraph 9 below or in the statistical analysis of trade in products subject to quantitative and other non-tariff barriers. Products covered by the LTA, like other manufactured and semi-manufactured products of particular interest to developing countries, should nonetheless be considered as falling within the purview of the liberalization programme outlined in chapter IV below, which calls for the urgent removal of quantitative and related restrictions, taking into account the more long-run objectives of the Arrangement.

---

[2] See, respectively, *Official Records of the Trade and Development Board, Eighth Session, Supplement No. 2* (TD/B/199/Rev.1), annex I; *ibid., Tenth Session, Supplement No. 2* (TD/B/295), annex I, and *ibid., Eleventh Session, Supplement No. 2* (TD/B/352), annex I.

[3] In connexion with the adoption of decision 1 (IV) see the summary record of the 62nd meeting of the Committee on Manufactures (TD/B/C.2/SR.62) and in connexion with the adoption of decision I (V) see the statement made at the Committee's 74th meeting by the representative of the USSR on behalf of the socialist countries of Eastern Europe (*Official Records of the Trade and Development Board, Eleventh Session, Supplement No. 2* (TD/B/352), annex III, B).

[4] For a list of these studies, see document TD/120, paragraph 4.

[5] See in particular the following documents prepared for the second session of the Conference: "Programme for the liberalization of non-tariff barriers in developed countries on products of export interest to developing countries" (TD/20 and Supp.1) and "An

analysis of existing quantitative restrictions in selected developed countries on selected products of export interest to the developing countries" (TD/20/Supp.4 and Corr.1, covering restrictions in the Federal Republic of Germany, France, Japan and the United Kingdom). For TD/20/Supp.1 see *Proceedings of the United Nations Conference on Trade and Development, Second Session*, vol. III, *Problems and Policies of Trade in Manufactures and Semi-manufactures* (United Nations publication, Sales No. E.68.II.D.16).

CHAPTER I

Identification of non-tariff barriers

8. Detailed studies of quantitative restrictions and other non-tariff barriers applied by developed market-economy countries to manufactures and semi-manufactures, including processed and semi-processed agricultural products, were prepared by the UNCTAD secretariat for the second session of the Conference as well as for subsequent

sessions of the Committee on Manufactures.[6] These studies discussed quantitative restrictions through quotas and licensing, export restraints,[7] import embargoes or prohibitions, state-trading, domestic procurement, domestic-content regulations, variable levies and supplementary import charges, advance deposit requirements, anti-dumping duties, countervailing charges, credit restrictions, direct and indirect subsidization, quantitative marketing obstacles, packaging and labelling regulations, safety standards and health requirements, tax measures, customs practices (including clearance, valuation, classification and related practices), as well as various other policies, programmes and practices applied by developed market-economy countries that affect imports. In many cases, owing to lack of information, it was not possible to determine precisely how, and to what extent, these trade regulations effectively constituted a non-tariff barrier to imports from developing countries.

9. In pursuance of decision 1(V) of the Committee on Manufactures, the secretariat has prepared a detailed inventory of non-tariff barriers, including quantitative restrictions, that are likely to be of serious concern to developing countries. It is based on information supplied by developed and developing countries or available in other international organizations, including GATT.[8]

---

[6] The following reports have been prepared by the UNCTAD secretariat for various sessions of the Committee on Manufactures: "An analysis of existing quantitative restrictions in selected developed countries on products of export interest to the developing countries" (TD/B/C.2/52 and Corr.1 and Add.1, covering restrictions in Austria, Denmark, Italy, Norway, Sweden and Switzerland); "Summary of the non-tariff barriers applied in selected developed countries on manufactures and semi-manufactures of export interest to developing countries" (TD/B/C.2/65); "An analysis of existing quantitative and other import restrictions in selected developed market-economy countries on products of export interest to the developing countries" (TD/B/C.2/83 and Corr.1 and TD/B/C.2/83/Add.1 and Add.1/Corr.1). In addition, the UNCTAD secretariat has prepared the following reports: "An analysis of non-tariff barriers in selected developed market economy countries on products of export interest to the developing countries" (TD/B/C.2/R.1 and Add.1); "An analysis of the effects of non-tariff barriers in developed market economy countries on selected products or product groups of export interest to developing countries" (TD/B/C.2/R.2); and "Products or product groups of export interest to developing countries subject to non-tariff barriers in developed market economy countries" (TD/B/C.2/R.3 and Corr.1 and Add.1-4, containing a preliminary itemized list of products, the barriers to imports and the developing countries affected by the barriers). For documents prepared for the second session of the Conference see footnote 5 above.

[7] These were formerly referred to in UNCTAD documents as "voluntary export restraints". They are applied by developing countries with regard to exports to certain developed market-economy countries, at the insistence of those countries among the latter which wish to restrict imports from the developing countries in question.

[8] The inventory, which excludes cotton textiles covered by the LTA, will be submitted to the Committee on Manufactures at its sixth session. Products were selected on the basis of their importance in the trade of developing countries as a whole (a minimum of $1 million of imports in 1968). Products of known particular interest to the 25 "hard core" least developed among the developing countries are included also, even if imports fell below this minimum. A further condition for inclusion was that the restriction related to a specific product. Products subject to non-tariff barriers of a more general nature, or which do not necessarily aim at restricting imports, are not included in the inventory—for example, those which are subject to automatic and liberal licensing, state monopolies, govern-

A. Product coverage and non-tariff barriers applied to main product categories

10. Total imports in 1968 into developed market-economy countries as a whole, from developing countries, of manufactures and semi-manufactures, including processed agricultural products and cotton textiles covered by the Long-Term Arrangement, amounted to $10.4 billion, of which about $2.3 billion (approximately 20 per cent) were subject to quantitative and related restrictions. Cotton textiles under the LTA accounted for $0.6 billion of this latter total.[9]

11. The inventory referred to above (para. 9) lists about 130 products (at the five-digit, or sometimes only four-digit, level of SITC or the corresponding BTN tariff headings or sub-headings), 55 of which[10] are of export interest to the least developed among the developing countries.[11]

12. The 130 products included in the UNCTAD secretariat's inventory are subject to one or more of the following non-tariff barriers: discretionary and unspecified licensing, quotas (global or bilateral), state-trading practices (in combination with other import restrictions), variable levies, export restraints, prohibition of certain imports, export restraints and import restrictions of an unspecified character. Total imports from developing countries in 1968 of these 130 products, by those developed market-economy countries which in 1971 applied any of the above restrictions, amounted to $1.7 billion, or 28.5 per cent of their imports of these products from all

---

ment procurement, packaging and labelling regulations, anti-dumping practices, health and sanitary regulations and standards and safety regulations.

[9] These estimates are based on data for 1968 covering imports of products falling within the BTN tariff headings or sub-headings affected by the restrictions under consideration that are applied by 18 developed market-economy countries. However, in some cases, restrictions are applied only to certain positions within the headings or sub-headings, so that the volume of imports affected by the restrictions is overstated. Total imports in 1968 by these 18 developed market-economy countries from developing countries of the products covered by the inventory amounted to $4.4 billion, or approximately 16 per cent of their imports of these products from all sources. Of this amount, products in BTN chapters 1-24 accounted for $676 million, or 15 per cent, and those in chapters 25-99 for $3.7 billion, or about 16 per cent, of the developed market-economy countries' total imports of the products in question. These figures of actual trade, and those mentioned in succeeding paragraphs, do not indicate (nor are they intended to indicate) the importance of the effects on trade of quantitative and related restrictions on the products in question. Clearly, the severer the restriction in a given country, the greater will be the volume of imports kept out.

[10] See the list in the annex to this report.

[11] Twenty-five "hard core" (least developed) countries were identified by the Committee for Development Planning (see *Official Records of the Economic and Social Council, Fifty-first Session, Supplement No. 7* (E/4990), para. 66) and by the UNCTAD *Ad Hoc* Group of Experts on special measures in favour of the least developed among the developing countries in its report (United Nations publication, Sales No. E.71.II.D.11), para. 19. This list was approved by the Trade and Development Board (resolution 82 (XI)) and subsequently by the General Assembly (resolution 2768 (XXVI)). The countries so identified are: *Africa:* Botswana, Burundi, Chad, Dahomey, Ethiopia, Guinea, Lesotho, Malawi, Mali, Niger, Rwanda, Somalia, Sudan, Uganda, United Republic of Tanzania, Upper Volta; *Asia and Oceania:* Afghanistan, Bhutan, Laos, Maldives, Nepal, Sikkim, Western Samoa, Yemen; *Latin America:* Haiti.

sources. Of this amount, products in BTN chapters 1-24 accounted for $414 million and those in BTN chapters 25-99 for $1.3 billion—respectively 20.2 per cent and 32.7 per cent of total imports of these products from all sources. From the above data it is evident that, quite apart from cotton textiles under the LTA, a considerable volume of exports of manufactures and semi-manufactures from developing countries is subject to import restrictions which are of concern to those countries.

13. The following paragraphs summarize the position regarding the main categories of products in the inventory and the non-tariff barriers applied to them.

1. SEMI-PROCESSED AND PROCESSED AGRICULTURAL PRODUCTS FALLING WITHIN BTN CHAPTERS 1-24

14. This category covers about 40 products in the UNCTAD inventory. On the basis of trade statistics for 1968, product groups of particular interest to developing countries that are subject to restrictive measures include processed vegetables and fruits, beverages, spirits, meat products and cereal preparations, and for all but a few items there is more than one type of restriction, applied by more than one developed market-economy country.

15. Restrictions applied to semi-processed and processed agricultural products falling within BTN chapters 1-24 are more numerous than those applied to manufactured and semi-manufactured products falling within BTN chapters 25-99. In consequence, although processed agricultural products constitute only one third of the total number of products included in the inventory, they account for about 64 per cent of the total frequency of import restrictions on all products in the inventory.[12]

16. Among the restrictions applied, discretionary licensing is the measure most frequently found in almost all the developed market-economy countries, the next most frequent being that of import quotas, either global or bilateral, in some cases both types of quota being applied simultaneously, in particular to meat products, processed vegetables and fruits, and cereal products and preparations.

17. With one exception, variable levies are applied only to products within the category under consideration and they affect in particular meat products and cereal products and preparations. Likewise, quantitative restrictions of an unspecified character are applied solely to this category of products, sometimes in combination with state trading.

2. MANUFACTURED AND SEMI-MANUFACTURED PRODUCTS FALLING WITHIN BTN CHAPTERS 25-99

18. There are about 90 products in this category which are included in the UNCTAD inventory. The products most subject to import restrictions, excluding cotton textiles covered by the LTA, are other textile products, petroleum products, ferro-alloys and ceramic products, jute products, leather and leather goods and woollen goods. Petroleum products comprise the bulk of these imports (see table 2 on page 148).

19. Within this category of products the textile sector (among sectors separately distinguished) shows the greatest frequency of restrictions (see table 2). Most of the other products face restrictions in one or two countries only.

20. Discretionary licensing and import quotas are the restrictive measures most frequently applied. Export restraints are applied to this category of products, mainly in connexion with trade with Canada. Specific products affected by this type of restriction are jute goods and other textile products not covered by the LTA. Imports into one or more of the developed market-economy countries are prohibited in the case of four products: organic or inorganic compounds, sodium glutamate, pyrotechnic articles and wrought plates and sheets of zinc.

B. Developed market-economy countries which most frequently apply non-tariff barriers[13]

21. Among the 18 developed market-economy countries covered by the inventory,[14] France, the Federal Republic of Germany, Italy and Japan[15] appear to apply the largest number of restrictive measures on products of particular export interest to developing countries, followed by Denmark, Finland and the Benelux countries. Austria, Ireland, Norway, the United Kingdom, Sweden, the United States and Switzerland maintain relatively few restrictions. The countries which maintain the fewest restrictions of all are Australia and Canada (see table 3 on page 148).

1. EEC COUNTRIES[16]

22. In France restrictions are maintained on 88 of the products in the inventory, of which 36 are processed agricultural products, 14 textiles and 11 petroleum products, the remainder being apparatus and machines and miscellaneous products falling within the relevant BTN chapters. The restrictions applied to processed agricultural products range from discretionary licensing to restrictions of an unspecified nature and various other measures affecting imports. With regard to textile goods other than cotton, they consist mainly of discretionary licensing or import quotas. For petroleum products the main restric-

---

[12] Estimate derived from table 1 (339 out of a total of 531) (see page 147).

[13] This section refers throughout to the products included in the UNCTAD secretariat's inventory. Thus it does not cover non-tariff barriers on cotton textiles that are covered by the LTA.

[14] Australia, Austria, Canada, Denmark, the EEC countries, Finland, Ireland, Japan, Norway, Sweden, Switzerland, the United Kingdom and the United States.

[15] At the fifth session of the Committee on Manufactures the representative of Japan, referring to his country's efforts at liberalization, stated that by the end of September 1971 the number of quantitative restrictions in force would be one third that prevailing two years earlier (*Official Records of the Trade and Development Board, Eleventh Session, Supplement No. 2* (TD/B/352), para. 110).

[16] The following paragraphs relate to restrictions applied in accordance with national policies of the EEC countries. In connexion with the variable levies applied by EEC, the spokesman on behalf of the Community, at the fifth session of the Committee on Manufactures, disagreed with their classification as a non-tariff barrier. He added that they were an instrument of the Common Agricultural Policy and had permitted the abolition of traditional protective measures such as quantitative restrictions and tariffs (*ibid.*, para. 137).

tion is discretionary licensing, in conjunction with state trading. Among the products subject to restrictions about 20 are subject to a discriminatory country classification whereby the restrictions are not applicable to developed market-economy countries or to certain developing countries.[17]

23. In the Federal Republic of Germany non-tariff barriers are applied to 26 processed agricultural products in the inventory and to 14 manufactured products, of which nine are textile products.

24. Italy maintains restrictions on 28 processed agricultural and seven other manufactured products, half of the latter being textile products and the remainder ethyl acetate, essential oils and cinematographic film.

25. The Benelux countries maintain restrictions on 22 processed agricultural products, mainly through the application of variable levies. In addition, restrictions are applied to three products: woven fabrics of jute, basketwork and "other" wrought plates of zinc.

2. EFTA COUNTRIES

26. In Austria, restrictions on meat products and cereal flours, groats and starches account for more than half of the 18 restrictions applied to processed agricultural products included in the inventory. Imports of four other manufactured products are also restricted, only one of these being a textile.

27. Denmark maintains restrictions on 21 processed agricultural products, mainly cereal products and fruit and vegetable preparations. Five other manufactured goods are also subject to restrictions.[18]

28. There are 26 products involved in the case of restrictions in Finland, of which 22 are processed agricultural products (mainly processed meat, wheat products and vegetable and fruit preparations). The other four relate largely to petroleum products within BTN chapter 27.

29. Norway applies import restrictions to 20 processed agricultural products in the inventory, of which seven are prepared vegetables and fruits falling within BTN chapter 20.

30. In Sweden 17 processed agricultural products are subject to restrictions, 16 of them through variable levies and one through licensing in accordance with the International Sugar Agreement of 1968.

31. Switzerland applies import restrictions to 12 processed agricultural products, mainly cereal flour, groats, starches, preserved fish, sugar confectionery, meat preparations and beverages. Other manufactured products subject to restrictions are casein, fireworks, other cinematographic film and chemical products and preparations.

32. The United Kingdom maintains restrictions on 17 products in the inventory; 12 are processed meat and

agricultural products and the remainder are manufactured goods, three of which are textile products.

3. OTHER DEVELOPED MARKET-ECONOMY COUNTRIES

33. Australia maintains restrictions on four manufactured products in the inventory, two of which are textiles. It was announced that imports of aluminium ingots were to be liberalized on 31 December 1971.

34. Apart from three cereal products, Canada applies no restrictions to processed agricultural products of particular export interest to developing countries. On the other hand, eight other manufactured goods are subject to restrictions, of which one is casein and the others all textile products.

35. In Ireland 21 items in the inventory are subject to restrictions, of which 14 are processed agricultural products while the remainder include fertilizers, rubber tyres, certain textiles and footwear products.

36. The restrictions maintained by Japan since the liberalization measures of October 1971 (see footnote 15 above) are far fewer, affecting 34 products in the inventory. Thirteen are processed agricultural products; cereal products and food preparations are especially affected. Petroleum products, chemical products, leather goods and mechanical appliances are the main products in BTN chapters 25-99 still subject to restrictions.

37. The United States applies import restrictions to 15 products: petroleum products, wheat products, chocolate and other food preparations, and knives, spoons and forks. Half the restrictions are in the form of global quotas on petroleum products within BTN chapter 27.[19] These petroleum products account for about 98 per cent of total imports into the United States from developing countries of manufactures and semi-manufactures included in the inventory.

C. Forms and frequency of specific non-tariff barriers

38. The specific non-tariff barriers covered by the UNCTAD secretariat's inventory are discretionary licensing, global and bilateral quotas, variable levies, unspecified licensing, export restraints, prohibition of imports and similar quantitative import restrictions. Table 1 indicates the frequency of these restrictions with regard to the products in the inventory.[20]

39. The type of non-tariff barrier most frequently encountered is that of discretionary licensing, applied either alone or in conjunction with other restrictions. Quantitative restrictions in the form of global or bilateral

---

[17] Countries falling within Zone I according to the French country classification.

[18] In addition to these restrictions, Denmark has applied, since 21 October 1971, a 10 per cent temporary import surcharge which covers about 50 per cent of total imports (see paras. 109-110 below).

[19] In addition to these restrictions, the United States also applied, from 16 August to 20 December 1971, a 10 per cent temporary import surcharge on all dutiable imports, except imports of goods subject to quantitative restrictions pursuant to United States law or goods not the subject of a trade concession by the United States (see also paras. 104-108 below).

[20] The various restrictions relate to individual products at the level of five or four digits of the SITC and four digits of the BTN. A measure is regarded as restrictive, and counted as a unit in the calculation of frequencies, irrespective of whether it covers all or only part of the relevant SITC or BTN heading or sub-heading.

TABLE 1

Frequency of major categories of specific non-tariff barriers[a]

	BTN chapter			Percentage of total
	1-24	25-99	1-99	
	Frequency			Frequency
1. Discretionary licensing	99[b]	86[c]	185[d]	34.7
2. *Quotas*				
Global import quotas	35	31	66	12.4
Bilateral import quotas	21	35	56	10.8
Bilateral quotas within global import quotas .	10	1	11	2.1
Total	66	67	133	25.3
3. *Other non-tariff barriers*				
Variable levies	132	2	134	24.9
Unspecified licensing	11	—	11	2.1
Export restraints	—	11	11	2.1
Prohibitions	6	6	12	2.4
Unspecified types of restriction	16	—	16	3.0
Other measures	9	20	29	5.5
Total	174	39	213	40.0
TOTAL	339	192	531	100.0

NOTE. The table covers the restrictions listed that are applied in one or more of the developed market-economy countries to products in the UNCTAD secretariat's inventory. A given restriction is counted once for each country applying it to a particular product or product group (whether to all items or only some of the items therein). For example, a given restriction is counted six times whether it affects six different products in one country or a single product in six different countries.

a At the five- or four-digit level of SITC or at the level of BTN tariff headings or sub-headings.
b Including 30 found in conjunction with other restrictions.
c Including 40 found in conjunction with other restrictions.
d Including 70 found in conjunction with other restrictions.

import quotas are the type found second in order of frequency. In a few countries (and mainly for processed agricultural products) global and bilateral import quotas are applied simultaneously to the same product. Sometimes, global quotas are applied only to a particular group of exporting countries, while imports from other countries are free of quotas. The allocation of licences within quotas can be discretionary, adding to the element of discrimination and uncertainty.

40. Variable import levies are applied principally to processed agricultural products within BTN chapters 1-24 by the EEC countries, Austria, Finland, Sweden, Switzerland and the United Kingdom. They affect 27 products in the UNCTAD secretariat's inventory.

41. Export restraints are applied most frequently in connexion with textile products other than cotton, and relate mainly to trade with Canada and the EEC countries. Unspecified licensing is applied mainly to processed agricultural products, often in conjunction with other measures. Prohibition of certain imports is the form of restriction least often applied. It may be resorted to, for example, for reasons of public health or national security.

42. Relatively few products are subject to state trading in developed market-economy countries, and the extent to which it constitutes a non-tariff barrier depends on the particular policies and practices of the state-trading enterprises.

D. Restrictions affecting products covered by GSP

43. About half the processed agricultural products in the UNCTAD secretariat's inventory are partly or wholly included in one or more of the following schemes in connexion with the GSP: those of Austria, Denmark, Japan, Norway, the United Kingdom, and EEC.[21] The EEC accords preferences to 19 products or product groups, for only four of which is coverage complete. Norway accords preferences to certain items under six products or product groups and Japan to certain items under five products. The United Kingdom grants preferences to all items in two groups and to certain items in two other groups. Denmark accords preferences to all items in one group and to some items in two others.

44. Out of the 90 products within BTN chapters 25-99 that are included in the UNCTAD secretariat's inventory, five already enjoy m.f.n. duty-free treatment and 74 are included in the schemes or offers of one or more of the countries applying import restrictions, namely, Austria, the Benelux countries, Canada, Denmark, the Federal Republic of Germany, France, Italy, Japan, Switzerland, the United Kingdom and the United States. The EEC

---

21 Preferential treatment is accorded in some cases for the whole tariff heading or sub-heading while in others only to certain items thereof.

TABLE 2

Frequency of restrictions applied, according to product group

Product group	Imports in 1968 by developed market-economy countries maintaining restrictions in 1971	Frequency of restrictions[a]
	(Million dollars)	(Percentage)
BTN chapters 1-24		
Processed meat products .	114.6	21.4
Processed cereal products and preparations	16.4	24.6
Processed fruit products . .	118.7	22.5
Processed vegetable products and edible preparations .	61.5	12.5
Sugar, sugar derivatives and chocolates	4.4	7.9
Beverages and alcohols . .	96.0	7.9
Tobacco manufactures . .	2.1	1.8
Other products	0.3	1.4
TOTAL	414.0	100.0
BTN chapters 25-99		
Woollen products	1.5	4.0
Jute products	25.9	4.9
Other textile products . . .	62.3	17.7
Petroleum products	1 199.9	16.1
Ceramic products	0.1	4.2
Leather and leather goods .	7.4	1.5
Electrical and mechanical appliances	4.0	9.4
Other products[b]	25.0	42.2
TOTAL	1 326.1	100.0

[a] See note to table 1.
[b] Including products of chemical and allied industries; basketwork; paper articles; base metals and articles thereof; optical, photographic and measuring instruments, toys, etc.

TABLE 3

Frequency of import restrictions applied in individual developed market-economy countries to products of export interest to developing countries

Importing country	Number of products affected by the restrictions	Frequency of restrictions applied[a]
France	88	140
Federal Republic of Germany	40	54
Italy	35	38
Benelux countries	25	27
Denmark	26	29
Finland	26	33
Austria	22	37
Norway	20	26
United Kingdom	17	19
Sweden	17	17
Switzerland	13	24
Japan	34	34
Ireland	21	21
United States	15	17
Canada	11	11
Australia	4	4
TOTAL NUMBER OF PRODUCTS AFFECTED	130[b]	531

[a] See note to table 1.
[b] About 50 per cent of these products are affected by restrictions applied in more than one country (see note to table 1).

accords preferences to all dutiable manufactured and semi-manufactured products in BTN chapters 25-99.[22] How-

[22] For coir and jute products customs exemption is also envisaged under specific measures to be arranged with the exporting developing countries (see TD/B/AC.5/34/Add.1, annex 1, p. 3).

ever, the number of products included in the EEC preferential scheme that are also subject to import restrictions varies from one country to another: in France there are 43 such products, in the Federal Republic of Germany 12, in Italy six and in the Benelux countries three. Of the products covered by their respective schemes or offers, Japan applies import restrictions to 17, the United Kingdom to five, Denmark and the United States to three, and Canada and Switzerland to one.

CHAPTER II

Effects of quantitative restrictions and variable levies on selected product groups

45. Previous studies by the UNCTAD secretariat have shown that the most restrictive non-tariff barriers are quantitative import restrictions on the one hand and measures which raise the cost to importers on the other.[23] In addition, the uncertainties created by such measures tend to depress trade even beyond the direct effects of the measures themselves, and bear particularly heavily on suppliers in developing countries.

46. In pursuance of decision 1(V) of the Committee on Manufactures the secretariat has examined particular non-tariff barriers applied to a limited number of product groups not covered by its previous studies—woven cotton

[23] See in particular documents TD/B/C.2/R.1 and TD/B/C.2/R.2.

fabrics (SITC 652/BTN 55.07, 55.08, 55.09 and 55.04A), leather footwear (SITC 851.0(2)/BTN 64.02), and tapioca and sago and substitutes (SITC 055.4(5)/BTN 19.04)—and has attempted on an illustrative basis to analyse their trade effects.[24] The main findings of these studies, which will be submitted in full to the Committee on Manufactures at its sixth session, are summarized in the following paragraphs.

[24] The criteria used for the selection of the further product groups to be studied and of the importing countries whose restrictions should be considered, as well as the various techniques used in the analysis (including their limitations and the assumptions involved) are discussed in detail in the study which will be presented to the Committee on Manufactures at its sixth session.

A. Quotas and discretionary licensing

47. The analysis of the trade effects of non-tariff barriers applied to woven cotton fabrics and leather footwear further illustrates the restrictive effects of quantitative import restrictions through quotas or discretionary licensing. The studies on both these product groups examine in depth trends in trade, production and consumption, investigate the quantitative import restrictions imposed by individual developed market-economy countries, and assess their impact.

48. Using the import elasticity of demand approach, the study on woven cotton fabrics estimates that differentials between external and internal prices resulting from quotas are likely to have reduced imports in 1969 into the Federal Republic of Germany by 17.8 per cent, into Sweden by 18.5 per cent, and into the United Kingdom by 21.6 per cent, below the level which would have obtained in the absence of quotas or licensing. These estimates are based on an estimated import elasticity of demand of 0.58, which is believed to be reasonably accurate, and on the assumption that import and export unit values are reasonable proxies for prevailing internal and external prices respectively.[25]

49. The study on leather footwear considers the impact of discretionary licensing applied by Japan as well as the potential impact of quantitative import growth limits proposed in the United States Congress in 1970. The consideration of the latter serves merely to illustrate the probable impact on exports from developing countries of, for example, limiting the growth of imports into the United States to 5 per cent per annum.

50. The evaluation of the restrictive effect of the discretionary licensing applied by Japan to leather footwear is difficult since this product has been subject to both high tariffs and very severe quantitative restrictions throughout the postwar period. In view of the strong protection afforded by quantitative restrictions there can be little doubt about their effectiveness. However, since at no time were these imports free of controls and actual imports have been very small, a quantitative assessment of the impact of the restrictions is extremely difficult to make.

51. Nevertheless, a number of interesting comparisons are possible. For example, from 1960 to 1969 Japan's imports of leather expanded from 2 913 tons to 17 341 tons (i.e. almost sixfold), while exports of non-rubber footwear declined from 52 049 tons to 47 953, which suggests that the larger imports of leather must have been devoted principally to domestic sales of footwear. During this period Japan's imports of leather from the developing countries increased about fivefold, from 2 497 tons to 12 400 tons.

52. On the assumption that imported leather footwear might, in the absence of quantitative restrictions, have captured up to 5 per cent of the market in 1969, imports during that year would have been 1 663 tons as compared with an actual figure of 710 tons—a difference of 57 per

cent. Moreover, if the developing countries had maintained their 1960 share of imports, namely, 24.5 per cent, imports into Japan from these countries in 1969 would have been 407 tons, whereas the actual figure was 174 tons.

53. A 5 per cent share in the market in 1969 would have resulted in imports of $10.5 million, some $6 million above actual imports, which amounted to $4.5 million. Again, applying the 1960 figure for the share of imports from developing countries, those countries would have earned some $736,000 of export revenue in excess of the actual figure. (The difference is proportionately smaller than when expressed in terms of volume because of the relatively low unit-value of imports of leather footwear from the developing countries.)

54. It is also relevant to compare the imports of leather footwear by Japan with those of major importers of leather footwear, such as the EEC countries. In 1969 imports of non-rubber footwear into the EEC countries (including intra-community trade) amounted to $365.7 million, of which $20.2 million (5.5 per cent) were from developing countries. This total may be compared with imports by Japan of $4.5 million of which $550,000 (12.2 per cent) were from the developing countries. EEC imports thus amounted to $1.97 *per capita* ($0.109 *per capita* from developing countries), which contrasts with imports by Japan of $0.044 *per capita* (and $0.0054 *per capita* from developing countries).[26]

55. If *per capita* imports by Japan in 1969 had been at the EEC level, Japan's imports of non-rubber footwear in that year would have totalled $201.6 million, and given the 1969 share of developing countries of 12.2 per cent, Japan's imports from those countries would have come to $24.6 million. Actual imports by Japan in 1969 of non-rubber footwear were only 2.2 per cent of these hypothetical values.

56. Imports of leather footwear into the United States are free of quantitative restrictions. However, in 1970 a proposal was placed before the United States Congress to limit the growth of imports to 5 per cent per year. It is of some interest, in considering the effect of such import ceilings, to assess what would have been the result if the proposed import control had been adopted by the United States Congress.

57. If such quantitative restrictions had been applied, they would have put a sharp brake on the expansion of United States imports of leather footwear. This can be illustrated by comparing the actual growth of imports since 1960 with the hypothetical growth on the assumption that imports during this period had been limited to a maximum annual growth of 5 per cent. On that assumption, imports would have amounted in 1969 to $83 million, instead of the actual figure of $377 million, i.e. only about 22 per cent of the actual 1969 level. Taking the same figure of 5 per cent, imports from developing countries would have been only $5.5 million, instead of $20.8 million (26 per cent). Alternatively, taking 1964 as the

---

[25] The price differential between external and internal prices resulting from tariffs was taken into account separately.

[26] The difference in *per capita* import levels, in the case of total imports, is, however, somewhat overstated, since trade in leather footwear among the EEC countries themselves is included in the EEC figure.

starting date for assumed import controls, imports from all sources in 1969 would have been reduced to $130 million, 66 per cent below the actual figure, and imports from developing countries would have been reduced to $5,650,000 representing a shortfall of 73 per cent.

58. Perhaps of more interest than this simple arithmetic are the effects such quantitative import controls would have had on production in the United States, assuming no change in consumption. It can be estimated that the imposition of quotas in 1964 would have reduced imports of shoes with leather uppers by some 49.2 million pairs in 1968, corresponding to 9.3 per cent of production in that year, which amounted to 529.5 million pairs. If the reduced imports had been fully offset by higher domestic production, the growth of production from 1964 to 1968 would have been about 2.6 per cent per annum instead of the actual rate of 0.4 per cent.[27] Thus, even with import quotas the growth of domestic production would have been small compared with most other industries, because of the underlying problem of the comparatively slow growth of demand for footwear.

B. Variable levies

59. The study on tapioca, sago and their substitutes examines the effects of the variable levy system applied by Austria and the EEC countries on imports of these products.

60. In the case of Austria, cross-sectional analysis comparing the import experience of Austria with that of the United States, which does not control imports of these products, suggests that actual imports into Austria in 1969 were less than 22 per cent of the hypothetical import value.[28] An alternative approach, based on actual Austrian imports during a representative pre-variable levy period, indicates that actual imports in 1969 were about 13 per cent of hypothetical imports. Of the over-all trade-restrictive effects of the Austrian levies, the variable component is estimated to account for about 85 per cent. Regardless of their estimated degree of restrictiveness, the very fact that variable levies can be used so as to limit imports to the volume necessary to make up for the difference between domestic output and demand implies that they restrict international trade and damage the export interests of the developing countries.

61. This is also the case for the EEC variable levies on tapioca, sago and their substitutes, applied since 1967. However, there did not result a notable increase in the degree of protection afforded to production in the various EEC countries. Nevertheless, the variable levies did constitute a different manner of protection, since by this means imports of these starch products were prevented from influencing Community support prices. Based on past EEC import patterns, it is estimated that actual 1969 imports of tapioca, sago and their substitutes were 60 per cent below hypothetical values. However, a comparison of internal and external prices and their respective implications for trade volumes suggests that exports to EEC of these products from developing countries in 1969 were only 7-10 per cent lower than they might otherwise have been.

C. Some more general findings on the impact of import restrictions

62. The above product studies support the findings of previous studies that for most manufactures and semi-manufactures, suppliers from developing countries account for only a small share of the total markets of developed countries and generally also for only a small proportion of imports of individual markets. The absolute level of their exports also is small. Where quantitative restrictions have been introduced it has usually been because of the pressures on import-competing producers resulting from rapid increases in imports from other developed countries.

63. Suppliers in developing countries are affected in several ways by these restrictions that are aimed primarily at imports from developed countries. First, the developing countries are normally not the source of the allegedly disruptive imports, and yet they must share the full consequences. Secondly, the quantitative restrictions are generally imposed across the board or in favour of major "traditional" suppliers so that the developing countries are tied to their frequently insignificant market shares and small absolute volumes of trade. Hence the rapid expansion of exports which they require in order to attain economic levels of output, increased shares of international trade and favourable competitive positions in the international market, is denied them. Thirdly, insufficient growth of export markets for products in which the developing countries may have a competitive advantage may oblige them to reallocate resources either to export industries for which markets are uncontrolled but where they have no real competitive advantage, or to the import-competing sector. Such a misallocation of resources impinges on the growth prospects of the developing countries concerned. Even if the import controls in the developed countries are not permanent, structural readjustment in the developing countries, when there is subsequent liberalization, may be very difficult and involve considerable capital outlay.

---

[27] In fact, this assumption is an extreme one, since imported and domestic shoes of equivalent price are not perfect substitutes on account of styling and other questions of taste and consumer preference.

[28] Since tapioca, sago and their substitutes have a relatively low income elasticity of demand, and since import-competing starches are produced efficiently both in the United States and in Austria, it seemed justified to compare United States *per capita* imports with those of Austria.

CHAPTER III

Efforts toward the relaxation and progressive elimination of non-tariff barriers

64. In recent years there has been much consideration and discussion at the international level of measures for the relaxation and progressive elimination of non-tariff barriers, including quantitative restrictions. The efforts made in this direction are described in the following paragraphs.

A. UNCTAD

65. Recommendation A.III.4 of the Conference at its first session, which was adopted without dissent, provided specific guidelines for policies in the field of non-tariff barriers affecting manufactures and semi-manufactures from developing countries. At the second session of the Conference, the question of a programme for the liberalization of non-tariff barriers affecting exports of manufactured and semi-manufactured goods by developing countries was considered on the basis of a report by the UNCTAD secretariat.[29] At that session the representatives of developing countries outlined the various elements of a programme for the liberalization of quantitative import restrictions and other non-tariff barriers, emphasizing the following: adherence to standstill provisions, the fixing of a time-table for the removal of quantitative restrictions, and the conversion of bilateral into global quotas to the extent possible. A draft resolution was submitted by 81 developing countries and put forward specific proposals.

66. However, the Conference did not reach agreement on this draft resolution,[30] and transmitted it to the Trade and Development Board for consideration.[31] At its third session, the Committee on Manufactures unanimously adopted decision 2 (III), on the liberalization of tariff and non-tariff barriers, in which the UNCTAD secretariat was requested to carry out a specified programme of work in the field of non-tariff barriers. It also decided to set up a sessional committee at its fourth session, if that were considered useful in the light of the secretariat documentation with a view to identifying non-tariff barriers of concern to the developing countries and to provide a forum for recommendations aimed at the removal of such barriers. The developing countries members of the Committee accepted this decision "as a practical way of carrying forward their aspirations of promoting greater access to markets for their exports, through the progressive liberalization of non-tariff barriers currently in existence in those markets". They stressed, however, that "in accepting this agreement at the third session, they have

not laid aside the draft resolution submitted by the 81 countries at the second session of the Conference; they look forward to its implementation; and they consequently reserve their right to return to it at subsequent sessions of the Board or the Committee on Manufactures".[32]

67. At its fourth session, the Committee on Manufactures had before it a report by the UNCTAD secretariat in which again a number of specific suggestions were made for a possible programme for the liberalization of quantitative restrictions on manufactures and semi-manufactures imported from developing countries.[33] These suggestions related to: a general standstill on the imposition or intensification of quantitative restrictions; provision of detailed information on existing restrictions; a more liberal administration of quantitative restrictions pending their final elimination; liberalization of the procedure for discretionary licensing in favour of developing countries; conversion of bilateral quotas and discretionary licensing practices into global quotas; elimination of global quotas which had not been fully utilized during a reasonable period of time; examination of licensing procedures required for price control, statistical or similar reasons with a view to ensuring that they do not tend to inhibit trade with developing countries; gradual enlargement of quotas; drawing up of a programme for the adaptation of domestic industries affected; discussions concerning the manner in which licenses are administered; and the possibility of exempting the developing countries from quantitative restrictions pending their elimination.

68. After a discussion of the matter, the Committee on Manufactures agreed, in decision 1 (IV), to establish a Sessional Committee on non-tariff barriers again at its fifth session. It further decided that "... the developed countries, in accordance with previous agreements in UNCTAD [recommendation in annex A.III.4 to the Final Act of the first session of the Conference], should endeavour not to raise existing quantitative restrictions and other non-tariff barriers to exports from developing countries nor establish new quantitative restrictions and other non-tariff barriers or take any discriminatory measures, where such action would have the effect of rendering less favourable the access to their markets for manufactured and semi-manufactured products of export interest to developing countries".[34]

69. By the same decision the Committee requested the UNCTAD secretariat, where necessary in the light of its work on the identification of non-tariff barriers, "to assist developing countries to identify non-tariff barriers of concern to them, particularly those countries which may

---

[29] See footnote 5 above.

[30] For the text of the draft resolution see *Proceedings of the United Nations Conference on Trade and Development, Second Session*, vol. I, *Report and Annexes* (United Nations publication, Sales No. E.68.II.D.14), annex VIII. For an account of the deliberations of the Conference, see annex VII, B of the same document, chapter II.

[31] At the first part of its eighth session, the Board decided to remit the draft resolution to the Committee on Manufactures at its fourth session. See *Official Records of the General Assembly, Twenty-fourth Session, Supplement No. 16* (A/7616), part one, paras. 80-83.

[32] See *Official Records of the Trade and Development Board, Eighth Session, Supplement No. 2* (TD/B/199/Rev.1), para. 23.

[33] See "An analysis of existing quantitative and other import restrictions in selected developed market economy countries on products of export interest to the developing countries" (TD/B/C.2/83), para. 129.

[34] See *Official Records of the Trade and Development Board, Tenth Session, Supplement No. 2* (TD/B/295), annex I, section F.

have special difficulties in identifying such barriers, such as the least developed of the developing countries".[35]

70. At the fifth session of the Committee on Manufactures the particular responsibilities of UNCTAD in the field of non-tariff barriers were reaffirmed and the secretariat was requested, by decision 1 (V), to continue its work on non-tariff barriers.[36] However, the Committee was unable to agree on a draft resolution submitted by the developing countries[37] recommending that the Board should establish an *ad hoc* intergovernmental group to carry out consultations and negotiations on the subject of non-tariff barriers affecting present and potential exports of products of interest to developing countries. It referred the draft resolution, together with a draft resolution prepared by the developed market-economy countries, to the Trade and Development Board. At its eleventh session the Board did not reach any decision on the substance of the two draft resolutions, but expressed the hope that efforts would be made by all to reach acceptable decisions at the third session of the Conference on the matters dealt with therein.[38]

B. GATT

71. Following the creation of its Committee on Trade in Industrial Products, in 1967, GATT established early in 1970, under the auspices of that Committee, five working groups on non-tariff barriers, the reports of which were examined by the GATT Committee in February 1971. Acting upon the recommendations of the Committee, the Council of Representatives, and subsequently the Contracting Parties at their twenty-sixth session, concluded that GATT's work on non-tariff barriers should be more selective and should move to the stage of elaborating solutions on an *ad referendum* basis. The topics which appeared to be most appropriate to start with were standards and their enforcement, problems associated with existing systems of customs valuation, and specific limitations on trade, where it was decided the work should initially focus on the operation of licensing systems.[39]

72. Similarly, GATT set up four working groups under the Agriculture Committee, to deal with the problems arising in the field of agricultural products. Based on the work of these groups, the Committee assembled a wide range of suggestions or proposals as to how the principal problems might be dealt with. It noted, however, that "among the wide range of possible solutions suggested,

none at the present stage commanded support wide enough for any solution to be described as mutually acceptable".[40]

73. Another GATT body, the Group on Residual Restrictions (a subsidiary body of the Committee on Trade and Development), has examined possibilities for the elimination of restrictions on 21 products or product groups. Manufactures and semi-manufactures covered by the examination included leather and leather products, leather footwear, cigars and cigarillos, fishmeal, coir mats and matting, certain preserved fruits and fruit juices, wine, molasses, ethyl alcohol, bran, menthol, and yarn, fabrics and garments of non-cotton fibres.[41]

74. At a meeting of the GATT Council in January 1970, a Joint Working Group on Import Restrictions was established as an *ad hoc* body to conduct consultations concerning quantitative import restrictions still in force, with regard to both agricultural and manufactured products. This Group has met twice, in April and December, 1970, and produced an inventory of all the remaining non-tariff barriers by GATT members, which is regularly up-dated. It is expected henceforth to act as a supervisory body that would meet every two years to take stock of progress towards the liberalization of the remaining import restrictions, mainly with regard to industrial products.

75. At the meeting of the GATT Committee on Trade and Development in January 1971, developing countries emphasized that serious efforts should be made to initiate positive action in respect to at least some of the most urgent problems already identified. To that end they believed that advance action to eliminate or reduce non-tariff barriers, especially on their products, could be applied without waiting for the results of a general negotiation. It was pointed out that there were many complexities in the area of tariff and non-tariff problems which would inevitably require that action would have to be taken in a comprehensive manner rather than on an individual basis. However, if it were possible to identify areas where specific problems of developing countries could be dealt with separately and on a priority basis, representatives from developed countries believed that careful and systematic consideration would be given to possible solutions.[42]

76. The GATT Committee on Trade and Development decided to establish a "Group of Three", composed of the chairmen of the contracting parties, the Council and the Committee on Trade and Development. The Group was requested to present proposals for concrete action that might be taken to deal with trade problems of developing countries, having regard to the provisions of GATT, the relevant conclusions of the contracting parties and past discussions in committees and the bodies of GATT.

77. The Group of Three issued an interim report at the end of April 1971. Drawing attention to that report at the eleventh session of the Trade and Development Board, the representatives of some developed market-economy

---

[35] *Ibid.*, section A.

[36] See the Committee's report on its fifth session, *Official Records of the Trade and Development Board, Eleventh Session, Supplement No. 2*, annex I. For the views of the socialist countries of Eastern Europe on the adoption of decisions 1 (IV) and 1 (V), see respectively the summary record of the Committee's 62nd meeting (TD/B/C.2/SR.62) and annex III, B of the above-mentioned report.

[37] For the texts of the draft resolution of developing countries on the liberalization of non-tariff barriers and of that of the developed market-economy countries on a further programme of work in UNCTAD in this field see annex II of the report referred to in the preceding footnote.

[38] See *Official Records of the General Assembly, Twenty-sixth Session, Supplement No. 15* (A/8415/Rev.1), part three, para. 232.

[39] See TD/B/C.2/108, para. 9.

[40] See *Official Records of the Trade and Development Board, Eleventh Session, Supplement No. 2* (TD/B/352), para. 96.

[41] See TD/B/C.2/108, para. 15.

[42] *Ibid.*, para. 16.

countries suggested that the suggestions contained therein might be of value to the work of UNCTAD.[43]

78. The Group of Three presented its final report in November 1971 to the Committee on Trade and Development and to the Contracting Parties. It expressed disappointment that, after a second series of consultations, the response to its very modest recommendations had been extremely meagre, and that, of the 16 developed countries to which the recommendations had been addressed, two, including the most important trading nation in the world, had taken backward steps.

79. In noting the progress so far made in the liberalization of tariff and non-tariff barriers, the Group drew attention to a number of "negative facts" that remained, observing that:

(*a*) Restrictions in the textile sector were being maintained and had a tendency to spread. There was no hope of progress unless a very determined multilateral effort were made;

(*b*) Restrictions and agricultural policies hampering access to developed countries of temperate zone products were maintained and there was no prospect of progress unless a very determined multilateral effort were made;

(*c*) The most important trading nation and another developed country had imposed import surcharges without exempting imports from developing countries;

(*d*) Two of the economically strongest developed countries in 1971 still maintained restrictions entailing less favourable treatment of a large number of developing countries than that given to highly developed countries.[44]

80. Further meetings are scheduled of the GATT working groups on customs valuation, industrial standards and import licensing. The working group on import licensing is still in a preparatory stage.

81. The question of adding new topics to the work programme of GATT in the field of non-tariff barriers was discussed in the Committee on Trade in Industrial Products in the summer of 1971. Among possible new topics mention was made of export subsidies and marking requirements.

82. In November 1971 the Committee on Trade in Industrial Products discussed the question of future work in the field of non-tariff barriers. It expressed the hope that a consensus with regard to new topics could be reached at the twenty-seventh session of the Contracting Parties.

83. At the twenty-seventh session of the Contracting Parties to GATT, held in November 1971, it was decided that the Group of Three should be continued in order to ensure follow-up action on its report. It was requested to explore with the Contracting Parties concerned the possibility of dealing with difficulties connected with the implementation of its recommendations and the progress made in implementing them, with freedom to make recommendations or suggestions aimed at facilitating the implementation of part IV of the General Agreement. With regard to the future work of the Committee on Trade in Industrial Products, there was general agreement that the main emphasis should be given to the work under way on industrial standards and licensing. There was consensus that work should be undertaken on export subsidies covered by article XVI, paragraph 4 of the General Agreement, on import documentation, consular formalities and problems of packaging and labelling. The GATT secretariat would compile, for individual developing countries, information showing the tariff and non-tariff barriers applying to their exports, indicating the volume of trade covered.

C. Other international organizations

84. Efforts with regard to the relaxation and progressive elimination of non-tariff barriers at a multilateral level have also been undertaken by OECD, ICC, ISO, and—in the field of documentation and procedures—by the regional economic commissions of the United Nations, in co-operation with UNCTAD.

85. The OECD has dealt with certain aspects of non-tariff barriers, such as government purchasing and import licensing and quantitative restrictions. The OECD Committee on Trade has carried out an enquiry into member countries' regulations, procedures and practices in the field of government purchasing, covering all procurement of supplies by central government authorities for governmental use.[45] It has also drawn up recommendations for uniform procedures for the application of licensing and quota schemes with a view to achieving uniformity and simplicity in these regulations.

86. The ICC Joint Committee on Non-Tariff Obstacles to Trade presented to the Congress of ICC in 1969 its survey of non-tariff obstacles and a set of recommendations relating to quantitative restrictions, import and export licensing, government procurement, monopolies and state-trading, subsidies, anti-dumping and countervailing duties, customs valuation and nomenclature and compulsory technical norms and standards.[46] At the XXIIIrd Congress of ICC (Vienna, 1971) the ICC Commission on the Expansion of International Trade presented a "Program for the Liberalization of International Trade", containing suggestions for the elimination of non-tariff obstacles.[47]

87. The ECE has been actively working for the simplification of trade documentation over the last ten years and this work has been extended to other regions, through the other economic commissions and—since 1970—through the establishment as a UNDP project, attached to UNCTAD, of advisory services on trade documentation. The aim is to reduce, simplify and standardize formalities,

---

[43] See *Official Records of the General Assembly, Twenty-sixth Session, Supplement No. 15* (A/8415/Rev.1), part three, para. 203.

[44] See GATT document L/3610 and Corr.1, 3 November 1971, section IV, paras. 58 to 60.

[45] OECD, *Government purchasing in Europe, North America, Japan: regulations and procedures.* Paris, 1966.

[46] *Non-tariff Obstacles to Trade*, report prepared by the ICC Joint Committee on Non-tariff Obstacles to Trade, Paris, May 1969.

[47] *XXIIIrd Congress of the International Chamber of Commerce, Program for the Liberalization of International Trade: Statement and Report*, Vienna, 1971.

procedures and documentation in all activities connected with international trade. The project has attracted great interest from developing as well as developed countries. The ECE will assume a co-ordinating role for the technical development work, through a special Working Party on Facilitation of International Trade Procedures, whereas UNCTAD, in collaboration with the other regional economic commissions, will continue to provide advisory services to developing countries.

D. Progress in liberalization at the national level and within economic groupings since the second session of the Conference

88. As is clear from the above, the recent efforts undertaken at the international level have not yet led to concrete action with a view to the substantial relaxation or removal of non-tariff barriers. At the national level, however, and within economic groupings of countries, the liberalization of non-tariff barriers has continued and a number of quantitative and other restrictions on products of export interest to developing countries have been removed since the second session of the Conference. This trend towards liberalization, however, did not take place without certain steps backward, some of which would appear to be of much wider scope than the measures of liberalization taken.

1. EEC

89. Virtually all quantitative restrictions on trade within the Community have been eliminated, and the effects of this liberalization are reflected in the rapid expansion of intra-Community trade, which by 1970 had reached a level about six and a half times that of 1958, the first year of the Common Market.[48] Imports of a number of products from third countries have also been liberalized, as described in the following paragraphs.

90. As a result of changes in import policies in Belgium-Luxembourg and the Netherlands, imports of penicillin, its salts and compounds and medicaments containing penicillin have been liberalized.

91. The Federal Republic of Germany has increased import quotas for industrial goods by one-fifth to one-third and lowered the value-added tax. It has also liberalized imports of sausages and similar products and, with a few exceptions, also fruit juices.

92. France has deleted a number of products, such as onions, inulin, lard for industrial purposes, flavoured sugars and syrups and molasses, glutanic acid, pocket watches, and clocks from its negative list. It has also removed restrictions on imports of hydrogenated fats and oils, margarine and related products and liberalized imports of silk fabrics and some undergarments. Imports of certain cereal products, bread and fine bakers' wares, some cotton items and fabrics, some special steels and certain optical elements have also been liberalized.

93. Italy has liberalized import restrictions on certain products such as molasses, sublimed sulphur and citric acid, and is considering further measures of liberalization.

94. In July 1969 the Community adopted, within the framework of its common commercial policy, procedures relating to quantitative restrictions applied by member States to imports from third countries. Common procedures have been established governing the administration of the restrictions and special procedures laid down for imports from third countries of certain products which are not subject to quantitative restrictions. A common import liberalization list, applying to all EEC member States, has been established and covers two-thirds of the items listed in the EEC common customs tariff.[49]

2. EFTA

95. Quantitative restrictions on industrial products have, with very few exceptions, been eliminated in the trade between the original members of EFTA. Iceland, which acceded to the Association on 1 March 1970, is an exception. Since its accession it has abolished quantitative restrictions on a number of products and will abolish gradually, in the manner provided by the Stockholm Convention,[50] the remaining restrictions (with a few exceptions) by the end of 1974.[51] In general, these liberalization measures have been or will be extended to third countries; cotton textiles are the principal exception. As in the case of EEC, the trade effects of liberalization in EFTA may be judged from the threefold increase in trade between EFTA countries, at an average annual rate of 11 per cent, during the ten-year period 1959-1969.

96. Austria has enacted new legislation, which provides for the liberalization of import restrictions, including those affecting products of export interest to developing countries, such as spices in processed and semi-processed form and most types of fruit juices. Quantitative restrictions have also been removed from chocolate and other food preparations containing cocoa. In addition, discrimination in the treatment of different developing countries has been abolished and the liberalization measures have in effect been extended to all developing countries by the inclusion of all of them in the list of countries to which liberalization measures apply.

97. In Denmark, in addition to the liberalization of certain agricultural products, quantitative restrictions have been lifted with respect to some vegetable prepara-

---

[48] *Commission of the European Communities, Fourth General Report on the Activities of the Communities, 1970*, Brussels-Luxembourg, February 1971, para. 311.

[49] The list relates to products for which commercial policy has not yet been harmonized, for example, some countries apply quantitative import restrictions to imports from third countries, while others have liberalized such imports. The member countries concerned can, on the basis of article 115 of the Treaty of Rome (treaty establishing the European Economic Community: see United Nations, *Treaty Series*, vol. 298 (1958), No. 4300), prohibit the entry of imports from third countries via other member countries, even if the necessary import formalities in the member countries which have liberalized these imports have been complied with.

[50] Convention establishing the European Free Trade Association, signed at Stockholm on 4 January 1960, United Nations, *Treaty Series*, vol. 370 (1960), No. 5266.

[51] *Tenth Annual Report of the European Free Trade Association, 1969-1970*, Geneva, September 1970, p. 26.

tions and fruit juices, wine and vermouth. Finland has liberalized virtually all non-agricultural goods and the remaining global quotas have been increased. Sweden abolished the special tax on fur skins on 1 January 1972, and the sales tax on carpets, pearls and precious stones is to be abolished on 1 July 1972.

98. Switzerland has liberalized imports of hand-made cotton fabrics. The United Kingdom has liberalized imports of jute products and, as of 1 January 1972, replaced quantitative restrictions on cotton textiles by tariffs.

3. LIBERALIZATION IN OTHER DEVELOPED MARKET-ECONOMY COUNTRIES

99. In pursuance of a new import policy concerning quantitative restrictions, Japan has liberalized a number of products, including vermouths and other wines of fresh grapes, brandy, liqueurs, woven fabrics of sheep or lamb's wool, certain sewing-machines, motor vehicles, certain kinds of sugar confectionery, chocolate and other food preparations containing cocoa, certain kinds of flour and meal of roots and tubers, etc. and certain medicaments. The new policy implied that by the end of 1971 half of the products still under the import quota system would be liberalized, bringing the number of restrictions to one-third of what they were in 1969. The Government of Japan has approved a plan to liberalize the imports of a further 20 items, with effect from 1 October 1971, among which are molasses, further kinds of sugar confectionery, steam turbines, electronic, telephonic and telegraphic switchboards, switch units of digital type and electronic computers. Japan is also planning to free imports of sulphur, heavy oil and gas oil, light airplanes, radar for aircraft and remote control devices for radio communication by the end of March 1972. Moreover, by that time, no restrictions will be applied to imports of cotton textiles.

100. New Zealand has brought the value of liberalized imports to more than 50 per cent of total imports.

E. Introduction of new import restrictions

1. EEC, FRANCE AND THE UNITED KINGDOM

101. Since the second session of the Conference, certain developed market-economy countries have introduced new, though partly temporary, non-tariff barriers, generally for balance-of-payments reasons. In addition, in July 1968, a common organization of the sugar market came into force in EEC whereby, for a number of products covered by the common agricultural policy, existing quantitative import restrictions were replaced by variable levies. Imports of processed fruits and vegetables containing added sugar were made subject to a levy covering the difference between the world market and the internal price for sugar. Practically all the major agricultural products and products processed from them are now covered by the common agricultural policy. In August 1971 EEC introduced temporary emergency measures for tomato concentrates, though they did not apply to exporting countries which guaranteed observance of the EEC minimum price.

102. France introduced emergency measures in July 1968, in the form of ceilings on imports from all sources of selected industrial products, including certain textiles of concern to developing countries. The measures were later revoked in accordance with the original schedule, the process being completed early in 1969.

103. The United Kingdom imposed advance deposits of 50 per cent of the value of imports, in November 1968, on products covering about 40 per cent of total imports; excluded from this requirement were basic foods, feeding stuffs, fuels and certain categories of goods imported mainly from developing countries. The rate of deposit was reduced in 1969, and abolished towards the end of 1970.

2. UNITED STATES TEMPORARY 10 PER CENT IMPORT SURCHARGE

104. In August 1971, the United States imposed, for balance of payments and other reasons, a temporary 10 per cent surcharge on all dutiable imports not subject to quantitative restrictions or not subject to trade concessions by the United States.[52] The surcharge was abolished on 20 December 1971, following negotiations among certain developed market-economy countries on the realignment of exchange rates. In October 1971 it was reported that the United States would be prepared to abolish the import surcharge, on a non-discriminatory basis, for man-made fibres, woollen textiles and apparel on the conclusion of new agreements with certain countries on voluntary quotas (for example, with Japan, the Republic of Korea and Hong Kong). Similarly, in return for restraints on exports of certain steel products by Japan and the EEC countries, and shoes by Italy and Spain, it would consider abolishing the surcharge on those products also.[53]

105. A precise estimate of the impact which the surcharge might have had on the exports of the developing countries, if it had been continued, is not possible in the absence of detailed information on the products, as listed in the United States tariff schedules, which were subject to the surcharge. However, on the basis of official trade data for the United States in 1970, it can be estimated that in that year imports of $3 billion would have been subject to the surcharge, corresponding to about 29 per cent of total most-favoured-nation imports from developing countries of $10.4 billion. The UNCTAD secretariat has estimated that on various assumptions, and on the basis of import elasticities available for 14 product groups, the reduction in exports from developing countries could have reached an annual rate of $500 million so long as the surcharge was applied, equivalent to 5 per cent of their total exports to the United States. This estimate made no

---

[52] An import surcharge should be considered as a non-tariff barrier, since it is a commercial policy measure, other than a tariff, which is under the direct control of the government and, by imposing an additional cost on importers, with the likelihood of reducing consumption of the goods subject to surcharge, tends to restrict imports.

[53] Japan has recently concluded a new agreement, for three years, with the United States, limiting the annual growth of exports of certain types of steel products to 2.5 per cent annually. The agreement includes specific quotas for stainless steels, tool steels and other alloy steels. (See *International Herald Tribune*, 19 January 1972.)

allowance for the indirect effects on the exports of developing countries of any decline in world trade that would have resulted from the continuation of the surcharge, or for the effects of any slowdown in business activity in Western Europe or Japan which might follow a major shift in the United States balance of payments.[54]

106. The effect which continuation of the surcharge would have had on the growth of trade of the developing countries and on the diversification of their exports is perhaps its most serious aspect. It is generally agreed that the developing countries must achieve such growth and diversification if the goals of the Second United Nations Development Decade are to be met.

107. The Working Party which was set up by GATT to examine the surcharge generally agreed that, in spite of the exemption of many raw materials and primary products normally exported by developing countries, it significantly affected their export interests.

---

[54] It did, however, allow for the impact of the expected rise in United States economic activity resulting from the totality of measures introduced, though not for the effect of any alternative measure that might have been adopted in the circumstances. The most important of the assumptions involved in this estimate are that: (a) no part of the surcharge would be absorbed by the exporters; (b) the currencies of the countries concerned would remain at par with the United States dollar; and (c) all commodities would be subject to the full amount of the surcharge. This last assumption is clearly incorrect, but no method was available to allow for the exceptions. (See "The international monetary situation: impact on world trade and development; preliminary report by the UNCTAD secretariat" (TD/B/C.3/98 and Corr.1) paras. 54-55.)

108. At the eleventh session of the Trade and Development Board the representatives of developing countries stated that, as a general principle, balance of payments difficulties among developed countries should not be used as a justification for imposing restrictions on the trade of developing countries, or for delaying the liberalization of trade by developed countries.[55]

3. DENMARK'S TEMPORARY 10 PER CENT IMPORT SURCHARGE

109. In October 1971, the Government of Denmark imposed an import surcharge, also for balance of payments reasons, to be progressively phased out by March 1973. From an initial rate of 10 per cent, the surcharge is to be reduced to 7 per cent in June 1972 and 4 per cent in November 1972. Raw materials, food, medical goods and other items which are exempt from the surcharge amount in all to 50 per cent of total imports into Denmark. As in the case of the United States import surcharge, the trade implications for developing countries are difficult to assess without more specific information on the products or items exempted.

110. The Government of Denmark, announcing its intention to implement its scheme of preferences under the GSP on 1 January 1972, indicated that it would exempt from the surcharge those products originating in preference-receiving countries.

---

[55] See *Official Records of the General Assembly, Twenty-sixth Session, Supplement No. 15* (A/8415/Rev.1), part three, annex II, para. 9.

CHAPTER IV

Possible approaches to a liberalization programme

111. In the light of the limited progress noted above, the need for establishing a consistent programme for the liberalization of non-tariff barriers has become even more important. The report by the UNCTAD secretariat prepared for the second session of the Conference, "Programme for the liberalization of non-tariff barriers in developed countries on products of export interest to developing countries"[56] discussed the various possible approaches to the reduction and elimination of quantitative and related restrictions. It would seem that the multilateral approach, on a product-by-product or product-group-by-product-group basis, is more likely to lead to a substantial liberalization than alternative approaches. If a liberalization programme is to be effective, it is essential that it be agreed upon and pursued in a multilateral forum, with the participation of the developed as well as the developing countries.

---

[56] TD/20/Supp.1, in *Proceedings of the United Nations Conference on Trade and Development, Second Session, vol. III, Problems and Policies of Trade in Manufactures and Semi-manufactures* (United Nations publication, Sales No. E.68.II.D.16).

112. In presenting the main elements of a possible programme in this field, pursuant to paragraphs 33-35 of the International Development Strategy, the UNCTAD secretariat has benefited from the discussions held and suggestions made in the various UNCTAD organs since the second session of the Conference and has also taken into account relevant material available in GATT. Many of the ideas and suggestions put forward are to be found in previous studies and reports by the UNCTAD secretariat or reflect discussions that have taken place in UNCTAD organs. However, few of the suggestions have ever been considered in depth or acted upon. The present document therefore brings together the main elements of a programme of liberalization in a comprehensive manner for consideration by the Conference.

A. Standstill

113. A standstill on the imposition of new barriers and on the intensification of existing barriers had been agreed upon in the recommendation in annex A.III.4 to the Final Act of the first session of the Conference and was

reaffirmed in decision 1 (IV) of the Committee on Manufactures and in paragraphs 33 and 34 of the International Development Strategy. It is essential that the standstill be strictly and fully observed and that appropriate consultation procedures be instituted within UNCTAD with a view to observing certain criteria by which departures from the standstill may be permitted and to ensuring that such departures are only temporary and the new restriction eliminated as early as possible. Strict adherence to the standstill has become even more important in view of the GSP and the possibility that the benefits accruing to the developing countries from the system could be nullified by the imposition of quantitative restrictions.

114. The following criteria for exceptions from the standstill in emergency situations are worthy of consideration:

(1) Any departure from the standstill should be due to compelling and exceptional circumstances and should be of short duration. Provision should be made for the removal of the restriction as early as possible.

(2) The exception should be justified by the injury to domestic industry which is eventually sustained rather than by an assumed extent of injury.

(3) In judging the extent of injury to domestic industry the government of a developed country should not artificially segregate products for the purpose of affording protection in a manner unrelated to the structure of the industry concerned.

(4) There should not result a reduction of imports from developing countries below the volume obtaining prior to introduction of the restriction. Indeed, so far as possible, the measure should allow for some further growth of imports.

(5) The relief provided to the domestic industries in the developed country should not be of a permanent character, while affording a reasonable period for the firms and workers concerned to carry out the necessary transfer of resources from non-competitive or uneconomic lines of production to those which have a comparative advantage.[57]

(6) The difficulties of domestic procedures must be demonstrably due to excessive imports from developing countries and not to other factors, unconnected with imports, such as backward technology or rigidities in marketing and competitive patterns.[58]

(7) So far as possible, there should be prior consultations with the developing countries concerned. Failing that, consultations with the developing countries affected should always take place as soon as possible after the restriction is imposed.

(8) Opportunities for consultations could also be provided, as appropriate, within the UNCTAD bodies concerned with non-tariff barriers.

115. The principle of standstill and the criteria set out above are equally relevant to products covered by the generalized system of preferences. Provisions for the application of safeguard measures in this connexion were agreed upon in the Special Committee on Preferences. The preliminary submission of the Nordic countries at the second part of the fourth session of that Committee contained specific suggestions concerning the application of safeguard arrangements and consultation procedures.[59] These suggestions included the following provisions. In critical circumstances limitations to imports may be introduced, but any level of limitation should not be lower than during a representative period prior to the market disruption, with due regard to reasonable growth rates while the limitations are in force; safeguard measures can be introduced against imports only from that country or those countries whose exports cause or threaten to cause market disruption; a donor country which has taken action unilaterally shall, as soon as possible, give notice of the measures taken to the international organ agreed upon to supervise the preference system and shall upon request offer adequate opportunity for consultations to developing countries having a substantial trading interest in the products concerned; and, a developed country having applied safeguard measures should periodically review the measures taken with the aim of relaxing and eliminating them as quickly as possible.

116. The standstill is no less relevant to action in restraint of exports, and departures from the standstill in this respect should also be subject to the preceding criteria. Provision for a notification procedure would also be desirable in order to secure proper surveillance of this restriction.

117. The application of the import surcharge by the United States was a serious deviation from the standstill on the imposition of non-tariff barriers. In view of the adverse effects of such measures on the export trade of the developing countries, and in accordance with the principle of standstill, consideration should be given to the exemption of imports from the developing countries from such surcharges in future. In this connexion, the GATT Group of Three, in its final report,[60] had recommended that, if the Government of the United States intended to maintain the surcharge beyond 1 January 1972, it should take steps to exempt imports from the developing countries.[61]

118. The effective observance of the standstill requires consultations among the countries concerned[62] in respect not only of the problems underlying the application of the measures departing from such standstill but also of: the modalities of their implementation; the anticipated effects on trade and national economies, particularly of the developing countries; and the conditions for their early elimination. Arrangements and procedures might therefore

---

[57] See in this connexion the report by the UNCTAD secretariat on adjustment assistance measures (TD/121).

[58] Where the cause is other than one of excessive imports from developing countries, the application of adjustment assistance measures would, of course, not be precluded.

[59] See TD/B/AC.5/24/Add.2, annex 2, section 4.

[60] See footnote 44 above.

[61] Developing countries have likewise urged that all products of export interest to developing countries should also be exempt in the case of the Danish import surcharge (see paras. 109-110 above), and not simply those covered by the Danish preferential scheme under the GSP.

[62] Such consultations have been recommended *inter alia* by the Conference in the recommendation in annex A.III.4 to the *Final Act and Report* of its first session.

be instituted within UNCTAD relating to both the nature of measures departing from the standstill and the conditions for phasing them out.

B. Measures for the reduction and removal of quantitative restrictions and related non-tariff barriers

1. ELIMINATION OF THE DISCRIMINATORY ASPECTS OF EXISTING RESTRICTIONS

119. Mainly for historical reasons, quantitative restrictions and licensing applied by some developed market-economy countries still have certain discriminatory features. For example, some countries maintain discriminatory country classifications whereby many developing countries receive less favourable treatment than others as regards imports of certain products. As a result, imports of certain products from some developing countries are treated less favourably than corresponding imports from other developing countries and from some developed countries. Moreover, in the allocation of quotas, some developed countries apply the criterion of importers' past performance, thereby favouring traditional suppliers to the exclusion of new ones, including those in developing countries. As a first step in the liberalization of quantitative restrictions consideration might be given to the elimination of remaining discriminating features of country classifications that affect developing countries.[63]

2. QUANTITATIVE RESTRICTIONS IN THE CONTEXT OF THE GSP

120. While the objective is eventual elimination of quantitative restrictions on all products of export interest to developing countries, consideration should be given to the early elimination of those applied to products covered by the GSP.[64] Tariff preferences on these products would by the same token take on greater significance. With regard to those products or product groups excluded from preferences because of their "sensitive" nature, there would appear to be virtually no justification for maintaining quantitative restrictions on them, since they already enjoy tariff protection. The need for liberalizing or eliminating the quantitative restrictions on these products is urgent, as pointed out below.

3. MORE LIBERAL ADMINISTRATION OF EXISTING QUANTITATIVE RESTRICTIONS, INCLUDING LICENSING

121. Specific practices connected with the application of licensing may further increase the restrictive effect of the restrictions themselves. For example, licences may be given to traders whose interest in importing is only marginal—or who have no interest in imports at all, such as domestic manufacturers of import-competing products. Indeed, in certain developed market-economy countries it is permissible to allocate licences and quotas to domestic producers of products similar to those subject to restriction.

122. Pending their complete elimination, import restrictions and licensing schemes could be administered more liberally, through measures that would ensure the full utilization of quotas. Licences, whether in connexion with or independent of quota schemes, should be issued at least cost or inconvenience to importers.

123. For products subject to quotas, licences or import permits the adoption of standard procedures[65] could be considered, and could comprise the following measures:

(a) All relevant information concerning quotas and the procedures for applying for licences or import permits should be made available to importers well in advance, through official publications and the news media.

(b) The authorities in the importing countries should take the necessary measures, when allocating quotas, to ensure that licences are issued, and imports effected, during the period prescribed. The validity of licences should be such as to ensure the full utilization of quotas.

(c) Importers should be given a reasonable period of time in which to apply for a licence.

(d) Applications for licences or permits should be made on a simple and standard form.

(e) The licensing authorities may seek the advice of other government departments or of technical and professional bodies regarding allocations, but should not limit consultations with the latter bodies to trade associations of producers.

(f) The requisite foreign exchange should be made available to the importer on presentation of the licence or permit, without further formality.

(g) In the case of bilateral quotas, arrangements might be made whereby the licensing is carried out in the exporting country.

124. For products not subject to quantitative restrictions but necessitating licences or import permits, the following measures could be considered:

(a) Licences should be issued automatically, and if not immediately, at least within a very short period following a request.

(b) Importers should not be required to provide any other documents and the requisite foreign exchange should be made available to them automatically.

125. It may be possible for developed countries using licensing for statistical, security and other purposes, which have no declared protective intent but nevertheless tend to cause inconvenience to importers, to apply less irksome measures for achieving the same objectives. Moreover, where licensing and quotas are based on past performance,

---

[63] The developed market-economy countries concerned are Austria, the Benelux countries, Denmark, Finland, France, the Federal Republic of Germany, Italy, Norway, Sweden, the United Kingdom and the United States.

[64] For the products covered by the GSP that are subject to quantitative restrictions, see paragraphs 43 and 44 above.

[65] In OECD standard procedures for the import of goods subject to global, bilateral or unilateral quotas were worked out in 1962 as part of standard procedures for imports in general.

consideration should be given to admitting new suppliers among developing countries.

4. LIBERALIZATION OF DISCRETIONARY LICENSING AND BILATERAL QUOTAS

126. Perhaps the most inherently damaging of all quantitative import controls is discretionary licensing. Its restrictive effects may exceed those of fixed quotas because of the greater element of uncertainty. Frequently the nature of any import restriction underlying the licensing is indeterminate. There may even be uncertainty as to whether an implicit or explicit quota exists or whether applications for licences are granted or denied on a purely discretionary basis to make up for shortfalls in domestic output. This undefined character of discretionary licensing makes business planning virtually impossible.

127. Licensing on a discretionary basis is employed by many developed market-economy countries and typically affects such products as processed food and beverages, motor fuels, aluminium products, construction equipment, textile fabrics, precious metals, electronic components, motorcycles, certain chemicals and pharmaceuticals, glassware and rubber manufactures.

128. Again, the developing countries are particularly vulnerable to discretionary licensing and tend to suffer from uncertainty over and variations in both the volume of imports permitted and their sources of supply. No reliance on stable export growth is possible for products subject to discretionary licensing, and indeed for any developing country to place reliance on markets where it is practised would be a highly risky proposition. Moreover, a developing country which accounts for only a very small share of the market of a developed country may find that its exports are subject to discretionary licensing as a result of rapidly increasing imports from suppliers in major developed countries. In that event the restrictions may be applied to all imports, regardless of origin, with the result that the developing country concerned suffers also, although it was in no way responsible for the surge of imports.

129. Discretionary licensing could be supplanted by global quotas, with adequate provision in favour of the growth of imports from developing countries. Pending the elimination of quotas, details of the maximum quantities for which licences will be issued should be published, in order to reduce uncertainty.

130. Bilateral quotas are also in general discriminatory. They are open to use against a particular country, as an exception to general liberalization or to a relatively liberal import régime. Moreover, since these quotas are normally established following negotiations, and may involve reciprocity, developing countries not able to offer reciprocal concessions are placed in a weak position. Where bilateral quotas are applied to a large number of countries their effect is similar to that of a global quota with fixed country allocations. Since bilateral quotas tend to keep out imports from suppliers in developing countries, particularly those from new or potentially new suppliers, and to limit trade for existing suppliers, consideration could be given to the conversion of bilateral quotas into global quotas, with adequate provision for new suppliers from developing countries.[66]

5. ELIMINATION OF QUOTAS NOT FULLY UTILIZED

131. Several developed market-economy countries publish the size of quotas in their official gazettes,[67] but for others such information is not readily available and it is therefore difficult to say just how the quotas are actually utilized. Some quota and licensing schemes provide for unused allocations to be added to quotas for the succeeding period,[68] while others do not. Consideration could be given to eliminating quotas which have not been fully utilized for a certain period. Where this is not easily possible, appropriate measures might be taken to ensure that quotas are fully utilized and that unused portions are carried over to the following period.

6. GRADUAL ENLARGEMENT OF QUOTAS

132. As a transitional step towards the complete elimination of import quotas, consideration could be given to their gradual enlargement, either automatically (by fixed annual percentage increases) or by drawing up a timetable retaining some flexibility regarding annual quota enlargements. The enlargement of the quotas could be related to the growth of the market and provide for a gradual increase in the market share of developing countries.[69] In this way an orderly phasing out of non-competitive domestic production would be ensured and the reallocation of resources to areas of comparative advantage would be encouraged.

133. Fixed annual percentage increases in quotas were formerly successfully operated by EEC and EFTA countries in their trade among themselves. At a broader international level, however, owing to wide differences among countries, the setting of a uniform percentage increase might be more difficult, and varying increases for different countries and different products might therefore have to be envisaged. In order to prevent undue difficulties for the importing developed countries, such as those arising from shifts in demand, and to ensure nevertheless appropriate benefits for the developing countries, periodic reviews of such quota increases could be made on a market-to-market basis, taking into account international developments in the products concerned and the interests of developing countries traditionally supplying the products in question, especially the least developed among them.

---

[66] Global quotas are sometimes administered on a "first come, first served" basis, while others are based on past performance, with the result that new importers may have difficulties in securing an allocation unless special provision is made.

[67] Among countries pursuing this practice are the Federal Republic of Germany, Italy, France, the Benelux countries, Finland, Norway, Denmark, Australia, the United Kingdom, the United States and Canada.

[68] Examples are Italy, Norway and Canada (dairy products only).

[69] This suggestion, originally made by the UNCTAD secretariat (in TD/20/Supp.1 and in TD/B/C.2/83), was subsequently taken up by the GATT Joint Working Group on Import Restrictions. One possible indicator of the growth of the market is domestic consumption of the product in question (or of the product group, if consumption of individual items is not known, owing to lack of data).

7. LIBERALIZATION OF VARIABLE LEVIES

134. The trade effects of variable levies have been discussed briefly in paragraphs 59-61 above. The most important application of variable levies is that of EEC, in the context of its common agricultural policy. By this means high internal prices are maintained for farm products, and imports which would bring down those prices are kept out. The EEC system involves: (a) fixing a level of prices that will ensure the attainment of certain economic, political and social objectives, which in turn determine the degree of self-sufficiency for a given product, and (b) applying a levy (with a fixed and a variable element) necessary to maintain this price level.

135. The variable levy system, as applied to manufactures and semi-manufactures incorporating agricultural commodities, is of major concern to the developing countries. In addition to their protective effects, such restrictions may have other important effects. The levy (or the variable element in the case of the EEC) may change frequently as a result of movements in world prices of the products concerned, thereby creating uncertainty for foreign suppliers. Moreover, changes in the rate of levy or in surcharges may not be announced properly or in good time, which creates particular difficulties for suppliers in developing countries. There may also be difficulties over the precise interpretation of EEC regulations concerning the rates, and changes in them, applicable to certain processed foods incorporating different amounts of the basic commodities subject to the variable levy system.

136. Agricultural self-sufficiency strikes at products in which the developing countries may have an important competitive advantage, and efforts towards more selective support programmes should be encouraged with a view to widening the opportunities for efficient outside suppliers. A clear-cut decision to reduce gradually high-cost, inefficient and uncompetitive agricultural production would lead to the liberalization of associated trade restrictions such as variable levies. Pending such liberalization, however, countries applying variable levies might consider exempting developing countries from such levies. The EEC could consider exempting them from the fixed element of the levy[70] and, where feasible, partly or wholly from the variable element.[71]

8. APPLICATION OF EXPORT RESTRAINTS

137. The limitation of imports through export restraints in the supplying country is also a quantitative restriction. The ultimate sanction is the threat by the importing country to resort to alternative protective devices, particularly quotas and import licensing, if export restraint is not exercised.

138. While the application of export restraints in developing countries has not, until recently, been as wide-spread as the use of quotas and licensing in developed countries, the nature of the products to which they are applied, and the competitive advantage of the suppliers affected by such restraints, suggest that this practice may pose a serious threat to trade in the future. With respect particularly to products which are considered "sensitive" in the developed market-economy countries concerned (owing to increasingly uncompetitive domestic production), but also to other products where labour cost differentials are important, the application of export restraints appears to be becoming more widespread, constituting a convenient alternative to more stringent import controls. Furthermore, pressure to restrain exports may be brought to bear on specific countries alleged to be the source of an unwelcome increase in imports, without this affecting supplies from other countries. This highly selective nature of export restraints is an inducement to their being employed in preference to other more broadly-based measures.

139. Developing countries that substantially expand their exports of manufactures and semi-manufactures thus run the risk of having to restrain such exports if the products are considered sensitive ones in the developed market-economy countries concerned.[72] They have little bargaining power when those countries threaten to apply import restrictions, and consequently have little choice but to agree to such export restraint, thus controlling the growth of exports. Furthermore, if their exports are simply diverted to other developed countries there is a risk that those countries, too, will take protective action.

140. Owing to the different degrees and kinds of pressure that can be brought to bear, and to the very nature of the measures themselves, it is difficult to devise direct methods of liberalization in the case of export restraints. The establishment of codes of behaviour or similar arrangements would appear to be beset by serious definitional and operational problems, although this in no way reduces the importance of the question.

141. The long-run solution lies in linking the liberalization measures applied to the import controls that are held in reserve, but in the meantime developed countries should refrain from requiring such restraints on the part of developing countries, and where they are at present applied (constituting a deviation from the standstill), should consider agreeing to their elimination as quickly as possible. Provision might also be made for a notification procedure in order to secure proper surveillance of this restriction.

9. PACKAGING, INDUSTRIAL STANDARDS AND HEALTH AND SANITARY REGULATIONS

142. Various manufactures and semi-manufactures of export interest to developing countries are affected by packaging and labelling regulations, safety standards, health requirements and related measures. Although some of these are hardly of a protective nature and most are fully justified in terms of their declared purpose, many are

---

[70] The fixed element of the levy in EEC is intended to protect the Community's processing industries.

[71] This could be done inter alia by reducing the variable element by a standard amount or by suspending it completely. For examples see the UNCTAD secretariat report "Study on processed and semi-processed agricultural products" (TD/B/AC.5/5), paras. 87 and 93.

[72] The application of any such restraints in emergency situations should be only temporary and governed by the criteria outlined in paragraph 114 above.

of concern to the developing countries, both because the products involved account for an important share of their total exports and because they tend to experience particular difficulty in complying with some of the regulations involved.

143. Alleviating the burden on developing countries does not mean eliminating the measures in question. Indeed, in many areas regulations are likely to be rather more rigorous in future, as a part of efforts to protect the consumer and control the environment. Rather, a number of steps may be undertaken, designed to facilitate compliance by the developing countries without diluting the measures themselves. In particular the following may be considered.

144. In setting and harmonizing standards and regulations, developed countries should ensure that the measures are not designed or implemented as a means of affording protection to domestic producers. They should also consider taking all appropriate measures to put into effect uniform standards and recommendations adopted by specialized international bodies. Through the participation of the appropriate national bodies in the work of international organizations concerned with standardization, they should ensure that account is taken of the need to avoid erecting new barriers to trade and to eliminate existing barriers. Governments of developed countries could, where necessary, encourage local authorities and appropriate private organizations to apply international standards and regulations. Where difficulties arise from discrepancies in national regulations or in standards, the Governments of the developed countries concerned might consult together in appropriate international forums. To enable all interested parties, including those in developing countries, to take cognizance of, and comment on, any proposed national regulations or standards, whether new or revised, sufficient publicity should be given such proposals, well in advance of their implementation. Developed countries should consider establishing a national service, available to interested parties, for assembling and disseminating comprehensive information on existing national standards and related regulations, including those elaborated by nationally recognized private organizations.

145. As regards the enforcement of standards or regulations, developed countries should endeavour to harmonize their testing methods and their procedures for quality control. Testing procedures for imported products should be applied expeditiously and regulations on product inspection and testing so formulated as not to impede access to the domestic market of the imported products. They should take into account measures adopted by developing countries to ensure adequate quality standards for their exports. With a view to providing effective access for imported goods, arrangements should be made for the clear definition and publicizing of testing requirements, so that foreign suppliers can comply with them; control and testing operations should be delegated to designated laboratories in exporting countries; facilities might be made available at designated points of entry to test products manufactured abroad; as evidence that products meet the requirements of the importing countries, certificates of foreign governments or recognized foreign institutions should be accepted; and prescribed documents should be simplified and adapted for easy completion, along the lines of other export documents.

146. For their part, developing countries should endeavour to participate more actively in the work of international organizations concerned with standardization, so that their special problems can be taken into account in the elaboration and harmonization, as well as enforcement, of international standards and regulations.

147. Developed countries and international organizations concerned with standardization should consider providing the requisite technical assistance to developing countries in this field.

148. Health regulations in some ways pose fewer problems than safety and technical standards, because there are fewer regulatory bodies involved and greater centralized control at the national level. In contrast, however, the problem of inspection poses far greater difficulties. The publicizing of information could be followed in this instance also, with respect to existing health requirements, inspection regulations, the time-lags and costs involved and clearance procedures, all on a country-by-country and product-by-product basis.

10. CUSTOMS CLEARANCE, VALUATION AND CLASSIFICATION

149. Significant deviations from standard customs procedures which add to importers' costs and uncertainties, create delays and result in inflated customs duties are a distinct form of non-tariff barrier. Customs procedures also provide ample scope for discretionary or arbitrary action which may be used in an *ad hoc* protective and discriminatory manner, sometimes creating a high degree of risk to traders.

150. There are several possible ways of ameliorating customs procedures and other transfer costs. In the case of customs clearance, the solution lies in simplifying and standardizing the documentation and procedures. Similarly, simplification may be possible for customs invoices, where standardized commercial invoices exist. Standard practices can be worked out for duty-free treatment of advertising matter and samples, as well as for goods destined for re-export and for the remission of duties paid on defective goods that are re-exported.

151. Developed countries should consider adhering strictly to the principle that valuation systems should be neutral in their effect and in no case used as a disguised means of providing additional protection through artificially inflating the value on which the rate of duty is assessed. Formalities should be kept to a minimum and valuations might be based normally on commercial documents. Developed countries should also ensure that their valuation systems and practices are sufficiently clear and precise to enable traders to estimate in advance, with a reasonable degree of certainty, the value of their goods for customs purposes. Moreover, the criteria used in determining the value should be published. Consideration could also be given to the harmonization of practices as regards the use of so-called "uplifts",[73] and developed

---

[73] In connexion with the assessment of the customs value, an uplift is an increase applied to the declared value for customs purposes in cases where this value does not represent the true value.

countries not already applying the valuation system of the Convention on the Valuation of Goods for Customs purposes[74] should do so.

C. Advance liberalization of quantitative and related restrictions affecting exports of developing countries

152. The slow progress of negotiations for the universal liberalization of quantitative restrictions and other non-tariff barriers makes it all the more urgent to take action to liberalize such restrictions specifically in favour of developing countries.[75] Action could be directed in the first instance toward the effective observance of the standstill and the reduction and elimination of quantitative and related restrictions affecting the exports of developing countries.

153. In particular, there seems to be a case for the advance liberalization of quantitative restrictions and variable levies affecting the exports of developing countries. The existing complex of quantitative restrictions on imports applied in developed market-economy countries appears to be *de facto* inequitable to the developing countries for several reasons.

154. For most manufactures and semi-manufactures supplies from developing countries are marginal (see paragraph 62 above). Where these products have been subject to quantitative restrictions this was usually because of pressures on import-competing producers arising from a rapid increase in imports from other developed countries.

155. As has been shown above and in other studies, quantitative restrictions tend disproportionately to affect suppliers in developing countries in that they appear to be applied with greatest intensity and frequency precisely to those products and product groups in which the developing countries have an actual or potential competitive advantage.[76] Competitiveness in these products is to a large extent determined by labour costs, and for this reason the products are considered "sensitive" ones in many developed market-economy countries. This consideration largely accounts for the disproportionately high incidence of non-tariff measures on the exports of developing countries.

156. The uncertainties, variations, delays and costs connected in particular with discretionary licensing and other variable import restrictions generally have a harsher impact on the smaller and newer suppliers in developing countries, who are thus placed at a disadvantage.[77]

157. The above features, which tend in a negative sense to distort international trade and prevent an optimum allocation of resources, also have a positive impact. Quantitative import restrictions interfere with the orderly growth of trade, either by preventing the growth of imports into developed countries or restricting it to specified annual increases, or by limiting the imports to a residual quantity designed to balance domestic supply and demand, often at predetermined price levels. On all three counts, the burden of the restrictions is particularly heavy on the developing countries. These countries are generally at an early stage of exporting manufactures and semi-manufactures, starting from a very low base. Consequently, they achieve relatively high export growth rates initially. They must thereafter attain a level of output at which they can become competitive in world markets and achieve a larger share of international trade in the products in which they have a competitive advantage. Developing countries therefore need a faster growth of exports than competing developed countries and so can less easily accept the consequences of quantitative restrictions.

158. These aspects of the incidence of quantitative restrictions and related non-tariff barriers thus tend to hamper the export performance of the developing countries, the efficient allocation of resources in those countries, and both the level and growth of their foreign trade and national income. As mentioned above, such discrimination against suppliers in developing countries is not normally the purpose of the quantitative restrictions, although there are some exceptions.

159. Unlike tariffs, quantitative and related import restrictions do not automatically raise import prices but act directly on the volume of imports by limiting the quantity (or value) of goods admitted into a country, irrespective of prices. They can easily discriminate, intentionally or otherwise, between imports from different sources, since the distribution of imports is determined not by the price mechanism but by administrative decisions. The trade-distorting effects of such discrimination could be highly detrimental to the most efficient potential

---

[74] Convention signed in Brussels on 15 December 1950 (United Nations, *Treaty Series*, vol. 171 (1953), No. 2234).

[75] At the fifth session of the Committee on Manufactures and at the eleventh session of the Trade and Development Board the developing countries urged that, in the liberalization of quantitative restrictions and other non-tariff barriers, they should be accorded preferential treatment in view of the serious nature, as well as the urgency, of the problems facing their countries in expanding exports of manufactures and semi-manufactures. The second Ministerial Meeting of the Group of 77, held at Lima in October/November 1971, recommended that immediate action be taken to eliminate non-tariff barriers affecting the exports of developing countries, on a preferential and non-reciprocal basis, in favour of all developing countries, without waiting for the results of any general multilateral negotiations (See *Proceedings of the United Nations Conference on Trade and Development, Third Session, vol. I, Report and Annexes* (United Nations publication, Sales No. E.73.II.D.4), annex VIII, F, part three, section C, III). The representatives of developed market-economy countries at the fifth session of the Committee on Manufactures and at the eleventh session of the Board had opposed the suggestion made by the developing countries that they be granted preferential treatment. It was pointed out that such treatment was impracticable, since such non-tariff barriers as health and sanitary regulations, customs valuation procedures, etc., required uniformity in application. Many practices identified as non-tariff barriers were based on legislation and could only be changed by legislation, which would be difficult to obtain. Furthermore, they pointed out, the liberalization of non-tariff barriers on a universal basis, which was the subject of negotiations in GATT, would also benefit developing countries, whose interests would receive special attention in GATT (see *Official Records of the General Assembly, Twenty-sixth Session, Supplement No. 15* (A/8415/Rev.1), part three, especially paragraph 204).

[76] See documents TD/B/C.2/83 and TD/B/C.2/R.1 and Add.1, as well as Ingo Walter, "Nontariff Barriers and the Export Performance of the Developing Economies", in *American Economic Review*, May 1971, p. 195.

[77] See document TD/B/C.2/R.2, containing an analysis of this question with respect to certain product groups of export interest to the developing countries.

exporters and also, through higher prices paid by the consumer and a less than optimal allocation of resources, to the countries applying the import restriction.

160. The liberalization of virtually all quantitative restrictions in the context of regional economic groupings of developed market-economy countries, in particular EEC, has been achieved in their trade with each other in industrial products and most agricultural goods. With the enlargement of the Community, such liberalization will encompass a larger number of developed market-economy countries, thus leading to a greater *de facto* discrimination against the developing countries, pending a more general liberalization of such barriers.

161. For these reasons, it appears fully justified that, pending liberalization on a universal basis, careful consideration be given to the advance liberalization of quantitative restrictions and variable levies affecting the exports of developing countries. Many of the products or product groups at present subject to such restrictions, and particularly the most "sensitive" ones, are likely to remain subject to restrictions for the foreseeable future. Hence advance liberalization in favour of developing countries, without waiting for liberalization applicable universally, is the only way in which these countries could substantially increase their exports of these products. Particular attention might be given in this context to those products that are of particular export interest to the least developed among the developing countries, those covered by the GSP, and those which are of major export interest to developing countries generally, such as cotton textiles and the products included in the UNCTAD secretariat's revised inventory of non-tariff barriers.[78] As regards processed and semi-processed agricultural products falling within BTN chapters 1-24, on which some developed countries still maintain an exceptionally large number of restrictions (particularly for non-tropical fruits and vegetables and other temperate zone products of export interest to developing countries), consideration might be given to the

early elimination of those restrictions also, in so far as they were intended essentially to provide protection against the products of other developed countries. The developing countries should not have to await or depend on agreements reached on a multilateral basis among the developed countries themselves for the liberalization of trade in these products.

162. Advance liberalization of quantitative and related restrictions in favour of the developing countries could be carried out within the framework of the relevant measures outlined in the preceding chapter, and if necessary could be achieved gradually. Consideration might be given in particular to the following:

(*a*) Developed market-economy countries still maintaining discriminatory country classifications should eliminate such classifications in so far as they are to the disadvantage of developing countries;

(*b*) Where discretionary licensing is supplanted by global quotas, a reasonable portion of such quotas should be allocated to developing countries, and there should be adequate provision for the growth of imports from those countries;

(*c*) In the gradual enlargement of quotas, provision should be made for relatively larger automatic or otherwise pre-determined increases in the quotas allocated to the developing countries;

(*d*) Developing countries should be exempted from the fixed element and, where possible, also from the variable element, of variable levies;[79]

(*e*) Developing countries should be freed from any obligation to apply export restraints.

163. In the case of those non-tariff barriers which clearly do not lend themselves to preferential liberalization, such as health and sanitary requirements, measures could be taken to alleviate their burden on the developing countries, as has been discussed above (paragraphs 143 and 144).

---

[78] See the annex to this report.

[79] In this connexion, see paragraph 136 above and the relevant footnotes.

CHAPTER V

The Long-Term Arrangement regarding International Trade in Cotton Textiles

164. The present LTA, which entered into force on 1 October 1962, supersedes the Short-Term Arrangement which was made for the period 1 October 1961 to 30 September 1962. The LTA has been extended twice, on the last occasion until 30 September 1973. Since its exceptional and transitional character has been recognized, it is reasonable to expect that further efforts will be made to phase out the Arrangement. In the meantime, it is important to improve and liberalize its working. In this context, cotton textiles under the Arrangement, like other manufactured and semi-manufactured products of particular export interest to developing countries, should be considered as falling within the purview of the liberalization programme outlined in chapter IV, calling for the removal or reduction of

quantitative and related restrictions, taking into account the objectives of the LTA.

165. Possible improvements in the Arrangement so long as it is in force, could be considered with a view to a more effective achievement of its objective of providing growing opportunities for exports of cotton textiles, so that trade takes place in a reasonable and orderly manner, without disruptive effects in individual markets and on individual lines of production in both importing and exporting countries. Co-operative action in this respect should be designed to facilitate and promote the economic expansion of the developing countries which have the requisite raw materials and technical skills. It would be appropriate for UNCTAD to consider the state of international trade in

cotton textiles and its development in the longer run (once the Arrangement lapses), particularly as regards the export interests of developing countries.

166. From available trade data it can be estimated that of total world imports in 1969 of cotton textile items covered by the LTA, amounting to $2,338 million, nearly 86 per cent ($2,006 million) originated in countries subscribing to the Arrangement, and of that amount 33.5 per cent ($673 million) was imported by developed market-economy countries.

1. RESTRAINTS ON GROUNDS OF MARKET DISRUPTION (LTA articles 3 and 6 (c))[80]

167. To ensure effective safeguards for both exporting and importing countries against extensive recourse to action under the escape clause, consideration should be given to revising articles 3 and 6 (c) of the Arrangement so as to allow for suitable multilateral procedures following the bilateral consultations that are provided for. The introduction and recognition of agreed criteria for the application of safeguard action would help to improve present procedures.[81]

168. Any relief afforded by the safeguard measures to domestic producers should be temporary and should not be designed to create a permanent exception to the liberalization target of the Arrangement. Annex B of the Arrangement could be modified to specify that the measures may be applied only for a limited and fixed period.[82] Should the importing countries consider it necessary to extend them for a further period, the time-limit should be progressively shortened, with a view to the complete elimination of import restrictions as soon as possible.

169. At the last periodic review by the GATT Cotton Textiles Committee of the implementation of the LTA, the representative of India pointed out that the Arrangement had been looked upon as a means of assisting importing developed countries in making the necessary adjustments in the cotton industry. In the view of his Government, these adjustments were not proceeding in the way in which the idea had been conceived, since in several developed countries it seemed that the cotton textile industry was actually expanding, taking advantage of the restraint imposed on cotton textile exports from developing countries.[83] In order to make adjustment measures in importing developed countries more effective, safeguard actions introduced by those countries might also be conditional upon the submission of satisfactory plans of adjustment assistance measures aimed at facilitating the transfer of firms and workers to industries or lines of production in which the importing developed market-economy countries have a comparative advantage.[84]

2. BILATERAL AGREEMENTS (LTA article 4)

170. The emphasis which importing developed countries have given to the negotiation of long-term bilateral agreements with exporting developing countries concerning access to their markets appears to be a source of some concern. Although these agreements generally provide for somewhat larger volumes of imports than the minimum commitments under the Arrangement, they would seem to run counter to the objective of the LTA regarding the elimination of quantitative restrictions as soon as possible. A developing country negotiating bilaterally with an importing country is not in a position to compare the quotas offered with those which the importing country may intend offering in bilateral negotiations with other countries. To the extent that trade in cotton textiles is organized on the basis of bilateral agreements, it might at least be ensured that (a) the duration of these agreements does not extend beyond that of the LTA, i.e., 30 September 1973 and (b) the quotas included in bilateral agreements are considered in a multilateral framework.

3. QUOTA FULFILMENT

171. The administration of quotas by many importing countries has frequently resulted in the under-utilization of export opportunities and thus created supplementary barriers to the export of cotton textiles from developing countries.[85] The impossibility of using the full quota deprives the exporting developing countries of part of their expected export revenue. In two instances (the United Kingdom and the United States), the importing developed market-economy country has entrusted the administration of quotas under the LTA to the exporting countries, once the total volume of exports has been agreed upon.[86] This practice has generally proved satisfactory and could be extended.[87]

172. In some developed market-economy countries quotas opened to exporting developing countries are broken down into a very large number of minor categories, and the countries concerned find it extremely difficult to utilize the quota for those items which cannot be produced efficiently.[88] Their opportunities would be increased if there were greater flexibility in administering quotas by allowing, for example, a change from one year to another in the proportions of different categories of cotton textiles within the quota, and by allowing a carry-over from one year to the next. The very fact that quotas for a given product are not fully used suggests that import restrictions are no longer necessary and could consequently be removed.

---

[80] For the relevant provisions of these articles see the report by the UNCTAD secretariat, "Study of the origins and operation of international arrangements relating to cotton textiles" (TD/20/Supp.3), paras. 39-43.

[81] See in this connexion the suggestions outlined in para. 114 above.

[82] For the relevant text of Annex B see TD/20/Supp.3, para. 39.

[83] See the report by the Cotton Textiles Committee (GATT document L/3288), paras. 99 and 100.

[84] For a fuller discussion of adjustment assistance measures, including those in the cotton textile industry, see the report by the UNCTAD secretariat, "Adjustment assistance measures" (TD/121/Supp.1, below).

[85] See TD/20/Supp.3, chap. IV.

[86] ibid., para. 17.

[87] See in this connexion GATT documents L/3120, para. 40, and L/3288, para. 31.

[88] See TD/20/Supp.3, paras. 185-187 and GATT documents L/3120, paras. 33 and 59, and L/3288, para. 42.

CHAPTER VI

Special measures in favour of the least developed among the developing countries[89]

173. In selecting products for the liberalization of quantitative restrictions and other non-tariff barriers, particular attention should be given, as suggested above, to those that are of current or potential interest to the least developed among the developing countries.[90] Many of these countries export only a small volume of manufactures and semi-manufactures, including processed agricultural products, and an expansion of their exports is unlikely to create market disruption in the developed market-economy countries. Special consideration should be given to the removal of quantitative restrictions applied to the export products of the least developed countries, if possible in advance of similar action in favour of other developing countries.[91]

174. Technical assistance could be provided by the UNCTAD secretariat and bilaterally, by both developed and developing countries, to those countries which lack the necessary technical and administrative resources for identifying the non-tariff barriers, including quantitative restrictions, which affect products of current or potential export interest. Consideration might also be given to assisting the least developed countries in any multilateral or bilateral negotiations on non-tariff barriers in which they might be engaged.

---

[89] Pursuant to Board resolution 82 (XI), the Secretary-General of UNCTAD submitted to the Conference a detailed and action-oriented programme for UNCTAD in favour of the least developed among the developing countries (see *Proceedings of the United Nations Conference on Trade and Development, Third Session*, vol. IV, *General Review and Special Issues* (United Nations publication, Sales No. E.73.II.D.7), document TD/135).

[90] Such products are indicated in the annex by an asterisk.

[91] See in this connexion the Action Programme in part III of the report of the Sixth ECA/OAU Joint Meeting on Trade and Devel-

opment circulated under cover of TD/B/L.267, which suggests (para. 139(ii)) that particular attention should be paid to the possibility of giving preferential treatment to the least developed among the developing countries in the liberalization of non-tariff barriers and that (para. 182 II.ii) highest priority should be accorded to the elimination of quantitative restrictions and other non-tariff barriers (e.g. border taxes and administration obstacles) affecting processed and semi-processed agricultural products of interest to the least developed countries. The second Ministerial Meeting of the Group of 77 held at Lima recommended the urgent elimination of quantitative restrictions and other non-tariff barriers affecting the processed and semi-processed products of the least developed countries (see *Proceedings of the United Nations Conference on Trade and Development, Third Session*, vol. I, *Report and Annexes* (United Nations publication, Sales No. E.73.II.D.4), annex VIII, F, part three, section C, III).

CHAPTER VII

Contribution of the socialist countries of Eastern Europe to the expansion of trade in manufactures and semi-manufactures of the developing countries

175. At its fifth session, the Committee on Manufactures, in decision 1(V), requested the UNCTAD secretariat to "Proceed expeditiously with further studies in conformity with section C of decision 1(IV) concerning measures for the expansion of trade of manufactures and semi-manufactures of the developing countries to the socialist countries of Eastern Europe, making suggestions in this respect ...".[92]

176. Pursuant to this request, the secretariat prepared studies analysing ways and means of expanding exports of manufactures from developing countries to the socialist countries of Eastern Europe. In a study prepared for the eleventh session of the Trade and Development Board, it drew attention to the new forms of industrial co-operation between the socialist countries of Eastern Europe and developing countries.[93] A second study reviewed the general policies, with special reference to two socialist countries, relating to the introduction of non-traditional new products from the developing countries into the

markets of the socialist countries of Eastern Europe.[94] A study entitled "Expansion of trade through the promotion of complementary economic structures"[95] was put before the Conference in connexion with item 18 of the agenda.

177. The Trade and Development Board normally establishes a sessional committee to deal with questions of trade relations between countries having different economic and social systems. During the sessions bilateral consultations are held on a confidential, voluntary and non-committal basis between individual developing countries and socialist countries of Eastern Europe to facilitate contacts and to contribute to the solution of any problems arising in trade between these two groups of countries. The Conference may wish to consider the possibilities of further developing and improving these mechanisms.

178. The socialist countries of Eastern Europe have taken action to standardize their foreign trade documents

---

[92] See *Official Records of the Trade and Development Board, Eleventh Session, Supplement No. 2* (TD/B/352), annex I.

[93] "Industrial co-operation in trade between socialist countries of Eastern Europe and the developing countries" (TD/B/350).

[94] "Ways and means of introducing new products from developing countries into the markets of selected socialist countries" (TD/B/351).

[95] See *Proceedings of the United Nations Conference on Trade and Development, Third Session*, vol. IV, *General Review and Special Issues* (United Nations Publication, Sales No. E.73.II.D.7), document TD/125.

and also, where appropriate, other documents drawn up by governments and international organizations as a result of developments in computer and communications techniques. These countries also disseminate information on trade possibilities and techniques specific to their markets.

179. In a joint declaration[96] made at the second part of the fourth session of the Special Committee on Preferences in 1970, five socialist countries of Eastern Europe stated that they intended to contribute to the promotion of exports of manufactures and semi-manufactures from the developing countries by granting tariff preferences (in the case of those of the countries having a customs tariff) and other special supplementary measures of a preferential nature, designed to expand their imports of those products from developing countries. In preparing their own plans, they would take into account the production and export potential of the developing countries. They further declared their intention of increasing the share of developing countries in their total imports of manufactures and semi-manufactures; of taking all practicable steps to create favourable conditions for imports from the developing countries and for the consumption of products imported; of according in their procurement policies preferential

treatment for imports from the developing countries; of continuing to take steps contributing to the creation in the developing countries of export production and the marketing of such production. These measures by the socialist countries parties to the declaration are to be achieved mainly through: the acceptance, in partial repayment of credits for complete plants and equipment, not only of traditional but also of new goods produced by those plants in the developing countries; by promoting industrial branch agreements; and by granting the developing countries technical assistance in the construction of national industrial undertakings and the training of national cadres.

180. Thus, as regards tariffs, the socialist countries of Eastern Europe have participated in the work of the Special Committee on Preferences and taken part in the mutually agreed arrangements for implementation of the GSP. The Conference may wish to consider, taking into account the discussions on this subject in the Committee on Manufactures and in the Trade and Development Board, as well as the views of the developing countries in the Declaration of Lima, whether similar procedures might be drawn up concerning the application of other measures by the socialist countries of Eastern Europe, in the context of Conference resolution 15 (II) and the joint declaration. Any such procedures might, in addition, take particular account of the interests of the least developed among the developing countries.

---

[96] For the text of the joint declaration see *Official Records of the Trade and Development Board, Tenth Session, Supplement No. 6A* (TD/B/329/Rev.1), para. 192.

CHAPTER VIII

Institutional machinery in UNCTAD for the consideration of non-tariff barriers

181. The question of establishing appropriate machinery in UNCTAD with regard to the liberalization of non-tariff barriers has been under consideration since the second session of the Conference. In a report submitted by the UNCTAD secretariat to that session,[97] the view was expressed that the drawing-up and carrying out of a programme of liberalization could be most effectively done "within the framework of an international organization whose membership comprises all the developed and developing countries concerned" and that it would therefore appear appropriate for UNCTAD to play the central role. The report also suggested that consideration might be given to the establishment within UNCTAD of a group on non-tariff barriers as a subsidiary body of the Committee on Manufactures and put forward suggestions for the functions of such a group.

182. At the second session of the Conference a draft resolution[98] was submitted by 81 developing countries which, *inter alia*, called for the establishment of an intergovernmental group on non-tariff barriers which should provide a forum for negotiations with a view to the elimination of

non-tariff barriers, especially quantitative restrictions, to the exports of manufactures and semi-manufactures, including processed and semi-processed primary products, from developing countries. The Conference was not able to reach a decision on this draft resolution and transmitted it to the Trade and Development Board for consideration. The Board in turn transmitted it to the Committee on Manufactures, which considered it at its third session (October 1968). At that session, the Committee on Manufactures decided[99] to set up a sessional committee at its fourth session to deal with the agenda item relating to non-tariff barriers.

183. At the Committee's fourth session the developing countries again presented a draft resolution[100] providing, *inter alia*, for the setting up of a working group on non-tariff barriers, which would consist of representatives of developed, developing and socialist countries and deal with the problem of non-tariff barriers affecting exports of developing countries on a product-by-product basis. The Committee did not agree on the establishment of the working group but decided that at its fifth session it would

---

[97] See *Proceedings of the United Nations Conference on Trade and Development, Second Session,* vol. III, *Problems and Policies of Trade in Manufactures and Semi-manufactures* (United Nations publication, Sales No. E.68.II.D.16), document TD/20/Supp.1, paras. 75-76.

[98] *Ibid.,* vol I (United Nations publication, Sales No. E.68.II.D.14), annex VIII, p. 400.

[99] See *Official Records of the Trade and Development Board, Eighth Session, Supplement No. 2* (TD/B/199/Rev.1), annex I, decision 2 (III).

[100] *Ibid., Tenth Session, Supplement No. 2* (TD/B/295), annex II(a).

once more set up a Sessional Committee on non-tariff barriers.[101]

184. At the Committee's fifth session the developing countries presented a draft resolution[102] recommending that the Board establish an *ad hoc* intergovernmental group of 17 members, open to all interested countries, "to carry out consultations and negotiations on the subject of non-tariff barriers affecting present and potential exports of products of interest to developing countries". These consultations and negotiations would be carried out between developed countries imposing non-tariff barriers on specific products and the developing countries affected, "with a view to establishing increasingly favourable conditions of access, on stable, lasting and equitable bases, leading to the complete and definite liberalization of non-tariff barriers affecting products of interest to the developing countries, in order to enable those countries to expand and diversify their exports. For this purpose, the group shall have the following functions:

"(*a*) To prepare a programme of work, on the basis of individual products and groups of products and having regard to both the countries applying non-tariff barriers and the countries affected thereby, for the reduction, attenuation and elimination of non-tariff barriers affecting the exports of developing countries;

"(*b*) To co-operate closely with the appropriate UNCTAD machinery with a view to ensuring that developing countries derive the maximum benefits from the generalized system of preferences".

185. The developing countries reiterated their view that the examination of non-tariff barriers affecting the trade of developing countries should take place in UNCTAD, in view of its more liberal and universal character. They pointed out that a large number of developing countries were not members of GATT and could not therefore have their special problems concerning non-tariff barriers given sufficient attention in that organization. Moreover, UNCTAD looked at the problem from the point of view of the needs of the developing countries, while GATT sought to liberalize non-tariff barriers on a global basis. UNCTAD was also the organization in the United Nations charged with the broader responsibilities of dealing with the trade and development problems of the developing countries, and with finding solutions to the problems of those countries.[103]

186. A draft resolution was also submitted by the developed market-economy countries, dealing with UNCTAD's further programme of work in the field of non-tariff barriers. While these countries recognized the particular responsibilities of UNCTAD in the field of non-tariff barriers, they considered that UNCTAD should avoid duplicating the detailed work which had been going on for some years in GATT and which UNCTAD was in any case not equipped to undertake.[104] They saw no valid reason for the establishment of an additional body and considered that further work in this field could continue in the Committee on Manufactures itself. The UNCTAD secretariat "should analyse, with the co-operation of the developing countries, the specific problems relating to quantitative import restrictions and other non-tariff barriers against specific products of substantial export interest to them, including the least developed among the developing countries".[105]

187. The Committee was unable to reach agreement on either of the two draft resolutions and decided to refer them to the Trade and Development Board for appropriate action at the Board's eleventh session. The Board did not reach any decision on the substance of the draft resolutions but expressed the hope that efforts would be made by all to reach acceptable decisions at the third session of the Conference on the matters dealt with therein.[106]

188. In the course of discussions in the Committee on Manufactures and the Trade and Development Board concerning the question of the establishment, within UNCTAD, of an appropriate institutional machinery on non-tariff barriers, the following three alternatives have thus been proposed:

(*a*) A sessional committee of the Committee on Manufactures;

(*b*) An *ad hoc* intergovernmental group which would be a subsidiary body of the Committee on Manufactures;

(*c*) An *ad hoc* intergovernmental group which would report directly to the Trade and Development Board.

189. Although no agreement has so far been reached on the question of machinery, there is consensus in UNCTAD on the following:

(*a*) UNCTAD has particular responsibilities in respect of non-tariff barriers affecting the trade of the developing countries and therefore it has a specific role to play in this field;

(*b*) The work programme of UNCTAD in the field of non-tariff barriers has been laid down in decisions 2 (III), 1 (IV) and 1 (V) of the Committee on Manufactures, and secretariat studies should be carried out in accordance with those decisions;

---

[101] *Ibid.*, annex I, decision I (IV).

[102] See *Official Records of the Trade and Development Board, Eleventh Session, Supplement No. 2* (TD/B/352), annex II, A.

[103] *Ibid.*, paras. 78-79. The second Ministerial Meeting of the Group of 77 (Lima, October/November 1971) recommended that at its third session the Conference should establish, as a subsidiary organ of the Trade and Development Board, an *ad hoc* intergovernmental group, open to all countries concerned, to perform the following functions: (*a*) to promote consultations and negotiations on non-tariff barriers affecting present and potential exports of products of interest to developing countries; (*b*) to propose measures, on the basis of individual products and groups of products and having regard both to the countries applying non-tariff barriers and to the countries affected thereby, for the reduction, relaxation and elimination, on a preferential and non-reciprocal basis, of non-tariff barriers affecting the exports of developing countries (see *Proceedings of the United Nations Conference on Trade and Development, Third Session*, vol. I, *Report and Annexes* (United Nations publication, Sales No. E.73.II.D.4), annex VIII, F.

[104] See *Official Records of the Trade and Development Board, Eleventh Session, Supplement No. 2* (TD/B/352), para. 75.

[105] *Ibid.*, para. 87.

[106] For the texts of the two draft resolutions and an account of the deliberations of the Board at its eleventh session see, respectively, *Official Records of the Trade and Development Board, Eleventh Session, Supplement No. 2* (TD/B/352), annex II, and *Official Records of the General Assembly, Twenty-sixth Session, Supplement No. 15* (A/8415/Rev.1), part three, paras. 195-210 and 227-232.

(c) The UNCTAD secretariat should provide technical assistance, as appropriate, to the developing countries, and in particular to the least developed among them, in the identification of non-tariff barriers of serious concern to those countries and affecting their exports.

190. The need for machinery in UNCTAD, which is based on a recognition of its special responsibilities with respect to developing countries, is strengthened by the fact that the States members of UNCTAD consist of the countries, both developed and developing, which are members of the United Nations or its specialized agencies. The membership is thus world-wide and UNCTAD is therefore a particularly appropriate organization to work for the liberalization of non-tariff barriers.

191. Whatever body may be set up for the purpose, it would be useful to indicate the functions which might be attributed to an UNCTAD body in the field of non-tariff barriers. The following functions or terms of reference of such a body are put forward on the basis of previous secretariat reports and of discussions in the Committee on Manufactures:

(a) To review periodically on a systematic basis, non-tariff barriers affecting manufactures and semi-manufactures of export interest to developing countries;

(b) To examine these restrictions as regards their extent and special characteristics, the justification for their maintenance and their effects on the economies of developing countries;

(c) To draw up, on the basis of (a) and (b) above and in the light of the recommendations and suggestions made at the second session of the Conference and subsequent sessions of the Trade and Development Board and the Committee on Manufactures, specific proposals for the liberalization of these restrictions on products of export interest to developing countries;

(d) To consider appropriate measures to help the adaptation of industries that might be affected by the liberalization of non-tariff barriers, thereby facilitating the implementation of the measures for liberalization;

(e) To review periodically, and on an *ad hoc* basis as necessary, the progress achieved in the liberalization of non-tariff barriers and to assess the effects of such liberalization on the export trade of developing countries; and

(f) In fulfilling the above functions to take into account and make full use of all relevant information in GATT as well as in other international organizations.

ANNEX

Product coverage of the UNCTAD secretariat's preliminary inventory of non-tariff barriers of concern to developing countries and affecting their exports

Description of product[a]	BTN	SITC
1. Meat, dried, salted, smoked, prepared or preserved	02.06.A & B*, 16.01*, 02*, 03* & 04*	012.1*, 012.9, 013.3*, 013.4*, 8*, 032.01*
2. Dried dehydrated or evaporated vegetables and fruits	07.04*, 08.01.D, 08.03.B, 04.B, 10, 11 & 12	052.01, 02, 03, 9, 053.61 & 63, 055.1*
3. Cereal flours, starches and milling products	11.01, 02, 06* & 08	046.01, 047.02, 055.44* & 599.51
4. Fatty acids, oils, alcohols and glycerol and glycerol lyes	15.10.A, 15.11*	431.31 & 512.26*
5. Sugar confectionery, syrups and molasses	17.04 & 17.05	062.01 & 062.02
6. Chocolate and other preparations containing cocoa	18.06	073.0
7. Preparations of flour and starches, macaroni, tapioca and pastry	19.02, 03, 04* & 08	048.42, 048.82, 048.3, 055.45*
8. Vegetable and fruit preparations	20.01, 02, 03, 04, 05, 06* & 07*, 21.04*,	053.2, 3, 5*, 62, 9*, 055.51, 52, 099.04*, 06* & 09
9. Non-alcoholic and alcoholic beverages	22.04, 05, 08* & 09*	112.11, 12, 4*, 512.24*
10. Manufactured tobacco, tobacco extracts and essences	24.02.A	122.1
11. Coal tar distilled products	27.07	521.4
12. Petroleum products	27.10.B*, C*, D, E*, F & G, 27.13, 27.14, A, 27.14.B & 27.16	332.1*, 2*, 3, 4*, 51, 62, 91.94, 95 & 96
13. Chemical elements and compounds	28.42.A, 28.52, 29.14, 23 & 44*	512.51, 72, 514.28, 515.3 & 541.3*
14. Medicaments, chemical fertilizers and essential oils	30.03*, 31.03.B, 33.01*	541.7*, 551.1*, 561.29
15. Lubricating preparations	34.03	332.52
16. Artificial waxes and casein	34.04, 35.01	599.71, 599.53
17. Pyrotechnic articles, powders and explosives and cinematographic film and other chemical products	36.05, 37.07*, 38.19.A	571.3, 599.99, 863.09*
18. Rubber and leather products	40.11*, 41.02.A*, 41.03*, 04*	611.3*, 91* & 92*, 629.1*
19. Basket work	46.03*	899.22*

Description of product[a]	BTN	SITC
20. Newsprint, books, periodicals, newspapers and pictures	48.01*, 49.01*, 02, 11*	641.1*, 892.11*, 892.2, 892.99*
21. Yarn and woven fabrics of silk	50.06, 07 and 09*	
22. Woven fabrics of synthetics, rayon, regenerated and man-made fibres	51.04.A, 56.07, 56.07.A & B	651.14, 22, 25, 3, 65, 92; 653.11*, 21, 4*, 51, 52 & 62
23. Yarn and woven fabrics of jute	57.06, 57.10*	
24. Yarn and woven fabrics of lamb's wool, sheep's wool, horsehair or animal hair	53.07, 10 & 11*	653.11, 21*, 4, 51, 52 & 62
25. Carpets not of cotton	ex 58.02*	657.6*
26. Knitted or crocheted fabrics—undergarments or outer-garments (not of cotton)	ex 60.02, 03, 04* & 05*	
27. Outergarments and undergarments and other fabrics (not of cotton)	ex 61.01*, 02*, 03*, 06* & 10	841.41, 42, 43*, 44*, 11*, 12*, 13*, 22*, 26
28. Bed linen, table linen, sacks and bags for packing (not of cotton)	ex 62.02*, 03*	656.1*, 656.91*
29. Footwear with outer soles of leather	64.02*	851.02*
30. Umbrellas and sunshades	66.01	899.41
31. Glazed sets, tableware of porcelain and other pottery and statuettes	69.08, 11 & 12	662.45, 666.4 & 5
32. Articles of jewellery and of precious metal	71.12 & 13*	897.11 & 12*
33. Coins, non-gold, non-currency	72.01.A*	961.0*
34. Pig iron, cast iron, ferro-alloys and ferro-manganese .	73.01.B, 02.A & 02.B*	671.2, 4 & 5*
35. Unwrought aluminium, waste and scrap	76.01.B	684.1
36. Wrought plates, sheets and strips of zinc	79.03.B	686.22
37. Cutlery	82.09, 82.14	696.01, 696.06
38. Office machines	84.53 ex, 84.55, ex 84.52	714.2, 3 & 92
39. Electrical, telecommunications machinery or appa-ratus, insulators and portable electric battery and mag-netic lamps	85.03, 10*, 15.A*, 15.B*, 15.C*, 19*, 20, 21, 25	722.2*, 723.21, 724.1*, 724.2*, 99*, 729.2, 729.3, 11, 812.43*
40. Telescopes, cinematographic cameras, cameras and electrical measuring instruments	90.05, 08*, 12, 28*	729.52*, 861.5*, 31, 34
41. Revolvers and pistols	93.02	899.24
42. Brooms and brushes	96.01, 96.02*	899.23, 899.24*
43. Other toys	97.03*	894.23*

NOTE. An asterisk (*) indicates a product or group of products of special interest to the least developed among the developing countries.
[a] Covering part of the BTN chapters or SITC headings mentioned. Product groups relate to one or more positions at the four-digit level of BTN and the five- or four-digit level of SITC. See also paragraphs 10 and 11 above and related footnotes.

ADJUSTMENT ASSISTANCE MEASURES

Report by the UNCTAD secretariat*

[Original text: English]

CONTENTS

LIST OF TABLES

---

* The text of this report was circulated to the Conference as document TD/121/Supp.1, dated 14 January 1972, and TD/121/Supp.1/Corr.1, dated 18 May 1972.

Introduction

1. The recommendation in annex A.III.6 to the Final Act of the first session of the Conference provides "that the developed countries should consider taking, among others, the following measures: . . . Arrangements for assisting the adaptation and adjustment of industries and workers in situations where particular industries and workers in those industries are adversely affected by increased imports of manufactures and semi-manufactures".[1]

2. The need for greater attention to adjustment assistance on the part of developed countries was further emphasized in General Assembly resolution 2626 (XXV) on the International Development Strategy for the Second United Nations Development Decade. Paragraph 35 of the Strategy states that "Developed countries, having in mind the importance of facilitating the expansion of their imports from developing countries, will consider adopting measures and where possible evolving a programme early in the Decade for assisting the adaptation and adjustment of industries and workers in situations where they are adversely affected or may be threatened to be adversely affected by increased imports of manufactures and semi-manufactures from developing countries".[2]

3. UNCTAD's work programme in the field of adjustment assistance was laid down in decisions 2 (III) and 1 (IV) of the Committee on Manufactures[3] in which the secretariat was requested to report upon and bring up to date, if necessary, the existing studies on adjustment assistance measures in force. In line with the Conference recommendation in annex A.III.6 and in pursuance of the decisions of the Committee on Manufactures, the secretariat prepared reports for the second session of the Conference, and for the subsequent sessions of the Committee on Manufactures, which reviewed developments in the field of adjustment assistance in the developed countries.[4] The Committee on Manufactures at its fifth session further requested the secretariat to undertake a more detailed review concerning the implementation of the various legislation in developed market-economy countries with a view to indicating the manner and extent to which adjustment assistance measures had facilitated increasing imports of manufactured and semi-manufactured products from developing countries, including the role of those measures in the context of the GSP.[5]

4. The present report takes into account the work done in UNCTAD since the first session of the Conference in 1964, as well as the activities of other international organizations, such as the ILO, GATT and OECD, in this field. In accordance with the request of the Committee on Manufactures, it reviews, in more detail, the implementation of existing adjustment assistance legislation in developed marked economy countries with a view to indicating the manner and extent to which such legislation facilitates the expansion of imports from developing countries, including its role in the context of the generalized system of preferences. The report also attempts to quantify, on a preliminary basis, the impact of this legislation on selected developed market-economy countries, and the implications for the character and extent of necessary adjustment assistance measures in the developed market-economy countries. It also suggests guidelines concerning the manner and extent to which adjustment assistance policies and programmes might be adapted to facilitate increasing imports into the developed market-economy countries from developing countries.

---

[1] See *Proceedings of the United Nations Conference on Trade and Development*, vol. I, *Final Act and Report* (United Nations publication, Sales No. 64.II.B.11), pp. 39-40.

[2] In this connexion see also paragraph 4 of the statement made by the representative of Belgium on behalf of the Group B countries, reproduced in annex III to the report of the Committee on Manufactures on its fifth session (*Official Records of the Trade and Development Board, Eleventh Session, Supplement No. 2* (TD/B/352)).

[3] See *Official Records of the Trade and Development Board, Eighth Session, Supplement No. 2* (TD/B/199/Rev.1), annex I; and *ibid., Tenth Session, Supplement No. 2* (TD/B/295), annex I.

[4] TD/19/Supp.2 and Supp.2/Corr.1, TD/B/C.2/86 and Corr.1, and TD/B/C.2/106.

[5] See the report of the Committee on Manufactures on its fifth session (*Official Records of the Trade and Development Board, Eleventh Session, Supplement No. 2* (TD/B/352)), paras. 150 and 161. See also TD/B/C.2/106, para. 21.

CHAPTER I

Activities of other international organizations in the field of adjustment assistance

A. GATT

5. The GATT Expert Group on Adjustment Assistance Measures met in November 1970 to review recent developments concerning adjustment assistance measures taken by Contracting Parties to the General Agreement and its own future work programme. The Group noted that there had been very little change in the situation since its meeting in May 1969 in the availability and use by Contracting Parties of specific adjustment assistance measures to facilitate increasing imports from developing countries.

6. The GATT Committee on Trade and Development, in considering the report of the Expert Group in November 1970, recommended that Contracting Parties should continue to give attention to appropriate measures of adjustment assistance as one important means of adaptation to increased imports from developing countries and that Governments should keep under review the possibilities of using either adjustment assistance measures or programmes to this end. It also recommended that account should continue to be taken of these possibilities in the work of the Group on Residual Restrictions and that the GATT secretariat should be requested to suggest what additional information concerning the present use of adjustment assistance measures would be helpful in exploring the possibilities of broader use of these measures.

7. The Expert Group met in May 1971 and considered, in the light of the above suggestions of the Committee on Trade and Development, additional information concerning adjustment assistance measures that might be requested of Contracting Parties. It drew up a questionnaire containing a number of points on which information was requested from Governments.[6] The information obtained through this questionnaire was to be considered by the Group at a meeting to be held prior to the twenty-seventh session of the Contracting Parties at the end of 1971.[7]

B. OECD

8. In pursuance of the work programme adopted by the OECD Industry Committee, the OECD secretariat has undertaken a survey of industrial policies in OECD countries[8] with a view to indicating the policies which would bring about the adaptation of structures to new economic and technological conditions, taking into account the main impediments to the successful restructuring of industry, the instruments available to Governments to facilitate the adjustment process and the role Governments play in promoting and facilitating structural adjustments, given the part which should be taken by financial institutions and industry in this report.

9. The OECD secretariat's work programme in this field includes studies on industrial policy, productivity of investments, multinational companies, small and medium-sized firms, industrial implantation in the context of regional development and a number of sectoral studies, e.g. on shipbuilding, the main branches of the engineering industries, iron and steel, textiles and pulp and paper.

C. ILO

10. The ILO Textiles Committee, which met in May 1968, had before it reports by the ILO secretariat on the effects of structural and technological changes on labour problems in the textile industry and on the labour problems connected with the development of the textile industry in countries undergoing industrialization. The conclusions reached by the Committee at that meeting emphasized the need to facilitate exports of textile goods from developing countries and the manpower adjustments, including retraining for employment in other industries, that would be necessary in developed countries. More recently, the ILO has prepared other studies on the quantitative effects of the removal or reduction of trade barriers against imports of manufactures and semi-manufactures from developing countries, on labour displacement in European and North American industrialized countries, and on trade, aid, employment and labour.

D. ICC

11. The ICC-UN-GATT Economic Consultative Committee, which met in Paris on 11 December 1970, considered the question of adjustment assistance in connexion with trade liberalization programmes. The Committee had before it a report of the ICC Commission on the Expansion of International Trade.[9] This report discussed the various means of providing adjustment assistance, the probable effects of such measures on industrial trade patterns and the structural adjustments carried out by industrialists themselves. The Consultative Committee stressed that efforts should be directed toward encouraging Governments to pursue liberal commercial policies and that adjustment assistance schemes could be a useful ingredient of such policies to increase export opportunities for manufactures originating in the developing countries. A renewed trade liberalization effort would require parallel action in the field of labour and social policy to reduce objections to such a programme and facilitate the necessary readjustments.

---

[6] See GATT document COM.TD/81, 22 June 1971.

[7] The meeting of the Group has been deferred until a large number of replies to the questionnaire has been received and circulated, and Governments have had sufficient time to study them.

[8] OECD, "A Survey of the Industrial Policies of 13 Member Countries" Paris, 1970; and "United States Industrial Policies", Paris, 1970.

[9] See TD/B/C.2/NGO/3.

Chapter II

The effects of increased imports from developing countries on employment in selected developed market-economy countries: a preliminary illustrative quantitative study

12. It is often maintained that liberalization by the developed market-economy countries of their tariff and non-tariff barriers to exports of developing countries would probably cause injury to many of the factors of production employed in affected import-competing industries in the developed world. In various cases, therefore, these interests exert pressure domestically against such liberalization. The GSP and other forms of trade liberalization have been curtailed in their scope by Governments of developed market-economy countries because of anticipated injury to domestic factors of production. Furthermore, it is possible that the actual intent of such liberalization measures as are undertaken may be at least partially offset by "escape clauses" and similar provisions designed to protect vulnerable factors of production in import-competing industries.

13. Adjustment assistance programmes can facilitate, in principle, the transfer of affected domestic factors into industries in which a country has a comparative advantage internationally. To the extent, therefore, that the developed market-economy countries can successfully implement adjustment assistance programmes, domestic pressures in these countries against trade liberalization should be lessened. This would then favour more rapid expansion of the exports of developing countries to the developed world.

14. In formulating or appraising adjustment assistance measures, a crucial question is the nature and extent of the impact of increased imports from the developing countries on different economic variables, particularly on employment, in the developed importing country. In what follows, an attempt has been made to quantify, to the extent possible, under certain simplifying assumptions, the employment effect in some developed countries of a faster increase in their imports of manufactures from the developing countries. The technical annex to this report indicates the methodology, statistical sources, assumptions and results of a preliminary illustrative quantitative study relating to the Federal Republic of Germany, the United Kingdom and the United States of America.

15. It is necessary to point out that, since the developing countries' present share of world trade in manufactures is very small, the over-all impact of an increase in imports of manufactures from the developing countries is not likely to constitute a serious problem. It may be noted in this connexion that year-to-year increases in the OECD countries' exports of manufactures to each other have ranged from $4 to $8 billion in recent years, and that the structural changes associated with this have been successfully absorbed by a combination of adjustment assistance and action on the part of the industries concerned.[10] The basic problem thus consists in the impact on particular sectors or industries. It is therefore considered important to study the impact of increased exports of manufactures from the developing countries on as disaggregated a level as the available statistics permit.

16. Another important aspect of the problem relates to the time period over which the impact is studied. In the very short term, in certain industries, especially where these are concentrated in particular regions or localities, the impact may be sizable or even severe. However, if the process of stuctural change is allowed to work itself out and is facilitated by the different measures discussed later in the present document, the adverse effects will be minimized. In fact, in the long term, these structural changes will bring about an increase in real wages and real incomes in the developed countries through a shift towards an optimal international division of labour.

17. Any discussion of the impact on the developed countries of increased imports of manufactures from the developing countries rests essentially on the assumptions relating to such increases. Ideally, a quantitative estimate of the likely impact of increased imports of manufactures from the developing countries on the developed countries should be based on a forecast of such trade taking into account the past export performance of the developing countries, income elasticities, price elasticities, elasticities of substitution and elasticities of supplies of the commodities concerned, changes in consumer tastes, technological changes as manifested by changes in input-output relationships, the degree of liberalization and the types of liberalization measures adopted by the developed countries with respect to such imports and the export policies of the developing countries.

18. Although quantification of the impact of increased imports of manufactures from the developing countries on the developed countries has not received the attention which it deserves, the existing studies clearly show that the displacement of labour caused by increased imports from the developing countries is typically small in comparison with other sources of labour displacement, such as increases in labour productivity and short-term fluctuations in business activity. For example, a study on the United States of America by Salant and Vaccara concludes that an increase of imports of manufactures from all sources of $1,000 million would cause a net decrease of 86,000 job opportunities in the country, which represents only one-eighth of 1 per cent of civilian employment in 1959.[11]

19. The Salant and Vaccara study also analysed the effects on employment, in 72 industries in the United States, of a $1 million increase in imports in each industry

---

[10] I. Little, T. Scitovsky and M. Scott, *Industry and Trade in Some Developing Countries* (London, 1970), p. 286.

[11] See W. S. Salant and B. N. Vaccara, *Import Liberalization and Employment: The Effects of Unilateral Reductions in the United States Import Barriers* (Washington, D.C., The Brookings Institution, 1961).

from all sources. Both primary and secondary effects were studied, with the use of an input-output table. A $1 million increase in imports for each industry represents very different rates of growth for the various items considered, depending on whether the manufactures imported already account for a significant share of the United States market (e.g., among imports from developing countries, textiles, clothing and footwear) or whether the market shares of imports are currently small. In the case of imports in the latter category, an increase of $1 million would represent a very high percentage increase.

20. Little, Scitovsky and Scott, using slightly different assumptions, show that a $744 million increase in imports of manufactures from the developing countries to the United States, the EEC countries and the United Kingdom, will cause the highest percentage of labour displacement (2.1 per cent) in the leather (excluding footwear) industry in the United States; and that labour displacement of around 1 per cent could occur in the clothing industry in those countries, while in all other industries the labour displacement would be less than 1 per cent.[12] Finally, the ILO study[13] concludes that the number of employment opportunities lost due to increased imports between 1961 and 1965 was only a small fraction of the labour displacement resulting from increased labour productivity during the same period.

21. None of the previous studies has specifically considered the time element. The increased imports were implicitly assumed to arrive suddenly and be a once-for-all phenomenon. This assumption makes the studies less valuable from the point of view of adjustment assistance measures accompanying the increased liberalization of imports of manufactures from the developing countries. This increase in imports will, by its very nature, be spread over a period of time and its effect on employment is therefore studied most appropriately over a number of years. The present study makes assumptions as to the future growth of imports over the period 1969-1973 which are related to the actual performance of imports from the developing countries during the preceding four-year period.

22. The choice of the four-year periods covering 1965-1969 and 1969-1973 was determined largely by statistical availability. Undoubtedly, it would have been more significant to extend the first period to 1970 and the second period to 1975, as the periods would then have corresponded to the last half of the first United Nations Development Decade and the first half of the Second Development Decade. However, as complete statistics for 1970 are not yet available, the periods 1965-1969 and 1969-1973 were used.

23. The estimates relating to the Federal Republic of Germany, the United Kingdom and the United States of America presented in the technical annex are based on the simplest assumptions with respect to the increase in imports of manufactures from developing countries by these three countries. The percentage increases of imports of manufactured goods from developing countries by these three countries were first calculated for the period 1965-1969. It was then assumed that the increases experienced during this period would double during the period 1969-1973. In the case of the recorded decline, it was assumed that the decline would halve. The assumption in some cases involves rates of growth that could hardly be attained even under the most favourable circumstances.

24. These assumptions tend to exaggerate the future importance of the traditional labour-intensive exports from developing countries which have grown quite rapidly in the recent past but whose future prospects may not be as favourable as, for instance, those of exports of dynamic products such as engineering goods. The study will therefore tend to exaggerate the adverse effects on the labour-intensive industries in developed countries such as textiles, clothing, leather, wood-manufactures etc. This is borne out in the results, which show much higher labour displacements in these industries than were recorded in any previous study.

25. It seems unlikely that there will be any large increase in imports of manufactures from the developing countries into developed countries where incomes and production are not growing, i.e. under the assumption of a static economy. This study, therefore, looks at the growth of apparent consumption in developed countries of each of the commodities selected. This provides a basis for taking into account the increased employment opportunities resulting from the growth of domestic consumption, as well as the labour diplacement resulting from increased imports, over the period 1969-1973.

26. The recognition that domestic markets will typically be growing has important implications for adjustment assistance measures. When the domestic market is growing, an increase in imports of manufactures will not cause an absolute contraction in domestic industry, but merely reduce the rate of expansion it might have attained. In such a case the practical problems of the required adjustment are of a different character and magnitude, and, to a certain extent, call for easier and less costly solutions. An expanding industry does not face the same difficulties as may occur when a static or declining industry faces increased competition from imports. It is therefore necessary to identify, on the one hand, those industries where increased imports are likely to cause an absolute decline in production and, on the other hand, those where, because of more rapidly rising home demand, the increased imports will result only in a somewhat reduced rate of expansion. Another possibility is that, despite increased imports from developing countries and an absolute decline in production for the home market, domestic industries may be able to expand their production by increased specialization leading to increased exports to third markets.

27. Before describing the results of the quantitative study, it is necessary to draw attention to the following underlying assumptions, which are not intended to be exhaustive. First, labour is completely immobile between

---

[12] Little, Scitovsky and Scott, op. cit.

[13] "Some labour implications of increased participation of developing countries in trade in manufactures and semi-manufactures: report by the International Labour Office" in *Proceedings of the United Nations Conference on Trade and Development, Second Session*, vol. III, *Problems and policies of trade in manufactures and semi-manufactures* (United Nations publication, Sales No. E.68.II.D.16), document TD/46/Rev.1.

industries, but mobile between firms in the same industry. Secondly, the product-mix of the output of domestic industries is identical to that of the competing imports from developing countries. This conditions has been met, to the extent possible, by the fairly high degree of disaggregation of industry data used in the study. Thirdly, a certain increase in the value of imports will involve an exactly equivalent cut-back in the production of the corresponding domestic industry. This is the 1:1 substitution relationship which is discussed in more detail in the technical annex. Fourthly, increased imports affect only the production of the industry with which they directly compete and do not affect the production of the inputs that are used internally by these industries. Fifthly, there are constant returns to scale and a constant ratio of inventories to sales in manufacturing industries. The demand for labour will therefore increase in proportion to the increase in consumption.

28. These assumptions and the fact that the calculations of the study have been based on an assumed increase in imports of manufactures from developing countries mean that the calculations are primarily of an illustrative nature. They illustrate some ways in which increased imports may cause labour displacement in the developed countries. In addition, they indicate the likely relative effects on different industries and, when large increases in imports are assumed, as in this case, they provide maximum estimates of the likely labour displacement in the various domestic industries. It is necessary to bear in mind that in reality it is not only imports from developing countries that are likely to grow that the domestic producers in the developed country concerned may compensate reduced outlets in the domestic markets by increased exports to third countries.

29. The results of the study, given in tables 1, 2 and 3, illustrate that when the effects of the growth of consumption are not taken into account, the number of employees in domestic manufacturing industries (ISIC major groups 20-39) displaced by the increased imports would, on average, amount to rather more than 93,000 per year for the United States of America, some 59,000 for the United Kingdom and some 47,000 for the Federal Republic of Germany. This would represent 0.5, 0.7 and 0.5 per cent respectively of the total employment in the manufacturing industries in these countries in 1969 for the Federal Republic of Germany and the United Kingdom and in 1967 for the United States of America.

30. The relative employment effects on the various industries can be seen by comparing average annual percentage rates of labour displacement amongst these industries. The yearly rate of labour displacement is typically below 1 per cent. The exceptions are the industries producing footwear, clothing, wood and cork products and electrical machinery in the United States of America; the industries producing food products, footwear, clothing, leather goods, non-metallic minerals, and basic metals in the United Kingdom, and the industries producing food products, footwear and clothing, leather and leather goods, non-metallic mineral products and basic metal manufactures in the Federal Republic of Germany. The employment effects in the industries producing beverages, tobacco products, textiles, furniture,

paper and paper products, metal products (excluding machinery) and transport equipment are small (below 0.5 per cent) in each of the countries studied.

31. It appears that footwear and clothing, leather and leather products, and to a lesser extent the electrical machinery and basic metal manufacturing industries, are generally the most sensitive to a large diversified increase of imports from developing countries, although the extent of the employment effect in each of these industries varies considerably from country to country. In the case of the United States if has been possible to study further the impact on some of these industries on a more disaggregated basis. The analysis in table 4 shows that most of the employment effect in the electrical machinery industry takes place in the sub-sectors producing radio and television equipment and communications equipment, while in the non-electrical machinery industry only the sub-sectors producing cutlery, hand-tools and office machines experience significant rates of labour displacement, varying between 0.5 and 0.9 per cent on a yearly basis. In the clothing and footwear industry, the percentage rate of labour displacement is considerably higher in the footwear than in the clothing sub-sectors, i.e. 4.2 per cent and 2.4 per cent respectively.

32. In table 5 the assumed increase in imports from developing countries during the period 1969-1973 is compared with the corresponding apparent domestic consumption of each of the products in 1969. It is necessary to point out that this comparison must be regarded as only approximate, owing to the different bases on which production statistics and foreign trade statistics are compiled in the three countries under consideration. It is difficult to forecast the increase in consumption in these three countries, and it has therefore been possible only to calculate the percentage increase in consumption which is equivalent to the assumed increase in imports (see column 6 in table 5). While in the case of some industries only small increases in consumption would be equivalent to the assumed increase in imports, in the case of some other fairly large increases in consumption seem to be involved. In general, these industries are the same as those that were identified as especially sensitive in tables 1-4, which did not consider the growth of domestic consumption (see paragraph 16 above). In the Federal Republic of Germany, output and employment will decline in the footwear and clothing, leather and leather goods, and basic metal manufacturing industries, following the assumed increase in imports, unless domestic demand for these products grows at an average annual rate of over 2 per cent (over 5 per cent in the case of leather and leather goods). In the United Kingdom the clothing and footwear, basic metal manufactures and miscellaneous manufactured goods industries require increases in domestic consumption of over 2 per cent per year, while in the United States of America the footwear and clothing, wood and cork products and leather and leather goods industries require growth rates significantly above 1 per cent. Since the income elasticity of demand for these products is known to be low in developed countries,[14] increased

---

[14] See "Leather and leather products: a summary report—a study by the UNCTAD secretariat" (TD/B/C.2/101), para. 8.

imports from developing countries are likely to cause actual labour displacement in these industries.

33. Labour productivity is an important determinant of industrial employment. It is pointed out, however, that an increase in labour productivity is likely to cause labour displacement only in specific industries or sectors. As an increase in labour productivity also represents technological change, increased production, better utilization of resources, higher incomes and growth of the economy, its over-all impact is likely to be the creation of new employment opportunities. The effects of recorded increases in labour productivity over the period 1965-1969 in reducing the labour requirements in the 20 industries of the three countries under study are shown in table 6. The results are comparable with those of a study undertaken by the ILO relating to eight industries in 15 developed market-economy countries and covering the period 1961-1965.[15] In the present study, data on employment and value added, disaggregated by 20 manufacturing industries, were supplied by ECE in the case of the Federal Republic of Germany and the United Kingdom. The U.S. Department of Commerce Census of Manufactures 1967 was used in the case of the United States of America.

34. Column 6 of table 6 compares the yearly labour displacement resulting from recorded changes in labour productivity and that which results from the very large assumed increase in imports of manufactures from the developing countries. In all but five out of the 60 industries (20 in each of the three countries) under study, labour displacement caused by changes in labour productivity[16] was found to be larger than that caused by the assumed increase in imports. However, in the leather and leather goods industry in the Federal Republic of Germany and in the clothing and footwear, the leather and leather goods, the basic metal manufacturing and miscellaneous manufacturing industries in the United Kingdom, the labour displacement effect of increased imports was greater than that of changes in labour productivity. In most other cases, labour productivity effects were considerably greater than those of assumed increased imports of manufactures from developing countries. These comparisons of the probable magnitudes involved show that the employment problems on an industry level resulting from increased competition from imports from developing countries are likely to be far more manageable than the employment problems presented by rising labour productivity.

[15] See footnote 13 above.

[16] There are three cases where the index of labour input per unit of value added appears to have increased (viz. the wood and cork products, furniture and leather, and leather goods industries in the United Kingdom).

35. The main conclusion to be drawn from tables 1-6 is that the adjustment problems that result from increased imports of manufactures from developing countries vary considerably from industry to industry. However, the over-all magnitudes, measured in terms of labour displacement, are not very large. Even in the case of the very large increases in imports of manufactures from developing countries assumed by this study, total labour displacement is no more than 0.7 per cent of total employment in manufacturing industry. Bearing in mind that industries have in the past adapted without too much difficulty, partly through their own effort and partly through government measures, to the much larger labour displacement created by rising labour productivity and increased imports from other developed countries, and taking into account the fact that some increases in domestic demand are likely to take place in the future, the over-all impact of the increased imports is not likely to present a serious problem. However, tables 1-5 also identify certain industries which appear to be more sensitive to imports from the developing countries. The sensitive industries seem to differ slightly from country to country, but will usually include the footwear and clothing industry, the leather and leather goods industry and, to a lesser extent, the basic metal manufacturing and electrical machinery industries.

36. In the post-war period, most developed market-economy countries have maintained high and relatively stable levels of employment associated with significant gains in productivity and increasing shares of exports in production and of imports in consumption, particularly in the case of manufactured goods. Seen against this background, rising levels of imports and productivity appear as essential elements in the dynamic process of economic growth and international specialization.

37. Developing countries should be allowed to participate fully in the move towards increasing specialization of production and trade in manufactured goods. Particular attention should be given to the need for making room for their exports in those areas where they have already gained competitive advantage. As is demonstrated by post-war economic history, the developed countries stand to gain from the adaptation of their industries to changes in the world economy. Problems may admittedly raise in the short run. Moreover, to the extent that changes in production and trade would reflect comparative advantages, certain industrial branches in the developed countries would tend to lose ground over time, since their economic characteristics are such that losses in the domestic market are not likely to be fully offset by gains in foreign markets through specialization efforts. However, it is precisely the objective of adjustment assistance to facilitate structural change in the interest of the world economy as a whole.

CHAPTER III

Review of existing adjustment assistance policies in the developed market-economy countries

A. Various types of adjustment assistance

38. Adjustment assistance in the developed market-economy countries is given to industry and/or labour either for their rehabilitation and modernization as productive factors within an industry, or for re-allocation into different and presumably more productive activities. While national, local or regional governments within these coun-

tries are usually the source of such assistance, there are cases in which aid is forthcoming principally from private industrial groups.

39. Adjustment assistance measures provided for industry may include capital grants, low-interest loans, loan guarantees, interest rebates or subsidies, various types of tax concessions, liberal depreciation allowances, engineering, marketing and management advice and provision of development sites and related infrastructure. Assistance to labour typically consists of one or more of the following: a supplement to, or an extension of ordinary unemployment insurance payments; funding and provision of vocational retraining services; and assistance in relocating, including reimbursement of removal expenses.

40. The arrangements for the administration of adjustment assistance programmes and the agency or authority that decides on the need for such assistance vary among the developed market-economy countries. Generally, in those countries, no single body has had responsibility for the administration of adjustment assistance programmes. The administration and implementation of such programmes involve a number of governmental agencies. Legislation provides for institutional arrangements within the existing administrative structure, through separate or specialized bodies or both. In many cases applications for adjustment assistance by firms and by workers are dealt with separately, the former by the Ministry of Industry and/or Commerce, and the latter by the Ministry of Labour, or similar bodies. In other countries, specialized bodies exist to deal with problems relating to specific industries, such as the textile and shipbuilding industries. In still other developed market-economy countries, the task of examining requests for adjustment assistance is carried out by a separate agency, which determines whether the applicant has met the eligibility criteria before further action is taken on the request.

41. Governmental adjustment assistance measures in the developed market-economy countries are typically available within the context of national programmes designed to help workers and firms adapt to economic dislocation, whatever its proximate cause. Furthermore, adjustment assistance may be provided within the framework of regional development programmes pursued by the national government, often in co-operation with local or regional development authorities. Adjustment assistance programmes geared specifically to economic dislocations caused by increased imports are the exception rather than the rule. Moreover, as has been discussed in earlier reports by the UNCTAD secretariat, none of the developed market-economy countries had available measures specifically designed to ease structural adjustment in industries in order to provide larger opportunities for imports from developing countries; however, it was likely that the implementation of adjustment assistance measures adopted under general or specific legislation had in some countries facilitated increases in imports from those countries.[17]

B. Costs and benefits of trade liberalization facilitated by adjustment assistance measures

42. Adjustment assistance programmes for the adaptation of domestic industries could eliminate inefficiency and waste throughout the industrial sector. Increased production and competitiveness of the industrial sector will facilitate trade liberalization particularly also with respect to relaxation and eventual elimination of tariff and non-tariff barriers applied to imports from the developing countries. Protection of existing production and structure of employment is applied in developed market-economy countries without due consideration being paid to its burden on the domestic economy.[18] It is important therefore to consider briefly the basic costs and benefits of structural adaptation of industry in these countries.

43. In the developed countries, adjustment assistance leading to trade liberalization would involve the re-allocation of production factors from less efficient into more efficient domestic industries. Temporary deterioration in the developed country's balance of payments following trade liberalization might be expected, since, even with very efficient adjustment assistance programmes, the immediate increase in imports following trade liberalization will normally occur before the affected factors have been fully retrained and re-allocated into more efficient export-oriented industries. Re-allocation may be expected to cause psychological and social hardships for the affected workers, as well as possible loss of income and other employment rights. The scrapping of not fully depreciated capital equipment likewise involves a cost for the affected firms.

44. The budgetary cost to the developed country undertaking adjustment assistance programmes must also be considered. Funds expended by the national Government to workers or to industry, the loss of tax revenues or interest income forgone on low-interest government loans — all these costs are reflected in the government budget and imply a greater tax burden on the tax-paying public.

45. But while there are, qualitatively speaking, definite "costs" to develop market-economy countries arising from adjustment assistance, there is reason to believe that these costs will be more than offset by the benefits flowing from trade liberalization.

46. The benefits arise principally from the more efficient allocation of world resources which follows upon trade liberalization. The effects of developed-country trade liberalization facilitated by adjustment assistance will be of obvious benefit to the developing countries which are able to take advantage of the increased export opportunities. Foreign exchange earnings from the export of manufactures and semi-manufactures in which they have a comparative advantage will be enhanced. This, in turn, will enable the developing countries to import capital equipment necessary for their further industrialization. Furthermore, to the extent that factors of production are mobile in the developing countries, the latter will benefit from the same type of re-allocative effect as the developed nations. The dynamic effects of new investment, brought

---

[17] See "Adjustment Assistance Measures: report by the UNCTAD secretariat" (TD/B/C.2/106), para. 4.

[18] See in this connexion OECD, *Inflation: The Present Problem— Report by the Secretary-General*, December 1970, pp. 41-56.

about by expansion of the more efficient industries, will be significant in both the developing and developed countries. The international community as a whole would also benefit from trade liberalization measures taken by the developed market-economy countries. As a result of the ensuing more efficient international division of labour, world prices of a number of internationally traded products may be expected to be lower. In addition, shifts in the production mix of the trade liberalizing developed countries and the developing countries would probably have implications for the optimal pattern of production in the rest of the world. Providing that factors of production in the rest of the world were mobile, further efficiency in the global allocation of resources would be possible. In the developed market-economy countries trade liberalization facilitated by structural adaptation of industry would make a positive contribution to their own consumer welfare and price stability. Furthermore, re-allocation of resources would tend to raise average productivity and hence increase return on factors of production. This would also allow the developed market-economy countries to reap benefits from an increased ability to export products of those industries in which they are internationally particularly competitive.

C. Some general considerations relating to adjustment assistance policies in the developed market-economy countries

47. Several general considerations with respect to adjustment assistance policies as a preferred alternative to protection in the developed market-economy countries should be emphasized. The shape of certain substantial parts of industry in these countries depends heavily upon government intervention, both through trade policies and through direct financial aid and administrative regulations such as those pertaining to government procurement and national standards. The tendency to think in terms of keeping alive declining industrial activities hardly justified under conditions of full employment and rapid growth has led to defensive and protectionist policies in several industries. During the Second United Nations Development Decade the emphasis should be shifted in developed market-economy countries to an outward-looking trade policy which no longer impedes imports, as well as to forward-looking employment and production policies which remove the causes of resource wastage in industry and identify and encourage those industries best fitted to exploit changing international trends in supply and demand. Increased advantage should be taken of the great potential supply possibilities in the developing countries, particularly for labour-intensive manufactured products.

48. The nature and scope of adjustment assistance policies and programmes to ease structural adaptation of industry, which in turn will facilitate increasing imports from the developing countries, vary among developed market-economy countries. One reason is the different degree to which import-competing industries in the developed countries are protected by tariff or non-tariff barriers. In the case of those countries with high trade barriers, there is room for significant trade liberalization and hence potentially significant injury to domestic factors

of production in the affected import-competing industries. Adequate adjustment assistance policies would be necessary in such countries, *ceteris paribus*, to facilitate the expansion of imports from the developed world. Furthermore, in the case of countries with relatively high trade barriers, the adequacy of general adjustment assistance programmes in regard to structural dislocations caused by factors other than increased imports cannot be taken necessarily to mean that these same programmes will be able to facilitate, and even to encourage, trade liberalization. Another reason is the difference in fundamental factor mobility in the various countries. In countries characterized by relatively high resource mobility, the need for formal adjustment assistance programmes to aid in resource re-allocations is not as great as it is in countries where such mobility is lower.

49. A second general consideration relates to the evidence of the preliminary quantitative study in chapter II that, for many of the developed market-economies, the aggregate labour displacement effects of a rapid expansion of imports from the developing countries would probably be insignificant compared to the continual labour displacement because of domestic productivity increases, and in the perspective of the very low annual growth rate in domestic consumption required to absorb these imports. This evidence underlines on the one hand the relative flexibility of developed-country adjustment assistance policies vis-à-vis imports from the developing countries, and shows on the other hand that the pressures in most developed market-economy countries favouring the retention or establishment of tariff and non-tariff barriers against exports from developing countries seem vastly disproportionate to the relative insignificance of these exports in the aggregate as a source of economic dislocation. The reason for this disproportion is basically twofold. First, import-competing industries in the developed countries are subject to competition from both other developed countries and the developing countries, and in many cases the increase in imports from the former outweighs the increase in imports from the latter countries. Since domestic protectionist pressures are typically aimed at the "total" import threat, the developing countries often face trade barriers in the developed world which are intended to restrict a much larger volume of potential imports from other developed market-economy countries.[19] Secondly, dislocations of the domestic economy arising from international competitive shifts or changes in trade policy typically encounter a much lower degree of acceptance than structural disturbances resulting from changes in domestic demand and technological advances. Structural adjustment is often left to market forces, although in recent years many developed market-economy countries have undertaken to facilitate this adjustment with general adjustment assistance policies and regional development programmes. Structural adjustments necessitated by

---

[19] Advance liberalization of import restrictions in favour of imports from developing countries only might encounter less domestic pressures. See on this subject the reports by the UNCTAD secretariat entitled "Programme for the liberalization of quantitative restrictions and other non-tariff barriers in developed countries on products of export interest to developing countries" (TD/120 and Supp.1). (For TD/120/Supp.1, see p. 141 above.)

increased imports, on the other hand, do not appear to receive the necessary attention, so that the threat of resource displacement due to increased imports tends to be met quite easily by means of tariff or non-tariff barriers. Domestic interests have been willing in many cases to forgo such protection only in return for governmental or private adjustment assistance measures designed to aid in their re-allocation to other industries or segments of industries.

50. A third consideration, which also follows from the quantitative study summarized in chapter II, relates to the evidence that only certain specific industries in the developed market-economy countries are likely to be materially affected as a result of significant trade liberalization in favour of the developing countries. While this is only a preliminary study, it does suggest that particular attention should be given to the adequacy of developed-country adjustment assistance programmes as they impinge on these more sensitive sectors. Furthermore, the developed market-economy industries most vulnerable to factor displacement from increased imports from the developing countries tend to be labour intensive in the developed countries. This indicates that special attention should also be devoted to determining whether the adjustment assistance programmes in the developed market-economy countries adequately facilitate labour mobility.

51. A further consideration relates to the observations following the present review of adjustment assistance policies in selected developed market-economy countries

in the context of facilitating an expansion of imports from the developing countries. None of the developed market-economy countries has available measures specifically designed to ease structural adjustment in industry in order to provide larger opportunities for imports from developing countries. Moreover, some countries have governmental programmes considered by them to be "adjustment assistance", but not so considered by others.

52. Among the developed market-economy countries, Canada and the United States of America are the only countries with specific, import-related adjustment assistance programmes. The United Kingdom has a programme of limited duration designed specifically to facilitate structural change in its cotton textile industry. Sweden, on the other hand, has relied almost exlusively on its national labour market policy as the instrument for promoting structural adjustment. In the Federal Republic of Germany considerable reliance is placed on the market as a mechanism for facilitating structural adjustment, but recently the Government has made a general policy commitment to promote domestic structural readjustment with a view to facilitating increased imports from the developing countries.

53. As to whether existing adjustment assistance policies and programmes do in fact facilitate increased imports from developing countries, this is not readily discernible from the information and data so far available concerning the application of these measures in the developed market-economy countries.

CHAPTER IV

Main aspects of adjustment assistance policies and programmes in selected developed market-economy countries

54. In the following sections the adjustment assistance policies and programmes of selected developed market-economy countries (Canada, the Federal Republic of Germany, Sweden, the United Kingdom and the United States of America)[20] are reviewed and the main aspects of these policies and programmes, including the manner and extent to which they facilitate increased imports from the developing countries, are analysed. The adjustment assistance policies of the European Communities are also reviewed to illustrate the application of adjustment assistance in a multilateral framework, based on the notion of sharing the adjustment costs arising from multilateral trade liberalization measures.

A. Canada

55. The basic policy of Canada concerning adjustment assistance is that the restructuring of the market economy is a natural and continuing process and that firms and

industries constantly adapt themselves to changes in market conditions and market prospects. The main aim of the Canadian adjustment assistance programme is to advance the developed, efficient and competitive industries, it being recognized that such programmes can and do facilitate adjustment to changing patterns of international production and trade.[21]

56. Canada has adopted a number of adjustment assistance policies designed to aid structural adjustment and over-all factor mobility. These policies cover general programmes designed to facilitate adjustment to dislocation, whatever the proximate cause, a regional development programme, and several programmes which are directly related to factor displacement caused by increased imports. None of these programmes is specifically designed to facilitate increased imports from the developing countries.

57. General adjustment assistance programmes in Canada include the following:

(a) The Technical and Vocational Training Assistance Act, under which financial assistance for the development of technical and vocational training facilities is provided;

---

[20] These countries were selected on the basis of the nature of their adjustment assistance policies and the extent to which information was available concerning implementation of these policies. As more information becomes available concerning the adjustment assistance policies of those and other developed market-economy countries, more detailed reviews will be undertaken.

[21] See GATT document COM.TD/H/3, 3 February 1966.

(b) The Manpower Mobility Program, which grants financial assistance to workers who are either unemployed or have been notified of permanent lay-off. These grants are designed to cover removal costs, resettlement and other incidental expenses connected with the relocation of a worker and his family, up to specified maximum amounts. Small grants are also extended to unemployed persons looking for work outside their home district. These grants include reimbursement of the job seeker's travel expenses, together with a small allowance for family support while he is away from home; and

(c) Canada Manpower Centres, which are distributed throughout the country and which, under the general supervision of the Department of Manpower and Immigration, act as a kind of clearing-house for information on employment opportunities throughout Canada.

58. Under the Regional Development Incentives Act (1969) financial assistance is available to firms proposing to establish a new facility or to expand or modernize an existing facility in a designated development region of the country. The amount of the development incentive, which is in the form of a capital grant, is related to the capital costs of establishing or expanding the facility and is, in part, dependent upon the number of jobs created by the new investment. Firms receiving such financial assistance are required to keep the Department of Manpower and Immigration informed of their prospective manpower needs and to co-operate with the Department in its employment counselling, training and placement activities.

59. Canada has three specifically foreign-trade-related adjustment assistance programmes: the Automotive Manufacturing Assistance Regulations, which accompanied the 1965 Canada-United States Agreement concerning Automotive Products; the more recent General Adjustment Assistance Programme, which is geared to the Kennedy Round tariff concessions; and the Textile and Clothing Board Act of 1971.

60. The 1965 Automotive Products Agreement was designed further to integrate and rationalize the North American automotive industry through the elimination of tariffs on trade in new automobiles, and also in parts and accessories for original equipment, between Canada and the United States. Since the objective was industry rationalization across national borders, economic dislocation in both countries was inevitable. Consequently, the domestic political feasibility of the Agreement depended upon the establishment of satisfactory adjustment assistance procedures for the affected factors in both Canada and the United States of America.

61. In Canada the Automotive Manufacturing Assistance Regulations[22] provided for an Adjustment Assistance Board to evaluate adjustment assistance petitions arising from injury allegedly caused by the 1965 Agreement and to administer loans granted to petitioning firms, after determination that such a loan would give the manufacturer a "reasonable prospect of a profitable operation that is not available through other sources of financing". Canadian automotive products manufacturers (excluding automobile manufacturers or subsidiaries of automobile manufacturers, which were predominantly American-owned) who could prove actual or potential injury as a result of the Agreement were eligible for such loans, on condition that they were used to modernize existing facilities or to convert into other lines.

62. Assistance for workers affected by the Automotive Products Agreement consisted of certain supplemental unemployment benefits. Petitioning employees had to satisfy the Board with respect to two criteria in order to qualify for assistance: (a) that 10 per cent of the work force or fifty employees, whichever is less, of an eligible automobile or automotive products manufacturer or branch or subdivision thereof, "have been or will be laid off for a period of four weeks or more", and (b) that "the lay-off, or a proportion thereof determined by the Board, was or will be caused by the termination or decrease of production, or other activity arising from the implementation of the automotive programme". Workers were potentially eligible for assistance regardless of whether they worked for a Canadian or a foreign-owned or foreign-controlled firm.

63. With respect to adjustment assistance under the Automotive Regulations it is of interest to note that, while workers dislocated as a result of the Automotive Products Agreement presumably were able to avail themselves of retraining and relocation assistance under Canada's general manpower mobility programme, there was no requirement that injured manufacturers had to re-allocate their capital into the production of different products. Yet substantial resource re-allocation evidently did occur in response to the elimination of tariffs under the Automotive Products Agreement. Two-way trade between Canada and the United States of America in the affected automotive products increased substantially faster than combined production by the two countries following implementation of the Agreement.[23]

64. While the principle was incorporated in the Automotive Regulations that petitioning firms and workers could base their petitions on *threatened* as well as on actual injury caused by implementation of the Agreement, information is not available as to whether assistance was actually granted on this basis. Under this programme, over $1 million in benefits were paid out to Canadian workers from 1965 to 1968.[24] Loans to manufacturers authorized under the provisions of this programme up to 30 June 1971 totalled $94 million.[25]

65. The General Adjustment Assistance Programme, as established in 1968 and revised in 1971, is designed to make assistance available to firms which establish that they have either received serious injury or are threatened with serious injury as a result of increased imports caused by Canadian tariff reductions under the Kennedy Round, or that they have significant new export opportunities as a result of Kennedy Round concessions by other coun-

---

[22] *Ibid.*, pp. 18-22.

[23] J. Jonish, "Adjustment assistance experience under the U.S.-Canadian Automotive Agreement", Seminar Discussion Paper 13, University of Michigan, 10 September 1969.

[24] Jonish, op. cit.

[25] Information supplied direct by the Canadian Government.

tries; eligibility also requires the submission by the petitioning firm to the General Adjustment Assistance Board of a satisfactory plan for the restructuring of its operations so as to improve its competitive position, as well as proof that "sufficient financing cannot be obtained on reasonable terms from other sources".[26] Assistance can include governmental insurance of up to 90 per cent of adjustment loans advanced by private lenders, direct governmental loans and governmental financial support for technical assistance to firms proposing to make improvements in their production, managerial, marketing and financial operations. It should be noted, however, that assistance to manufacturers under the Programme is not restricted to firms intending to shift their activities to different products. Indeed considerable emphasis is placed upon the re-organizing and re-equipping of firms to compete more effectively and "to survive". This would not, in principle, rule out assistance to manufacturers in declining industries that are attempting to maintain their share of the domestic market. Up to October 1971 the General Adjustment Assistance Board, operating under the Programme, authorized loan insurance of $37.9 million to assist 37 manufacturers and approved grants totalling $105,000 for the provision of consulting assistance to 17 firms. Fifteen of the 37 manufacturers to be assisted by loan insurance were in the textile, footwear and food products industries. None of the 11 firms in the textile industry qualifying for this assistance, however, based their petitions on injury received from increased imports.[27]

66. As a condition for receiving governmental guarantees or loans under the Programme, manufacturers are required to give three-months' notice of lay-offs to both the affected workers and the Board, where the lay-offs involve 20 or more workers and will last at least two months. The notice period is intended to be utilized for the retraining and relocation of the affected workers, in co-operation with the Department of Manpower and Immigration.[28]

67. Because of the close relationship between trade and domestic industrial development, the Department of Industry and the Department of Trade and Commerce were merged in 1970. The new Department of Industry, Trade and Commerce is "charged with developing and carrying out programmes, *inter alia*, to assist the adaptation of manufacturing industries to changing conditions in domestic and export markets and to change in the techniques of productions".[29] This department was instrumental in the introduction to and enactment by Parliament of the Textile and Clothing Board Act in May 1971. This legislation was a direct response to increased competition from imports in the textile and clothing industries. For instance, although Canada accepted no obligation automatically to increase access to the Canadian market under the LTA, imports of woven cotton textile products from developing countries, as a percentage of Canadian con-

sumption, increased from 7.1 per cent in 1960 to 12.5 per cent in 1965.[30] Over the period 1960-1967 the number of spindles and looms in place in the Canadian cotton textile industry declined by 6 per cent and 12 per cent respectively while employment in this sector fell by 8 per cent.[31]

68. The Textile and Clothing Board Act provides for a Textile and Clothing Board to evaluate temporary protection petitions from manufacturers and adjustment assistance petitions from worker's groups in the textile and clothing industries. (In this connexion it should also be noted that, under amendments made in January 1971 to the regulations governing the General Adjustment Assistance Programme, a manufacturer of textile or clothing goods or footwear who requires a loan to adapt efficiently to competition from textile or clothing goods or footwear "imported at such prices, in such quantities or under such conditions as to cause or threaten serious injury", and is unable to obtain this financing on reasonable terms from other sources, may qualify for an adjustment assistance loan from the general Adjustment Assistance Board without having to show that such injury is the result of increased imports attributable to Kennedy Round tariff reductions.)

69. A manufacturer may file a notice of complaint with the Textile and Clothing Board alleging that "the importation of the textile and clothing goods described in the notice is causing or threatening serious injury to his production in Canada of any textile and clothing goods". The petitioning firm is also required to file the Board a plan either for the "continued efficient development" of its operation or the phasing out of lines of production "that have no prospect of becoming internationally competitive". The plan must provide a means for the producer to compete in the Canadian market in the context of the prevailing tariff structure.

70. In reviewing the petitioning firm's complaint and adjustment plan, the Board is required to take into account any relevant manpower and regional considerations, provisions or international agreements, the "probable effect of any proposed special measures of protection on various classes of consumers", conditions prevailing in international trade and "the principle that special measures of protection are not to be implemented for the purpose of encouraging the maintenance of lines of production that have no prospects of becoming competitive with foreign goods in the market in Canada if the only protection to be provided" is that offered under the current structure of tariffs. On the basis of this review, the Board is to make a recommendation to the Minister of Industry, Trade and Commerce on whether "special measures of protection" should be implemented.

71. Groups of workers may likewise petition the Textile and Clothing Board for certification of eligibility for adjustment assistance benefits. The eligibility criteria for petitioning workers are similar to those operative under the Automotive Manufacturing Assistance Regulations, except that in this case the actual or threatened lay-

---

[26] GATT document COM.TD/W/88, 7 February 1969.

[27] Information supplied direct by the Canadian Government.

[28] See GATT document COM.TD/W/88.

[29] See "Adjustment assistance measures: report by the UNCTAD secretariat" (TD/B/C.2/106), para. 16.

[30] See GATT document COT/105, 26 September 1968, p. 90.

[31] See GATT document COT/W/115, 26 September 1969, table 10.

offs of workers need not be related to specific trade agreement concessions.

72. It is difficult to evaluate what the ultimate impact of the Act will be with respect to facilitating increased imports of textiles and clothing products from the developing countries. While the Act severs the tie between adjustment assistance and specific trade concessions, thereby in principle facilitating increased imports regardless of whether or not they arise from trade concessions or productivity advances abroad, it also incorporates a kind of escape-clause mechanism. This provision for "special measures of protection" is to be implemented only if the petitioning manufacturer plans ultimately to become competitive with foreign suppliers, but this increased competitiveness may well be achieved through modernization of productive facilities rather than through the phasing out of traditional productive activities. In this connexion it is worth mentioning that the Textile and Clothing Board did not find injury in the case of polyester-cotton yarns and, therefore, no quantitative restrictions were introduced in respect of this item. Bilateral agreements with 13 countries have been concluded with respect to the imposition of export restraints on cotton and cotton-polyester yarns.

B. Federal Republic of Germany

73. While the Federal Republic of Germany has no policy of adjustment assistance relating specifically to imports, there exist several general government programmes designed to facilitate structural adjustment, as well as Federal and *Länder* regional development programmes which may have the indirect effect of facilitating domestic adjustments to increases in imports.

74. The Federal Government has for some time granted limited financial assistance to unemployed workers for the purpose of retraining and relocation. More recently, with enactment of the Vocational Training Law of 1969 and the Law for the Promotion of Work, the Government has stepped up its financial support for vocational training, advanced training and retraining programmes. Displaced workers in the coal and iron ore mining sectors have been particularly heavy recipients of adjustment assistance from the Federal Government.[32]

75. Manufacturers in the Federal Republic of Germany are potentially eligible for Government guarantees of borrowing and direct credits at reduced interest rates for adjustment purposes.[33] Government policy is that direct credits are to be granted solely for the switching of production programmes to new items; no financial assistance for subsidizing existing production is contemplated. Adjustment credit facilities are made available under the European Recovery Programme Special Fund. Over the period 1958-1965, a total amount of DM99 million was made available but not utilized to the full. Certain forms of tax relief are also granted to facilitate the structural adaptation of industry. For instance, deferral of capital

gains taxes applicable to the sale of plant and equipment is provided for under the Income Tax Amendment Law of 1964.

76. Federal Government budgetary outlays in the form of capital grants and subsidies for industry adjustment designed to facilitate increased imports from developing countries would appear to be negligible in the Federal Republic. Funds allocated to the "promotion of industries, improvement of productivity and the Board of Rationalization" of the German economy in 1969 and 1970 amounted to only 1.5 per cent of total grants to industry. Indeed, principal recipients of such aid were traditional branches of industry such as coal and iron ore mining and shipbuilding, none of which compete significantly with imports of manufactures from the developing countries, and certain "new branches of industry", such as aviation, electronic data processing and atomic energy.[34]

77. The Regional Promotion Programme of the Federal Government apparently has assisted firms and workers within the Federal Republic to adapt to structural changes. An average of nearly 10,000 new jobs annually have been created in recent years as a result of investment subsidies provided under the Programme. Some of the individual *Land* development programmes have also assisted factor re-allocation by making available loans at reduced interest rates or interest subsidies to small and medium-sized firms undergoing structural adaptation.

78. The cotton textile industry in the Federal Republic has evidently undergone considerable structural adjustment in the recent years.[35] From 1960 to 1967 the number of spindles in place in the German cotton textile industry declined by 21 per cent, while the number of looms in place fell by 43 per cent. Cotton textile industry employment in the Federal Republic decreased by 34 per cent in the same period. While the textile industry has been the largest recipient of low interest credits under the Federal Government's European Recovery Programme Special Fund, and medium-sized textile firms in Baden-Würtemberg have received interest subsidies from the *Land* Government, most of the structural adjustment in this industry appears to have occurred without the assistance of governmental programmes. Consultations recently initiated between the Federal Government and the cotton textile industry concerning adoption of a specific programme to assist that sector, however, would seem to indicate that privately co-ordinated efforts at rationalization and adjustment in this industry are no longer adequate.

79. An evaluation of the extent to which the several adjustment assistance programmes in the Federal Republic have in the past facilitated increased imports from developing countries is not possible, given present data limitations. However, following guidelines[36] respecting the structural adjustment policy to be followed during the Second United

---

[32] See OECD, "A Survey of the Industrial Policies of 13 Member Countries"..., pp. 20-24 and 32-34.

[33] See GATT document COM.TD/H/3, pp. 26-33.

[34] Deutsches Institut für Wirtschaftsforschung, *Considerations concerning the problem of adjustment assistance measures*, memorandum, 4 August 1971.

[35] See GATT, *A Study on Cotton Textiles* (Geneva, July 1966), p.75; and GATT document COT/W/115, p. 35.

[36] Federal Republic of Germany, Government Press and Information Office, *Bulletin*, No. 25, 17 February 1971, pp. 263-274.

Nations Development Decade, recently issued by the Federal Government, are noteworthy in this regard:

"In the opinion of the Federal Government, structural adjustments constitute an indispensable requirement for sustained economic growth and improved international division of labour. Structural changes caused in the process of integrating the developing countries into the international division of labour should not be artificially delayed, but should, where necessary, be encouraged by appropriate structural adjustment measures. The migration of labour and capital from sectors which have to adjust to changing market conditions should not be prevented through support measures. Social hardships caused during the adjustment process should be counteracted through timely measures. Financial and fiscal incentives and investment guarantees against political risks should be applied to encourage the relocation of production (expansion of firms, establishment of new firms, joint ventures, investments in firms in developing countries).

"In its framework of growth-oriented structural policies, the Federal Government, in promoting the structural adjustment, retraining of labour for new jobs with better chances for the future, is taking into account the justified interests of the developing countries."*

C. Sweden

80. Adjustment assistance in Sweden is implemented principally within the context of that country's general labour market policy, although other measures are also available which relate specifically to structural adjustment of manufacturing and regional development objectives.[37] At present in Sweden there are no adjustment assistance programmes linked directly to increases in imports.

81. Swedish policy recognizes that "an important prerequisite for economic progress" is the re-allocation of resources from uncompetitive productive activities into more efficient sectors. An active labour market policy is seen as critical in facilitating this structural adjustment and overcoming demands for support or protection of uncompetitive industries. Measures to facilitate and stimulate the process of adjustment in the labour market have become an increasingly important element of Swedish economic policy in recent years.

82. The Swedish labour market policy is designed to promote general occupational and geographical mobility as well as regional development goals. With respect to general labour mobility the following measures are available under the direction of the National Labour Board:

(a) Travel allowances, which cover interview trip expenses for job-seeker and wife, together with removal costs;

(b) "Starting help", in the form of lump sum grants, the amount of which is tied to whether the new job is to be temporary or permanent;

(c) Resettlement allowances for entire families;

(d) Separation allowances to cover expense of maintaining two households (up to 12 months) in the event that a worker's family cannot immediately move to a new region;

(e) Government purchase of houses in depressed areas in the event that inability to sell his house prevents the worker from relocating to another area;

(f) Provision of dwellings in areas where jobs are available but housing scarce. Workers moving to such areas are given some priority in regard to housing;

(g) Workers participating in government-sponsored training courses receive a monthly subsistence allowance ordinarily ranging between 40 and 80 per cent of the average wage level for male workers in manufacturing industries;

(h) Subsidies to employers who operate vocational training programmes.

83. An attempt is being made to adapt these measures to changing conditions by means of 12-month forecasts of labour needs based on information collected by local offices of the national employment service, together with an "advance warning" system whereby employers are obliged to inform the employment service of planned lay-offs or plant close-downs. Furthermore, local employment offices in areas with acute unemployment problems can be temporarily reinforced. At all times adults have access to a national occupational counselling service.

84. Other Government measures designed principally to stimulate employment include public works projects, the placing of additional Government contracts with private industry, and fiscal provisions whereby during recession periods firms may set aside a certain portion of their profits free of tax for investment purposes.

85. Government-sponsored credit institutions have also been developed in Sweden with the specific aim of fostering structural adaptation of enterprises and the development of small and medium-sized firms. These institutions include the Swedish Investment Bank, which provides long-term financing for large, long-range, or particularly high-risk projects; the Industrial Credit Bank, the Business Credit Association and numerous trade development associations which provide financing for small and medium-sized enterprises.[38]

86. With respect to the promotion of regional development, Sweden's Industrial Location Policy provides for capital grants, generally not exceeding 35 per cent of construction costs, to firms locating in specified development areas.[39] In some cases, larger subsidies, covering in addition wage costs and training programmes of these firms, are available. The above-mentioned "advance

---

* Unofficial translation.

[37] See GATT document COM.TD/W/92/Add.3, 21 April 1969.

[38] See OECD, "A Survey of the Industrial Policies of 13 Member Countries"..., pp. 268-269.

[39] See OECD, The regional factor in economic development: policies in fifteen industrialised OECD countries (Paris, 1970), p. 83.

warning" system helps to cushion the impact of large worker lay-offs on the immediate community.

87. A recent Royal Commission has surveyed Sweden's labour market policy and concluded that it has been generally successful. In 1968, out of a labour force of 3.8 million, 53,000 individuals received travel allowances, and about half of those workers also received some form of "starting help". Approximately 100,000 people commenced retraining courses, of an average duration of four months. The total expenditure under the national labour market policy for the year 1971 is said to amount to more than $400 million.[40] With respect to geographical mobility, a 1964 investigation of 1,091 persons who had received "starting help" a year earlier showed that roughly 90 per cent had not returned to their home community and could therefore be regarded as successful cases. Another investigation was made in 1964 of individuals who had completed retraining courses a year earlier. This study of occupational mobility showed that only 48 per cent of those persons were employed in the occupation for which they had been retrained and that another 38 per cent were employed in other (usually allied) occupations. A follow-up study in late 1966 indicated that roughly one-third of those individuals were still employed in the occupation in which they had received training. The Royal Commission concluded that this relatively high "fall-out" among retrained workers was the result of a chronic labour shortage in Sweden in certain expanding industries together with generally full employment on a nationwide basis, which meant that the selection of applicants for retraining was limited, and to a great extent consisted of so-called "unemployables". The Commission therefore recommended that the retraining programme be extended to other than unemployed workers, since the problem was as much to alleviate manpower shortages as to eliminate unemployment.[41]

88. Evidence is also available with respect to the implementation of these general adjustment assistance measures in the context of communities particularly hard hit by increased foreign competition. In both of the cases concerned, the phasing out of a shipyard in the small town of Oskarshamn, and the reduction of productive activities of a textile firm in Borås, advance warning to the local Labour Board of imminent lay-offs facilitated the relocation of affected workers. Other adjustment assistance measures included retraining, attraction of new industry to the affected communities, and the awarding of new orders designed to slow the dismissal rate of the affected persons.[42]

89. The Swedish textile and clothing industries have been particularly affected by foreign competition in recent years. Imports of cotton textiles and clothing from all sources increased by 69 per cent between 1962 and 1968. The number of spindles and looms in place in the Swedish cotton textile industry fell by 51 per cent and 41 per cent respectively in the period 1960-1967. Employment in the domestic cotton textile industry declined by 35 per cent in the same time span.[43] While Sweden's textile import policy is more liberal than that of other western European countries with important textile sectors, the Government has from time to time been forced to impose temporary restrictions on these imports in order to deal with acute employment problems not amenable to rapid solution by the general labour market policy. A Government committee of inquiry has recently been appointed to examine the problem of foreign competition in the textile and clothing sectors and to recommend measures that might be taken to promote the competitiveness of the domestic industries.[44]

D. United Kingdom

90. The policy of the United Kingdom Government regarding adjustment assistance is that such measures should be viewed in a long-term perspective. It is prepared to consider such measures in particular cases of need, but prefers a pragmatic approach to the problem, whereby help for purposes of structural adjustment is made available as and when necessary, provided however that market forces are allowed to contribute toward achieving the necessary adjustments in the economy. Government policy allows a wide range of measures to assist localities suffering from unemployment for whatever reason, including increased competition from developing countries.[45]

91. With the exception of the Cotton Industry Act of 1959 and the Shipbuilding Industry Act of 1967, adjustment assistance policies in the United Kingdom have been geared solely to general structural adjustment and regional development objectives. Indeed, the policy of the United Kingdom with respect to changing competitive conditions in foreign trade has recently been expressed as "normally" allowing domestic industries to make their own adjustments to these changes, including adjustments necessitated by the introduction of the GSP, although the Government was prepared to consider such measures in "particular cases of need", as evidenced by the aforementioned Cotton Industry Act.

92. The more important general adjustment assistance policies in the United Kingdom[46] include the following:

(a) The Industrial Expansion Act of 1968, by which the Government is authorized to provide financial support, "through industrial investment schemes" for projects which are designed to promote efficiency, profitability, productive capacity or technological advance in an industry. This financial support, in the form of either

---

[40] See the report of the Committee on Manufactures on its fifth session (*Official Records of the Trade and Development Board, Eleventh Session, Supplement No. 2* (TD/B/352)), annex IV, para. 7.

[41] GATT document COM.TD/W/92/Add.3.

[42] *Ibid.*, and GATT document COM.TD/H/3.

[43] GATT document COT/W/115, pp. 20-26.

[44] OECD, "A Survey of the Industrial Policies of 13 Member Countries"..., p. 272.

[45] See the report of the Committee on Manufactures on its fifth session (*Official Records of the Trade and Development Board, Eleventh Session, Supplement No. 2* (TD/B/352)), annex IV, para 2.

[46] See OECD, "A Survey of the Industrial Policies of 13 Member Countries"..., pp. 223-242; and GATT document TD/W/96/Add.6, 30 April 1969.

capital grants or loans, is intended only for growth industries and is provided only when unavailability of funds from other sources would mean that the project would not be undertaken;

(*b*) Capital grants amounting to 20 per cent of investment (40 per cent in "development areas") in new plant and equipment for use in manufacturing, ship repairing, construction and mining industries are available from the Government. In the fiscal year 1970 the budgetary cost of such grants amounted to £590 million;

(*c*) The Industrial Training Act of 1964. under which the Government is empowered to establish industrial training boards with the following objectives: (i) to ensure an adequate supply of trained manpower at all levels in industry; (ii) to improve the quality and efficiency of industrial training, and (iii) to distribute training costs more evenly among firms. Retraining is undertaken both by Government training centres and private industry on a partially subsidized basis.

93. With respect to regional development in the United Kingdom, additional financial assistance for the costs of retraining is available to firms providing new jobs in the "development areas". Certain types of assistance are also available to workers relocating in those areas. The Government also provides loans (at moderate rather than preferential rates) and a smaller number of capital grants to enterprises locating in the "development areas". Furthermore, the Government, through the Board of Trade, has followed a policy of establishing industrial estates and constructing factories in these high priority areas. The factories are then sold or rented to industry at prices which effectively convey some element of governmental subsidy.[47]

94. As noted earlier, the United Kingdom has also embarked on several extensive adjustment assistance programmes relating to specific industries. The Shipbuilding Industry Act of 1967 (as amended) is a case in point. This act provides for a Shipbuilding Industry Board which is authorized to make various types of financial grants to shipbuilding enterprises for the purpose of consolidating into groups for re-equipping purposes. In addition, under this act the Minister of Technology is empowered to guarantee bank loans made to British shipowners for the purpose of ordering ships from British yards, provided that the Shipbuilding Industry Board recommends a guarantee on the basis of the shipbuilders' progress in reorganizing his productive establishment.

95. The cotton industry is another case in point.[48] Between 1912 and 1958 annual production of cotton fabrics in the United Kingdom fell by almost 75 per cent as a result of the decline in exports and substantial increases in imports. In order to facilitate the elimination of the resultant surplus capacity in the domestic cotton textile industry, the Government introduced a specific programme of adjustment assistance, embodied in the Cotton Industry Act of 1959. After extensive consultation with the industry, the Government contributed two-thirds of the

compensation for scrapping obsolete equipment in the spinning, doubling and weaving sections of the industry and about one-fourth in the finishing sector. The balance of the compensation was financed by bank loans which were to be repaid from the proceeds of a levy on firms remaining in the industry. Between 1959 and 1966 (when the provisions of the Act expired) the total amount of compensation paid for scrapping obsolete equipment was $59 million, of which $32 million was paid by the Government and $27 million by the industry. Under this Act the Government also agreed to pay 25 per cent of the cost of approved re-equipment schemes. The net value of the grant was much less than 25 per cent, however, because depreciation allowances had to be calculated on the basis of the net cost to the firm of machinery purchases. Grants by the Government over the period 1959-1966 for these purposes totalled about $38 million.

96. The Cotton Industry Act also included an innovation in that provision was made for compensation of employees losing their jobs as a result of the foregoing scrapping and re-equipping schemes. This compensation was to be financed entirely by a levy on firms remaining in the industry. Between 1959 and 1966 the cost of this compensation to displaced employees totalled $13 million and further levies were expected. More recently, additional assistance was provided to workers in this industry through the establishment of the Cotton and Allied Textiles Industrial Training Board in 1966. Training measures authorized by the Board, which potentially are available to approximately 250,000 workers in 8,000 individual establishments, are financed by a levy on all employers in the industry. Actual training grants are then made available to those firms operating training programmes approved by the Board.

97. The trend of United Kingdom exports and imports of cotton textiles and clothing observed for the period 1912-1958 has continued in the period following the Cotton Industry Act of 1959. United Kingdom exports of cotton textiles and clothing declined by 26 per cent in the period 1962-1968, while imports in the same period rose by 25 per cent. In response to this continued trend in foreign trade and the Government-supported scheme for eliminating surplus capacity, the number of spindles in place in the domestic cotton textile industry decreased by 53 per cent between 1960 and 1967, while the number of looms in place fell in the same period by 41 per cent. Cotton textile industry employment fell by 103,200 in this period, a decline of 32 per cent. In spite of the continued contraction of the domestic cotton textile industry, the Government has apparently avoided taking protectionist measures. On the contrary, it is planned that after 1 January 1972 imports of cotton textiles from the Commonwealth countries will be subject to tariff rather than quota barriers.

E. United States of America

98. Adjustment assistance measures in the United States of America are available under programmes designed to facilitate general structural adjustment and regional development, as well as under specifically import-related

[47] OECD, *The regional factor in economic development...*, pp. 75, 80-81 and 86.

[48] See GATT, *A Study on Cotton Textiles...*, pp. 72-73; and GATT document COT/W/115, p. 49.

programmes provided for under the Trade Expansion Act of 1962 and the Automotive Products Trade Act of 1965. The United States does not, however, employ adjustment assistance measures specifically intended to facilitate increased imports from the developing countries.

99. General adjustment assistance policies designed to improve labour mobility in the United States include:[49]

(a) The Manpower Development and Training Act of 1962, under which a nationwide programme of training for unemployed and under-employed workers has been established;

(b) The Job Corps, which provides training for young adults in rural conservation and urban training centres;

(c) The Neighbourhood Youth Corps, which provides full or part-time experience and training for youths;

(d) The Job Opportunities in the Business Sector program, in which the Department of Labour and co-operating firms share the expense of training and providing jobs for "hard-core" unemployed workers;

(e) The Adult Basic Education program, which provides pre-high-school-level classes to individuals whose employment potential is limited by severe educational deficiencies;

(f) The Vocational Education Act of 1963, under which the Government supports vocational training for occupations not requiring a college degree;

(g) The "New Careers" program, which trains disadvantaged adults in the context of public and non-profit agencies in certain areas of high social priority;

(h) The "Operation Mainstream" program, which provides experience for chronically unemployed adults, designed to prepare them for competitive employment;

(i) The Work Incentive program, under which employable persons 16 years and older receiving welfare assistance are referred to suitable jobs, training, or other pre-employment programmes to enable them to become economically independent.

100. General adjustment assistance policies primarily intended to aid small and medium-sized enterprises include:

(a) The Farmers' Home Administration program, which provides credits, guarantees and technical assistance to family farms affected by natural disasters or structural economic changes. Since 1964 this agency has also made loans to low-income farm and non-farm rural families and to co-operatives organized by such families;

(b) The Small Business Administration, which provides credits and counselling to small firms;

(c) The Economic Development Administration (formerly the Area Development Administration) provides a wide range of guarantees, loans and direct grants in connexion with regional development programmes.

101. Adjustment assistance policies in the United States that relate specifically to foreign trade date from passage of the Trade Expansion Act in 1962. The close association in United States policy between escape clause and adjustment assistance measures also originated with the particular provisions of that act.

102. Escape clause action was quite prevalent in the United States prior to 1962. Of 113 investigations into escape clause petitions between 1948 and 1962, the United States Tariff Commission decided in favour of escape clause action in 33 cases and was evenly divided in eight others.[50] Proponents of trade liberalization urged that more stringent escape clause criteria be incorporated in the Trade Expansion Act, so as to reassure United States negotiating partners that future trade concessions to be made by the United States would be more or less permanent; that is, free from escape clause action.[51]

103. Three basic eligibility criteria were embodied in the 1962 legislation:

(a) That imports of the article in question are entering the United States in increased quantities;

(b) That such increased imports are attributable "in major part" to trade agreement concessions; and

(c) That the increased imports are "the major factor" in causing, or threatening to cause, serious injury to the industry in question.

All these tests are more stringent than those provided under previous United States trade agreement legislation. Of particular importance, however, are the second and third criteria, inasmuch as the Tariff Commission, which is charged with investigating whether these criteria are being met, has generally interpreted the language "the major part" or "major factor" to mean a particularly high degree of causation.

104. While the tightening of the escape clause criteria served to improve the validity of United States offers of trade concessions, it was felt that wide domestic support for further trade liberalization depended upon the availability of adjustment assistance as an alternative to escape clause action.[52] Consequently, provision was also made under the Trade Expansion Act for adjustment assistance to factors of production displaced or facing dislocation as a result of trade concessions made under that act. The criteria by which petitioners' claims are evaluated have generally been interpreted by the Tariff Commission as being identical to those applying to escape clause petitions.

105. Under the Trade Expansion Act, firms and workers' groups may petition for either escape clause relief an adjustment assistance, or for both. In either case the Tariff Commission will undertake an industry investigation. If the Commission finds that the industry has been injured in accordance with the three eligibility criteria mentioned earlier, the President may provide tariff relief to the industry or refer the firms comprising the industry and/or the workers concerned to the appropriate executive departments for certification of eligibility to apply for adjustment assistance. Such firms or workers' groups are eligible for assistance if they can meet the foregoing eligi-

---

[49] GATT, documents COM.TD/W/92, 14 March 1969, and COM.TD/H/3.

[50] See T. W. Murray and M. R. Egmund, "Full employment, trade expansion and adjustment assistance", *The Southern Economic Journal*, vol. XXXVI, No. 4, April 1970.

[51] See S. D. Metzger, "The escape clause and adjustment assistance: proposals and assessments", *Law and Policy in International Business*, Summer 1970.

[52] *Ibid.*, and J. A. Manley, "Adjustment assistance: experience under the automotive Products Trade Act of 1965", *Harvard International Law Journal*, vol. 10, No. 2, Spring 1969.

bility criteria. If the Tariff Commission fails to find that the industry as a whole has been injured, or if a petition for adjustment assistance only has been filed, the President may still certify the petitioners as eligible to apply for adjustment assistance provided the firm or workers' group can show that the eligibility criteria are met in their respect. While escape clause relief is possible under this legislation, the President retains the discretion to provide adjustment assistance as an alternative to protection. Furthermore, while the Tariff Commission has six months within which to make its determination and report on escape clause relief, it is required to report its determination with respect to adjustment assistance petitions within 60 days after filing of the petition.

106. Firms that have been certified as eligible for adjustment assistance may formally apply for assistance at any time within two years after certification. Application is made to the Secretary of Commerce and must include a proposal by the firm for its economic adjustment. Adjustment assistance is provided only after it is determined that the proposal is reasonably calculated materially to contribute to the firm's economic adjustment, that it gives adequate consideration to the interests of workers employed by the firm, and that it demonstrates that the firm will make all reasonable efforts to utilize its own resources in the adjustment process.[53] Technical assistance is available to applicant firms in the preparation of their adjustment proposals. Financial assistance provided under the Trade Expansion Act includes loans bearing moderately low interest rates and loan guarantees. Tax relief is also available in the form of a special carry-back of operating losses.[54]

107. Workers who have been certified as eligible for adjustment assistance may apply for assistance at any time within two years after certification of eligibility by the Secretary of Labor. Application is made to a worker's state employment security agency, which must determine whether the applicant satisfies a number of specific criteria relating to his precise employment status before becoming unemployed. Assistance is available from these agencies in the form of one or more of the following:

(a) A cash allowance equal to 65 per cent of the worker's average weekly wage within a specified income limitation, usually for no more than 52 weeks;

(b) Testing, counselling, training and job placement services; and

(c) Cash relocation allowances.[55]

108. From 1962 to November 1969 the Tariff Commission made no affirmative findings of eligibility with respect to 27 separate adjustment assistance petitions. Of these 27 petitions, six had been filed by workers, eight by firms and 13 by industries. The study by Murray and Egmund has shown that the controlling test in the majority of investigations was the second criterion (that the increased imports are attributable "in major part"

to trade agreement concessions) and that the third test (that the increased imports are "the major factor" in causing, or threatening to cause, serious injury to the petitioners) was also important.[56]

109. It appears that changes in the composition of the Tariff Commission, whose members are appointed by the President, and changing interpretations as to the stringency of the foregoing criteria led to the first affirmative decisions by the Commission, in November 1969.[57] Between 1 November 1969 and 15 April 1971, the Commission made affirmative decisions with respect to 12 workers' group petitions for adjustment assistance and was divided on another 26 cases. Of the latter cases, the President had referred 21 for certification of eligibility, and five cases were pending. The Department of Labor had certified 21 cases, and 12 cases were still awaiting certification. With respect to the 13 petitions by firms in this period, adjustment assistance had been authorized in four cases and in three cases a decision was still pending.

110. In the same period there were three findings of injury to an entire industry in an escape-clause action and one case (leather shoes) was still pending. On the basis of these findings, eight workers' group petitions for adjustment assistance had been certified, as well as five petitions from firms. Over this period the Secretary of Labor issued certifications of eligibility involving nearly 12,000 workers, and it has been estimated that this figure might increase to 22,000 by the end of 1971.

111. Considerably expanded funding of adjustment assistance in the United States appears to be intended by the Administration in the fiscal year 1972. Loans to firms qualifying for adjustment assistance are expected to rise to $100 million, and eligible workers are expected to receive, in the aggregate, $20 million. Guarantees of loans from private financial institutions to eligible firms are also expected to increase to $100 million. Over-all, adjustment assistance disbursements would rise to approximately $130 million from the $26 million in benefits the Administration estimates it will disburse in the fiscal year 1971. In line with the expected rise in petitions for adjustment assistance, the Administration is requesting a 15 per cent increase in authorized personnel for the Tariff Commission and a $1 million rise in the Commission's operating budget.[58]

112. As to United States imports of non-rubber footwear,[59] these have grown substantially in recent years, climbing from 4.4 per cent of domestic production in 1960 to 33.7 per cent in 1969. While non-rubber imports from developing countries have been increasing rapidly, these imports still constitute less than 20 per cent of total imports. In the textile and clothing industries, total imports of the different fibre and apparel categories

[53] See GATT document COM.TD/H/3, p. 62.

[54] See "Adjustment assistance measures: report by the UNCTAD secretariat" (TD/B/C.2/86), para. 28.

[55] See GATT document COM.TD/H/3, p. 63.

[56] See Murray and Egmund, op. cit.

[57] See the report of the Committee on Manufactures on its fifth session (*Official Records of the Trade and Development Board, Eleventh Session, Supplement No. 2* (TD/B/352)), annex IV, para. 4.

[58] Journal of Commerce, New York, 1 February 1971.

[59] Information derived from *Hearings before the Committee on Ways and Means, House of Representatives, 91st Congress, 2nd Session* (Washington, D.C., 1970), Part 5, pp. 1362-1368, and Part 7, p. 2006.

accounted for less than 10 per cent in some cases, and less than 5 per cent in others, of apparent United States domestic consumption in 1969. Imports from developing countries in these product groups have also been increasing rapidly, however, with three developing countries in South-East Asia (India, Pakistan and Hong Kong) accounting for almost one-third of United States imports of cotton, wool and man-made fibre manufactures in 1970. These trends would seem to indicate that the developing countries increasingly have a comparative advantage in certain categories of non-rubber footwear, textiles and clothing sold in the United States market.

113. While increasing imports have undoubtedly contributed to structural disturbances in these industries, it is not all clear that they have constituted the major factor. Technological changes in production in both sectors, together with a growing emphasis on style changes, have resulted in increased vulnerability to imports but also increased vulnerability of the smaller, marginal producers to competition from the larger domestic firms within each industry.[60] Indeed, a 1969 Tariff Commission study of the textiles and apparel industries in the United States was unable to report to the President that increasing imports had resulted in any over-all injury to those industries. A similar study with respect to the non-rubber footwear industry, submitted to the President in January 1971, resulted in an even division of opinion in the Tariff Commission as to whether that sector was being injured in major part because of increased imports arising from trade agreement concessions. In any event, the past few years have seen steadily mounting pressures within these industries for protectionist measures designed to limit imports, although recent bilateral agreements with Italy and Spain, whereby those countries have agreed to restrain their export of footwear to the United States, may work to restrain these protectionist pressures in the footwear industry.

114. Since the Tariff Commission began to make affirmative decisions with respect to adjustment assistance petitions in late 1969, the following treatment has been accorded petitions arising from the textiles, footwear and radio and television equipment industries, i.e. the sectors which the quantitative study in chapter II suggests might be the most vulnerable to structural displacement in the event of new trade liberalization measures specifically benefiting the developing countries. Taking industry, firms' and workers' group petitions for the period November 1969 to April 1971 in the aggregate, affirmative decisions were made with respect to two out of four textile petitions and 13 footwear petitions were subject to affirmative decisions (20 petitions still pending, 16 resulted in negative decisions) and decisions on the four petitions arising from the radio and television equipment industry were still pending.[61]

115. It is too early to judge whether the partial success of the foregoing petitions will tend to ease protectionist pressures in these industries; thus far there is little evidence that it is having this effect. Of some importance perhaps in this connexion is the fact that adjustment assistance as provided under the Trade Expansion Act may be inadequate to solve the underlying problem.[62] A major part of the dislocation in the textiles and footwear industries involves marginal smaller firms which, for various reasons, are unable to respond to the rapid technological change and the general upward pressure on wage levels. The older and relatively inefficient segments of the footwear and the textile and apparel industries, both highly labour-intensive, are very vulnerable to increased competition and are less capable of withstanding the impact of larger imports than they are the other disruptive forces prevailing in these industries. The institution of quantitative import controls on their products would very probably change the longer-term prospects for survival of many of these smaller firms. It is questionable whether the poorly managed and capitalized firm or the inherently immobile workers of the regions in which these firms are often located will really be able to take advantage of the adjustment assistance measures provided under this act, in the sense of re-allocation into more productive activities. This raises the further question whether comprehensive guarantees against the normal risks arising from competition are a practicable or relevant aspect of adjustment assistance policy.

116. Before examining recent thinking with respect to formulation of adjustment assistance policies in the United States, it may be useful to review briefly the assistance programme instituted under the Automotive Products Trade Act of 1965 (APTA).[63] This act served as the United States legislative basis for implementation of the Canada-United States Automotive Products Trade Agreement mentioned earlier. Less stringent adjustment assistance eligibility criteria than those provided under the Trade Expansion Act were incorporated in APTA for four basic reasons: (1) under APTA the relevant tariff cuts would be 100 per cent, as opposed to 35 per cent (weighted by imports) tariff reductions resulting from the Kennedy Round negotiations; (2) it was foreseen that under APTA factor displacement would occur not only as a result of increased imports but also in some cases because of reduced exports from the United States to Canada; (3) resource re-allocation was a stated purpose, not just an expected by-product, of the Automotive Products Agreement; and (4) United States labour was unwilling to support APTA unless its adjustment assistance provisions were considerably more liberal than those embodied in the Trade Expansion Act.

117. Eligibility for adjustment assistance under APTA depended basically on whether the Automotive Agreement Adjustment Assistance Board created by APTA (consisting of the Secretaries of Commerce, Labor and the Treasury) determined that the operation of the Agreement had been "the primary factor" in causing or threatening to cause dislocation of the petitioning firm or groups of

---

[60] Information derived from preliminary work by the UNCTAD secretariat.

[61] Information derived from a study of adjustment assistance policies and programmes in the United States in the particular context of selected industries or sectors of industries, including the textile and clothing and non-rubber footwear industries, recently made by the UNCTAD secretariat for submission to the Committee on Manufactures at its sixth session.

[62] *Ibid.*

[63] See Manley, op. cit.

workers. APTA provided that the Tariff Commission should act only as "fact-finder" with respect to adjustment assistance petitions. The Board created by the legislation had complete discretion as to whether the operation of the Automotive Products Agreement had, in fact, been "the primary factor" in causing or threatening to cause the alleged factor dislocations. Contrary to the strategy of the Tariff Commission under the Trade Expansion Act, the Board published in advance of any petitions its interpretations of the APTA criteria. The Board interpreted "the primary factor" as meaning simply the single most important factor in causing factor displacement. This, of course, was significantly less stringent than the Tariff Commission's apparent interpretation (at least in the early years) of the "major factor" under the Trade Expansion Act. Furthermore, the Board load down a specific definition of "significant unemployment", the qualifying criterion for a statutory finding of worker "dislocation".

118. As in the case of the Trade Expansion Act, "eligible" workers received aid from the Department of Labor. Assistance under APTA was similar in nature to that provided under the adjustment assistance provisions of the Trade Expansion Act. Petitions for adjustment assistance under APTA were filed by 21 groups of workers and 14 of the petitions were ruled on favourably, resulting in certifications for assistance covering about 2,500 workers. Up to 1969, approximately 1,950 out of the 2,500 workers had received weekly payments totalling just under $4 million. Retraining and relocation allowances have amounted to significantly less, however, being some $60,000 and $1,000 respectively in the aggregate over the same period. No petitions were received by firms.[64]

119. In response to petitioner dissatisfaction with the stringency of adjustment assistance eligibility criteria under the Trade Expansion Act and rising protectionist sentiment in the United States,[65] the President's Message on trade to Congress of 18 November 1969 recommended elimination of the second eligibility criterion under that act (the tie between increased imports and prior trade agreement concessions) and relaxation of the third criterion (substitution of "primary cause" for the wording "major factor"). These changes, however, would presumably have made it easier to qualify for escape clause relief, as well as for adjustment assistance, than had formerly been the case, although the President did recommend that direct aid to those individually injured should be made more readily available than tariff relief to entire industries, citing the harmful side effects which escape clause action can have on over-all trade policy. It was further recommended in the President's Message that an inter-agency board within the Executive Branch, following the pattern of the APTA programme, should be responsible for applying the eligibility criteria, and that the Tariff Commission should act only as a "fact-finding" body. The Message also recommended that potential loss of workers' pension and seniority rights should be taken into account in framing adjustment assistance measures and that assistance should be made available to separate units of

multi-plant companies and to groups of workers in such facilities where injury to the unit but not to the parent firm was substantial.

120. The proposed trade legislation emerging in Congress in 1970 was nevertheless protectionist in intent. That legislation would have eliminated the second eligibility criterion and relaxed the third, in respect of both escape clause and adjustment assistance petitions, in accordance with the President's recommendations. Furthermore, it would have increased the readjustment allowances payable to eligible workers over and above the amount provided under the Trade Expansion Act. Most significant, however, it would have curtailed the President's discretion as regards refusing to accept an escape clause recommendation from the Tariff Commission and awarding adjustment assistance relief as an alternative. Under this bill adjustment assistance is no longer regarded as a preferred alternative to escape clause relief.[66]

121. In May 1970 the President established the Commission on International Trade and Investment Policy which was invited to examine the principal problems in the field of United States foreign trade and investment and to produce recommendations designed to meet the challenge of the changing world economy during the current decade. The report submitted to the President contains an important chapter on Governmental responses to competition from imports.[67]

122. At the outset the Commission stated that if increasing United States imports are a consequence of normal shifts in the international competitive position of various American industries, the Government should allow Americans to reap the benefits of cheaper goods from abroad, while seeking to prevent serious damage to the economic well-being of specific groups of workers, firms, industries or communities. The considerations of equity which justify assistance to those who are harmed by policies benefiting the general public are qualified by the assertion that although imports may have significant effects on specific industries, plants, and communities, the aggregate dislocation of United States production and employment from import competition is a relatively small part of a continual process of adjustment to economic change in the over-all American economy.

123. In analysing alternative approaches to import competition, the Commission emphasized that while adjustment assistance is focused on the particular firms or workers injured by increased imports, the impact of import restriction cannot be confined to those factors actually suffering injury. Use of adjustment assistance also avoids the adverse effects on costs of United States-produced goods in both domestic and foreign markets, the

[64] See Jonish, op. cit.

[65] See Metzer, op.cit.

[66] United States Congress, Proposed Trade Act of 1970 (H.R. 18970); H.R. Report No. 91-1435, 91st Congress, 2nd Session (Washington, D.C., 1970), p. 32; and Metzger, op. cit.

[67] See Commission on International Trade and Investment Policy, United States international economic policy in an interdependent world, report to the President (Washington, D.C., July 1971), chap. 3, pp. 45-69; also idem, Papers I, pp. 319-394, containing the contributions on adjustment assistance submitted to the Commission by S. D. Metzger, M. M. Fooks, and the Departments of Commerce and of Labor.

restrictions on access for those goods to markets abroad, and the strains on United States foreign relations that are associated with increased protection against imports. Hence in general the Government should encourage adjustment rather than impose restrictions. The purpose of escape-clause import restrictions should be to permit a seriously injured domestic industry again to become competitive without continuing restrictions, and such relief should be extended on a declining basis and for a limited period of time only; moreover, escape-clause relief should normally consist of a tariff increase instead of an import quota.

124. The Commission was of the opinion that the current adjustment assistance programme has rarely achieved its objectives and that consequently major reforms are necessary in order to strengthen materially the scope, content, and administration of adjustment assistance. Moreover, policies in response to import competition should be carried out with specific long-term objectives, rather than be required to operate under policy options dictated mainly by short-term circumstances. Such policies designed to ease adjustment to import competition can operate more effectively within the context of a co-ordinated industrial and manpower policy. Elements of such a policy would include, *inter alia*, provision of information on likely trends in American and foreign production and employment patterns, identification and government encouragement of promising new areas of productive activity and greater co-ordination of various government programmes. It is noted that industry, labour and Government collect data relating to economic adjustment, but that in most instances this information is made available only after the particular workers and firms undergoing adjustment have suffered hardships. It was therefore recommended that an industrial and manpower policy should be established which would co-ordinate and augment programmes for anticipating and assisting adjustments to economic change arising from international trade and investment.

F. The European Communities[68]

125. During the formation of the European Coal and Steel Community and the European Economic Community, adjustment assistance programmes were introduced to ease the problems of structural adjustment in the member countries, caused by the changing pattern of trade accompanying economic integration.

1. ECSC

126. Under the provisions of article 56 of the Treaty of Paris and section 23 of the Transitional Provisions annexed to the Treaty, the High Authority is empowered to assist

in the redeployment of redundant miners and steel workers. The re-adaptation arrangements are usually tailored to the particular circumstances of these workers within the country concerned. These arrangements are generally designed to aid workers who have lost their jobs in consequence of closures or production cutbacks, by providing them with a continuing income and facilities for retraining. More specifically, the workers (*a*) receive "tide-over" allowances to make up for temporary loss of wages; (*b*) are given occupational retraining courses at High Authority and Government expense; and (*c*) are reimbursed for the incidental expenses of moving to other jobs.

127. The beneficiaries of these programmes are in the majority of cases colliery workers in Belgium, the Federal Republic of Germany and France, displaced by the restructuring of the coal mining industry in those countries. During the period 1954-1970, the High Authority assisted more than 370,000 workers at a cost of over 146 million units of account. The scale of assistance operations has increased swiftly as a result of rapid structural changes in the coal mining, iron ore mining and iron and steel industries, and of the determination of the High Authority to keep its assistance in line with evolving requirements.

128. Under article 54 of the Treaty of Paris, the High Authority is empowered to assist in the financing of investment projects in the coal and steel industries, as well as schemes for building workers' housing and large power stations. Financial assistance is granted in the form of loans at more or less market rates of interest in the case of industrial programmes in the coal and steel sectors, and of loans at a very low rate of interest in the case of the construction of workers' housing. Under article 56 of the establishing Treaty, ECSC provides redevelopment loans designed to promote employment in various regions severely hit by economic displacements arising from economic integration. From the inception of these financial operations through 1970 the High Authority had extended credits totalling 1,033 million units of account under these loan programmes. It has been estimated that in 1970 some 11,680 new jobs were created in various coal- and steel-producing areas as a result of redevelopment loans granted by ECSC.

2. EEC

129. Article 123 of the Treaty of Rome established the European Social Fund to ensure employment and guarantee the income of wage-earners against the risks involved in the integration of the member countries' economies and also to promote the expansion of employment by measures which tend to prevent structural unemployment. Assistance to workers is given in the form of retraining, resettlement allowances and guaranteed wages during enterprise conversion. During its ten-year period of operation, ending in 1970, the Social Fund refunded to member countries for assistance to approximately 1,300,000 workers 153.8 million units of account, of which 145.4 million units of account was for retraining and 8.4 million units of account for resettlement purposes. The relatively small size of the latter sum is a result of difficulties encountered in reloca-

[68] Information derived from: Commission of the European Communities, *Fourth General Report on the Activities of the Communities, 1970* (Brussels-Luxembourg, Feb. 1971), p. 109, and preceding annual reports; *Journal officiel des Communautés européennes*, No. L.28, 4 Feb. 1971; and "Adjustment assistance measures: report by the UNCTAD secretariat" (TD/B/C.2/86 and Corr.1).

tion from country to country. Principal recipients of this assistance have been workers in Italy, the Federal Republic of Germany and France. By a Decision of the Council of Ministers dated 1 February 1971, the rules of the Social Fund were amended in order further to facilitate through community subsidies the better adaptation of labour supply and demand in these countries. Complementary action entrusted to the Social Fund also provides for interventions in anticipation of labour displacement.

130. Financial assistance in the form of loans (in some cases on very favourable terms) and recently also in the form of guarantees, has been provided by the European Investment Bank in connexion with industrial investment, infrastructure in less-developed regions and indirect lend-

ing to small and medium-sized firms, in both EEC member countries and associated countries. From the time of its establishment to 1 December 1970 the Bank signed 312 loan and guarantee contracts, totalling 1,758 million units of account.

131. While no attempt has been made here to evaluate the degree to which the various adjustment assistance programmes of ECSC and EEC may have facilitated increased imports from the developing countries, these programmes are nevertheless of interest, in the sense that they are an illustrative example of what can be done on a multilateral basis to ease the adjustment problems of countries undertaking significant trade liberalizations measures.

CHAPTER V

Conclusions

132. Current imports from developing countries by developed market-economy countries which compete with the products of relatively labour-intensive domestic industries are low compared to domestic consumption or to total imports. The basic conclusion of the quantitative study referred to in chapter II suggests that the aggregate labour displacement impact in the developed market-economy countries of significantly increased imports from the developing countries would be small, particularly if compared to the displacement effect resulting from increases in domestic labour productivity. Similarly, the aggregate costs of structural relocation to facilitate increased imports from developing countries and the budgetary costs of the required adjustment assistance programmes should be relatively moderate, especially since the need for assistance is centred on a few labour-intensive industries, such as textiles and clothing, footwear and leather and to a lesser degree, basic metal manufacturing and electrical machinery. On the other hand, because of the key role of the export sector in developing countries for fostering economic development, adequate adjustment assistance programmes with a view to liberalizing imports from the developing countries are particularly needed. Such trade liberalization will be of benefit not only to the developing countries, but also to the developed market-economy countries effecting such liberalization. Lower prices in developed market-economy countries, resulting from the expansion of imports of lower-cost products of the developing countries, will make a positive contribution to consumer welfare.[69] In the long term, structural changes in these countries will bring about an increase in real income through a shift towards an optimal international division of labour.

133. The review of the existing adjustment assistance policies of five developed market-economy countries shows that only Canada and the United States have adjust-

ment assistance programmes linked directly with trade liberalization. However, none of these countries has programmes which are specifically concerned with facilitating increased imports from developing countries.

134. While tying the availability of adjustment assistance to specific trade concessions in respect of products of particular interest to the developing countries will presumably facilitate expansion of the developing countries' exports to a greater extent than the absence of any adjustment assistance programme, the longer-term goal of the developing countries should involve adjustment assistance availability in the developed world which favours increased imports resulting from any cause, whether it be specific trade concessions or productivity advances in the developing countries. The recent Canadian legislation concerning the textile and clothing industries does not require requests for adjustment assistance to prove a link between increased imports arising from trade concessions and alleged injury. However, initial decisions taken in the framework of the administration of the programme embodied in this legislation had the immediate effect of introducing new trade barriers rather than facilitating developing-country access to the Canadian market. Similarly, the trade legislation proposed in the United States in 1970 would have severed this connexion, although, as has been shown, the result of this legislation, were it enacted, might well be easier industry access to escape-clause relief as well as to adjustment assistance.

135. The experience of Sweden with its general labour market policy would seem to indicate that anticipation of resource displacement helps to alleviate uncertainty and dissatisfaction among productive factors and therefore to discourage protectionist pressures. In this connexion, both Canada and the United States have incorporated in their various import-related adjustment assistance programmes anticipatory provisions which are designed to allow for adjustment assistance in cases where expected increased imports threaten to injure non-competitive domestic producers. There is no evidence, however, that in practice petitioning firms or workers have been able successfully to predicate their case solely on the basis of threatened injury.

---

[69] It appears that in the import policies of many developed countries the interests of the consumers are not taken adequately into account. As an example to the contrary, see certain provisions of the Textile and Clothing Board Act of Canada described in paragraph 70 above.

136. The Swedish experience further suggests that the over-all effectiveness of a developed market-economy country's adjustment assistance policies will depend to a large degree upon whether the various programmes, be they general or specifically import- or regional-development-related, are mutually compatible and complementary and in line with the objective of facilitating trade liberalization. This is particularly important in connexion with the administration of import-related and regional development adjustment assistance programmes which may work at cross purposes in cases where injury to an industry also means labour displacement problems in a particular region of a country. Action should therefore be taken to prevent the dependence of less prosperous regions of developed countries on industries without prospects of long-term viability and growth. As a rule, adjustment assistance programmes should lead to conversion of segments of industries to new lines of production rather than to modernization of existing lines.

137. With regard to implementation of existing adjustment assistance policies, the examination of the adjustment assistance policies embodied in the Trade Expansion Act of 1962 of the United States of America indicates that policy intent and implementation can be very far apart. Although the availability of adjustment assistance was envisaged as a cornerstone of United States trade liberalization policy in the 1960s, there were no successful petitions for assistance under this act until late in 1969. Lack of implementation of the adjustment assistance programmes probably helped contribute to the increasing protectionist pressures in the United States in the late 1960s and early 1970s. Furthermore, unclear eligibility criteria in an adjustment assistance programme may lead to diminished acceptance of the entire adjustment assistance effort. Moreover, changing interpretations of these eligibility criteria, as a result of changes in the membership of the reviewing board, probably also add to petitioner uncertainty, and therefore contribute to protectionist sentiment. Careful formulation and interpretation of these criteria may make a significant difference as to whether the goals of the programmes are achieved.

138. For the one industry for which substantial evidence is available, cotton textiles, the review of five major developed market-economy countries suggests that significant structural readjustment has occurred in the past decade in the Federal Republic of Germany, Sweden and the United Kingdom, and less readjustment (in percentage terms) in Canada and the United States of America. The pattern of response to increased imports of cotton textiles has differed from country to country: the Federal Republic of Germany has left most of the adjustment to private industry, although some assistance has been given in the form of credits; Sweden has chosen to rely on its general labour market policy, while the United Kingdom Government provided extensive financial aid to the industry in the context of the Cotton Industry Act of 1959, together with a scheme by which firms remaining in the industry compensated workers made unemployed by the scrapping and re-equipping programmes. In response to the government-supported scheme for eliminating surplus capacity, the number of spindles in place in the domestic cotton textiles industry decreased by more than half between 1960

and 1967, while the number of looms in place fell by two-fifths. In the same period employment in the cotton textiles industry declined by one-third. In Canada the Textile and Clothing Board under section 21 of the Governing Act certifies workers eligible for adjustment assistance benefits. Thus, assistance to workers is specifically provided for in the textile policy, in addition to that which is also available under the country's general manpower mobility programmes. The United States offered some financial support to the industry for research and development and also allowed increased accelerated depreciation for the purchase of textile machinery. In the past few years, however, there have been signs in most of these countries of the inadequacy of existing adjustment assistance measures. The Governments of the Federal Republic of Germany, Sweden and the United Kingdom have recently undertaken consultations with their respective cotton textile industries with regard to specific measures of assistance. Canada has recently passed the Textile and Clothing Board Act, which provides for a scheme of temporary protection for firms (pending adjustment) and adjustment assistance for workers. In the United States there has been increased pressure for a system of involuntary quotas on the import of various textile products.

139. The real benefits of trade liberalization facilitated by adjustment assistance arise from the expansion of the export of certain manufactures and semi-manufactures in which the developing countries have a comparative advantage, combined with a more effective resource allocation in both the developing and developed worlds, which leads to an increase in global productivity. This implies a re-allocation of resources out of those declining industries or declining segments of industries in the developed market-economy countries in which the developing countries have a competitive advantage. However, from the review of adjustment assistance programmes in five major developed countries discussed above, it appears that most of these programmes, at least in principle, provide assistance for the modernization and rehabilitation of productive factors that continue producing the same products, as well as for re-allocation into entirely new productive activities. Nevertheless, policy-makers in the Federal Republic of Germany and Sweden emphasize the need for re-allocation as opposed to mere modernization of resources.

140. In this connexion, it would be useful if Governments evaluated results obtained from adjustment assistance policies and programmes with a view to shifting adjustment assistance facilities from enterprises unable to take advantage of them in order to become more competitive, to more promising branches or segments of industries.

141. The steps that Governments take in order to facilitate structural adjustments are generally supplementary to the spontaneous adaptation of the industrial sector in developed market-economy countries to technical advances and changes in demand and external supply which affect the relative competitiveness of domestic producers. Adjustment assistance programmes are, in particular, intended to help small firms which cannot obtain sufficient financing on reasonable terms from other sources, and workers who for various reasons are unable

to respond to the rapid change characterizing certain industrial sectors. Specific and general adjustment assistance programmes which in fact respond to the objective of liberalization of imports, as well as to the needs of small-scale enterprises and relatively immobile workers, should be characterized by flexibility and provide for adequate incentives, so that enterprises and workers will really be able to take advantage of the measures provided.

142. Considering the effects of the available adjustment assistance programmes in these five developed market-economy countries, while it is possible that the programmes have facilitated or could, indirectly, facilitate imports, the continued existence of significant tariff and non-tariff

barriers to exports of developing countries and the exemption by many countries of "sensitive" items from the GSP are *prima facie* evidence that existing adjustment assistance policies and programmes are neither directed toward nor adequate to lead to greater liberalization of imports originating in the developing countries.

143. The extent of existing over-all government intervention in the industrial sector presents substantial opportunities for action. The main areas for possible action are reduced protection for uncompetitive industries or segments of existing industries, more active manpower and regional policies to ease structural adaptation, more extensive competition policies and more efficient public expenditure and social policies.

CHAPTER VI

Suggested policy guidelines for adjustment assistance measures in the context of facilitating increased exports from developing countries

144. Governments of developed market-economy countries influence production and trade in particular categories of manufactured goods not only through commercial policies but also by various types of fiscal, financial and regional policies, public procurement, training and research and development. Adequate use of these tools for the effective introduction of forward- and outward-looking policies, designed to result in appropriate domestic adjustment of the structure of industry and employment in those countries, will facilitate the acceptance of an improved international division of labour.

145. The following are some suggestions on possible specific guidelines for programmes aimed at assisting the adaptation and adjustment of industries and workers that might be adversely affected or threatened by increased imports into the developed market-economy countries of manufactures and semi-manufactures from developing countries.

(a) Adjustment assistance programmes should include an appropriate mechanism for anticipatory resource displacement in industries that are particularly vulnerable, owing to changing conditions in world production and trade. Anticipation of structural displacement would lessen the uncertainties felt by domestic producers following increased international competition. Successful anticipation of structural displacement, combined with efficient re-allocation measures, would weaken the psychological barriers to adjustment, as well as specific protectionist pressures, and would diminish the time-lag between an increase in imports and the increase in exports from expanding industry.

(b) The scope and operation of the GSP and the potential for reduction of non-tariff barriers would be enhanced by the application of such production and trade policies in the developed market-economy countries characterized by a forward and outward-looking nature. Import-related adjustment assistance programmes might at first be applied to those domestic industrial sectors which are most sensitive to increased imports from developing countries. Implementation of these specific

programmes would provide the developed countries with experience in formulating appropriate measures which would gradually be extended to other products of export interest to the developing countries.

(c) Adjustment assistance should be designed to facilitate the conversion of industrial activities to economically competitive production rather than the modernization of basically non-competitive lines of production. If such assistance is provided simply for the modernization of existing firms, which will produce the same products or very close substitutes for the traditional products, the basic purpose of structural improvement will not be attained and the potential for expansion of exports of manufactures and semi-manufactures from the developing countries will be correspondingly diminished. Enterprises in developed market-economy countries might, *inter alia*, seek to transfer the manufacture of non-economic traditional products to subsidiaries established in developing countries which may have a competitive advantage in producing those goods. Enterprises in developed market-economy countries might also consider relying on subcontracting to manufacturers in developing countries the production of those semi-manufactures for the production of which they are no longer competitive.

(d) Eligibility criteria for adjustment assistance should be explicit and liberal, in view of the basic purpose of the programmes, which is to help those weaker segments of the domestic economy that can be converted and thus be integrated into competitive industrial branches. In particular, the programmes should provide for measures designed to reduce significantly the burden of adjustment on workers and regions adversely affected by structural changes that are of benefit to the economy as a whole. Developed market-economy countries should also establish procedures to ensure consistency among specifically import-related and general and/or regional adjustment assistance programmes, in order to ensure that all efforts are complementary and in line with the common objective of restructuring the domestic industrial sector for a more rational integration in world production and trade.

(e) The present link in the legislation of certain developed market-economy countries between protectionist measures and adjustment assistance should be replaced by an approach that regards adjustment assistance as a preferred alternative to escape-clause measures. Experience demonstrates that ambiguity of existing programmes as between protectionist measures and trade liberalization has clouded the basic purpose of adjustment assistance and has currently resulted in the application of definitely more protectionist import trade policies.

146. The application of adjustment assistance policies and programmes in order to facilitate trade liberalization would be greatly assisted by the availability of relevant information, including that pertaining to foreign trade aspects of national development policies and programmes in the developing countries. Accordingly, it might be useful to consider the possibility of a more systematic exchange within UNCTAD, among developed and developing countries, of relevant specific information regarding adjustment assistance policies and programmes in relation to supply possibilities of manufactures and semi-manufactures in the developing countries which might assist in more dynamic adjustment measures in the developed countries. Such co-operation might be extended to seeking possibilities of production in developing countries of products which are needed by industries in developed countries and could be produced more competitively in developing countries.

TECHNICAL ANNEX

1. The purpose of this annex is to describe in detail the assumptions, methodology and sources of data utilized for the quantitative estimates of the likely impact of increased imports from the developing countries on employment in the Federal Republic of Germany, the United Kingdom and the United States of America.

Selection of commodity groups and industries

2. The model underlying the present exercise requires that the imports should be perfect substitutes for domestic products and that the cross-elasticities between the two should be infinite. This condition would hold if import/output sectors were fully disaggregated into their components in order to ensure that the composition of imports could be matched with the composition of domestic production.

3. The available statistics enables the manufacturing sector in the three countries studied to be disaggregated into 20 industries based on ISIC major groups 20-39. These include all the major industries producing manufactures and semi-manufactures. In the case of the United States of America, it was possible, for the industries that were shown to be among the most sensitive, i.e. textiles, clothing, footwear and leather goods, electrical machinery and non-electrical machinery, to obtain further disaggregation on the basis of the United States Industrial Code. This further disaggregation does not include every branch of the particular industry, but concentrates on the branches of particular, current or future export interest to the developing countries.

Sources of statistical data

4. The study relies on the United Nations *Commodity Trade Statistics* for all data on imports and exports. Employment and output statistics for the United States were obtained from that country's latest available census of manufactures, and are based on the ISIC classification. For the United Kingdom and the Federal Republic of Germany, employment and output data were supplied direct by ECE. The tables for each country studied are not exactly comparable as, *inter alia*, the import figures for the United States are calculated on an f.o.b. basis whereas those for the United Kingdom and the Federal Republic of Germany are on a c.i.f. basis.

Correspondence of statistical data

5. The major problem in the technique utilized for the present study has been to match the classification used in the United Nations *Commodity Trade Statistics* (SITC) with the breakdown of employment and output statistics in the importing countries (ISIC). The correspondence used is shown in the table below.

SITC CODE IDENTIFIED ACCORDING TO ISIC MAJOR GROUPS[a]

SITC	Description	ISIC
012, 013, 032, 046, 047, 048, 052, 053, 055, 062, 071.3, 072.2, 072.3, 073, 091, 099	Processed food	20
111, 112	Beverages	21
122	Tobacco manufactures	22
231.2, 231.3, 231.4	Synthetic rubber	31
243	Wood, shaped or simply worked	25
251	Pulp and waste paper	27
266	Synthetic and regenerated (artificial) fibres	23
267	Waste materials from textile fabrics	23
332	Petroleum products	32
431	Processed animal and vegetable oils	31
5	Chemicals	31
611, 612, 613	Leather and fur skins	29
621	Rubber products	30
63	Wood and cork manufactures	25
64	Paper and paper products	27
65	Textile yarn and fabrics	23
66	Non-metallic mineral manufactures, n.e.s.	33
67	Iron and steel	34
68	Non-ferrous metals	34
69	Manufactures of metal, n.e.s.	35
71	Machinery, other than electric	36
711	Power generating machinery other than electric	36
712	Agricultural machinery and implements	36
714	Office machines	36
715	Metalworking machinery	36
717	Textile and leather machinery	36
718	Machines for special industries	36
719	Machinery and appliances, other than electric	36
	Electrical machinery	
722	Electric power machinery and switchgear	37
723	Electric power distribution equipment	37
724	Telecommunications apparatus	37

SITC	Description	ISIC
725	Domestic electrical equipment	37
726	Electro-medical apparatus	37
729	Other electrical machinery and apparatus .	37
73	Transport equipment	38
81	Sanitary, plumbing, heating and lighting fixtures and fittings	35
82	Furniture	26
83	Travel goods, handbags	29
84	Clothing	24
85	Footwear	24
86	Professional and scientific instruments; photographic and optical goods, etc.	39
89	*Miscellaneous manufactured articles, n.e.s.*	
891	Musical instruments, sound recorders, etc. .	39
892	Printed matter	28
893	Articles of plastic	31
894	Perambulators, toys and sporting goods . .	39
895	Office stationery and supplies, n.e.s.	39
897	Gold and silverware and jewellery	39
899	Manufactured articles, n.e.s.	39
961.0	Coin (other than gold coin), not being legal tender	39

NOTE. SITC 896, "Works of art, collectors' pieces and antiques", although classified under manufactures, is not included here.

[a] United Nations, *Standard International Trade Classification, Revised, Statistical Papers*, Series M, No. 34 and *International Standard Industrial Classification of All Economic Activities, Statistical Papers*, Series M, No. 4, Rev.1 (United Nations publications, Sales Nos. 61.XVII.6 and 58.XVII.7, respectively).

Assumptions regarding the growth of imports from developing countries, 1969-1973

6. It has been assumed that the increase in imports from developing countries experienced in the period 1966-1969 will double in the period 1969-1973. This is obviously unrealistic when applied to all the imports under study. The past high rate of increase is more a consequence of the low initial base than an indication of the future possibilities for exports. For this reason, a limit of 500 per cent was imposed in the three cases where the increases would have exceeded this figure. Even when this limit is applied, the figures imply that imports in the categories concerned, i.e., imports of rubber products, non-electrical machinery and electrical machinery into the United States, would more than double in each of the four years of the period 1969-1973. Rates of growth of this magnitude have not been attained in the past for more than a few years and seem unlikely to be attained during the period 1969-1973, in view of several factors including supply elasticities in exporting countries, demand elasticities in importing countries and restrictions on imports, particularly quantitative restrictions.

7. Column 4 in tables 1, 2 and 3 shows the effects of these assumptions on the yearly increase in imports into the Federal Republic of Germany, the United Kingdom and the United States of America in 1973. The increase is distributed among the industries on the basis of the total amount of imports in 1969 in each industry and the growth of these imports in the period 1965-1969, according to the following formulae:

$$\Delta X_{1973} = X_{1969} \quad \alpha \frac{(\Delta X_{1969})}{(X_{1965})}$$

where subscript X equals total imports in the industry in the year and subscript ΔX equals the increase in imports in the industry in the previous five years.

8. It can readily be seen from the tables that the assumption involves much larger increases in imports than were assumed in any of the previous studies. Little, Scitovsky and Scott[a] assumed a diver-

sified increase of $744 million in total imports into the United States, the United Kingdom and the six countries of the Common Market. The present study assumes an average yearly increase of about $3,000 million for the Federal Republic of Germany, the United Kingdom and the United States alone. The Salant and Vaccara study[b] assumed a $1 million increase for each commodity. In the present study only paper and paper products, tobacco products, printing and publishing, and furniture in the United Kingdom, and tobacco products, printing and publishing and furniture in the Federal Republic of Germany have yearly import increases of less than $1 million, while the clothing and footwear industry in the Federal Republic of Germany, the United Kingdom and the United States records average yearly increases of $105 million, $70 million and $574 million, respectively. Increases of this size are implausible in the case of goods subject to quantitative restrictions.

Effect of increased imports on domestic industry output

9. In order to study the effect of increased imports on domestic production a 1:1 substitution relationship is assumed; in other words, it is assumed that a $1 million increase in imports will involve a $1 million cutback in the production of the corresponding domestic industry. This is a crucial assumption which implies that foreign and domestic goods are perfect substitutes for each other and that there is no difference in the product-mix of home output and competing imports. Even where the products considered are disaggregated to the level considered in the present study, foreign and domestic products will not be perfect substitutes and the product-mix of imported and domestically produced articles of the same nature is likely to vary. The 1:1 relationship is therefore a maximum assumption. In reality, we can expect the cutback in home production to be less than the increase in imports. This is another reason why the labour displacement figures in tables 1, 2, 3 and 4 are regarded as maximum estimates.

Effect of reduced output on employment

10. Measuring the effect of reduced output on employment involves the application of a labour productivity ratio, by industry, and the question arises whether a marginal or average ratio should be used. Logically, the marginal productivity should be used, because the marginal plant is the one that will close down in the face of increased competition from imports. At first sight it would seem that, as the marginal plant will be a relatively inefficient one, it is likely to be more labour-intensive than the average plant in the developed countries, as the comparative advantage lies in capital-intensive production. However, empirical studies concerning the United States and Japan[c] have shown that there is usually very little difference between the marginal and average labour/productivity ratios on an industry level. For this reason the simple average labour/productivity ratio has been used. It is pointed out, however, that despite aggregative empirical studies of particular countries, there are many industries in which differences in productivity as between firms are quite considerable. In these cases the adoption of an average labour/productivity ratio could distort the results obtained.

11. The figures for labour displacement shown in tables 1, 2, 3 and 4 have been estimated on the assumption that other factors remain constant. Therefore they cannot be interpreted as indicating the actual number of jobs or workers displaced over the period. In fact, the labour employment displacement data can be interpreted

---

[a] Little, Scitovsky and Scott, op. cit.

[b] Salant and Vaccara, op. cit.

[c] T. Watanabe, "Approaches to the problem of inter-country comparisons of input-output relations: a survey and suggestions for future research", in *Proceedings of UNIDO Conference on International Comparisons of Inter-Industry Data* (United Nations publication, Sales No. E.1968.II.B.14).

only as indicating the extent to which future employment will be below the employment levels which would have been recorded if imports from developing countries had remained constant throughout the period.

12. Table 5 shows that, if consumption is growing, the impact of increased imports from developing countries on employment in domestic industries will be reduced. Table 5 is essentially a first attempt to examine a situation in which both imports and consumption in each of the 20 manufacturing industries are growing over the four-year period 1969-1973.

Employment effect of increases in labour productivity

13. Table 6 estimates the employment displacement effects of changes in labour productivity defined as value-added per unit of labour. The data by industry on employment and value-added at constant prices for the period 1965-1969 were supplied by ECE. They cover the Federal Republic of Germany and the United Kingdom. For the United States of America comparable figures for 1963 and 1967, based on the ISIC, were obtained from the national census of manufactures. The following formulae were used to calculate the labour displacement due to the increase in labour productivity:

(1) Displacement of labour 1965-1969 $= L\,1969$:

$$\left(1 - \frac{L\,1969/P\,1969}{L\,1965/P\,1965}\right)$$

(2) Displacement of labour 1963-1967 $= L\,1967$

$$\left(1 - \frac{L\,1967/P\,1967}{L\,1963/P\,1963}\right)$$

where L equals wage and salary earners in the industry and P equals value added in the industry. The first formula refers to the Federal Republic of Germany and the United Kingdom, and the second to the United States of America. The study only treats observed movements of labour productivity which could have been caused by a large number of factors, including technological change, changes in managerial inputs, alterations in work patterns, increased use of excess capacity, effects of economies of scale etc.

TABLE 1

Federal Republic of Germany: employment effects of increased imports of manufactures from developing countries

No.	ISIC major group	Imports (thousands of dollars) 1965 (1)	Imports (thousands of dollars) 1969 (2)	Percentage change (per cent) (3)	Average yearly increase in imports 1969-1973 (thousand dollars) (4)	Gross output 1969[a] (million dollars) (5)	Number of employees 1969 (thousands) (6)	Gross output per employee[a] (dollars) (7)	Average yearly number of employees displaced by increased imports (8)	Average yearly rate of labour displacement (as per cent of employment in 1969) (9)
20	Food	70 567	93 533	32.5	15 199	11 264	548	20 554	740	0.135
21	Beverages	5 408	13 835	155.8	10 778	2 492	152	16 394	658	0.433
22	Tobacco products	98	185	88.8	82	267	32	8 344	10	0.080
23	Textiles	89 359	135 205	51.1	34 545	5 680	512	11 093	3 114	0.608
24	Footwear, wearing apparel and made-up textiles	92 589	193 073	108.5	104 742	4 038	515	7 937	13 197	2.563
25	Wood and cork products	36 051	56 297	56.2	15 820	1 192	71	16 789	942	1.327
26	Furniture	6 487	6 609	1.9	63	3 198	380	8 416	8	0.002
27	Paper and paper products	1 187	2 679	125.7	1 684	2 584	213	12 131	138	0.065
28	Printing and publishing	199	596	199.5	595	3 054	252	12 118	49	0.019
29	Leather and leather goods	15 158	41 761	175.5	36 645	611	57	10 719	3 419	5.998
30	Rubber products	1 257	3 174	152.5	2 420	1 209	143	8 455	286	0.200
31	Chemicals	25 535	42 104	64.9	13 663	9 339	580	16 101	849[b]	0.146
32	Petroleum products	51 555	28 383	-44.9	-1 593	1 157	37	31 270	-51[b]	-0.138[b]
33	Non-metallic mineral products	23 990	31 765	32.4	5 146	4 610	433	10 647	483	0.112
34	Basic metal manufactures	294 223	517 347	75.8	196 075	8 842	684	12 927	15 168	2.218
35	Metal products excluding machinery	5 608	7 026	25.3	889	7 961	854	9 322	95	0.011
36	Machinery other than electric	4 632	14 684	217.0	15 932	9 594	1 182	8 117	1 963	0.166
37	Electrical machinery, apparatus and appliances	5 852	18 721	219.9	20 584	8 872	1 019	8 707	2 364	0.232
38	Transport equipment	3 313	7 158	116.1	4 155	10 040	794	12 645	329	0.041
39	Miscellaneous manufactured articles	10 161	35 222	246.6	43 429	5 191	409	12 692	3 422	0.837
		743 229	1 249 357	—	520 863	101 195	8 867	—	47 183	—

Sources: United Nations, *Commodity Trade Statistics, Statistical Papers, Series D,* 1965 and 1969; and information supplied direct by ECE.

[a] Provisional figures.

[b] A minus sign (−) denotes a decrease in imports or an increase in employment.

TABLE 2

United Kingdom: employment effects of increased imports of manufactures from developing countries

No.	ISIC major group	Imports (thousands of dollars)		Percentage change (per cent) (3)	Average yearly increase in imports 1969-1973 (thousand dollars) (4)	Gross output 1969[a] (million dollars) (5)	Number of employees 1969 (thousands) (6)	Gross output per employee[a] (dollars) (7)	Average yearly number of employees displaced by increased imports (8)	Average yearly rate of labour displacement (as per cent of employment in 1969) (9)
		1965 (1)	1969 (2)							
20	Food	77 624	152 740	96.8	73 926	6 697	568	11 790	6 270	1.104
21	Beverages	8 707	11 350	30.4	1 725	2 025	134	15 112	114	0.085
22	Tobacco products	2 487	1 995	−19.8	−49	705	41	17 195	−3[b]	−0.007[b]
23	Textiles	143 180	145 204	1.4	1 017	5 377	611	8 800	116	0.019
24	Footwear, wearing apparel and made-up textiles	92 573	169 001	82.6	69 798	1 888	475	3 975	17 559	3.697
25	Wood and cork products	92 309	94 700	2.6	1 231	1 205	118	10 212	121	0.103
26	Furniture	4 223	2 242	−46.9	−132	725	137	5 292	−25[b]	−0.018[b]
27	Paper and paper products	324	282	−13.0	−5	2 102	220	9 554	−1[b]	..
28	Printing and publishing	1 653	2 786	68.5	954	2 371	367	6 460	148	0.040
29	Leather and leather goods	35 186	43 193	22.8	4 924	274	47	5 830	845	1.798
30	Rubber products	2 786	4 747	70.4	1 671	867	130	6 669	251	0.193
31	Chemicals	47 372	80 963	70.9	28 702	3 616	436	8 294	3 661	0.794
32	Petroleum products	233 169	169 405	−27.3	−5 781	1 357	47	28 872	−200[b]	−0.426[b]
33	Non-metallic mineral products	152 186	187 859	23.4	21 980	2 026	327	6 196	3 547	1.085
34	Basic metal manufactures	338 219	526 439	55.7	146 613	5 478	564	9 713	15 095	2.676
35	Metal products excluding machinery	8 172	11 939	46.1	2 752	3 751	519	7 241	380	0.073
36	Machinery other than electric	26 405	37 945	43.7	8 291	8 353	1 050	7 955	1 042	0.099
37	Electric machinery apparatus and appliances	18 282	28 262	54.6	7 716	4 488	831	5 401	1 429	0.172
38	Transport equipment	10 481	14 489	38.2	2 768	9 840	1 086	9 061	306	0.028
39	Miscellaneous manufactured articles	40 080	72 072	79.8	28 757	1 369	375	3 651	7 877	2.100
		1 335 418	1 757 613	—	396 858	64 514	8 083	—	58 532	—

Sources: As for table 1.

[a] Provisional figures.

[b] A minus sign (−) denotes a decrease in imports or an increase in employment.

TABLE 3

United States of America: employment effects of increased imports of manufactures from developing countries

No.	ISIC major group	Imports (thousands of dollars)		Percentage change (per cent) (3)	Average yearly increase in imports 1969-1973 (thousand dollars) (4)	Gross output[a] 1967 (million dollars) (5)	Number of employees 1967 (thousands) (6)	Gross output per employee[a] 1967 (dollars) (7)	Average yearly number of employees displaced by increased imports (8)	Average yearly rate of labour displacement (as per cent of employment in 1967) (9)
		1965 (1)	1969 (2)							
20	Food	133 163	273 855	105.7	144 732	74 916	1 432	52 316	2 767	0.193
21	Beverages	6 517	8 661	32.9	1 425	9 146	222	41 198	35	0.016
22	Tobacco products	1 017	2 011	97.7	982	4 914	75	65 520	15	0.020
23	Textiles	304 936	391 079	28.2	55 142	19 733	926	21 310	2 588	0.279
24	Footwear, wearing apparel and made-up textiles	203 483	595 836	192.8	574 386	24 533	1 583	15 498	37 062	2.341
25	Wood and cork products	117 444	267 804	128.0	171 395	11 217	556	20 174	8 496	1.528
26	Furniture	13 329	31 088	133.2	20 705	7 746	425	18 226	1 136	0.267
27	Paper and paper products	2 088	6 257	199.7	6 248	20 740	638	32 508	192	0.030
28	Printing and publishing	4 931	11 038	123.8	6 833	21 671	1 025	21 142	323	0.032
29	Leather and leather goods	41 458	69 877	68.5	23 933	-1 950	104	18 750	1 277	1.228
30	Rubber products	182	10 129	5 465.4	12 661	7 328	264	27 758	456	0.173
31	Chemicals	145 665	247 050	69.6	85 974	47 931	1 103	43 455	1 978	0.179
32	Petroleum products	932 825	1 070 555	14.8	79 221	22 042	142	155 225	510	0.359
33	Non-metallic mineral products	103 496	180 171	74.1	66 753	14 604	591	24 711	2 701	0.457
34	Basic metal manufactures	508 328	575 474	13.2	37 981	46 550	1 279	36 396	1 044	0.082
35	Metal products excluding machinery	23 638	55 343	134.1	37 108	34 398	1 340	25 670	1 446	0.108
36	Machinery other than electric	4 221	55 390	1 212.2	69 238	48 357	1 858	26 026	2 660	0.143
37	Electrical machinery apparatus and appliances	44 893	351 151	682.2	438 939	43 896	1 897	23 140	18 969	1.000
38	Transport equipment	4 931	11 247	128.0	7 198	68 238	1 824	37 411	192	0.011
39	Miscellaneous manufactured articles	103 069	282 130	173.7	245 030	27 855	1 224	22 757	10 767	0.880
		2 699 614	4 496 146	—	2 085 884	557 765	18 508	—	94 614	—

Sources: United Nations, Commodity Trade Statistics, Statistical Papers, Series D, 1965 and 1969; U.S. Department of Commerce, Statistical Abstracts; 1970 and Census of Manufactures, 1967.

TABLE 4

United States of America: employment effects in certain manufacturing industries of increased imports of manufactures from developing countries

Industry	National Industry Code	Increase in imports from developing countries 1965-1969 (per cent)	Average yearly increase in imports 1969-1973 (thousand dollars)	Employment 1967[a] (thousands)	Shipments 1967[a] (million dollars)	Shipments per employee 1967 (dollars)	Average yearly labour displacement 1969-1973	Average yearly rate of labour displacement 1969-1973 (as per cent of employment in 1967)
1. Textiles (ISIC 23)								
Yarn and thread	228	125.9	10 350	118	2 589	21 900	473	0.4
Weaving, cotton	221	28.2	11 342	204	3 346	16 400	690	0.3
Weaving, synthetics and wool .	222	22.1	24 742	150	3 372	22 500	1 098	0.7
Narrow fabrics	224	72.2	1 346	25	433	17 700	76	0.3
Floor coverings	227	56.1	6 875	44	1 776	40 400	140	0.4
2. Clothing and footwear (ISIC 24)								
Leather goods except footwear	31 less 314	49.0	893	118	2 213	18 800	448	0.4
Clothing except furs	23	186.6	500 112	1 349	20 964	15 500	32 265	2.4
Footwear	321	2 114.0	135 843	226	3 234	14 300	9 500	4.2
3. Electrical machinery (ISIC 37)								
Radio and television equipment	365	537.2	185 255	130	4 107	31 600	5 750	4.4
Communication equipment . .	366	658.5	56 681	537	11 447	21 400	2 648	0.5
Household appliances	363	942.5	2 241	168	5 279	31 400	71	—
Electric lighting and wiring . .	364	190.1	1 176	161	9 312	57 800	20	—
4. Non-electrical machinery (ISIC 36)								
Cutlery, handtools	342	592.1	18 262	157	3 722	23 700	771	0.5
Farm machinery	352	67.4	288	134	4 232	31 500	9	—
Office machines	337	2 790.3	46 970	190	5 717	30 100	1 560	0.9
Metalworking machinery . . .	354	237.0	2 078	334	7 422	22 200	49	—

Sources: As for table 3.

[a] Provisional figures.

TABLE 5

Percentage increase in apparent consumption required to absorb the assumed yearly increase in imports of manufactures
from developing countries

(Million dollars)

No.	ISIC major group	Domestic production 1969[a]	Imports 1969	Exports 1969	Apparent consumption 1969[b]	Average yearly increase in imports of manufactures from developing countries 1969-1973	Average yearly percentage increase in apparent consumption required to absorb the additional imports
	FEDERAL REPUBLIC OF GERMANY						
20	Food	11 264	621	202	11 683	15	0.13
21	Beverages	2 492	169	63	2 598	11	0.42
22	Tobacco products	267	9	36	240	—	—
23	Textiles	5 680	1 393	1 481	5 592	35	0.63
24	Footwear, wearing apparel and made-up textiles	4 088	1 020	462	4 646	105	2.26
25	Wood and cork products	1 192	353	132	1 413	16	1.13
26	Furniture	3 198	105	250	3 053	—	—
27	Paper and paper products	2 584	826	318	3 092	2	0.06
28	Printing and publishing	3 054	71	209	2 916	1	0.03
29	Leather and leather goods	611	233	169	675	37	5.48
30	Rubber products	1 209	180	223	1 166	2	0.17
31	Chemicals	9 339	1 706	3 839	7 206	14	0.19
32	Petroleum products	1 157	572	264	1 465	2	0.14
33	Non-metallic mineral products	4 610	450	601	4 459	5	0.11
34	Basic metal manufactures	8 842	3 156	2 783	9 215	196	2.13
35	Metal products excluding machinery	7 961	378	1 189	7 150	1	0.01
36	Machinery other than electrical	9 594	1 760	6 302	5 052	16	0.32
37	Electrical machinery, apparatus and appliances	8 872	995	2 404	7 463	21	0.28
38	Transport equipment	10 040	1 184	4 668	6 556	4	0.06
39	Miscellaneous manufactured articles	5 191	759	1 552	4 398	43	0.98
	UNITED KINGDOM						
20	Food	6 697	1 032	226	7 503	74	1.00
21	Beverages	2 025	166	456	1 735	2	0.12
22	Tobacco products	705	12	84	633	—	—
23	Textiles	5 377	612	946	5 043	1	0.02
24	Footwear, wearing apparel and made-up textiles	1 888	384	338	1 934	70	3.61
25	Wood and cork products	1 205	698	18	1 885	1	0.05
26	Furniture	725	32	56	701	—	—
27	Paper and paper products	2 102	886	194	2 794	—	—
28	Printing and publishing	2 371	102	195	2 278	1	0.04
29	Leather and leather goods	274	103	120	257	5	1.95
30	Rubber products	867	59	174	752	2	0.27
31	Chemicals	3 616	1 211	1 741	3 086	29	0.96
32	Petroleum products	1 357	525	342	1 540	6	0.39
33	Non-metallic mineral products	2 026	929	1 090	1 865	22	1.18
34	Basic metal manufactures	5 478	1 879	1 433	5 924	147	2.48
35	Metal products excluding machinery	3 751	200	556	3 395	3	0.09
36	Machinery other than electrical	8 353	1 635	3 402	6 586	8	0.12
37	Electrical machinery, apparatus and appliances	4 488	639	1 118	4 009	8	0.20
38	Transport equipment	9 840	892	2 571	8 161	3	0.04
39	Miscellaneous manufactured articles	1 369	661	851	1 179	29	2.46
	UNITED STATES OF AMERICA						
20	Food	74 916	807	588	75 135	145	0.19
21	Beverages	9 146	648	18	9 776	1	0.01
22	Tobacco products	4 914	13	156	4 771	1	0.02
23	Textiles	19 733	1 076	706	20 103	28	0.14

TABLE 5 *(continued)*

No.	ISIC major group	Domestic production 1969[a]	Imports 1969	Exports 1969	Apparent consumption 1969[b]	Average yearly increase in imports of manufactures from developing countries 1969 1973	Average yearly percentage increase in apparent consumption required to absorb the additional imports
24	Footwear, wearing apparel and made-up textiles	24 533	1 594	235	25 892	574	2.22
25	Wood and cork products	11 217	1 095	313	11 999	166	1.38
26	Furniture	7 746	192	55	7 883	21	0.27
27	Paper and paper products	20 740	1 588	891	21 437	6	0.03
28	Printing and publishing	21 671	126	312	21 485	7	0.03
29	Leather and leather goods	1 950	220	86	2 084	24	1.15
30	Rubber products	7 328	156	195	7 289	13	0.18
31	Chemicals	47 931	1 481	3 657	45 755	86	0.19
32	Petroleum products	22 042	1 115	428	22 729	79	0.35
33	Non-metallic mineral products	14 604	1 008	448	15 164	67	0.44
34	Basic metal manufactures	46 550	3 344	1 834	48 060	38	0.08
35	Metal products excluding machinery	34 398	749	774	34 373	37	0.11
36	Machinery other than electrical . . .	48 357	2 542	7 188	43 711	69	0.16
37	Electrical machinery, apparatus and appliances	43 896	1 947	2 678	43 165	439	1.02
38	Transport equipment	68 238	5 279	6 515	67 002	7	0.01
39	Miscellaneous manufactured articles .	27 855	1 862	1 671	28 046	245	0.87

Sources: Domestic production data: supplies direct by ECE or derived from U.S. Department of Commerce, *Statistical Abstracts, 1970*; foreign trade data: based on United Nations, *Commodity Trade Statistics, Statistical Papers, Series D, 1969*; data on yearly increase in imports of manufactures from developing countries: based on tables 1, 2 and 3.

[a] Provisional figures.

[b] Estimates.

TABLE 6

**Comparison of labour displacement due to changes in labour productivity, 1965-1969
or to an assumed increase in imports of manufactures from developing countries, 1969-1973**

No.	ISIC major group	Index of employment 1965-1969 (1965 = 100) (1)	Index of value added 1965-1969 (1965 = 100) (2)	Index of labour inputs per unit of value added (3)	Yearly labour displacement due to changes in labour productivity 1965-1969[a] (4)	Yearly labour displacement due to increased imports 1969-1973[a] (5)	Ratio 4 : 5[a] (6)
				FEDERAL REPUBLIC OF GERMANY			
20	Food	101.5	116.6	0.87	4 110	740	0.180
21	Beverages	96.2	111.0	0.87	4 940	858	0.133
22	Tobacco products	82.1	116.1	0.71	2 320	10	0.004
23	Textiles	92.8	118.0	0.79	26 880	3 114	0.116
24	Footwear, wearing apparel and made-up textiles	93.8	109.8	0.85	19 312	13 197	0.683
25	Wood and cork products	87.7	121.6	0.72	4 970	942	0.190
26	Furniture	99.2	124.6	0.80	19 000	8	—
27	Paper and paper products	101.4	126.9	0.80	10 650	138	0.013
28	Printing and publishing	100.8	126.9	0.79	13 230	49	0.004
29	Leather and leather goods	77.0	99.3	0.78	3 135	3 419	1.091
30	Rubber products	109.2	124.1	0.88	7 865	286	0.067
31	Chemicals	106.6	159.8	0.67	47 850	849	0.018
32	Petroleum products	97.4	135.2	0.72	2 590	51	0.020
33	Non-metallic mineral products . . .	91.2	110.2	0.83	18 403	483	0.026
34	Basic metal manufactures	92.3	125.0	0.74	44 460	15 170	0.341
35	Metal products excluding machinery	96.2	116.2	0.82	38 430	95	0.002
36	Machinery other than electrical	104.1	112.7	0.92	23 640	1 963	0.083
37	Electrical machinery, apparatus and appliances	104.3	133.3	0.78	56 045	2 365	0.042
38	Transport equipment	108.5	147.6	0.74	51 610	329	0.006
39	Miscellaneous manufactured articles .	110.2	146.4	0.75	25 563	3 422	0.134

TABLE 6 *(continued)*

No.	ISIC major group	Index of employment 1965-1969 (1965 = 100) (1)	Index of value added 1965-1969 (1965 = 100) (2)	Index of labour inputs per unit of value added (3)	Yearly labour displacement due to changes in labour productivity 1965-1969[a] (4)	Yearly labour displacement due to increased imports 1969-1973[a] (5)	Ratio 4:5[a] (6)
		UNITED KINGDOM					
20	Food	99.6	112.0	0.89	15 620	6 270	0.401
21	Beverages	94.4	116.0	0.81	6 365	114	0.018
22	Tobacco products	97.6	109.3	0.89	1 128	−3	−0.003
23	Textiles	91.9	108.6	0.85	22 913	166	0.007
24	Footwear, wearing apparel and made-up textiles	93.7	95.5	0.98	2 375	17 559	7.393
25	Wood and cork products	96.7	89.7	1.08	−2 360	121	−0.051
26	Furniture	95.1	93.4	1.02	−685	−25	−0.036
27	Paper and paper products	96.9	112.2	0.86	−7 700	−1	—
28	Printing and publishing	103.1	110.2	0.94	5 505	148	0.027
29	Leather and leather goods	92.2	89.6	1.03	−353	845	−2.394
30	Rubber products	100.8	118.1	0.85	4 875	251	0.051
31	Chemicals	99.1	127.0	0.78	−23 980	3 461	−0.144
32	Petroleum products	104.4	120.9	0.86	1 645	−200	−0.122
33	Non-metallic mineral products	95.9	110.2	0.87	10 628	3 547	0.333
34	Basic metal manufactures	92.8	96.3	0.96	5 640	15 095	2.676
35	Metal products excluding machinery	97.2	105.2	0.92	10 380	380	0.637
36	Machinery other than electrical	100.0	115.4	0.87	34 125	1 042	0.031
37	Electrical machinery, apparatus and appliances	102.2	129.7	0.79	43 628	1 429	0.033
38	Transport equipment	96.0	103.2	0.93	19 005	306	0.016
39	Miscellaneous manufactured articles	114.0	121.5	0.94	5 625	7 877	−1.400
		UNITED STATES OF AMERICA					
20	Food	99.7	120.5	0.83	60 860	2 767	0.045
21	Beverages	108.3	129.2	0.84	8 880	35	0.004
22	Tobacco products	96.2	120.9	0.80	3 750	15	0.004
23	Textiles	107.3	132.7	0.81	43 985	1 294	0.029
24	Footwear, wearing apparel and made-up textiles	105.1	128.0	0.82	71 235	37 062	0.520
25	Wood and cork products	98.9	124.0	0.80	27 800	8 248	0.297
26	Furniture	112.7	136.2	0.83	18 063	1 136	0.063
27	Paper and paper products	108.7	130.1	0.84	25 520	192	0.008
28	Printing and publishing	112.1	136.6	0.82	46 125	323	0.007
29	Leather and leather goods	104.0	126.4	0.82	4 680	1 277	0.273
30	Rubber products	106.5	127.8	0.83	11 220	456	0.041
31	Chemicals	122.1	139.1	0.88	33 090	1 979	0.060
32	Petroleum products	92.8	146.2	0.63	13 135	510	0.039
33	Non-metallic mineral products	103.1	119.7	0.86	20 685	2 701	0.131
34	Basic metal manufactures	113.7	130.9	0.87	41 568	1 044	0.025
35	Metal products excluding machinery	118.4	141.3	0.84	53 600	1 446	0.027
36	Machinery other than electrical	127.1	158.5	0.80	92 900	2 660	0.029
37	Electrical machinery, apparatus and appliances	125.5	146.1	0.86	66 395	18 969	0.286
38	Transport equipment	117.8	128.7	0.92	36 480	193	0.005
39	Miscellaneous manufactured articles	129.1	157.6	0.82	55 080	10 767	0.195

Sources: Employment and productivity data: supplies direct by ECE or derived from U.S. Department of Commerce, *Statisticals Abstracts, 1970* and *Census of Manufactures, 1967*; data on yearly labour displacement due to increased imports: based on tables 1, 2 and 3.

[a] A minus sign (−) denotes employments in opposite directions or an increase in employment.

RESTRICTIVE BUSINESS PRACTICES

Report by the UNCTAD secretariat*

[*Original text: English*]

CONTENTS

Introduction

1. It will be recalled that at its second session the Conference decided by resolution 25 (II) that a study should be undertaken on the question of restrictive business practices. Since then, a great deal of work has been done by the secretariat in collecting relevant information with the assistance of both developed and developing countries. At the fifth session of the Committee on Manufactures an interim report on restrictive business practices[1] was submitted, containing in a summary descriptive form certain information which had been collected up to then. The report described, in particular, the legal and factual situation with regard to certain restrictive business practices which can and, to some extent, do affect the export interests of developing countries. The practices concerned involved import and rebate cartels and agreements on standards in the developed market-economy countries, restrictions on export, in particular in licensing agreements, and restrictions resulting from the activities of export cartels in the developed market-economy countries.

2. The substantive background report (see document TD/122/Supp.1 below) submitted to the Conference at its third session contains a detailed study on the question of restrictive business practices. The report deals with:

(*a*) Cartel activity in the developed market-economy countries and contractual restrictions on export activity of firms in developing countries, in particular in the light of additional information which has been collected;

(*b*) The contribution which the multinational corporations make to the export efforts of the developing countries;

(*c*) Restrictive business practices in relation to patents and trademarks, especially from the angle of the extent to which the patent and trademark systems may contain inherent restrictions on the export ability of firms in developing countries;

(*d*) The question of collateral protection which may be provided for the export interests of developing countries through the application of restrictive business practice

---

* The text of this report was circulated to the Conference as document TD/122, dated 22 December 1971, and TD/122/Corr.1, dated 9 February 1972.

[1] United Nations publication, Sales No. E.72.II.D.10.

legislation in developed market-economy countries, notably in controlling cartel activity;

(e) The question of the extent to which developing countries may have adopted policies to provide a certain degree of protection for their export interests through laws, guidelines and codes to regulate foreign investment; the operation of screening procedures for such investment and for technical collaboration agreements; and the enactment of laws with regard to competition policy;

(f) The problems of conflicts which have arisen and which may arise between the policies of countries and firms relating to restrictive business practices; and

(g) Existing bilateral and multilateral arrangements which have been introduced to provide for consultations and the dealing with problems in this area.

Chapter I

Restrictive business practices in relation to the export interests of the developing countries

3. The known cases of import cartels in the developed market-economy countries would appear to be few, since in most of these countries they are either prohibited altogether or authorized in certain exceptional cases only, or are subject to a control of abuses under the relevant restrictive practices laws. However, from time to time illegal import cartels have been found to exist in developed market-economy countries and in certain cases these have involved trade with developing countries and have affected their export interests. Rebate cartels also exist in some developed market-economy countries, and certain of these cartels would seem to operate in such a manner as to discourage and prevent imports from the developing countries of the products covered by such arrangements. In the case of agreements on standards it is often difficult to draw a distinction between public and private standards, since the latter standards may become compulsory as a result of becoming gradually incorporated into the public safety regulations or specifications. Nevertheless, such agreements have on certain occasions had the effect of excluding trade from the developing countries because the norms set are difficult to adhere to or because certification is difficult to obtain.

4. Restrictions on export activity may be found to a greater or less extent in contracts and licensing agreements between firms in developing countries and firms in developed market-economy countries. These restrictions can and do in certain cases constitute an important barrier to export activity in developing countries and for this reason action has been taken in some of these countries to modify the agreements entered into. To estimate in precise terms the actual impact of restrictive provisions, such as clauses controlling or prohibiting exports and the tying of raw material inputs and the supply of components, would be extremely difficult, but that they can have an adverse effect cannot be contested.

5. Export cartels are usually exempted in developed market-economy countries from the provisions of the competition legislation. A large number of such cartels are known to exist in these countries, and in certain cases international export cartels exist. Such cartel activity involves exports to developing countries and concerns a wide range of products. To the extent that export cartels are successful, a by-product of such success could well be harm to the export interests of developing countries. Where the export cartel is an international arrangement involving the major producers and exporters in developed countries, such cartels would possess even greater power to harm the interests of developing countries than would be the case with national export cartels.

Chapter II

The multinational corporation[2]

6. During the 1960s investments by the multinational corporations in countries outside those of their domicile rose rapidly. A major part of this investment took place in the developed market-economy countries, and principally by corporations in the United States and the United Kingdom. The developing countries accounted for approximately one-third of the book value of the total investments of such corporations. Roughly half of this investment was made by United States firms and some 20-25 per cent by United Kingdom firms.

7. The manufacturing sector, excluding the petroleum and extractive industries, accounted for 20-25 per cent of the investments by United States and United Kingdom corporations. These are the only two countries about which detailed information is available. The United States corporations were by far the most important investors in the developing countries, their investments in these countries at the end of 1970 totalling $5.5 billion. Well over 80 per cent of this amount was invested in Latin America, and in particular in Argentina, Brazil and Mexico, these three countries accounting for almost 60 per cent of the total investments of United States corporations in manufacturing in developing countries. Of the total investments of United Kingdom corporations in the manufacturing sector in developing countries, estimated at approximately $1.4 billion in 1968, 30 per cent was invested in India and a further 30 per cent in Latin American countries and in particular Argentina, Brazil and Mexico and in Commonwealth countries in the Caribbean.

8. The multinational corporations have established themselves in a large number of developing countries. The parent companies of about 50 per cent of these corporations are located in the United States and those of about 25 per cent are located in the United Kingdom. Latin America accounts for 60 per cent of United States subsidiaries in developing countries and Africa and Asia for over 75 per cent of United Kingdom subsidiaries. Increasingly, corporations in the Federal Republic of Germany and Japan are investing in the developing countries, and during the 1960s there was a considerable increase in foreign investments by corporations in these two countries in the developing countries. In the case of corporations in the Federal Republic of Germany. such investment was

---

[2] The term "multinational corporation" is used in a broad sense to refer to any firm which has subsidiaries in more than one foreign country. In consequence the bulk of foreign investments would be made by such firms.

made mainly in Latin America and in the case of Japanese corporations in Latin America and Asia.

9. The activities of the multinational corporations in the developing countries are essentially of three types, namely:

(a) Those relating to plantation and extractive industries;

(b) Those undertaken to encourage imports of products from the parent companies and their affiliates and in certain cases to assemble the goods imported; and

(c) Those relating to manufacturing in the developing countries, in particular as a result of the import substitution policies of these countries.

During the 1960s, especially in the more advanced developing countries, the emphasis in the activities of the subsidiaries of the multinational corporations would seem to have passed from the second to the third category. Moreover, in the same period, exports by such firms as a percentage of their total sales have increased, especially in Latin America, within the framework of regional economic integration.

10. During the 1960s, an increasing proportion of world trade was concentrated in the hands of the multinational corporations. Trade between the various parts of the multinational corporation, both in developed and in developing countries, represented a significant proportion of those countries' total exports and imports. By the mid-1960s between a fifth and a quarter of the total exports of both the United States and the United Kingdom was accounted for by intra-company transactions. With regard to the manufacturing sector, it would seem that in certain of the developing countries some 40 to 50 per cent of their total exports of manufactures is accounted for by the exports of multinational corporations, and, in the case of Latin America, over 50 per cent of the exports by these corporations consists of intra-company transactions, and principally transactions involving motor vehicles and equipment, food products and chemicals and allied products. Generally, the proportion of total sales which is exported by affiliates in developing countries is significantly smaller than the proportion exported by affiliates in the developed countries. For example, manufacturing affiliates of United States corporations in Latin America and other regions exported only 9 to 10 per cent of their total sales in 1968, as compared with exports by affiliates in Canada and Europe of between 25 and 30 per cent of their total sales. This would in part reflect the more export-oriented nature of the activities of United States manufacturing affiliates in developed countries, and in the case of Canada the fact that certain industry sectors, such as that of motor vehicles, are more closely integrated with those in the United States.

11. In all the major developed market-economy countries, the 1960s saw a widespread increase in merger activities, and in Western European countries these particularly involved the multinational corporation. It would seem that in certain of these countries the stricter enforcement of restrictive business practices laws may have encouraged mergers for the purpose of avoiding prohibitions on certain activities. Another trend noticeable in this period was the increasing specialization within the various parts of the multinational corporations in the production of certain components and parts in sub-assembly, both in developed and in developing countries. Obviously, this trend has accounted in part for the growth in intra-company import/export transactions.

12. The multinational corporations have clearly become a dominant factor in determining the pattern of world exports. Their power grew rapidly in the course of the 1960s.[3] In the case of the leading multinational corporations the value of the total sales of each of them exceeds that of the individual gross national products of most of the developing countries and of a number of the smaller European countries. The combined gross national products of the developing countries of Africa, excluding Algeria, Egypt, Libya and Morocco, would be approximately equal to the total sales of the General Motors Corporation, $9.74 billion in 1969. Similarly, the sales of the Royal Dutch/Shell Group exceeded the individual gross national products of all developing countries in Africa, in Latin America, except for Argentina, Brazil and Mexico, and in Asia, except for India and Pakistan.

13. Despite the significant contribution which the multinational corporations have made to world trade and to that of the developing countries, the existence of restraints on the export activities of their subsidiaries and affiliates has increasingly attracted the attention of governments in certain countries, both developing and developed.[4] In a number of these countries there is evidence that such restrictions exist and that they could be an important barrier to increased export activity in developing countries. Obviously, not all subsidiaries are restricted in their export activity, and a number are probably restricted to a certain extent only. Another restriction which can affect their export activity and which, in part, may result from the patents used by the subsidiaries and affiliates in the developing countries, is the tying of the supply of certain raw materials and industrial intermediate goods to the parent company. In this connexion, the evidence would seem to suggest that in certain cases excessively high transfer prices have been charged for the supply of such inputs to the subsidiaries in developing countries.

14. Because of the increasing importance of the multinational corporations in world trade, and their large financial resources, the movement of their funds into and out of different currencies has become an important phenomenon and has, in certain cases, aggravated problems facing governments in periods of balance-of-payments crises.

15. A great deal of additional work is required to evaluate the full contribution which the multinational cor-

---

[3] The problems of the power of the multinational corporations is referred to in the secretariat report to the Conference entitled "Private foreign investment in its relationship to development". See *Proceedings of the United Nations Conference on Trade and Development, Third Session*, vol. III, *Financing and Invisibles* (United Nations publication, Sales No. E.73.II.D.6), document TD/134, paras. 23-28; this report will also be issued separately as a United Nations publication.

[4] Export restrictions on the activities of subsidiaries and associates of the multinational corporations in the developing countries may be explicit, in the form of restrictive clauses in agreements between the firms in question or they may result implicitly from the nature of the control by the parent company of the activities of the subsidiary or associate.

poration is making and can make in the future to the export efforts of the developing countries. The limitations on export activity which exist require further detailed analysis. In the developed market-economy countries, increasing attention is being paid to the phenomenon of the multinational corporation. However, at this stage, little attention would seem to have been paid to the question from the point of view of the developing countries, and especially to the question how to maximize the contribution of such corporations to the export efforts of the developing countries.

Chapter III

Restrictive business practices in relation to patents and trademarks

16. Both patents and trademarks involve certain inherent restrictions on exports and imports. In the case of patents, exports to countries in which the patentee has obtained corresponding patents for the product in question may be prohibited unless the patentee has given his authorization. Consequently, even if the relevant licensing arrangements or investment contracts do not specifically contain clauses restricting such exports, they automatically require the prior approval of the patentee. This inherent restriction applies irrespective of whether the licensee in the developing country is an independent firm or a subsidiary of the patentee.

17. In contrast, no specific restrictions on export are inherent in unpatented know-how acquired by firms in the developing countries, and the only restrictions possible are those which may be contained in relevant licensing contracts. However, if the licensing contracts involve both patents and unpatented know-how, restrictions on export may be more severe than those resulting inherently from the patent system. Contractual restrictions may also be placed on the use which a licensee can make of patents and of unpatented information supplied for the working of the patents after the termination of the contract. Contracts normally run for the unexpired term of the patents involved. Hence, such restrictions would relate essentially to their use after the expiry of the patent. In certain developed countries specific provisions have been included in their patent laws to declare such restriction on patents and know-how null and void by permitting the licensee to terminate the licence notwithstanding anything in the licence to the contrary. Developing countries may similarly wish to include such provisions in their legislation, given the unjustified nature of such restrictions.

18. Where corresponding patents in developing countries are held by the same patentee, this situation may result in restrictions both on the import and on the export of the patented product. Compulsory licensing provisions in the developing countries may be invoked when imports are prevented. However, normally when a licensee obtains a patent, he also obtains assistance from the patentee in putting the invention into effect, and this might not be the case where a compulsory licence is granted. Compulsory licensing procedures in the past have been little used even in developed countries, in part probably on account of this consideration and owing to the lengthiness and costliness of the procedures involved.

19. In the case of a trademark, the exclusive right of the owner relates not to particular products or services as such but only to the use of the mark in association with such products. In consequence the inherent restrictions on exports in trademarks are not as great as in the case of patents. The trademark owner is generally not authorized to prevent the importation of products which have originated in his own enterprise, that is, "genuine" products which have lawfully entered commerce abroad, perhaps through an affiliate firm or licensee. Only where the trade marked product originates from different sources, that is with different manufactures, does there appear to be no firmly established rule as to whether unauthorized imports violate the domestic trademark.

20. Since the function of a trademark is normally to identify the manufacturer of a product, it would appear illogical for the parent company to prevent imports which have originated with a subsidiary, since the manufacturer of the domestic article and of the imported article are the same enterprise, although the manufacturing has taken place in two different countries. In protecting the legitimate interests of the trademark owner and the consumer of the product in such cases, reliance should be placed not on the trademark system but on the laws of contract and the laws regarding unfair competition, including protection against consumer deception.

21. It is in particular in the fields of food preparations, chemicals, pharmaceuticals, automobiles and other finished durable consumer products that trademarks seem to have an important role in deciding consumer acceptance. Probably the most important trademarks in use belong to the enterprises of developed countries. Furthermore, it is in the industries mentioned above that the multinational corporations have invested notably in the developing countries. An important point to remember is that the owner of the trademark has a specific interest in ensuring that products bearing his mark maintain a uniform quality standard and for this reason he may often be willing to permit the use of the mark only by firms over which he has direct control, namely, subsidiaries or controlled affiliates.

22. There are three ways in which the developing countries can attempt to control restrictions relating to patents unpatented know-how and trademarks, namely, through the relevant laws on industrial property, through the use of restrictive business practice legislation, and through screening procedures for foreign investment and technical collaboration agreements. Which approach or approaches a developing country may adopt depends upon many factors, and where such controls should be located is, therefore, a matter of individual choice. The important consideration is the avoidance of a situation where no control can be administered over restrictions which adversely affect the interest of the country in question.

Chapter IV

Collateral protection in developed market-economy countries for the export interests of the developing countries

23. There is the possibility for some collateral protection to be given to the export interests of the developing

countries against restrictive business practices in the developed market-economy countries through the application of laws in the latter countries. The extent to which this has occurred, however, would seem limited.

24. Where cartel restrictions are applied in developed market-economy countries by firms located there, the location of the firms and their restrictive activities create no difficulties for action by the governments of these countries. In cases where restrictions affect both foreign suppliers and domestic independent suppliers, action to protect the latter is likely to protect the foreign suppliers also. The limitations upon such protection generally result from the limited scope of the laws.

25. Since import cartels are generally regarded as domestic cartels in developed market-economy countries, collateral protection for the export interests of the developing countries is available against the activities of import cartels to the same degree as it is available to the domestic consumer against the activities of domestic cartels. Such cartels are either prohibited or strictly controlled. Similarly, to the extent that rebate cartels are prohibited or their activities controlled, in particular through legislation prohibiting resale price maintenance, collateral protection is available against the activities of such cartels. The restrictive effects on foreign suppliers of agreements on standards in developed market-economy countries are generally outside the scope of these countries' cartel laws, except where such agreements are made for exclusionary or discriminatory purposes. In such circumstances, where action is taken it is likely to provide collateral protection for the developing countries' export interests. Where restrictions on exports from developing countries appear in contracts between firms in developed market-economy countries and firms in developing countries, the only collateral protection available at all is that afforded by the restrictive business practice laws in the developed market-economy countries. It is only in the case of the United States that action has from time to time been taken in this regard. When the export interests of the developing countries are harmed by the activities of export cartels in developed market-economy countries, there is little prospect of collateral protection being provided under the laws of these countries, for export cartels are usually exempted. In the case of international export cartels, only limited action would be possible, since the action of a particular country can reach only those firms which are within its jurisdiction. It would seem that only in the case of the United States has action been taken against international export cartels, and therefore the degree of collateral protection that has been afforded against the activities of such cartels has probably been minimal.

Chapter V

Action in developing countries to protect their export interests

26. In a number of developing countries some action has been taken to protect their export interests against restrictive business practices. Such action has been taken through foreign investment laws, guidelines and codes; procedures for the registration and screening of investment and contractual arrangements entered into by firms in their countries with foreign enterprises; and national competition laws controlling restrictive business practices.

27. Foreign investment laws, guidelines and codes exist in many developing countries. As with the developed countries, the policies of developing countries towards foreign investment vary considerably. It would seem that only a small number of these laws, guidelines and codes refer specifically to the encouragement of export activity by the foreign investor. In a number of these countries, the registration of new investments under technical collaboration agreements involving non-nationals is required. In certain cases, screening procedures exist and include provision for the examination of possible restrictions on export activity. In the case of some developing countries, notably Argentina, Brazil, Colombia, India, Mexico and Pakistan, laws have been enacted prohibiting certain restrictive business practices. These vary in scope, in the degree to which they cover various types of restrictive business practices and in the extent to which they apply to relations between a firm in a developing country and firms which are domiciled outside its sovereign jurisdiction, but whose activities nevertheless affect domestic trade. Most of these laws are of recent date, and therefore little experience or knowledge exists as to how far they might be used to protect the export interests of the countries concerned.

28. An important recent example of action by a group of developing countries to curb restrictive business practices is the harmonization of policies with regard to the operations of foreign enterprises and the use of imported technology in the Andean Group of countries. In Articles 20 and 25 of decision No. 24 of December 1970 of the Commission of the Cartagena Agreement it was agreed to prohibit certain restrictive business practices in relation to the use of patents and trademarks. Member States agreed not to authorize, save in exceptional cases, agreements which prohibit or limit the export of manufactured products, which require the purchase of raw materials, intermediary goods and equipment from a determined source, or which contain restrictions relating to sale and resale prices, obligations to pay royalties on non-used patents and trademarks, prohibitions on the use of competing technologies and restrictions on the volume and structure of production.

29. The ability of developing countries to control restrictions on their exports is limited by a number of factors. A major factor is their limited bargaining power in negotiations with foreign enterprises and governments, given their dependence on the import of foreign technology to accelerate their economic development. Other factors are: the absence in the majority of developing countries of laws or procedures aimed at controlling restrictions; difficulties in obtaining sufficient relevant information, even if they have such laws and procedures, as a basis for taking appropriate remedial action; a shortage of trained experts in this field; and their limited control over the activities of such enterprises as the multinational corporations. Despite these limitations, it is evident from observations made earlier in this report that a number of developing countries, and in particular the more advanced of these, are taking action to deal with problems in this field.

There could also be scope for similar action in other developing countries where circumstances might indicate a need. Nevertheless, the exact nature of the steps to be taken will obviously depend not only on the type or types of restrictive business practices to be dealt with, but also on the legislative provisions and economic circumstances of the developing countries concerned.

30. In the case of the least developed among the developing countries the limitations mentioned clearly pose greater problems. In particular, because they lack experience in the field of restrictive business practices they have considerable difficulty even in recognizing the practices which are adversely affecting their export interests. In negotiations with foreign enterprises their bargaining power is extremely limited, especially on account of the small size of their domestic markets and of competition from other countries for investments and technical know-how. Furthermore, the institution of registration and screening procedures for foreign investment in such countries may well serve to deter rather than to encourage new investments. Technical assistance should therefore be supplied to such countries at their request to assist them in determining where problems in the field of restrictive business practices have arisen and may arise, and in devising appropriate solutions.

Chapter VI

The problem of conflicts between policies of countries and firms relating to restrictive business practices

31. The policies of foreign enterprises, those of the governments of the home countries of the parent companies and those of the host countries in which such enterprises establish affiliates, do not necessarily coincide. As a result, conflicts can arise and have arisen.[5] One aspect of these conflicts is the claim of the extraterritorial application of national laws and policies. Such claims have essentially, though not exclusively, arisen in relations between developed market-economy countries. Such claims have concerned the application of competition policies, laws and regulations of the United States and of the EEC.

32. It has only been possible to give a preliminary look at this question and this preliminary examination provides no basis for forming any conclusions as to whether any actual problems or practical difficulties in regard to the question of extraterritoriality have arisen for the developing countries. The cases which have arisen have not generally concerned the developing countries, except in regard to maritime affairs. Furthermore, in the few developing countries having restrictive business practice legislation, there is no information available to suggest that they have so far encountered difficulties by reason of the extraterritorial application of their competition laws to foreign enterprises. It is recognized that the issues involved are very sensitive, and it is not surprising therefore that, as between developed countries which have encountered problems in this field, solutions are being sought on a prag-

matic basis through discussion at a bilateral and multilateral level.

33. The foregoing remarks should not, however, be taken to imply that such problems are irrelevant or theoretical from the point of view of developing countries. As an increasing number of developing countries enforce their own competition laws, establish screening procedures and negotiate improved access to foreign markets for their exports, similar problems to those encountered in the developed countries could well arise. Consequently, further study of this question, concentrating on the practical implications of the problem from the point of view of the developing countries, is required.

Chapter VII

Bilateral and multilateral arrangements in the field of restrictive business practices

34. Action has been taken at a bilateral and multilateral level to control restrictive business practices. In particular, the United States has concluded bilateral friendship, commerce and navigation treaties with a number of developed and developing countries, and such treaties contain clauses relating to appropriate action by each party in the field of restrictive business practices, where problems might arise. In addition, the United States has informal bilateral consultative arrangements with Canada regarding matters of interest to both countries in the field of restrictive business practices. Multilateral arrangements in the field of restrictive business practices vary from geographically limited arrangements, on a regional or subregional basis, such as those in EEC and EFTA, to arrangements on a more global basis such as those in OECD and GATT. By and large, the principal objective would seem to be to resolve conflicts and potential conflicts between developed market-economy countries in the area of their competition policies. Consequently, the main focus of past discussions and co-operation relating to restrictive business practices would seem to have taken place in the context of the creation of regional economic groups, such as EEC and EFTA, and in the framework of OECD.

35. This is understandable because by and large developing countries have in the past paid little attention to the question of restrictive business practices. Essentially, it is only now that the more advanced of these countries are becoming aware of the problems that can arise in this field.

36. Recently a number of proposals have been made by academics, lawyers, statesmen and international non-governmental organizations for strengthening existing multilateral arrangements or for creating new ones. Such proposals have to a large extent been formulated with the objective of controlling the activities of foreign enterprises and, to a lesser extent, of controlling cartel activity. A common element in most of these proposals is the establishment of a policy forum to resolve conflicts which may arise, in particular as a result of divergencies between the policies of the multinational corporations and the interests of the State. In addition, a number of the proposals have recognized the need for greater participation and interest

---

[5] This question is also referred to in paras. 57-59 of the report mentioned in footnote 3 above.

y developing countries in this area. In summary, the proposals suggest either the establishment of appropriate international machinery to deal with the problems and the definition initially of a limited and acceptable agreement regarding the responsibilities of this machinery, or the drawing up of a multilaterally agreed upon set of principles, codes or rules regarding the activities or conduct of foreign enterprises and especially of multinational corporations. The proposals are not mutually exclusive alternatives, and it is recognized that some combination of the two approaches might be the most effective and useful way of finding appropriate solutions.

Chapter VIII

Conclusions

37. As can be seen from the foregoing, continued research by the secretariat and by the governments of member states and discussion between developed and developing countries are required on the question of restrictive business practices. On the basis of the work that has been done so far it would seem that important gaps exist in the control of the restrictive business practices which can affect the trade interests of developing countries. As a result, some action at a multilateral level aimed at closing the gaps would seem appropriate. In particular, the gaps occur in the controls relating to certain cartel activities, certain activities of foreign enterprises such as multinational corporations and the extraterritorial application of laws and policies of developed countries.

38. A great deal of information has been gathered by the secretariat about restrictive business practices. There are, however, a number of technical issues, indicated in this document, which need further detailed consideration. Similarly, a number of specific policy issues require fuller discussion. In order to facilitate such consideration and discussion, the secretariat is collecting additional data and for this purpose it will require the continued co-operation of governments of both developed and developing countries. Discussions at a general level would not seem likely to lead, at this stage, to substantial progress in work in this field. In order that appropriate remedial measures can be considered, as called for in the International Development Strategy for the Second United Nations Development Decade, the establishment of an expert group would seem desirable. Such an expert group could examine a number of the technical issues involved and could formulate suggestions. In particular, it could examine the possibility of drawing up codes or guidelines for the conduct of foreign enterprises in relation to the export interests of the developing countries. The issues that could be examined in this regard are:

(a) Export restrictions, tied purchasing arrangements and transfer pricing;

(b) The supply of more detailed information to the developing countries about the activities of foreign enterprises operating in those countries;

(c) The laws and policies of the developed market-economy countries with regard to the different types of cartel activity;

(d) The WIPO[6] model laws for the developing countries on inventions and trade names, with the objective of specifically taking into account the export interests of the developing countries;

(e) The effects of restrictive business practices in relation to the patent and trademark systems on the export interests of developing countries;

(f) The possibilities for remedial action in the developing countries through the adoption of policies and measures on restrictive business practices and through the use of screening procedures for foreign investments; and

(g) The specific assistance that can be given to the least developed among the developing countries in dealing with problems confronting them in this respect.

39. Every effort should be made to reduce, and where possible eliminate, the impact of restrictive business practices adversely affecting the export interests of developing countries. In this connexion, attention is drawn to paragraph 37 of the International Development Strategy for the Second United Nations Development Decade, as follows:

"Restrictive business practices particularly affecting the trade and development of the developing countries will be identified with a view to the consideration of appropriate remedial measures, the aim being to reach concrete and significant results early in the Decade. Efforts will be made with a view to achieving these results before 31 December 1972."

If developing countries are to build up internationally competitive manufacturing industries, it is essential that they should be in a position to export and that their ability to export should not be hampered by the existence of unreasonable restrictions. Careful examination needs to be given to the following points:

(a) The extent to which certain restrictions can be regarded as reasonable in that they protect the legitimate interests of the licensor or parent company and licensees or subsidiaries in other countries;

(b) The extent to which restrictions may exceed the inherent restrictions on export resulting from the existence of corresponding patents in foreign countries;

(c) The extent to which use may be made of trademark rights by such foreign enterprises as multinational corporations to prevent imports of products manufactured by their subsidiaries or affiliates;

(d) The extent to which the tying of sources of supply of inputs to the licensees is justifiable, especially in the manufacture of particular patented products; and the extent to which the prices paid for such tied inputs exceed the market prices for such products; and

(e) The extent to which restrictions are placed on the use of patents and on unpatented know-how after the termination of contracts and the expiry of the patents involved.

---

[6] It will be recalled that at the fifth session of the Committee on Manufactures the representative of WIPO indicated his organization's willingness to assist the secretariat in its study on restrictive business practices (see *Official Records of the Trade and Development Board, Eleventh Session, Supplement No. 2* (TD/B/352), para. 179).

40. The problems referred to do not affect the developing countries only. Indeed, significant limitations have been found to exist in the ability of developed countries to control such restrictive business practices—even with their well-established laws and mechanisms in the field of competition policies. The fact that governments of developed market-economy countries have become aware of the need to find practical solutions to the problems involved is shown by the work going on in OECD. Undoubtedly, the problems facing the developing countries are even greater and the scope for remedial action is more limited. While some action is possible in the more advanced developing countries, for the least developed among the developing countries the problems are immense,

and careful consideration needs to be given to the interests.

41. For the purpose of dealing with these problems from the point of view of the developing countries what is needed is a detailed exchange of international experience and knowledge on the various issues involved. Only after such a full exchange of information and experience will it be possible to consider establishing or strengthening machinery for dealing at an international level with those restrictive business practices which affect the trade interests of developing countries. In order that this first step may be taken, the establishment of an expert group is recommended.

RESTRICTIVE BUSINESS PRACTICES

Report by the UNCTAD secretariat*

[Original text: English]

CONTENTS

---

* The text of this report was circulated to the Conference as document TD/122/Supp.1, dated 7 January 1972, and TD/122/Supp.1/Corr.1, dated 27 March 1972, in supplement to the report issued as TD/122 (see p. 205 above).

LIST OF TABLES

Introduction

1. The Conference at its second session decided, by resolution 25(II) of 27 March 1968, that a study should be carried out "on the question of the restrictive business practices adopted by private enterprises of developed countries, with special reference to the effects of such practices on the export interests of the developing countries, especially on the relatively least developed". The Trade and Development Board was to determine the nature, scope and characteristics of the study. Accordingly, the Board at its eighth session adopted resolution 51(VIII) of 5 February 1969, by which it decided that the initial work on the study outlined by the secretariat in its report, "Restrictive business practices",[1] should consist of "studies of particular problem areas based upon suggestions put forward by developing countries, especially the relatively least developed among them, of actual or suspected restrictive business practices adopted by enterprises in developed countries, which may be affecting their export interests".

2. Since that time, the secretariat has collected a large amount of information, with the assistance of developed and developing countries members of UNCTAD, about the restrictive business practices which can affect, and which in certain cases do affect, the export interests of the developing countries. This information, collected by means of studies of individual countries and through the replies to the note verbale/questionnaire sent by the Secretary-General of UNCTAD to States members, formed the basis for the description of the factual and legal situation with regard to restrictive business practices contained in the interim report submitted by the UNCTAD secretariat at the fifth session of the Committee on Manufactures.[2] In paragraph 19 of that document, the secretariat outlined its suggestions with regard to future work.

3. After considering the report, the Committee on Manufactures at its fifth session reached conclusion 2(V).[3] That conclusion gave the secretariat a fairly broad and flexible mandate with regard to the future work to be done on the question of restrictive business practices. In carrying out its mandate, the secretariat has borne in mind the views expressed during the fifth session of the Committee on Manufactures and at the eleventh session of the Trade and Development Board.

4. In the course of the discussions in the Trade and Development Board at its eleventh session on the question

---

[1] See *Official Records of the Trade and Development Board, Eighth Session, Annexes*, agenda item 6 (*d*), document TD/B/C.2/54.

[2] See *Restrictive business practices* (United Nations publication, Sales No. E.72.II.D.10).

[3] See *Official Records of the Trade and Development Board, Eleventh Session, Supplement No. 2* (TD/B/352), annex I.

f restrictive business practices, and at the request of tates members, the representative of the Secretary-General of UNCTAD indicated that additional work was proceeding in certain areas and that the results of this work would, to the extent possible, be included in the report to the third session of the Conference.[4] The areas indicated were:

(*a*) The collection of additional information about the operations of cartels in the developed countries;

(*b*) An analysis of the contribution of the multinational corporations to the export efforts of the developing countries;

(*c*) An examination of the inherent restrictions of the patent and trademark system on exports of the developing countries;

(*d*) An examination of the competition policies and the restrictive business practice legislation in developed and developing countries.

5. In the preparation of this report to the Conference, the secretariat has utilized to the extent possible, given the restraints on the size of the documentation, the additional information collected relating to these areas. However, the secretariat did not think it appropriate to examine in any great depth the purely technical issues involved, since it would seem that they could more appropriately be considered by the Committee on Manufactures and/or by any technical body which might be established at the expert level. In fact, the technical issues involved would seem to require careful examination at such a level. The secretariat is publishing a number of the studies which have been prepared on the subject of restrictive business practices. The following studies are in course of preparation and some of them should be available before the third session of the Conference:

(*a*) The interim report *Restrictive business practices*, submitted at the fifth session of the Committee on Manufactures (see para. 2 above);

(*b*) A study on restrictive business practices in the United States of America, prepared by Professor D. Greer, Department of Economics, University of Maryland, United States of America (in TD/B/390);[5]

(*c*) A study on restrictive business practices in the Federal Republic of Germany, prepared by Dr. K. Markert, of the Federal Cartel Office of the Federal Republic of Germany;

(*d*) A study on restrictive business practices in the United Kingdom, prepared by Professor D. Swann, Department of Social Sciences and Economics, University of Technology, Loughborough, England (in TD/B/390);[5]

(*e*) A study on the restrictions on exports in foreign collaboration agreements in India, prepared by the Indian Investment Centre, New Delhi, India (TD/B/389);[6] and

(*f*) A study on the restrictions on exports in foreign collaboration agreements in the Republic of the Philippines, prepared by Mr. C. Virata, Secretary of Finance, Republic of the Philippines, with the assistance of officials in the Board of Investments in the Philippines (TD/B/388).[7]

6. In addition to the above-mentioned countries, mention should be made of similar studies in preparation on Australia, Japan (in TD/B/390),[5] Mexico and Pakistan.

7. Studies on certain other specific aspects will be available for further examination of such aspects at an expert level. These are:

(*a*) A study on the operations of multinational United States enterprises in developing countries, prepared by Professor R. Vernon, Graduate School of Business Administration, Harvard University, Massachusetts, United States of America (TD/B/399);[8]

(*b*) A preliminary study on the multinational enterprise and trade flows in developing countries, in particular from the point of view of multinational corporations in the United Kingdom, prepared by Professor J. H. Dunning, Faculty of Letters and Social Sciences, University of Reading, England, in association with the Advisory Group of *The Economist*;

(*c*) A preliminary study on the protection of developing countries' export interests through restrictive business practice legislation, prepared by Professor C. Edwards, formerly of the Department of Economics, University of Oregon, United States of America; and

(*d*) *Restrictive business practices: An analysis of the World Intellectual Property Organization Model Laws for the Developing Countries*, from the point of view of the export interests of the developing countries, prepared by G. Tookey, Q.C. (TD/B/398).[9]

8. Studies on certain other aspects of the question of restrictive business practices are envisaged.

9. It should also be recalled that in paragraph 37 of the International Development Strategy for the Second United Nations Development Decade it was agreed that:

"Restrictive business practices particularly affecting the trade and development of the developing countries will be identified with a view to the consideration of appropriate remedial measures, the aim being to reach concrete and significant results early in the Decade. Efforts will be made with a view to achieving these results before 31 December 1972".

10. The following issues are discussed in the present report. Chapter I contains a brief description of restrictive business practices which could affect the export interests of the developing countries. Whilst it is essentially a summary of the practices described in detail in the interim report to the Committee on Manufactures, it also includes, to the extent possible, additional information so far collected. The chapter deals with the activities of import and rebate cartels and their effects on the export interests of the developing countries; the restrictive effects of private agreements on standards; the contractual restrictions on exports and on the export ability of firms in developing countries; and the activities of export cartels in developed countries.

---

[4] See *Official Records of the General Assembly, Twenty-sixth Session, Supplement No. 15* (A/8415/Rev.1), part three, para. 221.

[5] United Nations publication, Sales No. E.73.II.D.8.

[6] United Nations publication, Sales No. E.72.II.D.7.

[7] United Nations publication, Sales No. E.72.II.D.8.

[8] United Nations publication, Sales No. E.72.II.D.16.

[9] United Nations publication, Sales No. E.73.II.D.1.

Chapter II discusses the contribution that the multinational corporations make and might make to the exports of the developing countries. It examines the role of the multinational corporations in international trade; the growing specialization in the activities of such corporations in various developed and developing countries; the restrictions which exist and might exist on the export activities of subsidiaries and affiliates in developing countries; the effects of the tying of the supply of essential inputs and the related question of transfer pricing within the corporation; and the intra-company movement of funds into and out of different currencies. The subjects dealt with in this chapter were only briefly examined in the interim report. Chapter III deals with the question of patents and trademarks and, to the extent appropriate, with the WIPO model laws for developing countries on inventions and on trademarks, tradenames and acts of unfair competition. In chapter IV the discussion centres on the actual or possible protection of the export interests of the developing countries through the administration of laws and policies in developed market-economy countries in the field of restrictive business practices. Chapter V deals with the protection which developing countries may provide to their export interests through the administration of laws and policies governing foreign investments, including the use of registration and screening procedures for such investments, and restrictive business practices laws. Brief reference is made to the limitations on the effectiveness of remedial action being taken in developing countries. The conflicts and problems which may arise for developing countries from the extraterritorial application of national laws and policies in the field of restrictive business practices are considered in chapter VI. In this connexion particular attention is drawn to the application of competition policies, laws and regulations. Chapter VI describes the existing bilateral, regional and multilateral arrangements to the extent that these deal or might deal with the question of restrictive business practices. Brief reference is also made to a number of recent proposals for strengthening multilateral action in this field, with particular reference to the activities of the multinational corporation.

11. This report to the Conference largely concentrates therefore on issues which have not been discussed in any great depth in the interim report submitted at the fifth session of the Committee on Manufactures. However whilst the aim has been to make the present report as self-contained as possible, it should nevertheless still be read in conjunction with the interim report.

CHAPTER I

Restrictive business practices in relation to the export interests of the developing countries

12. As was indicated in the interim report, restrictive business practices that can affect the export interests of the developing countries can be divided into three general categories. The first category includes the concerted activities of firms in the developed market-economy countries to control the terms upon which certain imports enter the markets of these countries. The activities considered in this regard are those connected with import cartels, rebate cartels and private agreements on standards.

13. The second category of such practices consists of the implicit and explicit restrictions placed on the export activities of firms in developing countries. Implicit or non-contractual restrictions of this nature result from the control exercised by foreign firms, and in particular the multinational corporations, over the activities of their branches, subsidiaries and affiliates in developing countries. On the other hand, explicit restrictions on export are usually specified in contractual arrangements entered into between firms in the developed and developing countries and dealing in particular with the supply of patented and unpatented know-how to the developing countries. The contractual arrangements in question can take the form, *inter alia*, of licensing, management and turnkey contracts or agreements.

14. The third category of practices covers the concerted activities of firms in developed countries in the field of export which can affect the export potential of the developing countries. In this regard, the activities of national and international export cartels are considered.

15. The following brief description of these practices is based on the information contained in the interim report and on certain additional information which has become available since the preparation of that report. No detailed discussion of the legal situation in the developed market economy countries is contained in this chapter, since it is dealt with in chapter IV, which discusses the question of the collateral protection that may be afforded to the export interests of developing countries through the administration of the laws and policies in the developed market-economy countries in the field of restrictive business practices.

A. Import cartels

16. Import cartels involve agreements relating principally to imports concluded among competing firms in one or several countries. Such cartels may collectively limit the aggregate amount of specified imported goods, determine the sources of supply for such imports and/or fix the prices and terms of purchase the cartel members will pay for such imports. Such activities may be (*a*) a defensive measure to achieve lower purchase prices for imported products because their importers encounter aggressive export policies pursued by suppliers through "natural" monopolies or export cartels or centralized State selling agencies; (*b*) an aggressive measure aimed at preventing or limiting imports in order to protect members of the cartel from import competition, or to ensure that imports take place before rather than after the processing of the goods in question, or to minimize the buying prices paid by cartel members; (*c*) part of an exclusive dealing arrangement between exporters and importers of a particular product,

ith the purpose of excluding other firms from the busi-
ess. From the point of view of the developing countries,
a aggressive import cartel would appear to be a most
armful activity, since it could restrict the volume of
xports from the developing countries and the range of the
rices paid to them for the imports permitted.

17. The known cases of import cartels in the developed
market-economy countries appear to be few, since in most
f these countries they are either prohibited or authorized
a certain exceptional cases only, or are subject to a control
f abuses under the relevant restrictive practices laws.

18. At the end of 1970, there were in Japan three
uthorized import cartels with regard to the import of
ertain agricultural products from particular developing
ountries in Asia. In addition, Japan has two import-
xport cartels for trade in certain textile products with
eveloping countries, and six import-export cartels for
ade in certain other textile products with developing and
ther countries.[10] In the case of the United Kingdom, one
nport cartel has been approved with regard to imports of
ulphuric acid. In the Federal Republic of Germany there
sed to be two authorized import cartels; one of these,
oncerned with imports of molybdenum, has since con-
nued on an informal basis, and there exists a similar
rrangement by the same firms with regard to imports of
ungsten. In the case of the United Kingdom and the
'ederal Republic of Germany, the cartels were authorized
s defensive arrangements.[11] In the case of the United
tates there are no legal import cartels. No information is
vailable as to whether legal import cartels exist in other
ountries.

19. As was indicated in the interim report, from time to
ime illegal import cartels which affected trade with the
eveloping countries have been found to exist in the
eveloped market-economy countries.[12] In certain cases
hese arrangements have been aggressive in nature. In
ddition, similar illegal arrangements have been found to
xist in relation to trade amongst certain developed
narket-economy countries.

B. Rebate cartels

20. Rebate cartels in the developed market-economy
ountries can function in a manner tending to discourage
he purchase of goods that may be imported. This objective
an be achieved by structuring the rebates on purchase
rices in such a fashion that they provide a disincentive
o customers to purchase from sources outside the cartel.

21. The rebate may be (a) a quantity rebate, i.e., relating
o the quantity purchased; (b) a loyalty rebate, relating to
xclusive purchases from the cartel; or (c) a functional
ebate, i.e., relating to a particular function performed in
he distribution of the product (such as wholesaling). The
rebate may be forfeited by buyers who obtain their
purchases from independent suppliers; or the rebates may
be graduated to increase as purchases increase and in such
a way as to provide a substantial incentive to buyers to
buy their entire requirements from the cartel members.

22. In the United States, rebate cartels are *per se* prohibited. In certain other countries, whilst in principle they
may be prohibited, they may qualify for a general or
special exemption, and in other countries again they are
subject to specific authorization, or to abuse controls. In
respect of only one of these countries is detailed information available about the number and operations of rebate
cartels, namely the Federal Republic of Germany. In that
country, the law provides a special exemption for such
cartels, and at the end of 1970, 33 rebate cartels were in
operation. On the basis of the information available, it is
difficult to determine the extent to which these cartels affect
the export interests of the developing countries. Furthermore, it should be mentioned that the Federal Cartel
Office of the Federal Republic of Germany requires that
in principle all purchases made from outsiders be taken
into account in the calculation of the rebate. If this were
done, then developing country suppliers would be placed
on an equal footing with members of the cartel. The fact
that this requirement is not always observed is indicated
in the interim report.[13] The report also indicates that in
the period 1957 to 1968, twelve aggregated rebate-cartel
arrangements were examined and adjudicated as violating
French law by the French Technical Commission for
Cartels and Dominant Positions. Other known cases have
related to trade within EFTA and EEC. The report also
indicates that deferred rebate and dual rebate systems of
loyalty rebates are applied by a number of international
shipping conferences.[14]

23. Since the publication of the interim report, additional information about Australia has become available.
It appears that, before their termination in consequence of
consultations by the Commissioner of Trade Practices
with the firms concerned, rebate-cartel type arrangements
had existed in that country with regard to the sale of all
types of electric lamps, nails, metal central valves, soft
drinks, industrial safety products, insulation materials,
vitreous china, sanitary ware and asbestos cement products.[15] It should be noted that retail price maintenance
was recently made illegal in Australia by an amendment
to the Trade Practice Act. However, by a High Court
decision in September 1971, the Act was ruled invalid and
unconstitutional.[16] The necessary revisions to the Act
are believed to be in preparation.

C. Agreements on standards

24. It is generally recognized that standards applied in
one country may have the effect of hampering, making

---

[10] See *Restrictive business practices...*, annex III, C.3 and C.4.

[11] *Ibid.*, paras. 26-29.

[12] A case of a collective boycott by two manufacturers in Australia
f ceramic wall tiles against imports from countries other than Japan
occurred in November 1970. This import-cartel type arrangement
vas subsequently terminated. (See *Commissioner of Trade Practices,
Fourth Annual Report, Year ended 30 June 1971*, Commonwealth of
Australia, chap. 1).

[13] See *Restrictive business practices...*, para. 50.

[14] See *The liner conference system* (United Nations publication,
Sales No. E.70.II.D.9), chap. IV.

[15] See footnote 12 above.

[16] See the *Financial Times*, 6 September 1971, "Australian court
decision on Trade Act".

more costly, or even excluding exports from other countries. Such agreements among suppliers or users of goods in developed countries may, if they attain substantial acceptance among buyers or if they become legally obligatory, prevent or handicap sales of products from developing countries that are not recognized as conforming to the applicable standards. For the purposes of the study on restrictive business practices, only those standards which are voluntary and established by trade associations of the manufacturers concerned, or by direct agreement among the suppliers or buyers, are relevant. In general, agreements on standards are exempted from the scope of the laws governing cartels in the developed market-economy countries. In the case of the United States, there is no statutory exemption, but it appears that agreements which apply non-discriminatory standards are considered as "reasonable" and hence lawful.[17]

25. In the interim report certain information was given about a number of such agreements. It was pointed out, however, that it was often difficult to draw a clear distinction between public and private standards, since private standards may in fact become "compulsory", because either they become gradually written into the public safety regulations or specifications for public contracts, or they receive some less mandatory public approval, or receive consumer acceptance. Nevertheless, such agreements can have the effect of excluding trade from developing countries in that the norms set may be difficult to adhere to or certification may be difficult to obtain.[18]

D. Restrictions on export activity in licensing agreements

26. The second category of practices consists of implicit and explicit restrictions placed on the export activities of firms in developing countries. The discussion in the present section will concern only explicit restrictions on exports, since the question of implicit restrictions will be dealt with in more detail in chapter II, which describes the activities of the multinational corporations. Similarly, restrictions on exports which are inherent in the patent and trademark systems will not be discussed, since they are dealt with in chapter III.

27. Chapter II of the interim report indicated the existence of a considerable number and variety of restrictive provisions which can be and are included in licensing agreements and contracts. Such restrictions can be classified into two categories: restrictive provisions on exports, and other restrictive provisions affecting the export potential and activity of a firm in the developing country concerned. The restrictions that may be placed on export are: global bans; prohibition of exports to specified countries; permission to export only to specified countries; the requirement of prior approval from the licensor for exports; export quotas; price controls on exports; the restriction of exports to specified products; permission to export only to, or through, specified firms; and prohibition of exports of substitute products. Other potential

restrictive provisions deal with the tying of purchases of essential inputs to the licensor; restrictions on production patterns; payments of a minimum royalty; restrictions on the use of the acquired technology after the termination of the contract; restrictions on disclosure of the technology received; agreements not to challenge the validity of patents and trademarks transferred; and the mutual exchange, or unilateral grant-back, of technical improvements. The extent to which such provisions are restrictive varies from case to case.

28. The interim report indicated that such restrictions to a greater or less extent, featured in contracts and licensing agreements entered into between firms in developing countries and firms in the developed market-economy countries. The report also indicated, on the basis of studies carried out in certain developing countries, namely India, Mexico and the Philippines, that such restrictions constituted an important barrier to export activity in these countries, and that for this reason, to the extent possible, action had been taken in some of these countries to modify the agreements entered into. Subsequent studies on restrictive business practices in the developing countries—namely one on Pakistan carried out by the secretariat, another on Chile[19] prepared by the Chilean Production Development Corporation and a further study prepared on certain industry sectors in Mexico[20]—have confirmed the importance of such restrictions as a barrier to export activity.

29. It would be extremely difficult, and probably unnecessary, to estimate in precise terms the actual impact of restrictive provisions in licensing agreements and contracts on the export capabilities of developing countries. Obviously, it cannot automatically be assumed that a firm would export if the contractual restrictions on export were removed. It may not be able to compete effectively in export markets because of high production costs. However, this does not mean that the restriction is irrelevant. The existence of such restrictions can discourage a firm from developing an export capability. They can in part also account for the internationally non-competitive nature of the firm's activities, especially, for example, if the firm has to pay higher than world market prices for its tied inputs.

E. Export cartels

30. The third category of restrictive business practices covers the activities of export cartels. Such cartels can adversely affect the export potential of developing countries in three ways: (a) by discrimination against firms in

---

[17] See *Restrictive business practices ...*, para. 61.

[18] *Ibid.*, para. 67.

[19] A preliminary report has been prepared by the Chilean Production Development Corporation analysing contracts involving royalties that were in force in Chile between 1966 and 1969. It was found that out of 500 enterprises operating under foreign licences that were investigated, only 24 indicated that they effectively had the possibility of exporting their products abroad. Most of the $2.5 million of goods exported in 1969 by these firms was made up of exports effected under the motor vehicle exchange agreement of LAFTA. D. Tunik, "Criteria used in the selection of products for the export market", ST/ECLA/Conf.37/L.22.

[20] M. S. Wionczek, G. Bueno and J. E. Navarrete, "La transferencia internacional de tecnología al nivel de empresa: El Caso de México" (a draft report currently under revision).

eveloping countries, through limiting the amount or
aising the prices of inputs purchased (e.g., of equipment,
aw materials or semi-manufactured goods which are
ssential to the production for export); (*b*) by aggressive
ctivities against firms of developing countries, when the
artel meets competition from developing countries in
oreign markets; and (*c*) by requiring firms in developing
ountries that are subsidiaries or affiliates of cartel mem-
ers to conform to market allocations, export quotas and
imilar restrictions that are included in the cartel's pro-
ramme.

31. Export cartels are less strictly controlled in the
eveloped market-economy countries than cartels restrict-
ag competition on the domestic market. In the developed
aarket-economy countries such cartels are either exempted
y definition from the laws controlling cartel activity or
utside the scope of such laws, by virtue of an explicit
rovision. In consequence, information about such cartels
difficult to obtain in the case of most of the developed
aarket-economy countries. But according to the informa-
ion that is available, export cartels would seem to be the
aost frequent type of cartel activity in these countries.

32. Only four countries—the Federal Republic of Ger-
aany, Japan, the United Kingdom and the United States—
equire export cartels to be notified to the competent
overnmental authorities, and only in the Federal Republic
f Germany, Japan and the United States are data pub-
shed on the notified export cartels or associations. On
he basis of the latest statistics, there are 81 export cartels
a the Federal Republic of Germany (31 December 1970),
14 in Japan (31 March 1970) and 35 export associations
a the United States (31 October 1970). In the case of the
Jnited Kingdom, no comparable statistics are available,
ut it was estimated as of September 1963 that the number
f export cartels was 64.[21] This number may now be
ubstantially higher.

33. As has been indicated in the interim report, on the
asis of published information it would seem that firms
a other developed market-economy countries—namely in
Austria, Belgium, Italy, the Netherlands, Norway and
witzerland—participate in some of the export cartel
rrangements of firms in the United Kingdom and the
ederal Republic of Germany. As a result, such cartels are
nternational cartels rather than national cartels.[22] In
ddition, evidence exists that some domestic cartels in the
leveloped market-economy countries are also engaged in
xports, with the result that exports made by the members
f these cartels are probably as strictly controlled as those
overed by export cartels.[23]

34. The number of export cartels in itself provides no
ndication of the extent to which the export potential of
he developing countries may be affected. Nevertheless, on
the basis of the published information available in the
Federal Republic of Germany, Japan and the United
States, it can be seen that the majority of these cartels
involve exports to the developing countries. Of the activities of 214 export cartels, including eight import/export
cartels, in Japan the activities of 124 related to exports to
the developing countries. Twenty-five were purely export
cartels exclusively relating to exports to the developing
countries, and the bulk of these involved textile products.
Similarly, the activities of two of the export/import cartels
involved textile products and were exclusively concerned
with trade with the developing countries. With regard to
the activities of the pure export cartels which involved
exports both to developed and developing countries, over
50 per cent were in the industry sectors of textiles and
pharmaceuticals. In the case of the Federal Republic of
Germany, the activities of 58 of the 73 purely export
cartels would seem to concern exports to developing countries as well as to certain developed countries. The main
industry sectors were chemicals and allied products,
electrical products and apparatus and certain minerals
and mining products. With regard to the 35 export cartels
in the United States, over 22 per cent of their total exports
were shipped to developing countries in 1962, and the bulk
of the exports were industrial raw materials.[24] It would
seem reasonable to assume therefore that export cartel
activity in other developed market-economy countries
would also involve to a similar extent exports to the
developing countries. For example, in the case of the
allegations in the United Kingdom in early 1971 of unfair
pulp and paper pricing policies by Nordic producers, the
President of the Norwegian Paper Council was reported
as stating that the present "Scan" organizations, which
set Scandinavian paper prices, would have to be dis-
mantled if Norway joined the Common Market. Furthermore, it was indicated that in the President's view this was
likely to lead to a reduction in European paper prices for
a certain period. In addition he is reported to have stated
that Norway would be interested in starting another
organization grouping the Scandinavians, Britain and the
Six, to deal with markets outside Europe and thus beyond
the scope of the Rome Treaty.[25] In this connexion, the
markets of the Philippines and Indonesia were cited as
examples.[26]

35. The existence of export cartels affecting the interests
of developing countries cannot be contested. Undoubtedly,
to the extent that export cartels are successful in their
operations, a by-product of such success could well be
specific harm to the export interests of the developing
countries. Where the export cartel is an international
arrangement involving the major producers and exporters
in the developed market-economy countries, such cartels
would possess even greater power to harm the interests of
developing countries than would national export cartels.

---

[21] See C. D. Edwards, *Cartelization in Western Europe* (Washing-
on, D.C.: Washington External Research Staff, Bureau of Intelli-
ence and Research, U.S. Department of State, 1964), pp. 19 and 21.
See also *Restrictive business practices* ..., para. 185.

[22] See *Restrictive business practices* ..., paras. 193-199.

[23] *Ibid.*, paras. 213-221.

[24] *Ibid.*, paras. 185-190 and annex III.

[25] Treaty establishing the European Economic Community,
signed at Rome on 25 March 1957 (United Nations, *Treaty Series*,
vol. 298 (1958) No. 4300.

[26] R. Dale, "Norway denies paper-pricing allegations", in the
Financial Times, 26 April 1971.

CHAPTER II

Activities of the multinational corporation and the export efforts
of the developing countries and territories[27]

36. The multinational corporation has obviously become a powerful determinant of the pattern of world exports. Its power in the course of the 1960s has grown rapidly.[28] As regards the more important multinational corporations, the total sales of these corporations individually exceed the value of the individual GNP of most developing countries and of a number of the smaller European countries. The combined GNP of the developing countries of Africa, excluding Algeria, Egypt, Libya and Morocco, was approximately equal to the total sales of the General Motors Corporation at $24.30 billion in 1969. Similarly, the sales of the Royal Dutch/Shell Group at $9.74 billion exceed the individual GNP of any of the developing countries in Africa, of those in Latin America, except Argentina, Brazil and Mexico, and those in Asia except India and Pakistan.[29]

37. Many of the activities of the multinational corporation dealt with in this chapter involve aspects of policies of these corporations which are either strictly confidential or secret. They concern exports, and in particular, exports by its subsidiaries and affiliates; the purchasing of essential inputs from within the corporation, that is from the parent company or its other affiliates; the prices paid for such purchases; and the movement of funds into and out of currencies by and within the corporation. For this reason, only limited information is available either in the developed or the developing countries. The information contained in this document is drawn from a wide range of sources, including published and unpublished studies by private individuals and governments, special studies undertaken for the UNCTAD secretariat in certain developed and developing countries, and reports and papers submitted to a number of international conferences on the multinational corporation.

38. An additional problem that should be mentioned is that the level of detail in the statistics published on the operations of the multinational corporation varies, and essentially only in the case of the United States and, to a lesser extent, of the United Kingdom,[30] is sufficient infor-

mation available to provide a general indication of the activities of the multinational corporation, However, even these statistics mostly refer to the situation as at the mid 1960s and do not therefore fully reflect the constantly evolving nature of the activities of the multinational corporation during the full course of the past decade.

A. The foreign investment and trade
of the multinational corporations

39. During the 1960s, investments by multinational corporations in countries outside their domicile rose rapidly. A major part of this investment took place in the developed market-economy countries and was made principally by multinational corporations of the United States and the United Kingdom.[31] For example, in the United Kingdom the direct capital stake of foreign companies other than in the field of oil, insurance and banking, grew from £1,254 million in 1960 to £2,617 million in 1966. About 80 per cent of this latter figure was owned by North American companies, principally those of the United States. It is also estimated that the direct stake of United Kingdom companies in firms abroad grew in the same period from £3,783 million to £6,025 million ($16.8 billion).[32] Similarly, in Australia, the annual inflow of direct private foreign investment in companies grew from $357 million to $526 million in 1968. In the same period the annual inflow of portfolio investment grew from $70 million to $425 million. Between the years 1962 and 1967 the level of United States corporate investment in Australia more than doubled.[33]

40. Between 1960 and 1970 the net flow of private direct foreign investment to developing countries from the developed market-economy countries[34] increased from $1,76

---

[27] In this chapter the term "multinational corporation" is used in a broad sense to refer to any firm which has subsidiaries in more than one foreign country. In consequence, the bulk of foreign investments in developing countries would be investments made by such firms.

[28] The problems of the power of the multinational corporations are referred to in the UNCTAD secretariat's report to the Conference, "Private foreign investment in its relationship to development". (See *Proceedings of the United Nations Conference on Trade and Development, Third Session*, vol. III, *Financing and Invisibles* (United Nations publication, Sales No. E.73.II.D.6), document TD/134, paras. 23-28; this report will also be issued separately as a United Nations publication.)

[29] C. Tugendhat, *The Multinationals* (London: Eyre and Spottiswoode, 1971), p. 2, and based on gross national product figures at current prices for 1965—the latest year for which detailed figures are available for most countries, *Yearbook of National Accounts Statistics*, 1969 (United Nations publication, Sales No. E.71.XVII.3), vol. 2, pp. 15-21.

[30] In the *Financial Times* of 12 October 1971 (p. 33) it was indicated that Mr. John Davies, Secretary for Trade and Industry, hai-

revealed to the October meeting of the National Economic Development Council that multinational corporations operating in the United Kingdom were likely to have to increase the information they make available as a result of changes then under consideration by the Government in the Companies Act.

[31] It has been estimated that the book value of total foreign investments by OECD member countries in 1966 was $90 billion, of which $55 billion was accounted for by United States multinational corporations and the remaining $35 billion by multinational corporations of other countries, of which the major proportion came from the United Kingdom. Approximately one third of the total was invested in the developing countries. For further details see OECD DAC (68) 14, 23 April 1968; and S. E. Rolfe, "The International Corporation", XXIInd Congress of the International Chamber of Commerce, Istanbul, 31 May-7 June 1969.

[32] See J. H. Dunning, "Foreign Investment in the United Kingdom", in I. A. Litvak and C. J. Maule (eds.) *Foreign Investment: the Experience of Host Countries* (New York, Praeger, 1970), chap. 9.

[33] See D. T. Brash, "Australia as Host to the International Corporation", in C. P. Kindleberger (ed.) *The International Corporation* (Cambridge, Mass., and London, M.I.T. Press, 1970), part V chap. 12.

[34] Australia, Austria, Belgium, Canada, Denmark, France, the Federal Republic of Germany, Italy, Japan, the Netherlands, Norway, Portugal, Sweden, Switzerland, the United Kingdom and the United States of America.

TABLE 1

United States foreign direct investments in developing countries as at the end of 1970

(Million dollars)

Developing countries	Mining and smelting	Petroleum	Manufacturing	Other	Total
Latin America[a]	2 037	3 929	4 604	4 115	14 685
Africa	350	1 916	100	245	2 611
Middle East	3	1 466	86	90	1 645
Asia and the Pacific[b]	91	1 066	692	628	2 477
TOTAL	2 481	8 377	5 482	5 078	21 418

Source: U.S. Department of Commerce, Office of Business Economics, Survey of Current Business, October 1971, pp. 32 and 33.

a Including all Western Hemisphere countries except the United States and Canada.

b Not including Japan, Australia and New Zealand.

million to $3,412 million, and of the latter amount about 45 per cent came from the United States, and between 8 and 9 per cent each from the Federal Republic of Germany, the United Kingdom and Japan.[35] The following is a discussion, on the basis of the latest statistics available, of the private direct foreign investment in developing countries by each of the above-mentioned developed market-economy countries.

41. By 1970 the aggregate investments of United States enterprises in developing countries totalled more than $21 billion. As is indicated in table 1, almost 40 per cent of this amount was invested in petroleum, 25 per cent in manufacturing and 12 per cent in mining and smelting. Almost 70 per cent of all the investments were in Latin America, and this area accounted for almost 84 per cent of investments in the field of manufacturing. Argentina, Brazil and Mexico accounted for 60 per cent of United States manufacturing investments in developing countries.

42. Most of the investments in the field of mining and smelting were concentrated in the copper and aluminium industries, lesser amounts in the iron ore and a variety of nonferrous metals sectors. It should be noted that each of these industries and the petroleum industry are dominated by a relatively small number of United States multinational corporations. With regard to manufacturing, the bulk of such investment occurred in the late 1950s and in the 1960s. In Latin America, in 1957, investment in manufacturing facilities was equivalent to only $1,280 million but by 1970 this investment had increased to $4,604 million, and in Asia it increased in the same period from $118 million to $692 million.

43. It has been estimated, with regard to manufacturing subsidiaries of the 187 most important United States multinational corporations, that the number established in Latin America grew from 572 in 1959 to 950 in 1967, in Asia from 83 to 237, and in Africa from 17 to 73 in the same period.[36]

44. It would seem that such investments have been made particularly in those industries where import substitution

in the developing countries has entailed the mobilization of considerable amounts of capital or the creation of fairly complex organizations, such as the basic chemical, automobile and farm machinery industries. It is in these industrial sectors that the foreign-owned multinational corporations have been especially active in the developing countries, as well as in those sectors where trade names play an important part in buyer acceptance, namely in food preparations, cosmetics and drugs. Of the subsidiaries of the 187 most important United States multinational corporations in the developing countries in 1967, over 60 per cent were established in the preceding ten years. Almost half of the subsidiaries were wholly owned and of the remainder almost 30 per cent were majority-owned.[37]

45. The cumulative flow of investments by the Federal Republic of Germany in the developing countries in the period 1961 to 1970 increased rapidly from DM 1,364 million to DM 5,108 million ($1,400 million). As is indicated in table 2, over 70 per cent of these investments were made in Latin America and a major proportion of that amount was invested in Brazil. That country accounted for almost 30 per cent of the Federal Republic of Germany's investment in the developing countries. The other major countries of investment were Argentina and Mexico. On the basis of information available for investments up to 1964,[38] which provides a breakdown of the investment figures by country and industry, it would seem that the greater part of the investment in Latin America was made in the sectors of motor vehicles and machinery; electrical and optical equipment; chemicals; and iron and steel. Africa was the second most important area of investment, accounting for about one-fifth of the total investment in developing countries. Libya took almost 50 per cent of this amount, which was largely invested in the petroleum industry. Asia accounted for just over 10 per cent of total investments in 1964. No details are available concerning the specific industrial sectors in which the substantial increase in investments of the Federal Republic of Germany took place in the period 1964 to 1970.

---

[35] OECD press release PRESS/A (71) 22, Paris, 28 June 1971, tables 1 and 11.

[36] Harvard Multinational Enterprise Study.

[37] Ibid. "Wholly owned" refers to subsidiaries in which the parents hold 95 per cent or more of the voting stock; and "majority-owned" where they hold 50 to 94 per cent.

[38] Deutsche Bundesbank, Monthly Report, December 1965.

TABLE 2

Cumulative flow of investments by the Federal Republic of Germany
in developing countries, 1961-1970[a]

(Million Deutsche Marks)

Country or area	1961	1965	1970
Latin America	1 099.3	1 579.1	3 664.7
of which:			
Brazil	639.7	839.3	1 470.8
Argentina	159.7	299.0	458.2
Mexico	37.4	104.6	300.6
Africa	141.8	395.5	1 003.0
of which:			
Libya	—	51.5	438.7
Liberia	34.1	86.1	152.2
Asia	122.8	241.7	440.1
of which:			
India	60.2	125.9	170.0
TOTAL	1 363.9	2 216.3	5 107.8

Source: Circulars of the Federal Ministry of Economic Affairs, March 1968 and April 1971.
[a] Figures do not include reinvested earnings in the developing countries.

46. The only country, other than the United States, concerning which some detailed information is available relating to direct foreign investments in the developing countries is the United Kingdom. Surveys of foreign assets were undertaken by the Board of Trade in the United Kingdom for the years 1965 and 1968, and a summary of the position in 1968 is contained in table 3. The book values of net assets of the United Kingdom's direct investments, excluding petroleum, in developing countries grew from around £1,431 million in 1965 to £1,668 million ($3,977 million) in 1968. However, as a proportion of the United Kingdom's total foreign assets, the developing countries' share fell from 37 per cent in 1960 to 30 per cent in 1968, thus indicating a more rapid growth in investments in developed countries than in developing countries in this period. Around 70 per cent of such investments in the developing countries were made in countries belonging to the sterling area. Of total investments in developing countries in the sterling area the Commonwealth West Indies and India accounted for approximately 25 per cent each, Commonwealth Africa for 20 per cent and Malaysia for 15 per cent.

47. The manufacturing sector accounted for approximately 35 per cent of total investments. However, in the case of developing countries not in the sterling area, the proportion was much higher—just under 50 per cent. Of total investments in manufacturing in 1965—the latest year for which a full detailed breakdown is available by country[39]—India accounted for over 30 per cent (and almost 50 per cent of such investments in the sterling area). Commonwealth Africa (mainly Nigeria and Kenya) for 12 per cent, and Mexico, Brazil and Argentina for between 6 and 8 per cent each.

48. In addition, it would seem that approximately £770 million ($2,148 million) had been invested in the petroleum industry in developing countries by the end of 1966. Almost 50 per cent of these investments were in developing countries in the Middle East and a further 25 per cent in Latin America.

49. In 1970 the 250 largest United Kingdom companies had 2,094 affiliates in the developing countries. Of this number, in order of importance, 397 were industrial holding companies, 370 were in the engineering sector, 284 in chemicals and allied products industries, 205 in the petroleum and 199 in the food, drink and tobacco sectors. Of the total number of affiliates, around 70 per cent were subsidiaries. Some 161 of these companies operated in six

TABLE 3

Book values of net assets attributable to the United Kingdom
in the developing countries as at 1968

(Million pounds sterling)

Industry sector	Sterling area	Non-sterling area	Total
Agriculture	329.8	42.5	372.4
Mining	79.3	42.5	121.8
Manufacturing	340.0	242.0	582.0
Distribution	193.3	88.9	282.2
Other	213.9	96.1	309.9
TOTAL	1 156.3	512.0	1 668.3

Source: Board of Trade Journal, 23 September 1970, "Book Values of Overseas Direct Investments".

[39] See *Board of Trade Journal*, 26 January 1968, "Book Values of Overseas Investments", p. IX, table 4.

TABLE 4

Japan's cumulative direct foreign investment since 1951 in Latin America, South-East Asia and the Middle East

(Thousand dollars)

Area	1959		1967	
	Number of contracts	Value	Number of contracts	Value
Latin America . . .	143	62 037	446	372 620
South-East Asia . .	200	36 380	890	279 925
Middle East	10	20 185	22	240 417
TOTAL	353	118 602	1 358	892 962

Source: Japan, Economic Deliberation Council, *Shihon Jiyuka to Kaigai Kigyo Shinshitsu* (Liberalization of Capital Movements and Overseas Expansion of Business), Tokyo (1969), p. 137.

or more countries in the world and 74 of them in six or more developing countries.

50. As is indicated in table 4, aggregate direct foreign investment by Japan since 1951 in the developing countries of Latin America, South-East Asia and the Middle East, was $119 million in 1959. During the next eight years, such investment grew on average by about 30 per cent per annum, reaching $893 million in 1967. Whilst, in value terms, Latin America was the most important area for Japanese investment, taking over 40 per cent in terms of the number of contracts concluded, South-East Asia accounted for more than 65 per cent of the total number of contracts. Japanese investment contracts in Latin America would seem to have involved a higher degree of Japanese equity participation than those in South-East Asia; for example, in Brazil—which accounted for a significant proportion of Japan's investment in Latin America, in particular in a steel mill and a shipyard as well as automobile and machinery plants—over 50 per cent of Japanese investors owned more than 75 per cent of the capital in the investment ventures.[40]

51. In both Latin America and South-East Asia, Japanese investments were essentially in the field of manufacturing; however, in the Middle East the investment has mainly been in oil exploration. With regard to South-East Asia, Japan has invested primarily in Taiwan,* the Republic of Korea and India. Between 1953 and 1968 Japan had concluded 264 investment contracts in Taiwan,* involving almost $54 million.[41] The main characteristics of Japanese

investment in South-East Asia have been the relatively small shares of capital ownership by Japanese investors and the small-scale or less capital-intensive nature of the operations undertaken, in particular, the concentration in labour-intensive industries.

52. The "Big Ten" enterprises in Japan are responsible for about 80 per cent of Japan's investment contracts in foreign countries.[42] In 1969, these enterprises accounted for approximately 47 per cent of Japan's exports and 62 per cent of its imports. They were also responsible for an important part of Japan's domestic production and internal sales. In 1969 the sales of these ten enterprises were equivalent to 27 per cent of Japan's gross national product.[43] At the end of March 1970, the number of foreign ventures of these enterprises were: Mitsui, 96; Mitsubishi, 53; C. Itoh, 45; Kanematsu-Gosho, 28; Nissho-Iwai, 20; Toyo Menka, 18; Sumitomo, 15; Nichimen, 15; and Ataka, 6. These overseas ventures are mostly located in developing countries and territories, in particular: Taiwan,* 36; Thailand, 31; Brazil, 22; Malaysia, 20; Singapore, 19; and Hong Kong, 16.[44]

53. To give an estimate of the order of magnitude of the number of subsidiaries or associates of the multinational corporations in developing countries, table V indicates that in 1969 there were 7,762 such companies, of which the parents were located in the United States and the major Western European countries. Almost 50 per cent of the 7,762 subsidiaries had parent companies in the United States; a further 25 per cent had parent companies in the United Kingdom and about a further 10 per cent had parent companies in France. With regard to the various regions, Latin America accounted for 60 per cent of the subsidiaries of the United States parent companies and Asia for almost 30 per cent. Africa[45] accounted for 45 per cent of the United Kingdom parent companies' subsidiaries and Asia for just over 30 per cent. In the case of subsidiaries with French parent companies, 70 per cent of these were located in Africa.

54. Essentially, the activities of the multinational corporations in the developing countries can be classified into three categories. First, there are the corporations that have established plantations and extractive industries in the developing countries, for example rubber, copra and banana plantations, and the extractive industries of petroleum, bauxite and various metals. Most of these products are exported to world markets. The degree of processing of the raw materials in the developing countries before export depends on a number of factors. Secondly, there are the corporations that have established subsidiaries in developing countries primarily to import products manufactured by the parent companies and other affiliates, and, in certain cases, to assemble or package the products imported. The majority of the subsidiaries of the multi-

---

* In the present publication, references to "Taiwan" are to be understood in the light of General Assembly resolution 2758 (XXVI) of 28 October 1971. By that resolution, the General Assembly decided *inter alia* "to restore all its rights to the People's Republic of China and to recognize the representatives of its Government as the only legitimate representatives of China to the United Nations, and to expel forthwith the representatives of Chiang Kai-shek from the place which they unlawfully occupy at the United Nations and in all the organizations related to it".

[40] See T. Ozawa, *Transfer of Technology from Japan to Developing Countries*, UNITAR Research Reports (RR/7) (New York, 1971), p. 7.

[41] *Ibid.*, p. 9.

[42] *Ibid.*, p. 37.

[43] See "Las Empresas de Comercialización Integrada en el Japón", by the Trade Policy Division of ECLA, ST/ECLA/Conf.37/L.20, 20 July 1971, table 5.

[44] See T. Ozawa, op. cit., p. 32.

[45] For a discussion of the operations of multinational corporations in Africa, see P. Streeten, "The Role of Private Foreign Investment in African Industrial Development".

TABLE 5

**Number of parent companies in selected Western European countries and the United States
having subsidiaries or associates in developing countries or territories, 1969**

Country or territory of subsidiary or associate ↓ Country of parent →	Austria	Belgium	Denmark	France	Germany, Federal Republic of	Italy	Luxembourg	Netherlands	Norway	Sweden	Switzerland	United Kingdom	United States of America	Total
Africa														
Algeria	—	2	—	90	2	2	—	2	—	—	1	2	21	122
Angola	—	5	1	—	1	—	—	1	—	—	—	3	5	16
Burundi	—	4	1	1	—	—	—	1	—	—	—	1	4	12
Cameroon	—	1	—	33	2	1	—	—	—	—	1	4	5	47
Central African Republic	—	—	—	6	—	—	—	—	—	—	—	1	4	11
Congo (People's Republic)	—	3	—	2	—	—	—	—	—	—	—	—	6	11
Egypt	—	—	—	—	1	2	—	1	—	—	3	2	33	42
Ethiopia	—	1	—	2	3	4	—	2	2	—	—	6	11	31
Gabon	—	—	—	9	1	1	—	—	—	—	—	—	—	11
Ghana	—	1	1	—	3	2	—	3	—	—	1	43	12	66
Guinea	—	—	—	15	—	—	—	—	—	—	1	3	—	19
Ivory Coast	—	1	—	44	4	1	—	2	—	—	—	2	12	66
Kenya	—	—	1	2	5	2	—	5	1	1	1	119	23	160
Liberia	—	—	1	2	2	3	—	4	—	2	1	9	32	56
Libya	—	—	—	1	3	1	—	2	—	—	—	12	36	55
Malagasy Republic	—	1	—	22	2	1	—	1	—	—	—	2	4	33
Malawi	—	—	—	1	1	—	—	1	—	—	—	35	—	38
Morocco	—	8	1	117	10	2	1	5	—	5	4	9	26	188
Mozambique	—	2	—	—	—	—	—	2	—	—	—	10	—	14
Nigeria	—	—	1	8	13	5	—	9	2	—	3	134	47	222
Rhodesia (Southern)	—	1	1	1	4	1	—	7	1	2	—	181	40	239
Senegal	—	—	—	46	2	1	—	1	—	—	—	2	—	52
Sierra Leone	—	—	1	—	3	2	—	—	—	—	3	15	4	28
Sudan	—	—	—	1	2	2	—	—	—	—	—	12	6	23
Swaziland	—	—	—	—	—	—	—	—	—	—	—	12	—	12
Tanzania	—	—	1	1	4	1	—	7	1	—	—	44	—	59
Togo	—	—	—	4	4	1	—	—	—	—	—	1	—	10
Tunisia	—	1	—	38	3	1	—	1	—	2	1	2	15	64
Uganda	—	—	—	—	4	1	—	2	1	—	—	36	7	51
Zaire	—	86	1	18	6	4	—	6	—	4	3	10	—	138
Zambia	—	—	—	1	2	1	—	3	1	3	—	109	8	128
Other Africa	—	2	—	31	4	7	—	3	—	—	1	26	14	88
Sub-total	0	119	11	496	91	49	1	71	9	19	24	847	375	2 112
Latin America														
Argentina	4	6	2	38	37	16	3	8	—	21	22	63	215	435
Bahamas	—	—	—	2	6	—	—	1	—	1	1	54	11	76
Barbados	—	—	—	—	—	—	—	—	—	—	—	15	—	15
Bermuda	—	1	—	1	—	—	—	—	—	5	—	34	6	47
Bolivia	—	—	—	—	—	—	—	—	—	—	1	4	19	24
Brazil	3	9	7	45	68	16	1	9	5	21	22	60	344	610
Chile	—	1	1	—	12	4	—	1	—	8	6	18	87	138
Colombia	—	—	1	9	12	6	—	9	—	15	4	14	202	272
Costa Rica	—	—	—	8	1	—	—	—	—	—	1	2	30	42
Dominican Republic	—	—	—	—	—	—	—	3	—	—	—	1	36	40
Ecuador	—	—	—	1	2	4	—	1	—	2	—	5	37	52
El Salvador	—	—	—	1	3	—	—	2	—	—	—	2	32	40
Guatemala	—	—	—	—	3	1	—	1	—	1	1	—	46	53
Haiti	—	—	—	—	—	—	—	2	—	—	—	—	11	13
Honduras	—	—	—	1	—	—	—	—	—	—	—	1	23	25
Jamaica	—	—	—	1	—	—	—	1	—	—	2	42	51	97
Mexico	—	1	2	20	21	13	—	12	1	18	10	43	521	662
Netherlands Antilles	—	—	—	2	2	—	—	40	—	1	1	1	9	56
Nicaragua	—	—	—	—	1	—	—	1	—	—	—	1	28	31
Panama	—	2	—	4	4	—	2	—	—	2	6	11	86	117

Table 5 *(continued)*

**Number of parent companies in selected Western European countries and the United States
having subsidiaries or associates in developing countries or territories, 1969**

Country or territory of subsidiary or associate ↓	Austria	Belgium	Denmark	France	Germany, Federal Republic of	Italy	Luxembourg	Netherlands	Norway	Sweden	Switzerland	United Kingdom	United States of America	Total
Latin America (continued)														
Peru	1	1	—	6	9	9	—	6	2	12	7	18	135	206
Trinidad and Tobago	—	—	—	—	—	—	—	2	—	—	2	36	38	78
Uruguay	—	1	1	10	3	4	—	1	—	8	2	6	69	105
Venezuela	—	3	1	9	13	7	—	12	—	8	6	25	247	331
Other Latin America	—	—	—	8	2	2	—	2	—	—	2	25	33	74
Sub-total	8	25	15	166	199	82	6	114	8	123	96	481	2 316	3 639
Asia														
Afghanistan	—	—	—	—	3	—	—	—	—	—	—	2	5	10
Burma	—	—	1	—	—	—	—	—	—	2	—	2	11	16
Ceylon	—	—	3	—	—	—	—	—	—	1	1	25	13	43
Hong Kong	—	—	2	4	9	1	9	1	—	3	4	63	135	231
India	2	1	2	5	40	—	—	4	—	10	12	208	201	485
Indonesia	—	4	1	—	1	1	—	4	—	1	—	17	28	57
Iran	1	4	1	6	9	3	—	3	—	2	1	10	61	101
Iraq	1	—	—	—	—	—	—	1	1	—	—	7	11	21
Israel	—	—	—	4	2	—	—	1	—	—	2	19	40	68
Khmer Republic	—	—	1	5	—	—	—	—	—	—	—	2	4	12
Korea (Republic of)	—	—	—	—	—	—	—	—	—	—	—	—	21	21
Kuwait	1	—	—	—	—	—	—	—	—	—	—	6	8	15
Lebanon	—	—	—	7	2	1	—	2	—	—	2	10	51	75
Malaysia	—	3	1	1	4	1	—	6	1	1	1	71	46	136
Pakistan	1	—	1	2	8	—	—	5	—	2	4	63	80	166
Philippines	—	—	1	—	5	—	—	4	—	4	2	8	181	205
Singapore	—	—	1	—	2	—	—	7	—	—	2	52	53	117
Taiwan*	—	—	—	—	1	—	—	—	—	1	—	2	48	52
Thailand	—	—	2	1	5	2	—	5	1	1	1	10	59	87
Viet-Nam (Republic of)	—	—	1	14	—	—	—	—	—	—	—	3	19	37
Other Asia	1	—	1	1	—	—	—	4	—	—	—	25	24	56
Sub-total	7	12	19	50	91	9	9	47	3	28	32	605	1 099	2 011
Total	15	156	45	712	381	140	16	232	20	170	152	1 933	3 790	7 762

Source: Derived from *Yearbook of International Organizations, 1968-1969.*

* See footnote (*) to paragraph 51 above.

national corporations in the developing countries, in particular in the least developed among the developing countries, are probably in these first two categories. Thirdly, there are the multinational corporations that have established subsidiaries in developing countries to manufacture products similar to those previously imported, and perhaps, to a certain extent, to export. In the more advanced developing countries in Latin America and Asia an important number of the subsidiaries seem to have changed their operations from the second to the third category, that is from packaging and assembling to manufacture, partly in response to the import substitution policies of those countries and to the domestic legislation requiring a certain percentage of the content of specific manufactured products (for example, in the automotive industry) to be locally produced. Moreover in recent years exports by such firms have increased as a percentage of their total sales, especially in Latin America within the framework of regional economic integration.

55. The contribution of the multinational corporations to the total exports of manufactures of developing countries has undoubtedly increased during the sixties, in particular in the relatively more advanced developing countries. Detailed statistics are at present only available with regard to the exports of subsidiaries of United States multinational corporations located in Latin America. Table 6 indicates that in the period 1963-1968 such exports of manufactures increased from $390 million to $753 million, and that exports to the United States in particular increased from $37 million to $212 million. By 1968 such

TABLE 6

Exports of manufactures from Latin America by manufacturing
subsidiaries of United States enterprises

(Million dollars)

	Exports to the United States		Exports to other destinations		Total exports	
	1963	*1968*	*1963*	*1968*	*1963*	*1968*
Food products	10	122	244	238	254	360
Paper and allied products	a	5	10	17	10	22
Chemicals	21	47	53	162	74	209
Rubber products	0	2	a	6	a	8
Primary and fabricated metals . . .	1	a	20	13	21	13
Machinery, excluding electrical	4	8	10	32	14	40
Electrical machinery	1	3	9	38	10	41
Transportation equipment	a	8	2	13	2	21
Other	a	17	5	22	5	39
TOTAL	37	212	353	541	390	753

Source: R. D. Belli, "Sales of Foreign Affiliates of U.S. Firms, 1961-1965, 1967 and 1968", in U.S. Department of Commerce, Office of Business Economics, *Survey of Current Business*, October 1970, vol. 50, No. 10, p. 20; and "Sales of Foreign Affiliates of U.S. Firms in 1965", in *Survey of Current Business*, November 1966, vol. 46, No. 11, p. 9.

a Under $500 000.

exports accounted for about 40 per cent of all exports of manufactures from Latin America.

56. Almost 50 per cent of these total exports in 1968 were food products, and over 25 per cent were chemicals. The importance of the exports of manufactures of the multinational corporations in terms of a particular country's total exports of these products can be gauged from the statistics available regarding Brazil. Total exports of manufactures from Brazil increased in the period 1967 to 1969 from $121.5 million to $178.9 million. In that period, the exports of manufactures of multinational corporations rose from $41 to $78 million, resulting in an increase in the percentage share of such exports in Brazil's total exports from 32 per cent to 43 per cent. With regard to certain industry sectors, the percentage share of the multinational corporations in 1969 was substantially higher: almost 80 per cent in the case of pharmaceuticals and chemical preparations and over 75 per cent in the case of machinery and transport equipment.[46]

57. As can be seen from table 7, as a proportion of their total sales, exports by United States manufacturing affiliates operating in developed and developing countries represented 22 per cent. However, in the case of developing countries the percentage of total sales exported was far smaller. In Latin America, exports represented just under 10 per cent of the total sales of such companies, and only in the food products sector was a significant proportion of total sales exported—namely almost 25 per cent. For areas other than Canada, Europe and Latin America, exports were less than 9 per cent of total sales. Such exports were principally in two industry sectors, namely primary and fabricated metals (28 per cent) and food pro-

ducts (18 per cent). In Canada on the other hand United States manufacturing affiliates exported 28 per cent of their total sales and over 20 per cent of total sales went to the United States. Exports to the United States were made primarily by three industry sectors—paper and allied products (44 per cent), transport equipment (40 per cent), and primary and fabricated metals (15 per cent). In EEC, United States manufacturing affiliates exported 26 per cent of their total sales and in other countries of Western Europe, including the United Kingdom, 23 per cent. In the case of EEC, significant exports occurred in all industry sectors, and in "other Europe", in the industry sectors other than food and rubber products.

58. These figures would seem to indicate that the activities of United States manufacturing affiliates in Canada and Europe are more export-oriented than in developing countries, and that in the case of Canada they reflect the degree of integration of certain industry sectors, such as motor vehicles, with those in the United States.

59. It should be noted that exports by United States manufacturing affiliates in both developed and developing countries increased rapidly in the period 1965 to 1968, and as a proportion of their total sales exports grew from 18 per cent to 22 per cent. Whilst the proportion of exports to total sales grew from 7 per cent to 9 per cent in the case of United States affiliates in Latin America and areas other than Europe and Canada, a dramatic increase in exports as a percentage of total sales occurred in Canada—from 18 per cent to 28 per cent. This was largely a result of increased exports of transportation equipment, which grew from $200 million to $2,247 million.[47]

60. The extent to which the exports by the multinational corporations are intra-company transactions, that is,

[46] See ECLA study, F. Fajnzylber, *Sistema Industrial y Exportación de Manufacturas, Análisis de la Experiencia Brasileña*, November 1970, for the Ministry of Planning and General Co-ordination of the Government of Brazil, p. 214, table 6.5.

[47] For a discussion of the 1965 figures, see *Economic Survey of Latin America, 1970* (United Nations publication, Sales No. E.72.II. G.1), and in particular tables 33 and 34, p. 297.

TABLE 7

Percentage of total sales of United States foreign manufacturing affiliates sold locally and exported in 1968

	All products	Food products	Paper and allied products	Chemicals	Rubber products	Primary and fabrication metals	Machinery, excluding electric	Electrical machinery	Transportation equipment	Other products
All areas										
Local sales	77.9	85.6	56.0	83.2	91.6	73.7	75.3	87.9	71.6	79.1
Exports to United States . . .	7.9	3.9	29.4	1.9	1.4	8.5	4.1	1.7	17.1	3.8
Exports to other countries . .	14.2	10.5	14.6	15.0	7.0	17.8	20.6	10.4	11.3	17.1
Canada										
Local sales	72.1	93.4	38.2	92.7	95.9	62.0	83.6	92.6	55.7	85.9
Exports to United States . . .	20.4	1.8	44.0	4.0	2.9	15.2	11.0	2.0	39.7	9.2
Exports to other countries . .	7.5	4.8	17.9	3.3	1.2	22.8	5.4	5.4	4.6	4.8
Latin America										
Local sales	90.5	75.8	92.7	89.5	98.1	97.7	90.0	93.1	98.4	95.6
Exports to United States . . .	2.7	8.2	1.7	2.4	0.5	—	2.0	0.5	0.6	1.9
Exports to other countries . .	6.8	16.0	5.6	8.2	1.4	2.3	8.0	6.4	1.0	2.5
Europe										
(a) *EEC*										
Local sales	74.3	72.1	83.6	83.8	66.6	83.8	66.6	82.6	71.5	68.0
Exports to United States . .	2.1	2.2	0.9	0.6	1.1	0.2	2.3	1.6	4.7	1.4
Exports to other countries .	23.6	25.7	15.5	15.6	32.3	16.0	31.1	15.8	23.8	30.6
(b) *Other Europe, including United Kingdom*										
Local sales	76.8	91.3	87.4	80.0	89.5	73.6	67.8	87.1	76.5	66.2
Exports to United States .	2.0	1.4	—	0.6	1.0	2.8	3.3	1.3	3.0	1.6
Exports to other countries .	21.1	7.3	12.6	19.4	9.5	23.6	28.8	11.6	20.4	32.2
Other areas										
Local sales	91.3	82.2	97.0	91.1	95.7	71.7	92.1	87.5	97.1	93.6
Exports to United States . . .	2.6	8.5	—	1.0	1.1	19.3	1.1	4.1	—	1.1
Exports to other countries . .	6.1	9.3	3.0	7.9	3.2	9.0	6.8	8.4	2.9	5.3

Source: U.S. Department of Commerce, Office of Business Economics, *Survey of Current Business*, October 1970, vol. 50, No. 10, p. 20, table 3.

exports to the parent company or other affiliates, is difficult to estimate. The position will obviously vary from country to country, depending on the types of manufactured goods exported. Where the bulk of such exports are intermediate goods, such as motor vehicle parts and components, petrochemicals, raw aluminium and copper, on which affiliate industries in other countries depend for their supplies of these essential inputs, the percentage share of intra-company exports in total exports of manufactures of the multinational corporations is likely to be higher than in cases where the bulk of the products exported are final products or traditional exports, such as textiles or footwear. However, even with regard to the exports of final products, especially food products, the parent companies and other affiliates might well use their own marketing organizations to distribute the products of the affiliates in the developing countries. Taking Latin America once again as an example, of total exports of $501 million in 1966 by United States majority-owned subsidiaries having at least 100 employees, intra-company exports at $260 million accounted for more than 50 per cent of the total exports, and an additional $124 million were accounted for by exports to the United States. Of the intra-company exports, 40 per cent consisted of motor vehicles and equipment, almost all coming from Mexico; over 20 per cent of meat products, the bulk coming from Argentina; and a further 16 per cent of chemicals and allied products, essentially originating in the Caribbean.[48]

61. In a study carried out on the effects of the United Kingdom's overseas investments on its balance of payments in the period 1955-1964, it was found that exports from overseas subsidiaries of British parent companies were comparatively insignificant. They accounted for only $1\frac{1}{2}$ per cent of the total sales of the subsidiaries. This would seem to indicate that United Kingdom subsidiaries tend to produce the same products as their parents and could therefore be more import-substitution oriented than United States subsidiaries, in particular in Latin America.[49]

[48] See *Effects of United States and Other Foreign Investment in Latin America*, Council for Latin America (January 1970), tables 1 and 2.

[49] See W. B. Reddaway, in collaboration with S. J. Potter and C. T. Taylor, *Effects of United Kingdom Direct Investment Overseas, Final Report* (Cambridge University Press, Occasional Papers 15, 1968) p. 216.

62. The contribution of multinational corporations to the exports of developed market-economy countries, in particular through intra-firm trade, undoubtedly reached significant proportions in the course of the 1960s. In 1966, about half of the United Kingdom's total exports were by British-based firms with overseas interests, and a further 20 per cent were by British-controlled concerns overseas; and 14 per cent of these total exports were by United-States-controlled firms. Exports to related concerns in overseas countries, or intra-company exports, represented about 22 per cent of total exports in that year. In the case of branches and subsidiaries of United States companies, intra-company exports from the United Kingdom represented 56 per cent of those companies' total exports.[50] Similarly, in the case of the United States, it has been estimated that 25 per cent of all United States exports in 1964 were accounted for by exports to foreign affiliates of United States companies. The percentage varied considerably from area to area. Exports to affiliates accounted for 46 per cent of all United States exports to Canada in 1964 and for about one-third of all United States exports to Latin America.[51] With regard to the 266 most important foreign-owned companies in Canada, it was found that in 1965 imports accounted for just over 30 per cent of their total purchases. A significant proportion of those purchases consisted of transport equipment, reflecting the integration of the motor vehicle industry of the United States and Canada. Exports by the same group of companies in 1965 represented 18 per cent of their total sales, the main exports being pulp and paper, transport equipment and mining products.[52] It has been found in the case of United States subsidiaries in Australia that imports accounted for 19 per cent of their total sales and that 90 per cent of these were imports consigned by affiliated companies in the United States and elsewhere.[53]

63. From the available statistics regarding exports of manufactures of developing countries and regarding foreign investments in those countries, it would seem that it is in the relatively more advanced developing countries that, in many cases, the foreign-owned or foreign-controlled industries are producing the new export products. As was pointed out in the "Review of trade in manufactures of the developing countries, 1960-1970", by the UNCTAD secretariat,[54] the most dynamic sectors of world trade, in both developing and developed countries, have been engineering products and miscellaneous light manufactures. Such products include in particular motor vehicles, parts and components, and electronic equipment—sectors in which foreign investment by the multinational corporations in developing countries has been especially marked.

64. Case studies on the automotive and semiconductor industries have been issued by UNITAR in connexion with the question of the transfer of technology. The study on the semiconductor industry[55] indicates the establishment, primarily for export, of electronic fabrication and assembling industries in Hong Kong, Mexico, the Philippines, Taiwan* and the Republic of Korea, as well as in certain countries in the Caribbean. It also indicates that all the United States corporations operating in that industry have engaged in such investment activities, as have a number of the leading corporations in the same field in Western Europe and Japan. The study on the automotive industry[56] shows that most of the large multinational corporations in that industry have subsidiaries in the developing countries. In many of the more advanced of these countries, the subsidiaries in question were responsible for manufacturing a significant proportion of the content of the vehicles produced, rather than being engaged simply in assembling operations. In general, the parent companies procured only a limited amount of motor vehicles or parts from their affiliates in the developing countries, and a significant proportion of those purchases was made in order to provide the affiliates with foreign exchange to pay for necessary imports. The cases of India and Brazil were cited in this respect. Nevertheless, there has been a growing trend of increased exports by automotive subsidiaries in the developing countries. In Latin America, there has been considerable growth in exports of motor vehicles, parts and components within the context of LAFTA. In the case of a number of developing countries there has been a noticeable trend for certain of these industries to supply specialized parts to world markets. For example, it appears that India exports braking equipment to the United Kingdom and diesel engine parts; Mexico exports automobile lamps to the United States; and the Republic of Korea exports piston rings and cylinder linings to world markets. However, it could well be that in certain Latin-American countries there may be need for some reorganization of the motor vehicle industries if they are to export on a competitive basis. For example in Chile, in 1962, 22 companies produced 7 800 motor vehicles at roughly four times the cost of similar motor vehicles directly imported from abroad.[57]

B. Mergers and specialization of production within the multinational corporations

65. The 1960s were marked by a widespread growth in the merger movement amongst companies, principally within national boundaries, but not exclusively. The mer-

[50] See "Overseas Transactions in 1966—trade credit and exports", in *Board of Trade Journal*, August 1968, p. 471.

[51] See S. Pizer and F. Cutler, "U.S. Exports to Foreign Affiliates of U.S. Firms", in U.S. Department of Commerce, Office of Business Economics, *Survey of Current Business*, December 1965, vol. 45, No. 12.

[52] See A. E. Safarian, *The Performance of Foreign-owned Firms in Canada* (Canada, Canadian-American Committee, 1969), pp. 29-30.

[53] See D. T. Brash, *American Investment in Australian Industry* (Cambridge, Mass., Harvard University Press, 1966), pp. 203-211.

[54] TD/111, para. 5.

* See footnote (*) to paragraph 51 above.

[55] Y. S. Chang, *The Transfer of Technology: Economics of Offshore Assembly, the Case of Semiconductor Industry*, UNITAR Research Reports (RR/11) (New York, 1971).

[56] J. Baranson, *International Transfer of Automotive Technology to Developing Countries*, UNITAR Research Reports (RR/8) (New York, 1971).

[57] See The Economist Intelligence Unit, *The Growth and Spread of Multinational Companies*, QER Special No. 5 (new and revised edition, 1971), p. 47.

er of companies has been marked particularly in Western Europe and to a lesser extent in the United States and Japan. During 1967 and 1968 more than 5,000 United Kingdom companies were involved in mergers or acquisitions of one sort or another, and nearly 70 of that country's top hundred companies either entered bids or were bid for.[58] This led to the creation of such large multinational companies as the British Leyland Motor Corporation, which was made up of ten previously independent companies; International Computers Limited, which involved nine companies or divisions of companies; and the General Electric Company, which absorbed the other two major electrical engineering concerns in the United Kingdom.[59] In France, in 1968 and 1969, 4,000 corporate marriages of various sorts took place, with the result that in 1970 it was estimated that St. Gobain-Pont-à-Mousson, Rhône Poulenc and Pechiney employed one in every forty Frenchmen.[60] Similar developments have occurred in some other European countries.[61] In the United States, the number of acquisitions of firms was 4,550 in 1969, 3,932 in 1968 and 2,384 in 1967, compared with fewer than 2,000 a year for all previous years in the 1960s.[62] The majority of the mergers involved conglomerate acquisitions rather than horizontal or vertical acquisitions.[63] It would seem that in Japan mergers in the 1960s took place essentially between small and medium-sized firms and numbered for most of this period between 800 and 1,000 annually.[64]

66. It is sometimes stated that national and international cartels of the period from the 1930s to the 1950s were a step in the evolution of the multinational corporations. Such cartel activities are believed to have provided a training in co-operation for purposes of production and supply. Whilst some of the multinational companies that appeared during the 1960s resulted from national mergers, in a few cases they also resulted from mergers beyond national boundaries. The merger movement has most probably also strengthened the position of the multinational corporations in world trade and resulted in the concentration of an increasingly important proportion of world trade in the hands of a relatively small number of corporations. It should be mentioned that mergers involving corporations with subsidiaries in other countries are generally arranged without any form of discussion with the host countries in which such subsidiaries are located. The absence of such consultation may create problems for developing countries, particularly problems arising from the concentration of market power, if two previously unrelated subsidiaries are brought together—for example, the international merger of two independent tyre manufacturers which also carry on significant manufacturing activities in other unrelated industries.

67. The merger movement has involved both horizontal concentration and vertical integration in industry, as well as the creation of conglomerates, in particular in Western Europe. The vertical integration resulting from mergers is particularly apparent in such fields as the production of aluminium and its end-products, as for example in the United Kingdom.[65] Such vertical integration tends to preclude exports of raw materials and intermediate goods except through the structure of the multinational corporations in question.

68. In the industrial sectors of computers, agricultural machinery and motor vehicles, the multinational corporations are increasingly tending to produce components and parts in many different countries of the world, including in certain instances, as already mentioned, the developing countries. As a result, the finished product represents a culmination of an international co-operative effort involving extensive intra-company trading marked by cross-shipments of sub-assemblies of industrial intermediates and components. For example, in the motor vehicle industry, affiliates of United States multinational corporations in Mexico have specialized in the production of transmission engines, engine blocks and specialized tooling and dies, for export to parent and sister companies. In other Latin-American countries, specialization in motor vehicle production within the context of regional economic groupings is also taking place. To a lesser extent, a similar trend is occurring in South-East Asia.[66] In addition, increasing specialization is occurring in the production of certain finished goods. For example, Olivetti calculators are manufactured in Italy and Mexico and adding machines in Italy and Argentina.[67]

[58] For further details on the mergers which have taken place in the United Kingdom, see "A Survey of Mergers 1958-1968", paper prepared by the staff of the Monopolies Commission, Department of Trade and Industry (1970). According to a report in the *Financial Times* of 10 September 1971 (p. 23), the Director-General of the Panel on Take-overs and Mergers pointed out that mergers were currently running at about 400 a year, which he stated was a huge figure, given that there were only 3,200 British companies whose ordinary shares were quoted on the London Stock Exchange. He likened this trend in mergers to a "second industrial revolution".

[59] See C. Tugendhat, op. cit., p. 62.

[60] *The Guardian*, 27 January 1970.

[61] In Switzerland, the two chemical and pharmaceutical giants, Ciba and Geigy, have merged. In the Netherlands, the two biggest chemical companies, AKU and KZO, have merged. The new company AKZO also has substantial interests in the food and textile industry sectors in the Netherlands. In the *Financial Times* of 10 September 1971 (p. 22) it was indicated that a merger was being prepared in the Netherlands to create one of the largest fertilizer production companies in the world. It should be noted that about 70 per cent of the Netherlands total production of nitrogenous fertilizer is exported, much of it to developing countries.

[62] See J. R. Felton, "Conglomerate Mergers, Concentration and Competition", in *American Journal of Economics and Sociology*, vol. 30, July 1971, No. 3, p. 228. *Source:* Federal Trade Commission, *Current Trends in Merger Activity*, 1969 (Washington, D.C., 1970), p. 8.

[63] For a discussion of mergers in the United States and constraints on mergers, see J. W. Markham, "The Constraints imposed by anti-trust", in J. B. Heath (ed.), *International Conference on Monopolies, Mergers and Restrictive Practices: Papers and Reports*, Cambridge, 1969 (London, H.M. Stationery Office, 1971).

[64] Y. Kanazawa, "Firm Behaviour and Policy on Mergers in Japan", in *International Conference on Monopolies, Mergers and Restrictive Practices* (see footnote 63 above).

[65] See the *Financial Times*, 8 January 1971, "Alcan-Booth—RTZ pillar in aluminium shuffle"; and the *Financial Times*, 3 December 1970, Financial Times Survey, "Aluminium".

[66] See J. Baranson, op. cit., pp. 76-80.

[67] For further details see M. Z. Brooke and H. Lee Remmers, *The Strategy of Multinational Enterprises* (London, Longman, 1970), part I, chap. 3, and C. Tugendhat, op. cit., chap. 7.

C. Areas of possible conflict between the activities of multinational corporations and the export interests of the developing countries

69. A number of the subsidiaries of the multinational corporations in the developing countries are participating in export. The extent to which restrictions, placed by the parent companies on the export activity of their subsidiaries, may have limited the growth of such exports, is difficult to determine. To a large extent the subsidiaries established in the developing countries, in particular in manufacturing rather than extractive industries, have been located there primarily to service the domestic market. In many cases the high tariff walls in these countries were probably an important factor determining the initial investment, and in a number of cases the cost of production of the subsidiary, at least in the initial stages, may well have been higher than that of the parent companies or its sister affiliates.

70. Nevertheless, as the subsidiaries in the developing countries improved their production performance and so lowered costs, some of them have undoubtedly reached the position of being able to export on a competitive basis, and a number have already done so, as has been indicated in the previous section. In addition, in certain cases, if export orders were secured, these might well have led to a subsidiary's operations becoming more competitive.

71. The fact that restrictions exist in many cases on the export activities of subsidiaries, and even on parent companies, cannot be contested. Such restrictions relate in particular to the allocation of export markets between the subsidiaries or affiliates and the parent company within the multinational corporation, and, in certain cases, even between multinational corporations. They also relate to the prices for exports and imports for transactions within the structure of the multinational corporation—such prices being set arbitrarily, taking into account the interests of the multinational corporation as a whole, and, as such, do not necessarily coincide with the specific interests of a particular subsidiary or affiliate or the interests of the host country. The existence of such restrictions and their potential harmful effects on the trade of particular countries have been referred to on many occasions in both developed[68] and developing countries.[69]

1. RESTRICTIONS ON EXPORTS

72. Where restrictions exist on the export activities o subsidiaries, the precise nature of such restrictions i likely to vary from case to case, depending on the policie of the multinational corporations. In certain cases, th multinational corporation might well assign amongst it subsidiaries and the parent company specific areas i which they will be responsible for exports. Such a market sharing process is often called the territorial allocation o markets. In other cases, multinational corporations ma centralize their export activities in an international mar keting division and leave it to that division to decide whic of its subsidiaries will be responsible for particular expor orders. Or again, the parent company may retain th primary responsibility for the corporation's export activit and require that its prior approval be obtained for an exports by its subsidiaries.

73. Unlike the situation with regard to licensing arrange ments, where specific provisions are usually included in th agreements relating to export activity, in the case o arrangements for export within the multinational corpora tion, and, in particular, where the subsidiaries are con trolled by the parent company, such arrangements are generally not concluded on a formal, written and juridica basis. As such these arrangements can be easily modifie to take into account the constantly changing circumstance within the multinational corporation and, in particular in relation to its position in the world market. Further more, as the competitive positions of the subsidiarie improve, the scope for changes in export arrangements wil obiously be enlarged, since such changes would generall be in the over-all interest of the multinational corporation

74. Despite this situation, Governments of both devel oped and developing countries are becoming increasingl concerned about the ability of multinational corporation to allocate and assign export markets. Such concern i natural, in particular in those cases where a subsidiary occupies a prominent position in a domestic market, but i barred from exporting to other markets and especially t nearby markets which may already have been allocated t the parent or to another affiliate company.

75. In the interim report certain information was con tained on restrictive export franchises in Australia.[70] I a study carried out in Canada, it was indicated that a similar problem exists in that country with regard t arrangements restricting exports within some multi national corporations.[71] It was found that about 15 pe cent of the 238 foreign-owned firms studied in Canada were subject to three types of private trade restrictions namely, where the patent rights applied to Canada only where the affiliation was stated to be unfavourable with regard to exports, and where those subsidiaries which exported through the parent firm could not bid on exports. Such restrictions were highly concentrated in certain industries—machinery, electrical products and

---

[68] See, in particular, W. D. Rogers, "New and future antitrust laws: overview and critique", address to the International Antitrust Symposium, American Society of International Law, College of William and Mary, Williamsburg, Virginia, United States of America, 16 October 1970.

[69] At the second Ministerial Meeting of the Group of 77, held in Lima from 28 October to 7 November 1971, it was recommended, with regard to the question of restrictive business practices, that the Governments of developed market-economy countries should promote the elimination of such practices in the distribution of the market and the fixing of prices. It was also recommended that in order to eliminate restrictive business practices in the field of transfer of technology, including the practices adopted in this respect by multinational companies, the Secretary-General of UNCTAD should, *inter alia*, carry out a study concerning the review of patent legislation and elaborate the bases for new international legislation regularizing the transfer from developed to developing countries of patented and non-patented technology, including related commercial and legal aspects of such transfer. (See *Proceedings of the United Nations Conference on Trade and Development, Third Session*, vol. I,

Report and Annexes (United Nations publication, Sales No. E.73.II. D.4), annex VIII, F, part three, sect. A, V, para. 5. In connexion with this latter recommendation, see chapter III below.

[70] See *Restrictive business practices ...*, para. 77.

[71] See A. E. Safarian, op. cit., pp. 35-36.

TABLE 8

Types of restrictive clauses: India

| | Number of agreements with restrictive clauses | | | |
| | Effective agreements approved till March 1964[a] | | Effective agreements approved between April 1964 and March 1969[b] | |
Type of restrictive clause	Subsidiaries	Minority foreign capital participation	Subsidiaries	Minority foreign capital participation
I. *Export restrictions*	56	230	8	55
1. Global ban on exports	32	80	1	1
2. Exports prohibited to specified countries	3	17	1	21
3. Exports permitted to specified countries only	16	101	3	22
4. Prior approval for exports	3	15	1	—
5. Exports permitted to or through specified firms only . .	1	13	2	8
6. Restrictions on use of trademarks in exports	—	—	—	3
7. Other export restrictions	1	4	—	—
II. *Other restrictions*				
1. Tied purchases	14	46	2	8
2. Restrictions on production patterns	2	36	—	—
3. Payment of minimum royalty	1	14	—	1
4. Restriction on sales procedures	6	17	—	—
5. Other restrictions	1	1	—	1
A. Total number of agreements with restrictive clauses	63	251	9	58
B. Total number of effective agreements	144	445	12	136

[a] *Source:* Reserve Bank of India, *Foreign Collaboration in Indian Industry, Survey Report* (Bombay, The Examiner Press, 1968), p. 106.

[b] *Source:* Study carried out for UNCTAD relating to agreements which had become effective by the end of September 1970, after the obtaining of government approval between April 1964 and March 1969.

some branches of the chemical industries. Of the firms surveyed, almost two-thirds stated that affiliation had little or no effect on exports (for example, because transfer costs were prohibitive) or that the question was not applicable (for example, because the company had just been established). In 39 cases the reply was that the effect of affiliation had been favourable for reasons that included obtaining contacts with customers abroad, securing guaranteed purchases by affiliates, and using the name, the research, or the sales organization of the parent. On the other hand, 20 firms stated that the effect of affiliation had been unfavourable because the firms were restricted in their exports to specific countries or because exports had been reduced or could not be undertaken, owing to the existence of affiliates abroad.

76. In contrast to the situation in Australia and Canada, in a study on foreign investment in the United Kingdom it was indicated that there was no real evidence of any problem in this field, although it was acknowledged that export market-sharing agreements between foreign subsidiaries and their parent companies existed. It was indicated that in many cases foreign-owned firms in the United Kingdom were highly export-oriented, and often more so than domestically owned British firms.[72] It was found that in 1967, 17 per cent of the United Kingdom's manufactured exports were exports by United States-owned subsidiaries, although these firms accounted for

only 10 per cent of the total sales of manufacturing industries in the United Kingdom. In 1965, exports represented 25 per cent of total sales for United States-owned subsidiaries, compared with 14 per cent for all the United Kingdom manufacturing industries.[73] It would seem therefore that investments by the United States in the United Kingdom could well have been undertaken from the start with the intention of developing exports in certain other markets through the subsidiaries.

77. With regard to the developing countries, certain relevant information is available about India, the Philippines and Mexico.[74]

78. Table 8 indicates the restrictions on exports in agreements involving subsidiaries and firms with minority foreign capital participation in India in the period up to March 1964 and the period from April 1964 to March 1969.

79. As can be seen from the table, some 40 per cent of the agreements concluded by subsidiaries with foreign companies in the period up to March 1964 contained clauses restricting exports. In the subsequent period, the percentage of total agreements containing restrictions was higher, 75 per cent or 9 out of 12 of the agreements by the subsidiaries. In the earlier period, over half the

---

[72] J. H. Dunning, op. cit.

[73] See J. H. Dunning, "The Role of American Investment in the British Economy", PEP Broadsheet 507 (London, 1969), p. 148.

[74] For the details of the basis on which the surveys referred to in this and following paragraphs were carried out, see *Restrictive business practices...*, chap. II, sect. B.

restrictions related to prior approval for exports and another 30 per cent to the requirement that exports be made to certain specified countries only. In the later period, the emphasis of restrictions was on this latter category. With respect to industry sectors, it is noteworthy that in the electrical goods and machinery industry, where foreign-controlled companies had a predominant share, there was a general absence of restrictive clauses relating to exports in the period up to March 1964. However, in the subsequent period, three out of five agreements in this sector contained restrictions, one a total ban on exports, one the requirement that exports should take place through the collaborators' agents or distributors, while another provided that the collaborators' permission would be required for exports. In the earlier period, restrictions on exports were particularly marked in the sectors of machinery and machine tools and pharmaceuticals.

80. With respect to firms with foreign minority participation—that is, with less than 50 per cent of the equity—more than half of the agreements in the period to March 1964 contained restrictive clauses, but the proportion fell to 40 per cent in the subsequent period to March 1969. Whilst a large number of these restrictions stipulated prior permission for exports to certain specified countries only, in the later period an increasing proportion prohibited exports to certain specified countries. There was a marked decline in the requirement of prior permission for exports in the period April 1964 to March 1969, from 80 out of the 230 agreements in the earlier period, to one out of 55 agreements in the later period. These restrictions concerned a wide range of industries, in particular those of machinery and machine tools, electrical goods and machinery, and chemicals and allied products.

81. Similarly, table 9, relating to the Philippines, indicates that of the 129 agreements concluded by subsidiaries 35, or 27 per cent, contained restrictions on exports, and 14 of these prohibited exports and 13 required prior approval for exports. In the case of foreign-minority-owned firms, 11 out of 53 of the agreements, or 20 per cent, contained such restrictions, and eight of these prohibited exports. The industry sectors in which the restrictions were most marked were office and paper supplies, pharmaceuticals and petroleum products.

82. A report[75] on the transfer of technology at the level of the firm in Mexico examines in particular three industrial sectors—the automotive industry, pharmaceuticals and petrochemicals. The report provides certain information about restrictions on export activity in these industries. With respect to the automotive terminal industry (complete motor vehicles) in Mexico, 60 per cent of the industry is in the hands of foreign-majority-controlled companies and 40 per cent in those of foreign-minority-owned companies. It was found that most of the agreements entered into by those companies involved restrictions on export activity. With respect to firms with a foreign-minority participation in the capital, such restrictions were explicitly specified in the agreements, and in general there was more than one agreement with foreign firms for the supply of the technology. With respect to foreign-majority-owned firms, usually only one agreement

existed. The export restrictions stipulated in these agreements were embodied in clauses prohibiting the export of the final product or making exports subject to the prior approval of the parent company. With regard to the export of components, in most cases the prior approval of the parent company was required. The report indicates, however, that such restrictions were in general of little significance in view of the present internationally non-competitive nature of the Mexican industry and therefore the small likelihood of the industry's being able to export. By law, 60 per cent of motor vehicles in Mexico must incorporate locally produced components and parts. In consequence there is a well established auxiliary automotive industry which predominantly involves joint venture arrangements, with foreign capital participation ranging from 0 to 100 per cent. United States firms are the major partners in these joint ventures, but firms from Canada, France, the Federal Republic of Germany, Sweden and Switzerland have also entered into such arrangements. The contracts entered into include a number of restrictions on export, the most important of which concern the allocation of export markets. In more than half of the agreements the foreign collaborator's prior approval for exports is required. With regard to the pharmaceutical industry, the draft report indicates that certain difficulties were encountered in obtaining information. However, of four agreements involving some of the major pharmaceutical manufacturers in Mexico, two contained a prohibition on exports so as to avoid competition in overseas markets which had already been assigned to the parent company or other affiliates, one authorized exports to Central America only, and the other authorized exports to Latin America only.

83. It should be mentioned that with regard to the information about India, the Philippines and Mexico, these agreements were not necessarily all made with the parent companies. Nevertheless it can be seen that restrictions on export activities of subsidiaries and affiliates exist in both developed and developing countries. The full extent to which such restrictions operate cannot be estimated, since no information is available with regard to export arrangements, not involving contractual agreements, that might exist between foreign companies and subsidiaries. In those developing countries where registration and screening procedures operate with regard to new foreign investments, and in particular in those countries where a certain degree of local participation is required in such arrangements, contractual agreements, including in a number of instances provisions which may restrict exports, probably relate to the bulk of new investments. However, with regard to investments which pre-date such registration and screening procedures, the implicit non-contractual restrictions on exports are probably more significant. In other developing countries where foreign investment is not regulated, the existence of non-contractual restrictions on export may be the more general practice.

2. TYING OF RAW MATERIAL INPUTS AND THE SUPPLY OF COMPONENTS

84. Another aspect on which concern has been frequently expressed is that multinational corporations

---

[75] M. S. Wionczek, G. Bueno and J. E. Navarrete, op. cit.

TABLE 9

Types of restrictive clauses: the Philippines (1970)

Type of restrictive clause	Number of agreements with restrictive clauses	
	Subsidiaries	Minority foreign capital participation
I. *Export restrictions*	35	11
1. Global ban on exports	14	8
2. Exports prohibited to specified countries	2	—
3. Exports permitted to specified countries only	—	1
4. Prior approval for exports	13	2
5. Exports permitted to or through specified firms only	4	—
6. Restrictions on use of trademarks in exports	2	—
II. *Other restrictions*		
1. Tied purchases	12	13
2. Restrictions on production patterns	—	—
3. Payment of minimum royalty	5	7
4. Improvements of patent process to licensor	9	4
5. Non-Philippines law to settle disputes	9	4
6. Restriction on termination	2	1
Total number of restrictive agreements[a]	46	23
Total number of agreements	129	53

[a] The total number of export restrictions and other restrictions can exceed the total number of agreements with restrictions, because a given agreement can contain an export restriction as well as other types of restrictions. A given agreement may also contain one or more types of export restriction.

end to require their subsidiaries to import from within the corporation's structure the raw materials and intermediate goods required rather than utilize similar domestically produced goods where these are available.

85. As has already been indicated in the cases of Canada and Australia, it has been found that tied purchasing arrangements exist, though the precise extent of these arrangements has been difficult to determine. In general, it would seem that in both countries foreign-owned subsidiaries are more import-oriented than domestically owned firms.[76]

86. Table 8, on India, indicates that 14 of the 144 agreements in the period up to March 1964 involving subsidiaries in India contained restrictions on the source of supply of raw materials and plant machinery. Two of the 12 agreements in the period from April 1964 to March 1969 contained similar restrictions. In the case of firms with minority foreign capital participation, 46 of the 455 agreements contained such restrictions in the earlier period and eight of the 136 in the latter period. Such restrictions were particularly marked in the sectors of electric goods and machinery and machine tools. In the case of the Philippines, table 9 indicates that tied-in purchases of raw materials were required in 12 of the 129 agreements involving subsidiaries and in 13 of the 53 involving firms with minority foreign capital participation. The majority of such restrictions applied to the pharma-

ceutical industry. Again, from the draft report on Mexico it appears that, in the case of the automotive terminal industry, a common restriction on the activities of subsidiaries and affiliates related to the source of purchases of components and raw materials. The report indicates this restriction could have prevented the production of certain components in Mexico.

87. A question related to the tying of inputs is that of transfer pricing—the prices which the multinational corporations charge for the inputs that are supplied through the corporations.

88. In certain cases, transfer pricing is aimed at minimizing the tax liability of the corporation as a whole, and in certain cases it may also be aimed at limiting or increasing the profits made by the subsidiaries for tax and other fiscal policy reasons, for example, to avoid income taxes, to reduce the impact of customs duties and to accumulate surplus funds in "safe" currency areas. The policies adopted by multinational corporations in this respect are secret, and information is, therefore, difficult to obtain. In addition, in a number of industries where vertically integrated multinational corporations are important world producers of certain raw materials and intermediate goods, prices set for such products in the intra-firm transactions are to a large extent determined arbitrarily, given the absence of a world market price for such products. To substitute open-market prices for such internal prices, even when such prices may exist, may be of little use, since the open-market prices in an international oligopoly, such as those for copper, aluminium and petroleum, are far removed from a price established by negotiation at arm's length between independent buyers and sellers.

[76] See A. E. Safarian, op. cit., pp. 37-38; and D. T. Brash, *American Investment in Australian Industry* (Harvard University Press, 1966), pp. 203-211.

89. Further research is certainly needed to clarify and assess the phenomenon of transfer pricing and intra-firm transactions generally, from the point of view of developing countries. The practices used obviously vary from country to country, and in certain cases may even vary according to the size of the firm, which involves its organizational structure and the degree of organizational control. Where the multinational corporation's investment in developing countries is in the form of joint venture arrangements or of multiple foreign participation arrangements, such forms of control or interests seem likely to reduce the possibilities of any intra-firm policies aiming at distorting the prices of the transferred goods.

90. In the studies on foreign investment carried out in Australia and Canada, some limited evidence was collected that arbitrary transfer pricing, adjustment of royalties and service fees and the allocation of the administrative costs were devices used to some extent in a manner contrary to the interests of those countries. In Australia, the author of the study called for the careful policing by the taxation authorities of "the prices at which foreign-affiliated companies price their imports and exports".[77] As was pointed out in the study on Canada," … what may be fair and reasonable from the standpoint of an international company attempting to minimize its over-all tax burden may not be fair and reasonable from the standpoint of Canada". The author suggests that, for purposes of taxation, the prices of goods and services sold between affiliates in different countries should be placed on an "arm's length" basis, the prices being decided where possible by market prices for comparable goods and services. Where such comparable prices do not exist, the prices should then be decided in consultation with the Canadian tax authorities.[78]

91. On the other hand, in the case of the United Kingdom it was recognized in a study that undercharging for services provided a concealed subsidy. Insofar as these are not charged for at an appropriate cost—that is at arm's length prices—United States subsidiaries operating in the United Kingdom will enjoy higher profits than they otherwise would and would appear more efficient than domestic producers. The study furthermore stated that it was indeed entirely possible that an "appropriate" adjustment would reduce the profitability of United States firms below that of their British counterparts.[79]

92. With regard to the developing countries, certain information is available. A recent study on the pharmaceutical industry conducted by the Colombian Government provides some data on the magnitude of price differentials between the chemically equivalent raw materials produced by the multinational corporations and those produced by "other firms", primarily Italian. The data indicate striking price differentials. For example,

Chemical name	Price per kilogram (dollars)	
	Other	Multinational
Nitrazepan	108.70	2 088.00
Diazepan	30.00-45.55	2 500.00
Prometacina	17.75-21.00	140.00
Erytromycina	100.00-145.50	275.56

The reasons for such wide price differentials can be many and other costs incurred by or due to the parent company (such as royalties) may be included in these transfer prices. The UNITAR study on the pharmaceutical industry,[80] in commenting on these and other figures involving price differentials, states that, "when operating in a market in which there is inflation, the possibility of devaluation and the problem of dividend remission, the profit oriented firm will want to take as much of its profit at home and as little in the [developing country] as is possible. A high transfer price furthers this goal strongly".[81]

93. The report on Mexico referred to earlier (paragraph 82) indicates that it is virtually impossible to ascertain the extent to which price-fixing arrangements have resulted in higher production costs in Mexico in the automotive industry. However, it is indicated that in two cases prices for raw materials purchased were as much as 30 per cent higher than normal competitive prices.

3. MOVEMENT OF FUNDS INTO AND OUT OF CURRENCIES WITHIN THE CORPORATION

94. One aspect of the activities of the multinational corporations, which is particularly relevant in the context of current world monetary problems, concerns the various actions which the multinational corporations may take to protect themselves against devaluation when a currency or currencies are weak. It is often claimed that in such situations the movements of the funds of multinational corporations into and out of currencies tends to magnify the problems facing the government or governments concerned. For example, it was found in a survey of 113 foreign-owned subsidiaries in the United Kingdom that close to 30 per cent of such firms in 1964 and 1965, when devaluation of the pound sterling seemed imminent, remitted over 100 per cent of their earnings, whereas in the previous three or four years no dividends had been paid. In so doing, the subsidiaries in question paid dividends out of accumulated profits, and in a few cases virtually all of the retained earnings were remitted.[82]

95. In addition to the problem of the high levels of profit repatriation when there is a fear of devaluation in a country, a tactic which can be used by the multinational corporation is to defer payment from their affiliates to the subsidiary or perhaps even to the parent company in the country concerned for goods that had been purchased

[77] See D. T. Brash, "Australia as Host to the International Corporation", in C. P. Kindleberger (ed.) *The International Corporation* (Cambridge, Mass. and London, M.I.T. Press, 1970), part V, chap. 12, pp. 317 and 318.

[78] See A. E. Safarian, op. cit., p. 100.

[79] J. H. Dunning, "The Role of American Investment in the British Economy", PEP Broadsheet 507 (London, 1969).

[80] See L. H. Wortzel, *Technology Transfer in the Pharmaceutical Industry*, UNITAR Research Report (RR/14) (New York, 1971) table 13.

[81] *Ibid.*, p. 37.

[82] See M. Z. Brooke and H. Lee Remmers, op. cit., p. 168.

om it. In addition, the subsidiary could be required to ʌake virtually immediate payment for all purchases made ʼom affiliates, instead of permitting a normal 30- or 0-day payment period.[83] It has been reported in a news- ʌaper article that the Chairman and Chief Executive ꜒fficer of CPC International Inc., the eighty-second largest ʌdustrial company in the United States and a major ʌultinational manufacturer and distributor of food and ʌdustrial products, stated that the three major operating ʌctors in his corporation were "wages, commodities ꜒rices) and currencies". The article states that the "CPC ʌd other multinational companies try to maintain their ꜒perations in a 'net asset position' in countries with weak ʌrrencies... In Latin-American nations, for example, ʌhere currencies generally are weak, CPC will encourage ʌe speedy payment of bills by its customers by offering ʌem big discounts. In countries like Germany or Japan, ʌ will extend credit with a lavish hand".[84]

96. Furthermore, the multinational corporations tend ꜒ move funds into and out of currencies to maximize ʌeir profits by taking advantage of interest rate differ- ʌntials and tax advantages which are available in one ꜒untry as compared with another.

D. The activities of the multinational corporations and the developing countries

97. Although the discussion in the present section of ʌe report has concentrated primarily on the activities ꜒f the multinational corporation in relation to the export ʌterests of the developing countries, this emphasis should ʌot imply that all these practices are necessarily common ꜒ all the multinational corporations with activities in the ʌeveloping countries. The manner in which a multi- ʌational corporation operates in a developing country is ʌfluenced by the nature of the relationship between the ꜒arent enterprise and the subsidiary, and this in turn is ʌfluenced by the differing policies on foreign investment ʌ the developing countries. The important question with ʌegard to the activities of the multinational corporations ʌ the developing countries is how to maximize the ꜒ontribution which these corporations can make to the ꜒conomic development of these countries, and in particular, ʌ the context of this study, how to maximize their contri- ꜒ution in the field of exports. This aspect is especially ʌmportant in view of the increasing role of multinational ꜒orporations in world trade.

98. At the eleventh session of the Trade and Develop- ʌent Board, in the discussion on the subject of restrictive ꜒usiness practices, some representatives, of both develop- ʌg and developed countries, referred to the activities of ʌultinational corporations, which they maintained could affect world trade and the export interests of the develop- ing countries. The representative of one developing coun- try expressed the view that in a number of cases the restrictive business practices of multinational corporations had frustrated the efforts of developing countries to expand exports on a regional basis, thus bringing the export policies of their countries into conflict with those of the corporations. The representatives of some developed market-economy countries, while recognizing that prac- tices such as cost allocation among subsidiaries, sales pricing, and informal market-sharing agreements among subsidiaries might affect trade, stated that such alleged practices, even when they existed, were outside the observ- able market channels and often difficult for the public authorities to detect. The identification of such practices, if at all possible, would involve extremely difficult and time-consuming studies. The representative of a socialist country of Eastern Europe stated that the practices and activities of multinational corporations affected world trade and that they should be studied on the basis of priorities for such work.[85]

99. In this connexion, it is interesting to note that in a recent OECD report it was stated that "Multinational firms play an important role in the diffusion and transfer of technology across the national boundaries of the advanced countries and from these countries to the devel- oping countries. The growing power and the high flexibility of multinational firms give rise to problems and conflict between these firms and the host countries, whose authority is often reduced, and especially when the objectives of multinational firms do not accord with the socio-economic goals of the countries in which they operate. In such circumstances, there is need for reciprocal understanding between governments of the host countries and the management of multinational firms to harmonize the strategies of those firms with the goals of the countries in which they operate".[86] Furthermore, the report indicates that, "To a great extent, the multinational firm has made purely national policies in the economic and even the social sphere obsolescent, and there is therefore a growing need for agreement among the Member countries on the broad objectives of economic and social policy, and for concerting specific actions—harmonizing of corporation laws, patent laws, collective bargaining, social insurance, monopoly control, etc".[87]

100. At this stage, only extremely limited attention has been given to the question of the activities of the multi- national corporation from the point of view of the devel- oping countries. Moreover, it would seem essential from the point of view of world trade as a whole that any proposals for the solution of problems in this field should take into account the interests of the developing countries, and, furthermore, that the developing countries should actively participate in the formulation of such proposals.

---

[83] Examples of such practices are reported in C. Tugendhat, op. ꜓it., pp. 134 and 135.

[84] C. N. Stabler, "How multinational firm protects its flanks in ʌonetary dealings", *Wall Street Journal*, 20 August 1971.

[85] See *Official Records of the General Assembly, Twenty-sixth Session, Supplement No. 15* (A/8415/Rev.1), part three, para. 219.

[86] See OECD, *Science, Growth and Society: a new perspective*, report of the Secretary-General's *Ad Hoc* Group on New Concepts of Science Policy (Paris, 1971), p. 94.

[87] *Ibid.*, p. 101.

CHAPTER III

Restrictive business practices in relation to patents and trademarks

101. As mentioned in chapter I of the present report, the UNCTAD secretariat's interim report, *Restrictive business practices*, indicated the existence of a considerable number and variety of restrictive provisions which can be, and are, included in licensing agreements between the licensors from developed countries and licensees in developing countries. As was indicated in chapter II of the earlier report, a significant number of foreign collaboration agreements, most of which presumably involve some sort of licensing arrangement, have been entered into with firms in developing countries. These have involved independent firms or firms in which the foreign licensor had a minority participation, or firms which are subsidiaries of a foreign firm. Further, it was pointed out that regardless of these explicit contractual restrictions and implicit restrictions on export through equity control, certain restrictions on export are inherent in the present system of protection of industrial property (mainly patents and trademarks).[88]

102. Patent law generally confers, as a means of encouraging inventions and their exploitation, the right to preclude third parties from making and selling the patented product or, in the case of a process patent, from applying the patented process without the agreement of the patent owner. This right may give the patent owner a monopoly position to the extent that there are no competing products (substitutes). However, it is rare that a single patent gives its owner a monopoly position with regard to a specific product. Where, however, a large number of related patents are owned by one firm, or where the patents of the leading firms in an industry are pooled, patents are likely to result in monopoly positions in a market. Unpatented know-how has been defined as "technical knowledge of industrial significance which has been built up in one organization and is not in the public domain".[89] By contrast to the case of patents, there is at present no generally accepted view as to the scope of legal protection of unpatented know-how. But it is clear that the protection of know-how does not include a right to exclude others from utilizing the know-how concerned

and from selling the resultant products. Rather, the protection of unpatented know-how is limited to safeguarding against unlawful communication to others or disclosure to the public, and against "stealing".[90] The protection of unpatented know-how does not therefore involve inherent restrictions on exports. Such restrictions may, however, be stipulated in licensing agreements under which such know-how is made available. Licences frequently cover both patents and unpatented know-how, since in many cases the licensee would be unable to make use of the patent without having access to the related unpatented know-how. In such cases it is often the possession of the unpatented know-how rather than the patent itself which confers upon the licensor his strong bargaining position vis-à-vis the licensee. This situation may force the licensee to accept wider restrictions on his activities, in particular with regard to exports, than might be the case if only a patent were involved.

103. A trademark is "any visible sign serving to distinguish the goods of one enterprise from those of other enterprises".[91] Trademark laws generally give the owner of a trademark the right to preclude others from using that trademark in commerce for goods or services in respect of which the mark is registered. Like a patent, a trademark thus involves inherent restrictions on the sale of products, but the exclusive right applies only to the use of the particular mark in association with the goods or services concerned. The reputation of a trademark may, however, in particular cases, be so strong that other enterprises may have difficulties in selling the same or similar products without that mark or with a different mark. In consequence, they may be forced to enter into a licence agreement with the trademark owner. In such cases the trademark owner is often in as similarly strong a bargaining position as the licensor of important unpatented know-how, and may be able to impose substantial restrictions, such as export restrictions, on the licensee.

104. In considering possible ways and means of removing export restrictions, it is a fact of vital importance that, in the case of agreements involving patents and trademarks, not only do contractual restrictions exist, but also certain inherent restrictions resulting from these two forms of industrial property as to the production and/or marketing of goods. For example, if the Government of a developing country in which a patent licensee is restricted under the licensing contract from exporting to other countries attempts to prohibit or annul such contractual restric-

---

[88] Article 1 (2) of the Paris Convention for the Protection of Industrial Property of 20 March 1883, as revised in Lisbon in 1958, states: "The protection of industrial property has as its object patents, utility models, industrial designs, trade marks, trade names, indications of source or appelations of origin, and the repression of unfair competition". The term "intellectual property" is generally used in a broader sense. As defined in article 2 (viii) of the Convention Establishing The World Intellectual Property Organization (WIPO) of 14 July 1967, it includes the rights relating to: "literary, artistic and scientific works; performances of performing artists, phonograms and broadcasts; inventions in all fields of human endeavour; scientific discoveries; industrial designs; trademarks, service marks, and commercial names and designations; protection against unfair competition; and all other rights resulting from intellectual activity in the industrial, scientific, literary or artistic fields".

[89] *The British Patent System*, Report of the Committee to Examine the Patent System and Patent Law (1970) (London, H.M.S.O., Cmnd. 4407), para. 493. The *Model Law for Developing Countries on Inventions* (BIRPI publication No. 801 (E), Geneva, 1965), in section 53 (1), defines technical know-how as "manufacturing processes or knowledge concerning the use and application of industrial techniques".

[90] See, for example, section 54 of the BIRPI-WIPO *Model Law for Developing Countries on Inventions*. In view of the fundamental difference between patents and the protection of unpatented know-how, it appears to be questionable whether, as section 57 of this law implies, the violation of unpatented know-how can be equated with the infringement of a patent.

[91] Section 1 (1) (a) of the *Model Law for Developing Countries on Marks, Trade Names and Unfair Competition* (BIRPI publication No. 805 (E), Geneva, 1967). The term trademark often includes service marks which relate to services performed by an enterprise. Collective marks, trade names, indications of sources, and appellations of origin are not considered in this report.

ons, it would not automatically make exports by the censee legally possible. The reason is that the patent aws in the countries to which the licensee might wish to xport may treat such exports as patent infringement if the censor has obtained corresponding patents in those coun- ries and has not given his authorization for such exports. he right of a licensee to export to other countries is, herefore, also dependent upon the patent situation in the ountries in question. In these circumstances, it would nly be to those countries where the product concerned as no patent protection that the removal of contractual xport restrictions could enable the licensee to export egally.

105. In view of this close interrelation between, on the ne hand, the contractual export restrictions in licensing greements involving patents or trademarks and, on the ther, export restrictions resulting directly from the indus- rial property protection law, it is necessary to consider he latter type of restrictions in the context of this study f restrictive business practices that can affect the export nterests of developing countries.[92] For the purpose of etermining the scope of this latter type of restrictions in nore detail, the international trade aspects of these laws nd, in particular, of the legal situation and experiences of leveloped and developing countries, are briefly examined. n this context it appears to be relevant to take into consid- ration the model laws for developing countries, drawn up y BIRPI[93] and by WIPO,[94] and the intergovernmental o-operation and international action in this field. In iew of their special differing features, patents and trade- narks will be considered separately.

A. Patents

106. The present national and international patent ystem and its implications for the developing countries vere described in detail in the United Nations Secretariat's eport, *The role of patents in the transfer of technology to leveloping countries.*[95] The essential features of this system, vhich have not been basically changed by the more recent levelopments in international patent co-operation such as he *Patent Co-operation Treaty* of 19 June 1970,[96] are the ollowing. Patents are government grants and are effective only within the territory of the country concerned. Na- ional patent laws, as a rule, give the same protection to nationals and foreigners, with the consequence that the

same inventor may obtain corresponding patents for his invention in several countries. These patents are legally independent of each other and each is governed exclusively by the law of the country in which it was granted. There is at present no international patent system on a world-wide basis.[97] Industrial patent co-operation has so far con- centrated on the equal treatment of nationals and for- eigners,[98] on harmonizing national patent legislation,[99] and on simplifying and making more economical the obtaining of patent protection for the same invention in several countries.[100]

107. Patent protection at the international level there- fore rests upon the co-existence of corresponding national patents in different countries. Since the patentee can deter- mine in which country the patent is worked and can issue licences to restrict the use of the patent to the production of products for sale in the territory of a particular country, he can thereby control the production of and international trade in the patented product with regard to all countries where his invention enjoys the protection of a patent. This method of international allocation of production and trade may in certain cases be used by the multinational corporations. The restrictive effects of the international patent system particularly affect those countries where the majority of patents are granted to foreign inventors. This is the case in all developing countries, and in partic- ular in the least developed of them. For example, of 9,812 patents granted in Argentina in 1969, 7,504 were owned by foreigners and only 2,308 by nationals. Bolivia granted 173 patents to foreigners and 20 to nationals. Mexico granted 5,129 patents to foreigners and 412 to nationals, and of 600 patents granted in the African, Malagasy and Mauritian Common Organization 596 were owned by foreigners and 4 by nationals. With regard to India the

---

[92] At the Second Ministerial Meeting of the Group of 77, it was recommended that the Secretary-General of UNCTAD should *inter alia* carry out a study concerning the review of international patent legislation (See *Proceedings of the United Nations Conference on Trade and Development, Third Session*, vol. I, *Report and Annexes* (United Nations publication, Sales No. E.73.II.D.4), annex VIII, F, part three, sect. G, II, para. 6).

[93] *Model Law for Developing Countries on Inventions* (1965) and *Model Law for Developing Countries on Marks, Trade Names, and Acts of Unfair Competition* (1967). Both model laws are now spon- sored by WIPO, after the coming into force of the Convention in April 1970 by which BIRPI became the World Intellectual Property Organization.

[94] *Model Law for Developing Countries on Industrial Designs* (WIPO publication No. 808 (E), Geneva, 1970).

[95] United Nations publication, Sales No. 65.II.B.1.

[96] WIPO publication No. 274 (E), Geneva, 1970.

[97] An international patent on a regional basis is granted by the African and Malagasy Office for Industrial Property, and is provided for in the "First Preliminary Draft of a Convention relating to a European Patent for the Common Market" (1970). It would be effective in all member countries of EEC and be governed by a system of international patent law created by the Convention.

[98] See, for example, article 2 of the Paris Convention for the Protection of Industrial Property.

[99] The Paris Convention, in article 5, provides, for example, for a three-year period after the granting of a patent before a compulsory patent may be issued, and for a two-year period after the grant of a compulsory licence before the patent may be cancelled by reason of having been abused. The African, Malagasy and Mauritian Common Organization aims at the complete harmonization of the patent laws of its members. Greater harmonization of national patent laws is also the objective of the Council of Europe Convention on the Unification of Certain Points of Substantive Law on Patents for Invention, signed at Strasbourg in 1963. A further project to harmonize national patent legislation was initiated by the countries of the Andean region (Bolivia, Chile, Colombia, Ecuador and Peru).

[100] The Patent Co-operation Treaty (1970) provides for an inter- national patent application (art. 3), an international search to dis- cover prior art (art. 15), and an international preliminary examina- tion to discover whether the invention appears to be novel, to involve an inventive step (to be non-obvious), and to be industrially applic- able (art. 33). The African, Malagasy and Mauritian Common Organization has established a central system for the granting of patents by the Office for Industrial Property in Yaounde, Cameroon. Under the "First Preliminary Draft of a Convention Establishing a European System for the Grant of Patents" (1970) a European Patent Office would be established which, in addition to granting European patents for the Common Market, would act as a central search and examination office for member countries, including non- EEC countries.

number of patent grants in 1969 is not known, but the statistics on patent applications filed indicate that the situation is similar (1,288 applications by nationals, 4,158 by foreigners).[101] It should also be noted that some of the patents granted to nationals would be patents owned by national subsidiaries of foreign firms, so that, in reality, the number of foreign-controlled patents may be even higher.

108. Only three developed countries granted more patents to nationals than to foreigners—the Federal Republic of Germany, 12,432 compared with 10,191; Japan, 18,787 compared with 8,870; and the United States, 50,395 compared with 17,162. In the case of France the number of patents granted to nationals was 10,288 compared with 21,732 to foreigners, and in the United Kingdom the corresponding numbers were 9,807 compared with 28,983.

109. The less advanced of the developed countries seem to experience a pattern of distribution between patents granted to nationals and foreigners similar to that in the developing countries. For example, only 5 per cent of all Canadian patents granted in 1968/1969 were owned by inventors with a residence in Canada, whereas 67 per cent were issued to residents of the United States and 28 per cent to residents of other foreign countries.[102] It is interesting to note in this context that a recent survey made in Canada indicated that only 15 per cent of the patents granted in Canada have been worked there, while 48 per cent have been worked in other countries, and that only 12 per cent of the patents owned by foreign residents in Canada were licensed to Canadian firms.[103]

110. Where corresponding patents are held by the same patentee, the result may be, in a number of countries, that both the export and the import of a patented product in each of these countries are restricted. As far as imports are concerned, the restriction could have a direct effect on that country's ability to export, especially where the product is an essential input for the potential export industry. Such restrictions on imports are a result of the importing country's patent law. They are therefore within the territorial reach of the governmental authorities of that country and hence action can be taken, for example through compulsory licensing, to secure imports. On the other hand, the inherent patent restrictions as regards exports result from the laws in foreign countries and are consequently generally outside the reach and control of the governmental authorities of the potentially exporting country.

111. Where a product cannot be imported into a developing country on reasonable terms because of the patent protection afforded in that country, the issue of compulsory licences to interested national firms is a possible remedy. Patent laws of a number of developing countries (e.g., sections 84 and 86-88 of the Indian Patent Act, 1970, section 34 of Republic Act 165 of the Philippines) and the Model Law for Developing Countries on Inventions (sections 34-45) make provision for such licences. How-

ever, under article 5A (4) of the Paris Convention, compulsory licences for failure to work can in the case of countries party to the Convention normally be issued only after a period of three years from the grant of the patent.[104,105] In addition, a compulsory licence is normally granted only for the working of the patented invention (see, e.g., section 84 of the Indian Patent Act, 1970)[106] and the patent itself may not provide sufficient details to enable it to be worked. When a licensee obtains a patent from a patentee, he normally also obtains assistance from the patentee in putting the invention into effect. Where a compulsory licence is granted this may not happen. A further reason why normal compulsory licensing procedures are often not invoked is the lengthiness and costliness of the procedures involved.

112. For this latter reason a number of developing countries have attempted to accelerate and simplify the issuing of compulsory licences by including provisions in their patent laws to the effect that under certain conditions any interested person becomes automatically entitled to a compulsory licence.[107] For example, under section 86 of the Indian Patent Act, 1970, the Patent Office, upon a motion by the Central Government, may order that a patent be endorsed with the words "licences of right" if the Office is satisfied that the reasonable requirements of the public with respect to the patented invention have not been satisfied or that the patented invention is not available to the public at a reasonable price.[108] Where a patent has been so endorsed, any interested person has the right to require the licensee to grant him a licence. However, automatic licences of right can normally be issued only two or three years after the patent grant, and require that

---

[104] Brazil is apparently the only country with a two-year period (art. 42 of the Industrial Property Code of 21 October 1969).

[105] Article 5A (4) does not apply to compulsory licences granted for reasons other than failure to work (*vide* proceedings of the Lisbon revision Conference, 1958, and G. H. C. Bodenhausen, *Guide to the Application of the Paris Convention for the Protection of Industrial Property as revised at Stockholm in 1967* (BIRPI, Geneva, 1968), p. 70. For example, sections 46-49 of the United Kingdom Patents Acts, 1949, contain extensive provisions regarding the use of patents "for the services of the Crown". Crown user embraces the requirements of the State for defence purposes and the requirements of the National Health Service. Health Services and Public Health Act, 1968, S.59.

[106] Section 34 of the WIPO Model Law does not require "working" by the compulsory licensee, but excludes, on the other hand, that he imports the products. The explanation given in the commentary to section 34 is that "importation would defeat the purpose of the compulsory licence, which is working *in the country*". With regard to importation to supply the public needs for food and medicines, some developed and developing countries grant compulsory licences for the import of patented products.

[107] Compulsory "licences of right" exist in several developed and developing countries. Industrial Property Code of Brazil, 1969, art. 48; Federal Republic of Germany, 1968, art. 8; Indian Patent Act, 1970, sect. 86; Israel Patent Law, 1967, S.104; Patent Law of Switzerland, 1964, art. 32; United Kingdom Patents Act, 1949, S.41; Patent Law of Yugoslavia, 1960, art. 32.

[108] Section 90 of the Act provides that the reasonable requirements of the public shall be deemed not to have been satisfied where, by reason of the refusal to grant a licence on reasonable terms, "an existing trade or industry or the development thereof, or the establishment of any new trade or industry in India, or the trade or industry of any person or classes of persons trading or manufacturing in India is prejudiced", or "a market for the export of the patented article manufactured in India is not being supplied or developed".

---

[101] See *Industrial Property*, December 1970, annex to No. 12, p. 2.

[102] See Economic Council of Canada, *Report on Intellectual and Industrial Property* (1971), p. 54.

[103] *Ibid.*, pp. 62-63.

he patent must be worked in the country in question —which may not always be technically or economically easible if a developing country requires only limited quantities of the patented input for the manufacture of other products.

113. Where the objective is to secure imports of a particular product, section 35 of the compulsory licensing provisions of the Model Law for Developing Countries on inventions may provide an appropriate guide. This states that "the Minister responsible for industrial property may, by order, provide that, for certain patented products and processes, or for certain categories of such products and processes, which are declared by that order of vital importance for the defence or the economy of the country, or for public health, compulsory licences may be granted, in the conditions provided for in section 34, even before the expiration of the period mentioned in sub-section (1) of that Section and even for importation into the country". In particular the commentary to section 35 expressly states that "promotion of local manufacture [of the patented product] is not necessarily among the aims of the Section". It should also be noted, however, that this section of the Model Law, like section 34, to which it is linked, makes no reference to the issuing of compulsory licences for the manufacture of goods for export. On the other hand, the commentary to sub-paragraph 1 (*d*) of section 34 seems to indicate that manufacture for export might be the subject of a compulsory licence.

114. On the question of manufacture for exports, compulsory licensing provisions in the patent laws of the developing countries can generally be used only with the aim of ensuring that domestic firms are initially not prevented from manufacturing a particular product or products in these countries. It should be noted, however, that the laws of several countries regarding the grant of compulsory licences provide that a licence may be granted by the authorities in a case where, owing to the refusal of the patentee to grant a licence on reasonable terms, an export market for the patented product is not being supplied.[109] One of the objectives of issuing a compulsory licence may be to permit local manufacture for export purposes: for example, this is one of the stated aims of section 90 of the Indian Patent Act, 1970. Nevertheless, the issuing of a compulsory licence cannot remove the inherent restrictions on export resulting from the existence of corresponding patents in other countries. Control by the developing countries of restrictions in licensing agreements involving patents is limited to restrictions on exports to those countries in which the product concerned has no patent protection.

115. Such control can be exercised in several ways:

(*a*) By including appropriate provisions in the industrial property laws of the particular country;

(*b*) By bringing agreements involving patents within the scope of the country's restrictive business practice laws; and

(*c*) By instituting appropriate screening procedures for foreign investment and technical collaboration agreements. With regard to the first approach it would seem that no

developed country has included such provisions in its industrial property laws. So far as the developing countries are concerned the Andean group of countries has followed this approach, and this is referred to later (paragraph 117 below). The second approach has been adopted by a number of developed countries, for example Canada, the Federal Republic of Germany and the United States. However, Australia and the United Kingdom have specifically excluded patent agreements from the scope of their laws on restrictive business practices. Among the developing countries, India has similarly excluded patents from its restrictive business practices laws. In regard to screening procedures, these would seem to have been instituted only in the developing countries and Japan.

116. The first approach has been suggested in the BIRPI-WIPO Model Law on inventions. Under section 33 (1), "clauses in license contracts or relating to such contracts are null and void in so far as they impose upon the licensee, in the industrial or commercial field, restrictions not deriving from the rights conferred by the patent".[110] As indicated in the commentary to section 33, unlawful restrictions which are outside the scope of the patent grant may consist "for example, of a stipulation requiring the licensee to use, or purchase from the licensor, some unpatented materials or components. Another example may consist of stipulating that the licensee will not export to certain foreign countries when exportation is not already limited because of patents existing in such countries. Still another example may consist of stipulating that the licensee will not sell competing products not infringing the patent to which the licence relates".

117. A recent important development in the control of restrictions through patent laws is the formulation of article 20 of Decision No. 24 of the Commission of the Cartagena Agreement, which was approved for implementation in each of the member States of the Andean group of countries. Article 20 provides that:

Member Countries may not authorize the conclusion of agreements relating to the transfer of foreign technology or to patents if the agreements contain:

(*a*) Clauses whereby the provision of technology carries with it the obligation, for the recipient country or enterprise, to purchase capital goods, intermediate products, raw materials or other forms of technology from a particular source, or to make permanent use of staff designated by the enterprise supplying the technology. In exceptional cases, the recipient country may accept clauses of this kind relating to the purchase of capital goods, intermediate products or raw materials, provided that the price of the articles is consonant with current price levels in the world market;

(*b*) Clauses whereby the enterprise selling the technology reserves the right to fix the selling or resale price of the products manufactured on the basis of the technology in question;

(*c*) Clauses containing restrictions on the volume and structure of production;

---

[109] United Kingdom Patents Act, 1949-1961, sect. 37; Israel Patents Act, 1967, sect. 119.

[110] Section 33 (2) provides that "the following in particular shall be deemed not to constitute such restrictions:

"(*a*) Limitations concerning the degree, extent, quantity, territory or duration of exploitation of the subject of the patent;

(*b*) Limitations justified by the interest of the licensor in the technically flawless exploitation of the subject of the patent;

(*c*) The obligation imposed upon the licensee to abstain from all acts capable of impeding or preventing the grant of the patent or prejudicing its validity".

(*d*) Clauses prohibiting the use of competing technologies;

(*e*) Clauses establishing a total or partial purchasing option in favour of the supplier of the technology;

(*f*) Clauses requiring the purchaser of the technology to transfer to the supplier any invention or improvements obtained through the use of the technology;

(*g*) Clauses requiring the payment of royalties to patentees in respect of unexploited patents; and

(*h*) Other clauses of equivalent effect.

Save in exceptional cases duly defined by the competent body in the recipient country, clauses prohibiting or limiting in any way the export of products manufactured on the basis of the technology in question shall not be accepted.

In no case shall clauses of this kind be accepted in respect of subregional trade or the export of similar products to third countries.

It may be noted that article 20 covers additional restrictions to those referred to in the examples given in the commentary to section 33 (1) of the BIRPI-WIPO Model Law on inventions.

118. The second approach is to bring agreements involving patents within the scope of restrictive business legislation. This, as has been indicated, is the approach adopted by several developed countries, for example, Canada,[111] the Federal Republic of Germany,[112] and the United States.[113] On the other hand other developed countries, such as Australia[114] and the United Kingdom,[115] have expressly exempted restrictions in patent licensing agreements from their restrictive business legislation. Of the small number of developing countries which have adopted restrictive business practices legislation, India has also exempted patent licensing agreements from the coverage of its Monopolies and Restrictive Trade Practices Act (1969). Section 15 of this act states that "no order made under this Act with respect to any monopolistic or restrictive trade practice shall operate so as to restrict... (*b*) any person as to the condition which he attaches to a licence to do anything, the doing of which but for the licence would be an infringement of a patent granted in India".[116]

119. A third approach to controlling restrictions on export in licensing agreements is the institution of registration and screening procedures for such agreements. This is the approach adopted in a number of developing countries, for example, Brazil, Chile, Colombia, El Salvador, Ghana, India, Iran, Mexico, Pakistan and the Philippines; the relevant procedures were described in the interim report.[117]

120. Which of the three approaches mentioned the Government of a developing country may wish to adopt will depend on a number of factors, including the availability of trained specialists in this field. If a country has no restrictive business practice legislation and feels no need for such legislation, but has an established patent system, then it may regard it as preferable to build up a section within its patent office to deal with the question of restrictions in patent licensing agreements. However, many licensing agreements may not involve patents, and therefore a separate office or department may be required for such agreements. Where a country has restrictive business practice legislation and therefore trained expert in this area of work, it may consider it preferable to provide for the controlling of restrictions in licensing agreements by that administrative body.

121. Undoubtedly from the point of view of many developing countries which wish to ensure that unreasonable restraints are not placed on the export activity of their firms, some type of screening procedure for licensing arrangements will be required. Where such screening is located—and it may be in several places, such as the central bank, the patent office and the board of investments—is a matter of individual choice for the country concerned. The important consideration is that the various legislative provisions governing restrictive business practices, investments and patents should be in harmony and that a situation should not arise where no effective control can be exercised over restrictions which go beyond the scope of the patent grant and which are considered not to be in the interest of the country in question.

122. As was pointed out earlier, the restrictions on imports and exports inherent in the present international patent system arise from the fact that corresponding patents in different countries are legally independent of each other even if they have been granted to the same person. They also derive from the assumption that it is a violation of the patent owner's exclusive right in a particular country if a patented product is imported into that country without the patent owner's consent, even though it was lawfully brought into commerce abroad by the patent owner himself or, with his consent, by a foreign licensee. This interpretation of the patent monopoly has, for example, been accepted by the Supreme Court of the Netherlands when it held that: "The territorially limited applicability of the law of patents for inventions has as a result that marketing (of a product) by the patentee on a foreign market does not affect the rights derived from a (Dutch) patent. Thus, a 'lawful bringing into commerce within the meaning of article 30 (2) of the Patent Act takes place only if bringing an item into commerce occurs in the Netherlands".[118] On the other hand, it may be noted that the Economic Council of Canada recommended in its 1971 report "that the patent right should be so defined that neither the holder of a Canadian patent nor any licensee thereunder should have the right to prevent the importation into Canada by any person of the patented article, or an article made by the patented process, from other countries where the article or process enjoys patent protection".[119] This recommendation by the Economic Council of Canada would seem to involve a redefinition of patent monopoly rights. It would mean, with regard to licensees in developing countries, that their products could be legally exported to all other countries where the

---

[111] Section 30 of the Combines Investigation Act, R.S.C. 1952.

[112] Section 20 of the Act against Restraints of Competition, 1957.

[113] Section 1 of the Sherman Act, 1890.

[114] Section 58 (*f*) of the Trade Practices Act, 1965-1967.

[115] Section 8 (4) of the Restrictive Trade Practices Act, 1956.

[116] A similar exemption is provided for in section 5 of the Israel Restrictive Trade Practices Law.

[117] See *Restrictive business practices* ..., paras. 137-150.

[118] 1943 Nederlandse Jurisprudentie No. 519. A similar view was adopted by the Supreme Court of the Federal Republic of Germany in a judgement of 29 February 1968, 49 BGHZ 331, 196 GRUR Int. 129.

[119] See The Economic Council of Canada, *Report on Intellectual and Industrial Property* (1971), p. 90.

me invention enjoys patent protection, provided that
ıe products in question were being sold on the domestic
ıarket of the licensee concerned. It would also mean,
owever, that within the framework of the commercial
olicies of developing countries, patentees and licensees
ıanufacturing in other countries would be able to export
ı developing countries in competition with licensees in
ıose countries. This is a very complex issue and would
:quire careful examination in the light of the present
ıterpretation of patent rights.

. Agreements involving patents and unpatented know-how

123. As has already been indicated, there is at present
ıo generally accepted rule as to the scope of legal protec-
ıon of unpatented know-how. Also, unpatented know-
ow as such involves no inherent restrictions on exports,
y contrast with patents and trademarks. However, licens-
ıg agreements involving know-how often contain restric-
ons on export. In this regard, it was indicated in the
ıterim report that in licensing agreements involving both
atents and unpatented know-how, restrictions were
nown to be placed on the use of the patents and associa-
:d know-how on the termination of the contracts.[120]
ienerally, and certainly in developed countries, contracts
ormally run at least for the unexpired term of the patents
ıvolved. Hence such contractual restrictions on the use
f patents and the associated know-how would relate
ssentially to their use after the expiry of the patent. This
ould seem an unjustified restriction. For example, in
ertain developed countries such contractual restrictions
re regarded as null and void once the patents have
xpired. In the United Kingdom, section 58 of the Patents
ct provides that when all original patents have ceased to
e in force, the licensee may terminate the licence, not-
vithstanding anything in the licence to the contrary.[121]
ı consequence developing countries could consider
ıcluding a provision in their patent laws to the effect
hat once a patent has ceased to be in force, the licensee
hould be free to use not only the subject-matter of the
atent but also any associated, unpatented technical infor-
ıation which he has acquired under or by virtue of the
cence involving the patent. The legal restriction on unlaw-
ıl disclosure of such know-how would of course continue
ı effect. Clearly, every effort should be made to facilitate
he transfer of patents and unpatented know-how to the
eveloping countries. Careful consideration should be
iven by the appropriate international bodies, such as
JNCTAD, UNIDO and WIPO, to the drawing up of
pecific measures in this regard. Several proposals by
tates members have recently been made with this objective
ı mind.[122]

---

[120] See Restrictive business practices ..., paras. 106 and 107.

[121] Section 20 of the Federal Republic of Germany's Act against
Restraints of Competition (Gesetz gegen Wettbewerbsbeschränkun-
en), of 27 July 1957, contains the provision that certain restrictions
re considered to be reasonable only in so far as they do not extend
ı time beyond the duration of the legal protection afforded by the
atent.

[122] See in particular the proposal by Sweden for a Patent Licens-
ng Convention, and the proposal by Brazil for a multilateral round
f negotiations on technology, WIPO documents LC/I/1 PC/EC/VII

C. Trademarks

124. As was pointed out earlier in this chapter, in the
case of a trademark the exclusive right of the owner relates
not to particular products or services as such, but only to
the use of the mark in association with such products or
services. Other firms are always free to manufacture and/or
sell a similar type of product or service without a mark or
under a different mark. It would appear, therefore, that
the inherent restrictions on international trade of the
international trademark system resulting from the existence of corresponding, but legally independent trademarks of the same firm or its licensees in different countries will not, in general, have the same economic significance as in the case of patents. Nevertheless, the export
interests of developing countries may be adversely affected
by such restrictions in the following circumstances. First,
a trademark licensee in a developing country wishing to
export a trademarked product to other countries may not
legally be in a position to do so because the trade mark
owner or licensees in these countries might have, under the
laws of their countries, the right to invoke trademark
protection to prevent imports of such products. Under
such conditions, trademarks could also be used to prevent
subsidiaries of multinational corporations from exporting.
Secondly, in the case of a trademarked article which is
an important input for exporting industries in a developing
country, the foreign manufacturer may have obtained a
trademark in that developing country and either he himself
or a licensee in that country might invoke his trademark
right to prevent the marked product from being imported
on reasonable terms.

125. Contrary to what appears to be the currently
prevailing interpretation of the patent law, the interpretation given to the trademark law is not generally such as
to provide the trademark owner with the right to prevent
unauthorized imports of marked products which he himself or an affiliated firm or a licensee has put into commerce abroad.[123]

126. This would appear to be a well established rule in
a great number of countries, in cases where the trademark
owner's products ("genuine" products) are involved.[124]
It means, for example, that the foreign manufacturer of
a trademarked product cannot exclude imports of a
"genuine" product by invoking his rights under his trademark registered in such an importing country. Likewise,
a domestic distributing licensee of the foreign trademark
owner, even though he may have been appointed by the
latter as the exclusive importer and distributor in the
importing country, cannot invoke the trademark law to

16, and P/EC/VII/21, paras. 39-50. See also Proceedings of the United
Nations Conference on Trade and Development, Third Session, vol. I,
Report and Annexes (United Nations publication, Sales No. E.73.II.
D.4), annex VIII, F, part three, sect. G, II, para. 8.

[123] See generally F. K. Beier, "Territoriality of Trademark Law
and International Trade", in International Review of Industrial
Property and Copyright Law (IIC) (Verlag Chemie GMBH, Wein-
heim (Federal Republic of Germany), vol. 1, No. 1, 1970), pp. 48-72.

[124] In addition to the cases cited in F. K. Beier's article (see
preceding footnote), the following recent cases bear out this view:
Supreme Court of Austria of 30 November 1970, 1971 GRUR Int.
90 (Agfa films); District Court of Osaka, Japan, of 27 February 1970,
1971 GRUR Int. 276 (Parker Pens).

prevent "parallel" imports by other importers. The same rule apparently applies where the domestic trademark is registered by a distributing subsidiary of the foreign manufacturer and trademark owner, or by a domestic distributor.[125]

127. Only where the trademarked products do not originate from the same source does there seem to be no firmly established rule as to whether unauthorized imports of that same trademarked product violate the domestic trademark. This would be the case, for example, where the domestic trademark owner or licensee manufactures and markets the trademarked product domestically and the imported product is manufactured abroad either by the trademark owner or by another licensee. Another example would be the case where two products bearing the same trademark are imported from two different manufacturers.[126] Since the function of a trademark is normally to identify the manufacturer of the product, it may be desirable to permit imports, although unauthorized by the trademark owner, especially in those cases where the imported product is manufactured by various parts of the same multinational corporation, whether a subsidiary or affiliate or the parent company. The legitimate interests of the domestic trademark owner could in such cases be safeguarded by the law against unfair competition and deceptive practices in trade or by contract law.[127]

128. The interpretation of the exclusive right under trademark in the foregoing way would substantially narrow the scope of inherent restrictions on international trade that may result from trademark protection. The more such a rule was accepted, the more likely it would seem that trademark licensors would make greater use of contractual restrictions on exports and imports in their trademark licensing arrangements. Hence, contractual restraints could assume greater importance that at present when licensors may still to a considerable extent rely on the inherent restrictions in the trademark system to limit the export activities of licensees.

129. As in the case of patent licensing restrictions, there are three approaches which can be used to control restrictions in agreements involving trademarks. With regard to the first approach, namely the inclusion of appropriate provisions in the industrial property legislation, it would seem that the trademark laws of developing countries do not generally contain provisions relating to restrictions in licensing agreements. The BIRPI-WIPO Model Law on marks, trade names and acts of unfair competition provides in section 24 (1) that "clauses in license contracts or relating to such contracts are null and void in so far as they impose upon the licensee, in the industrial or commercial field, restrictions not deriving from the rights conferred by the registration of the mark or unnecessary for the safeguarding of these rights". This rule would seem, however, as far as export and import restrictions are concerned, to be practically overruled by section 24 (2) (a), which states that "limitations concerning the ... territory ... in connexion with which the mark may be used" do not constitute restrictions that fall under section 24 (1).[128] Section 24 of the Model Law would not therefore be applicable in cases where, in a developing country, a subsidiary of a multinational corporation is prevented by a trademark licensing arrangement from exporting to other countries in which the corporation or its licensees have trademark protection.[129]

130. On the other hand, section 28 of the Model Law provides that "the responsible Minister or other competent authority may, by order, provide that, on pain of invalidity, license contracts or certain categories of them

[125] In addition to cases cited in F. K. Beier's article, cf. Supreme Court of France of 17 April 1969, 1971 GRUR Int. 276 (Körting), Supreme Court of Finland of 23 January 1968, 1969 Nordisk Immateriellt Räätskydd 96 (FELICA). Section 20 of the BIRPI-WIPO Model Law for developing countries on marks, trade names and acts of unfair competition, is therefore not in line with current trademark law interpretation in the world in requiring that the sale must have taken place in the country in order to exhaust the owner's exclusive right in the products sold. In the commentary to section 20 it is pointed out: "In exceptional cases, which will probably not occur frequently in developing countries, namely, cases where the same registered owner of a trademark in different countries sells in these countries *wholly identical goods* under *exactly the same mark*, the Courts will determine whether the owner abuses his exclusive right to the mark if the objects to the use of the mark by third parties in one or more of these countries in relation to the goods which he has sold under his mark in another of the countries". It is questionable whether these cases are really exceptional as far as developing countries are concerned. In any case, trademark law in developing countries should not be made more restrictive than in other countries, particularly since it might be primarily multinational corporations from developed countries that benefit from such restrictions.

[126] An example of such a situation is the Cinzano case currently being litigated in the Federal Republic of Germany. In this case the plaintiff, the domestic subsidiary of the Italian Cinzano Company, is invoking trademark law to prevent a food chain-store in the Federal Republic of Germany from importing vermouth wine manufactured in France and Spain by other subsidiaries of Cinzano, Italy, and marketed in these two countries under the Cinzano trademark. The District Court of Hamburg, in a judgement of 10 March 1971, 1971 GRUR Int. 272, denied a violation of the Cinzano trademark registered in the Federal Republic of Germany, even though it had found that the imported wine was not physically identical with the wine marketed by the plaintiff. (This wine was manufacturered by Cinzano, Italy, and imported by the plaintiff from that company.) The Court held, however, that it would be a violation of unfair competition law if the vermouth imported from France and Spain was sold without its being made sufficiently clear to buyers that it is not identical with the vermouth marketed by the plaintiff. The case is at present being considered on appeal.

[127] This view is taken, for example, by F. K. Beier in the article cited above (see footnote 123), pp. 67-72. The Economic Council of Canada, in its *Report on Intellectual and Industrial Property*, made the

following recommendation: "No owner of a Canadian trademark should be able to allege that the importation of goods produced by a related company—that is, 'members of a group of two or more companies one of which, directly or indirectly, owns or controls a majority of the issued voting stock of the others' [The Trade Mark Act, Section 2 (r)]—constitutes infringement of his mark. Similarly, when owners of Canadian marks are linked, either directly or indirectly, to unrelated companies through licensing agreements, the Canadian owner of the mark should not be allowed to restrict the importation of goods produced by the other company". The implementation of these proposals would have the effect of allowing entry into Canada of goods produced abroad by a foreign parent, subsidiary or linked company, bearing a mark similar, if not identical, to that used on products of the same type and quality produced by the Canadian owner.

[128] Section 24 is part of chapter VI of the Model Law, which contains detailed provisions on licensing contracts. The provisions are largely identical with the provisions on patent licensing contracts in the Model Law on inventions. Whether this is appropriate in view of the substantial differences between patents and trademarks is open to question.

[129] Section 24 of the Model Law is therefore open to the same reservations that were expressed with regard to section 20 of this law.

ad amendments or renewals of such contracts, which involve the payment of royalties abroad, shall require the approval of ..., taking into account the needs of the country and its economic development." In the commentary it is pointed out that "the authority concerned will be able to protect the national interest against excessive foreign influence, and to protect the country's balance of payments". It would appear that the wording of section 28 would be sufficiently broad to permit control over undue restrictions on exports and imports of the trademarked article. However, such control would only be possible in cases involving payments abroad.

131. An example of the harmonization of control over such restrictions at a subregional level by developing countries is contained in article 25 of Decision No. 24 of the Commission of the Cartagena Agreement. This provides:

Licensing agreements for the use of foreign trademarks in the territory of member countries may not contain restrictive clauses of the following kinds:

(a) Clauses prohibiting or limiting the export or sale to specific countries of products manufactured under the trademark in question or of similar products;

(b) Clauses requiring the use of raw materials, intermediate goods and equipment supplied by the owner of the trademark or his affiliates. In exceptional cases, the recipient country may accept clauses of this kind provided that the price of the articles in question is in keeping with current world market prices;

(c) Clauses fixing the selling or resale price of products manufactured under the trademark;

(d) Clauses requiring the payment of royalties to the owner of a trademark in respect of trademarks;

(e) Clauses requiring the permanent use of staff provided or designated by the owner of the trademark; and

(f) Other clauses of equivalent effect.

132. With regard to the application of general restrictive business practices legislation, it would seem that, in those few instances where developing countries have enacted such legislation, no general exemption is provided for restrictions in trademark licensing agreements as is the case with restrictions in patent licensing agreements. However, the law may not be applicable to export restrictions in general.[130]

133. In those developing countries which have registration and screening procedures involving *inter alia* an examination of agreements containing restrictions on export, it may be possible to remove such restrictions concerning the use of trademarks.

134. As in the case of restrictions on export extending beyond the scope of a patent, the considerations mentioned in paragraphs 120 and 121 above will apply in determining the most appropriate mechanism for controlling restrictions relating to the use of trademarks. Likewise, with regard to the control of such restrictions, it would seem important that developing countries should avoid a situation arising where no effective control can be exercised over unreasonable restrictions relating to the use of trademarks in exports.

---

[130] For example, section 15 of the Indian Monopolies and Restrictive Trade Practices Act, 1969, provides that "no order made under this Act with respect to any monopolistic or restrictive trade practice shall operate so as to restrict ... (c) the right of any person to export goods from India, to the extent to which the monopolistic or restrictive trade practice relates exclusively to the production, supply, distribution or control of goods for such export". No information is at present available about whether this provision is interpreted to exempt from the controls under this Act export restrictions on domestic firms resulting from trademark licensing agreement's

CHAPTER IV

Collateral protection for the export interests of developing countries[131]

135. The possibility of protecting an enterprise in a developing country from restrictive practices through the application of national laws in developed market-economy countries is limited. The reason is that each law is applicable only within specified limits that depend upon (a) whether the restrictive practice took place or had effects in the country in question, or whether the practice restricted the foreign trade of that country; and (b) whether the law covers the practice in question.

136. National laws apply only to restrictions affecting the particular country's domestic or foreign trade. In no developed market-economy country do such laws seek to prevent enterprises engaged in business from restricting the domestic trade of other countries or international trade between other countries. The application of the national law of a developed market-economy country in cases where the trade of a developing country is or might be harmed becomes possible only if there is also harm to the trade of that developed market-economy country.

137. Even when a practice affects both the trade of a developing country and that of a developed market-economy country, the protection of the former's interests by action under the laws of the latter may be unavailable or only partly available because of gaps, differing from country to country, in the extent of the business activity covered by the law and the nature of the restriction covered by it. National laws frequently exempt the processing of and trade in agricultural products, financial institutions, transportation enterprises, State-owned enterprises, and regulated industries. Such laws may provide total or partial exemption for certain types of restrictive practices. They differ from one another in their applicability to various types of restriction, such as discrimination in prices or terms of sale or purchase, refusal to sell, exclusive dealing, tying requirements and resale price maintenance. What might be found unlawful in one developed country might

---

[131] The legal situation in the developed market-economy countries has been dealt with at length in the interim report, *Restrictive business practices*. Therefore only a brief summary of the legal situation is given in the present chapter in dealing with the question of collateral protection. This aspect was not explicitly dealt with in the interim report.

be beyond the scope of the law in a second or be covered by a special exemption in a third.

138. Where both the trade of a developing country and that of a developed market-economy country are affected by a particular restrictive business practice, it might be possible in certain circumstances for the laws of the developed market-economy country to be invoked by plaintiffs in a developing country.[132]

A. Import cartels

139. Proceedings involving the activities of import cartels have been infrequent in all developed market-economy countries.

140. In general, the laws of developed market-economy countries subject import cartels to the same rules as apply to purely domestic cartels. The rationale is that cartels, by excluding competitive alternative foreign products, restrict competition on the domestic market. Consequently, import cartels are *per se* prohibited in the United States and prohibited in principle in Canada, France, the Federal Republic of Germany, Japan and Norway. However, the Federal Republic of Germany and Japan have special provisions concerning the exemption of import cartels. In the Federal Republic of Germany import cartels may be authorized if there is no or only insignificant competition among foreign suppliers. In Japan import cartels may be authorized in the case (among others) where an imported product is subject to substantial restraint of competition at the place of export or to excessive competition among importers and if, as a result, price or other conditions of trade are extremely disadvantageous relative to those prevailing among importers in other countries or to the conditions of domestic trade in the exporting country. In other countries where the legislation contains a general exemption clause it would be possible for such exemptions to be given to import cartels. Insufficient evidence is available, however, to allow the drawing of any conclusion as to whether such general exemption clauses have been used to permit defensive import cartels, as is the case in the countries providing special exemptions.

141. In the two countries which require the registration of cartels as a precondition for making cartels a lawful practice (Austria and the United Kingdom), and in those countries which merely subject cartels to a control of abuses (Australia, Belgium, Denmark, Finland, Luxembourg, Netherlands, Sweden and Switzerland), there are no special provisions concerning the operations of import cartels.[133]

142. It is most improbable that cartels can exclude foreign imports or impose restrictions upon them without also imposing some sort of restrictions upon the domestic market. Accordingly, except when the cartel is deemed to be justified by its function as a domestic counter-measure against monopolistic conditions in the foreign market, or by a need to avert injury to domestic producers, protection against import cartels may be provided for foreign suppliers by a developed country's restrictive practices law even though that law takes no account of the cartel effect upon these suppliers.

B. Rebate cartels

143. Rebate cartels of suppliers in developed market-economy countries, unless they relate exclusively to export to foreign markets, are in principle subject to the same rules as apply to cartels generally. Rebate cartels are therefore, *per se* prohibited in the United States as a form of illegal price-fixing. In Canada, France, the Federal Republic of Germany, Japan and Norway they are prohibited in principle, but may qualify for a general or special exemption. In this connexion, the Federal Republic of Germany provides for a special exemption for rebate cartels, such cartels being exempted in individual cases if the agreed rebates are such as to constitute a genuine compensation for services rendered and if the cartel does not seriously damage outsider-suppliers or discriminate against customers. In order to meet these requirements, aggregated rebate cartels in practice must, *inter alia*, make provision that purchases from firms outside the cartel are included in calculating the basis for the rebates.[134] France normally regards aggregated rebate cartels as illegal, and Canada appears to prohibit rebate cartels *per se* as a form of price-fixing.

144. When loyalty discounts or aggregated rebate granted by a cartel are not applicable to purchases from independent suppliers, the effects might be felt by independent domestic suppliers as well as by foreign suppliers. Rebate cartels are not usually constituted solely to prevent imports. The governments that apply controls are primarily concerned with the cartel's impact upon domestic buyers and sellers. Whether or not remedial action taken will give collateral protection to exporters from developing countries will depend upon the extent to which imported products are taken into account.

C. Agreements on standards

145. The laws of the developed market-economy countries that are concerned specifically with standardization are designed, in general, to ensure that standards are devised with technical competence and with due regard for the interests of groups affected by the standards. In principle private agreements to apply uniform standards or to refuse to buy products which do not meet such standards are regarded as cartel practices. But, whilst theoretically coming within the scope of the control applying to cartels in the developed market-economy countries concerned, such agreements are exempted. In the United States there is no express exemption from the general prohibition of cartels in Section 1 of the Sherman Act, but it appears that agreements which apply objective and non-discriminatory standards are not considered as restrictive and hence are lawful. Of the countries where

---

[132] For a discussion of the possibilities of such action, see G. de Q. Walker, "The Australian Plaintiff and the Sherman Act", in *The Anti-trust Bulletin*, vol. XIV, Winter 1969, pp. 901-932.

[133] See *Restrictive business practices ...*, paras. 24 and 25.

[134] *Ibid.*, para. 48.

artels are in principle prohibited—Canada, France, the Federal Republic of Germany, Japan and Norway—two make provision for special exemptions for agreements on standards, namely, the Federal Republic of Germany and Japan. It would seem that in the other countries such agreements would normally come within the scope of the general exemptions. A number of the countries in which the laws require notification and registration of cartels —for example Australia and the United Kingdom—have exempted standardization agreements from this procedure. Moreover, it is very unlikely that action under relevant abuse laws would be taken in the case of an objective, non-discriminatory standards agreement.[135]

146. As in the case of the other types of exclusionary agreements, the Governments which subject standardization agreements to restrictive practice laws apply them where the particular country's trade is restricted. But misuse in excluding goods from the domestic market or subjecting them to discriminatory terms of sale may be regarded as a restriction of national trade, whether or not the excluded goods are of foreign origin. In such circumstances enforcement of national laws could afford collateral protection to exports from developing countries.

D. Licensing agreements

147. Where restrictions on the exports of developing countries appear in contracts between firms in developed market-economy countries and firms in developing countries to which they are not linked by ownership or management, the inducement for the latter's acceptance of restriction is almost always the fact that technological assistance is offered by the former only on restrictive terms.

148. Collateral protection, if available, is usually accorded through the restrictive practices laws of the developed market-economy countries. These laws can provide such protection only if they cover restrictions of the country's domestic or foreign trade embodied in contracts that impose restrictions abroad.

149. The anti-trust laws of the United States are capable of providing some collateral protection. Similar possibilities under the laws of other countries are both more limited and more uncertain. As regards the control of agreements with licensees, the law in the Federal Republic of Germany would appear to offer some possibility, since it explicitly covers acts committed abroad which produce domestic effects in the Federal Republic of Germany. The law of Japan would seem to offer some possibility, since it explicitly forbids international contracts in unreasonable restraint of trade. Though Norwegian law exempts activity in other countries, it includes provisions for report on and "supervision" of these activities, lest they detrimentally affect Norwegian interests. Thus, the laws of the developed market-economy countries provide, at the most, only limited collateral protection against direct restriction of exports from developing countries.[136]

150. From time to time, restrictions in agreements involving the transfer of patent rights or unpatented technical know-how between United States and foreign enterprises have been prohibited as a result of proceedings under the Sherman Act, on the grounds that they limited United States imports and exports and transcended the mere exercise of the patent rights of the United States. The law has been applied from time to time against contracts between enterprises in the United States and enterprises elsewhere, regardless of the nationality of the participants or the place where the contract was made, when these contracts restricted foreign exports to the United States, or restricted United States exports to foreign markets.[137]

151. In a recent speech, Mr. Richard W. McClaren, the United States Assistant Attorney General, Anti-trust Division, stated: "It is part of our [United States] anti-trust policy to help implement the [United States] free trade commitment by seeking out or prosecuting anti-competitive international business practices and relationships affecting the United States". He went on to say: "We will be alert to challenge barriers to entry erected by private corporations by means, for example, of unduly restrictive patent, know-how and technology licences". He ended his speech with the remark that the United States is aware "that some important foreign firms are entirely excluded from competing in the United States [and] we do not believe that this sort of anti-competitive effect can be justified in the guise of a know-how licence".[138]

E. Export cartels

152. When exports from developing countries are restricted by the activities of export cartels based in developed market-economy countries, there is little prospect of collateral protection under the laws of these countries. Export cartels are usually exempted. Export cartels have been specially exempted in the Federal Republic of Germany, Japan and the United States, and exempted by definition or by explicit provision defining them as outside the scope of laws governing cartels, in other countries. Only under the laws of two developed market-economy countries—Japan and the United States— might some collateral protection be provided for the export

---

[135] *Ibid.*, para. 61.

[136] See C. D. Edwards, *Trade Regulations Overseas: The National Laws* (Dobbs Ferry, New York, Oceana Press, 1966), chapters on the United States, the Federal Republic of Germany, Japan and Norway.

[137] In the case of *United States* v. *Imperial Chemical Industries Ltd.*, 100F. Supp. 504 (S.D.N.Y. 1951), the firms Dupont and Imperial Chemical Industries (ICI) were required to terminate a comprehensive arrangement by which each company conveyed to the other patents and relevant unpatented information which thereby effectively excluded exports to the United States from ICI. Again in a more recent case, *Zenith Radio Co.* v. *Hazeltine Research Inc.*, 395 US 100 (1969), the Supreme Court affirmed the lower court's holding of illegality in the participation by a United States company in a foreign patent tool which was designed for, and had the effect of, preventing United States exports of radio and television sets to Canada. For action by the Government of the United States in screening certain licensing agreements entered into by firms in their country with firms in foreign countries, see *Restrictive business practices* ..., paras. 130-133.

[138] Richard W. McClaren, "Anti-trust policy today", speech before the National Industrial Conference Board, New York, 5 March 1970.

interests of developing countries.[139] The Japanese Export and Import Trading Act provides for consideration of importing interests, and this might be interpreted as providing for the consideration of foreign competitor interests also. The Act provides in section 5 *bis*, subparagraph (ii), that the Minister of International Trade and Industry shall order agreements to be modified or prohibited, unless "the interests of importers or enterprises concerned at the destination are not injured and there is

[139] Recognition that export cartels can be effective in securing export orders and in competing for the world trade, has led to discussion in the United States on the desirability of restructuring its anti-trust laws so as to permit United States firms to form export associations that could compete with foreign cartels. In this connexion the Secretary of the Treasury, Mr. John B. Connolly, testifying before the newly formed special committee on international trade of the Senate Finance Committee, stated, "we are reaching the time when we may have to restructure our anti-trust laws as they apply both domestically and in business abroad." *Forbes*, 15 June 1971, p. 21.

no fear of gravely injuring international confidence i Japanese exporters". This provision would seem to requir that the interests of buyers be protected in export agree ments and perhaps also the interests of exporters fror other countries. To this extent it would seem to provid a statutory basis for taking up with the Japanese Govern ment complaints concerning restrictive practices by expor cartels of that country which adversely affect the interest of buyers and exporters in developing countries.

153. In the case of international export cartels, nationa laws could only, at best, be applied to a segment of th cartel's activity. Each country could within the limits o its laws take action against the domestic participants i such a cartel. The United States has taken action agains multinational cartels, and experience would seem t indicate that this kind of proceeding is difficult because o the problems of jurisdiction and access to information.

CHAPTER V

Possible protection of the export interests of developing countries by action in those countries

154. A number of developing countries have sought to protect their export interests by formulating specific policies with regard to foreign investment and licensing agreements, by instituting administrative procedures to give effect to such policies, and in certain cases by enacting statutory provisions. These policies, administrative procedures and legislative provisions fall into three categories: foreign investment guidelines and codes; procedures for the registration and screening of arrangements entered into with foreign enterprises by local firms; and competition laws controlling restrictive business practices. The success that developing countries will achieve in this regard will depend upon their bargaining and negotiating power,[140] on how effectively they can secure compliance with their laws, and on how effectively they can administer their registration and screening procedures and investment guidelines and codes.[141]

A. Foreign investment policies, guidelines and codes

155. Policies on foreign investment in developing countries pertain basically to the manner in which subsidiaries and affiliates of foreign enterprises can operate in these countries. There are some broad general elements in the policies that have been adopted in the following developing countries, though the specific aspects and details of application of the policies vary from country to country: Bolivia, Brazil, Chile, Colombia, Ecuador, India, Kenya, Liberia, Mexico, Pakistan and the Philippines. The broad general elements are: (a) foreign firms must offer evidence

[140] See C. V. Vaitsos, "Bargaining and the distribution of returns in the purchase of technology by developing countries", in *Bulletin of the Institute of Development Studies*, University of Sussex, vol. 3, No. 1 (October, 1970), pp. 16-23.

[141] For a general outline of this problem, see D. Seers, "Big companies and small countries: a practical proposal", in *Kyklos: Revue internationale des sciences sociales*, vol. XIV, No. 4 (1963), pp. 599-607.

that they are capable of operating on a sound and efficien basis, and that they will contribute to the national develop ment of the country involved; (b) foreign investment an technical collaboration will be permitted in specified indus tries but not in others; (c) there must be training o nationals; (d) foreign business enterprises must file periodic reports on their business activities; (e) foreign investmen must be limited to specified proportions of the total valu of such investments to provide for local capital participa tion; and (f) foreign investors' tax obligations are explici and agreed upon.

B. Registration and screening procedures

156. The registration of new investments and technica collaboration agreements involving non-nationals is required under the foreign investment policies of some o the developing countries.[142] The proposed arrangements are screened with the objective of determining that they will be in the best interests of the developing country. The registration and screening procedures contain certain common elements, which can in general be divided into three main areas: criteria for issuing permission to conduct business activity; factors against issuing such permission; and permissible action after authorization has been obtained. The specific aspects that are usually considered with regard to each of these areas are the following:

1. *Criteria for issuing permission to conduct business activities*

(a) There must be sufficient over-all benefits to the national economic development;

[142] Registration and screening procedures in the following countries were described in detail in the preliminary report: Brazil, Chile, Colombia, El Salvador, Ghana, India, Iran, Mexico, Pakistan and the Philippines; see *Restrictive business practices* ..., paras. 135-150 and tables 5 and 6.

(b) The balance-of-payments effects must, to the extent possible, be beneficial;

(c) The proposed arrangements must lead to an expansion of production and increased employment;

(d) The royalty payments must be within certain fixed ranges and regarded as reasonable.

2. *Factors against issuing permission to conduct business activities*

(a) Prohibitions and limitations on export activity;

(b) The tying of purchases to the suppliers of the technical know-how, especially where domestically produced similar goods are available;

(c) The setting of unreasonably low prices for exports;

(d) The setting of unreasonably high prices for imports of intermediate goods required to produce the final products exported;

(e) Restrictions on production or exports after the termination of the technical know-how agreement.

3. *Permissible action after authorization has been obtained*

(a) The remittance of all or an approved portion of the profits made; and

(b) The remittance of an approved portion of net proceeds from sales.

C. Restrictive business practices laws

157. Only a small number of developing countries, and generally the more advanced of these, have enacted specific restrictive business practices legislation. Before 1960, three developing countries in Latin America—Mexico, Argentina and Colombia—had enacted laws prohibiting specified restrictive business practices. In 1963 Brazil enacted such legislation, India did so in 1969, and Pakistan in 1970. The Philippines is understood to have draft legislation under consideration in this field.

158. Where policies governing competition exist in developing countries, they vary in scope, in the degree to which they cover various types of restrictive business practices, and in the extent to which they apply to relations between a firm in a developing country and firms that are domiciled outside its sovereign jurisdiction, but whose activities nevertheless affect domestic trade.

159. A detailed interpretation of the laws of the countries mentioned is not possible at the present stage, since most of them are of only recent enactment, and therefore little experience or knowledge exists as to the extent to which they might be used to protect the export interests of the developing countries concerned. In particular, from the absence of case law it seems that the boundaries of the laws have probably not yet been determined in a series of relevant proceedings.

160. If developing countries wish to enact legislation on restrictive business practices, such legislation will obviously vary considerably from country to country in its scope and objectives. These would be influenced by such factors as the level of economic development achieved, the degree of private enterprise in the country, the role of foreign enterprises in such development, and the concentration of economic power and wealth within the country.

161. As has already been mentioned, a detailed study on the question of restrictive business practices laws is projected and certain work has already commenced. This study will be available in due course.

D. Harmonization of policies within the Andean group of countries

162. The Commission of the Cartagena Agreement, at its session in December 1970, agreed upon the harmonization of the policies in the member states of the Andean Pact—Bolivia, Chile, Colombia, Ecuador, and Peru—at a subregional level with regard to foreign investment and technological agreements involving the use of patents and trademarks. The policies agreed upon have since been implemented. They provide *inter alia* for the establishment of registration and screening procedures for foreign investment in each of the member countries. Foreign owned enterprises, which are defined as those in which 50 per cent or more of the share-holding is held by foreigners, are only allowed to benefit from improved export opportunities within the larger market created by the Andean Pact if they sign agreements to become joint ventures (mixed companies) by transferring at least 51 per cent of the share capital to nationals of the host country within a period of fifteen to twenty years. The objective of this requirement is to ensure that the substantial benefits from the larger market created by the Andean countries will flow to nationals of these countries. The agreed common policy requires all foreign investments to be registered with the host country's appropriate authority, and new investment must obtain that authority's approval.

163. All agreements on the importation of technology and on patents and trademarks are to be reviewed and submitted for the approval of the appropriate authority in each of the member States of the Andean Pact to evaluate the effective contribution of the imported technology. Member States have agreed not to authorize, except in exceptional cases, agreements which prohibit or limit the export of manufactured products based on the imported technology or manufactured under the trademark in question. This also applies to similar manufactured products. In addition, restrictive clauses requiring the purchase of raw materials, intermediate goods and equipment from a specified source will not be permitted, except in exceptional cases and then only if the prices correspond to the current levels of the international market. Similarly restrictive clauses relating to sale and resale prices, obligations to pay royalties on non-used patents and trademarks, the prohibition of the use of competing technologies, and restrictions on the volume and structure of production are not permitted.[143]

---

[143] See in particular articles 20 and 25 of Decision No. 24 on transfer of technology of the Commission of the Cartagena Agreement. For a description of these articles of the decision see "Case study of Chile, Arrangements for the transfer of operative technology to developing countries", ESA/FF/AC.2/13 of 16 June 1971; see also the study, "Policies relating to technology of the countries of the Andean Pact: their foundations", in *Proceedings of the United Nations Conference on Trade and Development, Third Session*, vol. III, *Financing and Invisibles* (United Nations publication, Sales No. E.73.II.D.6), document TD/107.

164. The approach of the Andean group of countries has been to harmonize the policies in member States.

E. Policies of some developed market-economy countries

165. Before concluding this brief discussion on action in the developing countries in the field of restrictive business practices and, in particular, on restrictions on the export activity of firms in their countries, brief mention is made of the guidelines and codes in two developed market-economy countries, Canada and Japan. The Canadian Government in March 1966, issued a set of guiding principles for good corporate behaviour. The principles were sent to large and medium-sized Canadian subsidiaries of foreign parent companies. They consisted of twelve basic principles, four of which seem to relate specifically to the problems of restrictive business practices. As indicated in the interim report,[144] in June 1968 Japan, in liberalizing its policy on the introduction of foreign technology, established foreign investment guidelines containing provisions specifically relating to the problems of restrictive business practices.

166. The guiding principles in Canada are as follows:

1. Pursuit of sound growth and full realization of the company's productive potential, thereby sharing the national objective of full and effective use of the nation's resources;

2. Realization of maximum competitiveness through the most effective use of the company's own resources, recognizing the desirability of progressively achieving appropriate specialization of productive operations within the internationally affiliated group of companies;

3. Maximum development of market opportunities in other countries as well as Canada;

4. Where applicable, to extend the processing of natural resource products to the extent practicable on an economic basis;

5. Pursuit of a pricing policy designed to assure a fair and reasonable return to the company and to Canada for all goods and services sold abroad, including sales to the parent company and other foreign affiliates;

6. In matters of procurement, to search out and develop economic sources of supply in Canada;

7. To develop as an integral part of the Canadian operation, wherever practicable, the technological, research, and design capability necessary to enable the company to pursue appropriate product-development programmes so as to take full advantage of market opportunities domestically and abroad;

8. Retention of a sufficient share of earnings to give appropriate financial support to the growth requirements of the Canadian operation, having in mind a fair return to shareholders on capital invested;

9. To work towards a Canadian outlook within management through purposeful training programmes, promotion of qualified Canadian personnel, and inclusion of a major proportion of Canadian citizens on its board of directors;

10. To have the objective of a financial structure which provides opportunity for equity participation in the Canadian enterprise by the Canadian public;

11. Periodically to publish information on the financial position and operations of the company;

12. To give appropriate attention and support to recognized national objectives and established government programmes designed to further Canada's economic development and to encourage and support Canadian institutions directed towards the intellectual, social and cultural advancement of the community.[145]

167. The guiding principles in Japan are the following:

1. Seek co-existence and prosperity with Japanese enterprises through joint ventures on an equal partnership basis;

2. Avoid concentration of investment in specific industries;

3. Avoid suppressing small enterprises when entering into industries characterized by small firms;

4. Co-operate voluntarily with the Japanese effort to maintain proper industrial order;

5. Avoid entering into unduly restrictive arrangements with parent companies abroad, and do not resort to unreasonable restrictions concerning transactions or to unfair competition;

6. Take positive steps toward developing Japanese technology, and do not hamper the efforts of Japanese industries to develop their own technology;

7. Contribute to the improvement of the nation's balance of payments through exports and other means;

8. Appoint Japanese to the board of directors and top management positions and make shares of company stock available to the public;

9. Avoid closures of plants, or mass dismissal, and unnecessary confusion in employment and wage practices by paying due regard to the prevailing Japanese practices;

10. Conform to the Government economic policy.[146]

F. Limitations on action by developing countries

168. The ability of developing countries to take action to control restrictions on their export activity is limited by a number of factors. First, as has already been pointed out, the majority of developing countries lack laws or procedures aimed at controlling such restrictions. Secondly, developing countries will encounter considerable difficulties, even if they have such laws and procedures, in obtaining sufficient relevant information to evaluate fully the effects of such restrictions and to take appropriate remedial action. Thirdly, most developing countries suffer from a shortage of trained experts in this area of work. Fourthly, there is the problem of the inherent limitations on their bargaining power in negotiations with foreign enterprises, given their dependence on obtaining the required technical know-how from such enterprises. Finally, there is also the problem of the limited sovereignty of any one State over the activities of such enterprises as the multinational corporations.

169. However, the enumeration of the limitations on action by developing countries should not be taken to imply that any remedial action would be impossible. The effectiveness of action will to a large extent depend on the

---

[144] See *Restrictive business practices...*, para. 154.

[145] For a discussion of these guidelines, see A. E. Safarian, op. cit., pp. 98-101. It would seem that Canada may also be examining the possibilities of establishing a screening mechanism for foreign investment. See the *Financial Times*, 18 November 1971, p. 5.

[146] For a discussion of these guidelines, see M. Y. Yoshio, "Japan as Host to the International Corporation", in C. P. Kindleberger (ed.) *The International Corporation* (Cambridge, Mass. and London, M.I.T. Press, 1970), p. 361.

nature of the restrictive business practice in question and on whether such a practice takes place or has effects in developing countries. Especially in the more advanced developing countries, where restrictive business practices legislation and other appropriate administrative mechanisms, exist, it should be possible to take remedial action.

170. In the case of the least developed among the developing countries the limitations enumerated obviously pose greater difficulties. In particular, owing to the absence of experience in the field of restrictive business practices they have considerable difficulties even in becoming aware of the restrictive business practices adversely affecting their export interests. In the negotiations with large foreign enterprises their bargaining power is extremely limited, in view especially of the small size of their domestic markets and the competition from other countries for investments and technical know-how. Furthermore, the institution of registration and screening procedures in such countries for foreign investments may well act to deter rather than to encourage new investments. In consequence, technical assistance should be supplied to such countries at their request to assist them in evaluating actual or potential problems in the field of restrictive business practices and in devising appropriate solutions.

CHAPTER VI

The problem of extraterritoriality

171. As has already been indicated, there is not necessarily harmony between the policies of the multinational corporations, the policies of the country of the parent company and the policies of the country of the subsidiary.[147] However, the laws and policies of the country in which the parent is located will in many cases influence and affect to some extent the activities of a subsidiary, or an affiliate, of that parent company in a foreign country. It is in this respect that conflicts of interest may arise and claims of the extraterritorial application of national laws and policies are made.[148] It has been stated that "any unit of a multinational enterprise, when operating in a territory of a sovereign State, responds ... to a flow of commands from the outside, including the commands of the parent and the commands of other sovereigns".[149] As a result, lines of accountability may become blurred and, as one scholar phrases it, sovereign States "feel challenged by an entity having power [but] not clear responsibility to the people over whom it exercises that power".[150]

172. The problem of extraterritoriality is dealt with in the present chapter with regard to the application of policies, laws and regulations relating to competition. It is only a short description of the problems that might arise for the developing countries. It is not intended to be an exhaustive discussion of the question, but merely a first look at the issue from the point of view of the developing countries.

A. Application of policies, laws and regulations relating to competition

173. The policies, laws and regulations governing competition differ from country to country. A practice regarded as lawful in one country may be regarded as unlawful in another, and conflicts may therefore arise in the application of these policies, laws and regulations. In this connexion it may be debatable where a certain practice took place and where the practice produced effects.[151] For example, an agreement may be concluded between firms in country A to regulate the prices and the distribution of a specific product, yet the effects of the agreement may be felt not only in country A, but also in countries B and C, which buy the product in question. If, in such a case, country B or C were to apply the criterion of where the act was committed for the taking of action against such a practice, the laws of these countries would not be applicable. However, if the "effects" criterion is applied, their laws would be applicable; yet claims of extraterritoriality by other governments concerned may be made with regard to decisions that may be taken to terminate the restrictive practice so far as they produce effects in the countries of the governments concerned.

174. From the viewpoint of the developing countries, problems arising in this context would seem to call for examination from three angles. First, the extraterritorial application of laws of developed countries may be in conflict with the policies of developing countries. Secondly, and conversely, action taken in the developed countries to terminate certain practices may indirectly benefit the export interests of the developing countries—an aspect discussed in chapter IV. Thirdly, the experience of developed countries in applying their laws to restraints on international trade, in particular by multinational corporations, would seem relevant to any consideration of remedial action in developing countries under their own laws.

175. Claims of extraterritoriality have been made especially in relation to the application of decisions con-

---

[147] This problem has also been referred to in the UNCTAD secretariat's report to the Conference, "Private foreign investment in its relationship to development". [See *Proceedings of the United Nations Conference on Trade and Development, Third Session*, vol. III, *Financing and Invisibles* (United Nations publication, Sales No. E.73.II.D.6), document TD/134, paras. 57-59].

[148] In this context the extraterritorial application of national laws and policies refers to those decisions and actions which are taken by a Government of a particular country with regard to the activities of firms in that country, whether they are national or foreign-owned, and which have direct effects on the activities of these firms, be they subsidiaries, affiliates or parents, in other countries.

[149] See R. Vernon, "The multinational enterprise: Power versus sovereignty", in *Foreign Affairs*, vol. 49 (July 1971), p. 736.

[150] Statement by J. N. Behrman, "Government policy alternatives and the problem of international sharing", presented at the Conference on the Multinational Enterprise, University of Reading, England, 28-30 May 1970.

[151] For a discussion of this issue see C. D. Edwards, "The Internationality of Economic Interests", in *University of Pennsylvania Law Review*, vol. III, No. 2, December 1962.

cerning the competition policies of the United States and the EEC.

176. In the case of the United States, complaints have been made by a number of countries in regard to anti-trust actions by the United States. A large number of the recorded complaints both from developing and developed countries[152] have related to maritime affairs, in particular in connexion with the Grand Jury investigation of the shipping industry in 1960 and the Federal Maritime Commission Investigation in 1960/1961.[153] These complaints especially related to the question of the submission of documents concerning international maritime shipping by the countries concerned to United States judicial authorities.[154] A number of the complaining countries subsequently enacted legislation prohibiting the supply of such documents by firms in their countries without the permission of their Governments.

177. Complaints regarding anti-trust action in the United States other than in the field of maritime affairs are known to have emanated from Canada, the Netherlands, Switzerland and the United Kingdom.[155] As in the field of shipping, these complaints related in part to decisions of United States courts requiring the transmission of company records of firms in other countries to those courts. Protective legislation aimed at preventing the transmission of such documents has been enacted, for example, in certain provinces of Canada, in the Netherlands, and in the United Kingdom.[156]

178. In addition, the complaints in certain cases concerned the purported extraterritorial application of the decisions of United States courts to activities outside the United States. As a result of the complaints, the final decisions of the United States courts took into account the points of view of the foreign governments. For example, in an anti-trust prosecution by the United States involving various domestic and foreign manufacturers of electric bulbs, N.V. Philips Gloeilampenfabrieken of the Netherlands was one of the defendants. After a complaint had been lodged by the Government of the Netherlands with the State Department, the United States district court took cognizance of the objection raised and modified the decree in such a way as to exempt Philips from any duties that would cause the company to act in violation of the laws of the Netherlands or of any other foreign country.[157]

179. In order to avoid potential conflicts, United States courts have in certain cases from the outset inserted "saving" clauses in their decisions, recognizing the rights of foreign States of supranational authorities to regulate conduct that takes place in their territories.[158]

180. The problem of the extraterritorial application of anti-trust laws was recently considered by the United States Commission on International Trade and Investment Policy. In its report to the President of the United States, the Commission inter alia expressed the view that the extraterritorial application of the anti-trust laws should be restricted to the greatest extent possible by more narrowly limiting it to instances where a clear and substantial, not potential, impact on United States commerce could be shown. The Commission also suggested that consideration be given to the establishment of a permanent international body, perhaps under the aegis of OECD, open to all countries, to resolve jurisdictional conflicts in anti-trust matters.[159]

181. From the point of view of the developing countries it would seem important to note that under the anti-trust laws of the United States, a United States-controlled affiliate is debarred from making any restrictive arrangements with other firms if they substantially affect United States commerce, whether foreign or domestic.[160] These laws apply also to the activities of any firm operating in the United States, whether it be United States-owned or foreign-owned. From the standpoint of the developing countries, these laws have therefore a bearing upon any restrictive arrangements, such as the territorial allocation of markets, price-fixing and other cartel arrangements to which a United States affiliate, or its parent, may be a party, regardless of whether such restrictive arrangements are permitted under the laws of the developing countries in question. Several cases[161] which have occurred in the United States have shown that that country's courts have extended their jurisdiction to United States affiliates abroad through the parent, and to foreign companies

---

[152] Complaints are known to have emanated from Canada, Denmark, Finland, the Federal Republic of Germany, India, Italy, Japan, Netherlands, Norway, Sweden, the United Kingdom and Yugoslavia. For details of these complaints see "Extra-territorial application of restrictive trade legislation", in *International Law Association, Fifty-first Report*, Tokyo (1964), part I, pp. 577-592.

[153] *Montship Lines Limited*, et al. v. *Federal Maritime Board*, 295F.2d 147 (C. A. Dist. Col. 1961).

[154] See the UNCTAD secretariat's report to the third session of Conference, *The regulation of liner conferences* (United Nations publication, Sales No. E.72.II.D.13), para. 94.

[155] For details of these complaints see R. R. Baxter, "Settlement of Disputes", in *International Law Association, Committee on the Extra-territorial Application of Restrictive Trade Legislation Report*, The Hague Conference (1970), pp. 40-47.

[156] *Canada:* The Business Records Protection Act, 1947, II Geo. VI, chap. 10 (Ontario) as amended, 14 Geo. VI, chap. 7 (1950); and an act respecting the Records of Business Concerns in the Province, 6-7 Eliz. II, chap. 42 (1958) (Quebec).
  The Netherlands: Economic Competition Act of 28 June 1956, as amended by the Act of 16 July 1958, sec. 39.
  United Kingdom: The Shipping Contracts and Commercial Documents Act, 1964 (ch. 87), sect. 2.

[157] *United States* v. *General Electric Co.*, 115F. Supp. 835 (D.N.J.1953). A subsequent case in which the terms of the final decision were modified by a United States court to take into account the views of a foreign government occurred in 1965, when a complaint was made by Switzerland. The case in question was *United States* v. *Watchmakers of Switzerland Information Center*, 1965, Trade Cases, para. 71,352 (S.D.N.Y. 1965).

[158] For example, see *United States* v. *Standard Oil Co. (N.J.)*, 1969, Trade Cases, para. 72, 742 (S.D.N.Y. 1968).

[159] See "United States international economic policy in an interdependent world", report to the President submitted by the Commission on International Trade and Investment Policy, Washington, D.C., July 1971, paras. 9.3 and 9.4.

[160] The Sherman Anti-trust Act, 15 USC, ss/1 *et seq.* (1964).

[161] *United States* v. *Imperial Chemical Industries Ltd.* et al., 100 F. Supp.504 (S.D.N.Y. 1951); *United States* v. *Timken Roller Bearing Co.*, 83 F. Supp.284 (N.D. Ohio E.D. 1949), modified, 341 US 593 (1951); *United States* v. *General Electric Co.* et al., 82 F. Supp.753, (D.N.J. 1949), modified, 115 F. Supp.835 (D.N.J. 1953); *United States* v. *Minnesota Mining and Manufacturing Co.* et al., 92 F. Supp.947, (D. Mass. 1950). A later case under section 7 of the Clayton Act was *United States* v. *Monsanto Co.*, 1967 Trade Cases, para. 72, 001 (WD pa. 1967).

either directly or through their United States affiliates.[162] Some of these cases are referred to in the following paragraphs.

182. The outcome of some of the cases adjudicated in the United States would seem to have important implications for the developing countries. It would seem that joint venture arrangements involving restrictions on United States trade and commerce in which United States multinational corporations participate, be it a partnership between United States corporations or between a United States corporation and a local company, could be more vulnerable to anti-trust laws than would be the case if the firm established in the developing countries were a 100 per cent United States-owned subsidiary. The following two cases might be cited in this connexion.[163] In the Minnesota Mining case (1950),[164] where a joint venture between two United States companies was set up in order to manufacture in factories abroad and to forgo exports from the United States, it was held that such a combination not only restrained the export trade, but, more importantly, restrained the trade of competing United States domestic exporters and potential exporters, since the latter had to face the joint operation abroad. The joint ownership in the foreign factories was eliminated in the final judgement, the Court allowing one company to purchase the entire interests in the factory. In the Timken case[165] (1951), the United States company owned share-holdings in affiliated companies in the United Kingdom and France of 30 per cent and 50 per cent respectively. Agreements were concluded between the three companies providing, among other things, for the allocation of sales territories, and where sales were made in the territory of one of the companies by one of the others, it was agreed that such sales would be made only at prices agreed by the company located in that territory. The Supreme Court held that labelling the arrangement as a joint venture would not be a sufficient defence to the charge of having entered into agreements for price-fixing and division of territories. The Court also held that investment abroad would not justify restrictions upon import and export.

183. In the light of these and other cases it has been stated that: "A joint venture permits the courts to conclude that the U.S. partner has 'conspired' with the other partner to do an illegal act. But a wholly owned subsidiary is said to be inseparable from the parent; legal counsel argues that courts would find it difficult to conclude that a single entity can conspire with itself".[166]

184. Another problem that could arise in connexion with the United States competition policies through the extension of its laws extraterritorially concerns the rationalization and concentration of industry in other countries. As is mentioned in chapter II of the present report, the encouragement of certain mergers forms part of the policies of a number of countries for the rationalization and improvement of the domestic and internationally competitive position of industry. The report of the Task Force on the Structure of Canadian Industry refers to this aspect. The report indicates, "It is not beyond the realm of possibility that Canadian programmes to rationalize industries through merger would be suspect in certain circumstances where some of the firms involved were United States controlled".[167] From the point of view of the developing countries, problems might arise in this area when they wish certain firms, of which at least one is United States-owned, to merge in order to become more competitive and perhaps in order to export.

185. It has been claimed by the United Kingdom that the Commission of the European Economic Communities applied the EEC law on competition policies extraterritorially as a result of a decision in 1969. Under this decision the Commission imposed fines on several dyestuff manufacturers in EEC countries, the United Kingdom and Switzerland, as a result of an investigation into an agreement, allegedly concluded in Switzerland, involving these manufacturers and regarding the sale, in particular the prices, of certain dyestuffs.[168] In the case of the United Kingdom and Swiss firms, the fines were imposed on the parents and not on the domestic subsidiaries in the EEC, apparently because only the parent companies took part in the alleged conspiracy. The subsidiaries themselves did not produce dyestuffs but obtained them from their parent companies and sold them at prices according to their parents' instructions. This decision led to a complaint from the United Kingdom Government. The aide-mémoire states inter alia:

> The United Kingdom Government are of the view that certain of the "considerations" advanced in the decision of the Commission of 24 July 1969, conflict with the principles of public international law concerning the basis upon which personal and substantive jurisdiction may be exercised over foreign corporations in anti-trust matters. ... In particular, it will be noted that the method by which the decision of the Commission was purportedly notified to I.C.I. (Article 4 of the decision) ignores the clear legal distinction between a parent company and its subsidiaries and the separate legal personalities of the latter. The United Kingdom Government consider that this attempted "notification" of a parent company through its subsidiary is designed to support a doctrine of substantive jurisdiction which is itself open to objection as going beyond the limits imposed by the accepted principles of international law.[169]

---

[162] For a discussion of this aspect, see W. L. Fugate, "International aspects of the United States anti-trust laws", in *International Conference on Monopolies, Mergers and Restrictive Practices* (see footnote 63 above).

[163] For a more detailed discussion of these two cases, see H. W. Wertheimer, "The International Firm and International Aspects of Policies on Mergers", and W. L. Fugate, op. cit.

[164] *United States* v. *Minnesota Mining and Manufacturing Co.* et al., 92 F. Supp. 947 (D. Mass. 1950).

[165] *United States* v. *Timken Roller Bearing Co.*, 83 F. Supp. 284 (N.D. Ohio E.D. 1949), modified, 341 US 593 (1951).

[166] See J. N. Behrman, op. cit., p. 119, and W. L. Fugate, op. cit., p. 231.

[167] Report of the Task Force on the Structure of Canadian Industry, *Foreign Ownership and the Structure of Canadian Industry* (Ottawa, Privy Council Office, January 1968), pp. 328 and 329.

[168] Decision of the EEC Commission of 24 July 1969, CCH, COMM.MKT.REP. 9314. On this case see Rahl (ed.), *Common Market and American Anti-trust. Overlap and Conflict* (1970), pp. 135-139 and K. Markert, *The Dyestuff Case: A Contribution to the Relationship between the Anti-trust Laws of the European Economic Community and its Member States*, XIV Anti-trust Bill. 869 (1969).

[169] The United Kingdom Government submitted an aide-mémoire to the Commission of the European Communities accompanied by a "Statement of principles according to which, in the view of the United Kingdom Government, jurisdiction may be exercised over foreign corporations in anti-trust matters". Both these texts are

186. If the United Kingdom's claim is justified, i.e. that the Commission is exercising extraterritorial jurisdiction, then developing countries might indeed have difficulties in taking effective action under their own restrictive business practices legislation to regulate those activities of foreign-based multinational corporations which may adversely affect the export interests of their countries. In particular, such a difficulty could arise where it might not be possible to hold a subsidiary in a developing country responsible for acts entered into by its parent with other firms outside that developing country, but which nevertheless affect the export interests of that developing country.[170]

187. The foregoing analysis is limited to a preliminary look at the question of extraterritoriality and at some examples of cases which have arisen in that context. Clearly, it provides no basis for forming any conclusion as to whether any actual problems or practical difficulties of the types described have arisen for the developing countries in the application of competition policies and laws in the developed market-economy countries. These cases cited, except in regard to maritime affairs, have generally

---

reprinted in: *International Law Association, Committee on the Extraterritorial Application of Restrictive Trade Legislation, Report,* The Hague Conference (1970), pp. 11-14.

[170] It seems that the Canadian Government may be investigating the possibility of amending its laws on competition to hold a foreign-controlled firm in Canada liable when, under direction of its parent or affiliate, it acts pursuant to an unlawful conspiracy entred into by the parent or affiliate. See the *Financial Times,* 18 November 1971.

---

not concerned the developing countries directly. Furthermore, in those few developing countries which have restrictive business practices legislation there is no information available to suggest that they have so far encountered the kind of legal difficulties described, in seeking to apply their competition laws to foreign enterprises. Nor is any information available on the question whether particular mergers that may have been desired by developing countries have been impeded by the laws of developed countries. The issues involved are not only very complicated but also very sensitive, and therefore it is not surprising that, as between developed countries that have encountered problems in this field, solutions are being sought on a pragmatic basis through discussions on a bilateral and multilateral level.

188. This should not imply, however, that such problems are irrelevant or theoretical from the point of view of the developing countries. As an increasing number of developing countries implement their own competition laws, establish screening procedures and negotiate improved terms for foreign investments and improved access to foreign markets for their exports, similar problems could well be encountered. Accordingly, further study of this question, focusing attention on the practical dimensions of the problem from their point of view, is required. The suggestion mentioned earlier, for the establishment of a permanent international body to resolve conflicts of jurisdiction in anti-trust matters between parent and host country of multinational corporations, would also deserve particular attention.

CHAPTER VII

Bilateral and multilateral arrangements

189. Up to this point the discussion has been essentially on national or unilateral action, in both developed and developing countries, relevant to the control of restrictive business practices which might affect the export interests of the developing countries. Attention has been drawn to the limitations on such action as well as to the problems that might arise from the extraterritorial application of national laws and policies. In the present chapter the existing bilateral and multilateral arrangements are examined to the extent that these deal or may deal with the question of restrictive business practices. A number of proposals made recently for strengthening multilateral action are then summarized.

A. Bilateral arrangements

1. FRIENDSHIP, COMMERCE AND NAVIGATION TREATIES OF THE UNITED STATES

190. Clauses providing for bilateral consultations with a view to settling disputes in the area of restrictive business practices have frequently been contained in Friendship, Commerce and Navigation treaties negotiated by the United States with other countries. The following is an example of such a clause:

The two Parties agree that business practices which restrain competition, limit access to markets or foster monopolistic control, and which are engaged in or made effective by one or more private or public commercial enterprises or by combination, agreement or other arrangement among such enterprises, may have harmful effects upon commerce between their respective territories. Accordingly, each Government agrees upon the request of the other Government to consult with respect to any such practices and to take such measures, not precluded by its legislation, as it deems appropriate with a view to eliminating such harmful effect.[171]

Clauses along these lines have been included in Friendship, Commerce and Navigation treaties concluded by the United States with Denmark, the Federal Republic of Germany, Greece, Ireland, Israel, Japan, the Republic of Korea, Nicaragua and Pakistan.[172] No evidence is readily

---

[171] United States of America and Federal Republic of Germany, Treaty of Friendship, Commerce and Navigation, signed at Washington, 29 October 1954, article XVIII (United Nations, *Treaty Series,* vol. 273, No. 3943).

[172] Treaty of Friendship, Commerce and Navigation between the United States of America and the Kingdom of Denmark, signed at Copenhagen on 1 October 1951, art. XVIII (see United Nations, *Treaty Series,* vol. 421, No. 6056).

United States of America and Federal Republic of Germany,

available, however, to indicate that regular or frequent use has been made of these clauses.

2. UNITED STATES/CANADA ARRANGEMENTS

191. As a result of discussions between the United States and Canada on the extraterritorial application of United States anti-trust laws, an informal arrangement between the two countries was agreed upon in 1959. This arrangement specified that: "each country, in enforcing its own anti-trust or anti-combines laws, consults the other when it appears that the interests of the other country will be affected by such enforcement".[173]

Each country reserved the right to take whatever action it saw fit under its own laws, and neither country had a veto over the action of the other. Notification is given wherever possible during the investigating phase, and the two States keep each other informed about developments in individual cases, as well as about general anti-trust policy. The consultations are carried on quietly, without disclosure to the companies concerned.[174] In 1969 the two Governments agreed that the OECD arrangements (described in paragraph 196 below) would be actively implemented and that at the same time notification and consultations would continue to be carried out under the 1959 understanding. They agreed that:

A primary concern would be cartel and other restrictive agreements and restrictive business practices of multinational corporations affecting international trade. The enforcement agencies of the two countries, each within its own jurisdiction, will where possible co-ordinate the enforcement of the respective laws against such restrictive business practices.[175]

Treaty of Friendship, Commerce and Navigation (see footnote 171 above).

Greece and United States of America, Treaty of Friendship, Commerce and Navigation, signed at Athens on 3 August 1951, art. XIV (see United Nations, *Treaty Series*, vol. 224, No. 3080).

United States of America and Ireland, Treaty of Friendship, Commerce and Navigation, signed at Dublin on 21 January 1950, art. XV (see United Nations, *Treaty Series*, vol. 206, No. 2792).

Israel and United States of America, Treaty of Friendship, Commerce and Navigation, signed at Washington on 23 August 1951, art. XVIII (see United Nations, *Treaty Series*, vol. 219, No. 2979).

United States of America and Japan, Treaty of Friendship, Commerce and Navigation, signed at Tokyo on 2 April 1953, art. XVIII (see United Nations, *Treaty Series*, vol. 206, No. 2788).

Treaty of Friendship, Commerce and Navigation between the United States of America and the Republic of Korea, signed at Seoul on 28 November 1956, art. XVIII (see United Nations, *Treaty Series*, vol. 302, No. 4367).

Treaty of Friendship, Commerce and Navigation between the United States of America and the Republic of Nicaragua, signed at Managua on 21 January 1956, art. XVIII (see United Nations, *Treaty Series*, vol. 367, No. 5224).

Treaty of Friendship and Commerce between the United States of America and Pakistan, signed at Washington on 12 November 1959, art. XVIII (see United Nations, *Treaty Series*, vol. 404, No. 5816).

[173] Report of the Task Force on the Structure of Canadian Industry (see footnote 167 above), p. 327. The informal arrangement was termed the "anti-trust notification and consultation procedure".

[174] See R. R. Baxter, "Settlement of Disputes", op. cit., p. 45.

[175] Joint statement, United States Department of Justice press release, 3 November 1969.

B. Multilateral arrangements

192. Multilateral arrangements in the field of restrictive business practices vary from limited geographic arrangements on a regional or subregional basis, such as those in EEC and EFTA,[176] to arrangements on a more global basis, such as those in OECD and GATT. In the case of the Andean group of countries, it will be recalled that, unlike the arrangements in EEC and EFTA (described below), no subregional or area arrangement as such was established, but national policies of the member States were harmonized with regard to foreign investment and restrictive business practices which might occur in relation to such investment.

1. EEC AND EFTA ARRANGEMENTS

193. The aim of the arrangements within EEC and EFTA in the field of restrictive business practices is to promote effective competition within these areas, in particular with regard to trade between member States. Such arrangements are limited in their scope, in that they apply only to abuses of competition or restrictive business practices affecting trade between member States.

194. Articles 85 and 86 of the Treaty of Rome establishing EEC relate to rules governing competition, and in particular to rules applying to enterprises in the Community. Article 85 prohibits "... any agreements between enterprises, any decisions by associations of enterprises and any concerted practices which are likely to affect trade between the Member States and which have as their object or result the prevention, restriction or distortion of competition within the Common Market ..." Article 86 prohibits "... action by one or more enterprises to take improper advantage of a dominant position within the Common Market or within a substantial part of it ...". In ensuring observance of these articles the Commission of EEC has been empowered to collect information, hold hearings, and make recommendations for terminating violations and invoking sanctions.[177] It would appear that the bulk of the complaints received by the EEC Commission and of the lawsuits before the courts of the Six have involved complaints from a firm inside one country against other firms located inside the same country.[178]

195. Unlike the Rome Treaty, the EFTA Convention[179] does not contain rules governing competition, but states certain general principles of policy in the field of restrictive business practices. In article 15, member States recognize that restrictive business practices (these are the same as those specified in the Treaty establishing the EEC) are "incompatible" with the Convention "in so far as they frustrate the benefits expected from the removal or

---

[176] The arrangements under the European Coal and Steel Community Treaty (see United Nations, *Treaty Series*, vol. 261 (1957), No. 3729) are not dealt with in the present chapter, since the arrangements relate to an industrial sector only. Its arrangements are broadly similar to those in the Treaty establishing EEC.

[177] Articles 3, 11 and 15 of Council Regulation No. 17, *Official Gazette of the European Communities*, No. 13, 204/62.

[178] A. Szokoloczy-Syllaba, "EFTA—Restrictive Business Practices", *Journal of World Trade Law*, vol. 4: No. 1, January-February 1970, p. 94.

[179] See United Nations, *Treaty Series*, vol. 370 (1960), No. 5266.

absence of duties and quantitative restrictions on trade between Member States ...". In the application of this general principle to complaints of restrictive business practices within EFTA, consultations among the members are envisaged. If such consultations do not result in a satisfactory settlement, the EFTA Council, under article 31, "may, by majority vote, make to any member State such recommendations as it considers appropriate". If such recommendations are not complied with, the Council may, by majority decision, authorize any member State to suspend to the non-complying member State such obligations under the Convention as the Council considers appropriate. In 1965 the Ministers of member States reaffirmed their Governments' readiness to examine with care complaints about restrictive business practices infringing article 15 engaged in by firms in their own territory and brought to their attention by another member State. Ministers agreed that member States were ready to investigate cases wherever there was some *prima facie* evidence of an infringement of article 15, and to hold informal and confidential bilateral consultations. If agreement were reached that the practice was incompatible with article 15, the member State would use administrative means, and, if necessary and available, legal powers to end the practices involved. Reports on such discussions and action taken would be circulated to all member States through the EFTA secretariat in order to ensure harmonization of the interpretation of the Convention's provisions. The formal consultation procedures referred to earlier would only be used after the informal bilateral consultations had not led to agreement. The informal consultation procedures just described are known to have been used in particular with regard to cartel arrangements or the exclusive dealing type.[180]

2. OECD ARRANGEMENTS

196. In 1967 the OECD Council adopted[181] a recommendation concerning co-operation between member countries on restrictive business practices affecting international trade.[182] In the operative paragraphs the Council recommended that the Governments of member countries should:

1. (*a*) That in so far as their laws permit, when member countries undertake under their restrictive business practices laws an investigation or a proceeding involving important interests of another member country, they should notify such member country in a manner and at a time deemed appropriate. Notification should, where appropriate, take place in advance in order to enable the proceeding member country, while retaining full freedom of ultimate decision, to take account of such views as the other member country may wish to express and of such remedial action as the other member country

may find it feasible to take under its own laws to deal with the restrictive business practice.

(*b*) That where two or more member countries proceed against a restrictive business practice in international trade, they should endeavour to co-ordinate their action in so far as appropriate and practicable under national laws.

2. To supply each other with any information on restrictive business practices in international trade which their laws and legitimate interests permit them to disclose.

3. To co-operate in developing or applying mutually beneficial methods of dealing with restrictive business practices in international trade.

The OECD Committee of Experts on Restrictive Business Practices was instructed to review developments and to examine periodically the progress made in this field. It would seem that the OECD Committee has received reports from member countries of notifications of and consultations concerning anti-trust actions, and that there have also been exchanges of unclassified information reported to the Committee.[183,184] The OECD arrangements are of course limited in their application to member countries.

3. GATT PROCEDURES

197. In 1960 the Contracting Parties to GATT adopted *ad hoc* notification and consultation procedures for dealing with conflicts of interests between Contracting Parties in the area of restrictive business practices. The Contracting Parties recommended that:

... at the request of any contracting party a contracting party should enter into consultations on such practices on a bilateral or a multilateral basis as appropriate. The party addressed should accord sympathetic consideration to and should afford adequate opportunity for consultations with the requesting party, with a view to reaching mutually satisfactory conclusions, and if it agrees that such harmful effects are present it should take such measures as it deems appropriate to eliminate these effects,

and decided that:

(*a*) If the requesting party and the party addressed are able to reach a mutually satisfactory conclusion, they should jointly advise the secretariat of the nature of the complaint and the conclusions reached;

(*b*) If the requesting party and the party addressed are unable to reach a mutually satisfactory conclusion, they should advise the secretariat of the nature of the complaint and the fact that a mutually satisfactory conclusion cannot be reached;

(*c*) The secretariat shall convey the information referred to under (*a*) and (*b*) to the Contracting Parties.[185]

The procedures have not been used by Contracting Parties, and the reasons for this are not known.[186]

---

[180] For the text of the agreed Ministerial Statement on this question see annex to the Communiqué reproduced in *EFTA Bulletin*, vol. VI, No. 7, November 1965, pp. 2 and 16. For a more detailed discussion of the EFTA arrangements, see *EFTA Bulletin*, vol. VIII, No. 5, July 1967, pp. 4-6; and A. Szokoloczy-Syllaba, "EFTA—Restrictive Business Practices", in *Journal of World Trade Law*, vol. 4, No. 1, January-February 1970, pp. 90-96.

[181] The delegate of Switzerland abstained.

[182] OECD. "Recommendation of the Council concerning co-operation between member countries on restrictive business practices affecting international trade", 5 October 1967, OECD/C(67)53 (Final).

[183] R. R. Baxter, op. cit. p. 38, referring to a letter to the author from Mr. W. L. Fugate, Chief, Foreign Commerce Section, United States Department of Justice of 11 February 1970.

[184] For work in OECD on the question of restrictive business practices, see extract from note by the Secretary-General of OECD, dated 2 August 1968, sent to the Secretary-General of UNCTAD and reproduced in "Restrictive business practices" (TD/B/C.2/54/Add.1), annex 4.

[185] GATT, "Decisions of seventeenth session" (L/1397, 5 December 1960), section 14.

[186] For discussion in the period 1955 to 1960 in GATT on the question of restrictive business practices, see extract from letter from the Director-General of GATT, dated 4 July 1968, addressed to the Secretary-General of UNCTAD and reproduced in "Restrictive business practices" (TD/B/C.2/54/Add.1), annex I.

4. CONVENTION ON THE SETTLEMENT OF INVESTMENT DISPUTES

198. The Convention on the Settlement of Investment Disputes between States and Nationals of other States, concluded under the auspices of IBRD in March 1965, came into force on 14 October 1966.[187] As of 30 June 1971, there were sixty-two Contracting States parties to the Convention. In addition, as of that date four States had signed the Convention but had not ratified it.[188] More than two-thirds of the Contracting States are developing countries, mainly in Africa and Asia. However, not a single Latin-American country has signed the Convention. The Convention established the International Centre for Settlement of Investment Disputes, the purpose of the Centre being to provide facilities for the conciliation and arbitration of investment disputes between Contracting States and nationals of other Contracting States. Paragraph (4) of article 25 indicates that any Contracting State may at any time notify the Centre of the class or classes of disputes which it would or would not consider submitting to the jurisdiction of the Centre. No such notifications have been made to the Centre.[189] Under the Convention, if both parties were agreeable, such investment disputes might include those arising in the area of restrictive business practices, including restrictions on export. There is no evidence to indicate, however, that any disputes of this nature have been submitted to the jurisdiction of the Centre.

199. It may be noted that many of the important capital-important countries, for example Argentina, Australia, Brazil, Canada, Chile, Colombia, India, Mexico, the Philippines, South Africa and Venezuela, are not as yet parties to the Convention.

C. Conclusion

200. The foregoing description of existing bilateral and multilateral arrangements relating to restrictive business practices would seem to indicate that, by and large, the principal objective of the establishment of such arrangements has been the settling of actual or potential disputes between developed market-economy countries, in particular in the area of competition policies, and, to this end, the establishment of closer co-operation between these countries. As a result, past discussions and co-operation in the area of restrictive business practices would seem to have taken place mainly in the context of the creation of regional economic groupings, such as EEC and EFTA, and in the context of the work of OECD.

201. This is understandable, for by and large developing countries have in the past paid little attention to the question of restrictive business practices. Only now is it being realized by the more advanced of these countries that problems in the field of restrictive business practices can arise that affect their over-all economic development and their export interests.

202. In the belief that the existing multilateral arrangements have certain shortcomings, a number of academics, lawyers, statesmen and international non-governmental organizations have made proposals aimed either at strengthening certain of the existing multilateral arrangements or at creating new ones.[190] Such proposals have, to a large extent, been formulated with the object of controlling the activities of the multinational corporation, and to a lesser extent of controlling cartel activity. A common element in most of the proposals is the establishment of a forum for settling disputes which may arise, in particular when the activities of the multinational corporations are not in harmony with the interests of States. A number of the proposals have recognized the need for greater participation and interest of developing countries in this area of work.[191] In summary, the proposals advocate either (a) establishing appropriate international machinery to deal with the problems of restrictive business practices, and to define initially a limited and acceptable agreement regarding the responsibilities of this machinery, or (b) the drawing up of a multilaterally agreed set of principles, code or rules regarding the activities or conduct of the multinational corporation. The proposals are not mutually exclusive, and it is recognized that some combination of the two might be the most realistic approach.

---

[187] Convention on the settlement of investment disputes between States and nationals of other States (United Nations, *Treaty Series*, vol. 575 (1966), No. 8359).

[188] International Centre for Settlement of Investment Disputes, *Fifth Annual Report, 1970/1971*, annex 1, p. 6.

[189] *Ibid.*, p. 3.

[190] For details of these proposals see:

P. M. Goldberg and C. P. Kindleberger, "Toward a GATT for investment: a proposal for supervision of the international corporation", in *Law and Policy in International Business*, vol. 2 (Summer 1970);

S. J. Rubin, "Multinational enterprise and national sovereignty: a skeptic's analysis", in *Law and Policy in International Business*, Vol. 3:1 (Winter 1971), pp. 1-41;

International Chamber of Commerce, Commentary—reproduced in TD/B/NGO/10, 21 January 1969—on the report by the UNCTAD secretariat, "Restrictive business practices" (TD/B/C.2/54 and Add.1); D. Seers, op. cit.;

G. Ball, "Cosmocorp: The Importance of Being Stateless", in *Columbia Journal of World Business*, vol. II (November-December 1967), pp. 6-25;

E. T. Penrose, *The Large International Firm in Developing Countries—The International Petroleum Industry* (London, George Allen and Unwin, 1968), p. 273;

W. D. Rogers, "New and future anti-trust laws: an overview and critique", an address to the International Anti-trust Symposium, American Society of International Law. College of William and Mary, Williamsburg, Virginia, United States of America, 16 October 1970;

C. Tugendhat, *The Multinationals* (London, Eyre and Spottiswoode, 1971), pp. 216-220; and

C. D. Edwards, "The world of anti-trust", in *Colombia Journal of World Business*, vol. IV, No. 4, July-August 1969.

[191] See in particular W. D. Rogers and S. J. Rubin, op. cit.

EXPORT PROMOTION

Report by the UNCTAD secretariat*

[*Original text: English*]

CONTENTS

Introduction

1. The term "export promotion" in the context of a developing country is open to a variety of interpretations. For example, it could cover a wide range of policies and measures bearing on what might be broadly described as export development. It could also cover action designed to improve the economic climate for exports, for example, measures to curb inflation, to ensure a realistic exchange rate or to manage home demand. Such broad interpretations would embrace nearly all aspects of export-oriented economic development, including general economic development, and financial, fiscal and commercial policies.[1]

2. This report is based on a less comprehensive concept of export promotion. It focuses on measures related to a developing country's efforts to market its products abroad and to promote the sale of those products systematically and effectively. It therefore deals with the infrastructure of the export promotion institutions and services needed for a sustained export effort—an effort directed principally to identifying opportunities in foreign markets for products with export potential and adopting appropriate measures to exploit these opportunities through product adaptation, marketing and promotion. It also deals with special measures that governments of developing countries must take to encourage exports. Since the roles of the public and private sectors in a national export effort are complementary, measures relating to both sectors are discussed. Thus this report is concerned with a developing country's needs in formulating and carrying out an export promotion programme, on the assumption

---

* The text of this report was circulated to the Conference as Document TD/123, dated 10 March 1972.

[1] See "Review of the export policies for expansion and diversification of exports of manufactures and semi-manufactures from developing countries: report by the UNCTAD secretariat" (TD/111/Supp.1).

that the government has already decided to adopt appropriate general economic policies.

3. Since the infrastructure for export marketing and promotion must of necessity serve both primary commodities and manufactures and semi-manufactures, these products are not treated separately; to divide the report along these lines would result in much repetition.

Chapter I

Export promotion in developing countries

4. This section deals with the export promotion needs and problems of developing countries and the measures they are taking to build up their export capabilities.

5. Serious interest in export promotion in developing countries is of relatively recent origin. In the early 1950s, when commodity prices were by and large at remunerative levels and the burden of foreign debt servicing had not become a major element in the external financial situation of developing countries, the promotion of exports was not a high priority in most of these countries. The subsequent deterioration in the terms of trade, increasing import expenditures generated by developmental needs, and the mounting burden of debt servicing, stimulated developing countries at the end of the 1950s and during the First United Nations Development Decade to turn their attention to increasing their foreign exchange earnings through export promotion. Export promotion was given a further impetus when it was realized in many developing countries that import substitution was uneconomic or that savings of foreign exchange through import substitution could yield only marginal gains. Moreover, a number of developing countries that are free of serious balance-of-payments difficulties through special circumstances, such as revenue from petroleum products, are paying attention to export promotion since it generates employment opportunities for an expanding population. Today, the economic development plans of most developing countries reflect government recognition of export promotion as a major element in national economic development and employment strategy.

6. It will be recalled that the subject was extensively discussed at the first session of the Conference and that a number of resolutions were then adopted on measures to promote exports from developing countries. The high priority given to export promotion by the governments of developing countries is evident from the measures they are taking to improve their export performance and their steadily growing requests for international assistance in this field. Nevertheless, such recognition of the importance of export promotion has not led to a vigorous and systematic exploitation of the new export opportunities that exist for both primary commodities and manufactures and semi-manufactures. The efforts made to improve export performance are often *ad hoc* and dispersed, and hence lack the character of a concerted national export promotion drive capable of being sustained over a period of years.

7. In this connexion it may be pointed out that, if a government is not committed to clearly defined export objectives, a number of general economic policy elements that have a bearing on the success of a national export promotion effort, such as monetary and fiscal policies, the management of internal demand and investment and commercial policies, are dealt with in an incoherent manner, without due regard to their effects on the expansion of export earnings.

8. There is a growing awareness in developing countries that the institutional factor mainly responsible for this situation is the absence, in many cases, of government machinery capable of:

(*a*) Ensuring that the country's foreign trade goals are adequately defined and integrated into over-all economic development objectives, so that the priorities accorded by the government to the development of exports are clearly recognized;

(*b*) Contributing effectively to the formulation of policies and programmes through which the goals established for the foreign trade sector can be realized;

(*c*) Monitoring the implementation of these programmes to ensure that the government's targets are realized on time.

9. It is relevant to note that, whereas in most developed countries there is a tradition of exporting and the necessary export infrastructure and services exist in the private sector, in developing countries the government must play a key role in the development and promotion of exports —a relatively new field of endeavour for most developing countries.

10. For developing countries, therefore, the promotion of exports is as much a problem of restructuring certain vital links in the administrative machinery of government as it is a technical problem of product development for export or overseas sales promotion. Unless an effective focal point is established within the government machinery with over-all responsibility and authority for formulating export promotion programmes and mobilizing the public and private sector bodies concerned in implementing these programmes, a co-ordinated national export promotion effort will be difficult to initiate and sustain. From a long-term point of view, the building up of the institutional export infrastructure, especially at the government level, must be a priority objective in a developing country's export promotion effort, since the government will then be able to deal with its export promotion needs as they arise and strengthen its export capabilities.

11. A sustained national export promotion effort requires co-ordinated action by a number of bodies in both the public and the private sectors that are variously involved in the stages between the production of the product and its purchase by the consumer abroad. If the focal point is to act effectively, therefore, it is essential, first, that it be able to bring together the key sectors of the country which have activities bearing on export expansion, in order to ensure its close the participation both in planning exports and in carrying out export promotion programmes. Secondly, the focal point must have the necessary authority and prestige to enable it to exercise leadership and ensure co-ordination. Thirdly, it must have a specialized secretariat capable of providing expert advice on the development of the country's export potential and on the

measures needed at the national level to exploit market opportunities abroad.

12. Many developing countries are making serious efforts to establish such focal points in the form of foreign trade councils or similar institutions to serve as the principal national policy-making organs in all matters relating to the development of exports, and vested with the necessary authority for this purpose. The membership of these institutions comprises ministers or senior policy-making officials with responsibilities in fields such as foreign trade, agriculture, fisheries, forestry, mining, industry, customs, taxation and general economic policy, and senior representatives of trade and industry.

13. The specialized foreign trade secretariat required for the effective functioning of the high-level, decision-making focal point can also serve as the administrative agency responsible for the day-to-day supervision of the implementation of the government's foreign trade programmes. Many developing countries have in fact taken steps to improve the efficacy of their governmental organs dealing with foreign trade. In countries where there is already substantial diversification of export possibilities, the foreign trade secretariat needs to be greatly strengthened and improved; in countries with a narrower range of export capacities, and with a shortage of qualified personnel, more modest export bureaux may be envisaged. Indeed, the question has been raised whether the latter countries need to give priority to building up even very modest specialized secretariats to deal with foreign trade, since they are able to export only a few traditional primary products in respect of which they already have some knowledge of export markets and exporting know-how. Experience has shown, however, that a small but efficient secretariat staffed by officials with a knowledge of foreign trade can have a catalytic effect, stimulating exports even in the least developed countries. For example, a number of countries have in recent years built up an export trade in relatively unsophisticated products, the supply of which has been organized without much investment of technical know-how. In other cases, the newly-established foreign trade secretariat has initiated measures to improve the grading and quality standards of primary products or to promote the first stage in simple processing so that added value may be obtained from traditional products.

14. A specialized foreign trade secretariat would thus appear to be a necessity in any country, whatever the stage of economic development it has reached. The size and organization of the secretariat must, of course, vary according to the special situation and needs of the country concerned, and its location will depend on the country's administrative structure. This is perhaps the area where the demands of developing countries for technical assistance are heaviest.

15. Effective trade promotion requires complementarity of organization and co-ordination between the export promotion services at home and abroad. Government departments and private institutions promoting trade at the exporting end at home must rely heavily on trade intelligence and advice from trade representatives abroad. Without accurate and up-to-date information on market conditions abroad for the country's exportable products it would be difficult for the foreign trade secretariat to give proper advice either to planning authorities or to the high-level policy body responsible for foreign trade. Hence many developing countries are striving to improve the quality of their foreign trade services and expand them to exploit export opportunities in new markets. However, the simultaneous establishment of home and overseas organizations imposes a considerable burden on developing countries, especially owing to the shortage of trained personnel for the specialized tasks involved.

16. An added difficulty in organizing trade services at home and abroad is that, while the principal exports of developing countries for some years to come will continue to be traditional raw materials, it is at the same time necessary to promote the sale of a number of new manufactures and semi-manufactures that are becoming available for export. Since the type and techniques of trade promotion needed for marketing primary products on the one hand, and manufactures on the other, are very different, the trade services at home and abroad have to be equipped to cope with these varied tasks. Many countries are seeking new markets for their traditional primary products in an effort to combat the sagging demand for these products; others are endeavouring to improve grading and quality standards of primary products or adopting some measure of processing and product adaptation in order to take advantage of new market opportunities that would improve the foreign exchange earning capacity of these products. The markets sought for manufactures and semi-manufactures are often different from those in which primary products can be promoted, and the channels of trade and marketing techniques are also very different. This diversity in target markets and techniques of promotion and marketing poses serious organizational problems for developing countries, especially owing to the lack of trained staff and inadequacy of foreign exchange resources for promotional activities.

17. It should be noted that overseas trade representatives of developing countries are obliged to be more actively involved in sales promotion activities than their counterparts from developed countries, since developing country exporters, especially of non-traditional products, do not have established contacts in foreign markets. The trade representatives perform many functions, such as advising on the choice of sales channels, appointing agents and building up after-sales service facilities for certain types of products, as well as exploring and negotiating subcontracting arrangements under which exports can find assured outlets. Governments are endeavouring to equip their foreign trade services for these specialized tasks.

18. Because individual producing and exporting concerns in developing countries are not large enough to have their own export promotion and marketing services, governments have been obliged to play an active role in encouraging joint marketing and promotional activities. Joint export marketing entities are being established to assist small-scale producers and exporters, and export promotion bodies, which bring together exporters of like products, are being set up to carry out joint promotion abroad. In certain cases, where private sector bodies are unable to promote exports effectively to countries with State trading systems, governments have had to organize State trading bodies to encourage exports to such destina-

tions. Governments have also taken steps to enable these bodies to organize sales missions and market orientation tours abroad for groups of exporters.

19. Since chambers of commerce and associations of industries are not adequately developed in most developing countries, traders have increasingly relied on the government for the provision of reliable trade information to enable exporters to adapt their products to the needs of foreign markets and to take appropriate marketing and promotional action through the proper trade channels. The organization of trade information systems that would provide adequate service to exporters, especially with respect to non-traditional products, has proved to be one of the most difficult tasks in developing countries, and requests for expert assistance in this area are growing rapidly, since a trade information service is basic to any effort that a government makes to promote exports. The responsibilities of a trade information service include the provision of comprehensive market surveys and export marketing plans for products for which it has been decided to launch a major promotional effort, since, in contrast to developed countries, the business sector in most developing countries has neither the overseas contacts nor the foreign exchange resources necessary to carry out these tasks.

20. The emergence of new types of exports, especially of capital goods and consumer durables, has brought into focus the lack of export financing and export credit guarantee facilities in a number of developing countries. Here again, governments have had to take the initiative in setting up these services in collaboration with the banking system.

21. Governments of developing countries are endeavouring to encourage exports by means of a number of other special assistance measures designed to improve the internal climate for exporting. First, they are taking measures to remove discouragement to export—for example, by simplifying export documentation and procedures, reducing delays in the recovery of drawbacks of customs duty paid on raw materials or intermediate goods for production for export and expediting pre-shipment inspection procedures. Secondly, they are seeking to provide positive inducements to export through various types of export incentive schemes and other facilities, such as free-trade zones, to encourage production for export. These areas of endeavour are all relatively new to most developing countries. Consequently these countries desire to have the benefit of the expertise and experience of other countries, both developed and developing.

22. The improved access to markets provided for exports from developing countries under the GSP, and the tariff concessions resulting from the recently concluded trade negotiations among developing countries have created renewed interest in export promotion in a number of those countries, and they are actively seeking to determine the products that could benefit from these international commercial policy arrangements. In this connexion they need both market research to ascertain export opportunities and marketing assistance to promote the sale of selected products. In addition, a number of groups of developing countries are taking steps to promote exports among themselves under various special regional or sub-regional arrangements.

23. In recent years there has been growing recognition in many developing countries of the value of joint promotional action by groups of countries interested in the export of similar products, joint efforts being often more economical as well as more effective than action by individual countries. These countries have in the first instance initiated joint market research projects on selected products in target markets of common interest. They have next embarked upon joint promotional campaigns for a particular product in the most promising markets. They are now planning to build up more comprehensive multinational product promotion institutions that can carry out general promotion campaigns for individual products or groups of products, in particular for primary products facing competition from synthetic substitutes.

24. All these measures need trained personnel. The developing countries concerned are therefore seeking ways and means of training specialized cadres as quickly as possible so that they can man both the government export promotion services and the export marketing institutions in the private sector. Some developing countries have established national training institutions with technical assistance from abroad, and the more advanced of these will soon be in a position to provide training facilities for other developing countries. There has also been an interesting initiative by a group of countries in one subregion aimed at securing the establishment of a regional training institution to serve all the participating countries. Such collaboration among a group of developing countries to deal with common problems would be an economical way of meeting requests for assistance in training, which will continue to grow rapidly in number as more developing countries make greater efforts to expand their exports.

Chapter II

Review of on-going technical assistance activities

25. The many developing countries which in recent years have given priority to export promotion are progressively adopting a combination of the various measures referred to in chapter I, each in the light of its special needs. As a result, there has been a rapidly growing demand for international technical assistance in most of these fields. The ITC was established to meet such needs, in collaboration with other agencies in the United Nations system whose activities have a bearing on the expansion of exports from developing countries. Over the years the Centre has become the focal point of United Nations technical assistance efforts designed to help developing countries expand their exports. This chapter outlines the fields in which export promotion assistance is provided by UNCTAD and ITC in co-operation with the regional export promotion centres which are being set up by the United Nations regional economic commissions, ECA, ECAFE and ECLA, and by UNESOB. These assistance programmes are financed by UNDP and by voluntary contributions from individual countries, which together total $5 million in 1972.

26. Export promotion assistance programmes are for-
ulated to meet the specific priority needs of the develop-
g countries concerned, within the context of each coun-
y's over-all economic development aims. They are thus
tegrated programmes, involving many interlocking ele-
ents in each country. For the purposes of this report,
owever, the technical assistance now being provided may
e classified under the following main headings:

. Improvement of the national institutional infrastructure for
export promotion.

. Establishment of specialized export promotion and marketing
institutions and services.

. Identification of market opportunities and development and
adaptation of products for export through market research.

. Export marketing and promotional strategies.

. Multinational product promotion.

. General export promotion measures.

. Training in export promotion and export marketing.

A. IMPROVEMENT OF THE NATIONAL INSTITUTIONAL INFRASTRUCTURE FOR EXPORT PROMOTION

27. The main weakness of the export effort in most
eveloping countries is the absence of a coherent national
xport promotion programme. One of the primary objec-
ves of technical assistance, therefore, is to assist the
overnment of a developing country to formulate a
uitable export promotion strategy in the light of the coun-
y's current economic situation and development aims.
n the basis of assessments of a country's export potential,
xport promotion experts advise the government on a
rogramme of export expansion, at the same time drawing
ttention to the institutional infrastructure that will be
eeded to implement the programme.

28. Since few developing countries have the institu-
onal infrastructure that they need at the government level
o undertake a concerted export promotion effort, assist-
nce in building up such an infrastructure is a key element
n the programme of most of these countries. Once the
nfrastructure is established, a government should be able
rogressively to improve its capacity to deal with the
ountry's export promotion needs and problems.

29. In countries requesting broadly-based technical
ssistance in export promotion, the technique of high-level
ymposia has been usefully applied. The aim is to create
 more general awareness of the importance of exporting
nd to secure the participation of both the public and the
rivate sectors in a concerted national export promotion
rive. The symposia are designed to bring together senior
ersonnel at the decision-making level in government and
he business community to discuss, with the participation
f international experts, the country's export promotion
roblems and technical assistance requirements. This type
f symposium has facilitated the discussion of the export
romotion strategies recommended by international ex-
erts and has often proved of great value in fostering
nutual understanding and securing a more co-ordinated
ational export promotion effort.

30. For strengthening the institutional infrastructure
or export promotion at government level, assistance has
een provided to developing countries in establishing:

(a) High-level export development councils to co-
rdinate and supervise national export promotion efforts;

(b) Foreign trade secretariats or export promotion
bureaux to service export development councils and to
carry out basic studies and monitor the implementation
of export promotion programmes;

(c) Trade representational services abroad;

(d) Basic trade information services for exporters.

B. ESTABLISHMENT OF SPECIALIZED EXPORT PROMOTION AND MARKETING INSTITUTIONS AND SERVICES

31. While the establishment of effective machinery for
export promotion at the government level is an indispensable condition for the success of a developing country's
export promotion effort, it is only the first step towards the
implementation of an effective export promotion programme. Because of the many related measures that have
to be taken simultaneously for sales promotion in foreign
markets, a number of specialized services have to be provided for producers and exporters. As export promotion
efforts are strengthened and better organized, the need for
such services and for specialized institutions through
which these services can be provided becomes more evident. Furthermore, experience shows that specific problems can often be resolved by such institutions and that
export sales can thus be effected even if the over-all
national export promotion organization is still in its
formative stages.

32. Expert assistance has been provided to enable
developing countries to establish specialized services in
the following fields:

(a) Public export trade organizations,

(b) Joint export marketing organizations for small-scale
producers,

(c) Export promotion bodies for groups of similar
products,

(d) Packing and packaging,

(e) Export financing and export credit insurance,

(f) Export processing zones,

(g) Quality control, grading and standardization.

C. IDENTIFICATION OF MARKET OPPORTUNITIES AND DEVELOPMENT AND ADAPTATION OF PRODUCTS FOR EXPORT THROUGH MARKET RESEARCH

33. The very substantial assistance provided for developing countries in the field of market research has three
objectives:

(a) Identification of market opportunities for products
that developing countries are capable of exporting, given
their current production capacities;

(b) Feedback of market information to suppliers in
developing countries to enable them to adapt their products to the specific needs of foreign markets;

(c) Assessment of the market potential for products
to be developed for future export.

34. The identification of market opportunities includes
determining prospects for export promotion through
suitable international sub-contracting arrangements between buyers in developed countries and producers in
developing countries.

35. In addition, the major market surveys published by ITC cover a number of products of significant export interest to a large number of developing countries, for example, oil cakes, shrimps and prawns, rice, manioc, tropical sawnwood, plywood and veneer, parquet, citrus juices, canned meat, fresh and processed fruits and vegetables, leather, hides and skins, unmanufactured tobacco, soluble coffee, spices, wines and oriental carpets. These surveys deal with some of the most promising markets for the products concerned and provide comprehensive information of value to producers and exporters in developing countries. They cover such facets as the assessment of market potential in importing countries, distribution channels, product specifications required by buyers, and packaging requirements. The aim of these surveys is to provide exporters in developing countries with information and data of immediate utility to them in initiating commercial contacts with buyers abroad and in adapting their products to the special requirements of foreign markets.

36. At the same time, the market feasibility studies carried out by the ITC are designed to assist individual developing countries to make decisions on the expansion of production capacity for export. They involve more complex assessments of long-term market prospects for specific products, on the basis of which production and investment decisions can be made.

D. EXPORT MARKETING AND PROMOTIONAL STRATEGIES

37. Many developing countries lack export marketing know-how, particularly in connexion with non-traditional products and non-traditional markets. Assistance in this area and in promotional strategies has been provided through international marketing experts skilled in particular product fields. This is in fact an extension of the ITC market research work and involves:

(a) Export potential surveys in countries requesting assistance to identify supply factors with respect to products which the country desires to market abroad;

(b) Identification of the most promising markets in which an initial marketing effort could be launched;

(c) Mapping out an export marketing and promotional programme in collaboration with prospective buyers in the target market (this includes estimating the cost/benefit of alternative marketing methods and promotional devices).

The entire work is carried out by international marketing experts, with counterparts from the business sector in the developing countries concerned to ensure effective follow-up action.

38. Another technique currently employed to assist the export marketing efforts of developing countries is that of market orientation tours. The object of such tours is to enable exporters from industries with export prospects to visit specific markets in order to discover for themselves the opportunities for, as well as the complexities of, selling abroad. Such tours also enable exporters to meet importers and discuss with them appropriate trading arrangements, taking into account specific requirements of the various import markets. During these visits the participants also enter into direct contact with agents, freight forwarders, distributors and other persons and institutions whose activities

are considered relevant to the particular market orientation study.

39. A new type of marketing assistance, which is being carried out on an experimental basis, is provided by market development programmes focused upon individual developed countries. For example, a pilot project now in operation aims at assisting exporters from a selected number of developing countries to introduce and promote sales of their products in a Nordic country through a suitable combination of marketing efforts and product development and adaptation to meet the technical and commercial requirements of that market. The major components of such assistance are the following: preliminary market acceptability tests of products tentatively selected for promotion; sales discussions between exporters from developing countries and potential importers, agents and distributors; sales promotion activities for the products selected, using various communication media, and assistance in drawing up and implementing long-term development plans for the products finally selected. It is expected, following an evaluation of the pilot project, that similar schemes will be introduced to promote the exports of developing countries in other markets.

E. MULTINATIONAL PRODUCT PROMOTION

40. An activity which is steadily growing in importance is that of multinational product promotion. Developing countries are increasingly considering the possibilities of joint action to improve the export earnings of commodities of interest to them, particularly primary commodities, by raising the general level of consumption through promotional means. This development is due in part to the emphasis that is being placed by various international bodies on concerted promotional measures as a means both of stimulating consumer demand and of finding new markets and end users for a number of traditionally traded commodities. Discussions are under way in a number of international bodies on this matter, and several studies and surveys have been undertaken on promotional strategies that would provide the basis for a collective effort by interested governments. The object of these studies is to identify markets with the greatest potential for increased consumption, assess the possible impact of promotional action on consumption, and offer suggestions on the feasibility and chances of success of promoting programmes in selected areas.

41. One result of these efforts was the opening of a sales promotion office for groundnuts at Geneva in the autumn of 1969; a promotional and publicity programme is now being carried out. Preliminary steps have also been taken to establish a joint interim secretariat for the proposed international tropical timber bureau, and consideration has been given to appropriate promotional measures with respect to a number of other products such as tea, oilseeds, oils and fats, cotton, hard fibres, wine, natural rubber and sugar.

42. A further development in this field is the organization of seminars on the promotion and marketing of specific products. The object of such seminars is to assist the representatives of participating countries to promote such products by acquainting them with recent technical, commercial and market developments in the major

importing countries, and by initiating discussion on the implementation of marketing procedures between the seminar participants and selected importers. These seminars are intended for senior staff in business and government with executive or promotional responsibilities for the expansion of the export trade in the products under study.

F. GENERAL EXPORT PROMOTION MEASURES

43. A number of general export promotion measures may be grouped under the general heading, creation of export consciousness and improvement of the climate for exports. These include both the removal of discouragements and the provision of incentives by governments. Assistance has been provided to developing countries in the following fields:

(a) Financial and fiscal incentives for the development of exports;[2]

(b) Simplification of export documentation and export procedures, including simplification of procedures for obtaining refunds or drawbacks of taxes and duties;

(c) Organization of trade missions;

(d) Organization of trade exhibitions and displays and other forms of trade publicity.

44. To illustrate the demands of developing countries in this general area, reference may be made to the simplification of export documents. The volume of export documentation, combined with the complexity of the procedures for clearing these documents through numerous official and semi-official agencies, has been a significant deterrent to the expansion of exports in many developing countries. The governments of many developing countries are now fully aware of this problem and over 50 have to date requested technical assistance in organizing a simplified system of export documentation.

45. In addition to the expert assistance rendered to governments, information on these general export promotion measures is disseminated to help them improve their services to exporters. Such information includes studies on most of the subjects already noted above, such as export incentives, organization of trade missions, and organization of trade exhibitions.

G. TRAINING IN EXPORT PROMOTION AND EXPORT MARKETING

46. The provision of training facilities has to date been one of the major elements of technical assistance in export promotion, since it is generally accepted that shortage of suitably qualified personnel is a major impediment to the export promotion efforts of developing countries. The training programmes provided have become increasingly sophisticated to meet the varying requirements of different countries. They range from general training courses in export promotion and international marketing, through more specific courses focused on products or export techniques, to workshops on export promotion and international marketing for instructors in business education institutions in developing countries. A short account of the major types of training so far provided in this field is given below.

1. *Training courses in export promotion and international marketing*

47. The object of these training courses is to train participants in the organizational and operational management of trade service activities and in export marketing and promotional techniques of immediate relevance to the needs of the countries concerned. Participation is sought from officials and executives in the public sector and the business community having direct responsibility in matters affecting the country's export trade. Increasing emphasis is placed on the organization of such courses on a country or regional basis to ensure that participants will have a more or less similar background.

2. *Seminars on export promotion and marketing techniques*

48. The object of these seminars is to bring the latest developments in trade promotional activities to the attention of senior government and business participants with full-time responsibility for specific promotion activities in connexion with their country's foreign trade. The seminars are organized either on a product basis or in relation to a specific export promotion technique, such as export packaging or export publicity.

3. *In-service training*

49. In-service training is provided to meet the special requirements of individual trainees. The advisers and specialists sent to developing countries by international assistance agencies are entrusted with the responsibility of training their counterparts. In addition, individual fellowships are provided for officials and executives in developing countries to enable them to work in specialized organizations in developed countries engaged in activities of interest to them.

4. *Workshops for instructors in export promotion and international marketing*

50. These workshops are designed for staff members of universities and colleges in developing countries where specialized courses in export promotion and business administration are currently offered or may be introduced. The object is to give instructors in such institutions the opportunity to become familiar with the latest trends in export marketing and export promotion, and also to learn of recent developments in teaching methodology and learning theory.

H. GENERAL APPROACH TO TECHNICAL ASSISTANCE

51. The above classification of technical assistance activities has been adopted only for presentational purposes. In practice the tendency is to combine the provision of different types of assistance within the framework of a single integrated project, adapted to meet the specific export problems of individual developing countries. A typical integrated assistance project provides for general advisers on the institutional and organizational aspects of export promotion, as well as for specialist advisers in, for example, export potential surveys, market research, product adaptation and export marketing, together with various types of training programmes. The various inputs

---

[2] See *Incentives for industrial exports: study by the secretariat of UNCTAD* (United Nations publication, Sales No. E.70.II.D.8).

are then programmed and appropriately timed within the total duration of the project under the continuous direction of a project manager to ensure optimum efficiency and maximum impact of the technical assistance upon the export performance of the country in which the project is implemented. A beginning has also been made with inter-agency technical assistance projects, where an integrated programme of specialized inputs is made available by two or more international agencies in accordance with their respective fields of competence; such projects are expected to grow in number and scope.

52. The special difficulties facing the least developed of the developing countries have been highlighted by a number of international bodies, and the export promotion needs of these countries have consequently been receiving particular attention in the past two or three years. Because of the problems arising, *inter alia*, from their weak economic infrastructure and limited administrative capacity, the least developed countries require new forms of technical assistance in their export efforts. New techniques are being evolved, such as missions of buyers from developed countries to assist the least developed countries in sales promotion and product adaptation, and on-the-job training of trade representatives of the latter countries in commercial centres in developed areas. More conventional assistance is also provided, designed to strengthen the government infrastructure for export promotion.

53. Finally, the liaison function performed by the ITC in promoting more effective partnership between developing countries and developed market-economy and socialist countries should be recognized as another valuable form of technical assistance. Because of the diverse needs and complex problems of developing countries in the field of export promotion, it was evident from the inception of the Centre that demands for assistance from these countries would grow rapidly. It was soon realized that a task of this magnitude could not be effectively carried out even by drawing upon the resources and expertise of several organizations within the United Nations system. Hence the Centre has built up, over the years, a liaison network in developing, developed market-economy and socialist countries which embraces government agencies, semi-governmental organs, trade chambers and associations and individual enterprises engaged in international trade. The Centre uses this network to the greatest extent possible to meet its needs for trade information, for the provision of training facilities and for the location of experts.

54. This liaison network has had the effect of stimulating other bodies, especially those established in developed countries, to devote greater attention to the export promotion needs of developing countries. Thus, the technical assistance agencies of a number of developed countries have put trust funds at the disposal of ITC, which have now reached a level of $3 million per annum, to finance additional technical assistance programmes for developing countries. National liaison officers in national organs responsible for foreign trade in many developed market-economy and socialist countries are providing valuable support by arranging to make available market information, training facilities and experts, to enable the Centre to meet the developing countries' growing demands for technical assistance. Furthermore, several developed countries have at their own expense seconded qualified staff to assist the work of the Centre, notably in market research and in programming and fact-finding missions to developing countries.

55. A partnership between developing, developed market-economy and socialist countries has thus been gradually instituted through the activities of the Centre and this collaboration has considerably enhanced its ability to serve the developing countries.

Chapter III

Future needs for international assistance

56. A significant feature of the export promotion assistance provided so far is that it has been confined largely to technical assistance; hardly any financial assistance has been forthcoming through either multilateral or bilateral channels in this very important field of development activity. In order to implement their export promotion programmes, developing countries need not only expert advice and the training of specialist personnel but also considerable outlays of scarce foreign exchange resources to launch marketing and promotional efforts, to offer credit facilities to buyers abroad comparable with those offered by competitors elsewhere, to set up warehousing and packaging facilities abroad and to take many other such measures that are essential to an export promotion effort.

57. In considering the directions in which assistance to developing countries in export promotion could be improved and strengthened, reference is made below to certain priority needs of these countries where financial assistance would be useful. It is not intended that this discussion should be confined to assistance that could be provided through UNCTAD or the ITC but to focus attention on areas where there is also scope for direct assistance to developing countries from developed market-economy and socialist countries.

A. IMPORT PROMOTION INSTITUTIONS IN DEVELOPED MARKET-ECONOMY AND SOCIALIST COUNTRIES

58. The development of the liaison network between the ITC and developed market-economy and socialist countries, as mentioned earlier, has led to the provision of support for the Centre by a number of national liaison agencies, especially in market research and marketing. These liaison agencies have helped the Centre to organize market research and in some cases have also provided trade information and advice on market opportunities. A number of developed market-economy and socialist countries have signified their intention to provide such services to developing countries, covering their respective markets, in direct response to requests. Certain countries, especially the socialist countries, intend to provide these services through existing institutions such as national chambers of commerce, while a number of developed market-economy countries are considering the creation of special machinery for this purpose on the lines of the Centre for the Promotion of Imports from Developing

Countries established by the Government of the Netherlands on 1 January 1971 in Rotterdam.

59. While the institutional machinery in developed market-economy and socialist countries through which market research and marketing assistance could be provided to developing countries would vary from one country to another because of legal, administrative and other factors, it is suggested that governments might consider reaching a common understanding on the scope of the assistance to be provided. Having regard to the needs of developing countries in building up new markets for their products, import promotion institutions in developed market-economy and socialist countries might equip themselves to respond to requests for assistance from developing countries in the following fields:

(*a*) Information on market opportunities and assessment of market potential for specific products;

(*b*) Advice to exporters in developing countries on product adaptation to meet the requirements of buyers;

(*c*) Establishment of commercial contacts between exporters in developing countries and importers, agents, or wholesalers;

(*d*) Servicing of business visitors from developing countries;

(*e*) Assistance to trade representatives of developing countries in carrying out market investigations and trade promotional work;

(*f*) Organization of sales missions;

(*g*) Organization of trade publicity—e.g. participation in trade fairs, commercial displays, in-store promotions, etc.

B. Export promotion of primary products

60. For some years to come most developing countries will have to continue to rely heavily for their foreign currency earnings on exports of traditional primary products. Although many of these commodities are encountering serious difficulties in international trade, especially those facing competition from synthetic substitutes, and although a number of them are of common interest to groups of developing countries, concerted efforts on an adequate scale have not been made by the exporting countries to improve the export earnings of these products through new marketing strategies, promotional action or product development. These are fields in which collaboration among exporting developing countries with respect to selected products could significantly contribute to the export earnings of such products. As mentioned above, there is growing recognition in developing countries of the value of such collaboration, but few of them possess the institutional infrastructure, the know-how or the technical research facilities to organize joint action. Developing countries need assistance in carrying out the initial investigations required before institutional arrangements at home and abroad can be determined; they also need both technical and financial assistance in the early stages of the operation of joint programmes until a point of consolidation is reached.

61. Importing countries, both developed market-economy and socialist, could assist the efforts of developing countries to organize joint marketing and promotional action for certain traditional products by encouraging their importing institutions to collaborate with the developing countries in such marketing and promotional action and by offering the facilities of their research institutions for the investigation of new end uses and product development.

62. The proposed international tropical timber bureau is an example of joint action envisaged by developing countries exporting tropical timber, with the collaboration of a number of institutions in developed countries.

C. Training for export promotion

63. The lack of trained personnel in the various specialized tasks involved in the formulation and implementation of national export promotion programmes has been a serious obstacle to the improvement of the export performance of many developing countries. While a great deal is being done through international assistance to provide training programmes in export promotion and export marketing to developing countries, these programmes as at present constituted meet only a relatively small part of the training needs in a field that is so vast and embraces so many specializations. A significantly greater effort needs to be made to enable training to be provided to larger numbers from both government and business sectors.

64. A broadly-based regional approach to training is needed for this purpose. A number of developing countries have educational institutions and training centres in which programmes in export promotion and export marketing could be built up to serve the needs not only of individual countries but also of groups of countries within a region or subregion. Likewise, possibilities exist of utilizing the facilities in certain regional institutions to provide training in these fields.

65. Such an effort would initially require substantial international assistance, through both funds and specialist staff, to establish the basic facilities and programmes; once established, these training centres would be largely self-supporting.

66. It is suggested that developing countries should explore the possibilities of utilizing UNDP resources to establish such institutions. This is a field that would be of considerable interest also to donor countries which are providing export promotion assistance to developing countries, since investment in training would make a significant contribution to building up the capacity of the developing countries to deal with their own needs and problems.

D. Financing of exports

67. Far-reaching changes have taken place in the export structure of a number of developing countries in recent years. There has been a shift from heavy reliance on exports of traditional primary products and a steady increase in the share of manufactures in their export trade. This expansion of exports of industrial products has brought

into focus the inadequacies of existing export finance facilities for these new types of exports.

68. The successful promotion of exports of manufactures, especially capital and semi-capital goods and consumer durables, depends not only on quality, price, delivery and after-sales service, but also on the capacity of the supplier or exporting country to offer deferred payment terms. This is particularly relevant when products are to be promoted in developing countries, where, owing to constraints in the external financial situation, credit terms are a determining factor in most import transactions. Owing to increased competition among suppliers the world over, export credit maturities have lengthened and terms of credit have been liberalized. Hence the success of developing countries' efforts to promote exports of their manufactures and to increase trade among themselves will depend to a great extent upon their ability to provide competitive terms of credit.

69. The problem has to be dealt with at two levels, the domestic and the international. At the domestic level the solution lies in providing export financing and export credit facilities in local currency to exporters within the framework of a country's over-all export promotion programme. Many developing countries have already taken measures in this direction and many more are considering arrangements to be implemented in the future. Technical assistance is being provided to assist the efforts of developing countries in this field. Such action at the domestic level, however, resolves only part of the problem for it meets only the needs of individual exporters in local currency.

70. At the international level the problem is a collective one for the country as a whole, since the export credits granted by a country to buyers abroad amount in fact to the export of capital. Since developing countries urgently need to import capital from abroad, they find it particularly difficult to offer export credits on acceptable terms. In other words, the perennial foreign exchange problems of developing countries prevent those countries from extending competitive credit terms to importers abroad. A way has therefore to be found to enable a developing country to offer competitive credit terms to foreign buyers for a wide range of products, and at the same time to collect the foreign exchange value of such exports at the time of shipment, so that its weak external financial situation is not further strained.

71. One method is to raise funds in the international money market on the strength of export documents. However, developing countries have found it extremely difficult to obtain such funds, since many of them fail to meet certain basic conventional requirements of lending institutions, such as a developed local money market, a freely convertible currency and the stability which would ensure a climate of financial security. Moreover, such funds are expensive to raise in the open money market

unless the commercial papers are guaranteed by an international institution, since the interest rate at which the papers are accepted is affected by the quality of the cover provided. Such transactions also involve case-by-case negotiations on the amount of credit, the rate of interest, the period of maturity and other issues, and require the adoption of a number of measures by various agencies which are not always capable of reaching the speedy agreements that are so essential for successful export promotion.

72. Appropriate international machinery is therefore needed to assist developing countries overcome their foreign exchange difficulties in respect of export credits. Through such machinery developing countries would be enabled to provide credits to foreign buyers of certain classes of goods; such credits would be financed or re-financed, and they would be guaranteed in order to facilitate their re-financing in international capital markets. The precise nature of such assistance and the institutional machinery through which it should be provided require further study, but the general objectives would be:

(a) To provide refinancing for credit institutions in the exporting countries;

(b) To provide financing for buyers in the importing countries against the guarantees of their governments;

(c) To grant a line of credit to the exporting country to be utilized against export documents.

73. The object of the above listing of the more urgent needs of developing countries in respect of which international technical and financial assistance would be most useful is to draw the attention of the Conference to these issues, since the Conference presents an opportunity for consideration at the intergovernmental level of broad policy guidelines for future collaboration between the developed market-economy and socialist countries and the developing countries in the field of export promotion. These issues are not discussed in depth in all their technical aspects, since the Conference may not be the appropriate forum for a technical discussion; other organs exist for this purpose.

74. Considering the rapidly growing demands for assistance in the field of export promotion, it is inevitable that both bilateral and multilateral assistance programmes in this field will expand substantially over the coming years. It is essential that the international bodies through which the multilateral programmes are implemented should be equipped to deliver a programme of assistance considerably larger and more varied than the current programme. For effective implementation, such an expanded programme will require specialized manpower in addition to financial resources. The international agencies, therefore, would wish to be assured of the collaboration of developed market-economy and socialist countries, as well as of certain developing countries, where some expertise has already been developed in the exporting field.

PROCEEDINGS OF THE THIRD SESSION OF THE UNITED NATIONS CONFERENCE ON TRADE AND DEVELOPMENT

Contents of the series*

Volume I. Report and annexes

This volume contains the report of the United Nations Conference on Trade and Development on its third session.

The report provides an account of the setting and aims of the third session of the Conference as well as of the activities of UNCTAD's permanent machinery during the period between the second and third sessions of the Conference. It includes a summary of the general debate, the conclusions reached at the end of the session and guidelines for future work. The full texts of resolutions, other decisions adopted by the Confrence, and of observations and reservations by delegations relating to these decisions, are contained in annex I. The texts of reports submitted by Committees and other sessional bodies of the Conference are reproduced in annex VI. The texts of proposals referred by the Conference to the Trade and Development Board are reproduced in annex VII.

Annex VIII reproduces "Other basic documents", including the texts of statements made at the inaugural ceremony, other selected statements, and messages received from Heads of State and Government. The same annex also reproduces the texts of certain declarations by groups of countries and delegations made before or during the session.

United Nations publication, Sales No. E.73.I.D.4.

Volume IA (mimeographed)

Part one of this volume contains the summaries of the statements made by Heads of delegation at the plenary meetings of the Conference; part two contains the summary records of the 82nd to 119th plenary meetings of the Conference.

Volume II. Merchandise trade

Part one of this volume contains selected studies submitted to the Conference dealing with commodity problems and policies. These studies provide an account of developments in international commodity policy, access to markets, pricing policy; commodity diversification, competitiveness of natural products; one study deals with questions raised by mineral production from the sea-bed.

Part two of Volume II contains studies submitted to the Conference dealing with trade in manufactures and semi-manufactures. One of the papers describes the main features of the preferential arrangements drawn up in UNCTAD and of the schemes implemented so far by certain preference-giving countries. Other studies selected for publication in this volume discuss a programme for the liberalization of quantitative restrictions and other non-tariff barriers in developed countries on products of export interest to developing countries. Papers on adjustment assistance measures, restrictive business practices and export promotion are also included in part two.

United Nations publication, Sales No. E.73.II.D.5.

Volume III. Financing and invisibles

Part one of this volume contains studies submitted to the Conference dealing with various aspects of the mobilization of financial resources for development.

The studies selected for publication in this volume provide a review of issues related to economic growth and development finance; mobilization of resources for development; external development finance; the "link" and the outflow of financial resources fom developing countries. A report on private foreign investment in its relationship to development identifying the main problems in this field is also included in this volume.

Part two of this volume makes reference to three studies in the field of shipping, namely: *Shipping in the seventies*, *The regulation of liner conferences*, *A code of conduct for liner conferences* and *Multinational shipping enterprises*, which were submitted to the Conference and are published separately.[1]

One section contains reports on insurance and developing countries and tourism and developing countries which are condensed versions of previous studies submitted to the Committee on Invisibles and Financing related to Trade at its fifth session.

Part two also includes a report on the specific role of the transfer of technology in stimulating economic development and access to advanced technology and a report on policies relating to the transfer of technology of the countries of the Andean Pact.

United Nations publication, Sales No. E.73.II.D.6.

---

* Four printed volumes and one mimeographed volume.

[1] United Nations publications Sales Nos. E.72.II.D.15, E.72.II.D.13 and Corrigendum and E.72.II.D.17 respectively.

Volume IV. General review and special issues

This volume contains a review of international trade and development, providing basic information about the main policy developments and international measures since the second session of the United Nations Conference on Trade and Development. It also includes studies of long-term changes in terms of trade and main problems of trade expansion and economic integration among developing countries. Other studies selected for publication in this volume deal with a comparison of two major economic groupings: the Western European Groupings and th Council for Mutual Economic Assistance, and wit expansion of trade and economic co-operation betwee the socialist countries of Eastern Europe and the develop ing countries.

The latter part of this volume includes three reports o special measures for the least developed among the deve oping countries and other special measures related to th particular needs of the land-locked developing countrie.

United Nations publication, Sales No. E.73.II.D.7.

Printed in Belgium
34911—August 1973—1,464

Price $U.S. 7.00
(or equivalent in other currencies)

United Nations publication
Sales No.: E.73.II.D.5
TD/180/Rev.1

Printed in Belgium
3601—August 1973—3,635

Price $U.S. 7.00
(or equivalent in other currencies)

United Nations publication
Sales No. E.73.II.D.
TD/180, Vol. I